An Introduction to Criminological Theory

This book provides a comprehensive and up-to-date introduction to criminological theory for students taking courses in criminology at both undergraduate and postgraduate level. Building on previous editions, which broadened the debate on criminological theory, this book presents the latest research and theoretical developments.

The text is divided into five parts, the first three of which address ideal type models of criminal behaviour: the rational actor, predestined actor and victimized actor models. Within these, the various criminological theories are located chronologically in the context of one of these different traditions, and the strengths and weaknesses of each theory and model are clearly identified. The fourth part of the book looks closely at more recent attempts to integrate theoretical elements from both within and across models of criminal behaviour, while the fifth part addresses a number of key recent concerns of criminology: postmodernism, cultural criminology, globalization and communitarianism. All major theoretical perspectives are considered including:

- Classical criminology
- biological and psychological positivism
- labelling theories
- feminist criminology
- critical criminology and left realism
- social control theories
- the risk society.

The new edition also features comprehensive coverage of recent developments in criminology, including situational action theory, desistance theory, peacemaking criminology, Loïc Wacquant's thesis of the penal society, critical race theory and Southern theory. This revised and expanded fourth edition of *An Introduction to Criminological Theory* includes chapter summaries, critical thinking questions, a full glossary of terms and theories and a timeline of criminological theory, making it essential reading for those studying criminology.

Roger Hopkins Burke is Principal Lecturer and Criminology Subject Leader in the Division of Sociology at Nottingham Trent University.

This latest edition not only offers readers an exhaustive, accessible and up-to-date explanation of criminological theories but highlights their application and relevance to contemporary debates and developments. Essential reading for anyone seeking to understand theories of crime and why they matter.

Neil Chakraborti, Reader in Criminology, University of Leicester

An Introduction to Criminological Theory offers a sound introduction to key theories relevant to crime matters in the modern age. Accessible and informative, it is written with the reflective criminologist in mind. As such, it is a must for all students, and anyone interested in explaining crime and considering how we respond to its occurrence.

Tina Patel, Lecturer in Criminology, University of Salford

An Introduction to Criminological Theory

Fourth edition

Roger Hopkins Burke

Routledge
Taylor & Francis Group

LONDON AND NEW YORK

First published 2001
by Willan Publishing

Fourth edition published 2014
by Routledge
2 Park Square, Milton Park, Abingdon, Oxon OX14 4RN

and by Routledge
711 Third Avenue, New York, NY 10017

Routledge is an imprint of the Taylor & Francis Group, an informa business

British Library Cataloguing in Publication Data
A catalogue record for this book is available from the British Library

Library of Congress Cataloging in Publication Data
Burke, Roger Hopkins.
An introduction to criminological theory / Roger Hopkins Burke. – Fourth edition.
pages cm
Includes bibliographical references and index.
1. Criminology. I. Title.
HV6018.B87 2014
364–dc23

2013027213

ISBN: 978–0–415–50171–2 (hbk)
ISBN: 978–0–415–50173–6 (pbk)
ISBN: 978–0–203–49836–1 (ebk)

Typeset in Palatino
by RefineCatch Limited, Bungay, Suffolk

Printed and bound in Great Britain by
CPI Group (UK) Ltd, Croydon, CR0 4YY

For Kristan, Thomas and Oliver

Contents

Acknowledgements   *xiv*

1 Introduction: crime and modernity   **1**
  Pre-modern crime and criminal justice   2
  The rise of modern society   3
  Defining and the extent of crime   5
  The purpose of criminological theory   8
  The structure of the book   8
  Summary of main points   25
  Discussion questions   26
  Suggested further reading   26
  Note   27

Part One: The rational actor model of crime and criminal behaviour   *29*

2 Classical criminology   **35**
  The Classical theorists   35
  The limitations of Classicism   40
  The neo-Classical compromise   40
  The enduring influence of Classicism   42
  Policy implications of Classicism   43
  Summary of main points   44
  Discussion questions   45
  Suggested further reading   45

3 Populist conservative criminology   **46**
  The rise of the political new right   46
  James Q. Wilson and 'right realism'   48
  Right realism and social control   51
  Developments in conservative criminology   52
  Criticisms of populist conservative criminology   56
  Policy implications of populist conservative criminology   57

Summary of main points 58
Discussion questions 59
Suggested further reading 59
Notes 59

4 Contemporary rational actor theories **60**
Contemporary deterrence theories 60
Rational choice theory 63
Routine activities theory 67
The rational actor reconsidered 71
Policy implications of contemporary rational actor theories 73
Summary of main points 76
Discussion questions 76
Suggested further reading 77
Notes 77

Part Two: The predestined actor model of crime and criminal behaviour 79

5 Biological positivism **83**
Early biological theories 83
Inherited criminal characteristics 86
Genetic structure theories 90
Criminal body types 91
Psychoses and brain injuries 93
Autistic spectrum disorders 96
Biochemical theories 98
Altered biological state theories 100
Treating the offender 105
Conclusions 106
Policy implications of biological positivism 108
Summary of main points 109
Discussion questions 110
Suggested further reading 110

6 Psychological positivism **111**
Psychodynamic theories 111
Behavioural learning theories 116
Cognitive learning theories 122
Conclusions 127
Policy implications of psychological positivism 127
Summary of main points 128
Discussion questions 129
Suggested further reading 129

7 Sociological positivism **131**
Emile Durkheim and social disorganization theory 132

The Chicago School 137
Robert Merton and anomie theory 140
Deviant subculture theories 146
Conclusions 163
Policy implications of sociological positivism 163
Summary of main points 164
Discussion questions 165
Suggested further reading 165

8 **Women and positivism** 167
Biological positivism and women 167
Psychological positivism and women 170
Sociological positivism and women 176
Conclusions 180
Policy implications of women and positivism 181
Summary of main points 181
Discussion questions 182
Suggested further reading 182

Part Three: The victimized actor model of crime and criminal behaviour 185

9 **Labelling theories** 193
The social construction of crime 194
The recipients of deviant labels 196
The consequences of labelling for the recipients 198
Moral panics and deviance amplification 199
Criticisms of labelling theories 201
Labelling theories revisited 202
Policy implications of labelling theories 205
Summary of main points 205
Discussion questions 206
Suggested further reading 206

10 **Conflict and radical theories** 207
Conflict theories 207
Criticisms of conflict theories 210
Radical theories 211
Criticisms of radical theories 215
Peacemaking criminology 217
Policy implications of conflict and radical theories 224
Summary of main points 225
Discussion questions 226
Suggested further reading 226

11 **The gendered criminal** 227
Perspectives in feminist theory 228

The feminist critique of early explanations of female criminality 231
The impact of feminist critiques 233
Feminism and prostitution 235
Is there a feminist criminology? 238
Crime and masculinities 240
Policy implications of the gendered criminal 242
Summary of main points 243
Discussion questions 244
Suggested further reading 244

12 Critical criminology **245**
The origins of critical criminology 246
Crimes of the powerful 247
Crimes of the less powerful 249
Critical criminology or 'left idealism' 250
Critical race theory 251
Critical criminology and the challenge of zemiology 256
Critical criminology revisited 259
Policy implications of critical criminology 260
Summary of main points 261
Discussion questions 262
Suggested further reading 262

Part Four: Integrated theories of crime and criminal behaviour *263*

13 Sociobiological theories **267**
Biosocial theory 268
Biosocial theory and the 'new right' 270
Sociobiological theories of rape 272
Recent sociobiological explanations of childhood delinquency 274
Conclusions 275
Policy implications of sociobiological theories 276
Summary of main points 276
Discussion questions 277
Suggested further reading 277

14 Environmental theories **278**
Early environmental theories 278
British environmental theories 279
North American environmental theories 280
Environmental design 285
Environmental management 288
Policy implications of environmental theories 290
Summary of main points 291
Discussion questions 292
Suggested further reading 292

15 Social control theories   **293**
The origins of social control theories   293
Early social control theories   295
Later social control theories   298
Integrated theoretical perspectives   299
A general theory of crime   302
Developments in social control theories   304
Conclusions   308
Policy implications of social control theories   308
Summary of main points   309
Discussion questions   310
Suggested further reading   310

16 Situational action theories   **311**
Situational action theory   312
Crime as moral action   313
Rules and rule guidance   314
The role of motivation   315
Environment and exposure   317
The importance of causal interaction   317
Development and change   319
Broader social conditions   320
Reflections on situational action theories   321
Policy implications of situational action theories   323
Summary of main points   323
Discussion questions   324
Suggested further reading   324

17 Desistance theories   **325**
The ontogenetic paradigm   327
The sociogenic paradigm   329
Understanding change in adulthood   331
Personality traits   332
The narrative identity   334
Narratives of desistance and change   335
Agency and choice   335
Narrating desistance   337
Developments and reflections on desistance theories   338
Policy implications of desistance theories   341
Summary of main points   341
Discussion questions   342
Suggested further reading   342
Note   343

18 Left realism   **344**
The origins of left realism   344
A balance of intervention   348

Left realism and 'New' Labour   351
Social exclusion and the 'underclass': a case study   352
'New' Labour criminal justice policy revisited   354
Recent developments in left realism   357
Left realist theory revisited – the historical context   360
Policy implications of left realism   361
Summary of main points   361
Discussion questions   362
Suggested further reading   363

Part Five: Crime and criminal behaviour in the age of moral uncertainty   365

19 Crime and the postmodern condition   373
Constitutive criminology and postmodernism   375
Anarchist criminology   380
Policy implications of crime and the postmodern condition   384
Summary of main points   385
Discussion questions   385
Suggested further reading   386
Note   386

20 Cultural criminology and the schizophrenia of crime   387
The focus of cultural criminology   387
The seductions of crime   390
The carnival of crime   392
The schizophrenia of crime   392
Crime as normal and non-pathological   393
One planet under a groove   395
Cultural criminology and the mass media   399
Policy implications of cultural criminology   407
Summary of main points   407
Discussion questions   408
Suggested further reading   408
Notes   408

21 Crime, globalization and the risk society   410
New modes of governance   410
Crime and the risk society   412
Penal modernism and postmodernism   415
Globalization and crime   418
Southern theory   425
Terrorism and state violence   426
Terrorism and postmodernism revisited   432
Policy implications of crime, globalization and the risk society   432
Summary of main points   434
Discussion questions   435

Suggested further reading   435
Notes   435

22   **Radical moral communitarian criminology**   **437**
The communitarian agenda   440
Radical egalitarian communitarianism   443
The concept of community reconsidered   445
The development of the concept of individualism in
   Western Europe   447
The origins of Durkheim's social theory   450
Durkheim, social solidarity and the French conception of
   individualism   451
Radical moral communitarian criminology   452
Policy implications of radical moral communitarian criminology   453
Summary of main points   455
Discussion questions   456
Suggested further reading   456

23   **Living in penal society**   **457**
Four models of criminal justice development   457
Loïc Wacquant and the government of insecurity   470
Racial inequality and imprisonment in the contemporary USA   470
Four peculiar institutions   472
Carceral recruitment and authority   473
Conclusions   476
Policy implications of living in penal society   479
Summary of main points   480
Discussion questions   480
Suggested further reading   481
Notes   481

24   **Conclusions: criminology in an age of austerity**   **482**
Criminological theory revisited   485
Competing models of a criminological future   487
Two models of public criminology   488
An alternative: democratic criminology   493
Closing thoughts: moral communitarianism and
   democratic criminology   497
Summary of main points   497
Discussion questions   498
Suggested further reading   498

Criminological theory timeline   *499*
Glossary   *502*
Bibliography   *510*
Index   *567*

Acknowledgements

I would like to offer my sincerest thanks to those who have provided advice and support during the researching and writing of the fourth edition of *An Introduction to Criminological Theory*. It has been appreciated. Thanks to those staff at Nottingham Trent University who have been particularly supportive to me during what has been a very difficult couple of years with a special mention to Phil Hodgson, Mike Sutton, Chris Crowther-Dowey and Matt Long. Thanks to all the staff at Routledge for their support and gentle chivvying when there was danger that this project would fail to be delivered on time (it only slipped by a couple of weeks in the end). Last, and very far from least, my family. My wife Kristan and our extremely talented boys Thomas (now 15 and doing his GCSEs) and Oliver (now 12), who are both excellent musicians and have a wicked sense of humour. Now who do they get that from?

1. Introduction: crime and modernity

Key Issues

1. Different ways of explaining criminal behaviour
2. Definitions of crime and criminality
3. Crime associated with particular groups
4. Why theory is important
5. Structure of the book

This is a book about the different ways in which crime and criminal behaviour have been explained in predominantly modern times. It will be seen that there are different explanations – or theories – that have been proposed at various times during the past 200 years by, among others, legal philosophers, biologists, psychologists, sociologists and political scientists. Moreover, these theories – in particular the earlier variants – have tended to reflect the various concerns and professional interests of the discipline to which the theorist or theorists has belonged. For example, biologists sought explanations for criminality in terms of the physiology of the individual criminal, while psychologists directed our attention to the mind or personality of the person. Increasingly, explanations have come to incorporate elements from more than one discipline. Thus, for example, some biologists came to recognize that individuals with the same physiological profiles will behave differently depending on the circumstances of their socialization.

Most of the theories discussed in this book nevertheless share one common characteristic. They are all products of a time period – approximately the past two centuries – and a way of life that has come to be termed the modern age. As such, these different explanations of crime and criminal behaviour are themselves very much a reflection of the dominant ideas that have existed during this era. It is therefore a useful starting point to briefly consider how crime and criminal behaviour was explained and dealt with in the pre-modern period.

Pre-modern crime and criminal justice

Prior to the modern age, crime and criminal behaviour in Europe had been explained for over a thousand years by spiritualist notions (Vold *et al.*, 1998). The influential theologian St Thomas Aquinas (1225–74) had argued that there is a God-given 'natural law' that is revealed by observing – through the eyes of faith – the natural tendency of people to do good rather than evil. Those who violate the criminal law are therefore not only criminals but also 'sinners', and thus crime harms not only victims but also the offender because it damages their essential 'humanness' or natural tendency to do good (Bernard, 1983). Central to spiritualist thought was demonology, where it was proposed that criminals were possessed by demons that forced them to do wicked things beyond their control. These days, criminal activity is rarely attributed to the influence of devils from hell – well, at least not by criminologists and criminal justice system practitioners – but the logic underlying this idea that criminals are driven by forces beyond their control is still with us. What can arguably be regarded as a modified variant of this form of thought – but where the explanatory power of spirituality has been replaced by that of science – is the focus of the second part of this book.

Pre-modern European legal systems were founded on spiritualist explanations of crime, and what little written law that did exist was applied through judicial interpretation and caprice, and in the main to those who were not of the aristocracy. Because crime was identified with sin – and the criminal could therefore be considered to be possessed by demons – the state had the moral authority to use horrible tortures and punishments. Those accused of crime often faced secret accusations, torture and closed trials, with arbitrary and harsh sanctions applied to the convicted. The emphasis of punishment was moreover on the physical body of the accused, for the bulk of the population possessed little else on which the power to punish could be usefully exercised. Foucault provides an account of a public execution reserved for the greatest of all crimes under the French *ancien regime*, regicide:

> The flesh will be torn from the breasts, arms, thighs and calves with red-hot pincers, his right hand, holding the knife with which he committed the said parricide, burnt with sulphur, and, on those places where the flesh will be torn away, poured molten lead, boiling oil, burning resin, wax and sulphur melted together and then his body drawn and quartered by four horses and his limbs and body consumed by fire.
>
> (1977: 3)

Pre-modern punishment frequently involved torture, and in some jurisdictions the possibility of being tortured to death remained a penal option into the nineteenth century. Penal torture had not been used in England since the eighteenth century, except in exceptional cases for treason; Scotland, on the other hand, retained in legal theory, although certainly not in practice, hanging, drawing and quartering for treason until 1948.

Little use was made of imprisonment as a punishment in the pre-modern era. Prisons were most commonly places for holding suspects and offenders prior to trial or punishment, except in cases of debt when they were used to hold debtors until their financial affairs could be resolved. It would appear that those who framed and administrated the law enacted and exercised the criminal codes on the premise that it was only the threat of savage and cruel punishments, delivered in public and with theatrical emphasis, that would deter the dangerous materially dispossessed classes who constituted 'the mob'.

It seems that from the seventeenth to the early eighteenth century the English ruling class or aristocracy sought to protect their property interests through the exercise of the criminal law (Koestler and Rolph, 1961). Thus, a vast number of property crimes came to be punished by death in accordance with a body of legislation enacted during that period and which later came to be known as 'the bloody code'. Hanging was the standard form of execution and was the typical punishment for offences ranging from murder to stealing turnips, writing threatening letters or impersonating an outpatient of Greenwich Hospital (Radzinowicz, 1948). By 1800, there were more than 250 such capital offences and executions were usually carried out en masse (Lofland, 1973).

The full weight of the law was nevertheless not always applied. The rural aristocracy – who sat as judges and 'justices of the peace' – used their prerogative of clemency and leniency in order to demonstrate their power over the 'lower orders'. Hence, evidence of 'respectability' in the form of references from a benevolent landowner, confirmation of significant religious observance and piety, or the simple discretionary whim of a JP could lead to a lesser sentence. These alternatives included transportation to a colony, a nonfatal, if brutal, corporal punishment or even release (Thompson, 1975).

In short, the administration of criminal justice was chaotic, predominantly non-codified, irrational and irregular, and at the whim of individual judgement. It was the emergence and establishment of the modern era and the subsequent new ways of seeing and responding to the world that provided the preconditions for a major break in the way in which crime and criminal behaviour was both conceptualized and dealt with.

The rise of modern society

The idea of the modern originated as a description of the forms of thought and action that began to emerge with the decline of medieval society in Western Europe. The authority of the old aristocracies was being seriously questioned, both because of their claims to natural superiority and their corrupt political practices. A new and increasingly powerful middle class was benefiting from the profits of trade, industry and agricultural rationalization. In the interests of the latter, the enclosure movement dispossessed many of the rural poor from access to common lands and smallholding tenancies, causing great hardship to those involved, yet, at the same time, producing a readily available pool of cheap labour to satisfy the demands of the Industrial Revolution. The aggregate outcome of these fundamental social changes was that societies were becoming increasingly industrialized and urbanized, causing previous standard forms of human relationships based on familiarity, reputation and localism to give way to more fluid, often anonymous interactions, which significantly posed problems for existing forms of social control.

The notion of the modern essentially involved a secular rational tradition with the following origins. First, there was the emergence of humanist ideas and Protestantism in the sixteenth century. Previously, the common people had been encouraged by the established Church to unquestioningly accept their position in life and look for salvation in the afterlife. It was with the rise of the 'protestant ethic' that people came to expect success in return for hard work in this world. At the same time, assumptions about the natural superiority – or the divine right – of the powerful aristocracy came to be questioned. Second, there was the scientific revolution of the seventeenth century where our understanding of the world around us was first explained by reference to natural laws. Third, the eighteenth-century philosophical Enlightenment proposed that the social world could similarly be explained and regulated by natural laws and political systems should be developed that embraced new ideas of individual rationality and free will. Indeed, inspired by such ideas and responding to dramatically changing economic and political circumstances, revolutions occurred in the American colonies and in France. These were widely influential and ideas concerning human rights were championed in many European countries by the merchant, professional and middle classes. Subsequently, there were significant changes in the nature of systems of government, administration and law. Fourth, the increasingly evident power of industrial society and the prestige afforded to scientific explanation in the nineteenth and twentieth centuries seemed to confirm the superiority of the modernist intellectual tradition over all others (Harvey, 1989).

The principal features that characterize the idea of modern society can thus be identified in three main areas. First, in the area of economics, there was the development of a market economy involving the growth of production for profit, rather than immediate local use, the development of industrial technology with a considerable extension of the division of labour, and wage labour became the principal form of employment. Second, in the area of politics, there was the growth and consolidation of the centralized nation-state and the extension of bureaucratic forms of administration, systematic forms of surveillance and control, the development of representative democracy and political party systems. Third, in the area of culture, there was a challenge to tradition in the name of rationality with the emphasis on scientific and technical knowledge.

The modern world was consequently a very different place from its pre-modern predecessor. Not surprisingly, therefore, modern explanations of crime and criminal behaviour – and the nature of criminal justice interventions – were different from those that existed in pre-modern times. A word of caution should nevertheless be considered at this point. Contemporary criminologist David Garland notes similarities between traditional accounts of criminality – whether they were religious or otherwise – and those of the modern era:

> Stories of how the offender fell in with bad company, became lax in his habits and was sorely tried by temptation, was sickly, or tainted by bad

blood, or neglected by unloving parents, became too fond of drink or too idle to work, lost her reputation and found it hard to get employment, was driven by despair or poverty or simply driven to crime by avarice and lust – these seem to provide the well-worn templates from which our modern theories of crime are struck, even if we insist upon a more neutral language in which to tell the tale, and think that a story's plausibility should be borne out by evidence as well as intuition.

(1997: 22–3)

Garland notes that there were plenty of secular explanations of the roots of crime to place alongside the spiritual in pre-modern society. What was lacking was a developed sense of differential explanation. Crime was widely recognized as a universal temptation to which we are all susceptible, but, when it came to explaining why some of us succumb and others resist, explanations tended to drift off into the metaphysical and spiritual.

Furthermore, we should note that 'traditional' ways of explaining crime have not entirely disappeared with the triumph of modernity, though nowadays they may be accorded a different status in the hierarchy of credibility. Nevertheless, we continue to acknowledge the force of moral, religious and commonsensical ways of discussing crime.

Defining and the extent of crime

It will become increasingly apparent to the reader that developments in what has come to be termed criminological theorizing have tended to reflect the economic, political and cultural developments that have occurred in modern society. In fact, definitions of crime and thus criminality are also closely linked to such socio-political factors and how we view the nature of society.

Crime includes many different activities such as theft, fraud, robbery, corruption, assault, rape and murder. We might usefully ask what these disparate activities – and their even more disparate perpetrators – have in common. Some might simply define crime as 'the doing of wrong' and it is a commonly used approach related to notions of morality. Yet not all actions or activities that might be considered immoral are considered crimes. For example, poverty and social deprivation might be considered 'crimes against humanity' but are not usually seen to be crimes. Conversely, actions that are crimes, for example, parking on a yellow line or in some cases tax evasion, are not seen as immoral (Croall, 1998).

The simplest way of defining crime is that it is an act that contravenes the criminal law. This is nevertheless a problematic definition, for many people break the criminal law but are not considered to be 'criminals'. In English law, for example, some offences such as murder, theft or serious assaults are described as *mala in se* or wrong in themselves. These are often seen as 'real' crimes in contrast to acts that are *mala prohibita*, prohibited not because they are morally wrong but for the protection of the public (Lacey *et al.*, 1990). Thus, the criminal law is used to enforce regulations concerning public health or pollution not because they are morally wrong but because it is considered to be the most effective way of ensuring that regulations are enforced.

Legal definitions also change over time and vary across culture. Thus, for example, in some countries, the sale and consumption of alcohol is a crime, while, in others, the sale and consumption of opium, heroin or cannabis is perfectly legal. For some years, there have been arguments in Britain for the use of some soft drugs such as cannabis to be legalized, and in 2004 the latter was downgraded from Class B to Class C, which meant that the police could no longer automatically arrest those caught in possession, although it remained illegal (Crowther, 2007). The government subsequently reclassified cannabis from Class C to Class B in January 2009. They did this to reflect the fact that skunk, a much stronger version of the drug, now accounts for more than 80 per cent of cannabis available on our streets, compared to just 30 per cent in 2002 (Home Office, 2009). On the other hand, there has been a demand for other activities to be criminalized, and in recent years these have included 'stalking', racially motivated crime and knowingly passing on the Aids virus. The way that crime is defined is therefore a social construction and part of the political processes.

This construction can be exemplified by considering what is included and excluded. Thus, Mars (1982) observes that 'crime', 'theft' and 'offence' are 'hard' words that can be differentiated from 'softer' words such as 'fiddle' or 'perk' that are often used to describe and diminish criminal activities conducted in the workplace. In the same context, the terms 'creative accounting' or 'fiddling the books' do not sound quite as criminal as 'fraud'. Furthermore, incidents in which people are killed or injured in a train crash or as a result of using unsafe equipment are generally described as 'accidents' or 'disasters' rather than as 'crimes', albeit they often result from a failure of transport operators or managers to comply with safety regulations (Wells, 1993). Thus, different words denote different kinds of crime, with some activities being totally excluded from the social construction of crime (Croall, 1998).

Crime is usually associated with particular groups such as young men or the unemployed, some of whom become 'folk devils', and are identified with certain kinds of offences. This social construction of crime is reflected in media discussions and portrayals of what constitutes the 'crime problem'. Thus, for example, rising crime rates or policies are introduced to 'crack down' on crimes such as burglary or violent street crime rather than on environmental crimes such as pollution, corporate crimes or major frauds.

The vast majority of criminological research – and thus the explanations or theories of criminal behaviour that emanate from those studies and which are discussed in this book – has been conducted on those from the lower socio-economic groups and their activities. For it is concerns about this apparently 'dangerous class' that have dominated criminological thought since at least the beginning of modern society. The substitution of determinate prison sentences for those of capital punishment and transportation came to mean in reality the existence of a growing population of convicted criminals that frightened many in 'respectable society'. It is therefore perhaps not surprising that both the law and criminology have subsequently targeted this group.

The problem of 'white-collar', business or corporate crime has nevertheless been recognized since at least the beginning of the twentieth century, although it has continued to be neglected and under-researched by criminologists (Clinard and Yeager, 1980; Kramer, 1984; Croall, 1992, 2001). Moreover, there has also been a tendency for much of the research conducted in this area to be atheoretical with white-collar and corporate crime perceived as a phenomenon completely separate from the 'normal', that is, predatory 'street' crime. This criminological neglect does appear at first sight somewhat surprising.

It has been estimated that, for example, in the USA, the economic losses from various white-collar crimes are about ten times those from 'ordinary' economic crime (Conklin, 1977) with corporate crime killing and maiming more than any violence committed by the poor (Liazos, 1972). In the same country, 100,000 people have died each year from occupationally related diseases that have mostly been contracted as a result of wilful violation of laws designed to protect workers (Swartz, 1975), defective products have killed another 30,000 US citizens annually (Kramer, 1984), while US manufacturers have been observed to dump drugs and medical equipment in developing countries after they have been banned from the home market (Braithwaite, 1984). Croall (1992, 2001) observes that the activities of the corporate criminal are not only greater in impact than those of the ordinary offender, but they are also longer lasting in effect.

There has been a real problem in actually defining the concept of white-collar or corporate crime (Geis and Maier, 1977). Sutherland (1947) had proposed that 'white collar crime may be defined approximately as a crime committed by a person of respectability and high social status in the course of his occupation'. This is nevertheless a restricted definition. White-collar crime can occur when an individual commits crime against an organization within which they work or, for example, when a self-employed person evades income tax. Corporate crime, on the other hand, involves illegal acts carried out in the furtherance of the goals of an organization and is therefore a particular form of white-collar crime. Schraeger and Short propose that organizational crime should be defined as:

> illegal acts of omission of an individual or a group of individuals in a legitimate formal organisation in accordance with the operative goals of the organisation which have a serious physical or economic impact on employees, consumers or the general public.
>
> (1978: 409)

This is a definition that goes beyond that of economic impact and includes crimes of omission – failure to act – as well as those of commission. Others go further and include serious harms, which, though not proscribed, are in breach of human rights (Schwendinger and Schwendinger, 1970). In this book, we will consider how the various explanations – or theories – of criminal behaviour that have usually been developed and applied to the socio-economically less powerful can be – and have on occasion been – applied to these crimes of the powerful and the relatively powerful.

The purpose of criminological theory

Criminology students – and in reality students of other disciplines as well – are invariably overwhelmed by the word 'theory', which they seem to subconsciously associate with the esoteric or even the mythical and scary 'rocket science' with the outcome being an inherent resistance to the subject matter (Hopkins Burke, 2012). Theory nevertheless means nothing more than 'explanation' and is simply about how and, most importantly, 'why' we do some things and in the form that we do them.

While many students are intimidated with their very first encounter with theory, it is nevertheless used by all of us on an almost daily basis. You may be one who believes that theory is abstract and has no fundamental basis in the *real* world but, whether you realize it or not, you use theory almost all the time. We all make assumptions and generalizations about the world around us. We thus theorize.

Theories are logical constructions that explain natural phenomena. They are not in themselves always directly observable, but can be supported or refuted by empirical findings. Theory and empirical research are connected by means of hypotheses, which are testable propositions that are logically derived from theories. The testable part is very important because scientific hypotheses must be capable of being accepted or rejected.

Theories can be simple or complex; it depends on how relationships are made in formulating them. Theory can be fun, depending on how it is applied. If you spend the day in a shopping mall, you can see how much fun theory can be. So why do we study theory? The reality is that we need theory in order to function effectively, in order to better understand the world around us. Life would be pretty dull if we were unable to generalize or make assumptions about people and things, and, of course, most of our daily theories tend to be illogical and a product of our own selective observation. Thus, often we see what we want to see.

Human behaviour tends to be very complex, almost abstract. Criminological theories are also mostly complex. Most theories introduced and discussed in this book are derived from research, conducted both in the past and the present, on criminal behaviour, which reflects both systematic observation and very careful logic. Theories not only provide a framework for us to interpret the meanings of observed patterns but they help us to determine when these patterns are meaningful and when they are not.

The structure of the book

This book is divided into five parts. The first three parts consider a different model – or tradition – of explaining crime and criminal behaviour that has been developed during the modern era. Different explanations – or theories – can generally be located in terms of one of these models and these are here introduced chronologically in order of their emergence and development. It is shown how each later theory helped to revive, develop and/or rectify identified weaknesses in the ideas and prescriptions of their predecessors within that tradition.

A word of caution needs to be signposted at this juncture. Explanations of criminal behaviour have become increasingly complex as researchers have become aware that crime is a more complicated and perplexing matter than their criminological predecessors had previously recognized. Thus, some readers might consider that a particular theory introduced as being central to the development of a particular tradition might also be considered in terms of a different model. In such instances, attention is directed to that ambiguity. For, clearly, as each tradition has developed, there has been an increasing recognition by researchers of a need to address previously identified weaknesses internal to the model. The solution has invariably encompassed recognition of the at least partial strengths contained within alternative approaches. Hence, biologists have come increasingly to recognize the influence of environmental factors, while some psychologists have embraced the previously alien notion of individual choice. Some more recent theoretical initiatives are in fact impossible to locate in any one of the three models. In short, their proponents have consciously sought to cross model boundaries by developing integrated theoretical approaches. These developments provide the focus of the fourth part of the book. The fifth and final part of the book addresses a range of contemporary criminological issues, forms of deviance, criminality and the nature of the societal response, which do not fit easily in any one particular theoretical tradition but which are seen to arise during an age of moral uncertainty.

Part One introduces the rational actor model. Central to this tradition is the notion that people have free will and make the choice to commit crime in very much the same way as they choose to indulge in any other form of behaviour. It is a tradition with two central intellectual influences. First, social contract theories challenged the notion of the 'natural' political authority, which had previously been asserted by the aristocracy. Human beings were now viewed as freely choosing to enter into contracts with others to perform interpersonal or civic duties (Hobbes, 1968 originally 1651; Locke, 1970 originally 1686, 1975 originally 1689; Rousseau, 1964 originally 1762, 1978 originally 1775). Second, utilitarianism sought to assess the applicability of policies and legislation to promote the 'happiness' of those citizens affected by them (Bentham, 1970 originally 1789; Mill, 1963–84 originally 1859).

Chapter 2 considers the ideas of the Classical School that provides the central theoretical foundations of the rational actor tradition. From this perspective, it is argued that people are rational creatures who seek pleasure while avoiding pain, and, consequently, the level of punishment inflicted must outweigh any pleasure that might be derived from a criminal act in order to deter people from resorting to crime. It was nevertheless a model of criminal behaviour that was to go into steep decline for many years. The increasing recognition that children, 'idiots' and the insane do not enjoy the capacity of perfect rational decision-making seemed best explained by the predestined actor model of human behaviour – or positivism – that is the focus of the second part of this book. The Classical School has, however, had a major and enduring influence on the contemporary criminal justice process epitomized by notions of 'due process' (Packer, 1968) and 'just deserts' (Von Hirsch, 1976).

Chapter 3 considers the revival of the rational actor tradition, which arose with the rise of the political 'new right' (populist or neoconservatives) both in the USA and the UK during the 1970s. This emerging body of thought was highly critical of both the then orthodox predestined actor model with its prescriptions of treatment rather than punishment and the even more radical 'victimized' actor model (the focus of the third part of this book) with its proposals of forgiveness and non-intervention (Morgan, 1978; Dale, 1984; Scruton, 1980, 1985). These rational actor model revivalists argued that crime would be reduced if the costs of involvement were increased so that legal activities become comparatively more attractive (Wilson, 1975; Wilson and Herrnstein, 1985; Felson, 1998). The revival of conservative theories during the last decades of the twentieth century has involved two significant policy agendas, incapacitation and deterrence. Although incapacitation has made a comeback in forms such as the castration of sex offenders and the deterrence theme has manifested itself in a variety of approaches to crime prevention such as drug use prevention campaigns with tactics such as mandatory urine testing, the major policy agenda of the new conservative theorizing centres around the incarceration of larger numbers of offenders for longer periods with the outcome that the prison population of the USA more than doubled in the space of twenty years (Irwin and Austin, 1994).

Chapter 4 discusses those theories that have come to prominence with the revival of the rational actor tradition. First, modern deterrence theories have addressed the principles of certainty, severity and promptness in terms of the administration of criminal justice (Zimring and Hawkins, 1973; Gibbs, 1975; Wright, 1993). Second, contemporary rational choice theories have proposed that people make decisions to act based on the extent to which they expect that choice to maximize their profits or benefits and minimize the costs or losses. Hence, decisions to offend are based on expected effort and reward compared to the likelihood and severity of punishment and other costs of crime (Becker, 1968; Cornish and Clarke, 1986). Routine activities theorists have developed a more sophisticated variant of this argument to propose that the likelihood of a crime increases when there are one or more motivated persons present, a suitable target or potential victim available, and an absence of capable guardians to deter the offender (Cohen and Felson, 1979).

Part Two introduces the predestined actor model. Proponents of this perspective fundamentally reject the rational actor emphasis on free will and replace it with the doctrine of determinism. From this positivist standpoint, criminal behaviour is explained in terms of factors, either internal or external to the human being, that cause (or determine) people to act in ways over which they have little or no control. The individual is thus in some way predestined to be a criminal.

There are three basic formulations of the predestined actor model: biological, psychological and sociological. All three variants nevertheless incorporate the same fundamental assumptions, and, although each is discussed separately, it will become increasingly apparent to the reader that they are not mutually exclusive; for example, biologists came to embrace sociological factors, while at times it is often difficult to differentiate between biological and psychological explanations. Three factors were central to the emergence of the predestined actor model. First, there was the replacement of theology as the central explanation of the essence of humanity with science. In particular, the theory of evolution proposed that human beings were now subject to the same natural laws as all other animals (Darwin, 1871). Second, there was development of social evolutionism and the view that human beings develop as part of a process of interaction with the world they inhabit (Spencer, 1971 originally 1862–96). Third, there was the philosophical doctrine of positivism and the proposition that we may only obtain knowledge of human nature and society by using the methods of the natural sciences (Comte, 1976 originally 1830–42).

Chapter 5 considers biological variants of the predestined actor model and starts with an examination of the early theories of the 'Italian School' where the central focus is on the notion that the criminal is a physical type distinct from the non-criminal (Lombroso, 1875; Ferri, 1895; Garofalo, 1914). There follows consideration of increasingly sophisticated variants on that theme. First, there is an examination of those theories that consider criminal behaviour to be inherited in the same way as physical characteristics. Evidence to support that supposition has been obtained from three sources: studies of criminal families (Dugdale, 1877; Goddard, 1914; Goring, 1913), twins (Lange, 1930; Christiansen, 1968, 1974; Dalgard and Kringlen, 1976; Cloninger and Gottesman, 1987; Rowe and Rogers, 1989; Rowe, 1990) and adopted children (Hutchings and Mednick, 1977; Mednick et al., 1984). Second, consideration is given to those theories that link criminal behaviour to abnormalities in the genetic structure of the individual (Klinefelter et al., 1942; Price and Whatmore, 1967; Ellis, 1990; Jones, 1993) and, third, later versions of the body type thesis (Hooton, 1939; Sheldon, 1949; Glueck and Glueck, 1950; Gibbons, 1970; Cortes and Gatti, 1972). Fourth, neurological and brain injuries (Mark and Ervin, 1970; Mednick and Volavka, 1980; Volavka, 1987) and, fifth, different categories of biochemical explanation are examined (Schlapp and Smith 1928; Dalton, 1961, 1984; Rose et al., 1974; Keverne et al., 1982; Olwens, 1987; Schalling, 1987; Virkkunen, 1987; Ellis and Crontz, 1990; Baldwin, 1990; Fagan, 1990; Fishbein and Pease, 1990; Pihl and Peterson, 1993).

Biological explanations of criminality are in some circumstances still highly relevant in contemporary society. Thus, autism and Asperger's Syndrome are two of the five pervasive developmental disorders (PDD) relatively recently discovered that are more often referred to as autistic spectrum disorders and these can – but not always – predispose those with the condition to criminal behaviour (Wing, 1998; Frith, 2003; Rosaler, 2004). The use of alcohol has much closer links with crime and criminal behaviour than most other drugs and this is at least partially explained by the reality that alcohol is legal, readily available and in extremely common usage. Alcohol and young people have become closely linked in the contemporary UK with hazardous drinking now most prevalent in teenagers and young adults than in any other age groups (Saunders, 1984; Collins, 1988; Fagan, 1990; Ramsay, 1996; Walby and Allen, 2004; Ruparel, 2004; Jefferis et al., 2005). Drugs are chemicals and once taken alter the balance of the body and brain and this can clearly affect behaviour, but the way that this occurs varies according to the type and quantity taken. Cannabis and opiates such as heroin tend to reduce aggressive tendencies, while cocaine and its derivative crack are more closely associated with violence (Fishbein and Pease, 1990; Pihl and Peterson, 1993; Ruggiero and South, 1995).

Central to biological positivism is the perception that criminality arises from some physical disorder within the individual offender and it is proposed that treatment can cure them of an inclination to criminality. The policy implication is thus to treat the defect and protect society from the untreatable. The available treatments have included drugs, psychosurgery, plastic surgery, genetic counselling and eugenics for those deemed untreatable.

Chapter 6 considers psychological variants of the predestined actor model. These all have in common the proposition that there are patterns of reasoning and behaviour specific to offenders that remain constant regardless of the different environmental experiences of individuals. There is a criminal mind. Three different psychological perspectives are identified. First, the psychodynamic approach has its roots in the notion of psychosexual development and the idea of a number of complex stages of psychic development (Freud, 1920, 1927). This approach was later developed through latent delinquency theory, which proposed that the absence of an intimate attachment with parents could lead to later criminality (Aichhorn, 1925; Healy and Bronner, 1936). Maternal deprivation theory was to propose that a lack of a close mother–child relationship in the early years of life could lead to criminal behaviour (Bowlby, 1952). Other researchers have proposed that the nature of child-rearing practice is closely linked to later behavioural patterns (Glueck and Glueck, 1950; McCord et al., 1959; Bandura and Walters, 1959; Hoffman and Saltzstein, 1967), while other theories propose that much criminality is a product of 'broken families' (Burt, 1945; Mannheim, 1948; Wootton, 1959; West, 1969; Pitts, 1986; Kolvin et al., 1990; Farrington, 1992a). Second, behavioural learning theories have their origins in the notion that all behaviour is learned from an external stimulus (Skinner, 1938). Criminals thus develop abnormal, inadequate or specifically criminal personalities or personality traits that differentiate them from non-criminals. These theories – based on the concept of conditioned learning – propose that there are dimensions of personality that can be isolated and measured and thus criminal behaviour predicted (Eysenck, 1970, 1977; Smith and Smith, 1977; McEwan, 1983; McGurk and McDougall, 1981; Farrington, 1994). Antisocial personality disorder proposes that similar techniques can be used to detect individuals who are 'psychopaths' (Cleckley, 1976; Hare, 1980; Feldman, 1977; Hare and Jutari, 1986; Hollin, 1989) and predict future dangerousness (Kozol et al., 1972; Monahan, 1981; Loeber and Dishion, 1983; Holmes and De Burger, 1989; Omerod, 1996). Third, cognitive theories are explicitly critical of the determinist nature of the previous two psychological traditions (Tolman, 1959; Piaget, 1980; Skinner, 1981). Social learning theory thus proposes that behaviour is learned through watching what happens to other people and then making choices to behave in a particular way (Sutherland, 1947; Akers et al., 1979; Akers, 1985, 1992). In this way, psychology can be seen to have moved away from its roots in the predestined actor model to incorporate notions from the rational actor model.

Chapter 7 considers sociological variants of the predestined actor model. These provided a direct challenge to those variants of the tradition that had focused on the characteristics – whether biological or psychological – of the deviant individual. Thus, in contrast, crime is explained as being a product of the social environment, which provides cultural values and definitions that govern the behaviour of those who live within them. Deviant or criminal behaviour is said to occur when an individual – or a group of individuals – behave in accordance with definitions that conflict with those of the dominant culture. Moreover, such behaviour is transmitted to others – and later generations – by frequent contact with criminal traditions that have developed over time in disorganized areas of the city (Durkheim, 1933 originally 1893; Shaw and McKay, 1972 originally 1931). Later anomie or strain theories develop the positivist sociological tradition to propose that most members of society share a common value system that teaches us both the things we should strive for in life and the approved way in which we can achieve them. However, without reasonable access to the socially approved means, people will attempt to find some alternative way – including criminal behaviour – to resolve the pressure to achieve (Merton, 1938). Delinquent subculture theories develop that argument further by observing that lower-class values serve to create young male behaviours that are delinquent by middle-class standards but that are both normal and useful in lower-class life. Thus, crime committed by groups of young people – or gangs – that seriously victimizes the larger community is in part a by-product of efforts by lower-class youth to attain goals valued within their own subcultural social world (Cohen, 1955; Miller, 1958; Cloward and Ohlin, 1960; Spergel, 1964; Matza, 1964; Mays, 1954; Morris, 1957; Downes, 1966; Wilmott, 1966; Parker, 1974; Pryce, 1979). Later deviant subculture theorists – with clear theoretical foundations in the victimized actor model – propose that involvement in particular subcultures, whether these be 'mainstream' (Willis, 1977; Corrigan, 1979) or 'spectacular' (Hebdige, 1976, 1979; Brake, 1980, 1985), is determined by economic factors. Postmodern approaches develop that perspective but recognize an element of albeit limited and constrained choice for some young people (Hopkins Burke and Sunley, 1996, 1998).

Chapter 8 considers how proponents of the predestined actor model have considered female criminality. Lombroso and Ferrero (1885) provide a fundamentally biologically determinist account, and later studies in this tradition rely implicitly on their assumptions about the physiological and psychological nature of women (Thomas, 1907, 1923; Davis, 1961, originally 1937; Pollak, 1950). The Freudian perspective is fundamentally grounded in explicit biological assumptions about the nature of women encapsulated by his famous maxim that 'anatomy is destiny' (Lerner, 1998); while Kingsley Davis' (1961, originally 1937) influential structural functionalist study of prostitution is founded on crucial assumptions about the 'organic nature of man and woman'. Sociological theories tend to be explanations of male patterns of behaviour and appear to have at first sight little or no relevance for explaining female criminality (Leonard, 1983).

Part Three introduces the victimized actor model. This is a tradition that proposes – with increasingly radical variants – that the criminal is in some way the victim of an unjust and unequal society. Thus, it is the behaviour and activities of the poor and powerless sections of society that are targeted and criminalized, while the dubious activities of the rich and powerful are simply ignored or not even defined as criminal.

There are two factors central to the emergence of the victimized actor model. First, there emerged during the mid-twentieth century within the social sciences an influential critique of the predestined actor model of criminal behaviour. Symbolic interactionism (Mead, 1934), phenomenology (Schutz, 1962) and ethnomethodology (Garfinkel, 1967) all questioned the positivist insistence on identifying and analysing the compelling causes that drive individuals towards criminal behaviour, while at the same time being unable to describe the social world in a way that is meaningful to its participants. Positivists were observed to have a restricted notion of criminality that was based on a tendency to accept the conventional morality of rules and criminal laws as self-evident truths and where a particular action is defined as a crime because the state has decreed it to be so. Second, there developed a critique of the orthodox predestined actor model notion that society is fundamentally characterized by consensus. Pluralist conflict theorists proposed that society consists of numerous interest groups all involved in an essential struggle for resources and attention with other groups (Dahrendorf, 1958). More radical theories – informed by various interpretations of Marxist social and economic theory – view social conflict as having its roots in funda-mental discord between social classes struggling for control of material resources (Taylor et al., 1973).

Chapter 9 considers social reaction – or labelling – theories (Lemert, 1951; Kitsuse, 1962; Becker, 1963; Piliavin and Briar, 1964; Cicourel, 1968). These propose that no behaviour is inherently deviant or criminal, but only comes to be considered so when others confer this label upon the act. Thus, it is not the intrinsic nature of an act, but the nature of the social reaction that determines whether a 'crime' has taken place. Central to this perspective is the notion that being found out and stigmatized, as a consequence of rule-breaking conduct, may cause an individual to become committed to further deviance, often as part of a deviant subculture. The labelling perspective has also been applied at a group level, and the concept of 'deviancy amplification' suggests that the less tolerance there is of an initial act of group deviance, the more acts will be defined as deviant (Wilkins, 1964). This can lead to a media campaign that whips up a frenzy of popular societal indignation – or a 'moral panic' – about a particular activity that is seen to threaten the very fabric of civilization. For example, 'lager louts', 'football hooligans', 'new age travellers', 'ravers' and even 'dangerous dogs' have all been the subjects of moral panics in recent years. Once labelled as such, those engaged in the particular activity become ostracized and targeted as 'folk devils' by the criminal justice system reacting to popular pressure (Young, 1971; Cohen, 1973). Among the critics of these classic labelling theories are those who argue they do not go far enough. By concentrating their attention on the labelling powers of front-line agents of the state working in the criminal justice system, the capacity for powerful groups to make laws to their advantage and to the disadvantage of the poor and dispossessed is ignored.

In more recent years, the notions and concepts of labelling theories have been modified and developed with more attention devoted to the significant issue of informal labelling carried out by parents, peers and teachers, which, it is argued, has a greater effect on subsequent criminal behaviour than official labelling (Matsueda, 1992; Heimer and Matsueda, 1994). Some have observed a significant shift to have occurred around 1974 with labelling theorists retreating from their underdog focus, moving away from the study of 'nuts, sluts, and perverts' (Liazos, 1972) and coming to accommodate legalistic definitions and focus on state power. Others, more recently, have suggested that the criminal justice system and the public are increasing the stigmatization of – particularly young – offenders and thus heightening the most negative effects of labelling (De Haan, 2000; Triplett, 2000; Meossi, 2000; Halpern, 2001).

Chapter 10 considers conflict and radical theories. For both sets of theorists, laws are formulated to express the values and interests of the most powerful groups in society, while at the same time placing restrictions on the behaviour and activities common to the less powerful, thus disproportionately 'criminalizing' the members of these groups. The more radical variants propose that it is the very conditions generated by the capitalist political economy that generate crime (Vold, 1958; Turk, 1969; Quinney, 1970; Chambliss, 1975). These latter ideas were further developed in the UK in the late 1960s and early 1970s by the 'new criminology' that sought an explanation of criminal behaviour based on a theoretical synthesis of Marxism and labelling perspectives (Taylor et al., 1973; Hall et al., 1978).

Criticisms of radical criminology have originated from three primary sources. First, traditional Marxists have questioned the manipulation of this theoretical tradition to address the issue of crime (Hirst, 1980). Second, there was the important recognition by the populist conservatives – or right realists – that most predatory crime is committed by members of the poorer sections of society against their own kind which changed the whole nature of political debate on the crime problem. Third, there was the increasing recognition of this latter reality by sections of the political left and the consequent development of a populist socialist response that is the focus of the final chapter of the fourth part of this book.

Peacemaking criminology takes these issues further and reflects the position of many marginalized groups in society who realize that they are incapable of overcoming political opposition and have to reach an accommodation in a fundamentally unequal society (Pepinsky and Quinney, 1991). The general argument presented is that the whole of the US criminal justice system is based on the continuance of violence and oppression (as seen in the prison system), war (as seen in the 'war on crime' and the 'war on drugs') and the failure to account for how the larger social system contributes to the problem of crime (as seen in the failure to reduce poverty in society) (Fuller, 2003; Young, 2011). Peacemaking criminology, perhaps not surprisingly, has been the recipient of significant and often vitriolic criticism, having been viewed as 'utopian', 'soft on crime', 'unrealistic' and 'just not feasible' (Akers, 1997, 2000).

Chapter 11 considers the gendered criminal. Feminists propose that it is men who are the dominant group in society and it is privileged males who make and enforce the rules to the detriment of women. Feminism is nevertheless not a unitary body of thought and this chapter thus commences with a brief introduction to the different contemporary manifestations of feminism. There follows a feminist critique of the predestined actor model explanations of female criminality (Smart, 1977; Heidensohn, 1985) and an examination of the impact of feminist critiques in four critical areas: the female emancipation leads to crime debate (Adler, 1975; Simon, 1975), the invalidation of the leniency hypothesis (Pollak, 1950), the emergence of gender-based theories (Heidensohn, 1985) and the recognition and redefinition of previously non-problematic activities such as domestic violence and intrafamilial child molestation as serious crimes that need to be taken seriously (Hanmer and Saunders, 1984; Dobash and Dobash, 1992). The chapter concludes with an examination of the notion of masculinity that feminism has encouraged a small but growing group of male writers to 'take seriously' (Connell 1987, 1995; Messerschmidt, 1993; Jefferson, 1997).

Chapter 12 considers critical criminology, which is one of two contemporary variants of the radical tradition in criminology. There are a number of different versions but in general critical criminologists define crime in terms of oppression where it is members of the working class, women and ethnic minority groups who are the most likely to suffer the weight of oppressive social relations based upon class division, sexism and racism (Cohen, 1980; Box, 1983; Scraton, 1985; Sim *et al.*, 1987; Scraton and Chadwick, 1996 originally 1992). The contemporary notion of relative deprivation has been developed – with its roots in anomie theory – and its proposition that crime is committed by members of the poorer sections of society who are excluded from the material good things in life enjoyed by those with economic advantage. They have also importantly drawn our attention to the crimes of the powerful that – as we observed above – have been inadequately addressed by traditional explanations of crime and criminal behaviour.

Critical criminologists have nevertheless been criticized by the other contemporary wing of the radical tradition – the populist socialists or 'left realists' – who consider them to be 'left idealists' with romantic notions of criminals as revolutionaries or latter-day 'Robin Hoods' stealing from the rich to give to the poor, while failing adequately to address the reality that much crime is committed by the poor on their own kind. Critical criminologists have nonetheless widened the horizons of the discipline to embrace the study of zemiology or those social harms that are often far more damaging to society than those restricted activities that have been defined as criminal (Schwendinger and Schwendinger, 1970; Shearing, 1989; Tifft, 1995). Critical race theory addresses the construction of racialized justice as a social and discursive process in the USA. Since its emergence twenty years ago, it has grown in significance to provide a major challenge to the operation of social control agencies that produce and maintain conditions of racial injustice (Bell, 2004; Coyle, 2010).

Part Four introduces various attempts at integrating different theories both within one of the theoretical traditions outlined in the first three parts of this book and across model boundaries. It observes that there are three ways in which theories can be developed and evaluated. First, each theory can be considered on its own. Second, there can be a process of theory competition where there is a logical and comprehensive examination of two different perspectives and a consideration of which one most successfully fits the data at hand (Liska, 1987). The third way is by theoretical integration where the intention is to identify commonalities in two or more theories in order to produce a synthesis that is superior to any one individual theory (Farnsworth, 1989). Hirschi (1989) nevertheless cautions that what passes for theoretical integration in criminology invariably involves ignoring crucial differences between the theories undergoing integration and observes that some examples are merely oppositional theories – from the victimized actor model tradition – in disguise.

Chapter 13 considers those sociobiological theories that have attempted a synthesis of biological and sociological explanations. Biosocial theorists argue that the biological characteristics of an individual are only part of the explanation of criminal behaviour and, thus, factors in the physical and social environment of the offender are also influential. It is proposed that all individuals must learn to control natural urges towards antisocial and criminal behaviour (Mednick, 1977; Mednick *et al.*, 1987). Environmentally influenced behaviour explanations address those incidents where outside stimuli such as drug and alcohol use has instigated or enhanced a propensity towards certain forms of behaviour (Fishbein and Pease, 1996).

The sociobiological perspective has been developed by the 'right realist' criminological theorists Wilson and Herrnstein (1985), who have developed a theory combining gender, age, intelligence, body type and personality factors and have considered these in the context of the wider social environment of the offender. They propose that the interplay between these factors provides an explanation of why it is that crime rates have increased in periods of both economic boom and recession, observing that the relationship between the environment and the individual is a complex one. Among the most contentious sociobiological criminological theories to emerge in recent years have been those that propose that rape has evolved as a genetically advantageous behavioural adaptation (Thornhill and Palmer, 2000). Moreover, there has been significant recent interest by sociobiologists in the USA in antisocial behaviour that is seen to emerge early in childhood, persists into adulthood and that is difficult or even impossible to rehabilitate (Aguilar *et al.*, 2000).

Chapter 14 discusses environmental theories, which are part of a long-established tradition with their foundations firmly located in the sociological version of the predestined actor model. Later British area studies were to incorporate notions from the victimized actor model, primarily a consideration of the effects of labelling individuals and groups of residents as different or bad (Damer, 1974; Gill, 1977). Later North American studies sought to incorporate the discipline of geography to provide a more sophisticated analysis of the distribution of crime and criminals (Brantingham and Brantingham, 1981). However, this was not to be simply a geographical determinist account. For, in adopting the recognition that crime happens when the four elements of a law, an offender, a target and a place concur, the perspective is brought into contact with those contemporary opportunity theories that characterize recent developments within the rational actor model (Cohen and Felson, 1979). Environmental management theories certainly presuppose the existence of a rational calculating individual whose activities can be restricted or curtailed by changing his or her surroundings (Wilson and Kelling, 1982).

Chapter 15 examines social control theories, which again have a long and distinguished pedigree with their origins in both the rational actor and predestined actor models (Hobbes, 1968 originally 1651; Durkheim, 1951 originally

1897; Freud, 1927), with both social and psychological factors employed in order to explain conformity and deviance. Early social theory had proposed that inadequate forms of social control were more likely during periods of rapid modernization and social change because new forms of regulation could not evolve quickly enough to replace declining forms of social integration (Durkheim, 1951 originally 1897). Early social control theorists – such as the Chicago School – had taken this argument further and proposed that social disorganization causes a weakening of social control, making crime and deviance more possible. Other control theorists nevertheless attached more importance to psychological factors in their analysis of deviance and conformity (Nye, 1958; Matza, 1964; Reckless, 1967). Later control theories are based on the fundamental assumption that criminal acts take place when an individual has weakened or broken bonds with society (Hirschi, 1969).

In an attempt to remedy identified defects in control theory, different writers have sought to integrate control theory with other perspectives. First, a model expanding and synthesizing strain, social learning and control theories begins with the assumption that individuals have different early socialization experiences and that these lead to variable degrees of commitment to – and integration into – the conventional social order (Elliott *et al.*, 1979). Second, an integration of control theory with a labelling/conflict perspective – from the victimized actor tradition – seeks to show how 'primary' deviants become 'secondary' deviants. This, it is argued, is an outcome of the selective targeting of the most disadvantaged groups in society – by the criminal justice system – acting in the interests of powerful groups (Box, 1981, 1987). Third, a further highly influential approach builds upon and integrates elements of control, labelling, anomie and subcultural theory and proposes that criminal subcultures provide emotional support for those who have been stigmatized and rejected by conventional society (Braithwaite, 1989).

Gottfredson and Hirschi (1990) subsequently sought to produce a 'general theory of crime' that combines rational actor notions of crime with a predestined actor model – control – theory of criminality. In accordance with the rational actor tradition, crime is defined as acts of force or fraud undertaken in pursuit of self-interest, but it is the predestined actor notion of – or lack of – social control that provides the answer as to exactly who will make the choice to offend when appropriate circumstances arise.

More recent developments in the social control theory tradition have been power control theory, which has sought to combine social class and control theories in order to explain the effects of familial control on gender differences in criminality (Hagan *et al.*, 1985, 1987, 1990; Hagan, 1989); control balance theories that define deviancy as simply any activity that the majority find unacceptable and/or disapprove of and that occurs when a person has either a surplus or deficit of control in relation to others (Tittle, 1995, 1997, 1999, 2000); and differential coercion theory which seeks to extend our existing understanding of the coercion–crime relationship (Colvin, 2000).

Chapter 16 introduces situational action theory, which is a recently developed general theory of moral action and crime that aims to integrate person and environmental explanatory perspectives and is based on five key propositions

(Wikström, 2005). First, acts of crime are moral actions. Second, people engage in acts of crime because they see them as a viable action alternative. Third, the likelihood that a person will consider an act of crime a valid action alternative depends on their crime propensity. Fourth, the role of broader social conditions should be analysed as the wider causes of criminal involvement. Fifth, the relevant causes of crime are only those social conditions and aspects of life-histories that directly influence the development of the individual propensity to criminality. Situational action theory provides a sophisticated basis for discovering who is likely to offend and under what circumstances, and in doing so considers key predestined actor model motivational issues long neglected by rational choice theorists (Wikström, 2005, 2006, 2009; Wikström and Sampson, 2003; Wikström and Treiber, 2007, 2009; Wikström *et al.* 2011).

Chapter 17 introduces desistance theories, which address the psychosocial processes involved in 'going straight' or what it is that enables or helps offenders to desist from committing crime. Maruna (1997) observes that few phenomena in criminology have been as widely acknowledged and as poorly understood as why people desist from committing crime. It is observed that, for most individuals, participation in 'street crimes' generally begins in the early teenage years, peaks in late adolescence or young adulthood and ends before the person reaches 30 or 40 years of age. Moreover, at some stage in their life course, usually between 18 and 35 years of age, even serious offenders tend to cease criminal behaviour. Age is clearly a very strong correlate of desistance but criminologists have generally failed to 'unpack' the 'meaning' of age (Sampson and Laub, 1992). Maruna (1997) asserts that what seems to be missing from both the previously orthodox ontogenetic and sociogenic approaches to desistance is 'the person' or the wholeness and subjective agency of the individual. Thus, we find the use of personal autobiographies in social enquiry, occasionally referred to as 'narrative' (Maruna, 2001; Maruna and Immarigeon, 2004).

Chapter 18 concludes the fourth part of the book with a consideration of 'left realism', which is a perspective that arose as a direct response to two closely related factors. First, a reaction among some key radical criminologists on the political left to the perceived idealism of critical criminology and its inherent apology for criminals; and, second, the rise of the populist conservatives and their 'realist' approach to dealing with crime. Thus, 'left realists' came to acknowledge that crime is a real problem that seriously impinges on the quality of life of many poor people and must therefore be addressed. From this perspective, a comprehensive solution to the crime problem – a 'balance of intervention' – is proposed (Young, 1994). On the one hand, crime must be tackled and criminals must take responsibility for their actions; on the other hand, the social conditions that encourage crime must also be tackled.

Left realism is not really an integrated theory of crime but rather an approach that recognizes that there is something to be said for most theories of crime and for most forms of crime prevention with the distinct suggestion that insights can be incorporated from each of the three models of crime and criminal behaviour introduced in this book. It is a strategy that was very influential with the 'New' Labour Government elected in the UK in 1997, which was demonstrated by the oft-quoted remark of Prime Minister Tony Blair first made while he was previously the Shadow Home Secretary: 'tough on crime, tough on the causes of crime'.

The chapter includes a case study that considers the issue of social exclusion, criminality and the 'underclass' from different theoretical standpoints introduced in the book. First, the behavioural perspective – normally associated with the populist or neoconservatives – argues that state welfare erodes individual responsibility by giving people incentives not to work and provide for themselves and their family. Moreover, it is observed that those 'controls' that stop individuals and communities from behaving badly – such as stable family backgrounds and in particular positive male role models – have ceased to exist for many members of this identified 'underclass' (Murray, 1990, 1994). Second, structural explanations – normally associated with sociological variants of the predestined actor model, critical criminologists and left idealists – observe the collapse of the manufacturing industry, traditional working-class employment and the subsequent retreat of welfare provision in modernist societies as providing the structural preconditions for the creation of a socially excluded class (Dahrendorf, 1985; Campbell, 1993; Jordan, 1996; Crowther, 1998). Third, a process model – which has a resonance with left realism – suggests that we identify and address the structural preconditions for the emergence of a socially excluded underclass, while at the same time considering and responding to the behavioural subcultural strategies developed by those finding themselves located in that socio-economic position (Hopkins Burke, 1999a).

Developments in 'left realist' theory are introduced to demonstrate the validity and value of the approach in an historical context and its significant contribution to theorizing the development of the criminal justice system. Hopkins Burke (2012, 2013) has thus adapted and adopted left realist theory in an historical context as a significant component of his criminal justice theory, which seeks to explain the development of the criminal justice system in modern societies and in whose interest this has all happened.

Part Five considers the implications for explaining crime and criminal behaviour posed by the fragmentation of the modernity that had provided the socio-economic context for the theories we encounter in the first four parts of this book. The outcome of that fragmentation has been a new socio-economic context that has been termed the postmodern condition by some social scientists (Lyotard, 1984; Baudrillard, 1988; Bauman, 1989, 1991, 1993) where there is recognition of the complexity of contemporary society, the moral ambiguities and uncertainties that are inherent within it, and where it is proposed that there are a range of different discourses that can be legitimate and hence right for different people, at different times, in different contexts.

Chapter 19 considers the morally ambiguous nature of crime and criminal behaviour in the postmodern condition. It is observed that the essential problem for the development of legislation and legitimate explanations of criminality in this fragmented social formation and era of moral uncertainty is the difficulty of making any objective claims for truth, goodness and morality. The only well-developed attempt to rethink the central issues and themes of criminology in terms of postmodern theories is the constitutive criminology originally developed by Henry and Milovanovic (1996, 1999, 2000, 2001) and in which two main theoretical inputs can be identified: the post-Freudian Jacques Lacan and chaos theory. Henry and Milovanovic (1996) define crime as the power to deny others and they argue that conventional crime control strategies actually encourage criminality rather than discourage it. They seek the development of 'replacement discourses', which encourage positive social constructions and challenge the omnipresence of power (Henry and Milovanovic, 1996).

The chapter concludes with a consideration of anarchist criminology, which, unlike most modernist intellectual orientations, does not seek to incorporate reasoned or reasonable critiques of law and legal authority but, in contrast, argues that progressive social change requires the pursuit of the 'unreasonable' and the 'unthinkable' (Ferrell, 1998). Anarchist criminologists thus launch aggressive and 'unreasonable' critiques against a law and legal authority which they observe undermines human community and constrains human diversity (Mazor, 1978; Ferrell, 1996, 1998).

Chapter 20 considers cultural criminology and the schizophrenia of crime. The former seeks to explain crime and criminal behaviour and its control in terms of culture, and it is argued that the various agencies and institutions of crime control are cultural products that can only be understood in terms of the phenomenological meanings they carry (Presdee, 2004). Cultural criminology thus uses everyday existences, life histories, music, dance and performance in order to discover how and why it is that certain cultural forms become criminalized (O'Malley and Mugford, 1994; Ferrell and Sanders, 1995; Ferrell, 1999), while Katz (1988) writes about the 'seductions of crime' in which disorder becomes in itself a 'delight' to be sought after and savoured and argues that the causes of crime are constructed by the offenders themselves in ways that are compellingly seductive. Presdee (2000) develops this sense of the interrelationship between pleasure and pain with his notion of 'crime as carnival', where he argues that the latter is a site where the pleasures of playing at the boundaries of illegality are temporarily legitimated at the time of carnival.

Hopkins Burke (2007) uses the term 'the schizophrenia of crime' to refer to the apparently contradictory contemporary duality of attitude to criminal behaviour where there is both a widespread public demand for a rigorous intervention against criminality, while, at the same time, criminality is seen to be widespread to the virtual point of universality with most people having committed criminal offences at some stage in their life. It is observed that, in a world where crime has become 'normal and non-pathological' (Garland, 1996), the boundaries between criminals and non-criminals – and legal and illegal activities – have become increasingly difficult to disentangle (Young, 1999, 2001), while, at the same time, the classic crime control strategies of modernity have become more problematic not least with the increasing globalization of deviance.

The chapter then considers the globalization of deviant youth subcultures in the guise of a significant fast-growing club culture (Carrington and Wilson, 2002), which has clear identifiable roots in the notions of the postmodern condition, the carnival of crime and beyond. The chapter concludes with a discussion of crime and the mass media. It is recognized that there are essentially two kinds of media coverage and/or representation of crime: first, the more frequent inclusion of some type of felony or street crime often involving an act of violence; and, second, the less common insertion of white-collar offences, involving some type of public or private trust violation that usually concentrates its focus on individuals and their victims in contrast to societal institutions or social organizations and their victims (Barak, 2012). Steve Chibnall (1977) and Yvonne Jewkes (2004) have mapped out the news values that not only shape the reporting of crime but that also help to locate these within the larger practices of journalism. Thus, at the end of the newsmaking day, the mediated construction of crime and justice becomes the socially constructed reality when, in reality, this is the socially constructed subjective reality (Surette, 2007). Hayward and Young (2012) respond to the frequent criticism that cultural criminology has little potential for crime policy by observing that it is an appreciative approach that totally eschews 'correctionalism'.

Chapter 21 considers further the relationship between crime and the increasing globalization of crime in the context of what has come to be termed 'the risk society' (Beck, 1992). The chapter commences by considering new modes of governance, which in criminology is a concept that has been used to signify changes in the control of crime. It is observed that for most of the twentieth century crime control was dominated by the 'treatment model' prescribed by the predestined actor model of crime and criminal behaviour and closely aligned to the benevolent state, which was obliged to intervene in the lives of offenders and seek to diagnose and cure their criminal behaviour. It was the apparent failure of that interventionist modernist project epitomized by chronically high crime rates and the seeming inability of the criminal justice system to do anything about it that was to lead to a rediscovery of the rational actor model and an increased emphasis on preventive responses (Crawford, 1997; Garland, 2001). Feeley and Simon (1994) propose that these changes are part of a paradigm shift in the criminal justice process from the 'old penology' to a 'new penology', which is concerned with developing techniques for the identification, classification and management of groups and categorizing them in accordance with the levels of risk they pose to society. Some consider these trends to be indicative of a broader transition in the structural formation from an industrial society towards a risk society (Beck, 1992), and Ericson and Haggerty (1997) observe that in this context we are witnessing a transformation of legal forms and policing strategies characterized by surveillance. The risk society thesis is – like the postmodern thesis – far from universally accepted by academics, with some recognizing the survival of significant aspects of penal welfarism – penal modernism (Garland, 1996, 2001) – and rejecting the whole notion that we have seen a significant penological break with the modernist past. With the huge expansion in prison populations during the past thirty years, it has become increasingly apparent to many penologists and sociologists that the state has taken 'a punitive turn' away from penal welfarism, but other academics propose that recent developments in social control are largely benevolent or benign (O'Malley, 1999; Matthews, 2005; Penna and Yar, 2003; Meyer and O'Malley, 2005; Hannah-Moffat 2005; Van Swaaningen, 2007; Hallsworth and Lea, 2008).

The chapter further considers the issue of the globalization of crime and criminality and it is observed that dealing in illicit drugs, illegal trafficking in weapons and human beings, money laundering, corruption, violent crimes, including terrorism, and war crimes are characteristic of such developments (Braithwaite, 1979; UNDP, 1999; Bequai, 2002; Eduardo, 2002). The growing influence of global organized crime is estimated to gross $1.5 trillion a year and has provided a significant rival to multinational corporations as an economic power (UNDP, 1999). Findlay (2000) explains the global explosion in criminality in terms of the market conditions that he observes to be the outcome of the internationalization of capital, the generalization of consumerism and the unification of economies that are in a state of imbalance. He proposes that power and domination are simply criminogenic. A United Nations Office on Drugs and Crime (UNODC) (2013) audit of globalized criminality showed that the global crime trends identified previously are still very much in existence with new profitable crimes emerging all the time. Transnational organized crime continues to be big business.

The chapter then considers the Southern theory devised by the Australian academic Raewyn Connell[1] (2007), who has challenged the intellectual domination of social theory – and by implication criminological theory – by those in the metropoles of Europe and North America. She argues that this has entailed a view of the world from the skewed, minority perspective of the educated and the affluent, whose views are then perpetuated globally in educational curricula. The South merely appears in such global theories primarily as a source of data for Northern theorists.

Globalization has greatly facilitated the growth of international terrorism, with the development of international civil aviation having made hijacking possible, television and the Internet have given terrorists worldwide publicity and modern technology has provided an amazing range of weapons and explosives (Eduardo, 2002). The chapter thus concludes with an extensive discussion of terrorism and state violence and observes that the widespread development of terrorist activities throughout the world during the past fifteen years has signified the end of any positive notion of postmodernism. For such societies can only function effectively if there is a reciprocal acceptance of diverse values from all participant groups.

It is observed that most of the major theories that seek to explain terrorism are derived from theories of collective violence developed in the field of political science. Hoffman (1993) notes that about a quarter of all terrorist groups and about half of the most dangerous ones are primarily motivated by religious concerns, believing that God demands action. However, religious terrorism is not about extremism, fanaticism, sects or cults, but about a fundamentalist or militant interpretation of the basic tenets of the religion. Crenshaw (1998) argues that terrorism is not a pathological phenomenon and the focus of study should be on why it is that some groups find terrorism useful and other groups do not. Nassar (2004) argues that the processes of globalization contribute to dreams, fantasies and rising expectations, which leads to dashed hopes, broken dreams and unfulfilled achievements. Terrorism breeds in the gap between expectations and achievements.

Chapter 22 presents the case for radical moral communitarian criminology. While it is recognized that recent terrorist atrocities have ended any legitimate notion of a postmodern society, it is also observed that there is no justifiable basis for a return to the unquestioned moral certainty of high modernity. It is the work of Emile Durkheim (1933) and his observations on the moral component of the division of labour in society that provides the theoretical foundations of a 'new' liberalism – or radical moral communitarianism – that provides a legitimate political vision that actively promotes the rights and responsibilities of both individuals and communities in the context of an equal division of labour. The latter is a highly significant element that deviates significantly from the orthodox version of communitarianism promoted by Amitai Etzioni (1993, 1995a, 1995b) and that was embraced and distorted in the UK by New Labour with its enthusiasm for a strong dictatorial central state apparatus with which to enforce its agenda. Radical moral communitarianism proposed that policies should be introduced that recognize that people and communities have both rights and responsibilities and acknowledge the fine balance between them (Hopkins Burke, 2003).

Chapter 23 commences with a consideration of four different models of criminal justice development. First, the orthodox social progress model is the standard non-critical explanation that considers the development of law and the criminal justice system to be predominantly non-contentious with institutions operating neutrally in the interests of all. Second, proponents of the radical conflict model argue that society is inherently conflict-ridden and the new control system served more than adequately the requirements of the emerging capitalist order for the continued repression of recalcitrant members of the working class (Cohen, 1985). Third, proponents of the carceral society model do not totally disregard the arguments presented by either the proponents of the orthodox social progress model or the radical conflict model, but consider the situation to be far more complex. From this Foucauldian perspective, strategies of power are pervasive throughout society with the state only one location of the points of control and resistance. Power and knowledge are inseparable. Humanism, good intentions, professional knowledge and the rhetoric of reform are neither, in the idealist sense, the producers of change nor, in the materialist sense, the mere product of changes in the political economy (Foucault, 1977, 1980). Fourth, the left realist hybrid model provides a synthesis of the orthodox social progress, radical conflict and carceral surveillance society models but with the added recognition of our interest and collusion in the creation of the increasingly pervasive socio-control matrix of the carceral society.

The chapter then considers the work of Loïc Wacquant (2009a), who identifies a new 'government of social insecurity' targeted at shaping the conduct of the men and women caught up in the turbulence of economic deregulation in advanced societies. Crucial to this disciplinary-tutelage agenda in the USA has been the need to control an increasingly economically excluded but enduringly problematic and potentially dangerous black population (Wacquant, 1998a, 1998b, 2001). Wacquant (2009a) argues that workfare and prisonfare are simply two sides of the same coin in the contemporary USA and this double regulation of poverty – through workfare and prisonfare – has been exported to Europe. It is observed that many black people in the UK are the targets of tutelage and discipline strategies, but as part of a socially excluded underclass that incorporates people from all ethnic groups but which, at the same time, is invidious and pervasive. It has become increasingly apparent that the socio-control matrix of the carceral society continues to incrementally expand in close parallel with increasingly insurmountable economic pressures (Hopkins Burke, 2012, 2013).

Chapter 24 concludes the book and considers criminology in an age of austerity. The chapter commences with some reflections on the difference between the socio-economic conditions at the time the first edition was published and subsequent developments. It is observed that, at the time of writing, two influential think tanks have warned that austerity measures in the UK could still be in place when the 2020 election takes place in seven years' time. This is the future socio-economic context in which academic and professional (applied) criminology will operate. The criminological theories introduced and discussed in this book are then briefly reviewed before we proceed to consider the future of criminology in an age of austerity. We follow Fichtelberg and Kupchik (2011), who observe a recent debate among criminological scholars who have engaged with the idea of 'public criminology' (Chancer and McLaughlin, 2007; Garland and Sparks, 2000; Zahn, 1999) where the focus has been on the growing disjunction between criminological knowledge and criminal justice policy. The authors observe that there are numerous models for understanding how social scientists and their findings interact with broader society and briefly outline and critique two of these broad inclusive models before contrasting them with their notion of democratic criminology. First, the technocratic model posits that the social scientist is the expert whose knowledge should be used without wider societal critique or debate in order to formulate criminal justice policy. They can thus advise policymakers and help them to construct effective criminal justice policies based not on ideology or opinion, but instead rooted in scientific research. Second, the genealogical approach swings to the extreme opposite from the technocratic model. Rather than seeing the views of the criminologist as those of a trained expert who rationally and scientifically guides policy formation, for the genealogist, the contributions of the social scientist themselves, along with criminal justice policy, are a subject of analysis. Fichtelberg and Kupchik (2011) then provide us with a third approach, 'democratic criminology', which involves an exchange of ideas between the criminologist and the public, in which public concern helps direct criminological research while the latter influences public opinion and policy.

The chapter concludes with a few closing thoughts and recognizes the connections and accord between moral communitarianism and democratic criminology and proposes that a legitimate role for the progressive criminologist in the age of – protracted – austerity is in challenging policies that help to reinforce the disciplinary-control-matrix, particularly when these are being promoted by moral entrepreneurs who have little or no understanding of how their humble policy or strategy contributes to the overall surveillance schema.

Summary of main points

1. This is a book about the different ways in which crime and criminal behaviour have been explained in predominantly modern times.

2. There have been different explanations – or theories – proposed by, among others, legal philosophers, biologists, psychologists, sociologists and political scientists.
3. The simplest way of defining crime is that it is an act that contravenes the criminal law, but this definition is problematic: many people break the criminal law but are not considered to be 'criminals'.
4. Legal definitions change over time and vary across culture. They are a social construction and part of the political processes.
5. Crime is usually associated with particular groups, such as young men or the unemployed, who become identified with certain kinds of offences.
6. This social construction of crime is reflected in media discussions and portrayals of what constitutes the 'crime problem' and policies are introduced to 'crack down' on these crimes.
7. The problem of 'white-collar', business or corporate crime has continued to be neglected and under-researched by criminologists.
8. Criminology students are often overwhelmed by the word 'theory' but it means nothing more than 'explanation' and about how and 'why' we do some things and in the form that we do them.
9. Theories are logical constructions that explain natural phenomena. They can be simple or complex.
10. Theories provide a framework for us to interpret the meanings of observed patterns and help us to determine when these are meaningful and when they are not.

Discussion questions

1. How was crime explained in pre-modern times?
2. How did society respond to criminality in pre-modern times?
3. Discuss the issues involved in defining crime and criminal behaviour.
4. Why is criminological theory important?
5. Who are the 'usual suspects' when targeting crime and why is this problematic?

Suggested further reading

For some contrasting accounts from very different perspectives of pre-modern criminal justice and attempts to explain the causes of crime, see Foucault (1977), Hay (1981) and Thompson (1975). Garland (1997) provides something of a pragmatic antidote to those who seek to identify distinct ruptures between pre-modern and modern thinking. For an introduction to the notion of modern society and modernity, albeit in the context of his discussion of postmodernity, see Harvey (1989). Croall (1998) provides an excellent introduction to the different forms of crime in existence and the extent of criminality with a particular emphasis on business and corporate crime that is still highly relevant today.

Pontell and Geis are editors of the excellent *International Handbook of White-collar and Corporate Crime*.

Note

1 Raewyn Connell is a transsexual who was formerly Bob Connell.

Part One

The rational actor model of crime and criminal behaviour

The average citizen hardly needs to be persuaded of the view that crime will be more frequently committed if, other things being equal, crime becomes more profitable compared to other ways of spending one's time. Accordingly, the average citizen thinks it obvious that one major reason why crime has gone up is that people have discovered it is easier to get away with it; by the same token, the average citizen thinks a good way to reduce crime is to make the consequences of crime to the would-be offender more costly (by making penalties swifter, more certain, or more severe), or to make the value of alternatives to crime more attractive (by increasing the availability and pay of legitimate jobs), or both . . . These citizens may be surprised to learn that social scientists that study crime are deeply divided over the correctness of such views.

(Wilson, 1975: 117)

The first identifiable tradition of explaining crime and criminal behaviour to emerge in modern society is the rational actor model. It has its origins in a range of philosophical, political, economic and social ideas that were developed and articulated during the seventeenth and eighteenth centuries and that were fundamentally critical of the established order and its religious interpretations of the natural world. Two major sets of ideas provide the intellectual foundations of a major period of social change: social contract theories and utilitarianism.

The essence of social contract theories is the notion that legitimate government is only possible with the voluntary agreement of free human beings who are able to exercise free will. It was the key writers in this tradition – Thomas Hobbes, John Locke and Jean-Jacques Rousseau – and their criticisms of the exercise of arbitrary powers by monarchs, established churches and aristocratic interests that created the preconditions for the specific attacks on pre-modern legal systems and practices that were later mounted by Jeremy Bentham and Cesare Beccaria and that provided the foundations of the rational actor model of crime and criminal behaviour.

Thomas Hobbes (1588–1678) emphasized that it is the exercise of human free will that is the fundamental basis of a legitimate social contract. Compliance can be enforced by the fear of punishment, but only if entry into the contract and the promise to comply with it has been freely willed, given and subsequently broken. Hobbes held a rather negative view of humanity and proposed a need for social institutions – and we have here the origins of the very idea of modern criminal justice systems – to support social contracts and to enforce laws. He claimed that in a 'state of nature' – or without outside intervention in their lives – people would be engaged in a 'war of all against all' and life would tend to be 'nasty, brutish and short'. He thus proposed that people should freely subject themselves to the power of an absolute ruler or institution – a 'Leviathan' – which, as the result of a political-social contract, would be legitimately empowered to enforce the contracts that subjects make between themselves (Hobbes, 1968 originally 1651).

John Locke (1632–1704) had a more complex conception of what people are like 'in the state of nature' and argued that there is a natural law that constitutes and protects essential rights of life, liberty and property: key assumptions that, subsequently, were to significantly shape the constitutional arrangements of the USA. Locke proposed that the Christian God has presented all people with common access to the 'fruits of the earth', but at the same time individual property rights can be legitimately created when labour is mixed with the fruits of the earth, for example by cultivating crops or extracting minerals. People nevertheless have a natural duty not to accumulate more land or goods than they can use, and if this natural law is observed then a rough equality can be achieved in the distribution of natural resources. Unfortunately, this natural potential towards egalitarianism had been compromised by the development of a money economy that has made it possible for people to obtain control over more goods and land than they can use as individuals.

Locke saw the transition from a state of nature to the development of a political society as a response to desires, conflict and ethical uncertainty brought about by the growth of the use of money and the material inequalities that consequently arose. The expansion of political institutions is thus necessary to create a social contract to alleviate the problems of inequality generated by this distortion of natural law. For Locke, social contracts develop through three stages. First, people must agree unanimously to come together as a community, and to pool their natural powers, so as to act together to secure and uphold the natural rights of each other. Second, the members of this community must agree, by a majority vote, to set up legislative and other institutions. Third, the owners of property must agree, either personally or through political representatives, to whatever taxes that are imposed on them.

Locke disagreed with Hobbes' view that people should surrender themselves to the absolute rule of a Leviathan and argued that people gain their natural rights to life and liberty from the Christian God and hold them effectively in trust. These rights are not therefore theirs to transfer to the arbitrary power of another. Furthermore, he argued that government is established to protect rights to property and not to undermine them. It cannot therefore take or redistribute property without consent. It is not the task of human legislation to replace natural law and rights but to give them the precision, clarity and impartial enforceability that are unattainable in the state of nature. Although Locke had a relatively optimistic view of human potential in the state of nature, he nevertheless observed the inevitable potential for conflict and corruption that occurs with the increasing complexity of human endeavour and the 'invention' of money. If natural rights are to be preserved, what is required is the consensual development of institutions to clarify, codify and maintain these rights to life, liberty and property. In short, these institutions should constrain all equally in the interests of social harmony (Locke, 1970 originally 1686).

Jean-Jacques Rousseau (1712–1778) was a severe critic of some of the major aspects of the emerging modern world, arguing that the spread of scientific and literary activity was morally corrupting. He emphasized that human beings had evolved from an animal-like state of nature in which isolated, somewhat stupid individuals lived peacefully as 'noble savages'. Rousseau (1964 originally 1762) originally claimed that humans were naturally free and equal, animated by the principles of self-preservation and pity. However, as humans came together into groups and societies, engaging in communal activities that gave rise to rules and regulations, the 'natural man' evolved into a competitive and selfish 'social man', capable of rational calculation and of intentionally inflicting harm on others. Rousseau thus had a pessimistic view of social change and was unconvinced that the human species was progressing. Civilization was not a boon to humanity; it was 'unnatural' and would always be accompanied by costs that outweighed the benefits.

With his later work, Rousseau (1978 originally 1775) appeared a little more optimistic about the future of humanity. He still asserted that at the beginning of history people were admirable, fundamentally equal, free individuals and that moral corruption and injustice arose as people came to develop more complex forms of society and become dependent on one another, thus risking exploitation and disappointment. However, he was now prepared to propose political solutions to the moral corruption of society, arguing the necessity of establishing human laws that consider all individuals equally and give each a free vote on the enactment of legislation.

Rousseau developed the concept of the *general will*, observing that, in addition to individual self-interest, citizens have a collective interest in the well-being of the community. Indeed, he traced the foundations of the law and political society to this idea of the 'general will' – a citizen body, acting as a whole, and freely choosing to adopt laws that will apply equally to all citizens.

Rousseau's work presented a radical democratic challenge to the French monarchical *ancien regime*, proposing that it was the 'citizen body' – not kings – that were 'sovereign' and government should represent their interests. It was only in this way that individuals could freely vote for, and obey, the law as an expression of the common good, without contradicting their own interests and needs. Rousseau considered that he had resolved the dilemma of human selfishness and collective interests posed by Hobbes. Moreover, he had done this without denying the potential existence of a positive and active form of civic freedom, based on self-sacrifice for a legitimate political community.

Social contract theories provide an overwhelming critique of pre-modern forms of government and are highly relevant to the development of the rational actor model of crime and criminal behaviour. First, there is the claim that human beings once lived in a state of 'innocence', 'grace' or 'nature'. Second, there is the recognition that the emergence of humanity from its primitive state involved the application of reason – an appreciation of the meaning and consequences of actions – by responsible individuals. Third, the human 'will' is recognized as a psychological reality, a faculty of the individual that regulates and controls behaviour, and is generally free. Fourth, society has a 'right' to inflict punishment, although this right has been transferred to the political state, and a system of punishments for forbidden acts, or a 'code of criminal law'.

Thus, human beings are viewed as 'rational actors', freely choosing to enter into contracts with others to perform interpersonal or civic duties. Laws can legitimately be used to ensure compliance if they have been properly approved by citizens who are party to the social contract.

A further major intellectual contribution to the development of the rational actor model was the philosophical tradition termed utilitarianism. Essentially, this assesses the rightness of acts, policies, decisions and choices by their tendency to promote the 'happiness' of those affected by them. The two most closely associated adherents and developers of the approach were the political philosophers Jeremy Bentham and John Stuart Mill.

Jeremy Bentham (1748–1832) proposed that the actions of human beings are acceptable if they promote happiness, and they are unacceptable if they produce the opposite of happiness. This is the basis of morality. His most famous axiom is the call for society to produce 'the greatest happiness of the greatest number'. 'Happiness' is understood to be pleasure and unhappiness is pain, or the absence of pleasure. The moral principle arising from this perspective is that, if individuals use their reason to pursue their own pleasure, then a state of positive social equilibrium will naturally emerge.

For Bentham, pleasures and pains were to be assessed, or 'weighed', on the basis of their intensity, duration and proximity. Moreover, such a calculus was considered to be person-neutral – that is, capable of being applied to the different pleasures of different people. The extent of the pleasure – or the total number of people experiencing it – was also a part of the calculation of the rightness of the outcome of an act. The overall aim was to provide a calculation whereby the net balance of pleasure over pain could be determined as a measure of the rightness of an act or policy.

John Stuart Mill (1806–1873) generally accepted the position of Bentham, including his emphasis on hedonism as the basic human trait that governs and motivates the actions of every individual. Mill nevertheless wanted to distinguish qualities – as well as quantities – of pleasures and this posed problems. For it is unclear whether a distinction between qualities of pleasures – whether one can be considered more worthwhile than another – can be sustained or measured. Mill emphasized, first, that pure self-interest was an inadequate basis for utilitarianism, and suggested that we should take as the real criterion of good the social consequences of the act. Second, he proposed that some pleasures rank higher than others, with those of the intellect superior to those of the senses. Importantly, both social factors and the quality of the act were seen as important in seeking an explanation for human behaviour.

Mill has proved to be a formidable and influential philosophical force but it is Bentham who has had the greatest impact on the development of the rational actor model of crime and criminal behaviour. He essentially provided two central additions to social contract theory. First, there is his notion that the principal control over the unfettered exercise of free will is that of fear, especially the fear of pain. Second, there is the axiom that punishment is the main way of creating fear in order to influence the will and thus control behaviour.

2. Classical criminology

Key Issues

1. The Classical School of criminology
2. Essential components of the rational actor model
3. Limitations of Classicism
4. Neo-Classical compromise
5. Enduring influence of Classicism

Classical criminology emerged at a time when the naturalistic approach of the social contract theorists we encountered in the Introduction was challenging the previously dominant spiritualist approach to explaining crime and criminal behaviour. Cesare Beccaria in Italy and Jeremy Bentham in Britain, writing in the late eighteenth century, established the essential components of the rational actor model.

The Classical theorists

Cesare Beccaria (1738–94) was an Italian mathematician and the author of *Dei Delitti e Delle Pene* (*On Crimes and Punishment*) (1963 originally 1767), a highly influential book, which was translated into 22 languages and had an enormous impact on European and US legal thought. In common with many of his contemporary intellectuals – and inspired by social contract theories – Beccaria was strongly opposed to the many inconsistencies that existed in government and public affairs, and his major text was essentially the first attempt at presenting a systematic, consistent and logical penal system.

Beccaria considered that criminals owe a 'debt' to society and proposed that punishments should be fixed strictly in proportion to the seriousness of the crime. Torture was considered a useless method of criminal investigation, as well as being barbaric. Moreover, capital punishment was considered to be unnecessary with a life sentence of hard labour preferable, both as a punishment and deterrent. The use of imprisonment should thus be greatly extended, the conditions of prisons improved with better physical care provided and inmates should be segregated on the basis of gender, age and degree of criminality.

Beccaria was a very strong supporter of 'social contract' theory with its emphasis on the notion that individuals can only be legitimately bound to society if they have given their consent to the societal arrangements. It is nevertheless the law that provides the necessary conditions for the social contract and punishment exists only to defend the liberties of individuals against those who would interfere with them.

Beccaria's theory of criminal behaviour is based on the concepts of free will and hedonism where it is proposed that all human behaviour is essentially purposive and based on the pleasure–pain principle. He argues that punishment should reflect that principle and thus fixed sanctions for all offences must be written into the law and not be open to the interpretation, or the discretion, of judges. The law must apply equally to all citizens, while the sole function of the court is to determine guilt. No mitigation of guilt should be considered and all that are guilty of a particular offence should suffer the same prescribed penalty. This extremely influential essay can be summarized in the following thirteen propositions:

1. In order to escape social chaos, each member of society must sacrifice part of their liberty to the sovereignty of the nation-state.
2. To prevent individuals from infringing the liberty of others by breaking the law, it is necessary to introduce punishments for such breaches.
3. 'The despotic spirit' – or the tendency to offend – is in everyone.
4. Punishments should be decided by the legislature not by the courts.
5. Judges should only impose punishment established by the law in order to preserve consistency and the certainty of punishment.
6. The seriousness of the crime should be judged not by the intentions of the offender but by the harm that it does to society.
7. Punishment must be administered in proportion to the crime that has been committed and should be set on a scale – or a tariff – with the most severe penalties corresponding to offences that caused the most harm to society. The most serious crimes are considered to be those that threaten the stability of society.
8. Punishment that follows promptly after a crime is committed will be more just and effective.
9. Punishment has to be certain to be effective.
10. Laws and punishments have to be well publicized so that people are well aware of them.
11. Punishment is imposed for the purpose of deterrence and therefore capital punishment is unnecessary and should not be used.
12. The prevention of crime is better than punishment.
13. Activities that are not expressly prohibited by law are therefore not illegal and thus permissible.

It is important to recognize that Beccaria's ideas have had a profound effect on the establishment of the modern criminal law and, while they may not be expressed in quite the same way, it is easy to detect resonances of his views in any popular discussion on crime. The doctrine of free will is built into many legal codes and has strongly influenced popular conceptions of justice.

Jeremy Bentham was a leading disciple of Beccaria. As a philosopher – as we saw above – he is classed as a utilitarian, or a *hedonistic utilitarian*, due to his emphasis on the human pursuit of pleasure. He was very much influenced by the philosophical materialism of John Locke, which had denied the existence of innate ideas and traditional, established religious notions of original sin. He consequently ascribed criminal behaviour to incorrect upbringing or socialization rather than innate propensities to offend. For Bentham, criminals were not incorrigible monsters but 'forward children', 'persons of unsound mind', who lacked the self-discipline to control their passions according to the dictates of reason.

Bentham's ideas are very similar to those of Beccaria and his most famous principle – 'the greatest happiness of the greatest number' – is the fundamental axiom of all utilitarian philosophy. People are rational creatures who will seek pleasure while trying to avoid pain. Thus, punishment must outweigh any pleasure derived from criminal behaviour, but the law must not be as harsh and severe as to reduce the greatest happiness. Moreover, the law should not be used to regulate morality but only to control acts harmful to society that reduce the happiness of the majority. He agreed with Beccaria about capital punishment, that it was barbaric and unnecessary, but disagreed about torture, allowing that on occasion it might be 'necessary' and thus have utility. This is a significant point worth reflecting on. If the intention is to get someone – anyone – to admit to having committed a criminal act, then the use of torture will be useful, but, if the purpose is to ensure that you have found the right offender, then it is of no use. This seems to be the point being made by Beccaria. If, on the other hand, you wish to obtain urgently some important information from someone whom you have good reason to believe is withholding this – as, for example, in the case of a planned terrorist atrocity – then the rationale for torture is rather different. This seems to be the utilitarian point being made by Bentham.

We might note that, although Bentham believed in the doctrine of free will, there is a strong hint in his work that suggests criminality might be learned behaviour. Indeed, it would seem to be the case that neither Beccaria nor Bentham believed that human beings enjoyed complete free will. Beirne (1993: 51) questions the nature of the voluntarism in Beccaria's notion of will, suggesting that his 'is a determined will, rather than a free will'; while it is clearly Bentham's view that human behaviour is 'determined' by the categorical imperatives of pleasure and pain:

> Nature has placed mankind under the governance of two sovereign masters, pain and pleasure. It is for them alone to point out what we ought to do, as well as to determine what we shall do. On the one hand the standard of right and wrong, on the other the chain of causes and effects, are fastened to their throne. They govern us in all we do, in all we say, in all we think:

every effort we can make to throw off our subjection will demonstrate and confirm it.

(1970 originally 1765: 11)

Beirne (1993) suggests that it may be that free choice was believed to relate to the actions taken to satisfy what was a driven desire or need, rather than determining the desires or need *per se*. He notes that Beccaria's observation that 'every act of our will is always proportionate to the strength of the sense data from which it springs' (cited in Beirne, 1991: 808) does not so much deny the presence of free will but suggests that free will is not the only aspect of human beings that must be considered. He concludes that Beccaria 'subscribed to a notion of human agency simultaneously involving "free" rational calculation and "determined" action'. The early purist judicial application of the Classical School doctrines nevertheless clearly presumed free will and full rationality on the part of the offender and all were to be held fully responsible for their actions.

Bentham and the Panoptican

Bentham spent a considerable amount of time and energy designing a prison, an institution to reflect and operationalize his ideas on criminal justice. Prisons were not much used as a form of punishment in pre-modern times, being reserved for holding people awaiting trial, transportation or some other punishment. They were usually privately administered, chronically short of money, undisciplined and insanitary places.

In 1791, Bentham published his design for a new model prison called a Panoptican. The physical structure of this edifice was a circular tiered honeycomb of cells, ranged round a central inspection tower from which each could be seen by the gaolers. He proposed that the constant surveillance would make chains and other restraints superfluous. The prisoners would work sixteen hours a day in their cells and the profits of their labour would go to the owner of the Panoptican. Bentham described the prison as a 'mill for grinding rogues honest' and it was to be placed near the centre of the city so that it would be a visible reminder to all of the 'fruits of crime'. Furthermore, said Bentham, such an institution should act as a model for schools, asylums, workhouses, factories and hospitals that could all be run on the 'inspection principle' to ensure internal regulation, discipline and efficiency.

Underpinning all of these institutions of social control was a shared regime and common view of discipline and regimentation as mechanisms for changing the behaviour of the inmates. The rigorous regime proposed as the basis of these institutions was itself part of a more general discipline imposed on the working class in the factories and mills:

[The prison] took its place within a structure of institutions so interrelated in function, so similar in design, discipline and language of command that together the sheer massiveness of their presence in the Victorian landscape inhibited further challenge to their logic.

It was no accident that the penitentiaries, asylums, workhouses, monitorial schools, night refuges and reformatories looked alike or that their charges marched to the same disciplinary cadence. Since they made up a complementary and independent structure of control, it was essential that their diets and deprivations be calibrated in an ascending scale, school-workhouse-asylum-prison, with the pain of the last serving to undergird the pain of the first.

Nor was it accidental that these state institutions so closely resembled the factory ... the creators of the new factory discipline drew inspiration from the same discourse in authority as the makers of the prison: nonconformist asceticism, faith in human improvability through discipline, and the liberal theory of the state.

(Ignatieff, 1978: 214–15)

The Panoptican, in its strict interpretation, was never built in England, but two American prisons were built based on such a model, although these institutions did not prove to be a success in terms of the original intentions of the builders and they had to be taken down and rebuilt. A variation on the theme, London's Millbank Prison, built in 1812, was also poorly conceived, built and administered, and was eventually turned into a holding prison rather than a penitentiary. Bentham's proposal also called for the provision of industrial and religious training and pre-release schemes, and suggested the segregation and classification of prisoners in order to avoid 'criminal contamination'.

Michel Foucault (1977) and Michael Ignatieff (1978) have both traced the development of the prison as a concept and as a physical institution observing that it was one of many 'carceral' institutions developed around the time in order to rationalize and discipline human activity along the lines of early modern thought. Foucault provides the following extract from rules drawn up for the House of Young Prisoners in Paris:

At the first drum-roll, the prisoners must rise and dress in silence, as the supervisor opens the cell doors. At the second drum-roll, they must be dressed and make their bed. At the third, they must line and proceed to the chapel for Morning Prayer. There is a five-minute interval between each drum-roll.

(1977: 6)

These imposing new penal institutions soon competed for domination of the new urban skylines with the great palaces, cathedrals and churches, which had long provided the symbols of the concerns of an earlier age. While the original Panoptican idea was not widely implemented, a variation on the theme developed and built from the early part of the nineteenth century still forms a substantial part of the prison estate in many countries. After a number of aborted experimental institutions had failed, a new model prison was built in North London, inspired by the Quaker prison reformer John Howard. Pentonville prison provided a template for over fifty similar prisons in Britain and for many others throughout the world.

While his writings focused on reform of the penal system, Bentham was also concerned to see crime prevented rather than punished, and to this end made suggestions that alcoholism should be combated and that those with no means of sustenance should be cared for by the state.

The limitations of Classicism

The philosophy of the Classical theorists was reflected in the Declaration of the Rights of Man in 1789 and the French Penal Code of 1791, the body of criminal law introduced in the aftermath of the French Revolution. The authors of these documents had themselves been inspired by the writings of the major Enlightenment philosophers, notably Rousseau. It was nevertheless attempts such as these to put the ideas of the Classical School into practice that exposed the inherent problems of its philosophy of criminal justice. The Classical theorists had deliberately and completely ignored differences between individuals. First offenders and recidivists were treated exactly alike and solely on the basis of the particular act that had been committed. Children, the 'feeble-minded' and the insane were all treated as if they were fully rational and competent.

This appearance in court of people who were unable to comprehend the proceedings against them did little to legitimize the new French post-revolutionary criminal code and, consequently, this was revised in 1810, and again in 1819, to allow judges some latitude in deciding sentences. It was thus in this way that the strict, formal, philosophical elegance of the Classical model was to be breached. It was to become increasingly recognized that people are not equally responsible for their actions and, as a result, a whole range of experts gradually came to be invited into the courts to pass opinion on the degree of reason that could be expected of the accused. Judges were now able to vary sentences in accordance with the degree of individual culpability argued by these expert witnesses, and it was this theoretical compromise that was to lead to the emergence of a modified criminological perspective that came to be termed *the neo-Classical School*.

The neo-Classical compromise

Neo-Classicists such as Rossi (1787–1848), Garraud (1849–1930) and Joly (1839–1925) modified the rigorous doctrines of pure Classical theory by revising the doctrine of free will. In this modified form of the rational actor model, ordinary sane adults were still considered fully responsible for their actions and all equally capable of either criminal or non-criminal behaviour. It was nevertheless now recognized that children – and, in some circumstances, the elderly – were less capable of exercising free choice and were thus less responsible for their actions. Moreover, the insane and 'feeble-minded' might be even less responsible. We can thus observe here the beginnings of the recognition that various innate predisposing factors may actually determine human behaviour, which is a significant perception that was to provide the fundamental theoretical foundation of the predestined actor model that is the focus of the second part of this book.

It was these revisions to the penal code that admitted into the courts for the first time non-legal 'experts', including doctors, psychiatrists and, later, social workers. They were gradually introduced into the criminal justice system in order to identify the impact of individual biological, psychological and social differences with the purpose of deciding the extent to which offenders should be held responsible for their actions. The outcome of this encroachment was that sentences became more individualized, dependent on the perceived degree of responsibility of the offender and on mitigating circumstances.

It was now recognized that a particular punishment would have a different effect on different people and, as a result, punishment increasingly came to be expressed in terms of punishment appropriate to rehabilitation. However, as those eminent proponents of the more radical variant of the victimized actor model Taylor *et al.* were later to observe:

> There was, however, no radical departure from the free-will model of man involved in the earlier Classical premises. The criminal had to be punished in an environment conducive to his making the correct moral decisions. Choice was (and still is) seen to be a characteristic of the individual actor – but there is now recognition that certain structures are more conducive to free choice than others.
>
> (1973: 10)

The neo-Classicists thus retained the central rational choice actor model notion of free will, but with the modification that certain circumstances may be less conducive to the unfettered exercise of free choice than others. Indeed, it can be convincingly argued that most modern criminal justice systems are founded on this somewhat awkward theoretical compromise between the rational actor model of criminal behaviour and the predestined actor model that we will encounter in the second part of the book. This debate between free will and determinism is perhaps one of the most enduring in the human and social sciences.

In summary, it is possible to identify the following central attributes of the Classical and neo-Classical Schools that provide the central foundations of the rational actor model:

1. There is a fundamental focus on the criminal law and the simple adoption of a legal definition of crime. This leaves the perspective crucially exposed to the criticism that legal definitions of crime are social constructions that change over time and with geographical location.
2. There is the central concept that the punishment should fit the crime rather than the criminal. This leaves it exposed to the criticism that it fails to appreciate the impact of individual differences in terms of culpability and prospects for rehabilitation.
3. There is the doctrine of free will according to which all people are free to choose their actions, and this notion is often allied to the hedonistic utilitarian philosophy that all people will seek to optimize pleasure but avoid pain. From

this perspective, it is assumed that there is nothing 'different' or 'special' about a criminal that differentiates them from other people. It is a doctrine thus exposed to the criticism that it fails to appreciate that the exercise of free will may be constrained by biological, psychological or social circumstances.

4. There is the use of non-scientific 'armchair' methodology based on anecdote and imaginary illustrations in place of empirical research, and it was thus an administrative and legal criminology, concerned more with the uniformity of laws and punishment rather than really trying to explain criminal behaviour.

The rational actor model was to go out of fashion as an explanatory model of crime and criminal behaviour at the end of the nineteenth century and was to be replaced predominantly by the new orthodoxy of the predestined actor model in its various guises. It nevertheless continued to inform criminal justice systems throughout the world.

The enduring influence of Classicism

The enduring influence of the Classical School is evident in the legal doctrine that emphasizes conscious intent or choice, for example, the notion of *mens rea* or the guilty mind. In sentencing principles, for example, the idea of culpability or responsibility; and in the structure of punishment, for example, the progression of penalties according to the seriousness of the offence or what is more commonly known as the 'sentencing tariff'.

Philosophically, the ideas of the Classical School are reflected in the contemporary 'just deserts' approach to sentencing. This involves four basic principles. First, only a person found guilty by a court of law can be punished for a crime. Second, anyone found to be guilty of a crime must be punished. Third, punishment must not be more than a degree commensurate to – or proportional to – the nature or gravity of the offence and culpability of the offender. Fourth, punishment must not be less than a degree commensurate to – or proportional to – the nature or gravity of the offence and culpability of the criminal (von Hirsch, 1976).

Such principles have clear foundations in the theoretical tradition established by Beccaria and Bentham. There is an emphasis on notions of free will and rationality, as well as proportionality and equality, with an emphasis on criminal behaviour that focuses on the offence not the offender, in accordance with the pleasure–pain principle, and to ensure that justice is served by equal punishment for the same crime. 'Just deserts' philosophy eschews individual discretion and rehabilitation as legitimate aims of the justice system. Justice must be both done and seen to be done and is an approach that is closely linked with the traditional Classical School notion of 'due process'.

Packer (1968) observes that the whole contemporary criminal justice system is founded on a balance between the competing value systems of due process and crime control. The former maintains that it is the purpose of the criminal justice system to prove the guilt of a defendant beyond a reasonable doubt in a public trial as a condition for the imposition of a sentence. It is based on an idealized form of the rule of law where the state has a duty to seek out and punish the guilty but must prove the guilt of the accused (King, 1981). Central to this idea is the presumption of innocence until guilt is proved.

A due process model requires and enforces rules governing the powers of the police and the admissibility and utility of evidence. There is recognition of the power of the state in the application of the criminal law but there is a requirement for checks and balances to be in place to protect the interests of suspects and defendants. The use of informal or discretionary powers is seen to be contrary to this tradition.

A strict due process system acknowledges that some guilty people will go free and unpunished but this is considered acceptable in order to prevent wrongful conviction and punishment, while the arbitrary or excessive use of state power is seen to be a worse evil. Problematically, a high acquittal rate gives the impression that the criminal justice agencies are performing inadequately and the outcome could be a failure to deter others from indulging in criminal behaviour.

A crime control model, in contrast, prioritizes efficiency and getting results with the emphasis on catching, convicting and punishing the offender. There is almost an inherent 'presumption of guilt' (King, 1981) and less respect for legal controls that exist to protect the individual defendant. These are seen as practical obstacles that need to be overcome in order to get on with the control of crime and punishment. If occasionally some innocent individuals are sacrificed to the ultimate aim of crime control, then that is acceptable. Such errors should nevertheless be kept to a minimum and agents of the law should ensure through their professionalism that they apprehend the guilty and allow the innocent to go free.

In the crime control model, the interests of victims and society are given priority over those of the accused, and the justification for this stance is that swifter processing makes the system appear more efficient and that this will deter greater criminality. In other words, if you offend, you are likely to be caught and punished and it is therefore not worth becoming involved in criminality. The primary aim of crime control is thus to punish the guilty and deter criminals as a means of reducing crime and creating a safer society.

It was observed above that the rational actor model had gone out of fashion as an explanatory model of criminal behaviour with the rise of the predestined actor tradition at the end of the nineteenth century. However, it would return very much to favour with the rise of the 'new' political right – or populist conservatism – during the last quarter of the twentieth century. It was, however, a revival where the purist Classical tradition of 'due process' promoted in particular by Beccaria would be very much superseded by the interests of the proponents of the crime control model of criminal justice.

Policy implications of Classicism

From this perspective, human beings are rational calculating individuals who enjoy free will and choose to commit crime in the same way that they choose any other form of behaviour. The key issue for policy-makers is thus how to use the institutions of the state – or the criminal justice system – to influence people not to choose crime.

The theory emerged at the time of the European Enlightenment over two hundred years ago and its central focus on rationality. This was nevertheless problematic. The theory is lacking in sophistication and was thus operationalized in a simplistic fashion based on an assumption that there is a mathematics of deterrence, that is, a proportional calculation undertaken first by policy-makers and then by potential offenders.

The Classical School believed that there are constants of value in pain and gain that can influence a decision to offend or not to offend. Problematically, we are not all the same nor do we share the same view as to what constitutes a rational decision to offend. At the same time, the Classical School were somewhat idealistic in presuming that a professional policing system could rapidly expand and deliver an exemplary service of investigation and detection. This was not to be the case and thus, if the certainty of punishment is to be achieved, there must be a major investment in policing.

Summary of main points

1. The Classical School of criminology established the essential components of the rational actor model.
2. Classical School criminology is based on the concepts of free will and hedonism where all human behaviour is purposive and based on the pleasure–pain principle.
3. Punishment should reflect that principle with fixed sanctions for all offences written into the law and not be open to the interpretation, or discretion, of judges.
4. The law must apply equally to all citizens, and all found guilty of a particular offence should suffer the same prescribed penalty.
5. Punishment must outweigh any pleasure derived from criminal behaviour, but the law must not be as harsh and severe as to reduce the greatest happiness.
6. Jeremy Bentham designed a prison – the Panoptican – to reflect and operationalize his ideas on criminal justice and to act as a model for schools, asylums, workhouses, factories and hospitals.
7. It became increasingly apparent that people are not equally responsible for their actions, with the outcome that increasingly experts were introduced into the courtroom to pass opinion on the level of culpability of the accused and judges were able to vary sentences accordingly.
8. These revisions to the penal code led to sentences becoming more individualized, dependent on the extent of mitigating circumstances, with punishment increasingly expressed in terms of the possibilities for rehabilitation.
9. The rational actor model went out of fashion as an explanatory model of

criminal behaviour at the end of the nineteenth century but continued to inform criminal justice systems throughout the world and is reflected in the contemporary 'just deserts' approach to sentencing.

10. Packer (1968) observes that the whole contemporary criminal justice system is founded on a balance between the competing value systems of due process and crime control.

Discussion questions

1. What are the key components of the rational actor model?
2. What are the basic principles of punishment from this rational actor perspective?
3. What were the identified weaknesses of the rational actor?
4. What was the neo-Classical compromise?
5. What are the enduring influences of the Classical School?

Suggested further reading

The best exposition and introduction of the core ideas of the Classical School and the fundamental concepts of the rational actor model is still provided by the most accessible original account by Beccaria (1963). King (1981), Packer (1968) and Von Hirsch (1976) provide essential demonstrations of the enduring and revitalized influence of the Classical School and rational actor thinking on the contemporary legal system and jurisprudence.

3. Populist conservative criminology

Key Issues

1. The political new right and the rediscovery of the rational actor model
2. James Q. Wilson and 'right realism'
3. Right realism and social control
4. Developments in conservative criminology
5. Criticisms of populist conservative criminology

The rational actor model ceased to be a popular means of explaining crime and criminal behaviour for most of a twentieth century dominated by the predestined actor model of crime and criminal behaviour that we will encounter in the second part of this book. It was to return very much to favour with the emergence of the 'new political right' – populist or neoconservatives[1] – during the 1970s and 1980s.

The rise of the political new right

During the 1970s, conservative intellectuals in both the USA and the UK mounted a vigorous moral campaign against various forms of 'deviance', and in 1979 Margaret Thatcher was to make crime a major and successful election issue for the first time in post-war Britain. Her general concern was to re-establish what she considered to be 'Victorian values' and to this end targeted the supposed debilitating permissive society of the 1960s and its perceived legitimization in 'soft' social science. For this political 'new right', the economic, technological and managerial achievements of the modern world should be safeguarded and expanded, but at the same time there should be a comprehensive assault mounted on its cultural and ethical components. Indeed, it was perceived to be this modernist culture with its emphasis on subjective values and individual self-expression that was crucially undermining the motivational requirements of an efficient economy and rational state administration. In short, individuals were seen as increasingly unwilling to achieve and even less prepared to obey (Habermas, 1989). Populist conservatives thus sought a revival in past tradition, in the values of the state, schools, family and, implicitly, in the unquestioned acceptance of authority.

In criminology, this perceived liberal indulgence was epitomized by the other two explanatory models discussed in this book. First, there is the enduring dominant orthodoxy of the twentieth century – the 'predestined actor' model – with its focus on discovering the causes of crime and, having once located them, offering treatment and rehabilitation rather than punishment. Second, there are the more radical variants of the 'victimized actor' model with their critique of an unfair and unequal society and their policy assumptions of understanding, forgiveness and non-intervention that were gaining increasing popularity with the idealistic but at that time still electorally viable political left.

Moreover, right-wing intellectuals observed that it was not merely that left-wing and liberal thought had simply failed to see problems inherent in 'soft' approaches to crime, discipline, education, and so forth. This so-called progressive theorizing had itself provided a basis for the acceleration of the permissive syndromes in question. High levels of criminality and disorder were therefore blamed not only on the weakening sources of social authority, the family, schools, religion and other key institutions, but even more so on the corrosive influence of the surrounding culture with its emphasis on rights rather than obligations and the celebration of self-expression to the point of self-indulgence, instead of promoting self-control and self-constraint (Tzannetakis, 2001). The new right argued that, in such a spiralling, demoralizing culture, it was clear that crime and violence would inevitably increase. Thus, real problems and sociological apologies alike had to be confronted, and an attempt made to reassert the virtue and necessity of authority, order and discipline (Scruton, 1980, 1985).

In social policy in general (Morgan, 1978) and in the area of crime and deviance in particular (Dale, 1984), an assault was mounted on liberal and radical left trends. Empirical justification for this attack on the self-styled forces of socially progressive intervention came from the publication of an influential paper by Robert Martinson (1974), which purported to show that rehabilitation programmes in prison simply 'do not work' and thus the whole rationale for the existence of a welfare-oriented probation service, in particular, was called into question. Consequently, we were to see the enthusiastic reintroduction of the idea of retributive punishment – serious crimes are simply evil, after all – and arguments for the protection of society from danger. From this populist conservative perspective, punishment is essentially about devising penalties to fit the crime and ensuring that they are carried out, thus reinforcing social values.

In short, this concern to treat the wrongdoer as an offender against social morality and not as a candidate for reform can be seen as a contemporary form of the rational actor model – but one with a distinctly retributive edge.

James Q. Wilson and 'right realism'

James Q. Wilson first published *Thinking About Crime* in the USA in 1975 some years after the election of a Republican president, Richard M. Nixon, with a mandate to 'get tough' on offenders by strengthening the criminal justice system, installing a tough Attorney General and giving the police more powers. The foremost proponent of right realism, Wilson discusses crime from the standpoint of new right philosophy and politics but nevertheless – certainly in his earlier work – rejects much of the traditional conservative approach to crime control as well as that offered by the political left. Later, Republican President Ronald Reagan (1981–89) appointed Professor Wilson to be his special adviser on crime, and a harder, more retributive element can be detected in this later variant of 'right realism'.

Wilson accepts liberal arguments that increased police patrols, longer prison sentences for offenders and changes of personnel in central government posts could have little effect on crime levels but was scornful of those arguments that denied the existence of crime as a real problem. On the contrary – and this is a central contention of right realism – crime is quite simply an evil that requires a concerted and rigorous response.

Thus, Wilson and George Kelling (1982, 1989) argue that the police are most effectively used not to reduce crime but to maintain social order. Kelling (1999) subsequently summed up this position thus: 'you ignore minor offences at great cost' and 'disorder not only creates fear but . . . is a precursor to serious crime'. Conversely, the maintenance of order allows community control mechanisms to flourish and encourages law-abiding behaviour. It is therefore the constructive function of the police to provide an environment in which criminality is unable to flourish. The focus should be less on simple breaches of the criminal law but more on regulating street life and incivilities – such as prostitution, begging, gang fights, drunkenness and disorderly conduct – which in themselves may not be that harmful, but which in aggregate are detrimental to the community and therefore need to be controlled (see Hopkins Burke, 1998b, 2004b; Karmen, 2004).

Wilson is suspicious of those proponents of the predestined actor model who call for treatment, not punishment. Not that right realists abandon all such explanations of criminal behaviour. Wilson and Richard Herrnstein (1985) have thus devised a biosocial explanation including biological and psychological components to explain why some individuals are more prone to criminality. They propose that the inclination of people to commit crimes varies in accordance with the extent to which they have internalized a commitment to self-control. This is all dependent on the level of investment a society has made in promoting self-control, through its socialization mechanisms, as well as on the – not necessarily unchangeable – genetic and biological characteristics of individuals. This perspective attacks certain types of family – particularly the single-parent variant – for ineffective socialization, while at the same time the ability to learn is affected by the constitution of the individual and the effectiveness of the input from family, peers, school and work. The conclusion is that it is biology that establishes the population that are at risk of becoming criminal, while it is socialization, or its failure, that helps to decide whether this will be realized. This sociobiological argument is discussed in more detail in Chapter 13.

Wilson thus uses the predestined model factors we will encounter in the second part of the book – such as biology and conditioning – in his initial analysis of criminal behaviour but, because this perspective fails to offer pragmatic policy suggestions, does not pursue this line of reasoning. For, it is not – or at least not yet – possible to alter the biology of an individual to the extent that would be necessary were his assumptions to be correct. Moreover, it would not be easy to rapidly improve the socialization offered by families, or quickly rid society of single-parent families, although both in the UK and the USA this has been a policy objective of the populist conservatives, and one that has been tackled to some extent as part of the welfare agenda. Thus, the aim is to reduce criminality through pragmatic intervention and by making the benefits of leading an honest and considerate existence more attractive to those who would otherwise take the wrong direction in life.

Right realism emphasizes the findings of victim surveys that show that the burden of crime falls disproportionately on the poor, the disadvantaged and those least able to defend themselves. They, however, deny absolutely the notion – proposed by the radical variants of the victimized actor model that we will encounter in the third part of this book – of a struggle of an oppressed class against an unjust society. Right realists stress the point that both perpetrators and victims of predatory crime tend to come from the same community. Crime is committed by individuals – or groups of individuals – against other individuals or groups of individuals.

Wilson emphasizes the individualistic nature of offending and adopts a utilitarian explanation for human action:

> If the supply and value of legitimate opportunities (i.e. jobs) was declining at the very time that the cost of illegitimate opportunities (i.e. fines and jail terms) was also declining, a rational teenager might well have concluded that it made more sense to steal cars than to wash them.
>
> (1975: 21)

The implication of this utilitarian argument would seem to support both increasing the benefits of 'non-crime' (by providing more and better jobs) and increasing the costs of crime (by the use of imprisonment). Wilson nevertheless concentrates on the latter half of the equation. In short, populist conservative crime control strategies – as we shall see below – tend to place far more emphasis on the stick than the carrot.

Right realists also differ from previous conservatives in the way in which they believe that punishment should be applied. Recognizing that the USA imprisons a very large proportion of its population for longer periods than other countries which have far lower crime rates, Wilson stresses the certainty of punishment more than its severity. Thus, it is proposed that one of the reasons increased police activity does not itself reduce crime is that the value of an arrest depends on whether a conviction results and on the subsequent actions of the criminal justice system. Wilson observes that, once the chances of being caught, convicted and imprisoned are accounted for, a given robbery is four times more likely to result in imprisonment in the UK than in California and six times more likely in Japan.

It is argued that offenders do not decide to transgress on the basis of the length of sentence, but first of all on the probability of the sentence being applied and thus 'consequences gradually lose their ability to control behaviour in proportion to how delayed or improbable they are' (Wilson and Herrnstein, 1985: 49). Felson – another criminologist widely associated with right realism and whose work is discussed in more detail in the following chapter – provides a neat and often quoted analogy:

> What happens when you touch a hot stove: you receive a quick, certain, but minor pain. After being burned once, you will not touch a hot stove again. Now think of an imaginary hot stove that burns you only once every 500 times you touch it, with the burn not hurting until five months later. Psychological research and common sense alike tell us that the imaginary stove will not be as effective in punishing us as the real stove.
>
> (1998: 9)

The solution, according to Wilson, involves catching more offenders – by increasing police effectiveness – and improving the consistency of the criminal justice system. A poor police/public relationship in the very areas where crime is most prevalent compromises the effectiveness of the police. Poor relations lead to a blockage of information and cooperation flow from the public to the police, together with hostility, mistrust and even protection for offenders by their victims.

The US criminal justice system – although it passes longer prison sentences – convicts fewer of those it tries for predatory crime than do other countries. Wilson and Herrnstein (1985) consequently argue against long sentences, observing that undue severity might persuade the prisoner that he has been treated inequitably, and prompt him to exact revenge by further offending.

Moreover, the longer the available sentence, the less likely judges are to impose them, thus the certainty principle is flouted further.

On the issue of the deterrent value of sentencing, Wilson and Herrnstein adopt a traditional rational actor model stance. They lament the irrationality of the criminal justice system, which, they argue, reflects the view of judges that prison does not act as a deterrent and, in support of their argument, they cite the low proportion of recidivists who are sent to prison. They thus call for fixed-term sentences for offences, regardless of the age of the offender and other attributes, such as the scope for rehabilitation.

It is observed that differential sentences for the same crime reflect a wish to change the behaviour of the offender. If the aim is to deter others, the sentence must be fixed and certain. Moreover, differential sentencing causes a moral dilemma. Those who are perceived less likely to reoffend receive shorter sentences, which in practice means that young, poor black offenders from unstable family backgrounds are sent to prison for longer than older, white middle-class offenders from stable family backgrounds who have committed the same offence.

Right realists nevertheless argue for the use of imprisonment to incapacitate criminals. Recidivists, they note, commit most known crime and, therefore, if offenders in particular categories are certain to be locked up, even for a short period, then the rate of offending in those categories must fall. However, this loss of liberty need not necessarily take the form of conventional imprisonment. Incarceration overnight, or at weekends only, would have the same effect, just so long as it is certain to be applied and rigorously imposed. This neo-Classical approach to deterrence, sentencing and incapacitation is neatly encapsulated in the conclusion of *Thinking About Crime*:

> Wicked people exist. Nothing avails except to keep them apart from innocent people. And many people, neither wicked nor innocent, but watchful, dissembling, and calculating of their opportunities, ponder our reaction to wickedness as a cue to what they might profitably do.
>
> (Wilson, 1975: 235–6)

Right realism and social control

Right realism has emphasized the necessity of upholding public order and public morality in the fight against crime. In contrast to liberal demands for the legalization – or at least decriminalization – of apparently non-problematic street offences such as prostitution and recreational drug taking, right realists propose that these should be more rigorously controlled. Moreover, in the fight against drugs, they see little point in increased interventions against the dealers and the addicts who are beyond help, but propose a concerted intervention against small-time users identified as attacking the fibre of the community (Wilson, 1985).

Wilson and Kelling (1989) propose that the police should intervene against behaviour that in itself is not strictly criminal, advocating action against empty properties, rowdy children and groups of young people on the streets, litter, noise harassment, intimidation and other incivilities that they consider to be indicators of social decline. Such action is justified because such activities provide the welcoming preconditions for high crime rates. Thus, right realists make no demands for changes in the structural conditions in society but rather for the behaviour of individuals to be controlled because it is these incivilities that interfere most with the enjoyment of life for many – particularly poor – people.

It is argued that interventions designed to restore order – and to control crime – should focus on those areas at high risk of becoming, or just beginning to turn into, high crime rate areas. Those areas where crime is already endemic should not have resources devoted to them. The emphasis should be on areas where behaviour can be changed and there is still a possibility of restoring order. In the more problematic localities, there should be a more comprehensive assault on criminality itself. The police should detect and prosecute offenders, with a particularly vigorous response for repeat offenders advocated. It was this latter proposal that led to the 'three strikes and you're out' policy in the US whereby following a third offence – however trivial – an offender would receive a very long prison sentence. In 2002, a total of 6,700 people were serving 25 years to life under 'third strike' legislation. More than 3,350 of them were non-violent offenders, with 350 serving 25 years for petty theft; 44 per cent were black and 26 per cent Latino (Campbell, 2002).

Right realism can be considered very much a contemporary revival of the rational actor model of crime and criminal behaviour. It is the central proposition of their thesis that crime is the result of individual choice and can be prevented or contained by pragmatic means that make the choice of criminal behaviour less likely; reducing the opportunity; increasing the chances of detection; increasing perceptions of detection partly through rigorous policing, especially of disorder; and, most importantly, definite punishment; the threat of severe, certain and swiftly imposed punishment. Imprisonment is seen to be particularly effective in neutralizing or incapacitating offenders and frightening others into adopting law-abiding lifestyles.

Right realism and its propositions on incapacitation have been extremely influential in the USA as the following figures suggest: the prison population in the USA exceeded two million people for the first time in 2002; it is the biggest prison population in the world, and has the highest number of inmates as a proportion of its population. A report from the US Justice Department has estimated that 12 per cent of black men in their 20s and early 30s were in prison, but only 1.6 per cent of white males in the same age group. The overall increase – almost double the number in 1990 – has been credited to the 'get tough sentencing policy that has led to longer sentences for drug offenders and other criminals'. One in every 142 people living in the USA was in prison (BBC News, 2003). Penal incapacitation is moreover not restricted to the USA: on 30 January 2004, the prison population in England and Wales stood at 73,688, an increase of 2,729 over the previous year and 25,000 over the previous ten years (Prison Reform Trust, 2004). By March 2013, that figure had increased to 84,431 (Ministry of Justice, 2013), despite the onset of major economic cutbacks in the public sector and the election of a Coalition Government dominated by Conservatives and a commitment to reducing the prison population.

An enthusiasm for retribution in US criminal justice policy in recent years is epitomized by the reintroduction during the past thirty years of capital punishment. This policy shift is in itself contrary to the early rational actor tradition established by Beccaria, who considered such punishment to be uncivilized and inappropriate to a modern criminal justice system; nevertheless, the parallel predilection for responding to children as rational adults is undoubtedly vintage rational actor thinking. An Amnesty International report published in September 2002 observed that in the previous decade two-thirds of known executions of under-age offenders – or children – had been conducted in the USA. It was observed that, of the 190 member states of the United Nations, only the USA and Somalia had failed to ratify the Convention on the Rights of the Child, which bans such executions (BBC News, 2002).

Developments in conservative criminology

Conservative criminology has (as we have seen above) moved a long way from the purist proposals of the rational actor model and has become identified with the view that criminal law is a codification of certain moral precepts and that people who break the law are those who are in some way psychologically or morally defective. Crime is simply a threat to law-abiding members of society and to the social order on which their safety and security depend. The essential questions asked by contemporary conservative criminologists are: 'how are morally defective persons produced?' and 'how can society protect itself against them?'

The causes of crime are thus located in the characteristics of individuals with the solution expressed in terms of a return to basic values whereupon good is seen to triumph over evil. For example, the moderately conservative self-control theory developed by Gottfredson and Hirschi (1990) (and which is discussed in more detail in Chapter 15) proposes that individuals with low self-control are the people most likely to commit crime. The traits associated with low self-control are perceived to include: a short-time perspective; a low level of diligence, persistence and tenacity; a tendency to be 'adventuresome, active, and physical'; a tendency to be 'self-centred, indifferent, or insensitive to the suffering and needs of others'; and a tendency to have 'unstable marriages, friendships, and job profiles' (Gottfredson and Hirschi, 1990: 91). The major cause of low self-control is considered to be 'ineffective parenting', a claim that is much more widely supported in conservative than liberal circles. Until well into the twentieth century, most criminological thinking was conservative and this viewpoint enjoyed a considerable revival with the Reagan and Bush administrations, and to some extent during the Clinton era, in the USA; and during the Thatcher/Major years and to some extent the New Labour governments in the UK.

A note of caution needs to be posted at this juncture. Not all individualistic theories are inherently conservative and for that matter many of the authors of these theories would not consider themselves to be on the right of the political spectrum. For example, some of the psychological theories we will encounter in Chapter 6, in particular social learning theories, differ only in emphasis from sociological perspectives, the classic example being differential association theory (Sutherland and Cressey, 1978; Akers, 1985). At the same time, more than a few proponents of individualistic theories would favour using information on the apparent differences between criminals and non-criminals to create more effective rehabilitation programmes for offenders well-established in crime and to assist those families seen to be at serious risk of producing young offenders (see Andrews and Bonta, 1994).

Despite these qualifications, there are two reasons why the renaissance of individualistic theory can be considered conservative. First, by looking internally to people for the sources of crime, individualistic theories fail to consider external variables. There is a tendency to take the existing nature of society as a given and to see crime simply as the inability of deficient individuals to adjust to that society. There is no consideration of how long-standing patterns of power inequality and living conditions are implicated in these criminogenic 'deficiencies'. Crime as a social problem is thus transformed into a problem of individual pathology. Society is taken as good, offenders are bad. From this perspective, criminology relinquishes any claims to being 'critical'. It risks concealing, if not actually excusing, the inequities rooted in the social order.

Second, the revival of individualistic theories has not resulted in an era of progressive practices in criminal justice. Thus, although individualistic theories may not be inherently conservative, they often are used – or at times misused – to justify 'get tough' crime control policies.

The revival of conservative theories during the last decades of the twentieth century involved two significant policy agendas: incapacitation and deterrence. Although incapacitation has made a comeback in forms such as the castration of sex offenders and the deterrence theme has manifested itself in a variety of approaches to crime prevention, such as drug use prevention campaigns with tactics such as mandatory urine testing, the major policy agenda of the new conservative theorizing centres around the incarceration of larger numbers of offenders for longer periods with the outcome that the prison population of the USA more than doubled in the space of twenty years (Irwin and Austin, 1994).

There are two aspects of conservative theorizing that propose that incarceration is a utilitarian practice. First, in the process of revitalizing the rational actor model, conservatives emphasize the need to ensure that crime does not pay and therefore lengthy prison sentences are seen to be an effective means of increasing the costs of offending. The argument is that some people will pursue crime as long as the benefits outweigh the costs. We could, of course, interpret this as implying that everyone who has 'nothing to lose' will turn to crime and hence policies should be developed to ensure that citizens have a sufficient 'stake in conformity', that they are afraid to risk it all by involvement in criminal activity. With conservative thinking, that logic is nevertheless replaced by one that proposes that law-breakers will be best deterred from further criminal involvement by long incarceration experiences and that those contemplating crime will be deterred from acting on their criminal impulses by examples of stricter incarceration of offenders. Second, in revitalizing the predestined actor model of criminal behaviour, conservatives are expressing their belief that a *proportion* of offenders – whether this is due to a criminal mind or to a criminal nature, and we will consider the possibilities of this in the second part of this book – are beyond rehabilitation and must therefore be incapacitated in prison (Wilson, 1975, 1985). Such thinking has clearly justified, if not actively encouraged, the widespread use of prisons as a solution to crime.

In the USA, the shift to conservative criminal justice policies was to become the dominant penological orthodoxy; in the UK, it was to some extent moderated by the election of New Labour governments between 1997 and 2010 and the subsequent influence of the left realism we will encounter in Chapter 18.

The term 'liberal-authoritarian' has been used to evoke the schizophrenic nature of the politics adopted by the Labour Party in government after 1997 and by the Conservative Party when in opposition. In an attempt to regain the political centre ground, both parties had simultaneously presented themselves as the guardians of freedom and the advocates of personal responsibility. There is of course nothing new in this approach. Margaret Thatcher claimed to be advancing the cause of freedom through deregulation and the enhancement of consumer choice while using the power of the state to enforce personal responsibility – the paradox of what Andrew Gamble (1989) called the 'free economy and the strong state'.

Both New Labour and the Conservative Party elected to power (albeit in a Coalition Government with the Liberal Democrats) nevertheless represent a break from Thatcherism to the extent that they have, rhetorically at least, recognized the need to heal social divisions, although a more authoritarian approach has been adopted with regard to crime policy. Like their New Labour predecessors, the Conservatives have presented tackling crime as a branch of social policy, as a way of improving the lives of the poorest and most vulnerable members of the community.

David Cameron (2008) claimed, when the then Leader of the Conservative Opposition, that crime, knife crime in particular, is regarded as symptomatic of a 'broken society', along with a host of other social problems, such as family breakdown, welfare dependency, debt, drugs, inadequate housing and failing schools. According to Cameron, the source of all these problems is a state which denies personal responsibility and 'a concept of moral choice' (2008). He complained:

> We talk about people being 'at risk of obesity' instead of talking about people who eat too much and take too little exercise. We talk about people being at risk of poverty, or social exclusion: it's as if these things – obesity, alcohol abuse, drug addiction – are purely external events like a plague or bad weather. Of course, circumstances – where you are born, your neighbourhood, your school, and the choices your parents make – have a huge impact. But social problems are often the consequence of the choices that people make. . . . Imagine if there was a government that understood, really understood, that encouraging personal and social responsibility must be the cornerstone of everything that it did and that every move it took reinforced that view.

Cameron's notion of 'compassionate conservatism' is thus limited to an awareness of social problems and an acceptance that government should be concerned about these. It is about enabling individuals to make their own moral choices and to take responsibility for their own lives. This is rather similar to the view of Margaret Thatcher that encouraging welfare dependency is unkind since it renders the individual a 'moral cripple' (Thatcher, 1976, cited in Jenkins, 1989). Conservative Party crime policy is underpinned by purist conservative criminological theory and proposes that each individual should be held responsible for his or her actions and be severely punished when they transgress. The emphasis on deterrent sentences indeed clearly demonstrates an underlying presumption of rational choice on the part of the criminal. In his 'broken society' speech cited above, Cameron (2008) declared that 'anyone convicted of knife crime should expect to go to jail', saying that he does not believe that the government's 'presumption to prosecute is enough', explaining that 'It doesn't send a strong enough signal. We need a "presumption to prison".'

Personal responsibility (or significantly a lack of it) is also seen to explain criminal behaviour with Cameron and the Centre for Social Justice citing family breakdown as one of the main causes of crime. 'Dysfunctional families', primarily characterized by parental neglect, are considered responsible for problems of addiction and educational failure, which can in turn lead to crime (Duncan Smith,

2007). The need to reinforce personal parental responsibility is clearly prioritized by the Conservatives, with the emphasis being placed on encouraging marriage and in tackling other problems that may lead to family breakdown such as educational failure, addiction and economic dependency (Duncan Smith, 2007) and there is no question who is to blame. Although New Labour has been criticized for exacerbating these problems through wrong-headed intervention programmes, the responsibility of individuals and communities is clearly invoked. Indeed, the causes of crime and other symptoms of social breakdown are seen to be cultural rather than structural (Cameron, 2008). Thus, for example, there is seen to be a 'deliberate culture of worklessness in Britain' that must be tackled by the imposition of ever-tougher penalties for those who refuse to work (Cameron, 2008).

Criticisms of populist conservative criminology

There are clearly a number of significant criticisms that can be made of populist conservative criminology. First, the perspective prioritizes a total focus on street criminality and the maintenance of social order to the virtual exclusion of the white-collar and corporate crimes that are so costly to the economy (Conklin, 1977; Croall, 1992, 2001; see Chapter 1). There is an apparent assumption that most people only experience and have an awareness of street crimes, although it is important here to recognize that it is these very offences that are the most visible and impact most directly on individuals. Mis-sold pension plans, the sale of under-tested and unlicensed pharmaceuticals to distant developing nations and the dumping of polluted effluent into rivers are all examples of crimes that have a considerable aggregate impact on society,[2] but it is being robbed in the street and returning home to find it burgled and trashed that impacts most immediately on individuals and engenders the greatest 'fear of crime' (Kershaw et al., 2000). It is that reality that has been recognized by criminological realists and politicians of both right and left persuasions. Indeed, it could be argued that it is that very recognition that makes them 'realists'.

Second, in searching for explanations of criminal behaviour, populist conservatives ignore all social economic and structural variables – such as poverty and other measures of social exclusion – and focus their attention solely on the behavioural conditioning and inadequate socialization of the individual. Nonetheless, the proposed explanatory link between incivilities, disorder and criminality has been difficult to empirically substantiate. In the UK, for example, Matthews (1992) found that various social indicators such as levels of poverty and the general level of public services available were far more significant than incivilities to the process of urban decline.

Third, the areas with the worst social problems and highest levels of criminality are not deemed worth saving (Wilson and Kelling, 1989). When their inhabitants transgress against the law, they are nevertheless targeted with vigorous crime control strategies and given harsh punishments; when they do not, they are left unprotected in high-crime areas, further marginalized and disadvantaged. Moreover, populist conservatives consider that these people themselves are responsible for their own predicament because they have failed to both correctly socialize their children and use the appropriate controlling mechanism – that is, invariably, corporal punishment – to condition behaviour.

Fourth, the policing of public order offences such as begging and vagrancy allows intervention on the grounds of often dubious legality and is simply unfair because it is particularly disadvantaged groups such as homeless beggars that are targeted (Hopkins Burke, 1998c, 2000).

Fifth, it has been argued that crime clear-up rates are the only true indicators of police performance and moving towards a social order model reduces the possibility of accurately measuring their efficiency (Kinsey *et al.*, 1986). More worryingly, if the police are allowed a more flexible role to control a whole range of incivilities, it becomes very difficult to ensure their accountability and professionalism (see Smith, 2004).

Sixth, this populist conservative rediscovery and adaptation of the rational actor model, with its central proposition that criminal behaviour is simply a rational choice made by those brought up in a world bereft of correct moral values, has led to the targeting and demonization of whole groups of people – such as New Age travellers, drug users and groups of young 'marauding' males – it is argued, by an intrusive and punitive 'law and order' state response with all these aforementioned categories of humanity deemed worthy of severe and vindictive punishment (see Hogg and Brown, 1998).

An early right realist and contemporary of James Q. Wilson who indeed had proposed a similar set of ideas – Ernest Van Den Haag (1975) – was most implicit about the wider political significance of right realism and thus completely dismissive of the above six objections. A rigorous supporter and defender of the inevitability and indeed necessity of capitalism, Van Den Haag observes that the basic rationale of the system is the creation of 'winners' and 'losers'. If we accept that analysis, we then also have to accept that the winners must be allowed to enjoy the fruits of their enterprise and risk-taking without these rewards being illegally taken away by the losers. In short, for capitalism to continue as a (successful) form of economic production, those responsible for the creation/accumulation of wealth – and in its widest sense that includes all those significantly employed core members of a polarized society (Jordan, 1996) with ready access to the opportunities and rewards offered by a meritocratic society – must be protected from the activities of criminals and a socially excluded 'underclass', which is discussed in more detail later in this book and which threatens our well-being, material and otherwise. Moreover, it is members of this core group in society that provide electoral majorities for maintaining these policies.

Policy implications of populist conservative criminology

The crime control policy implications of populist conservatism can be summarized in the following ten propositions.

1. Crime is not determined by social conditions but by tendencies within individuals. Policies thus need to target those tendencies and not structural inequalities.
2. Searching for the causes of crime is an expensive distraction with no record of success and therefore a waste of time.
3. Individuals choose to commit crime. Thus fewer will choose criminal behaviour if governments create more effective and appropriate punishments that are certain to be administered.
4. Policies to improve social conditions will not reduce crime rates and are thus irrelevant.
5. Rehabilitation is an ineffective way of responding to offenders and should be avoided.
6. Crime is a real problem for ordinary people and 'the fear of crime' has a rational basis and should not be ignored.
7. We need to be realistic about what can be achieved in the war against crime and acknowledge the limitations of the current knowledge base.
8. We should not object to the implementation of policies that enable us to achieve pragmatic marginal gains but we should discount utopian grand solutions.
9. Crime is a violation of the law because the latter is an embodiment of the morals of society, which in turn reflects absolute religious notions of right and wrong. Crime is an offence against morality.
10. Crime may be prevented by the repeated assertion of strong social authority founded on traditional morality.

Summary of main points

1. The rational actor model returned to favour with the emergence of the 'new political right' during the last three decades of the twentieth century.
2. The 'nothing works' agenda significantly challenged the rationale for rehabilitation-focused interventions.
3. Retributive punishment was reintroduced with the purpose of protecting society from danger.
4. Crime is a real problem that requires a concerted and rigorous response.
5. The solution to the crime problem involves catching more offenders and improving the consistency of the criminal justice system.
6. The certainty of punishment is stressed more than its severity.
7. Right realists argue for the use of imprisonment as an incapacitator.
8. Conservative criminology argues that people who break the law are in some way psychologically or morally defective.
9. The need to reinforce personal parental responsibility is prioritized with the emphasis on encouraging marriage and tackling family breakdown.
10. Populist conservatives ignore all social economic and structural variables and focus their attention solely on the behavioural conditioning and inadequate socialization of the individual.

Discussion questions

1. Why did rational actor theories become popular again at the end of the twentieth century?
2. What solutions to the crime problem were proposed by the political new right?
3. How do right realists explain involvement in criminality?
4. Why is there an emphasis on children and families by conservative criminologists?
5. What are the identified problems with right realist criminology?

Suggested further reading

For a discussion of the failings of the then dominant predestined actor model and the – at the time – quite influential victimized actor model as a precursor to the rise of popular conservatism and right realism, see Dale (1984), Morgan (1978) and Scruton (1980). Wilson (1985), Wilson and Herrnstein (1985) and Wilson and Kelling (1982, 1989) are essential key texts associated with right realism. Good critiques of different aspects of the populist conservative criminological agenda are offered by Kinsey et al. (1986), Matthews and Young (eds) (1992) and Hogg and Brown (1998).

Notes

1 I have used the term populist conservatives here as that is more descriptive of the elec-torally successful new right politics of the Thatcher (and less so Major) governments during the period 1979–97. The term neoconservatives has gained considerable recognition in the USA but in both constituencies electoral success was based on widespread popularity with groups not previously considered conservative. Thus, the terms 'populist' and 'neo' conservative can be used here interchangeably.
2 Of course, corporate crimes do impact very much on individuals. For a discussion of the victims of mis-sold pensions, see Spalek (2004), while this is an extremely impor-tant contemporary issue in view of the continuing and deepening economic crisis that has enveloped the world since the 'credit crunch' seemingly instigated by highly dubious banking policies and strategies.

4. Contemporary rational actor theories

Key Issues

1. The rational actor model in contemporary society
2. Contemporary deterrence theories
3. Rational choice theory
4. Routine activities theory
5. The limitations of contemporary rational actor theories

Interest in the rational actor model of crime and criminal behaviour was revived both in the UK and the USA during the rise of the political new right – or populist conservatives – during the 1970s and 1980s. The second decade of that time period was to see the influential emergence of the 'nothing works' (Martinson, 1974) agenda at the British Home Office, which seriously questioned the effectiveness of rehabilitation – proposed by the then dominant paradigmatic orthodoxy of the predestined actor model of crime and criminal behaviour – as a crime control strategy. This chapter considers three groups of contemporary rational choice theories that have come to prominence with that revival: (i) contemporary deterrence theories; (ii) rational choice theories; and (iii) routine activities theory.

Contemporary deterrence theories

At the core of contemporary deterrence theories are the principles of certainty, severity and celerity (speed) of punishment, proportionality, specific and general deterrence (Zimring and Hawkins, 1973; Gibbs, 1975; Wright, 1993). The deterrence doctrine proposes that, in order to deter, punishment must be both swift and certain, the notion of celerity concerns the swiftness with which sanctions are applied after the commission of a crime, while certainty refers to the probability of apprehension and punishment. If the punishment is severe, certain and swift, people will, it is proposed, rationally calculate that there is more to be lost than there is to be gained from committing crime. Moreover, it is argued that certainty is more effective in deterring crime than severity of punishment. The more severe the available punishment, the less likely it is to be applied. On the other hand, the less certain the punishment, the more severe it will need to be to deter crime (Akers, 1997).

Deterrence is said to operate in one of two ways. First, in the case of 'general deterrence', the punishment of offenders by the state is seen to serve as an example to the general population who will be frightened into non-participation in criminal behaviour (Zimring and Hawkins, 1973). People will engage in criminal and deviant activities if they do not fear apprehension and punishment. Norms, laws and enforcement are thus to be designed and implemented to produce and maintain the image that 'negative' and disruptive behaviours will receive attention and punishment. Although specific individuals become the object of enforcement activities, general deterrence theory focuses on reducing the probability of deviance in the general population. Examples of control activities reflecting the concerns of this concept include: drink-driving crackdowns, special gang-related crime task forces and police units, publication and highly visible notices of laws and policies (Notice: Shoplifters will be prosecuted to the fullest extent of the law), and the death penalty.

Second, in the case of 'specific deterrence', it is proposed that the apprehended and punished offender will refrain from repeat offending because they realize that they are certain to be caught and severely punished. Specific deterrence thus focuses on punishing known deviants in order to prevent them from again violating the specific norms they have broken. The concern here is that motives and rationales that lie behind the original behaviour can, perhaps, never be explained, but, through the rational use of punishment as a negative sanction, problematic behaviour can be stopped. Examples include shock sentencing, corporal punishment, mandatory arrests for certain behaviours (for example, domestic violence). The ultimate form of individual deterrence is considered to be the death penalty, although research evidence on the deterrent effectiveness of capital punishment has remained ambiguous.

Among the earliest studies of deterrence were examinations of murder rates in various geographical localities before and after the abolition of capital punishment. Ehrlich (1975) used a subsequently much criticized econometric version of rational choice theory to propose that every execution carried out in the USA deterred seven or eight other murders. His findings were nevertheless in contrast to those of studies previously conducted in that country, which had found that the availability of the death penalty in state legislation had no effect on the murder rate (Sellin, 1959; Bedau, 1964). Moreover, following the abolition of capital punishment for murder in England and Wales in 1965, research suggested no identifiable impact on the rate of homicide (Beyleveld, 1979; Morris and Blom-Cooper, 1979).

It has often been suggested that murder – particularly in a domestic context – is a crime where the offender is highly unlikely to make a rational choice before committing the act. If that is the case, the potential consequences will be irrelevant and deterrence is unlikely. In this context, Walker (1985) argues that capital punishment is no more effective a deterrent than a sentence of life imprisonment. The situation might well be different in the case of contract killers – or other professional criminals – who apparently do make a rational choice to commit murder and thus deterrence might be a significant issue. Pfohl (1994) interestingly found that when states abolish the death penalty there is a corresponding drop in capital crimes reported. It is a finding worthy of some speculation.

There was a moratorium on the use of the death penalty in the USA for a period of four years during the 1970s until the case of Gary Gilmore, who actively sought death following his conviction for murder and refused all avenues of legal appeal to stay his execution. He was executed on 17 January 1977.[1] There are those on the (usually libertarian) political right that argue – contrary to the usual liberal mainstream view that capital punishment is no more than legalized state murder, which is contrary to the human/civil rights of the criminal – that it is indeed a more humane punishment than imprisonment for the rest of your life in what amounts to little more than a cage.

We have seen that proponents of the rational actor model assume that potential offenders calculate the rewards and risks associated with crime and research supports the suppositions of the right realists – discussed in the previous chapter – which suggest that the likelihood of detection is a more important part of that calculus than the potential level of punishment (Beyleveld, 1978, 1979). Certainly, the chances of being caught in the commission of an offence by a passing police patrol have been found to be extremely low in the UK (Bottomley and Coleman, 1981), while the detection rates for burglary, for example, have varied between 9 per cent and 46 per cent depending on the locality. The extent to which people believe that they might be caught is therefore probably a more important variable. Gill and Matthews (1994, see also Matthews, 1996) conducted a study of convicted bank robbers and interestingly found that none of their research subjects had even considered the possibility that they would be caught before setting out on their criminal enterprises, even though all had previous criminal convictions.

Even if punishment does deter effectively, a number of ethical objections can be raised to the use of sentences for this purpose. Beyleveld (1978) suggests that the types of punishment needed to deter a potential offender will vary substantially between different people, different crimes and different circumstances. Therefore, in order to deter crime, it might well be necessary to set sentences at a level totally out of all proportion to the seriousness of the offence (Wright, 1982) and this is rather at odds with the central rational choice actor model concept that the punishment should fit the crime. Moreover, when a particular offender has not been deterred, then he or she must receive the threatened punishment. The consequences of such punishment may be simply counterproductive (Wright, 1982).

Martin and Webster (1971) have argued that conviction and punishment may simply push an individual into a situation where he or she has little to lose from further offending. The opportunity to live by legitimate means may be reduced and the individual with previous convictions is pushed towards further illegitimate activity regardless of the consequences. This is an argument similar to that proposed by the labelling theorists working in the victimized actor model tradition that we will encounter in the third part of this book. Central to that perspective is the notion that being caught and stigmatized may lead to an offender becoming committed to further offending behaviour.

Wright (1982) suggests that the possibility of severe punishment encourages offenders to try harder to avoid detection and conviction, and this can lead to violent escapes and to time being wasted by not guilty pleas in court that have no realistic chance of success. Moreover, child sex offenders who could benefit from treatment might be deterred from seeking it.

The use of punishment as a deterrent is based on the core rational actor model assumption that people choose to commit crime. Imposing deterrent sentences on those individuals who have little or no control over their impulses – or who break the law unwittingly – would appear to be morally indefensible, although it can be legitimately argued that deterrence remains a valid option in the case of intentional calculating offenders (Walker, 1980), even though there remains considerable debate as to the existence of such individuals. Critics of contemporary deterrence theories focus on this limited conception of human action on which this perspective is founded and argue the need to develop a considerably more sophisticated theory of human behaviour, which explores the external and internal constraints on why people do or do not engage in criminal activity (see Piliavin *et al.*, 1986; Klepper and Nagin, 1989; Grasmick and Bursik, 1990; Matravers, 1999). For it is proposed that such a theory must recognize the significant number of motivational states – rational and irrational – that can result in the commission of a crime. It is clearly evident that many petty criminals are incapable of accurately balancing the costs and benefits of crime before committing an offence and many young men get involved in street fights with others like themselves without any thought for the consequences of their actions. Keane *et al.* (1993) argue that such people do not in any sense act in a rational manner because their low self-control – or overwhelming demand for immediate gratification – quite simply excludes the possibility of calculating behaviour. If this supposition is correct, then punishment in these circumstances is almost never likely to deter, no matter how certain, severe or quickly it is implemented.

The high recidivism rate further challenges the usefulness of contemporary deterrence theories. Reoffending rates for young people leaving custody are particularly high. Thus, for males aged 14–17, the rate of reconviction within two years of discharge from prison in 1998 was 84 per cent. Of those who were reconvicted, 36 per cent were again sentenced to custody for their first subsequent conviction (NACRO, 2003). Moreover, it would be incorrect to assume that no offences are committed by offenders while they are in custody. Assaults, both on other inmates and staff, are common. During 2000–1, there were 6,388 recorded assaults across the UK Prison Service, and by this measure the five worst-performing establishments were all young offender institutions (Prison Reform Trust, 2002). Similarly, the widespread use of drug testing within the 'secure estate' suggests that detention does not prevent access to illegal substances. Furthermore, the potential of incapacitation to reduce overall levels of crime is extremely limited. The Home Office (2001) has estimated that it would take a 15 per cent increase in the level of custody to effect a 1 per cent reduction in offending.

Rational choice theory

The considerable revival of interest in the rational actor model of crime and criminal behaviour has been clearly demonstrated by the significant government enthusiasm for situational crime prevention measures, which were energetically promoted as governments essentially lost patience with the failure of criminologists to solve the apparently never-ending explosion in the crime figures. Certainly, spending in the UK since the late 1970s was to become devoted more to finding and evaluating pragmatic solutions to particular offences than to developing criminological theory. At the same time, most professional crime prevention practitioners that were to enjoy government patronage came to accept the central notion that crime is an outcome of the opportunity to offend. Regardless of offender motivation, removal of that opportunity, it is argued, will reduce the incidence of crime. Consequently, whole ranges of measures were to be introduced in order to remove or reduce the opportunity to offend.

Situational crime prevention methods aim to reduce a wide range of crimes. Target hardening in its simplest form can amount to no more than closing a door after leaving a room or building unoccupied. At a more sophisticated level, it can take the form of toughened glass 'anti-bandit' screens, specially designed security fencing and armoured safes. If a target can be removed completely instead of simply being protected even more impressive results are possible. Such strategies include the centralization of cash transactions and the issue of tokens for use with gas and electricity meters. Where valuable targets cannot actually be removed, an alternative strategy lies in reducing their attraction to thieves. For example, credit and debit cards were much more attractive to thieves before the UK government-sponsored Chip and PIN system.[2] Some straightforward situational crime prevention initiatives can be remarkably cost-effective and successful, for example, Painter and Farrington (1999, 2001) demonstrated that a scheme to introduce street lamps both substantially reduced criminality and paid for itself within a year.

Proponents of the effectiveness of formal surveillance argue that potential offenders will be deterred by the threat of being seen, and propose that agencies – such as the police and private security companies – that engage in observation activities will deter offenders (Mayhew, 1984). On the other hand, the concept of natural surveillance is founded on the notion that, by observing their environment as they go about their everyday business, people can provide themselves with some protection against crime. Moreover, commercial organizations can seek to protect themselves by the careful positioning of their employees.

These pragmatic strategies for reducing the opportunity to offend are theoretically informed by more recent variants of the rational actor model. In his memoir of a criminal career in the early twentieth century USA, Jim Phelan observed that:

> The robber is a tradesman who, from economics or other motivation, chooses a trade with greater rewards and dangers than navvying. All men in dangerous jobs ... will readily understand the thief-convict ... Yet no one speaks of hereditary test-piloting. No semi-neurotics rush into print about the movie-stuntman's characteristic nose or jaw.
>
> (1940: 178)

From this perspective, involvement in crime – well, at least property crime – is the outcome of a career decision, it is a chosen way of life, a way of making your living, one of a range of options. There is no need for complex cultural and structural biological arguments – such as we will encounter in the second part of this book – to explain it. The key premises of rational choice theory can thus be summarized in the following five propositions.

1. Most criminals are normal-reasoning people. The mode of reasoning used by all adults – with perhaps the exception of the mentally ill, is rational.
2. Rationality is a mode of thinking in which individuals are able to accurately distinguish means and ends: what they want and the ways that are available to them for obtaining those ends. For example: ends – possessing a certain amount of money for a certain amount of work; and means – paid employment, buying a lottery ticket, stealing the money.
3. For each of the different means available to them, rational actors are also able to calculate the likely costs (things they do not want to happen) and benefits (how many or how much of their ends they can achieve) of following a course of action.
4. If benefits outweigh costs, do it. If costs outweigh benefits, don't do it.
5. So, according to rational choice theory, it is not necessary to consider prior causes, antecedents and structures. All that matters are the rational judgements and calculations facing a given person, with their particular set of ends and preferences, in a given situation.

Earlier and less sophisticated variants of rational choice theory had tended to follow the summarized key propositions above and compare the decision-making process adopted by offenders with straightforward economic choice. Thus, Gary Becker (1968) proposed that the potential offender calculates the legitimate opportunities of earning income available, the amount of reward they offer, the amounts offered by illegal methods, the probability of arrest and the likely punishment. The person chooses the activity – legal or illegal – that offers the best return. Suggested preventive strategies – such as those proposed by the right realists encountered in the previous chapter – would involve reform of the law and its administration in order to alter the equation and make crime appear less attractive.

It is perhaps not surprising that these early theories have been accused of implying too high a degree of rationality by comparing criminal choices too closely with marketplace decisions, and, at the same, failing to explain expressive non-economically motivated criminal activity such as vandalism (Trasler, 1986). In the first instance, it can nevertheless be argued that the amateurish criminal who makes wildly inaccurate estimates is no less a rational being than a consumer who runs up huge debts (Sullivan, 1973) and, in the second case, Clarke (1987) observes that, while the motivation behind some expressive crimes may be pathological, their planning and execution may be highly rational. Expressive crimes such as vandalism are actually well explained by the related concept of crime as a function of opportunity and routine activities (Cohen and Felson, 1979). Such offences are usually unplanned and most likely to occur in places where the potential perpetrators are likely to find themselves in the normal course of their lives. A crime such as arson, for example, may have a financial motive, but it is more likely to be committed for expressive reward, to gain the approval of peers, to 'get back at' a target (such as a school) (see Knights, 1998) or simply to alleviate boredom.

A more sophisticated and highly influential variant of rational choice theory has been subsequently developed notably through the work of Clarke and Cornish. From their perspective, crime is defined as 'the outcome of the offender's choices or decisions, however hasty or ill-considered these might be' (Clarke, 1987: 118). In other words, offenders invariably act in terms of a limited or bounded form of rationality. They will not always obtain all the facts needed to make a wise decision and the information available will not necessarily be weighed carefully but it is an approach that avoids the inherent tendency within the predestined actor model to treat criminals as a category of humanity apart from law-abiding citizens. As Paul Ekblom succinctly observes:

> [It is an approach] that does not rely on past improvements in society, treatment-regimes for offenders or early interventions in children's socialisation to reduce current criminality; or on the sheer aversive intensity of sanctions anticipated at some remote time in the future to deter or incapacitate present offending. It does not directly aim to change *offenders'* [emphasis in original] propensities or motives for crime at all. It takes these as given and, proceeding from an analysis of the circumstances engendering particular crimes, it introduces specific changes to influence the offender's *decision* or *ability* [emphasis in the original] to commit these crimes at given places and times.
>
> (2001: 264)

Thus, from the rational choice perspective, crime is simply rational action performed by fairly ordinary people in response to particular pressure, opportunities and situational inducements (Hough *et al.*, 1980; Trasler, 1986). Clarke (1987) is nonetheless not entirely dismissive of the predestined actor model, suggesting that most of the factors seen as predisposing an individual to commit crime can be interpreted in terms of their influence on offender cognitive decision-making. This suggestion that individuals respond to situations in different ways because they bring with them a different history of psychological conditioning is examined further in the final section of Chapter 6.

Bennett (1986) observes that an offence rarely happens because of a single decision to act. A series of decisions will probably be made, starting with the original choice to offend, somewhere at some time, and ending with the final decision to act against a particular target. Therefore, both dispositional and situational factors are involved. Others note the operation of a conscious selection process at the scene of burglaries (Brantingham and Brantingham, 1984; Mayhew, 1984), while situational factors would clearly be expected to exert more influence nearer the criminal event taking place (Bennett, 1986; Heal and Laycock, 1986). If these suppositions are correct, there are clear implications for crime prevention practitioners in deciding when and where to intervene in the sequence of decisions that the potential offender has to make.

Early variants of rational choice theory had considered the issue of offender motivation to be irrelevant, although later variations propose that offenders choose to act in a certain way because these actions appear to them rational in the circumstances in which they find themselves and in terms of their knowledge base and cognitive thought processes (Clarke, 1987, 1999). Sutton (1995, 1998) proposes that it is the existence of stolen goods markets that provides the crucial motivation for theft. Indeed, much of the motivation for seeking out those markets is invariably provided by the large increase in drug addiction in recent years. Bennett *et al.* (2001), for example, detected a considerable correlation between heroin and crack cocaine use and offending behaviour, finding that those who used both drugs regularly spent on average £290 a week or £15,000 a year, were rarely employed and invariably needed to steal to fund their habit.

Sutton (2004) observes that, while there is no doubt that supply to stolen goods markets is provided by those with a motivation to steal, the demand for the goods is – in at least many cases – stimulated by respectable people prepared to ask few questions in the right circumstances. He thus notes that many respectable members of society will be only too willing to buy a top of the range television set if offered for a totally unrealistic price as long as it comes unused in a box. If it has clearly been used and comes with a child's fingerprints visible on the screen, they will be far less enthusiastic. The suggestion is that goods apparently stolen from a factory or 'off the back of a lorry' are somehow acceptable to many 'respectable' members of society, but when they are clearly the outcome of a household burglary they are far less so.

The offence of handling stolen goods has long been a low priority for a resource-stretched public police service and the criminal justice system. Sutton (2004) suggests that judges and their advisers should consider the social harm stolen goods markets do in stimulating the incidence and prevalence of theft – and the unintended consequences of providing subsidies for the illicit sex and drugs industries – and that they should be considerably less tolerant of the local 'fence', thus substantially reducing criminal opportunity. We might nevertheless speculate whether the eradication of stolen goods markets would substantially reduce drug-addicted motivation or simply displace addicts to other means of obtaining cash such as prostitution – male as well as female – or armed robbery (Hopkins Burke, 2004b).

Routine activities theory

Routine activities theory is, to some extent, a development and subdivision of rational choice theory, which proposes that, for a personal or property crime to occur, there must be at the same time and place a perpetrator, a victim and/or an object of property (Felson, 1998). The crime event can take place if there are other persons or circumstances in the locality that encourage it to happen but, on the other hand, the offence can be prevented if the potential victim or another person is present who can take action to deter it.

Cohen and Felson (1979) took these basic elements of time, place, objects and persons to develop a 'routine activities' of crime events. They are placed into three categories of variables that increase or decrease the likelihood that persons will be victims of 'direct contact' predatory – personal or property – crime. The first variable is the presence in the locality of motivated offenders, which are perceived to be predominantly young males. Second, there is the necessity of available suitable targets, in the form of a person or property. The term 'target' was used in preference to that of 'victim' because the acquisition of property or money was seen to be the focus of the great majority of criminal behaviour. Suitability of the target is characterized by four attributes (VIVA):

- **V**alue calculated from the subjective rational perspective of the offender
- **I**nertia, the physical aspects of the person or property that impede or disrupt its suitability as a target
- **V**isibility, which identifies the person or property for attack
- **A**ccessibility, which increases the risk of attack.

The third variable is the absence of 'capable guardians' against crime. Thus, the likelihood of a crime taking place increases when there are one or more persons present who are motivated to commit a crime, a suitable target or potential victim that is available, and the absence of formal or informal guardians who could deter the potential offender. In short, 'the risk of criminal victimisation varies dramatically among the circumstances and locations in which people place themselves and their property' (Cohen and Felson, 1979: 595).

Cohen and Felson observe that it is the fundamental changes in daily activities related to work, school and leisure since the Second World War that have placed more people in particular places at particular times. This has both increased their accessibility as targets of crime and at the same time keeps them away from home as guardians of their own possessions and property.

In his more recent work, Felson (1998) has come to place less emphasis on the significance of formal guardians – such as the police – because he has reached the conclusion that crime is a private phenomenon largely unaffected by state intervention. He now emphasizes the natural crime prevention and deterrence that occurs in the informal control system, the 'quiet and natural method by which people prevent crime in the course of daily life' (Felson, 1998: xii–xiii). Ordinary people, oneself, friends, family or even strangers are the most likely capable guardians.

Felson (1998) has also subsequently applied routine activities theory to four crime categories other than the property variants:

- exploitative (robbery, rape)
- mutualistic (gambling, prostitution, selling and buying drugs)
- competitive (fighting)
- individualistic (individual drug use, suicide).

In doing so, he has identified a fourth variable that enables a criminal event to take place – the absence of an intimate handler, a significant other, for example, a parent or girlfriend – that can impose informal social control on the offender. A potential offender must escape the 'intimate handler' then find a crime target without being under the surveillance of this 'capable guardian'.

Cohen and Felson (1979) relate crime rates to a 'household activity ratio', that is, the percentage of all households that are not husband–wife families or where the wife is employed outside the home. Such households are considered more vulnerable to crime victimization because their members are away from home more and less able to function as guardians of their property. Moreover, they are more likely to possess more desirable goods to be stolen, while at the same time they are more exposed to personal crime away from home. Controlling for age composition and unemployment, Cohen and Felson found that the changes in household activity were correlated with changes in the rates of all major predatory violent and property crimes.

Cohen *et al.* (1981) have developed a more formalized version of routine activities theory and renamed it 'opportunity' theory. This considers elements of exposure, proximity, guardianship and target attractiveness as variables that increase the risk of criminal victimization. But these are not measured directly. These are assumed from variations in age, race, income, household consumption, labour force participation, and residence in different areas of the city obtained from US crime victimization surveys. Their findings nevertheless support most of their propositions.

Cromwell *et al.* (1995) studied the responses of the formal and informal control systems to the devastation of Hurricane Andrew that occurred in Florida in 1982 and they found that the natural disaster temporarily increased the vulnerability of persons and property as crime targets. For a short time, there was nearly a complete loss of police protection in some of the neighbourhoods and motivated offenders with previous records were attracted to the areas in the aftermath of the storm, while at the same time some local people took criminal advantage of the situation. There was, however, little looting and crime rates actually went down during the time when the community was most vulnerable, only to increase again after the initial impact period. Cromwell *et al.* explain these findings as being most likely the result of neighbours watching out for neighbours, citizens guarding their own and other property – sometimes with firearms – citizens' patrols, and other steps taken to aid one another in the absence of government and formal control.

The fact that some people may be motivated to commit crime when targets are made vulnerable by such events as natural disasters raises important questions about the concept of the motivated – or potential – offender that purist versions of the rational actor model are ill-equipped to answer. Quite simply, does the concept of motivated offender in routine activities theory refer only to someone who has an inherent predisposition to offend? Or does it include anyone who is enticed by the opportunity for quick gain itself, even though he or she may not have previously existing criminal intentions?

Mike Sutton (2014, forthcoming) questions the whole notion of 'opportunity' in routine activities theory (RAT), observing that this is seen to arise when a relatively more capable and sufficiently motivated 'likely' offender succeeds against a target or victim. This thus proves that they were capable offenders against relatively incapable or absent guardianship. Sutton argues that this crime as 'opportunity' explanation does not provide discoverable and measurable quantifiable values that would enable criminologists to predict and test individual or general victim or target vulnerability. This means that the capable and suitably motivated offender components of 'crime opportunity' cannot be discovered and objectively measured before a successful crime happens – only afterwards. It thus follows that until a crime is successfully completed – or fails in the attempt – the current notion of 'crime opportunity' cannot be known by offenders to exist in advance of the crime being completed or failing. This is because no potential thief could know for sure that they would be more capable than any guardian or that guardianship would remain absent. After all, if that was possible, there would be no reason for so many failed criminal attempts. Sutton (2014, forthcoming) argues that the widely cited claim that 'opportunity makes the thief' (Felson and Clarke, 1998) is logically flawed. The current classic RAT and situational crime prevention notion of 'crime opportunity' – Sutton suggests that 'ratortunity' is perhaps a better word for it – is an elegantly precise, perhaps perfect, post hoc description of any successfully *completed* criminal act. It is nothing more.

Akers (1997) furthermore observes that routine activities theory fails fundamentally to explain why it is that some people engage in criminal behaviour and others do not. There is a taken-for-granted assumption that such people exist and that they commit crimes in certain places and at times when the apparent opportunities and potential victims are available. It tells us absolutely nothing about these people and their motivations. The predestined actor model discussed in the following second part of this book offers numerous suggestions.

Regardless of the identified shortcomings of routine activities theory, there have been some useful and interesting applications and developments in its use both in the USA and the UK in recent years, which have been helpful in explaining why it is that certain groups are more likely to become victims of crime. Thus, Boudreaux *et al.* (2001) review existing research on the topics of child abduction and child homicide and identify and assess potential victim risk factors through a discussion of victim access, vulnerability and routine activities theory. Freisthler *et al.* (2004) use the concept to provide a partial explanation for the substantial growth in recorded cases of child abuse in the USA since the early 1970s, identifying a close correlation with a parallel growth in substance – in particular alcohol – abuse during the same time period. Pizarro *et al.* (2007) consider the journey to murder and show that there are statistically significant differences among homicide types in terms of the length of the journey of victims and suspects to the incident location and in their motives for actually going there. The findings of the researchers suggest that the demographic and lifestyle characteristics of victims and suspects have an impact on their journey to crime and victimization.

In the UK, Nick Tolson (2007) has used routine activities theory as the basis of his Clergy Lifestyle Theory, which he has used to assess the risk of violence to members of the clergy with the practical purpose of improving their safety and security. He found that since 1996 there had been a total of five vicars murdered and many others seriously injured. Gabe (2001) found that 12 per cent of clergy suffer from physical violence and that 70 per cent suffer from some form of violence and found these figures to be significantly higher than for other professional groups who work in the community. Moreover, while the majority of assaults inflicted on probation officers and GPs – other professional groups with a high rate of victimization – had occurred in their main place of work, the majority of assaults on members of the clergy were reported to have taken place in their homes, in the street or on local estates rather than in church buildings. At the same time, most GPs and probation officers knew their assailant, while almost half the clergy who had experienced an assault said that they did not know their assailant. Thus, an attack could occur at virtually any time or location in their everyday lives, while at the same time any stranger they encountered was potentially an assailant. Tolson (2006) found that 48 per cent of the clergy in his sample had suffered at least one violent incident in the preceding twelve months. He found that there is much similarity in how the clergy live their lives and almost all are on their own at certain points of the day; they travel, visit and, on occasion, pray on their own, which in certain situations can mean that they are at very high risk of violence should they encounter the 'motivated offender', whoever they might be (Tolson, 2007). Thus, while the notion of crime opportunity in routine activities theory might have limited value (Sutton, 2014, forthcoming), particularly in the case of certain economically motivated crimes, the concept is nevertheless very useful in helping to identify targets and victims at high *risk* of becoming completed crimes in other categories of crime as the above examples demonstrate.

The rational actor reconsidered

The Classical theorists had emphasized the rationally calculating, reasoning human being who could be deterred from choosing to commit criminal behaviour by the threat of fair and proportionate punishment. Moreover, they had proposed that all citizens should be treated equally in terms of a codified and rationalized legal system. In terms of the influential social contract theories of the time – epitomized and institutionalized by the initial aftermath of the French and American Revolutions at the end of the eighteenth century – human beings were (mostly) all seen to be equal citizens. In this purist initial version of the rational actor model of crime and criminal behaviour, the implicit emphasis was very much on a due process criminal justice model epitomized by such notions as the 'rights of man' and the 'rule of law'.

This purist version was both amended and fell into decline for three closely interlinked reasons. First, it became clear that not all are equally rational calculating human beings: a recognition that was to herald the end of what in practice had been a rather short-lived notion that all human beings are equal. Second, there was an increasing awareness that a rational due process criminal justice intervention was having little effect on the crime statistics, not least because there was a growing group of recidivists who were apparently not deterred by this strategy. Third, the latter discovery neatly coincided with the rise of the predestined actor model and its central supposition that criminals are a separate entity from law-abiding citizens. This is the focus of the second part of this book

Thus, the revised version of the rational actor model – that came to the fore with the rise of the political 'new right' in the last quarter of the twentieth century – implicitly accepted the predestined actor notion that there are different categories of human beings, while denying the central notion of that model that proposed treatment or rehabilitation in preference to punishment. Criminal motivation or the predisposition of the offender was immaterial.

The emphasis was now on deterrence and – if the person failed to heed that warning and was not to be deterred or scared off – punishment. The issue of motivation was of no importance as long as criminal behaviour ceased to occur. Hopkins Burke and Pollock (2004) nevertheless challenge the supposed irrelevance of addressing the issue of offender motivation in their discussion of hate – or bias – crime and they define the perpetrators of such offences to be:

> those unaccepting of the heterogeneous nature of the contemporary societies in which they live and primarily characterise social groups according to their visible ethnic, racial or sexual identity rather than their personal attributes. Thus, a key component of hate victimisation is the existence of bias and prejudice based upon 'what' someone is, rather than 'who' they actually are.
>
> (Hopkins Burke and Pollock: 2004: 2)

They acknowledge that the introduction of specific legislation and targeted situational crime prevention measures have had some considerable impact on reducing the incidence of hate crimes and recognize that for many – and this appears to be a widespread and influential discourse – the impact of this contemporary rational actor intervention strategy has brought a satisfactory outcome. The validity of ignoring hate motivation is, on the other hand, fundamentally questioned:

> An ethnic minority colleague of ours recently summed up this apparent contemporary race-relations orthodoxy by observing that 'if they aren't saying it and they aren't doing it then that's ok'. But is it ok? These dimensions of intervention [legal and situational crime prevention] do not eradicate hatred itself, and the colleague had undoubtedly also seen the look in their eyes which betrayed their real thoughts. It could well be that as an outcome of a change in structural circumstances – for example, the arrival of a group of immigrants or asylum seekers in the locality, the chance meeting of a new friend or colleague with similar latent views, perhaps while on holiday or after the consumption of a few 'social' drinks, or as the outcome of surfing the Internet – that latent hate crime motivation could well be transformed into something more insidious.
>
> (Hopkins Burke and Pollock, 2004: 18)

Hate crimes have not tended to be at the top of the crime control agenda of populist conservative politicians seeking election, but in dealing with offenders in general, and predatory street offenders in particular, they seem to be only too willing to accept the notion proposed by James Q. Wilson that there are simply evil people – or perhaps more accurately a class or underclass of evil people – who need to be rigorously targeted by the agencies of the criminal justice system. Thus, with this revised formulation of the rational actor model, there has been an emphasis on a crime control model criminal justice intervention that promotes the detection and punishment of those offenders who cannot be deterred as the main priority. The huge increase in the prison population in both the USA (BBC

News, 2003) and the UK (Prison Reform Trust, 2004) during the past twenty years appears to be testimony to the success of this crime prevention strategy.

If the prescriptions of the rational actor model are in any way accurate, then the prisons should be clearly full of people who have made (for them) rationally calculating decisions to commit criminal offences. Yet the reality is very different. Statistics suggest that prisons are full of people with (often chronic) mental health problems who seem incapable of making any rational choice. In the most recent large-scale survey of UK prisons, it was found that over one-third of men serving prison sentences had a significant mental health problem (such as anxiety or depression); nearly one in ten had experienced some form of psychosis, while one in four had attempted suicide in prison. Over three-quarters of men on remand and nearly two-thirds of male inmates met the diagnosis of having a personality disorder (Mind, 2006). The suicide rate among male prisoners is six times higher than among men in the general population, and in 2003 there were 94 suicides in prisons in England and Wales, 80 of which were men with 19 per cent under 21 years of age. Many aspects of prison life undermine the health and well-being of those in custody, and exacerbate pre-existing mental health problems. As Juliet Lyons (2005) from the Prison Reform Trust observes: 'If you had to invent a way to deepen mental health problems and create a health crisis, an overcrowded prison, and particularly the bleak isolation of its segregation unit, would be it.'

It is thus clear that prisons are full of prisoners who cannot be considered fully rational calculating actors and thus the limitations of the rational actor model first identified two hundred years ago are still relevant today. In the following second part of this book, we will consider the predestined actor model of criminal behaviour, which makes alternative suggestions as to how such people should be dealt with.

Policy implications of contemporary rational actor theories

All three categories of contemporary rational actor theories – contemporary deterrence theories, rational choice theories and routine activities theories – have their theoretical foundations in the Classical School theorists Cesare Beccaria and Jeremy Bentham (Chapter 1), which were revived and revitalized by the populist conservatives during the last three decades of the twentieth century (Chapter 2).

The central rational actor model concept of deterrence is based on the notion that people consciously try to avoid pain and seek pleasure. It logically follows that by making a choice painful enough – such as the choice of committing crime – individuals will choose not to engage in that particular activity. This perspective would predict that crime rates are the lowest in those places where offending evokes the most 'pain' (or costs) and highest in those places where offending brings the most 'pleasure' (or benefits). In short, deterrence theory seeks to explain why individuals do or do not offend and, moreover, why it is that certain places in society have higher or lower crime rates. This perspective has clear implications for criminal justice policy and practice. Crime can be reduced by organizing the criminal justice system to maximize the pain of doing crime and to minimize its benefits.

The whole aim of the criminal justice system from this perspective is to 'scare people straight', both those who have engaged in crime (specific deterrence) and those who are thinking about committing crime (general deterrence). Problematically, for the past three or four decades, the USA (and to a lesser extent UK) policy-makers have spent literally billions of dollars on a costly experiment that proposes that getting tough on crime – especially through mass incarceration – will reduce reoffending. Todd Clear (1994) has referred to this ongoing attempt to use the criminal justice system in the USA to be an instrument for inflicting pain as the 'penal harm movement' (see also Currie, 1998).

Rational choice and routine activities theory both propose that crime rates are a product of criminal opportunity (see the above critique of the concept from Sutton). It is thus thought that, by increasing the number of guardians, decreasing the suitability of targets or reducing the offender population, the crime rate should decline. A central implication of understanding offending in terms of a rational calculation means that the criminal justice system is capable of controlling crime, that aggressive law enforcement and severe punishment should deter offenders, and, consequently, produce a notable reduction in criminal offending.

The inherent problem with rational actor theories is that they are founded on the disputed assumption that offenders are rationally calculating individuals. Though there is some empirical support for the tenets of this theory, its primary weakness is the assumption that offenders think before acting, that they conduct a cost-benefit analysis before deciding to engage in crime. Despite the appearance of rationality in offending, the implications of assuming this to be the case, in terms of deterrence, is not strongly supported by research.

Deterrence comprises the certainty, severity and celerity of legal sanctions. Thus, it is proposed that rationally calculating offenders can be discouraged from committing offences if the chances of their being caught are high, the punishment is severe and justice is swift. Therefore, if criminals are indeed rational, an inverse relationship should exist between punishment and crime; as the sanctions for offending are increased, a threshold should be reached where it is no longer beneficial to the offender to engage in offending behaviour. By implication, it is held that crime rates are influenced and controlled by the threat and imminence of criminal punishment and commonly assumed that, if offenders were punished more severely, they, being rationally calculating individuals, would choose not to offend because the offence is not worth the punishment. Doob and Webster (2003) nevertheless conducted a comprehensive review of deterrence literature published in the last thirty years of the twentieth century and concluded that variations in sentence severity do not affect the level of crime in society. Thus, while deterrence may make intuitive sense, it is not supported by empirical research.

LeBlanc and Frechette (1989) argue that most offenders make almost no preparation for an offence and this is especially true for young offenders. This means that the illegal behaviour is not the outcome of a calculated or well-thought-out process. Ladouceur and Biron (1993) accept that some thought does go into offending but note that the plans tend to focus on the immediate offence, not the long-term consequences of that action. Doob and Cesaroni (2004) thus suggest that a distinction needs to be made between rational choice in the short term and consideration of the long-term implications. The young do not consider the long term; they are impulsive and focus on the immediacy of the rewards associated with offending. Even if they do think of the criminal justice consequences, they find them irrelevant as it is unlikely that they will be caught. Tunnell (1996) conducted interviews with convicted prisoners and found that all sixty respondents simply did not think about the criminal consequences of their actions. Though they knew their actions were criminal, and therefore tried to avoid capture, more than half were unaware of the severity of the punishment for the offence.

Since most offenders do not think they will be caught, and in fact it is unlikely that they will be caught, increasing the penalty has no prolonged effect on the crime rate. It is the perceived risk of apprehension, not the severity of punishment that holds the greatest power to deter, though this ability is limited as well. This is demonstrated by the Kansas City experiment, where it was found that variations in police patrol techniques had little effect on crime patterns (Kelling et al., 1974). Regardless of the actual likelihood of apprehension, most offenders simply do not think they will be caught. This finding is supported by Bursik et al. (1990), who failed to find a relationship between the likelihood of being arrested or imprisoned and corresponding crime rates.

Originally proposed by Oscar Newman in the 1970s, situational crime prevention is supposed to create defensible space, which suggests that crime can be prevented through the use of architectural designs that reduce opportunity (see Chapter 14). Situational crime prevention is aimed at convincing would-be criminals to avoid specific targets. It is thus held that criminal acts will be avoided if the potential targets are carefully guarded, if the means to commit crime are controlled, if potential offenders are carefully monitored, and if opportunities for crime are reduced (Siegel and McCormick, 2006: 135). The difficulty with situational crime prevention strategies in general, and closed-circuit television (CCTV) and public surveillance in particular, is that they tend to displace offending behaviour to locations that are not under surveillance. Instead of preventing crime, these often costly surveillance strategies simply move crime to another location (Barr and Pease, 1990). This is exemplified by the police crackdown on illicit drug use in Vancouver in 2003. Rather than reducing drug offending, the only 'success' of the intervention was to disperse drug activity over a larger area. Wood (2004) emphasizes that, since enforcement efforts do not address wider issues such as poverty, health, harm reduction, welfare and housing, they are incapable of producing real reductions in crime.

It would seem that assuming a rational basis for committing a crime overestimates the extent to which people consider the legal consequences of their actions. Contemporary rational actor theories also focus on individuals and their choices, while ignoring the social constraints and conditions that shape the circumstances in which they live, their thought processes and life chances. These exert considerable influence on people. Engaging in crime is not simply a rational decision. It is affected by the interaction of a number of factors and influences. Furthermore, increasing the penalty also assumes that offenders were aware of the original sanction and felt it was worth the risk, while the new, more punitive punishment makes it no longer worth the risk in a cost-benefit analysis. This, again, is assuming that offenders are aware of the change in the severity of the sentence and rationally calculate their choice of action. Since this assumption is not supported by the research literature, both specific and general deterrence strategies have not yielded the results predicted by rational choice theorists.

Summary of main points

1. At the core of contemporary deterrence theories are the principles of certainty, severity and celerity of punishment, proportionality, specific and general deterrence.
2. With 'general deterrence', the punishment of offenders serves as an example to the general population who will be frightened into non-participation in criminal behaviour.
3. With 'specific deterrence', the apprehended and punished offender will refrain from repeat offending because they realize that they are certain to be caught and severely punished.
4. Imposing deterrent sentences on individuals who have little or no control over their impulses would appear morally indefensible.
5. The high recidivism rate further challenges the usefulness of contemporary deterrence theories.
6. Earlier and less sophisticated variants of rational choice theory compared the decision-making process of offenders with straightforward economic choice.
7. Early variants of rational choice theory considered offender motivation to be irrelevant, although later variations propose that offenders choose to act in a certain way because these actions appear to them rational in the circumstances in which they find themselves.
8. Routine activities theory proposes that for a personal or property crime to occur there must be at the same time and place a perpetrator, a victim and/or an object of property.
9. The offence can be prevented if the potential victim or another person is present who can take action to deter it.
10. Ordinary people, ourselves, friends, family or even strangers are the most likely capable guardians.

Discussion questions

1. What are the differences between 'general' and 'specific' deterrence?
2. What are the identified weaknesses with contemporary deterrence theories?
3. Are rational choice theories of any value in explaining criminal behaviour?
4. How do routine activities explain criminal acts?
5. What are the weaknesses in routine activities theory?

Suggested further reading

For a comprehensive introduction to the notion of 'deterrence' in contemporary criminal justice and jurisprudence observed from a US perspective, see Gibbs (1975), Zimring and Hawkins (1973), and Piliavin *et al.* (1986). Walker (1980, 1985) and Grasmick and Bursik (1990) provide the equivalent in a UK context. Matravers (ed.) (1999) provides a series of essays on punishment and political theory. For further discussion of contemporary rational choice theory and situational crime prevention, see Clarke (1980, 1987, 1999), Clarke and Mayhew (1980), Cornish and Clarke (1986) and Mayhew *et al.* (1976). Cohen and Felson (1979) and Felson (1998) are key routine activities theory texts.

Notes

1 It was a case that received worldwide publicity and was immortalized by the British punk rock band The Adverts in their hit record 'Looking through Gary Gilmore's Eyes', which was banned by the BBC for being in bad taste.
2 Banks and retailers replaced magnetic stripe equipment with that based around smart-cards, which contain an embedded microchip and are authenticated automatically using a PIN. When a customer wishes to pay for goods using this system, the card is placed into a 'PIN pad' terminal (often by the customer themselves) or a modified swipe-card reader, which accesses the chip on the card. Once the card has been verified as authentic, the customer enters a 4-digit PIN, which is checked against the PIN stored on the card. If the two match, the transaction is completed. This technology is nevertheless not without its problems.

Part Two

The predestined actor model of crime and criminal behaviour

The method which we . . . have inaugurated is the following. Before we study crime from the point of view of a juristic phenomenon, we must study the causes to which the annual recurrence of crimes in all countries is due. These are natural causes, which I have classified under the three heads of anthropological, telluric and social. Every crime, from the smallest to the most atrocious, is the result of the interaction of these three causes, the anthropological condition of the criminal, the telluric environment in which he is living, and the social environment in which he is born, living and operating. It is a vain beginning to separate the meshes of this net of criminality.

(Ferri, 1968 originally 1901: 71–2)

It was shown in the first part of this book that the rational actor model of crime and criminal behaviour proposes that human beings possess free will, which enables them to make rational decisions about what actions they should take, whether these are legal or illegal. It is also proposed that, as rational calculating human beings, they should be held fully accountable for their actions. These ideas – as we have seen – had been highly influential in changing criminal justice policies during the late eighteenth and early nineteenth centuries particularly in France. However, with the publication of the first national crime statistics in that country in 1827, it became clear that these data were astonishingly regular. Furthermore, some places had higher rates than others and these differences remained relatively constant from year to year. Rational actor model proponents had expected random changes in the number of crimes. The regularity of the new crime statistics suggested that, rather than being entirely the product of free will, criminal behaviour must be influenced by other factors.

It was also clear that crime rates were increasing rather than decreasing and so was the rate of recidivism or repeat offending. People who had received the prompt proportionate punishment administered by the new French criminal code were committing more offences rather than fewer, which suggested that the rational actor model notion that changes in punishment policies alone could reduce crime was simply wrong.

These recognitions were to be highly influential in the rise of the predestined actor model of crime and criminal behaviour, which is a tradition with its origins in a very different view of society and human nature than that proposed by the rational actor model. It emerged in the nineteenth century during a period of rapid industrialization and the consolidation of capitalism as the dominant mode of production in Europe and – at that time – when there was a major concentration of previously rural-based peasants into the fast-expanding large cities, the creation and expansion of the factory system and the introduction of new productive technologies. These changes saw the flow of labour into employment in the industrial sphere and the emergence of a new social class – the working class or the proletariat.

The rise of the urban working class was accompanied by major industrial, social and political conflict. Life was hard and brutal for these people. Child labour was common and there was a thin dividing line between conditions experienced by those working for a living and those condemned to the poorhouse. Living and working conditions were harsh, dirty and crowded. At the same time, the capitalist class was amassing huge fortunes and adopting opulent lifestyles. The contrast in circumstances and opportunities between the two classes was immense.

It was at this time that the working class began to organize itself industrially and politically and, although banned by law, workers began to combine into trade unions, while there was a growing sympathy for fledgling socialist notions of a 'classless society'. This was all reflected in the proliferation of alternative working-class publications, pamphlets and daily press, and in the formation of socialist parties. It was also a time of new thinking about the nature of human beings and of society in general.

Proponents of the predestined actor model – or positivist school of criminology – rejected the rational actor model emphasis on free will and replaced it with the doctrine of determinism, and from this perspective it was argued that criminal behaviour could be explained in terms of factors, either internal or external to the human being, which cause people to act in a way over which they have little or no control. Thus, in some way, it is the destiny of the individual to become a criminal.

There are three basic formulations of the predestined actor model: biological positivism (the focus of Chapter 5), psychological positivism (Chapter 6) and sociological positivism (Chapter 7). All three versions are nevertheless founded on the same fundamental assumptions, and, although each is discussed separately, it will become increasingly apparent to the reader that they are not mutually exclusive. Chapter 8 considers how each of these three formulations has explained female criminal behaviour.

Three sets of ideas provide the intellectual foundations of the predestined actor model. First, there is the notion of evolution and science. Before the latter half of the nineteenth century, explanations of the essence of humanity had been fundamentally provided by theology, but from that time onwards such questions became increasingly the preserve of science, in particular biology.

The biggest influence on the development of biology was the work of the great English naturalist Charles Darwin (1809–82), whose major works *The Origin of Species* (1968 originally 1859), *The Descent of Man* (1871) and *The Expression of Emotion in Man and Animals* (1872) are widely considered to mark the end of 'pre-scientific' thinking about the causes of human behaviour.

In a world dominated by religious stricture and biblical explanation, it was simply assumed that human beings are a species distinct from the rest of the animal world with the free will to choose a course of action based on their assessment of the pleasures and pains that various alternatives are likely to provide. It was Darwin's theory of evolution that was to first seriously challenge such views.

According to evolutionary biology, humans are animals subject to the laws of nature like all other animals and it is these rather than free will or choice that must therefore govern human behaviour. The task of scientists interested in criminal behaviour is to isolate and identify those causal forces that determine conduct and, inevitably, the first place they looked for such forces was in the biological constitution of the offender.

The second set of ideas was provided by social evolutionism, of which Herbert Spencer (1820–1903) was the major theorist. In the 1850s, he had produced a series of essays – especially 'The Development Hypothesis' and 'Progress: Its Law and Cause' that drew from biology the elements of a general evolutionary *Naturphilosophie*. This was to be the basis of his multivolume *System of Synthetic Philosophy* (1862–96), which first expounded a set of general evolutionary principles that he then applied to biology, psychology, sociology and ethics. In sociology, in particular, Spencer broke new ground in comparative data collection and synthesis.

Spencer was an evolutionist before Darwin. He had always held the view that human characteristics are inherited and it was this aspect of his work that was to be the biggest influence on the development of the predestined actor model of crime and criminal behaviour. Spencer nevertheless went much further than Darwin, explaining evolution as the product of the progressive adaptation of the individual character to the 'social state' or society, and in this respect his sociology rests on definite psychological foundations. His major contribution to the development of sociology is, however, his recognition that human beings develop as part of a process of interaction with the social world they inhabit. This significant thesis that environmental factors influence the development of the human being was – as we shall see – to be increasingly important and latterly fundamental to the development of the predestined actor model.

The third set of ideas focused on the positivist method devised by the philosopher and social visionary Auguste Comte (1798–1857), who perhaps is best known for giving a name to the discipline of sociology, which he nevertheless outlined rather than practised. The foundation of his thought was his search in chaotic times – exemplified by the major transition from predominantly agrarian to urban societies throughout Western Europe – for principles of cultural and political order that were consistent with this apparently forward march of society. In his later writings, especially *the Discours sur L'esprit Positif* ('Discourse on the Positive Spirit'), the *Systeme de la Politique Positif* ('System of Positive Polity') and the *Catechism of Positive Religion*, Comte provided the design for a new social order. This work provides the theoretical foundations of the social positivism that is the focus of Chapter 7.

For Comte (1976), positivism is the doctrine that the methods of the natural sciences provide the only means of obtaining knowledge of human nature and society. This knowledge has to be constructed out of evidence obtained from the senses – from empirical data – although there is to be a role for theoretical conceptualization in order to make sense of this data. Thus, from the positivist standpoint, truth can never be attained through abstract speculation or pure intellectual philosophizing. On the contrary, the laws that govern all events in the world – for all are caused in regular discoverable ways – are available to the rigorous observer. Having obtained their empirical data, the scientist can then formulate these laws in order to subject them to test and verification. None of this was new – British empirical philosophers, such as David Hume, had said as much for two hundred years – but what was radical was the application of positivism to the discovery of social laws. The implications of this theoretical revolution were colossal, for the application of positivist knowledge could provide the means for the peaceful reconstruction of the social order by the elite of enlightened scientists and intellectuals. It was this aspect of his work that undoubtedly influenced the early biological criminologists discussed in the following chapter.

5. Biological positivism

Key Issues

1. The Italian School and early biological theories
2. Inherited criminal characteristics
3. Genetic structure theories
4. Autistic spectrum disorders
5. Altered biological state theories

The foundations of the biological variant of the predestined actor model of crime and criminal behaviour – or biological positivism – can be located primarily in the work of Cesare Lombroso, Enrico Ferri and Raffaele Garofalo. These early and highly influential biological criminologists – or the Italian School as they are usually collectively known – argued that criminology should focus primarily on the scientific study of criminals and criminal behaviour. Both their methodology and clearly some of their findings might seem highly simplistic and even laughable by the standards of today, but they nevertheless established an enduring scientific tradition, which has become increasingly sophisticated over the years and has enjoyed something of an explanatory renaissance in recent years.

Early biological theories

Cesare Lombroso (1836–1909) was both a psychiatrist at the University of Turin and a physician employed in the Italian penal system. In 1875, he published his most famous work *L'Uomo Delinquente* (*On Criminal Man*) and the primary – and most significant – theme in this early work is that criminals represent a physical type distinct from non-criminals. Said to represent a form of degeneracy apparent in physical characteristics suggestive of earlier forms of evolution, criminals are *atavistic*, throwbacks to earlier forms of evolutionary life. Ears of unusual size, sloping foreheads, excessively long arms, receding chins and twisted noses are indicative signs of criminality. Although essentially a biological positivist, we should nevertheless note that, in the later editions of his work, Lombroso came increasingly to pay attention to environmental factors such as climate, poverty, immigration and urbanization.

Lombroso now classified criminals in four main categories. First, *born criminals* are simply those who can be distinguished by their physical atavistic characteristics. Second, *insane criminals* are those including idiots, imbeciles, paranoiacs, epileptics and alcoholics. Third, *occasional criminals* or *criminaloids* are those who commit crimes in response to opportunities when these might be available – as identified by rational actor theorists – but importantly, in contrast to that alternative tradition, have innate traits that predispose them to commit criminal behaviour. Fourth, *criminals of passion* are those motivated to commit crime because of anger, love or honour.

Lombroso made little reference to female offenders and considered their criminality to be predominantly restricted to prostitution and abortion, and observed that a man was invariably responsible for instigating their involvement in these crimes. This stereotypical view – that women engage in prostitution because of their sexual nature – totally disregarded the obvious motivation of economic necessity but was to remain an enduring and influential explanation of female criminal behaviour until very recently and is discussed in more detail in Chapters 8 and 11.

Lombroso undoubtedly used primitive methodology based on very limited data and a very simplistic use of statistics. Moreover, he did not have a general theory of crime that would enable him to organize his data in any meaningful way (Taylor *et al.*, 1973). Criminals were simply those who had broken the law and the problem thus appeared deceptively straightforward. All one needed to do was locate the differences between people that produce variances in their tendencies to violate the law.

Early biological proponents of the predestined actor model fundamentally assumed that offenders differ in some way from non-offenders. They then problematically observed that offenders appeared to differ among themselves and committed different types of crime. Moreover, offenders who committed the same type of crime appeared alike in terms of important characteristics. The solution to this problem was to subdivide the criminal population into types – each of which would be internally comparable with respect to the causes of crime – and different from other types on the same dimensions.

Most today consider the approach of Lombroso to have been simplistic and naive but we should observe that he did make three important contributions to the development of modern criminological theory. First, he directed the study of crime away from the armchair theorizing that had characterized the early proponents of the rational actor model towards the scientific study of the criminal. Second, although his methodology was rather primitive, he demonstrated the importance of examining clinical and historical records. Third, and most significantly, he recognized the need for multi-factor explanations of crime that include not only hereditary, but also social, cultural and economic factors. These latter important factors were also emphasized by his successors in the early biological tradition Enrico Ferri and Raffaele Garofalo.

Enrico Ferri (1856–1929) was thus not simply a biological positivist but significantly argued that criminal behaviour could be explained by studying the interaction of a range of factors: *physical factors*, such as race, geography and temperature; *individual factors*, such as age, sex and psychological variables; and *social factors*, such as population, religion and culture (Ferri, 1895). He rather radically proposed that crime could be controlled by improving the social conditions of the poor and, to that end, advocated the provision of subsidized housing, birth control and public recreation facilities and it was a vision that fitted well with the socialist views of Ferri. In the 1920s, he was invited to write a new penal code for Mussolini's fascist state, but his positivistic approach was rejected for being too much of a departure from rational actor model legal reasoning. Sellin (1973) observes that Ferri was attracted to fascism because it offered a reaffirmation of the authority of the state over the excessive individualism that he had always rejected.

Raffaele Garofalo (1852–1934) was both an academic and a practising lawyer remembered for his doctrine of 'natural crimes' where he argued that, because society is a 'natural body', crimes are offences 'against the law of nature'. Criminal behaviour is therefore unnatural. The 'rules of nature' are the rules of right conduct revealed to human beings through their powers of reasoning. For Garofalo, the proper rules of conduct come from thinking about what rules should be allowed or prohibited, and he identified acts that he argued no society could refuse to recognize as criminal and, consequently, repress by punishment.

Garofalo argued that these *natural crimes* violated two basic human sentiments that are found among people of all ages, namely the sentiments of *probity* and *pity*. Pity is the sentiment of revulsion against the voluntary infliction of suffering on others, while probity refers to respect for the property rights of others. Garofalo argued that these sentiments are basic moral sensibilities that appear in the more advanced forms of civilized society and proposed that some members may have a higher than average sense of morality because they are superior members of the group. True criminals, on the other hand, lack properly developed altruistic sentiments and have psychic or moral anomalies that can be inherited.

Garofalo identified four criminal categories, each one distinct from the others because of deficiencies in the basic sentiments of pity and probity. The first category, *murderers*, are totally lacking in both pity and probity and will kill and steal whenever the opportunity arises. Lesser criminals are more difficult to identify and this category is subdivided on the basis of whether criminals lack sentiments of either pity or probity. Thus, the second category, *violent criminals*, lack pity and can be influenced by environmental factors, such as the consumption of alcohol, or the fact that criminality is endemic to their particular population. The third category, *thieves*, suffer from a lack of probity, a condition that might be more the product of social factors than is the case for criminals in the other categories. His fourth category contains sexual criminals, some of whom will be classified among the violent criminals because they lack pity. Others require a separate category because their actions stem from a low level of moral energy rather than a lack of pity.

The penological implications of the respective theories of Lombroso and Garofalo are substantially different. Lombroso had wanted to provide treatment for – and change – deviants so that they could be reintegrated into society. Garofalo reasoned that criminal behaviour demonstrated a failure to live by the basic human sentiments necessary for the survival of society. Criminals should therefore be eliminated in order to secure that survival. Life imprisonment or overseas transportation was proposed for lesser criminals. Significantly, both Garofalo and Ferri were prepared to sacrifice basic human rights to the opinion of 'scientific experts' whose decisions would take no account of the opinions of either the person on whom they were passing judgement or the wider general public. Their work was thus acceptable to the Mussolini regime in Italy, because it provided scientific legitimization to ideas of racial purity, national strength and authoritarian leadership (Vold, 1958). It will be seen in the following sections that later biological explanations of crime and criminal behaviour became – and indeed have become – increasingly more sophisticated. The logical conclusions that can be reached from the implications of the tradition established by Garofalo and Ferri nevertheless remain the same. If an incurable criminal type exists and can be identified, then the logical solution is surely to isolate and remove such individuals permanently from society. Some would indeed suggest that this process of isolation take place before the individual has the opportunity to offend. The notion of treatment should not be automatically assumed to be a soft option to the punishment intervention advocated by proponents of the rational actor model. The term 'treatment' can have much more sinister connotations with serious civil rights implications. We should thus perhaps be grateful that the latter apparently more sophisticated biological variants of the predestined actor model remain inherently problematic.

Inherited criminal characteristics

An idea arose at the end of the nineteenth century that criminality is inherited in the same way as physical characteristics, and evidence to support this supposition has subsequently been obtained from three sources: (i) criminal family studies; (ii) twin studies; and (iii) adopted children studies.

Criminal family studies

Criminal family studies have their origins in the work of Dugdale (1877), who traced 709 members of the Juke family and found that the great majority were either criminals or paupers. Goddard (1914) subsequently traced 480 members of the Kallikak family and found that a large number of them had been criminals. Interestingly, while both researchers had observed social as well as inherited criminal characteristics as causes of crime, both emphasized the link between criminality and 'feeblemindedness'. Indeed, following the invention of intelligence tests (IQ tests) by Alfred Binet in 1905, inherited feeblemindedness was commonly proposed as a principal cause of crime, although it was to go out of fashion for some considerable time from the 1920s onwards.

Goring (1913) reported a fairly sophisticated study of 3,000 prisoners, with a history of long and frequent sentences, and a control group of apparently non-criminals. The prisoners were found to be inferior to the control group in terms of physical size and mental ability, while strong associations between the criminality of the children and their parents and between brothers were found. Moreover, it was found that children who were separated from their parents at an early age, because the latter were imprisoned, were as likely, or more likely, to become criminals compared with other children not separated in this way. Thus, contact with a criminal parent did not seem a significant factor associated with criminal conduct. Goring thus claimed that the primary source of criminal behaviour is inherited characteristics rather than environmental factors.

Three principal weaknesses can be identified in Goring's study. First, there is a failure to measure satisfactorily the influence of environmental effects on criminal behaviour. Second, a comparison of stealing and sex offences is based on the assumption that parental contagion is restricted entirely to techniques of crimes and fails to consider the possibility that the transmission of values is more important. Third, the study was restricted to male criminals, although the ratio of 102 brothers to 6 sisters imprisoned is mentioned. It would seem logical that, if criminality is inherited, females should be affected to a similar extent as males unless it is a sex-linked condition. Twin and adoption studies have attempted to provide a more sophisticated examination of the relationship between criminality and heredity (Sutherland and Cressey, 1978).

Twin studies

There are clear genetic differences between identical (monozygotic) twins and fraternal (dizygotic) twins. Identical twins occur when a single fertilized egg produces two embryos. They are thus genetically identical. Fraternal twins are the outcome of two different eggs being fertilized at the same time and they are as genetically different as children born after separate pregnancies. It is obvious that differences in the behaviour of identical twins cannot be explained by different inherited characteristics but, on the other hand, various studies have proposed that similarities in their conduct can be explained by shared heredity.

Lange (1930) examined a group of 30 men, comprising 13 identical twins and 17 fraternal twins, all of whom had a prison record and found that, in 77 per cent of cases for the identical twins, the other brother had such a record. However, for the fraternal twins, only 12 per cent of the second twins had a prison record. This percentaged relationship is referred to as a criminal concordance. Two hundred pairs of ordinary brothers – near to each other in age – were also compared. Where one brother had a criminal record, the same applied to the other brother in only 8 per cent of cases. Lange thus concluded that heredity plays a major part in the causation of criminal behaviour.

Christiansen (1968) examined official registers to discover how many of 6,000 pairs of twins born in Denmark between 1881 and 1910 had acquired a criminal record and found that in the 67 pairs of identical male twins – where at least one brother had a criminal record – the criminal concordance was 35.8 per cent. There were 114 pairs of fraternal male twins where at least one brother was a convicted criminal, but the criminal concordance was only 12.3 per cent. The criminal concordance was found to be higher for both categories where more serious offences had been committed.

A problem with twin studies is a lack of clarity about the sort of characteristics that are supposed to be passed on and this is important, as variations might reveal themselves in quite different forms of behaviour (Trasler, 1967). For example, some pairs of twins in Lange's study had committed very different types of offences from each other and it could well be the case that a predisposition to offend is inherited but the actual form of offending is determined by other factors. Christiansen did not, however, claim that inherited characteristics were the only – or for that matter the dominant – factor that led to the higher concordance for identical twins. He was of the opinion that twin studies could increase our understanding of the interaction between the environment and biological traits and, in fact, he used variations in concordance rates in urban and rural areas to suggest that environmental factors might play a greater part in an urban setting. It is, nevertheless, a central criticism of such studies that they cannot accurately assess the balance between the effects of inherited characteristics and those of the environment. Twins are more likely than ordinary siblings to share similar experiences in relation to family and peers and it is possible that such similarities will be greater in the cases of identical twins.

Dalgard and Kringlen (1976) studied 139 pairs of male twins where at least one brother had a criminal conviction and concordances of 25.8 per cent and 14.9 per cent were found for identical and fraternal twins, respectively. However, when the researchers controlled for mutual closeness, no appreciable difference in concordance rates was found between the types of twins and they thus concluded that hereditary factors were not significant in explaining crime. However, Cloninger and Gottesman (1987) reviewed the same data and reached a very different conclusion, observing that, if Dalgard and Kringlen had been correct, then the environmental effects would cause psychologically close identical twins to act the same as each other, and psychologically distant identical twins to act differently. This did not happen.

A more recent twin study supports both inherited characteristics and environmental explanations of criminality. Rowe and Rogers (1989) collected data from self-report questionnaires involving 308 sets of twins in the Ohio State school system in the USA and concluded that inherited characteristics partly determine the similarity of behaviour of same-sex and identical twins. They nevertheless recognized that interaction between siblings could cause initially discordant siblings to become concordant in their levels of offending. Moreover, as twins are brought up together as a general rule, it becomes virtually impossible to reach any firm conclusion as to the role of inherited characteristics alone (Rowe, 1990). Studies of adopted children have sought to overcome that inherent methodological problem.

Adopted children studies

In the case of adopted children – where contact with a criminal parent has obviously been limited – any association between criminal behaviour can be attributed to inherited characteristics with a greater degree of certainty. Hutchings and Mednick (1977) carried out a study of male adoptees born in Copenhagen between 1927 and 1941 and found that 48 per cent of young males with a criminal record and 37.7 per cent with a record of minor offences had a birth father with a criminal record. Among young males without a criminal record, 31.1 per cent had a birth father with such a record. The study discovered that an adoptee was more likely to have a record where both the birth and adoptive father had previous convictions.

In a further comparison, 143 of the adoptees with criminal records were matched with a control group containing the same number of adoptees without convictions. Among the sample group, 49 per cent were found to have criminal birth fathers, 18 per cent had criminal birth mothers and 23 per cent had criminal adoptive fathers. Among the control group, 28 per cent were found to have criminal birth fathers, 7 per cent had criminal birth mothers and 9.8 per cent had criminal adoptive fathers. On the basis of these findings, a very strong link between inherited characteristics and criminal behaviour was proposed.

The research was later replicated in a wider study that encompassed all non-familial adoptions in Denmark between 1924 and 1947 (Mednick *et al.*, 1984). A similar though slightly less strong correlation between birth parents and their adopted children was found and again the most significant results were when both birth and adoptive parents were criminal. The researchers concluded that there was an inherited characteristic element that was transmitted from the criminal parents to their children that increased the likelihood of the children becoming involved in criminal behaviour. It is nevertheless important to note that adoption agencies try to place children in homes situated in similar environments to those from which they came and it remains a possibility that it is upbringing not inherited characteristics that cause criminal behaviour. On the other hand, some people may be genetically endowed with characteristics that render them more likely to 'succumb to crime' (Hutchings and Mednick, 1977: 140). Exactly what these inherited crime-inducing characteristics might actually be is not really considered.

Intelligence and criminal behaviour

In more recent years, there have been attempts to rehabilitate notions of a link between intelligence and criminal behaviour. This interest in intelligence is based on a controversial position – taken in the late 1960s – that proposed intelligence to be genetically based, and that differences in IQ can be used to explain different criminal propensities between ethnic groups (see Shockley, 1967; Jensen, 1969). Robert Gordon (1986) argued from this perspective that IQ is actually the best predictor of offending behaviour among various groups.

Hirschi and Hindelang (1977) reviewed studies on IQ and offending behaviour and found that – as a predictor of offending behaviour – IQ is at least as good as any of the other major social variables. Furthermore, they noted that IQ is also strongly related to social class and ethnic group. Because offending behaviour is viewed as the province of lower-class young people from ethnic minorities, this relationship implies that such people have lower IQs and this argument has received a great deal of understandable criticism. For example, Menard and Morse (1984) observed that IQ is merely one of the ways in which juveniles are disadvantaged in US society and proposed that it is the societal and institutional response to these disadvantages that are the real explanation for offending behaviour.

In general, critics of IQ tests have noted that the way in which the tests are constructed provides advantages to those who are middle class and white, while it is argued that the tests do not measure innate intelligence, but rather some other ability, such as a facility in language or cultural concepts.

Genetic structure theories

A further category of biological explanations of crime and criminal behaviour considers abnormalities in the genetic structure of the offender. Crucial abnormalities identified are those related to the sex chromosomes. People usually have 23 pairs of chromosomes, 46 in all, and the sex of a person is determined by one of these pairs. The normal complement in a female is XX and in a male XY but in some men an extra chromosome has been found to be present.

Klinefelter *et al.* (1942) found that sterile males often display a marked degree of feminization and sometimes with low intelligence and increased stature. It was subsequently discovered that these men with 'Klinefelter's syndrome' had an extra X chromosome. In 1962, Court Brown conducted a study of Klinefelter males in psychiatric institutions and discovered an abnormally high incidence of criminal behaviour among his subjects and suggested that these men are over-represented among the population of homosexuals, transvestites and transsexuals. It is, of course, important to recognize that such activities are no longer illegal.

Later studies considered incarcerated criminals and focused on individuals with an XYY complement of sex chromosomes, in order to test the hypothesis that they might be characterized by 'extra maleness', and thus be more aggressive. Casey in 1965 and Neilson in 1968 conducted the first major studies at the Rampton and Moss Side secure hospitals, respectively, and found that men with an extra Y chromosome tend to be very tall, generally of low intelligence and often present EEG abnormalities (EEG is discussed below). Moreover, many of these early examples were found to have histories of criminal and aggressive behaviour with theft and violent assault their characteristic offences.

Price and Whatmore (1967) noted that subjects with an extra Y chromosome tend to be convicted at an earlier age than other offenders, come from families with no history of criminality, tend to be unstable and immature without displaying remorse and have a marked tendency to commit a succession of apparently motiveless property crimes. Witkin *et al.* (1977) explain the over-representation of such men in institutions to be the result of their slight mental retardation.

A range of criticisms has been made of these genetic structure theories. First, almost all the research has been concentrated on inmates in special hospitals and has revealed more evidence of psychiatric disorder than criminality. Second, there does not appear to be any fixed and identifiable XYY syndrome, which means the concept is not useful in predicting criminal behaviour. Third, the offending behaviour of some young males with an extra X chromosome may be due to anxiety in adolescence about an apparent lack of masculinity. Fourth, all the young male offenders with an identified extra Y chromosome have come from working-class backgrounds. It is thus possible that because young males with an extra Y chromosome are usually tall and well built, they may be defined as 'dangerous' by judges and psychiatrists, and more likely to be incarcerated than fined. Finally, and crucially, there are thousands of perfectly normal and harmless people in the general population who have either an extra X or Y chromosome.

Advances in genetic science in recent years have led to a revival of claims that aspects of criminality can be accounted for by genetic factors. Ellis (1990) thus looked to processes of natural selection operating on genetic evolution to explain some aspects of criminal behaviour and has argued that some criminal activities – especially rape, assault, child abuse and property offences – are linked to powerful genetic forces. He nevertheless offers no proof of genetic connections with crime and criminal behaviour, merely presenting a hypothesis based on assumptions of inherent animal-like behaviour.

It has however become increasingly apparent that a tendency to contract many diseases is strongly affected by inherited factors and the particular genes related to specific ailments are currently being identified. Moreover, there have been suggestions in recent years that insurance companies might wish to examine the genetic characteristics of potential clients. Geneticists have been cautious in claiming that human behaviour is primarily determined by inherited characteristics but the discovery that some personality traits can be explained by a genetic component (Jones, 1993) does greatly strengthen the possibility that some criminal behaviour can be explained by a genetic susceptibility triggered by environmental factors and this point is revisited in Chapter 13.

Criminal body types

A further category of the biological variant of the predestined actor model has its foundations directly in the Lombrosian tradition of concentrating on body type. Kretschmer (1964 originally 1921) identified four criminal body types: first, asthenics are lean and narrowly built, flat-chested and skinny with their ribs easily counted; second, athletics have broad shoulders, deep chests, flat stomachs and powerful legs; third, pyknics are of medium build with an inclination to be rotund with rounded shoulders, broad faces and short stubby hands; and fourth, mixed types are those which are unclassifiable. Kretschmer argued that the asthenic and athletic builds are associated with schizophrenic personalities, while pyknics are manic-depressives.

Hooton (1939) conducted a detailed analysis of the measurements of more than 17,000 criminals and non-criminals and concluded that the former are organically inferior to other people, that low foreheads indicate inferiority, and that 'a depressed physical and social environment determines Negro and Negroid delinquency to a much greater extent than it does in the case of Whites' (Hooton, 1939, Vol.1: 329). Hooton was not surprisingly widely condemned for the racist overtones of his work and his failure to recognize that the prisoners he studied represented only those who had been caught, convicted or imprisoned. Moreover, his control group appeared to be representative of no known population of humanity.

Sheldon (1949) produced the first modern systematic linking of body traits with criminal behaviour but was at the same time highly influenced by his predecessors in this tradition. He significantly shifted attention from adults to offending male youths, studying 200 between 15 and 21 years of age in an attempt to link physique to temperament, intelligence and offending behaviour, classifying the physiques of the boys by measuring the degree to which they possessed a combination of three different body components. First, endomorphs tended to be soft, fat people; second, mesomorphs were of muscular and athletic build; and third, ectomorphs had a skinny, flat and fragile physique. Sheldon concluded that most offenders tended towards mesomorphy and, because the youths came from parents who were offenders, the factors that produce criminal behaviour are inherited.

Glueck and Glueck (1950) conducted a comparative study of offenders and non-offenders and gave considerable support to the work of Sheldon, finding that, as a group, offenders tended to have narrower faces, wider chests, larger and broader waists and bigger forearms than non-offenders. Approximately 60 per cent of the offenders were found to be predominantly mesomorphic but the researchers – like their predecessors – failed to establish whether this group were offenders because of their build and disposition, or because their physique and dispositions are socially conceived to be associated with offending. Or indeed whether a third set of factors associated with poverty and deprivation affected both their body build and offending behaviour.

Body type theories can be criticized for ignoring different aspects of the interaction between the physical characteristics of the person and their social circumstances. People from poorer backgrounds will tend to have a poorer diet and thus be small in stature, while young people in manual occupations are likely to acquire an athletic build. The over-representation of such people among convicted criminals may thus be explained by a variety of sociocultural – rather than biological – factors.

Gibbons (1970) argues that the high proportion of mesomorphy among offenders is due to a process of social selection and the nature of their activities is such that deviants will be drawn from the more athletic members of that age group. Cortes and Gatti (1972), in contrast, propose that such arguments falsely accuse biological explanations of criminal behaviour of being more determinist than they actually are. They propose that, as physical factors are essential to the social selection process, human behaviour has both biological and social causes.

Hartl et al. (1982) conducted a thirty-year follow-up of Sheldon's research subjects and found that the criminal group still showed significant signs of mesomorphy, but, on the other hand, the highly influential longitudinal Cambridge

Study in Delinquent Development found no evidence that offenders were in any way physically different from non-offenders (West, 1982). There thus remains much ambiguity in the findings from body type research, although researchers continue to pursue this approach with Raine *et al.* (2000) finding that three-year-old children (boys or girls) who were just half an inch taller than their peers had a greater than average chance of becoming classroom bullies with the ambitious suggestion that they would go on to be violent criminals.

Psychoses and brain injuries

This category of the biological variant of the predestined actor model addresses neurological conditions that supposedly *cause* criminal behaviour but there is little evidence that brain injuries actually lead to criminal behaviour. There have been cases reported, but these are very rare, and studies suggest that the original personality and social background of the person are of greater significance. A brain injury might, however, accentuate an underlying trend to aggression if it occurs in a specific area of the brain.

There is some evidence of association between criminality and 'minimal brain dysfunction' (MBD), which is a condition that can lead to learning disabilities in school and thus – by various routes – to offending behaviour, although there is little evidence of neurological malfunction in these cases. The usual personality changes associated with brain injury are forgetfulness, impaired concentration and diminished spontaneity in thought.

There are some organic psychoses that are associated with brain lesions or malfunctions. First, *epidemic encephalitis* is a condition that was widespread among children in the 1920s and was often linked to destructiveness, impulsiveness, arson and abnormal sexual behaviour. Second, *senile dementia* is a general organically based deterioration of the personality that affects some old people and may be accompanied by arson, paranoid delusions and deviant sexual behaviour. Third, *Huntingdon's chorea* is an inherited disease involving brain decay – characterized by involuntary and disorganized movements, apathy and depression – that may result in vicious assaults in a fit of uncontrollable temper. Fourth, *brain tumours* – especially in the temporal lobe region – can activate the neural systems linked to aggressive behaviour that can result in outbursts of rage, violence and even murder but the condition is reversed with the surgical removal of the tumour. Fifth, much attention has been devoted in the criminological literature – from Lombroso onwards – towards *epilepsy*, particularly temporal lobe epilepsy and it has been found that some, but by no means all, victims of this illness do sometimes make violent assaults on people during and occasionally between seizures (Mark and Ervin, 1970).

There does appear to be a relationship between violent and aggressive behaviour and malfunctions of the limbic system, which is that part of the brain concerned with mediating the expression of a broad range of emotional and vegetative behaviours, such as hunger, pleasure, fear, sex and anger. Various studies have shown that it is possible, by electrical stimulation of the brain, to induce aggressive behaviour in otherwise placid subjects (see Shah and Roth, 1974) and removing or burning out that part of the brain that appears to be responsible for aggression can also control it. It is also possible to electrically stimulate other parts of the brain to produce docility.

In a study of unprovoked 'abnormal' killers, Stafford Clark and Taylor (1949, cited in Shah and Roth, 1974) found that 73 per cent had abnormal EEG readings and, among 'clearly insane' murderers, the incidence was 86 per cent. EEG – electroencephalogram – is a record of the rhythmical waves of electrical potential occurring in the vertebrate brain, mainly in the central cortex. Other studies have also shown that EEG abnormalities are highest among aggressive psychopathic criminals and lowest among emotionally stable groups (see Mednick and Volavka, 1980; Volavka, 1987).

EEG abnormality is often associated with chromosomal abnormality. Thus, the majority of people who have an extra X or Y chromosome also have EEG abnormalities. Epileptics always have EEG abnormalities and so very frequently do those with a psychiatric condition known as psychopathy, a condition discussed more fully in the following chapter. There are three possible explanations of the link between EEG abnormality and psychopathy: first, psychopaths do not have the same levels of sensory perception as other people; second, the condition may be associated with the malfunction of specific brain mechanisms, particularly those concerned with emotion; and third, the pattern of brainwaves is different in children and adults and thus what may be normal for the child is abnormal for the adult.

It is this last possible explanation that has led to the development of the concept of EEG motivation, and it seems probable that this proceeds in parallel with psychological motivation. Much of the psychiatric abnormality shown in the behaviour disorders of early adult life can be related to emotional immaturity and this tends to significantly reduce or disappear as an individual passes into his or her 30s and 40s. It is among persons of this type that EEG abnormality is most commonly found.

There is undoubtedly a *correlation* between psychopathy and abnormal EEG but, on the one hand, there are criminals diagnosed as psychopathic but with normal EEG patterns, while, at the same time, there are many non-criminal people with bizarre EEG patterns. Moreover, anticonvulsant drugs that stabilize brain rhythms have no effect on psychopaths. EEG patterns are therefore extremely difficult to *interpret* and quite often 'experts' will disagree totally. It has thus not been possible to produce the foundations of a general explanation of crime and criminal behaviour from studies of the brain and the central nervous system. Hans Eysenck has, however, attempted to develop a general theory based on the autonomic nervous system but his work, which is discussed in the following chapter, is overwhelmingly psychological.

Much of this earlier work has been more recently developed and incorporated under the term *forensic neuropsychology*, which is predominantly biological in orientation. Neuropsychologists try to show how behaviour (including criminal behaviour) is paralleled in brain functions. It is a field of study that is relatively young and research-based but it is still of rather uncertain practical value (but yet it is very promising). Especially in the USA, increasing attention has been drawn to the field, mostly regarding its application to insanity defence cases (Tallis, 2007). While neuroimaging may one day help us determine criminal responsibility, the overarching question remains an ethical and philosophical one. Thus, should individuals with brain-based disorders be held responsible for their antisocial behaviour and, indeed, is it possible to alleviate responsibility for certain disorders? At the time of writing, these questions are philosophical as the neuronal basis of criminal/antisocial conduct has yet to be discovered (Perlin and McClaln, 2010).

Studies conducted to date suggest that there might be some connection between impairment found within certain areas of the brain and antisocial personality disorder (APD) or psychopathy. Brain damage may also contribute to an inability to control anger or disorganized thought. Even if the meaning of this connection is not yet understood, the results of neuropsychological assessments may still serve as an important factor when determining risk to reoffend and overall functioning. Brain structures/areas commonly associated with APD or psychopathy include a) the prefrontal cortex (primarily medial and ventromedial sections); b) the amygdala and hippocampus; c) the temporal lobe; and, to a lesser extent d) the corpus callosum and e) the angular gyrus (Raine and Yang, 2006).

The ventromedial prefrontal and limbic areas especially have received much attention. It is also worth noting that psychopathy is defined by two factors: antisocial behaviour (which is associated with prefrontal areas and problems with inhibition) and lack of emotions (associated with amygdale and the limbic system). Research indicating that psychopaths often do not respond to treatment further strengthens this association between brain dysfunction and psychopathy. Psychopathy is often cited as the single greatest predictor of repeat offending (Hare, 2003), especially violent offending (Wahlund and Kristiansson, 2009), and increased knowledge into the biological basis of antisocial behaviour disorder could be incredibly informative for psychologists and the legal system (Harris and Rice, 2006). This condition is discussed in more detail below.

Some childhood behaviour disorders are thought to be caused by brain dysfunction resulting from complications in pregnancy, birth or childhood and this issue is discussed in Chapter 13. A mild form of dysfunction that has been discussed in recent years is attention deficit disorder, which is sometimes identified in conjunction with hyperactivity, the symptoms including behavioural problems and poor cognitive responses. Mannuzza *et al.* (1989) tested a sample for hyperactivity both in childhood and later in young adulthood and found that a significantly greater number of hyperactive children than the controls had been arrested, convicted and imprisoned. The researchers found that this difference could be almost entirely explained by the presence of an antisocial conduct disorder in young adulthood. Hyperactivity alone could not be considered responsible for the onset of the later criminal behaviour.

The Cambridge Study in Delinquent Development tested a cohort of young males at regular intervals from the age of eight and data was collected on attention deficit, hyperactivity, home background and delinquency (Farrington *et al.*, 1990) and found that both attention deficit and behavioural problems were associated with high rates of offending. The problems from the former could be linked to a low IQ, an early record of offending, being a member of a large family and having criminal parents. Behavioural problems were thus linked to deficient parenting. The researchers nevertheless considered that the connection between attention deficit and crime was not necessarily biological, considering that environmental and social factors could have been influential.

Certain learning disabilities – allegedly arising from a dysfunction in the central nervous system – have also been linked to offending behaviour. There is, however, a problem in concluding whether such disabilities arise out of biological or social factors. It is not difficult to see how children with learning difficulties can be perceived as being disruptive or lazy at school and such inappropriate behaviour may also serve to alienate potential friends with the outcome that the young person can come to feel rejected, alienated and isolated. At that point, they may well stop going to school – either through truancy or exclusion – and start to mix with other disaffected young people on the streets with the disastrous consequences outlined in the discussion of deviant subculture theories in Chapter 7. Ignoring biologically founded conditions in children and young people can be very much to their disadvantage as is suggested by the relatively recent discovery of the large number of children with autistic spectrum disorders.

Autistic spectrum disorders

Eugen Bleuler first used the term 'autism' at the beginning of the twentieth century to refer to what he thought to be a variant of schizophrenia characterized by 'a narrowing of relationships to people and the outside world, a narrowing so extreme that it seemed to exclude everything except the person's own self' (Frith, 2003: 5). In 1943, Leo Kanner distinguished autism from childhood schizophrenia, observing the crucial distinction that 'people with schizophrenia withdrew from social relationships while children with autism never developed them in the first place' (cited in Mesibov *et al.*, 2001: 7).

In 1944, Hans Asperger, a Viennese paediatrician, introduced the term 'autistic psychopathy', emphasizing the peculiarities of communication and the difficulties in social adaptation of children with autism (Frith, 2003). However, while Kanner had described children with a more extreme debilitating variant of autism, Asperger described more able, indeed sometimes gifted, children (Attwood, 1998). However, while the variant of autism identified by Kanner was to gain worldwide recognition, the condition identified by Asperger was to remain virtually unknown outside of Germany until it was introduced to the English-speaking world by Lorna Wing in 1981 (Rosaler, 2004).

Wing and Gould (1979, cited in Wing 1998) concluded that children with Kanner's autism and Asperger's Syndrome have in common a triad of impairments affecting social interaction, communication and imagination, accompanied by a narrow, rigid, repetitive pattern of activities, and they developed from this discovery the notion of a continuum or spectrum of disorders held together by this triad. This spectrum runs from clear-cut autism through to subtle variants that shade into traits found within the normal (neurotypical) population. Moreover, it is now thought that 'autistic traits are widely distributed in the normal population and many "normal people" show isolated autistic traits' (Thambirajah, 2007: 133).

Autism and Asperger's Syndrome are two of the five pervasive developmental disorders (PDD), which are more often referred to today as autistic spectrum disorders. They have a 'neurological basis in the brain and genetic causes play a major role. However, precise causes are still not known' (Hill and Frith, 2004: 1). Thus, they are 'defined using behavioural criteria because, so far, no specific biological markers are known' (Hill and Frith, 2004: 2), which demonstrates that the non-specific and variable nature of the autistic spectrum makes it difficult to diagnose. The risk of becoming an offender is statistically more probable if any child experiences certain risk factors such as peer rejection, low popularity, social isolation (Farrington, 2005), poor social functioning and impulsivity (Pakes and Winstone, 2007), which are common among children and young people on the autistic spectrum. Johnston significantly observes that 'Those people who fall within the autistic spectrum . . . have very particular difficulties which markedly impair their understanding of the social world, and they may be more prone to problem behaviour and therefore to offending' (1997: 270).

There are thus a number of features of autistic spectrum disorders that can predispose those with the condition to criminal behaviour (Berney, 2004). First, some have narrow obsessions and are unaware of the effect that their behaviour has on others. Howlin (1997) cites the case of a young man fascinated by washing machines from a very young age who would enter any house where he could hear one in action without any appreciation of the alarm this would cause the occupant. Second, some have problems with the interpretation of rules, particularly social ones, and as a result of this may 'find themselves unwittingly embroiled in offences such as date rape' (Berney, 2004: 347). It is a misinterpretation of social rules that can be linked to social naivety and social relationships. Often eager to be accepted, such children can be very 'easy prey' (Howlin, 2004) and, as the National Autistic Society (2005) observes, this has led some to be befriended by, and become the unwitting accomplices of, criminals. They simply do not understand the motives of other people. Third, children on the autistic spectrum like routine and are resistant to changes. If unexpected changes occur, 'it can be so distressing to a person with autism that they may react with an aggressive outburst' (National Autistic Society, 2005: 9) (see also Baron-Cohen, 1988; Ghaziuddin, 2005).

Asperger himself first suggested a possible association between the condition he described as 'autistic psychopathy' and violence, while several other studies have documented examples of violence in those with autistic spectrum disorders (see Baron-Cohen, 1988). Howlin nevertheless pertinently observes that:

Although there is little evidence of any significant association between autism and criminal offending, occasional and sometimes lurid publicity has led to suggestions that there may be an excess of violent crime amongst more able people with autism or those diagnosed as having Asperger's syndrome.

(2004: 301)

This all becomes evident with the case of a thirteen-year-old autistic boy who killed his baby brother by cutting off his left hand and stabbing him seventeen times (BBC News, 2001). When asked by the police why he did it, he replied, 'I wanted to be with my mum' (BBC News, 2001). Kelly (2006) reports the case of a 21-year-old male who stabbed to death his 57-year-old boss because he thought she was to blame for getting him sacked. Despite the gravity of this offence, it was observed that 'even now [he] believes he acted appropriately'.

There is, however, a significant possibility that other factors could have influenced the offending behaviour in the above cases and in others involving people on the autistic spectrum. Ghaziuddin (2005) observes that factors such as poor parental control, a chaotic environment and a family history of poor mental health and criminality could predispose such a person to violence.

It is clear that there are many people located somewhere on the autistic spectrum and many of these have symptoms that can clearly dispose them to criminal behaviour. It is thus important that society becomes aware of this condition and the various difficulties that it can pose for those who are on the spectrum. On the other hand, it is important to recognize that many – if not the great majority – of the people on the spectrum do not become involved in criminal behaviour and indeed there are many very famous people past and present who are on the autistic spectrum and it is extremely likely that this condition has actually contributed to their success. The crucial issue here would again seem to be the specific interaction of predisposing biological factors in a particular social context.

Biochemical theories

Biochemical explanations of criminal behaviour are similar to the altered biological state theories discussed in the following section. The difference lies in the fact that biochemical explanations involve substances – or chemical processes – already present in the body, while altered state explanations involve the introduction of outside agents. In this section, we will consider sexual hormones, blood sugar levels and adrenaline sensitivity.

Sexual hormones

Glands such as the pituitary, adrenals, gonads, pancreas and thyroid produce hormones. They control – and are themselves controlled by – certain anatomical features that affect the thresholds for various types of responses and have extensive feedback loops with the central nervous system. Schlapp and Smith (1928) first suggested a causal relationship between hormones and criminal behaviour, arguing that either an excess or underproduction of hormones by the ductless glands could lead to emotional disturbance followed by criminal behaviour.

It has long been recognized that male animals – of most species – are more aggressive than females and this has been linked to the male sex hormone testosterone (Rose et al., 1974; Keverne et al., 1982). The relationship between sex hormones and human behaviour does appear more complex, even though testosterone has been linked with aggressive crime such as murder and rape.

However, it does seem that in most men testosterone levels do not significantly affect levels of aggression (Persky *et al.*, 1971; Scarmella and Brown, 1978). Studies of violent male prisoners suggest that testosterone levels have had an effect on aggressive behaviour. However, these results were not as strong as had been expected from the studies of animals (Kreuz and Rose, 1972; Ehrenkranz *et al.*, 1974).

Problematically, these studies of humans have not differentiated between different forms of aggression, although later studies sought to address this issue. Olwens (1987) thus conducted a study of young men with no marked criminal record and found a clear link between testosterone and both verbal and physical aggression with a further distinction between provoked and unprovoked aggressive behaviour: provoked aggressive behaviour tended to be more verbal than physical and was in response to unfair or threatening behaviour by another person; unprovoked aggressive behaviour, in contrast, was violent, destructive and involved activities such as starting fights and making provocative comments. The relationship between testosterone and unprovoked violence was nevertheless found to be indirect and would depend on other factors, such as how irritable the particular individual was. Schalling (1987) discovered that high testosterone levels in young males were associated with verbal aggression but not with actual physical aggression, which suggests a concern to protect status by the use of threats. Low-testosterone-level boys would tend not to protect their position, preferring to remain silent. Neither study suggests a direct link between testosterone and aggression, but in a provocative situation those with the highest levels of testosterone were found more likely to resort to violence.

Ellis and Crontz (1990) note that testosterone levels peak during puberty and the early 20s and this correlates with the highest crime rates. It is a finding that they claim provides persuasive evidence for a biological explanation of criminal behaviour and argue that it explains both aggressive and property crime, observing that sociological researchers have failed to explain why this distribution exists across all societies and cultures. There is nevertheless no evidence of a causal relationship between criminal behaviour and the level of testosterone. The link may be more tenuous, with testosterone merely providing the environment necessary for aggressive behaviour to take place.

McBurnett *et al.* (2000) propose that violent behaviour in male children may be associated with low saliva levels of the stress hormone cortisol, finding those with low concentration were three times more likely to show indications of aggression.

Blood sugar levels

Hypoglycaemia or low blood sugar levels – sometimes related to diabetes mellitus – may result in irritable, aggressive reactions, and may culminate in sexual offences, assaults and motiveless murder (see Shah and Roth, 1974). Schoenthaler (1982) conducted experiments where it was discovered that, by lowering the daily sucrose intake of young offenders held in detention, it was possible to reduce the level of their antisocial behaviour. A discussion of the effects of undernutrition on the central nervous system and thus on aggression can be found in J. Smart (1981). Virkkunen (1987) has linked hypoglycaemia with other activities often defined as antisocial, such as truancy, low verbal IQ, tattooing and stealing from home during childhood and alcohol abuse. If alcohol is drunk regularly and in large quantities, the ethanol produced can induce hypoglycaemia and increase aggression.

Clapham (1989) cites the case of a man who stabbed his wife to death and attempted suicide but was acquitted of murder. The man had been on a strict diet for two months preceding the fatal incident – losing three stone in weight – and had been starved of all sugar, bread, potatoes and fried food. On the fateful morning, he had consumed two glasses of whisky and was found immediately after the killing to be suffering from amnesia. Blood tests were conducted in prison several weeks later and he was found to be still suffering from reactive hypoglycaemia. The jury accepted the expert medical opinion that the man had been reduced to an automaton and could not be held responsible for his actions.

Adrenaline sensitivity

The relationship between adrenaline and aggressive behaviour is a similar area of study to that involving testosterone with each involving the relationship between a hormonal level and aggressive antisocial behaviour. Schachter (cited in Shah and Roth, 1974) thus found that injections of adrenaline made no difference to the behaviour of normal prisoners but a great difference to psychopaths; while Hare (1982) found that, when threatened with pain, criminals exhibit fewer signs of stress than other people. Mednick *et al.* (1982) discovered that not only do certain – particularly violent – criminals take stronger stimuli to arouse them, but also, once they are in a stressed state, they recover more slowly to their normal levels than do non-criminals. Eysenck (1959) had offered a logical explanation for this relationship some years previously. An individual with low stress levels is easily bored, becomes quickly disinterested in things and craves exciting experiences. Thus, for such individuals, normal stressful situations are not disturbing, they are exciting and enjoyable, something to be savoured and sought after.

Baldwin (1990) suggests that the link between age and crime rates can be partially explained by considering arousal rates, observing that children can quickly become used to stimuli that had previously excited them and thus seek ever more thrilling inputs. The stimulus received from criminal-type activities does nevertheless decline with age, as does the level of physical fitness, strength and agility required to perform many such activities. Baldwin interestingly explains both the learning of criminal behaviour and its subsequent decline in terms of stimuli in the environment, which does then pose the question as to whether the production of adrenaline is biologically or socially dictated.

Altered biological state theories

Altered biological state theories are those that link behavioural changes in an individual with the introduction of an external chemical agent. These are here divided into the following categories: allergies and diet, alcohol and illegal drugs.

Allergies and diet

Links have been proposed between irritability and aggression that may lead individuals in some circumstances to commit criminal assault, and allergic reactions to such things as pollen, inhalants, drugs and food. Research on the criminological implications of allergies continues but studies indicate two main reactions in these patients. First, *emotional immaturity* is characterized by temper tantrums, screaming episodes, whining and impatience, while, second, *antisocial behaviour* is characterized by sulkiness and cruelty.

More recent research has attempted to bring together earlier work on blood sugar levels, allergies and other biochemical imbalances. The basic premise of the theory of 'biochemical individuality' is that each person has an absolutely unique internal biochemistry and we all vary in our daily need for each of the forty-odd nutrients – minerals, vitamins, carbohydrates, etc. – required to stay alive and healthy. From this idea flows the concept of 'orthomolecular medicine' that proposes that many diseases are preventable and treatable by the proper diagnosis, vitamin supplementation and avoidance of substances that would bring on an illness or preclude a cure. Prinz *et al.* (1980) proposed that some foods – and in particular certain additives – have effects that may lead to hyperactivity and even criminality. A low level of cholesterol has been linked with hypoglycaemia, particularly when alcohol use has been involved (see Virkkunen, 1987).

At first sight, it might appear strange to link criminal behaviour with vitamin deficiency but the evidence for an active role for biochemical disturbance in some offences of violence is too great to be ignored. Indeed, some quite impressive results have been obtained in the orthomolecular treatment of some mental disorders. For example, Vitamin B3 (niacin) has been used successfully to treat some forms of schizophrenia (see Lesser, 1980; Pihl, 1982; Raloff, 1983) and there is some evidence that addiction to both drugs and alcohol may be related to unmet biochemical individual needs.

Substance abuse is usually brought about by the intake of drugs in the widest sense. Some of these drugs are legal and freely available, such as alcohol, which is drunk, and glues and lighter fluids, which are inhaled. The medical profession prescribes some such as barbiturates, while others – such as cannabis, amphetamines, LSD, MDMA or 'Ecstasy', opiates (usually cocaine or heroin) – are only available illegally.

Alcohol use

The use of alcohol has probably much closer links with crime and criminal behaviour than most other drugs – with the contemporary exception of crack cocaine and possibly heroin – and this highly significant link is at least partially explained by the reality that alcohol is legal, readily available and in extremely common usage. In short, alcohol has long been associated with antisocial activity, crime and criminality. Saunders (1984) calculated that alcohol was a significant factor in about 1,000 arrests per day or over 350,000 a year; Flanzer (1981) estimated that 80 per cent of all cases of family violence in the USA involved the consumption of alcohol, while De Luca (1981) estimated that almost a third of the cases of violence against children in the home were alcohol related. Other studies have discovered a strong link between alcohol and general levels of violence (Collins, 1988; Fagan, 1990), while Collins (1988) shows that considerable numbers of non-violent offenders claim to have been drinking when they offended. Rada (1975) found that half his study of convicted rapists had been drinking when they had offended. Collins (1986) concluded that prisoners with drinking problems had committed more assaults than those without such problems. Lindqvist (1986) found that two-thirds of convicted murderers in Sweden had been drinking at the time they had committed their offences.

There are significant problems with assuming a direct causal link between alcohol use and crime because alcohol does not have the same effect on all people, for example, Native Americans and Eskimos have been found to metabolize more slowly than white people. Goodwin *et al.* (1973) propose that a predisposition to alcoholism can be genetically transmitted and any drug – including alcohol – can accentuate psychological symptoms in individuals. Ramsay (1996) observes that it is necessary to consider the lifestyle and sub-culture of an alcoholic as these might well be more relevant to their criminal activities than their drinking. Abram (1989) suggests that both alcohol use and criminal behaviour may be the outcome of a third factor such as antisocial personality disorder.

Research suggests that victims of crime are also likely to have been drinking. Gottfredson (1984) found that in the UK the chances of becoming a crime victim increased from 5 per cent among non-drinkers to 15 per cent among heavy drinkers and this was particularly so in the case of the young (see also Mott, 1990). Hodge (1993) found that two-thirds of a sample of assailants and 50 per cent of their victims said they had been drinking immediately before the offence occurred. The British Crime Survey 1996 found that victims of domestic violence had far higher levels of alcohol consumption than non-victims (Mirrlees-Black, 1999).

Alcohol and young people have become closely linked in the contemporary UK, although this has certainly not always been the case. In the interwar period, young people aged 18–24 were the lightest drinkers in the adult population and the group most likely to abstain. Nor did alcohol play a significant part in the youth culture that came into existence in the 1950s, this being more likely to involve the coffee bar than the pub. It was not until the 1960s that pubs and drinking became an integral part of the youth scene and, by the 1980s, those aged 18–24 years had become the heaviest consumers of alcohol in the population and the group least likely to abstain (Institute of Alcohol Studies, 2005).

By the year 2002, hazardous drinking, that is, a pattern of drinking that brings with it the risk of physical or psychological harm now or in the future, was most prevalent in teenagers and young adults. Among females, hazardous drinking reached its peak in the 16–19 age group, with just under one-third (32 per cent) having a hazardous drinking pattern. Among males, the peak was found in the 20–24 age group, with just under two-thirds (62 per cent) having a hazardous drinking pattern (Office for National Statistics, 2001). These changes were accompanied by a decline in the age of regular drinking. Thus, nowadays, most young people are drinking regularly – though not necessarily frequently – by the age of 14 or 15. One survey found that more than a quarter of boys aged 9–10 and a third of those a year older reported drinking alcohol at least once in the previous week, normally at home (Balding and Shelley, 1993).

Most surveys suggest that there is a growing trend of drinking for effect and to intoxication, with a related aspect being the partial merging of the alcohol and drug scenes in the context of youth culture. A large survey of teenagers in England, Wales and Scotland found that, by the age 15–16, binge drinking is common, as is being 'seriously drunk' (Beinart et al., 2002). In this study, binge drinking was defined as consuming five or more alcohol drinks in a single session. The growth in binge drinking may be regarded as particularly significant as there is evidence that drinking – and especially heavier drinking – in adolescence increases the likelihood of binge drinking continuing through adult life (Jefferis et al., 2005).

Alcohol is associated with a wide range of criminal offences in addition to drink-driving and drunkenness in which drinking or excessive consumption defines the offence. Alcohol-related crime has thus become a matter of great public concern and, in England and Wales, approximately 70 per cent of crime audits published in 1998 and 1999 identified alcohol to be an issue, particularly in relation to public disorder (Home Office, 2000).

The term 'alcohol-related crime' normally refers to offences a) involving a combination of criminal damage offences, drunk and disorderly and other public disorder offences; b) involving young males, typically 18–30; and c) occurring in the entertainment areas of town and city centres. However, a whole range of offences are linked to alcohol and these do not necessarily occur in the context of the night-time economy. A study conducted for the Home Office in 1990 found that the growth in beer consumption was the single most important factor in explaining crimes of violence against the person, while research also shows that a high proportion of victims of violent crime are drinking or under the influence of alcohol at the time of their assault and a minimum of one in five people arrested by police test positive for alcohol (Bennett, 2000).

An All-Party Group of MPs investigating alcohol and crime was advised by the British Medical Association that alcohol is a factor in 60–70 per cent of homicides, 75 per cent of stabbings, 70 per cent of beatings and 50 per cent of fights and domestic assaults; the Police Superintendents Association reported that alcohol is a factor in 50 per cent of all crimes committed; and the National Association of Probation Officers advised that 30 per cent of offenders on probation and 58 per cent of prisoners have severe alcohol problems which are a significant factor in their offence or pattern of offending (All-Party Group on Alcohol Misuse, 1995).

Being under the influence of alcohol increases the likelihood of a person becoming a victim of crime as well as increasing the likelihood they will become a perpetrator. Women who have consumed alcohol are more at risk of stranger and acquaintance rape than are rape victims in general. BCS figures suggest that 15 per cent of female rape victims were too drunk to be capable of giving consent (Walby and Allen, 2004), while a study of female rape victims in the Metropolitan Police District found that 27 per cent had been drinking around the time of the offence (Ruparel, 2004).

Illegal drug use

Illegal drug taking does not have as long an association with criminal behaviour as alcohol consumption and it was only at the beginning of the twentieth century that drugs were labelled as a major social problem and came to be regulated. Drugs are chemicals and once taken alter the chemical balance of the body and brain and this can clearly affect behaviour, but the way that this occurs varies according to the type and quantity of the drug taken (see Fishbein and Pease, 1990; Pihl and Peterson, 1993). The biological effects of cannabis and opiates such as heroin tend to reduce aggressive hostile tendencies, while cocaine and its derivative crack are more closely associated with violence. Interestingly, some see both alcohol and drug misuse as intrinsically wrong and thus in need of punishment, while others see them as social and personal problems requiring understanding and treatment. The first solution has generally been applied in the case of (illegal) drugs, while the second has tended to be more acceptable in

the case of (legal) alcohol.

In 2001/2, 15 per cent of men and 9 per cent of women aged 16–59 in England and Wales said that they had taken an illicit drug in the previous year. Among those aged 16–24, 35 per cent of males and 24 per cent of females said they had done so in the previous year. The drug most commonly used by young people was cannabis, which had been used by 33 per cent of young men and 22 per cent of young women during that time period. Ecstasy was the most commonly used Class A drug, with higher use among the 16–24-year-olds than those aged 25–59. In 2001/2, 9 per cent of males and 4 per cent of females aged 16–24 had used Ecstasy in the previous year. Since 1996, there has been an increase in the use of cocaine among young people, especially among males; while, in contrast, the use of amphetamines and LSD has declined (Institute of Alcohol Studies, 2005). Drug use has been found to be widespread among school pupils, although there has been a decrease in prevalence since 2003. In that year, 21 per cent of pupils admitted having taken a drug during the previous year; this figure had decreased to 18 per cent by 2004 (Department of Health, 2005).

Breaking the link between drugs and other criminal behaviour has been a key feature of government anti-drug strategies since the mid-1990s (CDCU, 1995; UKADCU, 1998). Studies estimate the cost of drug offences to the criminal justice system as £1.2 billion (Brand and Price, 2000) and the social costs of Class A drugs have been estimated to be nearly £12 billion (Godfrey *et al.*, 2002). Research on offender populations in the UK reveals that acquisitive crime (particularly shoplifting, burglary and fraud) is the primary means of funding drug consumption (Bennett 2000; Coid *et al.*, 2000; Edmunds *et al.*, 1999). The evidence points to users of heroin and cocaine (particularly crack) as the most likely to be prolific offenders (Bennett 2000; Stewart *et al.*, 2000).

The NEW-ADAM research programme has found that those who report using heroin, crack or cocaine commit between five and ten times as many offences as offenders who do not report using drugs. Although users of heroin and cocaine/ crack represent only a quarter of offenders, they are responsible for more than half (by value) of acquisitive crime (Bennett *et al.*, 2001). Links between problematic drug use and crime are nonetheless complex. Edmunds *et al.* (1999) suggest that experimental drug use can pre-date contact with the criminal justice system and become problematic after extensive criminal activity. For those engaged in crime prior to drug use, their offending behaviour can increase sharply.

There are at least five ways in which drugs can be identified as being linked with crime. First, drug users may commit offences – including violent ones – in order to fund their activities, particularly if they are addicted to heroin (Jarvis and Parker, 1989) and in more recent years crack cocaine. Most drug-related offending nevertheless falls into the category of non-violent property offences (Chaiken and Chaiken, 1991) or prostitution (Plant, 1990). Second, there is a possibility that drug use and other criminal behaviour simply occur alongside each other because of the presence of a third factor such as mental health problems (McBride and McCoy, 1982; Auld *et al.*, 1986). Third, drug dealers have a tendency to protect their business interests by whatever means necessary and this is increasingly likely to mean violence (Ruggiero and South, 1995). Fourth, drugs are chemicals, which alter the balance of both body and brain and can significantly change behaviour (Fishbein and Pease, 1990; Pihl and Peterson, 1993). Fifth, there can be state involvement in the drugs trade and it has been suggested by Dorn and South (1990) that in the USA the Central Intelligence Agency (CIA) has been involved in the illegal drugs trade.

Treating the offender

Central to the biological variant of the predestined actor model of crime and criminal behaviour is the perception that criminality arises from some physical disorder within the individual offender and it is argued that, by following a course of treatment, individuals can be cured of the predisposing condition that causes their criminality. We will now briefly consider three forms of individualized treatment: surgical intervention, chemotherapy and electrocontrol.

Surgical intervention often means prefrontal leucotomy, a technique that severs the connection between the frontal lobes and the thalamus. It causes some degree of character change – mainly a reduced anxiety level – and has been used with some success to treat the paranoid and paraphrenic types of schizophrenia, but has now been largely replaced by neuroleptic drugs. It has also been used on 'sexually motivated' and 'spontaneously violent' criminals. Castration has been used on sex offenders in Denmark and the USA with indecisive results. Stürup in Denmark claimed 'acceptable' results with sex offenders, but Mueller (1972, cited in Menard and Morse, 1984) tells of a rapist in California who – following castration – turned from rape to child molesting and murder.

Chemotherapy involves the use of drugs in treatment programmes and also for control purposes. Some drugs are used for the treatment of specific behaviour patterns, for example, antabuse has been used in the treatment of alcoholics, cyclozocine for heroin addicts (both are blocking agents), benperidol (cyproterone acetate), an anti-libidinal drug, and stilboestrol (a female hormone) for sex offenders.

Benperidol and stilboestrol constitute 'chemical castration' and their use on prisoners in the UK and USA instigated widespread intense debate. Proponents insist that these chemicals can only be ethically used on people who freely offer their services as volunteers but there is considerable doubt as to whether one can ever find 'free volunteers' in prison. These drugs also have unpleasant side effects, for example, stilboestrol causes atrophy of the genitals, female breast development, nausea, feminization, obesity and serious psychiatric disorders.

Some drugs are used exclusively for control purposes. Mace and CS gas are routinely used for riot control. Sedatives and tranquillizers are frequently used to keep potential troublesome prisoners calm. In nineteenth-century prisons, opium was used for this purpose and, in the contemporary UK, Valium, Librium and Largactil are generally used. In the USA, a heavy tranquillizer (prolixin) is used, which reduces hostility, anxiety, agitation and hyperactivity but often produces a zombie-like effect. It has some other unpleasant side effects, which according to the manufacturers include automatic reactions, blurred vision, bladder paralysis, glaucoma, faecal impaction, tachycardia, liver damage, skin disorders and death. It is extensively used in prisons for the sole purpose of keeping troublemakers quiet.

Electro-control is still a little futuristic since the research programme is still ongoing in the USA with the idea being to plant a telemetric device on – or in – the prisoner. This will transmit data about the physical state of the subject to a central computer programmed to assess the mental state of the subject from the information. If the indications are that he or she is about to commit an offence, an impulse is sent to a receiver planted in the brain that has the potential to cause pain, paralysis or even death. These devices could enable a dangerous offender to be safely released from prison. The two main obstacles to the implementation of such schemes have been the limited range of the equipment and ethical concerns raised by civil liberty groups.

Conclusions

Each of the attempts to explain crime and criminal behaviour discussed in this chapter follows directly in the biological predestined actor model tradition established by Lombroso. Each theory has sought explanations in the measurable, organic part of individuals, their bodies and their brains and it is certainly impossible to deny that some of these studies really do explain the criminality of a tiny minority of offenders. Closer investigation of individual cases nevertheless demonstrates that social and environmental factors have been equally important. Indeed, it is important to note that most of the researchers – from Lombroso onwards – increasingly came to recognize that reality.

The early biological positivists had proposed that discoveries about the natural world – and natural laws – would find a counterpart within human behaviour. The criminological emphasis of this approach has thus been on the scientist as the detached objective neutral observer who has the task of identifying natural laws that regulate criminal behaviour. Once these natural laws have been discovered, a reduction in offending behaviour is seen as possible by the use of treatment programmes aimed at ameliorating or eliminating the causes of that behaviour. It has also been proposed that investigations should be extended into the lives of individuals who are deemed to be 'at risk' of offending in order that treatment might be instigated and many offences be prevented before they occur. In short, criminal behaviour is perceived to be a sickness – an inherently problematic analysis – that has led to treatments that are intrusive, in some cases unethical, and on occasion with horrendous wider implications.

The early biological positivists replaced the rational calculating individual of the rational actor model with an organism subject to the forces of biological heredity and impulsive behaviour beyond conscious control. From this same source, however, came Social Darwinism, a mode of thought based on the notion that *The Origin of Species* offered a new evolutionary and scientific basis for the social sciences as well as for biology. It was an idea highly compatible with interests in the wider world and was soon used to give 'scientific' legitimacy to an old idea, namely that the capacity for rational judgement, moral behaviour and, above all, business success was not equally distributed among the various races and divisions of humanity.

Quite prominent figures of late nineteenth-century social science began to argue that Africans, Indians, the 'negroes' of North America, paupers, criminals and even women had inherited smaller brains and a reduced capacity for rational thought and moral conduct than everyone else. Such ideas were particularly appealing in the USA, which was experiencing an influx of immigrants of diverse ethnic background and where people were particularly ready to equate the biological processes of natural selection with the competition of an unrestricted market. In both Britain and the USA, programmes of selective breeding were proposed to encourage progress or to prevent civilization from degenerating (Jones, 1980). It was a view that was to remain popular into the early decades of the twentieth century and that was to obtain support from the 'science' of eugenics and its supporters who were concerned with 'improving' the genetic selection of the human race.

The biological variant of the predestined actor model of crime and criminal behaviour was highly compatible with this viewpoint. Goring (1913) was convinced that criminality was passed down through inherited genes and, in order to reduce crime, recommended that people with such characteristics should not be allowed to reproduce. The more recent and rigorous research in search of the 'criminal gene' has rather similar implications.

In 1994, a new Centre for Social, Genetic and Development Psychiatry was opened at the Maudsley Hospital in south London to examine what role genetic structure plays in determining patterns of behaviour, including crime (Muncie, 1999). The following year, a major conference was held behind closed doors to discuss the possibility of isolating a criminal gene – the basis of which rested on the study of twins and adoptees (Ciba Foundation Symposium, 1996).

Moreover, one of the best-selling social science books of the 1990s, *The Bell Curve* (Herrnstein and Murray, 1994), claimed that black people and Latinos are over-represented among the ranks of the poor in the USA because they are less intelligent. The suggestion is that inherited genes mainly determine IQ and that people with low intelligence are more likely to commit crime because they lack foresight and are unable to distinguish right from wrong. Muncie (1999) observes that such theories continue to be attractive – at least to some – because they seem to provide scientific evidence that clearly differentiates us from 'them', an out group we feel legitimately entitled to target, outlaw and, in the final instance, eradicate. It is an argument that Einstadter and Henry (1995) note to be characteristic of totalitarian regimes, whether they are Nazi Germany or the former USSR, and by extension of the more recent forced therapy programmes in the USA.

Morrison (1995) observes that the Holocaust – the systematic extermination of over six million people by Nazi Germany during the Second World War – was undoubtedly the crime of the twentieth century, yet it had provided such a great problem for criminology that it had not previously been mentioned in any textbook. For he observes the essential question to be whether the Holocaust is at odds with modernity or simply the logical consequence of a project of which we might note the biological variant of the predestined actor model of crime and criminal behaviour to simply be a component. There is certainly strong available evidence to support the latter proposition. The Jewish social theorist Hannah Arendt argues that the Holocaust destroyed the semblance of any belief that evil must be motivated by evil and conducted by evil people. She observes that 'the sad truth of the matter is that most evil is done by people who never made up their mind to be either good or bad' (Arendt, 1964: 438). Morrison observes that this horrendous and unsurpassable crime can only be explained by 'the weakness of individual judgement in the face of reason, in the face of the claims of organisation, in the face of claims of the normal, in the face of claims for progress' (1995: 203).

The outcome was to destroy our belief in the right of experts – whether they are scientists, social engineers or managerial politicians – to think for us unquestioned. It was suddenly no longer possible to take the notion of modernist civilization for granted or to accept a unilinear image of social progress in human affairs. The biological variant of the predestined actor model had led to the plausibility of ideas such as sterilization, genetic selection and even death for the biologically untreatable. Such work was now unpalatable for many in the context of the mid-twentieth century experience of mass systematic extermination in death camps of outsider groups whether based on their ethnicity (in the case of the Jews, Slavs and Gypsies), their sexuality (in the case of homosexuals), their health (in the case of the disabled and seriously ill) or their behaviour (in the case of whole categories of criminals).

In more recent years, there has been a sustained campaign to rehabilitate biological theories with the recognition that physical and social environment factors are more closely linked. There remain, however, serious ethical implications surrounding possible treatment regimes and these issues are revisited in Chapter 13.

Policy implications of biological positivism

The fundamental explanation of crime and criminal behaviour for biological positivists is that there is some form of biological inferiority, which is indicated by physical or genetic characteristics that in some way distinguish criminals from non-criminals. The policy implications of the biological theories explored in this chapter include isolation from other human beings, the use of sterilization to ensure that certain categories of biological defectives do not breed and reproduce, or even execution. Biological theorists have also advocated brain surgery, chemical treatment including castration, improved diets and treatment programmes to eliminate dependency on – or even the social use of – alcohol and drugs.

In short, the policy implication of the biological variant of the predestined actor model is to treat the defect and protect society from the untreatable. The available treatments have included drugs, psychosurgery, plastic surgery, genetic counselling and eugenics for those deemed untreatable. Protection of the public has included the use of experts as decision-makers, individualized diagnosis, prediction of risk, the use of indeterminate sentencing and keeping incurable offenders incarcerated for life for the protection of society. There has been a tendency to medicalize criminal justice issues with a parallel potential for misuse by government (and its agencies) as a form of social control with discrimination against different social groups based on the presence of biological risk indicators.

Summary of main points

1. Biological positivists argue that criminology should focus primarily on the scientific study of criminals and criminal behaviour.
2. Early advocates proposed that offenders differ in some way from non-offenders and differed among themselves and committed different types of crime.
3. Inherited criminal characteristics propose that criminality is hereditary and evidence has been obtained from: (i) criminal family studies; (ii) twin studies; and (iii) adopted children studies.
4. A further category of biological explanations considers abnormalities in the genetic structure of the offender, such as those related to the sex chromosomes.
5. Advances in genetic science in recent years have revitalized claims that aspects of criminality can be accounted for by genetic factors.
6. Autism and Asperger's Syndrome are two of the five pervasive developmental disorders (PDD) that are more often referred to as autistic spectrum disorders and these can predispose those with the condition to criminal behaviour.
7. Biochemical explanations of criminal behaviour involve substances – or chemical processes – already present in the body and include sexual hormones, blood sugar levels and adrenaline sensitivity.

8. Altered biological state theories link behavioural changes with the introduction of an external chemical agent, such as allergies, diet, alcohol and illegal drugs.
9. Links have been proposed between irritability and aggression that may lead individuals in some circumstances to commit criminal assault, and allergic reactions to such things as pollen, inhalants, drugs and food.
10. The use of alcohol has much closer links with crime and criminal behaviour than most other drugs and this is at least partially explained by the reality that alcohol is legal, readily available and in extremely common usage.

Discussion questions

1. How do inherited characteristic theories seek to explain criminal behaviour?
2. How do sex chromosome theories explain criminal behaviour?
3. In what circumstances are people on the autistic spectrum likely to commit criminal offences?
4. Which drugs are most linked to criminal behaviour and in what way?
5. Discuss some of the ethical issues linked with biological theories of crime.

Suggested further reading

Biological positivism is an extremely wide subject area and there are thus many relevant texts. Students are therefore advised to use the references in the text as a guide to specific interests. Ferri (1968) is nonetheless a timeless original still worth considering as a general introduction to early criminological positivism *per se*, while Shah and Roth (1974) provide an overview of some of the crucial albeit earlier research in this tradition. For some more recent and very different examples of biological positivism, see Herrnstein and Murray (1994), from a right realist perspective, and Jones (1993), an eminent contemporary geneticist. For a discussion of the wider implications of biological positivism in modern society, see Bauman (1989), Morrison (1995) and Taylor *et al.* (1973), who provide very different but essential accounts.

6. Psychological positivism

Key Issues

1. The criminal mind
2. Freud and psychodynamic theories
3. Behavioural learning theories
4. Cognitive learning theories
5. Cognitive behavioural methods

We saw in the previous chapter that proponents of the biological variant of the predestined actor model argue that criminal behaviour is the outcome of factors internal to the physical body of the individual human being that predisposes them to criminality. For psychological positivists, the search for the causes of crime is directed to the mind and thus we encounter notions of the 'criminal mind' or 'criminal personality'. For purist proponents of this perspective, there are patterns of reasoning and behaviour that are specific to offenders and these remain constant regardless of their different social experiences.

There are three broad categories of psychological theories of crimes and the first two groupings – psychodynamic and behavioural learning theories – are firmly rooted in the predestined actor tradition. The third group – cognitive learning theories – reject much of that positivist tradition by incorporating notions of creative thinking and thus choice, in many ways more akin to the rational actor model.

Psychodynamic theories

Psychodynamic explanations of crime and criminal behaviour have their origins in the extremely influential work of Sigmund Freud (1856–1939). His assertion that sexuality is present from birth and has a subsequent course of development is the fundamental basis of psychoanalysis and one that has aroused a great deal of controversy. Freud had originally proposed that experiences of sexual seduction in childhood are the basis of all later neurosis but, subsequently, he was to change his mind and conclude that the seductions had not actually taken place, they were fantasies. It is this notion of the repressed fantasy – pushed to the back of our mind and forgotten – that is the core tenet of the psychoanalytic tradition.

Within the psychoanalytical model, developed by Freud, the human personality has three sets of interacting forces. First, there is the id or primitive biological drives. Second, there is the superego – or conscience – that operates in the unconsciousness but which is comprised of values internalized through the early interactions of the person, in particular with their parents. Third, there is the ego or the conscious personality and this has the task of balancing the demands of the id against the inhibitions imposed by the superego, as a person responds to external influences (Freud, 1927).

Freud himself proposed two different models of criminal behaviour. The first views certain forms of criminal activity – for example arson, shoplifting and some sexual offences – as essentially reflecting a state of mental disturbance or illness. His theory of psychosexual development proposes a number of complex stages of psychic development that may easily be disrupted, leading to neuroses or severe difficulties in adults. Crucially, a disturbance at one or more of these stages in childhood can lead to criminal behaviour in later life. Of essential importance to the psychosexual development of the child is the influence of the parents and, importantly, many of these influences are unconscious. Neither parents nor children are in fact aware of how they are influencing each other. This is an important recognition for, in a sense, it reduces the responsibility of parents for producing children that offend.

The second model proposes that offenders possess a 'weak conscience'. Hence, for Freud, the development of the conscience is of fundamental importance in the upbringing of the child. A sense of morality is closely linked to guilt, and those possessing the greatest degree of unconscious 'guilt' are likely to be those with the strictest consciences and the most unlikely to engage in criminal behaviour. Guilt is significantly something that results not from committing crimes, but rather from a deeply embedded feeling that develops in childhood, the outcome of the way in which the parents respond to the transgressions of the child. It is an approach that was to lead to a proliferation of tests attempting to measure conscience or levels of guilt, with the belief that this would allow a prediction of whether the child would later become a criminal.

The Freudian approach is clearly firmly embedded in the predestined actor model. Unconscious conflicts or tensions determine all actions and it is the purpose of the conscious (ego) to resolve these tensions by finding ways of satisfying the basic inner urges by engaging in activities sanctioned by society. The later Freudian tradition was more concerned with elaborating on the development of the ego.

Aichhorn (1925) argued that at birth a child has certain instinctive drives that demand satisfaction, and that it is unaware of – and obviously unaffected by – the norms of society around it. It is thus in an 'asocial state' and the task is to bring it into a social state. When the child's development is ineffective, it remains asocial. Crucially, if the instinctive drives are not acted out, they become suppressed and the child is said to be in a state of 'latent delinquency'. When given outside provocation, this 'latent delinquency' can be activated and translated into actual offending behaviour.

Aichhorn concluded that many of the offenders with whom he had worked had underdeveloped consciences which were the result of the absence of an intimate attachment with their parents when they were children. The proposed solution was to locate such children and place them in a happy environment where they could identify with adults in a way they had previously not experienced with the intention of developing their superego.

Aichhorn identified two further categories of criminal. First, there were those with fully developed consciences but who had identified and indeed might well have very close relationships with parents who were themselves criminals. Second, there were those who had been allowed to do whatever they liked by overindulgent parents.

Healy and Bronner (1936) conducted a study of 105 pairs of brothers where one was a persistent offender and the other a non-offender and found that only 19 of the former and 30 of the latter had experienced good-quality family conditions. These findings suggest that circumstances within a household may well be favourable for one child but not the sibling. It was proposed that the latter had not made an emotional attachment to a 'good parent', hence impeding the development of a superego.

Healy and Bronner also found that siblings exposed to similar unfavourable circumstances might react differently. Thus, one might become an offender, while the others do not. The proposed explanation was that offenders are more emotionally disturbed and express their frustrated needs through deviant activities, while the thwarted needs of the non-offenders were channelled into other socially accepted activities. Healy and Bronner emphasized that the growth and effect of conscience are complicated matters that vary between individuals, thus, one might condemn stealing but condone lying, or vice versa.

Friedlander (1947, 1949) argued that some children develop antisocial behaviour or a faulty character that can leave them susceptible to deviant behaviour. Redl and Wineman (1951) similarly argued that some children develop a delinquent ego, the outcome of which is a hostile attitude towards authority because the child has not developed a good ego and superego.

John Bowlby (1952) influentially argued that offending behaviour takes place when a child has not enjoyed a close and continuous relationship with its mother during its formative years. He studied 44 juveniles convicted of stealing and referred to the child guidance clinic where he worked and compared them with a control group of children – matched for age and intelligence – which had been referred to the same clinic, but not in connection with offending behaviour. Problematically, no attempt was made to check for the presence of criminal elements in the control group, thus exposing the study to criticism on methodological grounds (Morgan, 1975). Bowlby found that seventeen of those with convictions for stealing had been separated from their mothers for extended periods before the age of five, in contrast to only two of the control group. Fourteen of the convicted group were found to be 'affectionless characters' – persons deemed to have difficulty in forming close personal relationships – while none of the controls was thus labelled.

Maternal deprivation theory was to have a major and lasting influence on the training of social workers (Morgan, 1975). While other researchers have sought to test it empirically, their findings have tended to suggest that the separation of a child from its mother is not, in itself, significant in predicting criminal behaviour. Andry (1957) and Grygier (1969) both indicated a need to take account of the roles of both parents. Naess (1959, 1962) found that offenders were no more likely to have been separated from their mothers than non-offenders. Little (1963) found, however, that 80 per cent of a sample of boys who had received custodial sentences had been separated from at least one parent for varying periods; in fact, separations from the father were found to be more common.

Wootton (1959, 1962) argued that there was no evidence that any effects of separation of the child from its mother will be irreversible and she observed that, while only a small proportion of offenders may be affected in this way, there was also a lack of information about the extent of maternal deprivation among non-offenders in general. Rutter (1981), in one of the most comprehensive reviews of the maternal deprivation thesis, considered the stability of the child/mother relationship to be more important than the absence of breaks and argued that a small number of substitutes can carry out mothering functions – without adverse effect – provided that such care is of good quality. Rutter considered the quality of child-rearing practices to be the crucial issue.

Glueck and Glueck (1950) found that the fathers of offenders provided discipline that was generally lax and inconsistent with the use of physical punishment by both parents being common and the giving of praise rare. The parents of non-offenders, on the other hand, were found to use physical punishment more sparingly and were more consistent in their use of discipline. McCord *et al.* (1959) agreed with the Gluecks that the consistency of discipline was more important than the degree of strictness. Bandura and Walters (1959) found that the fathers of aggressive boys are more likely to punish such behaviour in the home, while approving of it outside, and also used physical punishments more than the fathers of their control group.

Hoffman and Saltzstein (1967) identified and categorized three types of child-rearing techniques. First, power assertion was found to involve the parental use of – or threats to use – physical punishment and/or the withdrawal of material privileges. Second, love withdrawal is where the parent withdraws – or threatens to withdraw – affection from the child, for example, by paying no attention to it. Third, induction entails letting the child know how its actions have affected the parent, thus encouraging a sympathetic or empathetic response. Essentially, the first technique primarily relies on the instillation of fear, while the other two depend on fostering guilt feelings in the child.

Hoffman and Saltzstein offer five explanations for the association to be found between moral development and the use of child-rearing techniques. First, an open display of anger and aggression by a parent when disciplining a child increases the dependence of the latter on external control. Punishment connected with power assertion dissolves both the anger of the parent and the guilt of the child more rapidly. Second, love withdrawal and induction, and the anxiety associated with them, has a longer-lasting effect so that the development of internal controls are more likely. Third, where love withdrawal is used, the punishment ends when the child confesses or makes reparation, which is referred to as engaging in a corrective act. In the case of physical punishment, there is likely to be a lapse of time between it being carried out and the child performing a corrective act. Fourth, withholding love intensifies the resolve of the child to behave in an approved manner in order to retain love. Fifth, the use of induction is particularly effective in enabling the child to examine and correct the behaviour that has been disapproved of.

Hoffman and Saltzstein propose that it is people who have been raised through the use of love withdrawal or induction techniques that are less likely to engage in offending behaviour because of the greater effect of internalized controls. People raised on the power assertion method depend on the threat of external punishment to control their behaviour and thus will only remain controlled as long as that risk is present, certain and sufficiently intense. It is of course only internal controls that are likely to be ever present.

A number of studies have gone beyond child-rearing practices to assess the relevance of more general features of the family unit in the causation of criminal behaviour and some of these conducted in both the USA and the UK have suggested that a 'broken home' – where one of the birth parents is not present – may be a factor in the development of offending behaviour.

Glueck and Glueck (1950) measured the frequency of broken homes among its samples and found that 60 per cent of the offenders came from such a home, compared with only 34 per cent of the control group. In Britain, Burt (1945) and Mannheim (1948) found that a high proportion of offenders came from such homes. Others note that the 'broken home' is not a homogenous category and that a range of different factors need to be considered (Bowlby, 1952; Mannheim, 1955; Tappan, 1960). Nye (1958) and Gibbens (1963) observed that offending behaviour is more likely to occur among children from intact but unhappy homes.

While West (1969) echoed the observations of Wootton (1959) about the difficulties of defining a broken home, his study with Farrington (1973) found that about twice as many offenders – compared with controls – came from homes broken by parental separation before the child was ten years old. Comparing children from a home broken by separation with those broken by the death of a parent, more children from the former were found to be offenders. Moreover, 20 per cent of the former group became recidivists, whereas none of those from the second group did.

Monahan (1957) suggested that broken homes were found far more among black than white offenders; while Pitts (1986) claimed a link between criminality and homelessness and found that African-Caribbean youths tend to become homeless more than their white counterparts. Chilton and Markle (1972) had previously observed that the rate of family breakdown is in general much higher in the case of black than white families and this may explain why it is that more black young offenders come from broken homes.

Two studies conducted more recently in the UK have reported that broken homes and early separation predicted convictions up to age 33 where the separation occurred before age 5 (Kolvin *et al.*, 1990) and that it predicted convictions and self-reported offending behaviour (Farrington, 1992a). Morash and Rucker (1989) found that, although it was single-parent families who had children with the highest rates of deviancy, these were also the lowest-income families. Thus, the nature of the problem – broken home, parental supervision, low income – was unclear. In a review of research conducted in the USA, Maginnis (1997) is far less unequivocal and concludes that children from single-parent families are more likely to have behavioural problems because they tend to lack economic security and adequate time with parents with the most reliable indicator of violent crime in a community being the proportion of fatherless families. Fathers, it is observed, typically offer economic stability, a role model for boys, greater household security and reduced stress for mothers. This is especially true for families with adolescent boys, the most crime-prone group of young people. It was found that children from single-parent families are more prone than children from two-parent families to use drugs, be involved in 'gangs', be expelled from school, be committed to young offender institutions and become juvenile murderers. It was concluded that single parenthood inevitably reduces the amount of time a child has in interaction with someone who is attentive to the needs of the child, including the provision of moral guidance and discipline. These possible explanations of crime and criminal behaviour are revisited in more detail in later chapters.

Behavioural learning theories

The second category of psychological theories we will consider – behavioural learning theories – have their origins in the work of Ivan Petrovich Pavlov and B.F. Skinner. Pavlov famously studied the processes involved in very simple, automatic animal behaviours, for example, salivation in the presence of food, and found that those responses that occur spontaneously to a natural (*unconditioned*) stimulus could be made to happen (*conditioned*) to a stimulus that was previously neutral, for example, a light. Thus, if you consistently turn the light on just before feeding the animal, then eventually the animal will salivate when the light comes on, even though no food is present. This conditioning can of course be undone. Thus, if you continue to present the light without the food, eventually the animal will stop salivating, a contrary process that is called *extinction*.

To some extent, the conditioning process is specific to the stimulus that is presented but it can also be generalized to other similar stimuli. Thus, if the animal has been conditioned to salivate to a red light, for example, it would salivate slightly if a blue light is turned on. However, you could train it to salivate only to the red light, by never rewarding it with food when presented with the blue light. For behaviourists, it is this notion of differential conditioning that is the key to understanding how learning works.

Pavlov carried out his work on automatic behaviours occurring in response to stimuli; B.F. Skinner extended the principle to active learning, where the animal has to do something in order to obtain a reward or avoid punishment.

The same principle nevertheless applies. The occurrence of the desired behaviour is increased by positive reinforcement and eventually extinguished by non-reinforcement.

Learned behaviours are much more resistant to extinction if the reinforcement has only occasionally been used during learning. This makes sense. If you put money in a ticket machine and no ticket comes out, you stop using the machine. On the other hand, many people put money in gaming machines even though they pay out prizes infrequently.

Behaviour can be differentially conditioned so that it occurs in response to one stimulus and not another. Indeed, in a sense all operant conditioning – as this type of learning is called – is differential conditioning. The animal learns to produce certain behaviours and not others, by the fact that only these receive reinforcement.

One further process has to be considered in order to explain the behaviour of the animals in conditioning experiments. If learning really happened as described, then the excitation produced by reinforcement would continue to build up over repeated trials, and a rat, for example, would continually press a bar for food, more and more frequently, until it died of exhaustion. What actually happens is that responses to the stimulus become less frequent as it is repeated – eventually stopping altogether – but start again at their old level if there is a break between presentations. To explain this phenomenon, behavioural learning theorists have presumed a 'quantity' of inhibition that builds up as the response is repeated, until it exceeds the level of excitation and stops the responses occurring. It reduces when the animal is not responding, leaving the level of excitation unchanged and so the response recommences.

Hans Eysenck (1970, 1977) sought to build a general theory of criminal behaviour based on the psychological concept of conditioning and central to his thesis is the human conscience, which he considers to be a conditioned reflex. We saw above that the Freudians have been interested in the notion of conscience but Eysenck viewed the concept very differently.

Eysenck's theory is not easy to compartmentalize. He argues from the biological predestined actor perspective that individuals are genetically endowed with certain learning abilities that are conditioned by stimuli in the environment but he accepts the rational actor model premise that crime can be a natural and rational choice activity where individuals maximize pleasure and minimize pain. People are said to learn the rules and norms of society through the development of a conscience, which is acquired through learning what happens when you take part in certain activities. In short, the virtuous receive rewards, while the deviant is punished.

Eysenck describes three dimensions of personality: *extroversion* – which itself consists of two different components, impulsiveness and sociability, and which are themselves partly independent of each other: *neuroticism* and *psychoticism*. Each dimension takes the form of a continuum that runs from high to low. Low extroversion is sometimes termed introversion and, in the case of neuroticism, a person with a high score would be regarded as neurotic and someone with a low score stable. Scores are usually obtained by the administration of a personality questionnaire, of which there are several versions, and it is usual to abbreviate the descriptions of a person's score, for example, high N (neuroticism), high E (extroversion) and high P (psychoticism).

Each of these personality dimensions has distinct characteristics. Thus, someone with a high E score would be outgoing and sociable, optimistic and impulsive, a high N person is anxious, moody and highly sensitive, while those with low scores on these continuums present the very opposite of these traits. Insensitivity to others, a liking for solitude, sensation seeking and lack of regard for danger are all linked with psychoticism (Eysenck, 1970). Feldman (1977) observes a similarity between this description of psychoticism and antisocial personality disorder – or psychopathy – which is discussed below.

Eysenck (1977) argues that various combinations of the different personality dimensions within an individual affect their ability to learn not to offend and consequently the level of offending. Someone with a high E and a high N score – a neurotic extrovert – will not condition well. A low E and a low N score – a stable introvert – is the most effectively conditioned. Stable extroverts and neurotic introverts come somewhere between the two extremes in terms of conditioning.

Various researchers have sought to test Eysenck's theory. Little (1963) compared the scores for convicted young offenders on the extroversion and neuroticism dimensions with those for non-offenders and found no difference in relation to extroversion but the offenders scored higher on the neuroticism scale. Neither dimension nevertheless appeared to be related to repeat offending. Hoghughi and Forrest (1970) compared scores for neuroticism and extroversion between a sample of convicted youths and a control group of supposedly non-offenders – or at least those with no convictions – and found that the offenders were rated higher on the neuroticism scale but were actually less extroverted than their controls. This finding could of course be explained by the possibility that it is the experience of detention itself that could make a young person neurotic.

Hans and Sybil Eysenck (1970) tested 178 incarcerated young offenders on all three personality dimensions and followed up this research on their release finding that 122 had been reconvicted and all of these scored significantly higher in relation to extroversion than the others. Allsopp and Feldman (1975) conducted a self-report study and found a significant and positive association between scores for E, N and P levels of antisocial behaviour among girls between 11 and 15 years of age with the strongest association found in relation to psychoticism. Their study of schoolboys conducted the following year reached similar conclusions (Allsopp and Feldman, 1976).

Less research has been conducted in relation to adult criminals but, where E and N scores for prisoners have been compared with those for non-prisoners, the former have received higher scores for neuroticism, and repeat offenders have been found to be more neurotic than first offenders. Little evidence has been found to suggest that adult criminals are more extrovert than non-criminals (Feldman, 1977). Eysenck has nevertheless responded to his critics by pointing out that extroversion has two components, sociability and impulsiveness, and argues that it is the latter that is more significantly associated with criminal behaviour (Eysenck, 1970). Many personality tests simply provide a score for extroversion that combines those for the two components, which means that a person who is highly impulsive but very unsociable will receive an E score midway on the personality continuum.

The association between psychoticism and criminal behaviour has been the subject of very little research but Smith and Smith (1977) and McEwan (1983) found a positive relationship between psychoticism and repeat offending. However, the work of Allsopp and Feldman (1975, 1976) and McGurk and McDougall (1981) suggests that combinations or clusters of scores for the three dimensions are more important than scores for individual dimensions.

Research has been conducted in order to test for a relationship between personality types and offence type. Hindelang and Weis (1972) found that with minor offences – such as vandalism and traffic offences – the descending order of offending was as they had predicted; thus, high E plus high N, high E and low N, or low E and high N, then low E and low N. However, this was found not to be the case with offences involving theft or aggression.

Eysenck *et al.* (1977) found that thieves or violent offenders had lower N scores than other groups, conmen had lower P scores, and there was no variation for E scores. McEwan and Knowles (1984) simply found no association between offence type and personality cluster. There thus seems to be considerable uncertainty and ambiguity about the validity and veracity of Eysenck's theory. Farrington (1994) nevertheless suggests that this approach seems to at least identify a distinct link between offending and impulsiveness but he found no significant links with personality.

Antisocial personality disorder appears to be a relatively recent term that is interchangeable with that of psychopathy. There are various and not always consistent definitions of this condition but in general these emphasize such traits as an incapacity for loyalty, selfishness, irresponsibility, impulsiveness, inability to feel guilt and failure to learn from experience. One feature common to all descriptions is a lack of empathy or affection (Blackburn and Maybury, 1985). The American Psychiatric Association (1968) had proposed that a person should be diagnosed as having 'antisocial personality disorder' when the above characteristics are 'inflexible, maladaptive, and persistent, and cause significant functional impairment or subjective distress'. Explanations are nevertheless many and varied.

McCord and McCord (1964) had suggested a lack of parental affection to be one of the key contributory factors. Robins (1966) found that children who behaved in a psychopathic manner were more likely to have fathers who were psychopathic or alcoholics but, on the other hand, Cleckley (1976) found that many of his psychopathic patients came from a happy and supportive family background. Indeed, Hare (1970) observes that most people from a disturbed background do not develop antisocial personality disorder.

Some researchers have studied the functioning of the central nervous system by using the electroencephalogram (EEG), which tests for abnormalities in the electrical activity of the brain in psychopaths. Syndulko (1978) suggested that irregularities are frequently shown in the EEG testing of those with antisocial personality disorder, but Hare and Jutari (1986) found that the EEGs of psychopaths were normal while they were active but abnormal while they were resting.

Other studies have examined the functioning of the autonomic nervous system (ANS) in those diagnosed as having antisocial personality disorder. The level of activity in the ANS is assessed by measuring the conductivity of the skin (electrodermal reactivity) and the level of cardiac reactivity. Hare and Jutari (1986) found that when psychopaths are resting their level of electrodermal reactivity is exceptionally low, and Hollin (1989) suggests that fast heart rate may be a sign that the psychopath is lowering the level of cortical arousal by 'gating out' the sensory input related to unpleasant situational stimuli.

Eysenck (1963) had found that those diagnosed with antisocial personality disorder are mostly extroverted, which suggests the possible relevance of the personality characteristics of psychopaths in explaining their antisocial behaviour. Extroverts are said to be more difficult to socialize because of difficulties in learning; this might well apply to psychopaths and their difficulties may well have a physiological foundation. If this is the case, then we might assume that psychopaths will be very poor at learning to avoid the unpleasant stimuli associated with particular acts, but Hollin (1989) observes that the findings from such studies vary according to the type of unpleasant stimulus used. Thus, when poor performance was met with physical pain or by disapproval, psychopaths obtained worse results than controls but were found to be better learners when the consequences were a financial penalty.

Some studies have examined the responsiveness of psychopaths to reward learning where correct responses are rewarded by social approval. The findings are mixed but there is no evidence that psychopaths are less amenable than other people to reward learning (Feldman, 1977).

Feldman (1977) observes that the subjects of antisocial personality disorder research may be unrepresentative, merely being those who have been brought to the attention of the authorities. Psychopathic behaviours may be extremely widespread throughout the population and psychopaths might well be found in legitimate occupations such as business, medicine and psychiatry (Cleckley, 1976). It is only when they engage in proscribed activities that the individuals will come to the attention of the authorities. Considering the findings of the different types of learning studies, there is nevertheless some evidence that psychopaths may be undersocialized because of the way that they learn and, moreover, it is also possible that these difficulties arise from physiological factors.

Vold et al. (1998) suggest that the term 'psychopath' is simply a useful term employed by psychiatrists who wish to describe a certain type of person who exhibits particular types of behaviour and attitudes. They argue that, when it is applied to criminals, the term seems to be merely a label attached to particularly serious offenders. It does nothing to help recognize such offenders in advance, to explain their behaviour or prescribe suitable treatment.

Some psychiatrists who have argued that they are able to identify future dangerous offenders have disputed this notion. Vold et al. have responded by noting that, 'if that is their claim, then their track record so far has been poor' (1998: 101). Kozol et al. (1972) sought to predict the future dangerousness of a group of high-risk offenders prior to their release from prison but failed to predict two-thirds of the violent crime that subsequently occurred. Monahan (1981) comprehensively reviewed the clinical techniques used for predicting violent behaviour and concluded that it can only be done within very restricted circumstances, arguing that it is not possible to predict violence over an extended period or when a person is moving from one situation to another, for example, being released from prison.

Researchers have subsequently moved away from trying to predict future violent behaviour towards the more general possibility that individuals might engage in any form of offending behaviour (Vold *et al.*, 1998). Most of this research has focused on juveniles rather than adults with the strongest predictor of later offending behaviour found to be early childhood problem behaviours such as disruptive classroom conduct, aggressiveness, lying and dishonesty (Loeber and Dishion, 1983). The stability of these behavioural problems over time suggests that these people may have certain personality characteristics associated with antisocial behaviour even if they do not show up on personality tests.

In recent years, personality typing – or offender profiling – has been used, particularly in the USA, to help detect particular types of criminals and it is a method found to have been most useful in the detection of serial murders, although we should note that offender profiling is not that new. Dr Thomas Bond produced a profile of Jack the Ripper in 1888 (Rumbelow, 1987). Serial murder is a repetitive event where the perpetrator kills on a number of different occasions, frequently spanning a matter of months or years, and often at different locations. The murders are often brutal and sadistic and the victims strangers. Most people consider such killers to be simply mad. Holmes and De Burger (1989), on the other hand, argue that such murderers are not suffering from any psychological illness, for in this type of case there is characteristically a motive, and proceed to describe four main types of serial killer. First, there is the *visionary motive type* where the killer commits crimes because they hear voices or see visions. The act itself is usually spontaneous and disorganized and committed only in response to the voices. Second, there is the *mission-oriented motive type* where the killer has a goal, usually to rid the world of a particular type of person such as prostitutes or vagrants – indeed, terrorists might well be included in this category – but they are not psychotic and have a strong wish to solve a particular problem. The victims are usually strangers, chosen because they fit into a certain category, of what the perpetrator considers to be legitimate targets, and the act is usually well planned and efficiently carried out. Third, there is the *hedonistic type* who kills basically for pleasure and the enjoyment of the act and there are two subcategories of this typology. The *thrill-orientated killer* enjoys the excitement of killing and so kills for pleasure; random strangers with no specific characteristics are chosen as victims with the killing spontaneous and disorganized. The lust killer, on the other hand, kills for a sexual motive, obtaining gratification by abusing others, with the victim usually a stranger who possesses the required characteristics. Fourth, there is the *power/control-oriented* type who is very difficult to distinguish from the lust or thrill-seeking types. In order to prove control, the killer may well carry out sexual acts, but the sex is only a form of power over the victim who is a stranger with specific characteristics and the crime – which is often very sadistic – will be organized and planned.

The psychological profile is, however, only one of many ways of finding a solution to a murder. The science on which it is based is not an exact one and this fact is often overlooked. Omerod (1996) notes the limitations of the methodology and argues that offender profiling is only useful in a few cases such as rape, killing or arson because the profile only describes a type of person and does not identify an individual. The profile can thus only usefully supplement other investigative methods.

Cognitive learning theories

Both psychodynamic and behavioural learning theories have clear foundations in the predestined actor model, although later more sophisticated variants of those traditions became more readily accepting of rational actor model notions of albeit limited choice. They both remained nevertheless committed to the central notion of psychological positivism that proposes that there are patterns of reasoning and behaviour specific to offenders that remain constant regardless of their different social experiences. The third psychological tradition has its foundations in a fundamental critique of the predestined actor model.

The behavioural learning theorists had emphasized the role of environmental stimuli and overt behavioural response but failed to satisfactorily explain why people attempt to organize, make sense of and often alter the information they learn. There thus emerged a growing recognition that mental events – or cognition – could no longer be ignored (Kendler, 1985). Cognitive psychologists proposed that, by observing the responses made by individuals to different stimuli, it is possible to draw inferences about the nature of the internal cognitive processes that produce those responses.

Many of the ideas and assumptions of cognitivism have their origins in the work of the Gestalt psychologists of Germany, Edward Tolman of the USA and Jean Piaget of Switzerland. Gestalt psychologists emphasized the importance of organizational processes in perception, learning and problem-solving, and proposed that individuals were predisposed to organize information in particular ways (Henle, 1985). Tolman (1959) had been a prominent learning theorist at the time of the behavioural movement but later – influenced by the Gestalt theorists – developed a distinctively cognitive perspective where he included internal mental phenomena in his perspective of how learning occurs. Piaget (1980) was a Swiss biologist and psychologist renowned for constructing a highly influential model founded on the idea that the developing child builds cognitive structures – mental 'maps', schema or networked concepts – for under-standing and responding to physical experiences within their environment. He proposed that the cognitive structure of a child increases in sophistication with development, moving from a few innate reflexes such as crying and sucking to highly complex mental activities. Four developmental stages of cognitive development were identified with each influenced by physiological maturation and interaction with the environment and characterized by qualitatively different forms of thought.

B.F. Skinner (1938) – as we have seen above – had argued from an operant conditioning perspective that the person must actively respond if they are to learn. Cognitivists share that view with Skinner but shift the emphasis to mental rather than physical activity. This social learning theory emphasizes that behaviour may be reinforced not only through actual rewards and punishments, but also through expectations that are learned by watching what happens to other people. Ultimately, the person will make a choice as to what they will learn and how.

An early proponent of the notion that crime is simply a normal learned behaviour was Gabriel Tarde (1843–1904), who argued that criminals are primarily normal people who – by accident of birth – are brought up in an atmosphere in which they learn crime as a way of life. His 'laws of imitation' were essentially a cognitive theory in which the individual learns ideas through an association with others. Behaviour follows from the incorporation of those ideas. Tarde's first law proposes that people imitate one another in proportion to how much contact they have with each other and this is more frequent and changes more rapidly in urban areas. His second law proposes that the inferior usually imitates the superior, suggesting that such offences as drunkenness and murder had originated as crimes committed by royalty but had been subsequently imitated by other social classes, while those in rural areas later imitated crimes originating in the city. His third law suggests that newer fashions replace older ones, for example, murder by shooting has come to replace that by knifing. This is an important theoretical development because it is the first attempt to describe criminal behaviour in terms of normal learned behaviour rather than in terms of biological or psychological defects albeit that the model of learning on which the theory is based is relatively simple (Vold *et al.*, 1998). Tarde was to significantly influence Edwin H. Sutherland's later differential association theory and the latter was to have a subsequently huge and enduring impact on criminology, particularly in the USA.

Sutherland had originally embarked on this line of enquiry with his research reported in *The Professional Thief* (1937), which consisted of a description of the criminal profession of theft as related to him by a thief with the alias 'Chic Conwell'. Sutherland thus discovered that thieving has its own techniques, codes, status, organization and traditions, which were imitated in other groups considered non-criminal.

Sutherland first used the term 'differential association' to explain interaction patterns by which thieves were restricted in their physical and social contacts to association with like-minded others and it was at this stage of its development more or less a synonym for a criminal subculture. In 1939, the concept was used to develop a theory of criminal behaviour where it was proposed that crime is a learned activity much like any other. Sutherland argued that it is the frequency and consistency of contacts with patterns of criminality that determine the chance that a person will participate in systematic criminal behaviour. The basic cause of such behaviour is thus the existence of different cultural groups with different normative structures within the same society that have produced a situation of *differential social organization*.

Certain shortcomings were identified with this early version of differential association theory. Fundamentally, it said little about the processes through which this 'contamination through exposure' could be resisted through a variety of personal or social differences. It was moreover a rather narrow and deterministic version of learning theory particularly as it tended to rule out such psychological factors as conscience and moral understanding.

Sutherland (1947) consequently revised his theory to now argue that criminal behaviour occurs when individuals acquire sufficient sentiments in favour of law violation to outweigh their association with non-criminal tendencies. Those associations or contacts that have the greatest impact are those that are frequent, early in point of origin or are the most intense. He argued that, at this level of explanation, it was not necessary to explain why a person has particular associations, for this involved a complex of social interactions and relationships, but he maintained that it was the existence of differential social organization that exposed people to varied associational ties. Differential association also remains in contrast to other psychological explanations, in that it retains a dominant sociological argument that the primary groups to which people belong exert the strongest influence on them. This formulation won wide acceptance because it was considered sufficient to explain the occurrence of all criminal conduct.

Some key questions were nevertheless to remain unanswered. Thus, what kind of associations can be considered intense? What if criminal attitudes are more compelling than others and thus are able to overcome a primary affiliation to conformist behaviour, even though criminal association ties are fewer? It can be argued, moreover, that the theory neglects personality traits, provides no place for variations in opportunities to engage in law-breaking and cannot explain spontaneous crimes of passion. It will nevertheless be seen in the following chapter that sociological delinquent subcultural theories have their foundations in Sutherland's arguments about the content of what is learned.

Sutherland is particularly remembered for his attempts to apply differential association theory to white-collar crime or crimes of the powerful. He noted that the vast majority of criminological data had been compiled in relation to offenders from the lower classes but observed that businessmen committed enormous amounts of crime, although this was invariably invisible (Sutherland, 1940). He thus considered traditional explanations of criminality to be based on a false premise and thus misleading. Indeed, there is some empirical support for this position. Geis (1967) examined evidence given to hearings into the illegal price-fixing activities of some companies in the USA and found that people taking up new posts tended to find price-fixing to be an established practice and routinely became involved as part of learning their new job. Baumhart (1961) had previously found unethical behaviour on the part of businessmen to be influenced by superiors and peers, with both he and Geis suggesting that the learning process is reinforced by 'rewards' and 'punishments'. Clinard (1952) noted, however, that differential association does not explain why it is that some individuals exposed to the same processes do not deviate and proposed that the theory be adapted to consider personality traits.

Others have maintained the view that crime is normal learned behaviour and have sought to explain that this knowledge acquisition does not have to take place in intimate personal groups. These later theories argue that learning can take place through direct interactions with the environment, independent of associations with other people, through the principles of operant learning.

Burgess and Akers (1968) thus rewrote the principles of differential association in the language of operant conditioning and proposed that criminal behaviour could be learned both in non-social situations that are reinforcing and through social interaction in which the behaviour of other persons helps to reinforce that behaviour.

Akers (1985) later revised the theory and it now focused on four central concepts. First, *differential association*, which is considered the most important source of social learning and refers to the patterns of interactions with others that are the source of social learning either favourable or unfavourable to offending behaviour. At the same time, the indirect influence of more distant reference groups – such as the media – is now also recognized. Second, *definitions* reflect the meanings that a person applies to their own behaviour, for example, the wider reference group might not define recreational drug use as deviant. Third, *differential reinforcement* refers to the actual or anticipated consequences of a particular behaviour where it is proposed that people will do things that they think will result in rewards and avoid activities that they think will result in punishment. Fourth, *imitation* involves observing what others do. Whether they actually choose to imitate that behaviour will nevertheless depend on the characteristics of the person being observed, the behaviour the person engages in and the observed consequences of that behaviour for others.

Akers *et al.* (1979) propose that the learning of criminal behaviour takes place through a specific sequence of events. This process starts with the differential association of the individual with other persons who have favourable definitions of criminal behaviour and they thus provide a model of criminal behaviour to be imitated and social reinforcements for that behaviour. Thus, primarily differential association, definitions, imitation and social reinforcements explain the initial participation of the individual in criminal behaviour. After the individual has commenced offending behaviour, differential reinforcements determine whether the person will continue with that behaviour.

Akers (1992) argues that the social learning process explains the link between social structural conditions and individual behaviours, for example, the modernization process and social disorganization, strain conditions and economic inequality that have all been linked with criminal behaviour affect the differential associations of the individual, definitions, models and reinforcements. These issues are further discussed in the following chapter and the third part of this book.

The emergence of the early learning theories had led to the development of a range of *behaviour modification* treatment strategies introduced with the intention of changing behaviour. As the early theorists had proposed that behaviour is related both to the setting in which the offence takes place and the consequences of involvement in such activities, strategies were developed to modify both the environment in which the offence took place and the outcomes of the behaviour. Bringing about change through modification of the environment is called *stimulus control* and is a standard technique in behaviour modification (Martin and Pear, 1992); it is most apparent in situational crime prevention where the intention is to reduce offending by either reducing the opportunity to commit an offence or increasing the chances of detection. Similarly, there are a range of established methods that seek to modify the consequences that follow a given behaviour. The concept of *token economies* is a significant one where positive acceptable behaviour is rewarded by the award of tokens to be later exchanged for something the person finds rewarding. Behaviour modification techniques are widely used not just with convicted offenders, but in most mainstream schools as a means of controlling children, encouraged by books on positive parenting – 'praise is much more potent than criticism or punishment' – and the training of pet dogs, among many applications.

Strategies that focus explicitly on overt behaviour are often termed *behaviour therapy*, although the basic underpinning theory is the same as that which informs behaviour modification. In the 1970s, the notion of skills training in health services was developed and quickly became widespread in the form of assertion, life and social skills training, the latter becoming widely used with a range of offenders (Hollin, 1990a).

A number of particular techniques have become associated with more recent cognitive behavioural practice, including self-instructional training, 'thought stopping', emotional control training and problem-solving training (Sheldon, 1995). The rationale underpinning this approach is that, by bringing about change of internal – psychological and/or physiological – states and processes, this covert change will, in turn, mediate change at an overt behavioural level. Changes in overt behaviour will then elicit new patterns of reinforcement from the environment and so maintain behaviour change.

These cognitive behavioural methods have been widely used with offender groups and, in particular, with young offenders (Hollin, 1990b) where social skills training, training in problem-solving and moral reasoning techniques have been popular and have been shown to have some success in reducing offending (Maguire, 2001).

The main concerns about the use of cognitive behavioural methods have focused on the abuse – and potential for abuse – of the methods used. First, there is an issue of powerful methods being used inappropriately by untrained – or poorly trained – personnel. Second, there are ethical issues of these methods being used with people such as prisoners – and in particular young offenders – who are in no position to give free and informed consent.

A particularly interesting example of the application of behaviour modification strategies – and the legitimacy of the aforementioned concerns – exists in Tranquility Bay, Jamaica, where 250 children, almost all from the USA, are incarcerated. They have not, however, been sent to the centre by a court of law or any welfare organization. Their parents have paid to have them kidnapped and flown there against their will, to be incarcerated for up to three years, sometimes even longer. They will not be released until they are judged to be respectful, polite and obedient enough to rejoin their families.

Parents sign a legal contract with the centre granting 49 per cent custody rights. It permits the Jamaican staff – whose qualifications are not required to exceed a high-school education – to use whatever physical force they feel necessary to control the child. The cost of sending a child there ranges from $25,000 to $40,000 a year (*The Observer*, 2003).

Conclusions

Psychological explanations of crime and criminal behaviour have firm foundations in the predestined actor model of crime and criminal behaviour and it is the implication of both the psychodynamic and behaviourist learning traditions that there is such a thing as the criminal mind or personality, which in some way determines the behaviour of the individual. The causes are dysfunctional, abnormal emotional adjustment or deviant personality traits formed in early socialization and childhood development, and the individual is, as a result of these factors, destined to become a criminal. The only way to avoid that destiny is to identify the predisposing condition and provide some form of psychiatric intervention that will in some way ameliorate or preferably remove those factors and enable the individual to become a normal law-abiding citizen.

The more recent cognitive learning approach involves a retreat from the purist predestined actor model approach. First, there is recognition of the links between the psychology of the individual and important predisposing influences or stimuli available in the social environment, but the behavioural learning theorists accept that point. It is the second recognition that is the important one. For criminals are now seen to have some degree of choice.

They can choose to imitate the behaviours of others or they can choose not to. There may be a substantial range of factors influencing their decision and these may suggest to the individual that in the particular circumstances – when the opportunity arises – criminal behaviour is a rational choice to make. Thus, we can see the links between recent cognitive learning theories and contemporary variants of the rational actor model. In short, the active criminal can, in favourable circumstances, make the choice to change their behaviour and cease offending or, alternatively, the individual living in circumstances where criminal behaviour is the norm can choose not to take that course of action in the first place. From this perspective, crime is not inevitably destiny. There are nevertheless considerable ethical issues raised by the use of some behavioural modification techniques that seek to influence the cognitive decision-making processes of offenders and indeed of others who have not been convicted of any crime.

Policy implications of psychological positivism

Psychological positivism shifts the focus of criminological enquiry and research from 'why is there crime in society?' to 'why is this individual a criminal?' and targets the latter. The criminal is a patient and crime is a disease where rehabilitation and reformation are the primary motive of intervention, which is epitomized by a change in terminology from penology to corrections particularly in the USA.

Psychological theories propose that crime results from mental or emotional disturbances in individuals, an inability to empathize with others, an inability to legally satisfy their basic needs, or the oppressive circumstances of their life. To combat crime, psychological positivists would thus (like biological positivists) isolate, sterilize or execute offenders not responsive to treatment. For treatable offenders, psychotherapy or psychoanalysis may prove effective. Other policy implications are to help people satisfy their basic needs legally, to eliminate sources of oppression and to provide legal ways of coping with oppression. Some of these apparently harmless low-level cognitive behavioural interventions can nevertheless have significant negative outcomes for their targets not least because they do not appear to be based on properly evaluated research evidence.

'Scared Straight' is a cognitive behavioural influenced programme designed in the USA to deter juvenile participants from future criminal offences and demonstrates the close theoretical links with contemporary rational actor model thinking and the influence of both on criminal justice policy-making. Participants visit inmates, observe first-hand prison life and have interaction with adult inmates, and these programmes have become extremely popular in many parts of the world. The basic premise is that juveniles who see what prison is like will be deterred from future violations of the law – in other words, 'scared straight'. Problematically, these programmes emphasize severity of punishment, but neglect the two other key components of deterrence theory – certainty and swiftness (Mears, 2007).

Petrosino et al. (2002) investigated the effects of programmes comprising organized visits to prisons by juvenile delinquents (officially adjudicated or convicted by a juvenile court) or pre-delinquents (children in trouble but not officially adjudicated as delinquents) and found intervention to be actually more harmful than doing nothing. Lilienfeld (2005) showed that such interventions could possibly worsen conduct-disorder symptoms, while Aos et al. (2001) found that 'Scared Straight' and similar programmes produced substantial increases in recidivism. Evidence indicates that these interventions are simply not effective in deterring criminal activity. In fact, they may be harmful and increase delinquency relative to no intervention at all with the same youths.

Critics of such policies argue that the media has capitalized on the intuitive appeal of this type of strategy. They observe that television talk shows often promote the efficacy, in a sensational manner, of 'Scared Straight' and similar interventions, noting that criminal policy is often based on intuition, rather than research evidence, and argue for the implementation of policies based on the latter (Mears, 2007; Marion and Oliver, 2006).

Summary of main points

1. Psychodynamic explanations of crime and criminal behaviour have their origins in the extremely influential work of Sigmund Freud and his assertion that sexuality is present from birth, which is the fundamental basis of psychoanalysis.
2. Freud proposed two different models of criminal behaviour: the first proposes that criminality reflects a state of mental disturbance or illness; the second that offenders possess a 'weak conscience'.
3. John Bowlby (1952) influentially argued that offending behaviour takes place when a child has not enjoyed a close and continuous relationship with its mother during its formative years.

4. Maginnis (1997) concludes that the most reliable indicator of violent crime in a community is the proportion of fatherless families.
5. Behavioural learning theories have their origins in the work of I.P. Pavlov and B.F. Skinner, and Hans Eysenck (1970, 1977) sought to build a general theory of criminal behaviour based on their psychological concept of conditioning.
6. Definitions of psychopathy in general emphasize such traits as an incapacity for loyalty, selfishness, irresponsibility, impulsiveness, inability to feel guilt and failure to learn from experience.
7. Personality typing (or offender profiling) has been used to help detect particular types of criminals and is a method found to have been most useful in the detection of serial murders.
8. Cognitive learning theories have their foundations in a fundamental critique of the predestined actor model proposing that, by observing the responses made by individuals to different stimuli, it is possible to draw inferences about the nature of the internal cognitive processes that produce those responses.
9. E.H. Sutherland first used the term 'differential association' to explain interaction patterns by which thieves were restricted in their physical and social contacts to association with like-minded others.
10. The emergence of cognitive learning theories led to the development of a range of behaviour modification treatment strategies introduced with the intention of changing behaviour.

Discussion questions

1. How do psychoanalytic theories explain criminal behaviour?
2. Discuss whether maternal deprivation theories continue to be a legitimate explanation of criminal behaviour.
3. Does Eysenck's theory of criminal personality provide an adequate explanation of criminal behaviour?
4. What is a psychopath and how do we know?
5. Discuss the range of available cognitive behavioural interventions and in what circumstances we might use them.

Suggested further reading

Psychological positivism is again an extremely wide subject area and there are thus many relevant texts. Students are therefore advised to use the references in the text as a guide to specific interests. However, for a general but comprehensive psychological account of criminal behaviour, see Feldman (1977) and Hollin (1989). Freud (1920) still provides an excellent introduction to the main tenets of psychoanalysis; while for a discussion and critique of the psychoanalytic tradition of explaining criminal behaviour, see Farrington (1992b, 1994). For a comprehensive discussion of the research on maternal deprivation theory, see Rutter (1981). Eysenck (1977) gives a comprehensive introduction to his notion of the criminal personality. The cognitive psychology perspective is well represented by Sutherland (1947) for the original and highly influential differential association theory and Akers (1985) for more contemporary social learning theory. Holmes and De Burger (1989) is essential reading for those interested in serial killers, while Omerod (1996) is worthy of consultation on offender profiling. Hollin (1990b) provides a comprehensive discussion of cognitive behavioural interventions with young offenders.

7. Sociological positivism

Key Issues

1. Emile Durkheim and social disorganization theory
2. The Chicago School and social theory
3. Robert Merton and anomie theory
4. Early deviant subcultural theories
5. Later deviant subcultural theories

We have seen in the previous two chapters that both the biological and psychological variants of the predestined actor model of crime and criminal behaviour locate the primary impulse for criminal behaviour in the individual. The sociological version rejects these individualist explanations and proposes those behaviours defined as criminal behaviour are simply those that deviate from the norms acceptable to the consensus of opinion in society. This perspective should not be confused with that of the victimized actor model – the focus of the third part of this book – which proposes that it is the weak and powerless who are defined as criminal and targeted by the rich and powerful in an inherently unequal and unfair society. Sociological positivists recognize that crime is a socially constructed entity but at the same time acknowledge that it poses a real threat to the continuance of that society and thus needs to be controlled in some way.

The sociological variant of the predestined actor model involves the 'scientific' measurement of indicators of 'social disorganization' – such as rates of crime, drunkenness and suicide – in specified urban areas. Proponents recommend that, once the whereabouts of existing and potential 'trouble spots' are identified, these must be 'treated', controlled or, in future, 'prevented', if serious social disorder is to be avoided. It is a long-established tradition with its roots in the work of the nineteenth-century 'moral statisticians', Quételet (in Belgium) and Guerry (in France) and their social campaigning counterparts in England – Mayhew, Colquhoun, Fletcher and others – who used early empirical methods to investigate the urban slums where crime and deviance flourished. It is an enduring tradition that owes much to the important contribution to sociology established by Emile Durkheim.

Emile Durkheim and social disorganization theory

Emile Durkheim was the founding father of academic sociology in France and a major social theorist working at the turn of the twentieth century. It was because of the strength and rigour of his large and complex sociological theory that he was able to assert powerfully the merits of social factors in explaining individual and group action. For Durkheim, it was not just the psychological and biological versions of the predestined actor model that were unable to provide an adequate explanation of social action, he was also strongly opposed to those theoretical ideas – social contract theory and utilitarianism – that had provided the foundations of the rational actor model. In short, a society that is divided into different interest groups on an unequal basis is not one in which 'just contracts between individuals and society could be made' (Durkheim, 1933 originally 1893: 202).

At this point, a few words of caution should be indicated. Durkheim is often misrepresented as a conservative indistinguishable from his French predecessor Auguste Comte. Taylor, Walton and Young (1973) – the eminent radical criminologists discussed fully in the third part of this book – and the present author (Hopkins Burke, 1998b, 1999b) consider this orthodox interpretation to be a gross simplification of a significant, radical, social and criminological theorist. Indeed, much of what has been said about Durkheim is more appropriate to the work of Auguste Comte.

Comte had argued that the process whereby with industrialization people have become increasingly separated into different places of residence and employment has subverted the moral authority of a previously united society. Thus, from this perspective, people are seen to commit criminal acts not so much because it is in their material interests to do so, but because there is no strong moral authority influencing them to do otherwise. It is the purpose of positivist social science to create this higher moral authority.

The essential difference between Comte and Durkheim lies in their differing views of human nature. For the former, the human being has a natural and inherent desire to reach perfection and it is the creation of a moral authority by social scientists that can create the ordered society that will bring about that state of being. Durkheim simply rejects this view. It is utopian and idealistic to argue that a higher moral authority could restrain human desires at all times in history. Thus, Durkheim, in contrast to Comte, proposes a 'dualistic' view of human nature: a duality between the needs of the body and the soul. Human instincts are biologically given, while it is the task of the social world to develop through the human 'soul' an adherence to a moral consensus that is the basis of social order and control. With the changing nature of complex modern society, that consensus is a shifting and adaptable entity.

It is possible to observe here a similarity between Durkheim and Freud, for both argue that an increased repression of the individual conscience is the basis of the development of a civilized society, but there are nevertheless substantial differences in their positions. For Durkheim, individual desires have to be regulated not simply because they have certain biological needs and predispositions, but also because the failure to control this aspect of the person can lead to a situation of disharmony and despair, culminating in what he terms egoism and anomie. Durkheim did agree with Freud that individuals were not really human until they had been socialized. Freud, however, saw socialization and the development of a conscience as necessary for individual well-being. For Durkheim, the lack of socialization and a conscience leads to conflict between the individual and society.

Durkheim was opposed to the utilitarians – because he considered them to be idealists rather than social scientists – and argued that moral authority can only be acceptable to men and women if it is relevant to their particular position in a changing society. If people are caught up in occupations that are unsuitable to their talents – and they recognize this underachievement – they can have little enthusiasm for moral authority. Central to his social theory is a concern with social change and his keenness to eradicate the 'forced division of labour'.

It was in *The Division of Labour in Society*, first published in 1893, that Durkheim described the processes of social change that accompany the industrial development of society, arguing that earlier forms of society had high levels of mechanical solidarity, while the more developed industrial societies are characterized by an advanced stage of 'organic' solidarity. However, a further note of caution needs to be indicated here: no society is entirely mechanical or organic with any social formation being in a state of development between the two extremes. Indeed, there may well be many pockets of intense mechanical solidarity in highly developed organic societies and this important observation is discussed below.

For Durkheim, societies with high levels of mechanical solidarity are characterized by the conformity of the group. There is thus a likeness and a similarity between individuals and they hold common attitudes and beliefs that bind one person to another. Now this is a form of social solidarity that may at first sight appear attractive – suggesting popular notions of the close-knit community – but at the same time severe restrictions are placed on the ability of an individual to develop a sense of personal identity or uniqueness. Thus, cooperation between individual members of the group is restricted to what can be achieved through the close conformity of each member to a single stereotype.

Durkheim argues that such societies can further be identified by a very intense and rigid collective conscience where members hold very precise shared ideas of what is right and wrong. There are, however, individuals within that group who differ from the uniform ideal and in these cases the law is used as an instrument to maintain that uniformity. Moreover, repressive and summary punishments are used against individuals and minority groups that transgress against the collective conscience of the majority. This punishment of dissenters usefully emphasizes their inferiority, while at the same time encouraging commitment to the majority viewpoint. In this sense, crime is a normal feature of a society with high levels of mechanical solidarity. Punishment performs a necessary function by reinforcing the moral consensus – or world view – of the group where a reduction in behaviour designated as criminal would as a necessity lead to other previously non-criminal activities becoming criminalized. Indeed, Durkheim takes this argument a step further and claims that a society with no crime would be abnormal. The imposition of tight controls that make crime impossible would seriously restrict the potential for innovation and social progress.

Durkheim argues that with greater industrialization societies develop greater levels of organic solidarity where there is a more developed division of labour and different groups become dependent on each other. Social solidarity now relies less on the maintenance of uniformity between individuals, and more on the management of the diverse functions of different groups. Nevertheless, a certain degree of uniformity remains essential.

It is time to indicate a further cautionary note. There has been a tendency – encouraged by some influential introductory sociology textbooks – for students to confuse the arguments presented by Durkheim on the increasing development of organic society, with those put forward by nineteenth-century conservatives, and the German sociologist Ferdinand Tönnies. For those writers, it was precisely this increasing fragmentation of communal beliefs and values that was the problem and the proposed solution thus lies in re-establishing the moral certainties of a society with high levels of mechanical solidarity. This is not the argument presented by Durkheim.

For Durkheim, the division of labour is a progressive phenomenon. Its appearance signals not the inevitable collapse of morality, but the emergence of a new content for the collective conscience. In societies dominated by mechanical solidarity, the emphasis is on the obligation of the individual to society: with organic formations, the focus is increasingly on the obligation of society to the individual person. Now to give the maximum possible encouragement to individual rights does not mean that altruism – that is, self-sacrifice for others – will disappear; on the contrary, moral individualism is not unregulated self-interest but the imposition of a set of reciprocal obligations that binds together individuals (Durkheim, 1933 originally 1893). Here lies the essential originality of Durkheim's interpretation of the division of labour.

For Adam Smith (1910 originally 1776), the founder of free-market economics, and the utilitarians, the specialization of economic exchange is simply an effect of the growth of wealth and the free play of economic self-interest. For Durkheim, the true significance of the division of labour lies in its moral role. It is a source of restraint upon self-interest and thereby renders society cohesive. The idea that unbridled egoism – or competitive individualism – could ever become the basis of a civilized order is for Durkheim quite absurd. In short, Durkheim regarded the cohesion of nineteenth-century laissez-faire society, with its wholly unregulated markets, its arbitrary inequalities, its restrictions on social mobility and its 'class' wars, as a dangerous condition. Such imperfect social regulation leads to a variety of different social problems, including crime and deviance.

Durkheim provided a threefold typology of deviants. The first typology is the *biological deviant* who is explained by the physiological or psychological malfunctioning we encountered in the previous two chapters and who can be present in a normal division of labour. The other two typologies are linked to the nature and condition of the social system and are present in those societies that are characterized by an abnormal or forced division of labour. The second typology, the *functional rebel*, is, therefore, a 'normal' person who is reacting to a pathological society, rebelling against the existing, inappropriate and unfair division of society and indicating the existence of strains in the social system. For Durkheim, such a person expresses the true 'spontaneous' or 'normal' collective consciousness as opposed to the artificial 'forced' or 'pathological' one currently in operation (Taylor *et al.*, 1973). The third typology, *skewed deviants*, involves those who have been socialized into a disorganized pathological society and are the usual focus of the student of deviance and criminal behaviour.

Durkheim proposed two central arguments to explain the growth of crime and criminal behaviour in modern industrial societies. First, such societies encourage a state of unbridled 'egoism' that is contrary to the maintenance of social solidarity and conformity to the law. Second, the likelihood of inefficient regulation is greater at a time of rapid modernization, because new forms of control have not evolved sufficiently to replace the older and now less appropriate means of maintaining solidarity. In such a period, society is in a state of normlessness or 'anomie', a condition characterized by a breakdown in norms and common understandings.

Durkheim claimed that, without external controls, a human being has unlimited needs and society thus has a right to regulate these by indicating the appropriate rewards that should accrue to the individual. Except in times of crisis, everyone has at least a vague perception of what they can expect to earn for their endeavours but, at a time of economic upheaval, society cannot exert controls on the aspirations of individuals. During a depression, people are forced to lower their sights, a situation that some will find intolerable, but, on the other hand, when there is a sudden improvement in economic conditions, social equilibrium will also break down and there is now no limit on aspirations.

A fundamental recurring criticism of Durkheim emphasized in virtually any introductory sociology text refers to his apparently unassailable methodological collectivism, or over-determinism as it is usually termed. Individuals, apparently, seem to have little – indeed no – choice in their actions, or in terms of the terminology used in this text their lives appear predestined because of the social conditions in which they live. It is without doubt this interpretation of Durkheim – where it appears impossible to locate any acceptable mechanism to explain social change – that has led to his work being almost universally dismissed as methodologically and politically conservative. A more recent methodological individualist reinterpretation of Durkheim contained in the work of his French compatriot Raymond Boudon (1980) recognizes that individuals do have choices, come together with others and form coalitions of interest on which they act and that it is in this way that social change can and does occur. Opportunities for conceiving of, and carrying out, that action are nonetheless invariably *constrained* by – sometimes overwhelmingly – structural constraints, not least the more strongly asserted, believed and enforced *conscience collectives* that are the products of the ultra, or intense, mechanical solidarities that dominate not only simple societies but also pockets of varying size within more complex contemporary societies. In short, individual choice – or acceptance or rejection of a particular way of life or apparent destiny – is possible, from this perspective, but the choices available may be limited, or, in some cases, virtually non-existent (Hopkins Burke and Pollock, 2004: 9).

Hopkins Burke and Pollock (2004) adopt this methodological individualist interpretation of Durkheim in their discussion of hate crime motivation – hate crimes being criminal acts motivated by hatred, bias or prejudice against a person or property based on the actual or perceived race, ethnicity, gender, religion or sexual orientation of the victim – and observe that, even in a complex post-industrial society characterized by high levels of organic solidarity, and multifarious interdependencies, the concept of mechanical solidarity retains considerable explanatory power. The authors observe that, even within complex and diverse societies, mechanical solidarities continue to significantly exist at three levels in the social world. First, there is the *macro* societal level of national identities that may be particularly strong in those societies where the collective conscience is rigidly enforced by reference to a fundamentalist religious or political belief system. Second, there is the *mezzo* or intermediate level of the organization and institution, for example, organized hate groups. Third, there is the *micro* level of the small group or gang, such as a 'football firm' in Britain or Europe or localized less organized hate groupings.

Hopkins Burke and Pollock (2004) observe that many contemporary hate groups have philosophies based on the notion of a collective society, consisting of common values, culture, identity, attitude and homogeneity. Those who deviate – or are in some way different from the perceived norm – are defined and labelled as being deviant and outsiders. Deviance is a necessary function of any mechanical solidarity – whether it be at the macro, mezzo or micro level – inhabited by hate groups because its existence and endurance tests the boundaries of tolerance leading to an ongoing evaluation of prevailing norms and values. Transgressors against the dominant world view – 'subaltern' (Perry, 2001) or subordinate groups, those whose sexual, racial, gendered, or ethnic, identities are different from the traditional white, male, heterosexual identity that exists in a 'normal' society – are perceived to have contravened the mechanical solidarity and are consequently censured.

Hopkins Burke and Pollock (2004) observe that this situation whereby a number of mezzo and micro mechanical solidarities co-exist alongside each other in the same geographical space provides a fertile enabling environment for racist hate as a sense of insecurity and uncertainty can arise among at least certain sections of the traditional white majority. Both Enoch Powell (in Britain) and Jean-Marie Le Pen (in France) have successfully taken advantage of the political opportunities proffered by this insecurity and dissent during the latter decades of the twentieth century by claiming that non-white immigration would pose a threat to tradition, culture and opportunity for the traditional 'white' community (Heywood, 1992). Thus, hate crime perpetrators, motivated by fears of cultural change, construct themselves as victims and demand first-class preferential citizenship as they feel alienated from their traditional community or mechanical solidarity.

In concluding this section, we might note that, although there continues to be controversy about the accuracy of Durkheim's disorganization theory taken as a whole, his notion that crime is linked to a breakdown in social controls has been a major inspiration to different sociologists in the twentieth century. In particular, his concept of anomie had a marked influence on the later work of Robert Merton discussed below. Moreover, the twin notions of anomie and egoism are extremely useful in helping to explain the nature of crime and criminal behaviour that occurred in the UK during the 1980s and the early 1990s, a more recent period of severe economic and social disruption. The aftermath of that period is still with us and will be examined in later chapters of this book. It is of enduring importance not least because, at the time of writing, we are undergoing a major, apparently long-term, worldwide economic downturn with likely significant changes in the pattern of crime and criminality linked to social disruption. In the meantime, we will consider the more readily recognized influence that is apparent in the work of the Chicago School.

The Chicago School

In the early part of the twentieth century, the USA underwent a major transition from a predominantly rural and agricultural society to one based on industrial and metropolitan centres. Chicago, for example, grew from a town of 10,000 inhabitants in 1860 to a large city with a population of over two million by 1910. Life was nevertheless hard, wages were low, hours were long, factory conditions were appalling and living in slum tenements created serious health problems (see Lilly et al., 1986).

Sociologists working at the University of Chicago reached the conclusion that growing up and living in such negative conditions undoubtedly influenced the outcome of people's lives. Moreover, crime and criminal behaviour in such an environment could not simply be explained in the individualist terms proposed by the biological and psychological versions of the predestined actor model. It made more 'sense' when viewed as a social problem and it was argued that the poor are not simply born into a life of crime but are driven by the conditions of their social environment. Thus, by changing their surroundings it would be possible to reverse the negative effects of the city and transform these people into law-abiding citizens.

Robert Park (1921) contributed two central ideas to the work of the Chicago School. First, he proposed that, like any ecological system, the development and organization of the city is neither random nor idiosyncratic but patterned; human communities, like plants, live together symbiotically. In other words, different kinds of human beings share the same environment and are mutually dependent on each other. At the same time, patterns of change in the city are comparable to changes in the balance of nature, the human population in US cities was migratory, rather than fixed, with new immigrants moving into the poor areas and replacing the previous inhabitants as they moved out to the suburbs. Second, Park observed that the nature of these social processes had their impact on human behaviours like crime, and these could be ascertained only through the careful study of city life. It was a research agenda that several researchers were to embrace.

Ernest Burgess (1928) produced a model of the city that provided a framework for understanding the social roots of crime and argued that, as cities expand in size, the development is patterned socially. They grow radially in a series of concentric zones or rings. Burgess outlined five different zones and proposed that a competitive process decided how people were distributed spatially among these: commercial enterprises were located in the central business district (or loop) in close proximity to the transport systems; the most expensive residential areas were in the outer commuter zones or suburbs, away from the bustle of the city centre, the pollution of the factories and the homes of the poor.

It was the 'zone in transition' – containing rows of deteriorating tenements and often built in the shadow of ageing factories – that was the particular focus of study. The outward expansion of the business district led to the constant displacement of residents. As the least desirable living area, the zone was the focus for the influx of waves of immigrants who were too poor to reside elsewhere. Burgess observed that these social patterns weakened family and communal ties and resulted in 'social disorganization'. It was this disorganization thesis that was influentially presented as the primary explanation of criminal behaviour.

Clifford Shaw and Henry McKay (1972, originally 1931) set out to empirically test concentric zone theory, collating juvenile court statistics in order to map the spatial distribution of juvenile offending throughout the city and their analysis confirmed the hypothesis that offending behaviour flourished in the zone in transition and was inversely related to the affluence of the area and corresponding distance from the central business district. They studied court records over several decades and were able to show that crime levels were highest in slum neighbourhoods, regardless of which racial or ethnic group resided there and, moreover, as these groups moved to other zones, their offending rates correspondingly decreased. It was this observation that led Shaw and McKay to conclude that it was the nature of the neighbourhoods – not the nature of the individuals who lived within them – that regulated involvement in crime.

Shaw and McKay emphasized the importance of neighbourhood organization in allowing or preventing offending behaviour by children and young people. In more affluent communities, parents fulfilled the needs of their offspring and carefully supervised their activities but in the zone of transition families and other conventional institutions – schools, churches, and voluntary associations – were strained, if not destroyed, by rapid urban growth, migration and poverty. Left to their own devices, young people in this zone were not subject to the social constraints placed on their contemporaries in the more affluent areas and were more likely to seek excitement and friends in the streets of the city.

Shaw actively promoted appreciative studies of the deviant, using the criminal's 'own story' by means of participant observation in their particular deviant world, which became known as the ethnographic or 'life-history' method and led to the publication of titles like *The Jack Roller: A Delinquent Boy's Own Story*, *The Natural History of a Delinquent Career* and *Brothers in Crime* (Shaw, 1930, 1931, 1938). These studies showed that young people were often recruited into offending behaviour through their association with older siblings or gang members.

Shaw and McKay concluded that disorganized neighbourhoods help produce and sustain 'criminal traditions' that compete with conventional values and can be 'transmitted down through successive generations of boys, much the same way that language and other social forms are transmitted' (Shaw and McKay, 1972: 174). Thus, young people growing up in socially disorganized inner-city slum areas characterized by the existence of a value system that condones criminal behaviour could readily learn these values in their daily interactions with older adolescents. On the other hand, youths in organized areas – where the dominance of conventional institutions had precluded the development of criminal traditions – remains insulated from deviant values and peers. Thus, for them, an offending career is an unlikely option.

Shaw and McKay fundamentally argued that juvenile offending can only be understood by reference to the social context in which young people live and, in turn, this context itself is a product of major societal transformations brought about by rapid urbanization and massive population shifts. Young people born and brought up in the socially disorganized zone of transition are particularly vulnerable to the temptations of crime; as conventional institutions disintegrate around them, they are given little supervision and are free to roam the streets where they are likely to become the next generation of carriers of the area's criminal tradition. It was this aspect of their work that provided crucial theoretical foundations for Edwin Sutherland's theory of 'differential association', which was discussed in the previous chapter.

The work of the Chicago School has been criticized from a number of standpoints. First, it has been observed that, while the deterministic importance of the transmission of a 'criminal culture' is emphasized, there is substantially less detail provided on the origins of that culture. Second, there have been criticisms of a tendency to see the spatial distribution of groups in the city as a 'natural' social process. The role that power and class domination can play in the creation and perpetuation of slums and the enormous economic inequality that permeates such areas is ignored. Third, it has been proposed that they provide only a partial explanation of criminality that seems best able to explain involvement in stable criminal roles and in group-based offending behaviour.

The Chicago School criminologists have nevertheless rightly had a substantial influence on the development of sociological explanations of crime and criminal behaviour. Particularly influential has been the recognition that where people grow up – and the people with whom they associate – is closely linked to a propensity for involvement in criminal activity.

The Chicago School has also had a further practical influence. In the 1930s, Clifford Shaw established the 'Chicago Area Project' (CAP). The intention was to allow local residents in socially deprived areas the autonomy to organize neighbourhood committees in the fight against crime and the project encompassed several approaches to crime prevention. First, a strong emphasis was placed on the creation of recreational programmes that would divert young people from criminal activity. Second, efforts were made to have residents take pride in their community by improving the physical appearance of the area. Third, CAP staff members would attempt to mediate on behalf of young people in trouble with those in authority, such as schoolteachers. Fourth, local people were employed as 'street credible' workers in an attempt to persuade youths that education and a conventional lifestyle was in their best interest. Schlossman *et al.* (1984) conducted an evaluation of fifty years of the CAP project and reached the conclusion that it had long been effective in reducing rates of reported juvenile offending.

In summary, social disorganization theory – as developed by Shaw and McKay – called for efforts to reorganize communities. The emphasis on cultural learning suggests that treatment programmes that attempt to reverse the criminal learning of offenders can counteract involvement in crime. Young offenders should thus be placed in settings where they will receive pro-social reinforcement, for example, through the use of positive peer counselling.

Robert Merton and anomie theory

Robert Merton's anomie – or strain – theory attempts to explain the occurrence of not only crime but also wider deviance and disorder, and in this sense it is a wide-ranging, essentially sociological explanation that promises a comprehensive account of crime and deviance causation, but – while it provides a major contribution to this endeavour – it ultimately fails to fulfil this ambition.

Merton borrowed the term anomie from Emile Durkheim in an attempt to explain the social upheaval that accompanied the Great Depression of the 1930s and later the social conflicts that occurred in the USA during the 1960s. His writings are particularly significant because they challenged the orthodoxy of the time that saw the USA as characterized by the term 'the American Dream', a vision of a meritocratic society in which hard work and endeavour – in the context of conservative values – would supposedly distribute social and economic rewards equitably.

Merton essentially followed the Chicago School sociologists in rejecting individualistic explanations of crime and criminal behaviour but at the same time took his sociological argument a step further than Durkheim. Whereas his predecessor had considered human aspirations to be naturally given, Merton argued that they are usually socially learned. Moreover, there are – and this is the central component of his argument – social structural limitations imposed on access to the means to achieve these goals. His work therefore focuses upon the position of the individual within the social structure rather than on personality characteristics and, in his words, 'our primary aim lies in discovering how some social structures exert a definite pressure upon certain persons in the society to engage in nonconformist conduct' (Merton, 1938: 672).

Merton proposed that this central aim could be achieved by distinguishing between *cultural goals* and *institutionalized means*. The former are those material possessions, symbols of status, accomplishment and esteem that established norms and values encourage us to aspire to, and are, therefore, socially learned; the latter are the distribution of opportunities to achieve these goals in socially acceptable ways. Merton observes that it is possible to overemphasize either the goals or the means to achieve them and that it is this that leads to social strains, or 'anomie'.

Merton was mainly concerned with the application of his theory to the USA and proposed that in that society there is an overemphasis on the achievement of goals such as monetary success and material goods, without sufficient attention paid to the institutional means of achievement, and it is this cultural imbalance that leads to people being prepared to use any means, regardless of their legality, to achieve that goal (Merton, 1938: 674). The ideal situation would be where there is a balance between goals and means and in such circumstances individuals who conform will feel that they are justly rewarded.

Deviant, especially criminal, behaviour results when cultural goals are accepted, for example, and people would generally like to be financially successful, but where access to the means to achieve that goal is limited by the position of a person in the social structure. Merton outlined five possible reactions – or adaptations – that can occur when people are not in a position to legitimately attain internalized social goals.

Conformity

Conformity is a largely self-explanatory adaptation whereupon people tend to accept both the cultural goals of society and the means of achieving them. Even if they find their social ascent to be limited, they still tend not to 'deviate'. Merton claimed that, in most societies, this is the standard form of adaptation, for, if this were not the case, society would be extremely unstable. He did nevertheless note that, for many people whose access to the socially dictated 'good things in life' through established institutionalized means is in some way more difficult than conventionally portrayed, the 'strain' to achieve might well become intolerable. People could alleviate the strain in such instances by either changing their cultural goal and/or by withdrawing their allegiance to the institutionalized means. In following either or both courses, people would be deviating from norms prescribing what should be desired (success) or how this should be achieved (legitimate means such as education, approved entrepreneurship or conscientious employment). The following four 'modes of adaptation' describe various ways of alleviating 'strain' generated by social inequalities.

Retreatism

Merton considered retreatism to be the least common adaptation. Retreatists are those who reject both social goals and the means of obtaining them, and these are true 'aliens': they are 'in the society but not of it' (Merton, 1938: 677). It is a category of social 'dropouts' that includes, among others, drug addicts, psychotics, vagrants, tramps and chronic alcoholics.

Ritualism

Merton identifies many similarities between 'ritualists' and 'conformists' with an example of the former a person who adheres to rules for their own sake. Bureaucrats who accept and observe the rules of their organizations uncritically provide the classic example. Those in rule-bound positions in the armed services, social control institutions or the public service may be particularly susceptible to this form of adaptation where the emphasis is on the means of achievement rather than the goals. These people, or groups, need not of course be particularly successful in attaining their conventional goals but their overemphasis on the 'means' clouds their judgement on the desirability of appreciating the goals.

Innovation

The innovator – the usual focus for the student of crime and criminal behaviour – is keen to achieve the standard goals of society, wealth, fame or admiration, but, probably due to blocked opportunities to obtain these by socially approved means, embarks on novel, or innovative, routes. Many 'innovative' routes exist in complex organic societies, so much so that some innovators may be seen to overlap with 'conformists'. For example, the sports, arts and entertainment industries frequently attract, develop and absorb 'innovators', celebrating their novelty in contrast to the conformist or ritualist, and providing opportunities for those whose circumstances may frustrate their social ascent through conventionally prescribed and approved routes.

The innovator may be exceptionally talented, or may develop talents, in a field that is restricted or unusual and conventionally deemed worthy of celebration for its novelty but these individuals are relatively unthreatening to conventional views of the acceptable means of social achievement. There are others, on the other hand, who appear to pose a distinctly destabilizing influence on conventional definitions of socially acceptable means of achievement and it is, therefore, one of the strengths of anomie – or strain theories – that they appreciate that some of these 'innovations' are merely 'deviant', and subjectable to informal social controls and censure, while others are proscribed by the criminal law.

Some activities are usually seen as 'criminally' censurable in most societies, although they may be excusable in certain circumstances. Robbery is usually seen as an offence when committed against an individual or an institution such as a bank. However, this might not be the case when committed in wartime against the persons or institutions of an 'enemy' state. Homicide is regarded as a serious offence in most jurisdictions, yet it is acceptable when promoted by socially or politically powerful interests in times of war. Similarly, where does the financial 'entrepreneur' stretch the bounds of legality or previously established 'acceptable' business means to the achievement of previously determined goals? Lilly *et al.* (1986) provide the example of stock exchange regulation abusers in the 1980s as an example of innovative business deviants. At a time when business deregulation had generated many fortunes, some people were encouraged by the prevailing economic circumstances to take opportunities to shorten the means to the social goal of wealth through 'insider dealing' and similar practices.

In short, the innovator may be seen to overemphasize the goals of achievement over the means. Conventionally regarded success may be achieved by any means that seem appropriate to the innovator, who strives to overcome barriers to achievement by adopting any available strategies for achieving established goals.

Rebellion

For Merton, rebellious people are those who not merely reject but also wish to change the existing social system and its goals. Rebels thus reject both the socially approved means and goals of their society. The emergence of popular images of the potential of both innovative and rebellious modes of adaptation to the standard social and economic patterns of Western life in the 1960s did much to renew an interest in Merton's approach to crime and deviance.

Three main criticisms have been made of anomie theory. First, it has been observed to be a self-acknowledged 'theory of the middle range' that does little to trace the origins of criminogenic circumstances. Merton is thus accused of being a 'cautious rebel' who fails to explain either the initial existence of inequality, or the exaggerated emphasis in society on making money (Taylor et al., 1973). Indeed, it was criticisms of this kind that instigated the search for a more totalizing, historically and politically aware criminology – or 'sociology of deviance' – in the late 1960s and 1970s. The rise – and indeed fall – of this mode of explaining criminal behaviour is the central focus of the third part of this book.

Anomie theory is not as comprehensive an account of crime and deviance as it may at first look for it fails to explain certain behaviours that are commonly labelled 'deviant' – such as recreational drug use – and which are often under-taken by people who otherwise accept the standard cultural goals and the institutionalized means of achieving them.

The second criticism is targeted at Merton's assumption that cultural goals and values are known and shared by all members of society. Lemert (1972), for example, argued that society is more accurately characterized by the notion of a plurality of values and, if this is the case, then Merton's 'ends–means' approach becomes problematic and generally insufficient in explaining crime and deviance. He can be partially defended in that he did state that different goals are possible within his scheme, but he does not give sufficient emphasis to different groups and different values. Moreover, the assumption that it is the 'lower classes' who are most likely to suffer from frustrated aspirations and who are subject to strain and commit criminal or deviant acts may not be accurate. Later criminological studies reveal that there is a great deal more deviant behaviour in society than Merton's formula suggests. Anomie theory – we are told – is hard-pressed to account for business fraud and other 'white-collar' crimes, and also for 'lower-class' conformity. Thus, anomie theory predicts both too few deviant activities among the more privileged members of society and too many among those potentially most subject to strain.

In defence of Merton, it would seem that he was motivated to explain those forms of highly visible and immediately apparent crime that have traditionally been committed by the poorer sections of society and that have been of immediate concern to the public and hence politicians and inevitably criminologists. Indeed, later researchers – predominantly working in the victimized actor tradition, which is the focus of the third part of this book – have sought to use the concept of anomie in an attempt to explain corporate crime. From this perspective, it has been argued that explanations based on individual motivations are inadequate and that it is necessary to consider these in the context of corporate goals, the essential one of which is to maximize profit over a long period (Etzioni, 1961; Box, 1983). Box thus identifies five potential sources of 'environmental uncertainty' for the corporation that represent obstacles to the lawful attainment of its main goal. These are: competitors, the government, employees, consumers and the public, especially as represented by protectionists. Box observes that, confronted with such obstacles, the corporation adopts tactics that frequently involve breaking the law in order to achieve its goal.

Staw and Szwajkowski (1975) compared the financial performance of 105 large firms subject to litigation involving illegal competition with those of 395 similar firms not so involved and concluded that environmental scarcity did appear linked to a whole range of trade violations. Box (1983) goes further and argues that adherence to the profit motive renders the corporation inherently criminogenic with the bulk of corporate crime initiated by high-ranking officials and he suggests, moreover, that the very factors connected with career success in corporations – and the consequences of such success – are themselves criminogenic.

Gross (1978) conducted a survey of several studies of corporate career mobility and noted the relevance of personality differences. He thus found senior managers to be ambitious, easily accepting of a non-demanding moral code, and to regard their own success at goal attainment as being linked to the success of the organization. Box (1983) took this notion a step further and argued that the very nature of the corporate promotion system means that those who reach the top are likely to have the very personal characteristics required to commit business crime, the greater success they achieve, the more free they feel from the bind of conventional values. In this way, we might observe that Box's interpretation of anomie seems to be closer to that of Durkheim than Merton.

Financial profit is not the only goal relevant to anomie. Braithwaite has described fraud as 'an illegitimate means to achieving any one of a wide range of organisational and personal goals when legitimate means . . . are blocked' (1984: 94), for example, he found a widespread willingness among pharmacologists to fabricate the results of safety tests. This behaviour could sometimes be attributed to financial greed but there were other explanations. Some scientists, for example, have an intense commitment to their work and when the value of this is threatened by test results there could be considerable temptation to cover this up in order to defend professional prestige.

Levin and McDevitt (1993) and Perry (2001) have observed the tendency for hate crime offenders to blame their economic instability or lack of job opportunities on the immigration of 'foreigners', while Hopkins Burke and Pollock (2004) argue that it is the actual adaptation of conformity that is problematic in this context. Central to the whole notion of conformity is the sense that adherents in some way buy into the legitimacy of the whole social order and exactly why they do this is not questioned by Merton, but adherence to the law, the influence of macro or localized 'correct' thinking, perhaps in the work context in the case of the latter, and a lack of opportunity could all be legitimate reasons why a person with latent – hidden or suppressed – hate crime motivation keeps this under control. It could well be that as an outcome of a change in structural circumstances – for example, the arrival of a group of immigrants or asylum seekers in the locality, the chance meeting of a new friend or colleague with similar latent views, perhaps while on holiday or after the consumption of a few 'social' drinks, or as the outcome of surfing the Internet – that latent hate crime motivation could well be transformed into something more insidious.

These observations suggest a fundamental premise that hate crime motivation is essentially a pathological deviation from societal norms. Hopkins Burke and Pollock (2004) nevertheless argue the converse and observe that hate crime motivation is simply normal and unremarkable in society as currently constituted. The powerful macro, mezzo and micro mechanical solidarities that exist in even the most complex contemporary organic societies – absorbed and internalized during a socialization process that may well have prioritized notions of hard work, law-abiding behaviour and indeed conformity to the group – legitimate hate motivation as normal. Given the opportunity in the right venue among 'our own kind' where such views are very much the norm, it is possible that latent hate motivation might well be actualized, where the at least tacit approval of the (perhaps) silent majority of conformists might provide succour, support and legitimization for those prepared to act upon their hate motivation.

The third criticism of Merton is that he made no attempt to apply his typology to women and, at first sight, it seems totally inapplicable to them. Leonard (1983) proposes that the main goal of US women is to achieve successful relationships with others, not the attainment of material wealth, and this is an argument to which we return in the following chapter.

Anomie theory has been subjected to many criticisms but is generally sympathetically regarded in the fields of sociology and criminology. Merton did a great deal to broaden the study of crime and criminal behaviour and to introduce the importance of social structure in shaping the life choices of individuals. Some have argued that he did not go far enough with this endeavour; however, it would seem that Merton – along with many liberal or social democratic critics of unrestrained egoism and conservative values both in his native USA and Britain – had no inclination to see a socialist transformation of society. The latter tends to be the ultimate goal of his critics working at the more radical end of the spectrum in the victimized actor model tradition. To criticize the substantial elements of his theoretical concerns on that basis is therefore rather unfair, particularly as many of those critics have since radically modified their views and come themselves to accept the explanatory potential of Merton's notion of anomie (see Chapter 18). In short, his work has provided a useful starting point for subsequent researchers.

Messner and Rosenfeld (1994) have developed an institutional anomie theory where they observe that the 'American Dream' is a broad, cultural ethos that entails a commitment to the goal of material success, to be pursued by everyone, in a mass society dominated by huge multinational corporations. They argue that not only has economics come to dominate our culture but the non-economic institutions in society have become subservient to the economy, for example, the entire educational system appears to have become driven by the employment market (nobody wants to go to college just for the sake of education any more), politicians get elected on the strength of the economy, and, despite widespread political discourses promoting the sanctity of family values, executives are expected to uproot their families at the behest of the corporation. Goals other than material success (such as parenting, teaching and serving the community) are simply secondary to the needs of the economy.

Messner and Rosenfeld (1994) argue that the dominant cause of crime is anomie, which is promoted and endorsed by the American Dream and where the emphasis is on seeking the most efficient way to achieve economic success. In this context, crime is invariably the most effective and efficient way to achieve immediate monetary gain. Beliefs, values and commitments are the causal variables, and the closer they are linked to those of the marketplace, the more likely the logic of the economy (competitive, individualistic and materialistic) will dictate a powerful social force that motivates the pursuit of money 'by any means necessary'. Moreover, since this lawlessness-producing emphasis is caught up in the structural emphasis society places on the economy (and little else), none of the many 'wars' on crime (for example, the war against drugs) will ever be successful (since they indirectly attack the economy).

Messner and Rosenfeld (1994) observe that, while commitment to the goal of material success is the main causal variable there are significant others such as values and beliefs. The two values that constitute the American Dream are those of achievement and individualism. Achievement involves the use of material success to measure self-worth with individualism referring to the notion of intense personal competition to achieve material success. Other beliefs related to the American Dream include universalism – the idea that chances for success are open to everyone – and this belief creates an intense fear of failure. Another belief, the 'fetishism' of money, refers, in this instance, to the notion that there are no rules for establishing when one has enough money (Messner and Rosenfeld, 1994). An area where the enduring influence of anomie theories is most apparent is in the discussion of deviant subcultures below.

Deviant subculture theories

There are different deviant subculture explanations of crime and criminal behaviour but all share a common perception that certain social groups have values and attitudes that enable or encourage delinquency. The highly influential US subcultural tradition was at its peak during the 1940s and 1950s and incorporated five main explanatory inputs.

First, there was Merton's concept of anomie with its proposition that people may either turn to various kinds of deviant conduct in order to gain otherwise unobtainable material rewards or, failing that, seek alternative goals.

Second, there were the case studies conducted by the Chicago School that had suggested that young males living in socially 'disorganized' areas had different moral standards from other people and these helped facilitate their willingness to become involved in offending behaviour. Moreover, some of these patterns of conduct were passed on – or 'culturally transmitted' – from one generation to the next.

Third, there was the 'masculine identity crisis theory' outlined by the then highly influential functionalist sociologist Talcott Parsons (1937) during a period when his work was highly influenced by Freud. Parsons argued that the primary social role of the adult male is job-centred, while that of the adult female is home-centred. Consequently, the father is absent from the family home for much of the time and is unable therefore to function as a masculine role model for his children. The outcome is that children of both sexes identify with their mother to the exclusion of their father and this is particularly problematic for the male child who encounters strong cultural expectations that he adopt a masculine role but has no real concept of what this involves. But he has, during his childhood, discovered that stealing, violence and destruction provoke the disapproval of his mother and hence identifies these as non-feminine and therefore masculine characteristics. Offending behaviour satisfies these criteria of masculinity.

Fourth, there was the 'differential association theory' that Edwin Sutherland had developed from the social disorganization thesis of the Chicago School – discussed in the previous chapter – and which proposed that a person was more likely to offend if they had frequent and consistent contact with others involved in such activities. Offending behaviour was likely to occur when individuals acquired sufficient inclinations towards law-breaking which came to eclipse their associations with non-criminal tendencies.

Fifth, there were the early sociological studies of adolescent gangs carried out in the social disorganization–cultural transmission tradition developed by the Chicago School. Thrasher (1947) thus argued that the adolescent gang emerged out of spontaneous street playgroups of young children in relatively permissive and socially disorganized slum areas but the young males involved were neither 'disturbed' or 'psychopathic' nor 'driven' by socio-economic forces beyond their control, they were simply looking for excitement, adventure and fun. This could be found on the streets but not at school or home.

Later studies of adolescent gangs followed in the tradition established by Thrasher and all argued that involvement in the young male gang was a natural response to a socially disorganized environment and deviant behaviour when it did occur had been learned from previous generations of adolescents (see, for example, Yablonsky, 1962). These studies continued throughout the 1930s, 1940s and 1950s in the USA with a few minor examples in the UK. At the same time, the concept of the 'delinquent subculture' was emerging in the USA.

Early US deviant subculture theories

Albert Cohen (1955) observed that previous research had tended to focus on the process through which individual young males had come to adopt deviant values and had either ignored – or taken for granted – the existence of deviant subcultures or gangs. By analysing the structure of such subcultures, Cohen argued that juvenile offending was rarely motivated by striving for financial success as proposed by Merton. In contrast, he argued that juvenile gang members in fact stole for the fun of it and took pride in their acquired reputations for being tough and 'hard'. The gang – or subculture – offers possibilities for *status* and the acquisition of respect that are denied elsewhere.

Involvement in gang culture is to use contemporary terminology simply cool.

Cohen noted that, although society is stratified into socio-economic classes, it is the norms and values of the middle class that are dominant and employed to judge the success and status of everybody in society. The young working-class male nevertheless experiences a different form of upbringing and is unlikely to internalize these norms and values. He is thrust into a competitive social system founded on alien and incomprehensible middle-class norms and values with the outcome that he experiences a deficit of respect and *status frustration*.

Since the young male is involved in a process of interaction with others who are faced with the same difficulties, a mutually agreed solution may be reached and a separate subculture with alternative norms and values with which young males can relate is formed. In this way, he can achieve status and respect for involvement in all the things the official culture rejects: hedonism, aggression, dishonesty and vandalism. In short, there is a conscious and *active* rejection of middle-class norms and values.

Cohen's delinquent subculture theory has attracted its share of criticism not least because he failed to base his theoretical formulation on empirical data and, indeed, all attempts to test it have failed and it can be argued that it is inherently untestable. Kitsuse and Dietrick (1959) showed there was no real basis for the assertion that the young working-class male experiences 'problems of adjustment' to middle-class values. They observe that middle-class norms and values are simply *irrelevant* to young working-class men because they have absolutely no interest in acquiring status within the dominant social system. Their aspirations are thus *not frustrated*. They simply resent the intrusion of middle-class outsiders who try to impose their irrelevant way of life upon them and offending behaviour should therefore be considered rational and utilitarian in the context of working-class culture.

Walter Miller (1958) develops this theme and argues that offending is simply the product of long-established traditions of working-class life and it is the very structure of that culture that generates offending behaviour, not conflicts with middle-class values. The *focal concerns* of working-class society – toughness, smartness, excitement, fate and autonomy – combine in several ways to produce criminality. Those who respond to such concerns automatically violate the law through their behaviour and, thus, the very fact of being working class places the individual in a situation that contains a variety of direct incitements towards deviant conduct. Implicit in this formulation is a significant attack on the notion that subcultures originate as a response to lack of status or thwarted aspirations. On the contrary, delinquency is simply a way of life and a response to the realities of their particular lives.

Miller himself problematically offers no explanation for the origins of these highly deterministic working-class values from which there appears to be no escape. All he does is note their existence and explain that conforming to them will lead to criminal behaviour. His work was strongly influenced by Parson's (1937) masculinity identity crisis where it had been noted that it is common in lower-class households for the father to be absent, often because he has transgressed against the criminal law. The home life is thus a female-dominated environment that leads working-class males to look for 'suitable' role models outside the home and these could be readily found in the street gangs – termed by Miller 'one-sex peer units' – where the adolescent male could take part in activities that uphold working-class 'focal concerns' and give him a sense of belonging, status and respect.

Richard Cloward and Lloyd Ohlin's *Delinquency and Opportunity* (1960) was a major development in deviant subculture theory and provided one of the central foundations of labelling theory, which itself is a central element of the victimized actor tradition we will encounter in the third part of this book. They essentially argue that it is necessary to have two theories in order to fully explain adolescent criminal behaviour: first, there is a need for a 'push' theory to explain why it is that large numbers of young people offend and, second, a 'pull' theory to explain the continuance of this behaviour and how it becomes passed on to others. The originality of their work lies in their use of a combination of Merton's anomie theory to explain the 'push' and Sutherland's differential association theory to explain the 'pull'.

Cloward and Ohlin observe that there is a discrepancy between the aspirations of working-class adolescent males and the opportunities available to them. When an individual recognizes that membership of a particular ethnic group or social class and/or lack of a suitable education has seriously restricted his access to legitimate opportunities, he will blame an unfair society for his failure and withdraw his belief in the legitimacy of the social order. It is this awareness that leads to a rejection of conventional codes of behaviour.

Cloward and Ohlin followed Cohen in stressing that individuals have to actively seek out and join with others who face the same problems and together these young males will devise a collective solution to their predicament, for surrounded by hostile adults they need all the support that they can get from each other. Moreover, they need to develop techniques to neutralize the guilt they feel and this is easier to achieve as the member of a like-minded group.

Underlying this reformulation of anomie theory is the assumption that illegitimate routes to success are freely available to those individuals who 'need' them. Cloward and Ohlin combine the cultural transmission theory of Shaw with the differential association theory of Sutherland to create an 'illegitimate opportunity structure' concept that parallels the 'legitimate opportunity structure' of Merton. From this theory, the existence of three separate delinquent subcultures was predicted. First, *criminal delinquent* subcultures are said to exist where there are available illegitimate opportunities for learning the motivations, attitudes and techniques necessary in order to commit crimes. Second, a *conflict* subculture exists where adolescent males – denied access to the legitimate opportunity structure because of their social class, ethnic origin, etc. – have no available criminal opportunity structure and, in this scenario, young males work off their frustrations by attacking people (assault), property (vandalism) and each other (gang fights). Third, *retreatist* subcultures tend to exist where drugs are freely available and membership is composed of those who have failed to gain access to either the legitimate or criminal subcultures. These young males retreat into drug misuse and alcoholism and are considered to be 'double failures'.

Cloward and Ohlin predicted – and this was 1960 – that, because the organization within poor inner cities was collapsing and adult crime was becoming too sophisticated for adolescent males to learn easily, the criminal delinquent subculture would decline. The conflict or retreatist subcultures would, on the other hand, expand, with increased adolescent violence, 'muggings', vandalism and drug addiction.

Three main criticisms have been made of Cloward and Ohlin's work. First, it is observed that their notion of the criminal subculture is modelled on the fairly stable and structured adolescent gangs of the Chicago slum areas of the 1920s and 1930s and which had long since ceased to exist (Jacobs, 1961). Second, there is an inherent assumption that the working class is a relatively homogeneous group and this is simply not the case. Third, they, like their predecessors, provide a grossly simplistic explanation of drug misuse, which is, in reality, fairly common among successful middle-class professional people, particularly if alcohol consumption is included under the generic term 'drugs'.

Cloward and Ohlin's theory was nevertheless the focus of considerable academic debate with a major issue being the extent to which the actions of young males in delinquent gangs are determined by their socialization and the extent to which they are committed to the delinquent norms of the group.

Ivan Spergel (1964) provided at least a partial answer to these questions, identifying an 'anomie gap' between aspirations measured in terms of aspired to and expected occupation and weekly wage, finding that the size of this gap differed significantly between offenders and non-offenders and between one subculture and another. Spergel consequently rejected Cloward and Ohlin's subculture categories and replaced them with his own three-part typology: first, a *racket subculture* is said to develop in areas where organized adult criminality is already in existence and highly visible; second, a *theft subculture* – involving offences such as burglary, shoplifting, taking and driving away cars – would develop where a criminal subculture was already in existence but not very well established; and, third, *conflict subcultures* – involving gang fighting and 'rep'(utation) would develop where there is limited or no access to either criminal or conventional activities.

Spergel significantly found that drug misuse was common to all subcultures as part of the transition from adolescent delinquent activity to either conventional or fully developed criminal activity among older adolescents and young adults, while people involved in drug misuse do not in themselves constitute a subculture. Moreover, the common form of deviant behaviour specific to a particular area depends on the idiosyncratic features of that particular district and not, as Merton – and Cloward and Ohlin – imply, on national characteristics.

The general conclusion reached by critics of early US deviant subculture theories is that they fail to provide an adequate explanation of adolescent offending behaviour, while a number of more specific criticisms can also be identified. First, descriptions of the 'typical' offender where they are portrayed as being in some way different from non-offenders and driven into offending behaviour by grim social and economic forces beyond their control make little sense. There is simply no attempt to explain why it is that many, if not most, young males faced with the same 'problems of adjustment' *do not* join delinquent gangs. Second, virtually all deviant subculture explanations consider adolescent offending to be a gang phenomenon, where, in reality, this is a very doubtful proposition. A lot of adolescent offending behaviour is a solitary activity or involves, at the most, two or three young males together. The fairly stable gangs identified by the deviant subculture theorists were certainly at that time very difficult to find. Third, none of these explanations takes into account the roles of authority figures – the police, parents, social workers and teachers – in labelling these young people as offenders. Fourth, no adequate explanations are provided of how it is that many young males appear to simply outgrow offending behaviour. Fifth, no explanation is provided for the offending behaviour of adolescent females. Sixth, there is an inherent assumption that offending is the preserve of the young male lower working classes and this is clearly not the case.

The deviant subculture concept has nevertheless been subsequently successfully applied elsewhere in the study of deviant and criminal behaviour with some researchers usefully utilizing it to explain corporate – or business – crime. Aubert (1952) examined the attitudes of certain Swedish citizens towards violation of wartime rationing regulations and found that two sorts of obligation influenced the behaviour of each research subject. First, 'universalistic' obligations affected their behaviour as a law-abiding citizen and these should have provided sufficient motivation to obey the law, but sanctions against those who transgressed were found to be invariably weak. Second, 'particularistic' obligations were considered to be due to business colleagues, and these were supported by a philosophy that demanded only avoidance of certain 'blatant offences'. The groups to which white-collar criminals belong were described as having 'an elaborate and widely accepted ideological rationalisation for the offences and ... great social significance outside the sphere of criminal activity' (Aubert, 1952: 267). Corporate crimes were found to be sometimes acceptable and endorsed by group norms with certain types of illegal activity seen as normal. Braithwaite (1984) similarly found that bribing health inspectors was normal and acceptable business practice in the pharmaceutical industry.

These subcultural influences are nevertheless not fully deterministic. Executives who violate laws are not pressured into action by irresistible forces beyond their control. Deviance may be encouraged and condoned but it is not automatic or uncontested destiny. Both Geis (1967) and Faberman (1975) found that, even within industries where criminal practices are common, some employees were not prepared to get involved in spite of often quite extensive pressure from senior managers. It seems that individual characteristics, variations between groups within a subculture and the degree of exposure to subcultural values seem to be relevant in this context.

Hopkins Burke and Pollock (2004) note the value of the deviant subculture concept in helping to account for hate crime motivation, for being part of a particular ethnic group with its additional transmitted traditions and mechanical solidarities can undoubtedly act as a particular focus for collective belonging and can undoubtedly provide both the fulcrum for the actualization of hate crime behaviour and protection against it. The authors also note that it is a particularly useful theoretical tool for helping to explain the kind of institutional racist police behaviour identified in the London Metropolitan Constabulary by the Macpherson Report in 1999.

There has long been a tough working-class police culture – 'canteen culture' as it has been termed (see Holdaway, 1983; Fielding, 1988; Reiner, 2000) – that has been transmitted and adapted to changing circumstances across the generations. Working in a hard, tough environment, invariably at risk of serious violence, notions of always looking after your colleagues in the face of external censure and senior management has made considerable sense to serving officers brought together in a perceived shared adversity and has rather inevitably led to them looking inwards to the group for a supportive shared world view. The outcome has been a 'stereotyping', separating and labelling of the public into categories deemed worthy of police assistance – the community or 'those like us' – and the 'others', the 'toe-rags', 'slags', 'scrotes', 'scum' and 'animals'. Some have argued that these stereotypes drive the day-to-day nature and pattern of police work (Smith and Gray, 1986; Young, 1991, 1993) and the Macpherson Report of 1999 clearly identified a significant issue of institutional racism within the Metropolitan Police where young black males were apparently not deemed worthy of victim status even when murdered.

Hopkins Burke (2004b) observes that this subculture was undoubtedly *relatively* non-problematic during an era when police intervention against the rougher elements of a predominantly white mono-cultural working class had undoubted support from most elements of society, including the socially aspiring respectable elements within that class who lived cheek-by-jowl with the roughs and sought protection from them. It was with the fragmentation of that society and the emergence of the ethnic and sexual preference diversity discussed in the final part of this book that this macho police subculture became increasingly problematic.

This early US deviant subcultural tradition has been widely accused of being overly determinist in its apparent rejection of free will, and in this variant of the predestined actor model deviants are seen to be not only different from non-deviants but in some way committed to an alternative 'ethical' code that makes involvement in deviant activity appear somewhat mandatory. While it is extremely likely that some young people, or police officers and business personnel, for that matter, are so strongly socialized into the mores of a particular world view – or mechanical solidarity – through membership of a particular ethnic group, the upbringing of their parents and the reinforcing influences of neighbourhood groups or gangs that they do not challenge this heritage in any way, it is also likely that many others have less consistent socialization experiences and have a far more tangential relationship to such deviant behaviour, although they may be at considerable risk of being drawn into a far deeper involvement.

David Matza and the anti-determinist critique

The best and most comprehensive critique of the highly determinist early deviant subculture tradition is provided by David Matza and, in doing so, he provides an influential and crucial link with the later non-determinist explanations discussed in the third part of this book. Matza (1964) observed that all criminologists working in the predestined actor tradition – from Lombroso onwards – have made three basic assumptions about crime, which, although they have some validity, have simply been taken too far. First, there has been a focus on the criminal and their behaviour, while the role of the criminal justice system – a significant part of the environment of the criminal – is ignored. Second, the predestined actor model is overly determinist in its rejection of the notion of rational free will and simply fails to recognize that human beings are capable of making rational choices but these are limited by structural constraints. Third, the predestined actor model considers criminals to be fundamentally different types of people from non-criminals, although there are, of course, substantial variations on this theme. Lombroso, for example, considered the criminal to have been 'born bad', while the deviant subculture theorist, on the other hand, considered the actions of the offender to be determined by a commitment to an alternative 'ethical' code that makes involvement in delinquent activity seem mandatory.

Matza notes that those working in the predestined actor tradition have simply failed to explain why it is that most young offenders 'grow out' of offending behaviour. From that determinist perspective, offenders would presumably continue to offend all the time, except of course when they have been incarcerated. This is clearly not the case but it is the logical deduction that can be made from the position taken by such writers as Cohen, and Cloward and Ohlin. In response, Matza proposes that delinquency is a status and delinquents are role players who intermittently act out a delinquent role.

These young men are perfectly capable of engaging in conventional activity and, therefore, the alleged forces that compel them to be delinquent are somehow rendered inactive for most of their lives. They simply 'drift' between delinquent and conventional behaviour. The young person is neither compelled nor committed to delinquent activity but freely chooses it sometimes and on other occasions does not do so.

Matza accepted the existence of subcultures whose members engage in delinquency but, on the other hand, denied the existence of a specific deviant subculture. Theories that propose the existence of such a subculture assume that this involves a contra culture, one that deliberately runs counter to the values of the dominant culture. Matza argued that this position is problematic for the following reasons. First, there is the implication that the young person does not experience feelings of guilt and this is not the case. Second, there is an assumption that young offenders have no respect for conventional morality, whereas, in reality, most young people involved in offending behaviour recognize the legitimacy of the dominant social order and the validity of its moral standards. Third, it is argued that young offenders define all people outside their 'delinquent subculture' as potential victims, whereas they distinguish special groups – mostly other delinquents – as legitimate targets to victimize. Fourth, it is proposed that delinquents are immune from the demands of the larger culture, whereas, in reality, the members of these supposed 'delinquent subcultures' are *children* and cannot escape from disapproving adults, and their condemnation of delinquent behaviour must therefore be taken into consideration with the strong probability that their demands for conformity will be internalized.

Matza found that young males could moreover remain within the 'subculture of delinquency' *without* actually taking part in offending behaviour. Thus, when he showed a sample of photographs of various criminal acts to a group of delinquents – some of which they themselves had committed – their reactions ranged from mild disapproval to righteous indignation.

Matza argued that juveniles go through three stages in a process of becoming deviant. The first stage is the nearest the young male comes to being part of an oppositional subculture and such a situation arises when he is in the company of other young males and where there appears to be an 'ideology of delinquency' implicit in their actions and remarks. In these circumstances, he is motivated by his anxiety to be accepted as a member of the group and his concerns about his own masculinity and 'grown-up' status. In this condition of anxiety, he reaches conclusions, in his own mind, about what will be the 'correct' form of behaviour to adopt, the 'correct' attitude to present and the 'correct' motives for engaging in a particular form of behaviour from the remarks, gestures and behaviour of the other adolescents. He hears and perhaps sees others in the group approving of or doing daring, but illegal, acts and assumes that, to be accepted, he must join in and show that he is just as good (or bad) as, if not better than, all the others. So he steals things, vandalizes things, hits people not because he 'really' wants to but because he feels he 'ought' to want to, because that is what being 'grown up' is all about.

Matza observes that what this young man fails to realize is that the other members of the group feel exactly the same as he does. The others are also plagued by doubts about acceptance, masculinity and adulthood and, indeed, may be taking *their* cues from him. In other words, all the members of the group are trapped in a vicious circle of mutual misunderstandings. This circle can be broken when two young men confess to each other that they do not like offending or when the particular individual is sufficiently old to stop feeling anxieties about masculinity and adult status. At this stage of maturity, a young man can decide to leave the group and cease involvement in deviant activity or to continue.

The second stage thus occurs when the young man, having overcome his original anxieties about masculinity, is faced with another problem: he must overcome his initial socialization that has taught him not to be deviant and hence protect himself from feelings of guilt. He must find extenuating circumstances that will release him from conventional control and leave him free to choose to drift into deviancy and thus, in this way, young males utilize 'techniques of neutralization' to justify their behaviour. Matza identifies five major types of neutralization:

- denial of responsibility (I didn't mean it);
- denial of injury (I didn't really harm him);
- denial of the victim (he deserved it);
- condemnation of the condemners (they always pick on us); and
- appeals to higher loyalties (you've got to help your mates).

These techniques are by themselves merely excuses and not explanations of deviant behaviour. Matza argued that at a deeper level there is a commitment to 'subterranean values', which – like Miller's 'focal concerns', which they resemble – exist in the wider culture of normal society. The most important of these values is what psychologists refer to as the 'need for stimulation', which means, in this context, the search for excitement. Young males commit deliberate criminal acts because they *are* criminal, quite simply, being deviant is better than being bored, deviancy is fun, it is exciting.

Matza argued that the operation of the criminal justice system and the actions of social workers might actually convince young people that deviant behaviour does not really matter. Deviant young males are not stupid; they are aware that many social workers, police officers, teachers and magistrates think that the young person is not fully responsible for their actions but will go ahead and punish – or rather 'treat' – them just the same. Deviant children are as quick as – or even quicker than – non-deviants to recognize this contradiction and to exploit it to their own advantage.

The third stage in a deviant career has now been reached with the young male now in a situation of 'drift' where he knows what is required of him and has learned the techniques of neutralization that justify his deviant behaviour. On the other hand, he is not automatically *committed* to deviant behaviour and he *could* just boast about previous and unverifiable exploits, much as other young people boast about imaginary sexual encounters.

The missing impetus that makes actual deviant behaviour possible is 'free will' and it is this recognition that distinguishes Matza completely from those working in the predestined actor tradition. The deviant is responsible for their behaviour. They *know* that their activities are against the law. They *know* that they may be caught and they *know* that they may be punished. They probably accept that they *should* be punished. It is one of the rules of the game. If this is the case, the question that remains to be asked is why the young person should continue to be involved in criminal behaviour.

In the first place, the young person has acquired certain skills partly from their older friends and partly from the mass media, for example television, which has made involvement in criminal behaviour possible. They will have learned from their friends how to manage guilt and discount the possibility of capture. They assume that they will not be caught and criminal statistics suggest that they are likely to be correct in this supposition. This state of *preparation* allows the young person to repeat an offence that they have committed before. Less frequently, the young person falls into a condition of *desperation* derived from a mood of *fatalism*, a feeling of being 'pushed around'. This feeling of being pushed around is sufficient for them to lose their precarious concept of their self as a 'real man' and, at that point, they need to 'make something happen' in order to prove that they are a cause, not merely an effect, and it is this feeling that leads them directly to become involved in more serious, previously untried, delinquent behaviour where, even if caught, they have still made something happen. The whole apparatus of police, juvenile court and social work department is concerned with them and has been activated by what they *themselves* did. In a state of desperation, the young person needs to do more than simply repeat an old offence. After all, as his or her peers would say, 'anyone can do that'. In the state of desperation, they need to do something that they have not tried before.

Matza's theoretical schema has also been usefully applied to the study of business crime. Corporate executives have thus been found to use 'techniques of neutralisation' to rationalize deviant acts and violate the law without feeling guilty (Box, 1983). Officials can deny responsibility by pleading ignorance, accident or that they were acting under orders. Vague laws that rest on ambiguous definitions and permit meanings and interpretation to fluctuate help facilitate this and, as a result, it is difficult to distinguish praiseworthy corporate behaviour from illegal actions. Box observes that, in these circumstances, 'it is convenient for corporate officials to pull the cloak of honest ignorance over their heads and proceed under its darkness to stumble blindly and unwittingly over the thin line between what is condoned and what is condemned' (1983: 55).

Bandura (1973: 13) found that shared decision-making in an organization allows people to contribute 'to cruel practices . . . without feeling personally responsible'. 'Denial of the victim' may also be used. The nature of much corporate crime permits an illusion that there is no real person suffering, particularly when the victims are other corporations or people in far-off countries, especially if they are less developed countries (Braithwaite, 1984).

Swartz (1975) has noted that company spokespersons have been prepared to blame industrial accidents on 'careless and lazy' workers or the development of brown lung in black workers on their 'racial inferiority'. The corporate criminal often denies that any harm has been caused. Geis quotes an executive who described his activities as 'illegal . . . but not criminal . . . I assumed that criminal action meant damaging someone, and we did not do that' (1968: 108). Moreover, the corporate employee can 'condemn the condemners', by pointing to political corruption, or describing laws as unwarranted constraints on free enterprise. Acting for the good of the company – or following widespread but illegal business practices – is seen as more important than obeying the law.

Hopkins Burke and Pollock discuss how techniques of neutralization can be used by hate crime offenders to excuse, justify and legitimate their actions and use the following all-inclusive and somewhat 'upmarket' illustration to make their point:

> Well I know it is rather unpleasant and one doesn't really like getting involved in these things, but they are different from us. They have a different way of life and it is not really what we want here. You really wouldn't want your children to mix with them now would you? I don't really approve of this sort of thing but something has to be done.

> (2004: 31)

The authors note that having absorbed experiences and knowledge at each stage of their socialization from parents and friends and having had these values reinforced by access to media – however self-selecting this might be – provides the race-hate perpetrator with choices that for them are very much rational. In a study conducted for the British Home Office, Rae Sibbitt (1999) found that the views held by all kinds of race-hate perpetrators are shared very much by the communities to which they belong and perpetrators very much see this as legitimizing their actions. In turn, the wider community not only spawns such perpetrators, but also fails to condemn them and thus actively reinforces their behaviour. Hate crime perpetrators are invariably very much part of their local deviant subculture or mechanical solidarity.

Early British deviant subcultural studies

Early British deviant subcultural studies tended to follow the lead of the US theories discussed above. The main influences were the work of Miller and Cohen, with the work of Cloward and Ohlin appearing to have had little or no application in Britain, well at least at that time.

John Mays (1954) argued that, in certain – particularly older urban – areas, the residents share a number of attitudes and ways of behaving that predispose them to criminality. These attitudes have existed for years and are passed on to newcomers. Working-class culture is not intentionally criminal. It is just a different socialization, which, at times, happens to be contrary to the legal rules. Criminal behaviour – particularly adolescent criminal behaviour – is not therefore a conscious rebellion against middle-class values but arises from an alternative working-class subculture that has been adopted over the years in a haphazard sort of way.

Terence Morris (1957) argued that social deviants are common among the working classes and that it is the actual characteristics of that class that creates the criminality. Forms of antisocial behaviour exist throughout society and in all classes, but the way in which the behaviour is expressed differs. He considered criminal behaviour to be largely a working-class expression. The family controls middle-class socialization, it is very ordered and almost all activities are centred on the home and the family. In the working classes, in contrast, the socialization of the child tends to be divided between family, peer group and street acquaintances with the outcome that the latter child is likely to have a less ordered and regulated upbringing. The peer group is a much stronger influence from a much earlier age and they encounter controls only after they commit a crime and when they are processed by the criminal justice system. The whole ethos of the working class, according to Morris, is oriented towards antisocial and criminal, rather than 'conventional', behaviour.

David Downes (1966) conducted a study among young offenders in the East End of London and found that a considerable amount of offending behaviour took place, but this mostly happened in street-corner groups, rather than organized gangs. Status frustration did not occur to a significant degree among these young males and their typical response to a lack of success at school or work was one of 'dissociation', a process of opting out rather than reaction formation. The emphasis was on leisure activities – not on school or work – with commercial forms of entertainment the main focus of interest, not youth clubs with their middle-class orientation. Access to leisure pursuits was nevertheless restricted by a lack of money and, as an alternative means of entertainment, youths would take part in offending. Peter Wilmott (1966) also conducted a study of teenagers in the East End of London and reached much the same conclusions as Miller, finding that adolescent offending behaviour was simply part of a general lower working-class subculture. Teenagers became involved in petty crime simply for the fun and 'togetherness' of the shared activity experience.

Howard Parker (1974) conducted a survey of unskilled adolescents in an area of Liverpool that official statistics suggested had a high rate of adolescent offending and found that there was a pattern of loosely knit peer groups, not one of tightly structured gangs. Offending behaviour was not a central activity. Young males shared common problems, such as unemployment, and leisure opportunities were limited. Some youths had developed a temporary solution in the form of stealing car radios. Furthermore, the community in which the young males lived was one that largely condoned theft, as long as the victims were from outside the area.

Ken Pryce (1979) studied African-Caribbean youngsters in the St Paul's area of Bristol and suggested that the first African-Caribbeans to arrive in the 1950s came to Britain with high aspirations but found on arrival that they were relegated to a force of cheap labour, while they and their children were subject to racism and discrimination, which contributed to a pattern of 'endless pressure'. Pryce suggested there were two types of adaptation to this pressure: one was to be stable, conformist and law-abiding, while the other was to adopt an expressive, disreputable rebellious attitude. Second and third generation African-Caribbeans were more likely – but not bound – to adopt the second response.

These earlier British deviant subculture studies were important because they drew our attention to specific historical factors, in particular the level of economic activity, and to the importance of a structural class analysis in the explanation of subcultural delinquency (Hopkins Burke and Sunley, 1996, 1998). They also demonstrated that different groups within the working class had identified distinct problems in terms of negative status and had developed their own solutions to their perceived problems. They, moreover, tended to neglect the involvement of young women in offending behaviour. Thus, where young women are discussed, they tended to be dismissed as 'sex objects' or adjuncts to male offending behaviour, merely 'hangers-on'.

Studies of deviant youth subcultures carried out in the USA since the late 1960s have predominantly focused on issues of violence, ethnicity, poverty and the close links between all three. Wolfgang and Ferracuti (1967) identified forty years ago a 'sub-culture of violence' where there was an expectation that the receipt of a trivial insult should be met with violence. Failure to respond in this way – and thus walk away from trouble – was greeted with social censure from the peer group. Curtis (1975) adapted this theory to explain violence among American Blacks and found that the maintenance of a manly image was the most important attribute in the subculture with individuals unable to resolve conflicts verbally and more likely to resort to violence in order to assert their masculinity. Behaviour is seen to be partly a response to social conditions, and partly the result of an individual's acceptance of the ideas and values that he has absorbed from the subculture of violence. Maxson and Klein (1990) more recently recognized that certain youth groups, for example, racist 'skinheads' and neo-Nazi organizations, engage in group-related violent behaviour for ideological – including political and religious – ends.

Later US deviant subcultural studies

Later research in the USA has proposed that poverty is basically the root cause of gangs and the violence they produce. Miller (1958) had argued that lower-class delinquency was a normal response to sociocultural demands but in his later writings he essentially adopts a 'culture of poverty' view to explain the self-perpetuation of gang life, a view that emphasizes the adaptational aspects of the gang to changing socio-economic circumstances (Miller, 1990). However, the most popular current theory to explain criminal behaviour among poor young people in the US inner city is William Julius Wilson's 'underclass theory' where it is suggested that groups in socially isolated neighbourhoods have few legitimate employment opportunities. Inadequate job information networks and poor schools not only lead to weak labour force attachment but also significantly increases the likelihood that people will turn to illegal or deviant activities for income (Wilson, 1991).

Wilson has been accused of failing to address the issues of gang formation and explain the development of specific types of gang problems (Hagedorn, 1992) but a number of other observers assume a close correlation between gangs, gang violence and the development of a socially excluded underclass (Krisberg, 1974; Anderson, 1990; Taylor, 1990). Poverty is central to the underclass thesis and various writers recognize that the absence of economic resources leads to compensatory efforts to achieve some form of economic and successful social adjustment (Williams, 1989; Moore, 1991; Hopkins Burke, 1999a). It is in this context that Spergel argues that 'a subculture arises out of efforts of people to solve social, economic, psychological, developmental, and even political problems' (1995: 149). This is an argument to which we return in Chapter 18.

Radical deviant subculture theories

The concept of deviant subculture was subsequently revised and revitalized by radical neo-Marxist sociologists and criminologists – working in the 'victimized actor' tradition – and based at the Birmingham University's Centre for Contemporary Cultural Studies (CCCS) during the 1970s (see Cohen, 1972; Cohen, 1973; Hebdige, 1976, 1979; Brake, 1985). These researchers observed that 'spectacular' youth subcultures – such as Teddy Boys, mods, skinheads and punks – arise at particular historical 'moments' as cultural solutions to the same structural economic problems created by rapid social change identified by Durkheim – and Merton in a rather different way – as an anomic condition.

These researchers recognize that, in contemporary societies, the major cultural configurations – or, we might observe, macro mechanical solidarities – are cultures based on social class, but within these larger entities are subcultures which are defined as 'smaller, more localised and differentiated structures, within one or other of the larger cultural networks' (Hall and Jefferson, 1976: 13). These subcultures have different focal concerns than the larger cultural configuration from which they are derived but will share some common aspects or core values with the 'parent culture'. Some, like deviant subcultures, are persistent features of the parent culture, but others appear only at certain historical moments and then fade away. These latter subcultures are highly visible and, indeed, 'spectacular', and, although their members may well look very 'different' from their parents or peers, they will still share the same class position, the same life experiences, and generally the same world view or core values of the parent culture. All they are doing, through their distinctive dress, lifestyle, music etc., is producing a different cultural 'solution' to the problems posed for them by their material and social class position and experience. They are invariably articulating a contemporary variant of the parent culture that is in accord with their changed socio-economic circumstances.

The central concern of that collection of studies was to locate the historical and environmental context in which particular youth subcultures arose and the details of 'style' adopted by these. Central to their argument is the notion that style is a form of resistance to subordination, which is essentially ritualistic, symbolic or magical, as it is not, actually, a successful solution to the problem of subordination. Resistance is not a desperate 'lashing out' or a passive adaptation to an anomic situation of disjunction, but a collective response designed to resist or transform dominant values and defend or recapture working class or ethnic group values – to win space, to reclaim community and reassert traditional values. This resistance is nevertheless symbolic rather than real.

Stan Cohen (1973) notes three contexts in which the concepts of ritual, myth, metaphor, magic and allegory are invoked. First, the target for attack is inappropriate or irrational in the sense of not being logically connected with the source of the problem, for example, it is argued that skinheads beating up Asian and gay people is actually a reaction to other things, such as perceived threats to community, homogeneity or traditional stereotypes of masculinity. Second, when the solution does not confront the real material basis of subordination and is not a genuinely political response, the activities are seen as merely, albeit violent, 'gestures'. Third, when the subcultural style denotes something beyond its surface appearance, for example, the boots worn by skinheads, the young people are making oblique coded statements about their relationships to a particular – in that example, white working-class – past or present.

The Birmingham researchers focused on two broad but overlapping areas: mainstream youth and delinquency, especially the transition from school to work and expressive or spectacular youth subcultures. The two major studies of mainstream youth subcultures are those of Willis (1977) and Corrigan (1979) and both are concerned with the transition from school to work among urban lower working-class adolescent boys. Their 'problem' is an alien or irrelevant education system followed by the prospect of a boring and dead-end job – or, nowadays, training and the benefits queue (see Hopkins Burke, 1999a) – and the 'solution' is a 'culture of resistance' manifested in truancy and petty offending. Actions are ritualistic (or magical) but they can never solve the problem. 'Spectacular' youth subcultures involve the adoption, by young people of both sexes, of a distinctive style of dress and way of using material artefacts combined, usually, with distinctive lifestyles, behaviour patterns and musical preferences. Both variants of subculture invariably involve a contemporary manifestation of parent culture values that have been adapted to the changed socio-economic circumstances in which the group finds itself.

The Birmingham studies represented an important development of the earlier deviant subcultural tradition – which had recognized that deviance often occurs in response to economic or status deprivation – and identified that particular subcultures or status groups have arisen in response to the perceived economic problems of distinct groups. Hopkins Burke and Sunley (1996, 1998) nevertheless observe that these studies presume a linear development of history where different subcultures arise, coalesce, fade and are replaced as economic circumstances change. Thus, for example, the 'Mods' were a product of the upwardly mobile working classes during the optimistic 1960s (Hebdige, 1976; 1979; Brake, 1980), whereas, on the other hand, the punks were a product of the 'dole-queue' despondency of the late 1970s (Hebdige, 1979; Brake, 1980, 1985).

Hopkins Burke and Sunley (1996, 1998) observed the co-existence of a number of different subcultures and propose this to be an outcome of a fragmented society where specific groups of young people have coalesced to create solutions to their specific socio-economic problems and central to this account is the possibility of choice. The simultaneous existence of different subcultures enables some young people to choose the solution to their problem from the various subcultures available, although that choice will undoubtedly be constrained by structural factors.

The early deviant subcultural studies – and indeed the work of the Birmingham School – tended to suggest that young people had limited choices, if any, between the subculture available at a particular time and in that geographical location and a life of conventionality. This more contemporary – or postmodernist – interpretation of youth subcultures enables us to recognize that individuals, and different groups of young people, not all members of the traditional working class but in existence concurrently at the same historical moment, have had very different experiences of the radical economic change that has engulfed British society since the late 1970s. This is a theoretical approach that is seemingly challenged by post-subcultural theorists.

Post-subcultural theory

In recent years, there has been a reaction to the Birmingham CCCS radical subcultural approach, which has been termed 'post-subcultural' (Muggleton, 2000). Initiated by Redhead (1993) and further developed by Muggleton (1997, 2000), this perspective proposes that the structurally grounded concept of subculture has become increasingly redundant in relation to contemporary youth culture. Underlying the move towards post-subcultural analysis is an argument that, as the relationship between style, musical taste and identity has become progressively weaker and articulated with more fluidity, subcultural divisions have broken down. This alleged breakdown was first noted by Redhead in his study of the early British rave scene, which he observed was 'notorious for mixing all kinds of styles on the same dance floor and attracting a range of previously opposed subcultures' (1993: 3–4). He argued that the combined effects of post-industrialization and the increasing amount of free time available to young people gave rise to a new 'clubbing culture', which supposedly dissolved previous structural divisions, such as class, race and gender, because the dance crowds became mixed in these respects. Redhead emphasized the influence of the market and media, as well as the increasing buying power of young people in the construction of their lifestyles. Reviews of the literature on youth culture or lifestyle research recognize this shift as a movement from a more structural approach towards one which emphasizes both the agency of young people and the influence of the marketplace as a site for socialization (Bennett, 1999, 2000; Besley, 2003; Chatterton and Hollands, 2002; MacRae, 2004; Miles, 2000). This approach takes a rational actor model of human behaviour perspective and views young people as social agents who are free to engage in consumer practices.

Muggleton, for example, argued that subcultural style is constituted solely through consumption, and is 'no longer articulated around the structural relations of class, gender, ethnicity or even the span of youth' (1997: 173). In post-subcultural studies, there is, it is argued, less attention paid to social divisions or stratified youth cultures. Indeed, in direct contrast to the class-based youth cultures identified by the Birmingham CCCS, contemporary youth cultures are said to be more fleeting and organized around individual lifestyle and consumption choices.

In order to capture these elements of choice and self-determination, researchers have tried to come up with new concepts, like 'neotribes' (Bennett, 1999), 'post-subculturalist' (Muggleton, 2000), lifestyle (Miles, 2000), taste culture (Thornton, 1995) and club culture (Redhead *et al.*, 1997). Bennett proposes that the phrase neotribes provides 'a better understanding of the series of temporal gatherings characterised by fluid boundaries and floating membership of young people' (1999: 600). He argues that the framework of neotribes is related to the concept of lifestyle, which he defines as: 'the sensibilities employed by the individual in choosing certain commodities and patterns of consumption and in articulating these cultural resources as modes of cultural expression' (1999: 607). What these researchers do agree upon is that the study of subcultures, as conducted at the Birmingham CCCS, no longer applies to the current globalized and commercialized times. In this postmodern, global era, youngsters are regarded as consumers with specific interests, desires and buying power. Now more than ever, children and young people find their identities and values in the marketplace, rather than in traditional sources such as the family, church and school.

In reaction to these changes, those involved in youth culture research began to engage with theories of globalization (Miles, 2000; Nayak, 2003) and, at the turn of the century, with the notion of global youth culture. It is the hedonistic vibe celebrated in the clubbing scene that appears to have been taken over by the researchers; clubbing is all about forgetting the problems of the week and, instead of social structures, cultural features (dress code, dance, pose) are centralized as the dividing and hierarchy-creating elements. In this approach, young people are viewed as free-floating consumers who can easily move in and out of styles according to the 'tastes of the day'.

Critiques of post-subcultural studies

Problematically, post-subcultural studies pay little attention to the importance of social divisions and inequalities in contemporary youth culture (Shildrick and MacDonald, 2006: 125). Although subculture theorists are criticized for focusing on one social group of young people, most post-subcultural studies likewise concentrate on the nightlife activities of just a single group, namely predominantly white middle-class urban youth. Indeed, they largely ignore questions of accessibility or inequality and spatial separation among different groups of (ethnic) consumers. Shildrick and MacDonald (2006) correctly highlight the tendency of many post-subcultural researchers to ignore the cultural lives and identities of less advantaged young people, forgetting that, for some, particularly among the many young people experiencing multiple factors of social exclusion, social divisions still shape their cultural identity. Most post-subcultural research focuses on nightlife and the capacity of young people to participate in different scenes by changing their style and musical preferences. However, the accessibility of this nightlife is not self-evident for all social groups of young people. Carrington and Wilson note the lack of attention paid by contemporary post-subcultural scholars to issues of 'racial formation, ethnic identity construction and the articulation of racism within and between "subcultures"' (2004: 71). The dance music subculture is undoubtedly a worldwide subcultural phenomenon and we return to this phenomenon in the discussion of cultural criminology in Chapter 20. It does seem, however, that the proposition subcultural theory is no longer a useful explanatory tool for explaining the behaviour of young people – or other groups of people in the social world – is rather wide of the mark.

Conclusions

The early sociological variants of the predestined actor model of crime and criminal behaviour have – like the early biological and psychological versions – been accused of being overly determinist. It is nevertheless a form of criminological explanation that has been extremely influential in informing the direction of later – less determinist – approaches. Furthermore, the recognition that social factors external to the human being place significant constraints on that person's choice of action has been particularly influential and, indeed, would be considered by many today to be an almost common-sense, if partial, explanation of criminal behaviour.

We have seen that the later subculture theorists came increasingly to recognize that human beings are able to make choices about the course of action that they will take but it is a recognition that does not signify a return to unbridled purist variants of the rational actor model. From the perspective of these later and more sophisticated versions of the predestined actor model, there is recognition of limited constrained human choice. Thus, the choices available to the individual are restricted by their life chances, such as their education, training and skills, place of upbringing, membership of ethnic group, gender and differential access to material resources. Thus, people do not enjoy free will – as in the rational choice actor conceptualization – for no human being is ever totally free and they simply make choices that are constrained by their social circumstances. These issues are developed more fully in the third part of this book.

Policy implications of sociological positivism

Sociological theories of crime and criminal behaviour propose that people commit crime because it is a normal activity in the geographical locations where they live and among the people in the neighbourhood. As Durkheim put it, 'crime is normal'. Social disorganization theories recognise the breakdown, or serious dilution, of the power of informal community rules to regulate conduct. The mix of peoples with limited resources, bringing with them a wide variety of cultural traditions sometimes at odds with traditional middle-class norms of behaviour, is not conducive to developing and/or maintaining a sense of legitimate community. The policy implications for reversing these trends include acculturation and assimilation along with community empowerment to help immigrants and isolated subcultures feel like part of mainstream society. This will sometimes require moving people to different parts of town and urban renewal. Community empowerment policies should include strengthening grass-roots organizations, and integrating networks with wider political, social and economic resources.

The implication of Mertonian anomie theories is to introduce policies that will bring about social change and enhance equal opportunities. Social change policies will involve reorganizing socio-economic roles available in society; realigning salaries in accordance with the contribution people make to society, so that professional sportspeople do not make more than teachers, for example, and eliminate greed, jealousy and excessive economic aspiration. Equal opportunity policies will include a focus on entitlements, of legitimate options through a better educational system, improved management practices in the workplace, the creation of fulfilling jobs, welfare floors, a war on poverty, head start/early intervention programmes, and better aptitude–career planning. In short, if the cause of crime is a disjunction between cultural values that emphasize material success for all and a social structure that denies access to the legitimate means of achieving it to some, then the cure for crime is to increase opportunities or to dampen aspirations.

Policy recommendations derived from subcultural theory would not differ in any significant ways from those derived from the social organization or anomie theories, but would emphasize the need to improve the life chances and enhance the legitimate cultural capital of young people by providing better education and employment opportunities while providing exciting recreational activities that compete with the excitement and pleasures of 'doing crime'.

Summary of main points

1. Emile Durkheim presents two arguments to explain the growth of crime in modern industrial societies: (1) such societies encourage a state of unbridled 'egoism' that is contrary to the maintenance of social solidarity and conformity to the law; (2) the likelihood of inefficient regulation is greater at a time of rapid modernization and social change.
2. The Chicago School argued that the poor are not simply born into a life of crime but are driven by the conditions of their social environment. By changing their surroundings, it is possible to transform these people into law-abiding citizens.
3. Shaw and McKay argued that disorganized neighbourhoods help produce and sustain 'criminal traditions' that compete with conventional values and can be 'transmitted down through successive generations'.

4. Robert Merton's anomie theory focused on the position of the individual within the social structure and distinguished between cultural goals and institutionalized means. The ideal situation is where there is a balance between goals and means so that those who conform feel that they are justly rewarded.

5. Merton outlined five possible reactions – or adaptations – that can occur when people are not in a position to legitimately attain internalized social goals.

6. There are different deviant subculture explanations of criminality but all share a common perception that certain social groups have values and attitudes that enable or encourage delinquency.

7. The early US deviant subcultural tradition (and its British followers) has been widely accused of being overly determinist.

8. David Matza provides an influential and crucial link with later non-determinist explanations and argues that juvenile males simply 'drift' between delinquent and conventional behaviour.

9. The concept of deviant subculture was subsequently revised and revitalized by radical neo-Marxist sociologists and criminologists based at the Birmingham CCCS during the 1970s who argued that particular subcultures have arisen in response to the perceived economic problems of distinct groups.

10. Post-subcultural theorists propose that the structurally grounded concept of youth subculture has become increasingly redundant.

Discussion questions

1. Does the work of Emile Durkheim have any relevance to contemporary society and, if so, in what way?
2. What are the policy implications of the work of the Chicago School and are these relevant in the twenty-first century?
3. What are the five adaptations to social strain or anomie outlined by Merton?
4. Discuss the relevance of deviant subcultural theory to the study of white-collar or business crime.
5. Is the concept of deviant subcultural theory still applicable to the study of groups of young people?

Suggested further reading

Sociological positivism is an extremely wide subject area and there are thus many relevant texts. Students are therefore again advised to use the references in the text as a guide to specific interests. However, for a comprehensive introduction to the increasingly rediscovered and currently highly influential social theory of Emile Durkheim, it is well worth consulting the original text, Durkheim (1933). Shaw and McKay (1972) provide a thorough introduction to the work of the

Chicago School. Merton (1938) – subsequently reprinted in many different collections – provides a still essential introduction to anomie theory. The early US deviant subculture tradition is well represented by Cloward and Ohlin (1960), Cohen (1955), Miller (1958) and Spergel (1964). Matza (1964) provides, in a text widely regarded as one of the best criminology books ever written, both an outstanding critique of that tradition and an excellent link with both the rational actor and victimized actor models. Spergel (1995) provides a comprehensive overview of more recent US work in that tradition. Early UK research is well represented by Downes (1966), Mays (1954), Morris (1957), Parker (1974) and Pryce (1979). A key text representing the later Marxist-influenced Birmingham CCCS approach is Hall and Jefferson (eds) (1976), while Hopkins Burke and Sunley (1998) provide a comprehensive but concise overview of the various formulations of deviant subculture theory, while introducing the notion of post-modernism into the debate. Hopkins Burke and Pollock (2004) provide a comprehensive and easily available discussion of the relevance of sociologically informed criminological theories for explaining hate crime motivation.

8. Women and positivism

Key Issues

1. Women and positivism
2. Women and biological positivism
3. Women and psychological positivism
4. Women and sociological positivism
5. Advances in sociological explanation of female offending

Explaining female criminal behaviour was for many years a neglected area of criminology, and a significant justification for that lack of attention centres on their apparently low levels of involvement in crime with the associated assumption that women are predominantly law-abiding. By the age of 28, 33 per cent of males and 6 per cent of females have been convicted of a serious offence and this ratio has remained similar over the years (Coleman and Moynihan, 1996). Even in the case of shoplifting – an offence traditionally associated with women – more males than females are convicted. In Britain, 80 per cent of those convicted of serious crimes are male, while only 3 per cent of the prison population consists of women. There are similar ratios in the USA.

The explanations of female criminality that did exist were founded very much in the predestined actor model of crime and criminal behaviour, and this chapter considers how each of the three variants discussed in the previous chapters – biological, psychological and sociological positivisms – have sought to explain female crime.

Biological positivism and women

The works of Lombroso – particularly *The Female Offender* – provide a fundamentally biologically determinist account of female criminality and, while his methodology and conclusions have long been discredited, later biological and psychological writings on female crime (see Thomas, 1907, 1923; Davis, 1961 originally 1937; Pollak, 1950, and others discussed here) have relied at least implicitly on assumptions about the physiological and psychological nature of women to be found in his work (Klein, 1973).

Lombroso – as we saw in Chapter 5 – proposed that crime is an atavism explained by the survival of primitive traits in individuals. Based on this assumption, he compared the physical characteristics of convicted female criminals and prostitutes with those women considered to be normal. Traits found to be more common in the 'criminal' group were defined as atavistic and those found to possess a number of these were considered potentially criminal. Moreover, it was argued that women share many common traits because there are fewer variations in their mental capacities: 'even the female criminal is monotonous and uniform compared with her male companion, just as in general woman is inferior to man' (Lombroso and Ferrero, 1885: 122) and furthermore this is explained by her being 'atavistically nearer to her origin than the male' (Lombroso and Ferrero, 1885: 107). Lower rates of female criminality were thus attributed to women in general having fewer anomalies – or variations – than men and this was explained by their being close to the lower forms of less differentiated life.

Lombroso proposed that women are inherently passive and conservative because their traditional sex role in the family inherently prepares them for a more sedentary existence, although he did propose a biological basis for this passivity as being related to the nature of the sex act between men and women. He argued that the great majority of women are constrained from involvement in criminal activity by a lack of intelligence and passion, qualities he associates with *criminal* women and all men. In other words, the female offender is seen – within this indisputably biologically determinist characterization – to be *masculine* and the normal woman *feminine*. Lombroso observed that the skull anomalies he found in female criminals are closer to those of men – either normal or criminal – than they are to normal women. The female offender often has a 'virile cranium' and considerable body hair but this masculinity is in itself an anomaly rather than a sign of development (Lombroso and Ferrero, 1885: 120).

Finally, Lombroso and Ferrero note that women have a lack of property sense, which, they argue, contributes to their criminality:

> in their eyes theft is . . . an audacity for which compensation is due to the owner . . . as an individual rather than a social crime, just as it was regarded in the primitive periods of human evolution and is still regarded by many uncivilised nations.
>
> (1885: 217)

This is a notion that has been challenged on different levels: first, there is the simple assumption that women have a different sense of property than men; second, if there is any credibility in that supposition, then this must be explained by the lack of female property ownership and non-participation in capitalist wealth accumulation; indeed, women have been considered property themselves (Klein, 1973).

Lombroso has nevertheless provided an enduring – albeit invariably implicit – influence on the biological study of female criminality. Many later biological positivists commented on the passivity and lack of aggression on the part of women and readily proposed this as an explanation for their non-involvement in criminal behaviour. Money and Ernhardt (1972) and Rose *et al.* (1971) propose – on the basis of studies conducted with rats in cages – that female passivity is related to the fact that men and women have both different brains and hormones, while behaviourists such as Marsh (1978) argued, in contrast, that differences in behaviour between the sexes is purely the outcome of socialization. In reality, it is very difficult to ascertain which – if either – of the social or the genetic has the greatest influence.

The generative phases of women theory is based on biological changes connected to the menstrual cycle and, from this perspective, it is proposed that, at times of menstruation, women are reminded that they can never become men and the subsequent distress this engenders makes them increasingly susceptible to offending behaviour. The most well-known proponent of this thesis is Otto Pollak (1950) – whose predominantly psychological work is discussed in the next section – and who also proposes that the hormonal disturbance resulting from pregnancy and the menopause may be a cause of female criminality. Dalton (1961) discovered that 59.8 per cent of imprisoned women she studied had committed their offences in the sixteen-day period covering pre- and postmenstrual hormone imbalance. On the other hand, 40.2 per cent – or nearly half of the women – had committed crimes during the other twelve days. The results therefore appear inconclusive.

While it remains unclear whether women engage in a higher incidence of criminal behaviour during their generative phases, it is clear that the law has accepted the condition as constituting mitigating circumstances in some instances. Susan Edwards (1988) notes that, in the nineteenth century, premenstrual tension (PMT) was frequently discussed as being an important element of a defence in cases of violence, killing, arson and theft. Both she and Luckhaus (1985) refer to cases in the early 1980s where PMT was successfully pleaded in mitigation with the outcome that murder charges were reduced to manslaughter. This is an interesting finding because medical evidence is divided about the existence of any such syndrome. If there are effects, they appear to be mainly psychological – such as tension, irritability, depression, tiredness, mood swings and feelings of loneliness, although Dalton (1984) includes some relevant physical effects such as epilepsy, fainting and even hypoglycaemia. Rose (2000) proposes that women who have such conditions should receive treatment at an early stage to avoid both later criminal behaviour and the need to admit this type of evidence in court.

In the case of post-natal depression, there is the special defence of infanticide. If a mother kills her child within its first year as a result of post-natal depression or breastfeeding, she has a partial defence to murder, which renders it infanticide. Interestingly, this defence is only available to women and is the only sex-specific defence recognized in the criminal law. It is nevertheless clear that some of these killings might possibly be the outcome of exhaustion through caring for the child, guilt through not feeling affection for it, or the effect of other social pressures, all of which could equally be suffered by a man with primary care of a child. Marks and Kumar (1993) show that the rates of killing of children under one have remained constant since 1957 at about 45 per million per year, which is higher than for any other age group. They found that women who kill such children are dealt with much more leniently than men even when the level of violence used by the women is greater. Dell (1984) has shown that in cases of manslaughter sentences have become increasingly punitive, but Maier-Katkin and Ogle (1993) suggest that even when women are convicted of manslaughter they are treated leniently – often with probation – which suggests that it is not so much about a special defence being available but more about a greater compassion for these women.

Men were found to receive considerably harsher sentences in relatively similar cases. Hormonal imbalances suffered by men – and discussed in Chapter 5 – do not normally influence either their conviction or their sentence. Women, on the other hand, can successfully plead such imbalances even in the most serious cases where they kill another human being. This situation is undoubtedly advantageous for the individual woman involved, but for women in general it allows the continuation of the enduring biologically positivist notion that has been in existence since at least Lombroso that they are incapable of controlling themselves and that their actions can be explained through – either physical or psychological – medical reasoning (see Wilczynski and Morris, 1993). The implication of this widely used reasoning would be that women should be treated for this 'sickness' rather than being punished. It thus removes from women the possibility that they might rationally choose to commit criminal behaviour in the socio-economic circumstances in which they find themselves.

Psychological positivism and women

The work of W.I. Thomas is significant because it marks a transition from purely biological explanations of female criminality to a more sophisticated variant that embraces physiological, psychological and even sociological factors. These theories are nevertheless founded on implicit assumptions about the biological nature of women that are heavily influenced by the work of Lombroso. Thomas (1907) thus explains the inferior status of women based on physiological assumptions that attribute to men high levels of sexual energy, which leads them to pursue women for their sex, and to women maternal feelings, which lead them to exchange sex for domesticity. The outcome is that women – who are also the property of men – are domesticated, while men assume leadership. The conduct of the two sexes is moreover regulated and controlled in different ways.

Thomas argued that, because women occupy a marginal position in the productive sphere outside the home, they consequently occupy a subsidiary position with regard to 'contractual' law, which regulates property and production. They simply do not constitute a threat to the commercial world and are therefore treated more leniently than men by the authorities in cases involving property. In matters of sexual conduct, the opposite is very much the case and women are rigorously prosecuted by the law.

In *The Unadjusted Girl* (1923), Thomas identified four basic 'wishes', which he proposed to be fundamental to human nature – the desire for new experience, for security, for response and for recognition – and proposed that these are derived from the biological instincts of anger, fear, love and the will to gain power and status. These instincts are channelled towards gender-appropriate goals through socialization, with women having a stronger desire for the biological instinct of love than men. It is this intense need to give and feel love that leads women into crime, particularly sexual offences like prostitution. Significantly, the activities of an individual – although driven by these basic 'wishes' – are controlled by the socialization processes and can thus be made to serve social or antisocial needs. In short, behaviour can be changed and the individual rehabilitated:

> There is no individual energy, no unrest, no type of wish, which cannot be sublimated and made socially useful. From this standpoint, the problem is not the right of society to protect itself from the disorderly and antisocial person, but the right of the disorderly and antisocial person to be made orderly and socially valuable. . . . The problem of society is to produce the right attitudes in its members.
>
> (Thomas, 1923: 232–3)

There is here a significant rejection of the Lombrosian biological perspective, which proposes that there are criminally predestined individuals who must be incarcerated, sterilized or otherwise incapacitated. Thomas alternatively proposes the manipulation of individuals to prevent antisocial attitudes and to correct the poor socialization provided in 'slum' families. The response to a criminal woman who is dissatisfied with her conventional sexual roles is not therefore to change the roles – which would of course involve substantial social transformations – but to change her attitudes.

Thomas (1923) proposes that middle-class women commit little crime because they are socialized to control their natural desires and to behave well, treasuring their chastity as an investment. The poor woman, conversely, is not immoral but simply amoral. She is not driven to commit crime as the purist predestined actor model proponent might suggest, but simply to seek it, motivated by the desire for excitement or 'new experience', and has no interest in middle-class notions of 'security'. Thomas thus uses a market analogy to define female virtue. Good women keep their bodies as capital to sell in exchange for marriage and security, while bad women trade their bodies for excitement. Klein (1973) observes that this is an astonishing – nay, obscene – statement to have been made in an era of mass starvation and illness. Thomas nevertheless simply rejects the possibility of economic explanations of female criminality with as much certainty as Lombroso and Freud, Davis and Pollak, to whom we now turn our attention.

The Freudian theory of the position of women is grounded in explicit biological assumptions about their nature and this is unequivocally expressed in his famous dictum that 'anatomy is destiny' (see Lerner, 1998). Women are seen to be anatomically inferior to men with a consequential inferior destiny as wives and mothers. At the root of this inferiority is the inferior nature of female sex organs, which is apparently recognized by children universally. Thus, girls assume that they have lost their penis as a punishment, become traumatized and grow up envious and revengeful. Boys noting that girls have lost their penis fear their envy and vengeance. In the Freudian schema, feminine traits are explained by inferior female genitals. Women are exhibitionistic and narcissistic, and attempt to compensate for their lack of a penis by being well dressed and physically beautiful. They are also masochistic – as Lombroso and Thomas also noted – because their sexual role is one of receptor, and their sexual pleasure consists of pain. In contrast, men are aggressive and pain inflicting (see Millett, 1970).

Women are also considered inferior because they are preoccupied with personal matters and have little sense of the wider world. Freud proposes that civilization is based on our repression of the sex drive and it is thus the duty of men to repress their strong instincts in order to get on with the worldly business of civilization. On the other hand, women

> have little sense of justice, and this is no doubt connected with the preponderance of envy in their mental life, for the demands of justice are a modification of envy; they lay down the conditions under which one is willing to part with it. We also say of women that their actual interests are weaker than those of men and that their capacity for the sublimation of their instincts is less.
>
> (Freud, 1933: 183)

Men are capable of sublimating their individual needs because they are rational and capable of understanding the need to control their urges in the interests of wider society. Women, in contrast, are emotional and incapable of making rational judgements. It is therefore appropriate that women should only have a marginal relationship to production and property. The deviant woman in this schema is thus one deemed to be going against her inherent nature and trying to be a man. She is thus aggressive and rebellious, and her drive for success is simply indicative of her longing for a penis. This is of course a hopeless ambition and the only outcome for the woman can be neurosis. The solution to her predicament is treatment and help so that she can adjust to her natural sex role.

Klein (1973) observes that Freudian notions of the repression of sexual instincts, the sexual passivity of women and the sanctity of the nuclear family were conservative even in the early twentieth century when they were developed. They were, however, developed into a remarkably enduring and virtually hegemonic perspective in the USA and beyond, which helped facilitate the return of women to the home and out of a productive economy with no capacity for them during the depression and post-war years (Millett, 1970). It was given even greater credibility by the status accorded to John Bowlby's (1952) 'maternal deprivation thesis' – published by the United Nations – which proposed that, to ensure the successful socialization of a law-abiding citizen, the child needs to be looked after closely and predominantly by its mother during its formative years.

Freud also significantly influenced such writers on female deviance as Kingsley Davis (1961 originally 1937), Otto Pollak (1950) and Gisela Konopka (1966), who used concepts of sexual maladjustment and neurosis to explain the criminality of women. These writers were to define healthy women as masochistic, passive and sexually indifferent, criminal women as sexual misfits, and significantly use psychological factors to explain female criminal activity while completely ignoring socio-economic factors.

Kingsley Davis' (1961 originally 1937) influential structural functionalist study of prostitution is significantly founded on crucial assumptions about the 'organic nature of man and woman' that have clear origins in the work of Thomas and Freud. Davis argues that prostitution is a structural necessity with its foundations in the sexual nature of human beings and concludes that prostitution is universally inevitable and that there will always be a class of 'bad' women available to provide their services as prostitutes. Prostitution is universal because sexual repression is essential to the functioning of society.

At the time Davis was writing – in the mid-twentieth century – sexuality was only legitimately permitted within the structure of the nuclear family, an institution of social stability and a bulwark of morality:

> The norms of every society tend to harness and control the sexual appetite, and one of the ways of doing this is to link the sexual act to some stable or potentially stable social relationship ... Men dominate women in all economic, sexual and familial relationships and consider them to some extent as sexual property, to be prohibited to other males. They therefore find promiscuity on the part of women repugnant.
>
> (Davis, 1961: 264)

The concept of prostitution is thus linked to promiscuity and defined as a sexual crime with prostitutes themselves perceived not as economically motivated but as sexual transgressors taking advantage of marital restraints on sexuality. Davis argues that there will always be a demand for prostitution as long as men seek women. Only the liberalization of sexual mores could bring about the eradication of prostitution and he was not optimistic that such a situation would ever arise:

> We can imagine a social system in which the motive for prostitution would be completely absent, but we cannot imagine that the system will ever come to pass. It would be a regime of absolute sexual freedom with intercourse practised solely for pleasure by both parties. There would be no institutional control of sexual expression ... All sexual desire would have to be mutually complementary ... Since the basic causes of prostitution – the institutional control of sex, the unequal scale of unattractiveness, and the presence of economic and social inequalities between classes and between males and females – are not likely to disappear, prostitution is not likely to disappear either.
>
> (Davis, 1961: 286)

Thus, men unable to attract women to engage in sexual activity for mutual pleasure – or (and Davis does not discuss this point) who do not have the time, predilection or social skills required to engage in the precursors to this activity – may become frustrated and thus sustain the demand for prostitution.

Davis argues that women become prostitutes for good pay and sexual pleasure and there thus exists a functional system beneficial for everyone. He denies the economic oppression of the women involved. They are on the streets through autonomous, individual choice. Klein (1973) observes that the women are merely adjusting to their feminine role in an illegitimate fashion – as Thomas theorized – they are not attempting to be rebels or to be men as Lombroso and Freud would suggest. At a level of generality, Davis observes the main difference between wives and prostitutes to be between legal and illegal roles; in a personal individualized sense, he sees the women who choose to become involved in prostitution as maladjusted and neurotic. However, given the universal necessity for prostitution, this analysis seems to imply the necessity of having a perpetually ill and maladjusted class of women, which Davis is not prepared to question let alone challenge.

Otto Pollak's *The Criminality of Women* (1950) – a further substantially influential text in the immediate post-Second World War period – proposes the theory of 'hidden' female crime to account for what he considers to be unreasonably low official female crime rates. It is – he argues – the very nature of women themselves that accounts for this subterranean criminality. They are simply the instigators rather than the perpetrators of much criminal activity. Pollak acknowledges a partly socially enforced role but insists that women are inherently deceitful for physiological reasons:

> Man must achieve an erection in order to perform the sex act and he will not be able to hide his failure. His lack of positive emotion in the sexual sphere must become overt to the partner, and pretense of sexual response is impossible for him, if it is lacking. Woman's body, however, permits such pretense to a certain degree and lack of an orgasm does not prevent her ability to participate in the sex act.
>
> (Pollak, 1950: 10)

The nature of women is therefore reduced to the sex act – as with Freud – and women are considered to be inherently more capable of manipulation, accustomed to being sly, passive and passionless. Moreover, women are innately deceitful on another level:

> Our sex mores force women to conceal every four weeks the period of menstruation ... They thus make concealment and misrepresentation in the eyes of women socially required and must condition them to a different attitude towards veracity than men.
>
> (Pollak, 1950: 11)

A second factor in hidden crime are the roles played by women that provide them with opportunities as domestics, nurses, teachers and housewives to commit undetectable crimes. Pollak, moreover, argues that the kinds of crimes committed by women are a reflection of their nature. False accusation, for example, is a consequence of treachery, spite or fear and is a sign of neurosis. Shoplifting, it is proposed, can be traced in many cases to a specific psychiatric disorder called kleptomania. Female criminality is thus explained in terms of socio-psychological factors – economic conditions are considered virtually inconsequential – female crime is personalized and a product of mental illness.

The third factor proposed by Pollak to explain the enigma of hidden female crime is the existence of 'chivalry' in the criminal justice system. Developing from Thomas the theme that women are differentially treated by the law, he argues that:

> One of the outstanding concomitants of the existing inequality . . . is chivalry, and the general protective attitude of man toward women . . . Men hate to accuse women and thus indirectly to send them to their punishment, police officers dislike to arrest them, district attorneys to prosecute them, judges and juries to find them guilty, and so on.
>
> (Pollak, 1950: 151)

Klein (1973) observes that the women who become the clients of the criminal justice system are likely to be poor, from ethnic minority backgrounds – or, if white middle-class women, those who have stepped outside acceptable definitions of female behaviour – and chivalry is unlikely to be extended to them. She observes that chivalry is a racist and classist concept founded on the notion of women as 'ladies' and this only applies to wealthy white women. These 'ladies', however, are the least likely women to ever come into contact with the criminal justice system in the first place. In these various and different psychological positivist explanations of female crime, crime defined as masculine appears to mean violent, overt crime, whereas 'ladylike' crime refers to sexual violations and shoplifting.

Klein observes that women are neatly categorized no matter what kind of crime they commit. If they are violent, they are 'masculine' and suffering from chromosomal deficiencies, penis envy or atavisms. If they conform, they are manipulative, sexually maladjusted and promiscuous. The economic and social realities of crime – that it is predominantly poor women who commit criminal offences and that most crimes they commit are property offences – are simply overlooked. The behaviour of women must be sexually defined before it will be considered, for women only count in the sexual sphere. We have thus seen that the theme of sexuality is a unifying thread in the various – invariably contradictory – psychological and biologically determinist theories considered above. Moreover, it was to be an enduring influence.

Campbell (1981) observes how women shoplifters – but not men who are responsible for the great majority of these offences – have been explained with reference to psychiatric problems and sexuality. Women are supposed to obtain sexual excitement from the act, or commit the crime to appease repressed sexual desires, or in order to be punished for such feelings. The prevalence of these explanations was to continue because of the number of single, divorced or widowed women found to be committing such offences.

The possibility that these very groups could be exposed to particularly harsh economic circumstances was ignored. Gibbens and Prince (1962) studied shoplifting and explained young male working-class involvement by reference to the gang or peer group pressure. In the case of a small group of middle-class boys, the researchers suggested that these suffered from homosexual tendencies, which enabled them to apply the sexuality-based explanations they had used to explain female involvement to this group.

The actions of criminal women have been invariably explained – as we have seen above – with reference to their having breached the dominant societal definition of female behaviour and some claim that this deviation from the norm justifies subjecting them to increasing sanctions as they move through the system (see Carlen, 1983). Most studies have found no evidence of gender bias in sentencing (see Daly, 1994a; Heidensohn, 1996), but Kennedy (1992) has documented a criminal justice system that she observes to be generally biased against women. She found that, in the case of young female offenders, the system appears ostensibly to want to help them by showing them the error of their ways and to this end attempts to resocialize them into a socially acceptable gender role. The welfare interventions applied to these young women are nevertheless considerably more invasive of their private lives than any applied to young men and they tend to be treated more as sexual miscreants than criminals. It is apparent – from the above discussion – that clinical and sexual explanations of female criminality have been widely accepted even when those crimes have no clear sexual basis. In the case of male criminality, such explanations have long been rejected – sometimes even when there is a clear sexual link – and there would appear to be different standards applied to explaining male and female criminality.

Sociological positivism and women

In this section, we consider the applicability of sociological positivist theories of crime and criminal behaviour to female criminality. We shall see that, although these theories claim to be general explanations of criminal behaviour, they invariably tend to be explanations of male patterns of behaviour and appear – at least at first sight – to have little or no relevance for explaining female criminality (Leonard, 1983).

Robert Merton's influential anomie theory sought – as we saw in the previous chapter – to provide a comprehensive explanation of crime and deviance, proposing that social structures pressure certain individuals to engage in nonconformist behaviour. He argues that US society overemphasizes its cultural goals without paying sufficient attention to the paucity of institutionalized means of obtaining these ambitions in a legitimate fashion and specifically refers to the overwhelming desire for financial success and material goods in US society and the willingness of some to use any means to obtain these goals.

Merton (1957) later acknowledged that wealth is not the only success symbol in US society, although he continued to emphasize its centrality. He also now recognized that more affluent people can experience pressure to 'innovate', since one can never have enough money, but he continued to insist that it is the lower classes who commit the most crime because they experience the greatest levels of strain. He also expanded his thoughts on ritualism and now claimed that this is most often found in the lower middle class, where children are socialized to obey rules but have limited opportunities for success.

Merton (1966) later acknowledged that people in power exercise a crucial role in determining what particular behaviour violates social standards and that punishment may be differentially imposed in terms of class, race or age. He nevertheless made no attempt to apply his theory to women and, at first sight, it does not appear applicable to them. Eileen Leonard (1983) observes that it is arguable whether the dominant goal in US society of monetary success is applicable in the case of women. Ruth Morris (1964) had earlier argued that women and girls aim for successful relationships with others rather than the traditional financial goals of men. More specifically, women were socialized to seek marriage and children more than a lucrative career and, while a quarter of a century later more women may aspire to careers, marriage and family remain an equally important goal.

Leonard (1983) acknowledges that many women marry and have children and perhaps in doing so avoid the anomic pressure men experience when unable to achieve social goals. It is also possible that anomie theory may help to explain increases in female criminality if the goals of women shift towards those of males with their greater involvement in the world external to the family. The problem with that possibility is that it presupposes a common goal for all women without any consideration of differential – or subcultural – socialization (Ladner, 1972; Anderson and Collins, 1992). Thus, anomie theory directs our thinking towards common goals, not class, race or ethnic variations.

Leonard (1983) also observes that anomie appears an inappropriate explanation of the crime that does occur among women. It is certainly difficult – in terms of the key concept of innovation – to conceive of an illegal means to the goal of marriage and the family. Theft and prostitution are not alternative means to marriage, while many women convicted of criminal offences are married with children.

Thus, anomie theory fails to explain why women deviate in the way that they do or what type of strain actually leads to each outcome. The theory – as Leonard observes – applies largely to men and mainly to the goal of financial success. It ignores social variations in terms of gender, race or ethnicity, and, when a group as significant as women is examined, it is not a matter of making minor revisions. The theory fails in important respects and, thus, Merton's 'common' symbols of success may not be so common after all (Leonard, 1983).

Theorists of deviant subcultures have played a central role in developing theoretical explanations of criminal behaviour that consider the differential socialization experiences of separate groups even though these were primarily concerned with urban, working-class male delinquency. Cohen (1955) thus proposes that males and females have different problems that require different solutions. Boys are mainly concerned with comparing their achievements with other males, while girls are more concerned about their relationship with males. Cohen does not regard this situation as 'natural' – as was the case with the biological and psychological positivists – but he does propose that girls are mainly fulfilled through their relationships with the opposite sex. He concludes that the problems of adjustment that lead to the formation of delinquent gangs are fundamentally male and that the delinquent subculture is completely inappropriate for addressing female needs.

Cohen argues that a female's 'peace of mind' depends on her assurance of sexual attractiveness and that sexual delinquency is one response to the central female problem of establishing satisfying relationships with men. Leonard (1983) observes that it is unclear how female sexual delinquency provides a solution to establishing satisfactory relationships with males. Moreover, it fails to explain why so many women who have not married successful males, or whose personal relationships are less than satisfactory, do not commit crime.

Miller (1958) makes no attempt to consider criminal activity among women and his arguments appear inapplicable to them. His focal concerns are supposed to apply to lower-class life in general, but, if this were so, male and female offending rates would be similar. It would seem that trouble, toughness, smartness, excitement, fate and autonomy are predominantly male preoccupations and are far less relevant to the lives of women.

Differential opportunity theory nevertheless appears more amenable to a consideration of gender because it addresses the unavailability of both legitimate and illegitimate opportunities. Thus, the lower participation of women in crime may be explained by their limited access to illegitimate opportunities (Harris, 1977). Cloward (1959) acknowledged that women are frequently excluded from criminal activities, although he proposed that class is a more important differential than gender. Other researchers have observed that girls are less likely to have subcultural support for delinquent behaviour when compared with boys (Morris, 1965; Campbell, 1984; Figueira-McDonough, 1984; McCormack et al., 1986; Chesney-Lind, 1989). Cloward and Ohlin's theory is enhanced by their consideration of the availability of illegitimate opportunity, but Leonard (1983) observes that they simply ignore societal reactions and fail to explain criminal behaviour among women who have achieved their social goals. Moreover, they do not question – let alone explain – why such profound structural differences exist in the behaviour and expectations of males and females.

Edwin Sutherland contributed substantially to the development of criminology with his theory of differential dissociation where he argued that involvement in crime was similar to any other learned behaviour (Sutherland and Cressey, 1960). Thus, individuals learn to rob a bank in very much the same way that they learn to fix a car: someone teaches them. In short, people become criminal because of frequent contact with criminal rather than law-abiding people. Cohen et al. (1956) observe that, if the primary group for most females is a relatively restrictive family, they may simply be less likely than males to learn criminal behaviour. Females also lack the opportunity for contact with adolescent gangs – or groups that generate white-collar crime – and this further limits the possibility of involvement in criminal behaviour. Even within the same groups as males – for example, the family – their social position is unequal and they are frequently taught dissimilar attitudes. The differential treatment of males and females may culminate, then, with women exposed to an excessive number of definitions of behaviour unfavourable to violating the law. Sutherland indicates this in a discussion of the sex ratio in crime when he states that 'probably the most important difference is that girls are supervised more carefully and behave in accordance with anti-criminal behaviour patterns taught to them with greater care and consistency than in the case of boys' (Sutherland and Cressey, 1960: 115).

Females encounter more anti-criminal patterns (within the family, where they are isolated and controlled) over a longer period of time (owing to external supervision) than males. Sutherland suggests these differences might have originated because females become pregnant and, hence, require more supervision. Thus, differential association interprets the low crime rate among women in terms of their associations, which tend to ensure that they will learn patterns of behaviour favouring adherence to the law.

The differential association approach is compatible with the sex role – or masculinity/femininity – theories that first appeared in the USA during the late 1940s and that propose that proper socialization is explained purely as a function of the physical sexual nature of the individual. In other words, maleness equals masculinity and femaleness equals femininity. It is when this 'natural' process breaks down that women become criminal. Again, these writers – like many of their biologically and psychologically determinist predecessors – have a tendency to portray women as passive, gentle, dependent, conventional and motherly.

Talcott Parsons (1947, 1954) – at the time the pre-eminent sociologist – explained different levels of offending behaviour between males and females as the outcome of the social and family structure prevailing in the USA at the time. The father worked outside the home to provide economically for the family, while the mother was involved with the care and upbringing of the children and looking after the home. Boys were expected to grow up like their fathers and consequently assumed that passivity, conformity and being good are behavioural traits that should be avoided. The outcome is an aggressive attitude that can lead to antisocial, rebellious and criminal activities. Girls, however, have a close adult model – their mother – which allows them to mature emotionally and become feminine.

Grosser (1951) argues that boys become interested in power and money, which might lead them to steal, while girls see that they will become carers and homemakers and so close relationships are more important to them. Girls are thus more likely to become involved in sexual promiscuity and any criminality – such as theft of clothes and make-up – that will make them more attractive to the opposite sex. Reiss (1960) takes up this theme and argues that young women may be willing to participate in sexual activity because having a close relationship with a male can bring prestige. However, if the girl becomes pregnant or contracts a sexually transmitted disease, she will lose all prestige from her male and female friends. Hoffman Bustamante (1973) notes that females are rewarded for conforming behaviour; males, on the other hand, although taught to conform, are often rewarded when they breach the rules. She argues that this teaches men – but not women – that, although conformity is generally desirable, it can be rational to breach the rules in some cases. Women, in contrast, are shown that the only legitimate way forward is conformity. Sex role skills are said to be important because they will determine the type of crimes an individual will be capable of committing. Thus, weapons are less likely to be used by women because they rarely learn how to use them but they may use household implements to threaten their victims.

Hoffman Bustamante notes that, among children and teenagers in the USA, girls are more likely than boys to be arrested for juvenile crimes such as 'breach of curfew' and 'running away'. She explains this by saying that girls are more likely to be noticed than boys if they are out alone, while parents worry more about their daughters than they do their sons. Subsequent research has found little evidence to show that either property or aggressive crimes are related to masculinity traits but it has been found that women are more likely to be aggressive if less feminine (see Cullen *et al.*, 1979; Shover *et al.*, 1979; Widom, 1979).

More recent research has alerted us to the possibility that some women may actually learn criminal behaviour within the family (Miller, 1986) and that the home is often a site of violence against women (Dobash and Dobash, 1980; Stanko, 1985). Cressey (1964) noted fifty years ago that the sex ratio is decreasing and that changes have occurred over time, and he proposed that, as the social position of women begins to approach that of men, the male–female differential will decline. Increasing employment and education for women has brought them into contact with more groups, while weakening restrictions on females, combined with the growing number of broken families and increasing urbanization, may play a role in increasing female crime.

More recently, Giordano and Rockwell (2000) have reconsidered the link between differential association and female criminality and proposed that it is the decisive factor. They observe that, although many women have suffered social deprivation or physical abuse without turning to offending behaviour, they suggest that all female criminals have had close associations with positive depictions of deviant lifestyles. From a young age, many of the women were 'immersed' in these definitions, which they learned from mothers, fathers, aunts, cousins and siblings who might be caught up in these activities. Giordano and Rockwell thus suggest that learning theory and differential associations may explain much female activity.

In concluding this section, we should note that the role of many women in society has changed radically from the vision of the happily married and economically dependent housewife on which most of the theories discussed in this chapter have focused. It seems that more women than ever are the only, the major or the joint breadwinner, and therefore the pressures of economic success are placed on them. As women often inhabit low-paid and insecure areas of the labour market – or are unemployed – they have tremendous pressures placed upon them to provide (Box, 1987). These increased strains may help to explain some of the recent increased female criminality, especially that which takes place in traditional male criminal areas (see Box and Hale, 1983). Certainly, there are certain offences that have risen dramatically and that are associated with female poverty, with evasion of payment for television licences probably the most dramatic example (Pantazis and Gordon, 1997). The reality is that women still commit substantially less crime than men, even in those social classes overly represented in the official crime statistics.

Conclusions

We should note that there have been no conclusive scientific tests that have been able to establish – or for that matter completely dismiss – any biological or psychological link with crime and criminal behaviour. Thus, while theories based on these ideas have been widely criticized – and may seem to the reader to be both nonsensical and sexist – they cannot be totally dismissed. Behavioural scientists and others in the social sciences have tried to establish other explanations for criminal behaviour and claim that either socialization or environment has accentuated a previously very small or non-existent biological difference. In general, it seems that biological arguments appear to have little contemporary credibility and the more sociologically based theories seem to offer more plausible explanations.

Sociological explanations have nevertheless failed to provide particularly plausible explanations of either female involvement in criminality or why it is that women are more conforming than men. It may be that the tendency to see male crime as normal necessarily overshadows the study of the much less common female offending (Heidensohn, 1996). Studies implicitly based on masculinity and on presumptions that the offender will be male mean that the behaviour of women, if included at all, is – unconsciously – considered from a masculine or 'malestream' perspective. These issues are revisited from a feminist perspective in Chapter 11.

Policy implications of women and positivism

The policy implications of positivism for women are clearly highly problematic. Biological positivism has been extremely influential and enduring in explaining female criminality, with policy implications of treatment and mitigation being central to such initiatives. The enduring suggestion from this perspective is that women are in some way the prisoners of their biology and act accordingly. Thus, treatment to rectify or alleviate this situation would be recommended. This position is nevertheless problematic for some women. Infanticide and indeed the pre- (or post)-menstrual tension defence can be appropriate mitigating factors for the defence in some cases and it is important not to lose sight of that reality. The same policy predicaments are clearly the case for psychological positivism, which would also point to the immense psychological pressures brought to bear upon women in the aftermath of their giving birth. The long-standing defence of infanticide would thus seem to be highly appropriate when such mothers kill their child in the first year of its life. The logical sociological positivist policy implication would nevertheless be to improve the living conditions and improve the support mechanisms to mothers and children in the aftermath of birth, thereby alleviating the need for mitigation when things go wrong.

Summary of main points

1. Explaining female criminal behaviour was for many years a neglected area of criminology not least because of the apparently low levels of female involvement in crime.
2. Early explanations of female criminality were founded very much in the predestined actor model tradition and in particular biological positivism.
3. Lombroso proposed that women are inherently passive and conservative because their traditional sex role in the family prepares them for a more sedentary existence. Many later biological positivists proposed this to be the key explanation for their non-involvement in criminal behaviour.

4. The work of W.I. Thomas is significant because it marks a transition from purely biological explanations of female criminality to a more sophisticated variant that embraces physiological, psychological and even sociological factors.
5. The Freudian theory of the position of women is grounded in explicit biological assumptions about their nature, which is expressed in his famous dictum 'anatomy is destiny'.
6. Freud significantly influenced such writers on female deviance as Kingsley Davis (1961 originally 1937), Otto Pollak (1950) and Gisela Konopka (1966), who used concepts of sexual maladjustment and neurosis to explain the criminality of women.
7. The actions of criminal women have been invariably explained with reference to their having breached the dominant societal definition of female behaviour and some claim that this deviation from the norm justifies subjecting them to increasing sanctions.
8. Sutherland argued that females encounter more anti-criminal patterns (within the family, where they are isolated and controlled) over a longer period of time (owing to external supervision) than males.
9. More recent research has suggested that some women may actually learn criminal behaviour within the family.
10. The role of many women in society has changed radically from the vision of the happily married and economically dependent housewife (if that role ever existed for many women) with many now the joint or sole breadwinner with the pressures of economic success placed on them.

Discussion questions

1. Is there any validity in biological explanations of female criminality in the twenty-first century?
2. What impact has the Freudian psychoanalytical tradition had on explaining female involvement in crime?
3. How have sociological positivists (or functionalists) explained female involvement in prostitution? Do you think that such explanations have any value in contemporary society?
4. Do you agree with the view that anomie theories have no relevance to explaining female involvement in crime?
5. Does sex role theory make a valid contribution to explaining female criminality?

Suggested further reading

Klein (1973) and Leonard (1983) provide excellent and enduring feminist critiques and overviews of biological, psychological and sociological positivism. For those who wish to consult the original theorists, the following will be considered useful: Lombroso (1920) for the foundations of biological positivism, which have influenced so many later theorists albeit often implicitly; Thomas (1923) and Pollak (1950) establish the main parameters of psychological positivism; while Parsons (1947, 1954) provides an – albeit difficult – but classic account of sex role theory and the division of labour within the nuclear family.

Part Three

The victimized actor model of crime and criminal behaviour

Definitions of serious crime are essentially ideological constructs. They do not refer to those behaviours which objectively and avoidably cause us the most harm, injury and suffering. Instead they refer only to a sub-section of these behaviours, a sub-section which is more likely to be committed by young, poorly educated males who are often unemployed, live in working-class impoverished neighbourhoods, and frequently belong to an ethnic minority.

(Box, 1983: 10)

We saw in the first part of this book that the rational actor model of crime and criminal behaviour understands human beings to possess free will and they therefore have the capacity to make rational decisions to engage in activities of their choice. Criminal behaviour is simply a rationally chosen activity. The predestined actor model, on the other hand, proposes that crime emanates from factors – be they biological, psychological or social – that are outside the control of the offender and that determine their behaviour. Thus, the major concern of this tradition is to identify and analyse what is considered to be the causes that drive individuals to commit criminal acts. A major criticism of that tradition has centred on its acceptance of the conventional morality and criminal laws as self-evident truths. In other words, if a particular action is defined as a crime, it is necessarily wrong because the state decreed it to be so.

The third model of crime and criminal behaviour provides a challenge to the predestined actor notion of determined human behaviour and its uncritical acceptance of the socio-political status quo. Thus, the victimized actor model proposes that the criminal is in some way the victim of an unjust and unequal society and it is the behaviour and activities of the poor and disadvantaged that are targeted and criminalized, while the actions of the rich and powerful are simply ignored or not even defined as criminal.

The victimized actor model has two theoretical foundations. First, there is the critique of the predestined actor model of human behaviour offered by symbolic interactionists and which was to become increasingly influential during the latter half of the twentieth century. The labelling theories that provide the first and earliest component of the victimized model tradition – and which are the focus of the following chapter – have their roots in symbolic interactionism in general and the work of George Herbert Mead (1934) in particular.

Symbolic interactionism primarily analyses the way individuals conceptualize themselves and others around them with whom they interact. Of central importance in that analysis is the concept of the 'procedural self'. This broadly speaking is the view that a person's self-identity is continuously constructed and reconstructed in interaction with 'significant others' – those who have an influence on the individual – and that human behaviour can only be understood by reference to this process. Moreover, it is proposed that meanings do not reside within objects or within the psychological elements of the individual person, but rather emerge out of the social processes of interpretation by which definitions of objects are created and used (Plummer, 1975).

Symbolic interactionists conclude that deviance is not a property *inherent* in certain forms of behaviour but one that is *conferred* on certain forms of behaviour by an audience. Thus, in this way, the focus of criminological enquiry was to shift away from the qualities and characteristics of the deviant actor and towards that of the audience, that is, the *response* of society to the deviant act. Of particular relevance here are the responses of the various agencies of social control, such as the police, courts, psychiatrists, social workers and teachers.

The work of those writers most closely identified with the labelling/ interactionist perspective, such as Lemert (1951), Becker (1963) and, in particular, Erikson (1962, 1966), Kitsuse (1962) and Cicourel (1968), was also influenced by phenomenological and ethnomethodological approaches.

Phenomenology is a philosophical approach that arose out of a general debate about the character, scope and certainty of knowledge. The most influential proponent of the sociological variant was Alfred Schutz, who argued that sociology should not attempt to establish the 'reality' of social phenomena. Such phenomena are only 'real' if they are defined as such by individuals who then act on the basis of those definitions. Since the reality that lies behind the way individuals interpret the world can never be penetrated, the positivist goal of objectivity should be abandoned in favour of a quest to ascertain *subjective* meaning. The focus on deviant meanings involved the recognition that negative or stigmatic responses to a deviant act may well affect the way that deviants see themselves. This in turn led to widening of the focus to include the creation of deviant meanings by agencies of social control (Rock, 1973).

Ethnomethodology draws on and further develops these phenomenological concepts and methods in order to describe social reality. It is a method of sociological study concerned with how individuals experience and make sense of social interaction. Central to this approach is the notion that *all* expressions of reality are 'indexical'; that is, they are based upon a set of assumptions specific only to the social context in which they are used. Perhaps the major significance of this approach to criminology lies in its profound questioning of the utility of criminal statistics. Unlike other perspectives, which viewed these as reasonably objective and independent of theory, ethnomethodologists treated them as social constructions produced, as are all phenomena, by interpretative work and social organization.

The second theoretical foundation of the victimized actor model is a critique of the orthodox predestined actor model notion that society is fundamentally characterized by consensus (Parsons, 1951). That orthodox view was based on the simple assumption that there is fundamental agreement concerning the goals of social life and the norms, rules and laws that should govern the pursuit of these objectives. There is, however, another long-established tradition in the social sciences that considers society to be fundamentally conflict-ridden.

Max Weber (1864–1920) had influentially argued that conflict arises in society from the inevitable battle within the economic marketplace over the distribution of scarce resources, and his model and its implications for criminal behaviour is both pluralistic and pessimistic. Societies are seen to develop in episodic ways, conditioned by historically contingent circumstances, the most important of these being inward – or outward – worldly orientation. Weber (1964) held structuralist ideas about political and economic stratification, distinguishing between class, party and *status*, the last being most strongly related to perception of life chances, but conflict is not limited to these structural features, as people also fight over ideas and values. This focus provides an explanatory space for socialization and motivational theories, which are based on resistance to the *iron cage of rationalization* or *bureaucracy*, an increasingly pervasive trend in society where every area of life becomes subject to calculation and administration. His emphasis on the behaviour of authorities makes the struggle over political, especially legislative, power (to improve the life chances of the status group) his central contribution to conflict criminology. Weber's approach is pessimistic in the sense that capitalism can only hope to remain flexible and constantly adjust in response to the permanence of conflict and its tendency to become routinized.

Georg Simmel (1908) wrote extensively on the sources of conflict and is a neglected founding father of sociology (Frisby, 1984). Some of his perspective can be identified as providing part of the basic foundations of symbolic interactionism, but he also fostered a conflict tradition unique for its idealistic tendencies and spontaneous natural tendencies. Simmel considered the basis of human relationships to be one of *homo homini lupus* where people are seen to be wolves by others (Wolff, 1950). Their true selves are only visible as fragments that emerge during the course of group involvement, that is, when they wish to obtain something from somebody. The self is always situated in context and there are as many selves as there are layers of situations or groups in society. Moreover, because the self is social there can be no antisocial interests because this would be simply self-destructive. People experience feelings like love and contempt at the same time and any time they think they are being a loner or outsider they are actually thinking of others. These insights led Simmel to focus on group conflicts where envies, wants and desires are expressed. Groups thus provide more or less enduring interaction and relative constancy of pattern but they do not consume all there is about an individual.

Form, rather than content, is important for Simmel (1900), who studied money and found that the comparison of quite different contexts yielded a number of stable and recurring social types, such as the *stranger*, the *enemy*, the *criminal* and the *pauper*. It is strangers – or immigrants – who are often the scapegoats of society. Content varies, but forms are the stable, permanent patterns of interaction. Intuitionism is used to find the inner nature of things without being distracted by sensory observation of what goes on in the context in which this is all taking place (Simmel, 1908).

Sociation is the real object of society and is viewed as an art, a game or play. Social groups are thus everywhere in (internal) conflict because no one group could exhaust their individuality and are therefore constantly in (external) conflict because of boundary-crossing allegiances. Collins refers to this rather unsympathetically as 'the grid-lock model of social conflict' (1988: 123) but it could be more positively seen as the ongoing expression of selves and thus not a conception of conflict. Simmel (1906) proposed that, because people deceive themselves and others every time they try to express their individuality, social structures are distinguished by the relative permissibility of lying and society itself is thus a lie and a fiction. A criminal is thus one who has given up too much integrity and lost their real self, or, on the contrary, one who is seeking too much individuality or anonymity is the criminal social type (Simmel, 1900).

Karl Marx (1818–83) had taken a much more radical stance and argued that conflict involves an inherent struggle by people to abolish the social divisions imposed by the material arrangements within society. Marxism as a social scientific tradition is best distinguished by a particular ontology (view of human nature) and epistemology (way of knowing). Marx considered humanity to be *homo faber* not *homo sapiens* (Engels, 1845), and Quinney (1965) explains this as the idea of human nature being essentially unfinished and constantly seeking to realize its potential. Explanations of crime based on socialization experiences, normative structures and cultural demands are therefore incompatible with Marxism because humans are never completely socialized, claim higher loyalties than societal norms and are culture builders, not the products of culture. This ontology thus involves a rejection of both the rational actor model (free will) and predestined actor model (determinism) traditions. It is also part of the deep structure of romantic thought in Western philosophy (Gouldner, 1970).

Marxist epistemology is realism but not the philosophical kind of Plato, rather the scepticism or disenchantment of the legal realist tradition that exists in jurisprudence. It is a mature epistemological perspective that seeks to make sense of the facts of constant change and the inevitable loss of idealism that emanates from this position, and this scepticism is the basis of the idea that nothing is morally neutral, that people retain the right to critique, expose, pass judgement and demystify (Quinney, 1974). Critique for the sake of critique is thus important to followers of Marx.

The methodology of Marxism is dialectical historical materialism. Hegel was the idealist philosopher who first popularized this method and was interested in looking forward to a progressive future when the final conflict between thesis and antithesis would result in synthesis. Marx famously 'turned Hegel on his head', which means that the starting point for Marxist analysis involves looking backward, and tracing the centuries-old conflict between the group that produces the means of material survival and the group that has appropriated that production (Chambliss and Mankoff, 1976; Reiman and Headlee, 1981). This methodology thus seeks to discover the total, fundamental and indispensable source of conflict, which is observed to be economic class relations. Such economic reductionism is thus at the centre of the Marxist tradition with the emergence of capitalism seen to be inherently contradictory and the point in history where the forces of production (equipment, technology) increases, while the relations of production (means of distributing produced goods) remained fixed (Marx, 1859).

For Marxists, social institutions embodied in the state – such as the criminal justice system – as well as ideas and ideologies – are only reflections of economic realities. Because the surplus population created by an increasingly efficient capitalism is seen as a threat to the capitalist mode of production, the economically powerful use the laws and state to protect their interests, while the converse is also true and economic powerlessness translates into political powerlessness. In response to the expropriation of their labour and the exploitation of their potential in commercialized relationships, criminals come to recognize their true objective interests and engage in proto-revolutionary action to bring about the end of capitalism and the guaranteed freedom from want and misery, which will be brought about by the establishment of a socialist society. Marxist scholars tend to be strongly committed to humanistic values (Kramer, 1985), keenly aware of the dangers of having ideas co-opted by other reformists (Platt, 1974), and thoroughly partisan inasmuch as their theorizing is intended to bring about the politicization of criminals who have not yet recognized their rightful place in history (Quinney, 1977). Treating criminals as proto-revolutionaries is sometimes called the primitive rebellion thesis, while Marx summed up this perspective thus:

The proletariat created by the breaking up of feudalism and the forcible expropriation of people from the soil could not possibly be absorbed by the newly-created capitalist manufacturers. At the same time, the proletariat could not suddenly adapt to the discipline of their new conditions, and so were turned into beggars, robbers, and vagabonds, partly from inclination, but in most cases from the stress of circumstances. Hence, by the end of the 16th century, the whole of Europe engaged in a bloody war against vagrancy, and legislation was created to treat them as criminals. It was also assumed that their criminal behaviour was voluntary and the result of free will, when in actuality it was because they could not adapt to the new economic conditions.

(Marx, 1867)

The conflict theorists – who are the focus of the earlier sections of Chapter 9 – had little conscious and explicit recourse to these traditions in sociology and preferred to concentrate on examining and commenting on the world around them, even though their explanations are often strongly resonant of this heritage. The one acknowledged influence is the work of the German sociologist Ralph Dahrendorf, whose work follows very much in the tradition established by Weber.

Dahrendorf (1959) proposes that there is conflict in society over the control of authority. Writing at a time when there were spectacular signs of disorder emerging in many economically developed countries in both Eastern and Western Europe, and in the USA, he accepted the inevitability of conflict but was confident that new accommodations could emerge to moderate and ameliorate the resulting disorder. Conflict in this formulation was seen positively as a motor for change, towards the development of more effective mechanisms and structures to integrate people and groups into society. While he was keen to distance himself from consensus thinkers who refused to accept the validity, and indeed utility, of conflict in society, Dahrendorf was at the same time critical of those 'utopian' Marxist modes of thought that promised an end to crime with the arrival of socialism (Dahrendorf, 1958).

Dahrendorf fundamentally held a pluralist view of society, which recognizes the many and varied interest groups in society and that these may conflict over who should hold authority. The challenge for the pluralist is to develop institutions that can best accommodate these varied interests. Dahrendorf fundamentally disagreed with Marxism on the question of inequality and located the source of inequity in the power and authority relationships within a society; he did not see these factors as necessarily linked to injustices in economic systems. Unlike Marx, who had argued for the abolition of inequality, Dahrendorf was of the view that, because cultural norms always exist and have to depend on sanctions if they are to be enforced, some people must have more power than others so as to make these sanctions work. Thus, it is not the economic inequality resulting from capitalism that produces social inequality, but it is an inescapable reality of any society where the basic units, the family or institutions such as the criminal justice system, necessarily involve dominance–subjection relationships.

Many of the founding principles of the USA have led to a deep-rooted aversion to socialist or Marxist forms of analysis and evidence of this can be found in the manner in which many European immigrants to the United States were screened for 'radical sympathies', most notably following the Bolshevik revolution in Russia in 1917. Subsequently, the post-Second World War 'witch hunt' for radical socialist and communist sympathizers in public life spearheaded by Senator Joseph McCarthy produced a climate hostile to theories based on class conflict.

By the late 1950s, there was nevertheless clear evidence of conflict in the USA, despite a high level of general; with the Black Civil Rights movement and a steadily rising crime rate were but two examples. In this context, a theoretical approach that offered a non-socialist or non-Marxist explanation for conflict appeared welcome to many American social theorists and criminologists. It was at the time that Dahrendorf was writing that George Vold presented his version of conflict theory, and, subsequently, Austin Turk developed the approach with direct reliance on the work of Dahrendorf. Richard Quinney was to follow. Their work is the focus of the earlier part of Chapter 9.

The later radical criminology tradition has its roots in an attempt to develop an understanding of crime in response to the rapidly changing and chaotic circumstances of the late 1960s and 1970s. Criticisms of Western societies as being overly concerned with wealth creation and material consumption were hardly new in the 1960s, but the decade saw evidence in the West that the apparent political consensus that had typified post-war politics was disintegrating. Concern began to emerge about the quality of life in societies that encourage the pursuit of material acquisition above the fulfilment of human need and satisfaction. The burgeoning student movement was at the forefront of this criticism, although many of its claims could be traced back to the concerns of social reformers and philosophers over the whole of recorded history. Alternative lifestyles were embraced and celebrated and these concerns were reflected in the arts and entertainment industries, making anti-materialism appear interesting and even fashionable.

It was a period characterized by anti-authoritarianism with its roots in an increasing recognition of the failings of the modern state in Western countries to cure human ills and address human needs. In countries such as the UK – and to a lesser extent the USA – there had been a dramatic post-war shift towards an acceptance of the role of the state in the provision of welfare services to ameliorate poverty, ill health, poor educational provision and other human wants. Undoubtedly, major improvements had been made, but none of these had fully met public expectations. In most cases, welfare benefits were distributed according to strict entitlement rules that attached conditions to the delivery of services. Many argued that benefits should be received as rights due to any citizen, rather than being conditional on obeying lifestyle rules. Hence, radical critics came to see the welfare states of many Western countries as being oppressive.

Many critics of the socio-political consensus came to search for broad political, economic and social theories to explain how Western societies had come to be as they were. Hence, there emerged a complex range of minority interest groups concerned with attempting to explain the circumstances in which social inequality came about. These groups began by mounting protests to push for the fulfilment of equal rights in society and gradually developed historical, political, social and economic theories to support their efforts to argue for change. The Black Civil

Rights movement in the USA developed and then fragmented into different wings, each holding differing views on the origins of and solutions to the problems that faced black people. The Northern Ireland Civil Rights movement similarly began with an assertion of equal rights for Catholic citizens in Northern Ireland, before different interpretations of the nature of the problems facing this group led to divisions based on differing views concerning the range of possible solutions.

The movement to secure equal rights for women also began to take on a new momentum in the late 1960s. More recently, we have seen further issues being raised and fragmentation caused by varying interpretations of the problems within the peace movement, animal rights, the environmental movement and an increasing array of interest groups.

9. Labelling theories

Key Issues

1. The social construction of crime
2. The recipients of deviant labels
3. The consequences of labelling for the recipients
4. Moral panics and deviance amplification
5. Recent developments in labelling theories

Labelling theories have their foundations in the various concepts and insights provided by interactionism, phenomenology and ethnomethodology – which we encountered above – and focus on three central concerns. First, there is a consideration of why and how it is that some acts come to be defined as deviant or criminal while others do not. Thus, to this end, there is an examination of legal codes and practices, and the social and professional interest groups that shape the criminal law. Second, it is recognized that certain people and groups are more likely to attract deviant, criminal and stigmatizing labels than others. There is thus an examination of the differential applications of laws and labels by the various social control agencies and the relationship of this to organizational context. Unfortunately, these early, well-known and highly influential labelling theorists – with the limited exception of Becker (1963), Kitsuse (1962), Piliavin and Briar (1964) and Cicourel (1968) – did not address these concerns as thoroughly as they might have done, although they contributed significantly to the development of the radical criminology discussed in the following chapter, while the later far less well-known and significantly less influential labelling theorists such as Hartjen (1974), Ditton (1979) and Arvanites (1992) focus very much on the issue of state power. Most of the energy of the most active phase of the highly influential earlier labelling theory was nevertheless directed towards the third concern that assesses the experience of being labelled for the recipients of the label. We will consider each of these concerns in turn.

The social construction of crime

Before labelling theories achieved prominence, most criminologists had a non-problematic conception of crime. Criminal behaviour was simply a form of activity that violates the criminal law. Once crime was thus defined, theorists – working in the predestined actor model tradition – could concentrate on their main concern of identifying and analysing its causes. This whole approach was nevertheless far too simplistic for proponents of the labelling perspective who argued that what is defined as 'criminal' is not fixed but varies across time, culture and even from one situation to the next. From this perspective, the conventional morality of rules and criminal laws in any given society should be studied and questioned and not merely accepted as self-evident.

Labelling theorists fundamentally argue that no behaviour is *inherently* deviant or criminal, but only comes to be considered so when others confer this label upon the act. Thus, it is not the intrinsic nature of an act but the nature of the societal reaction that determines whether a 'crime' has taken place. Even the most commonly recognized and serious crime of murder is not universally defined in the sense that anyone who kills another is everywhere and always guilty of murder. The essence of this position is neatly summarized in a well-known passage by Becker who, unlike most other labelling theorists, was concerned with the creators and enforcers of criminal labels and categories:

> Social groups create deviance by making the rules whose infraction constitutes deviance, and by applying those rules to particular people and labelling them as outsiders. From this point of view . . . the deviant is one to whom the label has been successfully applied; deviant behaviour is behaviour that people so label.
>
> (1963: 4)

Becker argued that rules – including criminal laws – are made by people with power and enforced upon people without power. Thus, even on an everyday level, rules are made by the old for the young, by men for women, by whites for blacks, by the middle class for the working class and, we might add here, by schools for their students and parents for their children, an observation to which we return later in this chapter. These rules are often imposed upon the recipients against their will and their own best interests, and are legitimized by an ideology that is transmitted to the less powerful in the course of primary and secondary socialization. As a result of this process, most people internalize and obey the rules without realizing – or questioning – the extent to which their behaviour is being decided for them.

Becker also argues that some rules may be cynically designed to keep the less powerful in their place, while others may have simply been introduced as the outcome of a sincere – albeit irrational and mistaken – belief on the part of high-status individuals that the creation of a new rule will be beneficial for its intended subjects. Becker termed the people who create new rules for the 'benefit' of the less fortunate 'moral entrepreneurs'.

Becker noted two closely interrelated outcomes of a successful 'moral crusade': first, there is the creation of a new group of 'outsiders', those who infringe the new rule; second, a social control agency emerges charged with enforcing the rule and with the power to impose labels on transgressors, although more often this simply means an extension of police work and power. Eventually, the new rule, control agency and 'deviant' social role come to permeate the collective consciousness and are taken for granted with the outcome being the creation of negative stereotypes of those labelled 'deviant'.

Becker (1963) cites the campaign by the US Federal Bureau of Narcotics (FBN) to outlaw marijuana use through the Marijuana Tax Act of 1937, which was justified on the grounds of protecting society – particularly young people – from the ill effects of this drug and relied heavily on propaganda of one sort or another to get its message across. In Becker's view, the campaign was undertaken primarily as a means of advancing the organizational interests of the FBN. Moreover, the successful conclusion of the campaign led to 'the creation of a new fragment of the moral constitution of society, its code of right and wrong' (Becker, 1963: 145).

Other studies have looked at the process whereby previously 'acceptable' forms of behaviour have been brought within the remit of the criminal law. Platt (1969) showed how contemporary approaches to 'juvenile delinquency' – indeed, even the very concept itself – were the outcome of a nineteenth-century moral crusade undertaken by largely upper-class women. This successful campaign established juveniles as a separate category of offender with their own courts, which, in turn, enabled the scope of the powers of intervention enjoyed by the state to be extended beyond mere breaches of the criminal law to cover 'status offences' such as truancy and promiscuity.

Tierney's (1982) analysis of domestic violence also provides evidence of the process of criminalization. She argues that 'wife battering' only emerged as an important social issue worthy of criminal justice intervention after the mid-1970s, mainly because of the increasing strength of the women's movement and the determination to secure the provision of refuges, legislation and other measures aimed at protecting women.

In short, what these and similar studies show is not the inherent harm of behaviour or its extensiveness that prompts changes in the law, but rather the concerted efforts of sufficiently motivated and powerful social groups to redefine the boundaries of what is considered acceptable and legal.

Others have adopted a macro perspective in order to explain these processes. Thus, Erikson (1962) draws upon Durkheim in arguing that all social systems place certain boundaries on culturally permissible behaviour and deviancy is simply that which is defined as crossing these parameters. Indeed, deviant behaviour may be the only way of *marking* these boundaries. Thus, transactions between deviants and social control agents are 'boundary maintenance mechanisms', which attract a good deal of publicity, and by acting outside of these system boundaries deviants demonstrate to society where the perimeters lie, while, at the same time, giving those inside a sense of identity or 'belongingness'. These processes in turn help to preserve social stability. Thus, in viewing deviance as essentially 'boundary maintenance activity', the work of Erikson marks a point of convergence between the labelling perspective and the functionalism of Durkheim.

Quinney (1970) also employed a macro sociological perspective but one that combined labelling theory with conflict theory, differential association and deviant subculture theories. He was also influenced by Durkheim's notion of mechanical and organic solidarity in proposing two ideal types of society (or social organization): *singular* and *segmental*. According to Quinney, in a singular or homogeneous society, all crime must necessarily occur outside any value system, since by definition all members of the society adhere to this value system. In a segmental or heterogeneous society, some segments will share common values with others, but, because there is unlikely to be a complete consensus, value systems will be in conflict to a certain extent. Thus, the criminal laws and their enforcement are a product of this conflict and the associated unequal distribution of political power.

Quinney argues that society is segmentally organized or pluralistic and, therefore, the criminal law tends to represent the values of politically powerful sections of society. Moreover, he suggests a direct relation between the possibility of someone being labelled as criminal and their relative position in the social structure.

The recipients of deviant labels

It is conventional wisdom that those who break the law will be labelled as criminal. Becker (1963) nevertheless exposed the inadequacy of this perception, noting that the innocent are sometimes falsely accused, and, more importantly, only some of those who violate the criminal law are eventually arrested and processed through the system. Kitsuse (1962) found – in a study of homosexuality that has much wider criminological ramifications – that it is not the behaviour *per se* that is the central issue. It is the interactional process through which behaviour is both defined as deviant and through which sanctions are initiated. Thus, distinguishing deviants from non-deviants is not primarily a matter of behaviour but is contingent upon 'circumstance or situation, social and personal biography, and the bureaucratically organised activities of social control' (Kitsuse, 1962: 256).

A number of important studies conducted in the USA confirmed that the actual behaviour is not the only factor in determining whether a deviant or criminal label is conferred. Official responses are shaped by a range of extra-legal variables, such as appearance, demeanour, ethnic group and age; for example, Piliavin and Briar (1964) looked at police encounters with juveniles and found that arrest decisions were based largely on physical cues – manner, dress and general appearance – from which the officer inferred the character of the youth. *Structural* factors, such as gender, social class, ethnic group and time of day, were also significant, thus a young, working-class, black male in a 'high delinquency area' at night was seen to have a very high chance of being at least stopped and questioned, if not arrested. The young man is quite simply *assumed* to be delinquent unless he can prove otherwise (Piliavin and Briar, 1964: 206). More recent studies undertaken in the UK have also shown that some police officers show class and/or race bias in the performance of their duties (see, for example, Smith and Gray, 1986; Institute of Race Relations, 1987).

Cicourel (1968) found that, in the course of their interactions with juveniles, the 'background expectations' of the police – that is, their commonsensical theories as to the typical delinquent – led them to concentrate on certain 'types' of individuals. A further factor in determining how that encounter developed was found to be dependent on how the individual officer defined his or her own role. Those who defined their role in terms of a 'due process' model that emphasizes the rights of the defendant attempted to follow the *letter* of the law and, therefore, tended to react only to specific, concrete evidence of the commission of a crime. In contrast, when officers perceived their role primarily in terms of a 'crime control' model that considers the control of crime to be of primary importance, they were more concerned with the *spirit* of the law. Thus, they were more likely to respond on the basis of their subjective definition of a situation and the personalities involved.

Cicourel found this process to be essentially class-biased, as it was generally working-class areas and their inhabitants that most closely mirrored the typifications and expectations of the police. Moreover, other criminal justice practitioners, such as probation officers, social workers and court officials, and the organizational context within which they work reinforced such practices. Cicourel found probation officers and social workers subscribed to a theory of delinquency causation that focused on factors such as 'broken homes', 'permissive parenting' or 'poverty'. Thus, juveniles with this sort of background were seen as the likeliest candidates for a delinquent career and were often, albeit unwittingly, launched upon one. These findings had serious implications for the validity of crime statistics.

Many criminologists from quite different perspectives had previously acknowledged that official statistics were not a wholly accurate reflection of the reality of crime, for example, there was much concern over the hidden figure of unrecorded crime. Official statistics had been widely viewed as reasonably objective and thus providing a reliable basis for discerning patterns in crime and suggesting associations. From a labelling perspective, official statistics were seen to be just another interpretation of the world and their only utility lay in the light they inadvertently shed on the agencies of social control that 'constructed' them. Quinney (1970) suggested four societal structures – age, gender, class and ethnic group – that would enhance the likelihood of someone receiving a criminal label and, thus, there is a high probability that a young, black, working-class male will be defined as deviant. Moreover, the reality that this group is over-represented in the official crime statistics is not surprising, since these figures are produced by agencies whose personnel, operating criteria and rationale are drawn from the more politically powerful segments of society. What Quinney was essentially arguing is that some people have the facilities for applying stigmatizing labels to other people, ostensibly because these other people violate norms the labellers wish to uphold. This is only possible because these others are identified as members of society with little or no political power.

The consequences of labelling for the recipients

It was noted earlier that labelling theories have for the most part concentrated on their third area of concern, which is assessing the consequences of the labelling process for the future conduct of the recipient and this aspect is certainly the most widely discussed and best documented. Frank Tannenbaum (1938) – who is usually regarded as the founder of the labelling perspective – noted that of the many young males who break the law only some are apprehended. His 'dramatization of evil' hypothesis described the process whereby a community first defines the actions of an individual as evil, but eventually goes on to define the individual himself as evil, thus casting suspicion on all his future actions. The evil is further 'dramatized' by separating the individual from his usual group and administering specialized treatment to 'punish' or 'cure' the evil. This leads to further isolation and the confirmation and internalization of his new 'tag'. Eventually, he will redefine his self-image in line with the opinions and expectations of others in the community and thereby come to perceive himself as criminal. This idea that, in reacting to people as 'criminal', society actually encourages them to become so, and that criminal justice intervention can deepen criminality, is the central contention of the labelling approach.

Edwin Lemert (1951) made a crucial distinction between *primary* and *secondary* deviance. The former – with affiliations to the predestined actor model – could arise out of a variety of sociocultural, psychological or even physiological factors. However, because these initial acts are often extremely tentative and certainly not part of an organized way of life, offenders can easily rationalize them as a temporary aberration or see it as part of a socially acceptable role, for example, a worker may observe that everyone pilfers a little from work. Thus, such behaviour will be of only marginal significance in terms of the status and self-concept of the individual concerned. In short, primary deviants do not view their deviance as central to themselves and do not consider themselves to be deviant.

If, however, these initial activities are subject to societal reaction – and with each act of primary deviance the offender becomes progressively more stigmatized through 'name calling, labelling or stereotyping' – then a crisis may occur. One way of resolving this crisis is for the individual to accept their deviant status and organize their life and identity around the facts of deviance, and it is at this stage that the person becomes a 'secondary deviant'. In short, it is proposed that a youth who steals something and is not caught may be less likely to persist in this behaviour than one that is apprehended and officially sanctioned. Deviance is simply the end result of a process of human interaction. Primary deviance may or may not develop into secondary deviance. It is the number of criminal transgressions and the intensity and hostility of societal reaction that determines the outcome.

It was with the influential work of Becker (1963), Erikson (1966) and Kitsuse (1962) – and their use of Merton's concept of the 'self-fulfilling prophecy': a false definition of a situation, evoking a new behaviour that makes the original false assumption come true – that the labelling perspective was to gain widespread popularity. These writers argued that most offenders are falsely defined as criminal. That is not to say that they are innocent in the sense of having not committed offences, but rather that the system, and thus society, not only judges their actions as criminal and 'bad', but extends this judgement to them as people. The consequences are that, once someone has been deemed by society to be 'bad', there is an expectation that this 'badness' must again find expression in some way or another, leading to the commission of further offences. Armed with these stereotypes of offenders as wholly criminal and incapable of law-abiding behaviour, the general population reacts to them on this basis and treats them accordingly. Consequently, offenders may face discrimination in employment, often even where their offence bears no relation to the type of work being sought. Moreover, a person's previous social status, such as parent, spouse or worker, is hidden under the criminal label until that becomes their 'master status' or controlling public identification.

In summary, labelling theorists claim that the false definition of offenders as uncompromisingly criminal fulfils this very prophecy by evoking hostile and negative societal reactions that render conformity difficult, and criminality attractive. Thus, the processes and means of social control that are intended to induce law-abiding behaviour can have the ironic and unintended consequence of achieving the very opposite. It would be meaningless to suggest that, in general, labelling theorists view the processes outlined above as in any way deterministic or unavoidable. It is quite possible that some offenders may react to being labelled and stigmatized by refraining from the type of conduct that elicited such a reaction, but as Downes and Rock pertinently observe:

> Interactionism casts deviance as a process which may continue over a lifetime, which has no necessary end, which is anything but inexorable, and which may be built around false starts, diversions and returns. The trajectory of a deviant career cannot always be predicted. However constrained they may seem to be, people can choose not to err further.
>
> (1998: 183)

The key point from a labelling perspective is that many offenders do internalize their criminal labels and, thus, stable or career criminality arises out of the reaction of society to them.

Moral panics and deviance amplification

The labelling perspective has also been applied at the group level and a useful analytical tool in this context is that of the deviancy amplification feedback or spiral (Wilkins, 1964), where it is argued that the less tolerance there is to an initial act of deviance, the more similar acts will be defined as deviant. This process will give rise to more reactions against offenders, resulting in more social *alienation* or *marginalization* of deviants. This state of affairs will generate more crime by deviant groups, leading to decreasing tolerance of deviants by conforming groups.

Deviancy amplification feedback is central to the phenomenon known as the 'moral panic', which Jock Young (1971) first used in his study of recreational drug users in north London and which was later developed by Stanley Cohen (1973) in his study of the societal reaction to the 'mods and rockers' disturbances of 1964. These studies marked a significant break with those approaches to delinquency – favoured by proponents of the predestined actor model – that were primarily concerned with finding the causes of delinquent behaviour. By contrast, definitional and structural questions relating to why certain groups define certain acts as deviant, and the consequences of this process, were asked.

Cohen (1973) found the press to be guilty of exaggeration and distortion in their reporting of the events in Clacton over the Easter bank holiday weekend in 1964. The sense of outrage communicated by such misrepresentation had set in motion a series of interrelated responses. First, there was increased public concern about the issue, to which the police responded by increasing their surveillance of the groups in question – mods and rockers. This resulted in more frequent arrests, which, in turn, appeared to confirm the validity of the original media reaction. Second, by emphasizing the stylistic differences and antagonisms between the groups, the press reaction encouraged polarization and further clashes between the groups.

Various moral entrepreneurs call for action to be taken against the groups involved in the outbreaks of lawlessness and usually pronounce that current controls are inadequate. Cohen (1973) shows that these entrepreneurs exaggerate the problem in order to make local events seem ones of pressing national concern and an index of the decline of morality and social standards. The extension of control leads to further marginalization and stigmatization of deviants, which, in turn, leads to more demands for police action and so on into a deviancy amplification spiral. Cohen located the nature and extent of reaction to the mods and rockers in the social context of Britain during the 1960s. In particular, ambivalence about social change in the post-war period, the new affluence and freedom of young people and their apparent rejection of traditional social norms such as employment and the family are used as a context for the panic.

The concept of moral panic is also central to Hall et al.'s (1978) study of 'mugging', although the concept is used within a very different theoretical framework. While conceding that there can be no deviance without an agency of condemnation and control, it is argued that the notion of moral panic is limited if employed without reference to the social and political structures that empower a dominant minority to construct and implement the process of labelling. Within labelling theories, moral panic is thus expressed in terms of a 'society' that creates rules and, within the Marxism that informs Hall et al.'s approach, it is expressed in terms of a 'state' that has the power to criminalize (Cohen, 1985: 272). Given its theoretical basis, this analysis falls more within the scope of the radical theories discussed in the following chapter.

Goode and Ben-Yehuda (1994) have more recently challenged the assumption of earlier theorists that moral panics are in some way engineered at the behest – and in the interests – of dominant elites and distinguish three different models. First, there is the grass-roots model where a panic has its origins within the general public and which expresses a genuinely felt – albeit objectively mistaken – concern about a perceived threat. Second, the elite-engineered model is where dominant groups deliberately and consciously generate concerns and fears that resonate with their wider political interests. Third, the interest-group model is where rule creators and moral entrepreneurs launch crusades that coincide neatly with their own professional concerns and interests. Goode and Ben-Yehuda (1994) identify the following five characteristics of a moral panic: (i) a disproportionate reaction; (ii) concern about the threat; (iii) hostility to the objects of the panic; (iv) widespread agreement or consensus that the threat is real; and (v) the unpredictability – or volatility – of moral panics in terms of scale and intensity.

Others have criticized the whole notion of moral panics as a conceptualization of social reaction. Left realists – the subject of Chapter 18 – maintain that crime and the fear of crime should be taken seriously and not dismissed as just an expression of media over-reaction or panic. For example, Waddington (1986) criticized the empirical basis of Hall *et al.*'s (1978) influential study of street robberies, arguing that incidents of 'mugging' were increasing at the time and therefore asked what a proportionate response to the problem should have involved. Others have identified problems with the use of the concept of moral panic to capture reaction to diverse themes or issues. For example, Watney (1987) has questioned the use of the concept to characterize media and policy reactions to HIV/Aids. McRobbie and Thornton (1995) argue that the whole idea of a moral panic needs to be reconsidered in an environment where there may be an institutionalized need for the media to generate 'good stories' and that these can easily become part of a promotional culture that 'ironically' uses sensationalism for commercial purposes.

Criticisms of labelling theories

As the labelling approach became more influential during the 1960s and early 1970s, it attracted criticism from a variety of sources. Plummer (1979) noted that, because the perspective is so loosely defined, it could harbour several diverse theoretical positions and therefore leave itself open to internal contradiction and criticism from all theoretical sides. Such ambiguity and eclecticism thus led some critics to claim that labelling is at best a vague perspective that does not contain consistent and interrelated concepts and that fails to make precise distinctions between mere description and causal statements (Taylor *et al.*, 1973). On the other hand, proponents of labelling theory such as Schur (1971) contend that the strength of the approach lies in its ability to analyse aspects of social reality that have been neglected, offer directions for research and thus complement other theoretical approaches.

Others argue that labelling theories fail to clearly define deviance. According to Gibbs (1966), labelling theorists claim that an act is deviant only if a certain reaction follows, yet at the same time refer to 'secret deviants' and 'primary deviants', and suggest that certain groups of people are licensed to engage in deviant behaviour without negative reactions. This implies, it is argued, that deviance can be identified not merely in terms of societal reactions to it but in terms of *existing social norms*. There may be ambiguity about certain kinds of 'soft' deviance – where criminal definitions are relative to time and place – but there can be no such ambiguity regarding 'hard' deviance, such as violent assault, robbery and burglary, which have always been universally condemned. 'Hard' deviants at least are fully aware that what they are doing is deviant or criminal but freely choose this course of action because it is profitable or exciting. Labelling is therefore an irrelevance.

Taylor *et al*. (1973) accept the notion that deviance is not simply an inherent property of an act but they do not agree that it is as arbitrary as labelling theorists imply. They take the view that the deviant is not a passive actor but a decision-maker whose rule-breaking reflects initial motives and choices, and thus has meaning. This approach overlaps with a further criticism that observes the emphasis to be on the negative repercussions of labelling, which implies an individual totally at the mercy of official labellers. A consequence of this overemphasis on societal reaction at the expense of individual choice has been the tendency to elevate the offender to the status of victim. Labelling theories have 'the paradoxical consequence of inviting us to view the deviant as a passive nonentity who is responsible neither for his suffering nor its alleviation – who is more "sinned" against than sinning' (Gouldner, 1968: 108). Yet, as previously noted, labelling theories do not on the whole argue that the effects of labelling are determinant, but rather that negative societal reaction can, and in many cases will, deepen criminality. Thus, as Downes and Rock quite correctly observe, 'criticisms of the species offered by Gouldner really reflect a response to only the most narrow versions of interactionism' (1998: 190). As for the charge that labelling theorists take the side of the deviant and overlook the 'real' victims of crime, some, most notably Becker (1967), make no apologies for this and argue that they are merely balancing out traditional approaches within criminology that are severely biased *against* the deviant.

Many of the criticisms of labelling theories would seem more justified had the approach been promoted as a developed theory rather than as a perspective comprising loosely connected themes. In the light of this, perhaps the most telling criticism of the perspective is that, though it focused on societal reaction, it stopped short of offering a systematic analysis of social structure and power relations. While acknowledging that political interest and social disadvantage influenced societal reaction, labelling theorists failed to make explicit the connection of the criminal justice system to the underlying capitalist economic order and the inequalities of wealth and power rooted therein. Some of these issues are addressed by later more recent labelling theorists and by the radical theorists we will encounter in the following chapter.

Labelling theories revisited

In more recent years, the notions and concepts of labelling theories have been modified and developed. First, more recent attention has been devoted to the significant issue of *informal* labelling, such as that carried out by parents, peers and teachers, which, it is argued, has a greater effect on subsequent criminal behaviour than official labelling. Ross Matsueda (1992) and Heimer and Matsueda (1994) discuss the reasons why individuals may be informally labelled as delinquents and note that such labels are not simply an outcome of interaction with the criminal justice system – for example, arrest – but are crucially influenced by the individual's offending behaviour *and* their position in society. Powerless individuals such as urban, ethnic-minority, lower-class adolescents are far more likely to be negatively labelled by parents and peers than more affluent middle-class young people. Matsueda (1992) also argues that informal labels affect the subsequent level of crime committed by individuals because these help shape their perceptions of how others see them. Thus, if they believe that others see them as delinquents and troublemakers, they are more likely to act in accordance with this perception and engage in offending behaviour.

Some have observed that a shift seems to have occurred around 1974, in which labelling theorists came to retreat from their underdog focus, moving away from the study of 'nuts, sluts, and perverts' (Liazos, 1972), and came to accommodate legalistic definitions and focus on state power. Thus, modern labelling theorists came to recognize that societies socially construct and create crime by passing legislation, and, therefore, the substantive nature of the law is a legitimate object of study. These are sometimes referred to as criminalization theories (Hartjen, 1974), and, while they have some resemblance to societal reaction – or labelling perspectives – they are more closely linked to a field of study that some call the sociology of law perspective or the study of law as a mechanism of social control. Labelling theories that focus on state power can be considered as branches of controlology (Ditton, 1979), which refers to a group of theories with some interest in crime waves and moral panics but mostly taking the view that criminal justice agencies are part of broader social control mechanisms, like welfare, mental health, education, the military and the mass media, all of which are used by the state to control 'problem' populations (Arvanites, 1992). Controlology has its theoretical foundations in the work of Foucault (1971, 1977), who argued that various instruments of social control (more humane, enlightened, reasonable responses to deviance) are packaged and sold by the state to cover up the inherent coercion and power in the system. The state is thus always trying to portray a 'velvet glove', where its ultimate goal is to exercise its 'iron fist' to control troublesome populations, in other words, the pervasive 'hard' and 'soft' 'policing' strategies that constitute the 'disciplinary-control-matrix' of the surveillance society (Hopkins Burke, 2004b, 2008, 2012, 2013) and which is discussed in more detail in the third part of this book.

Link (1987), Link *et al.* (1987) and Link *et al.* (1989) have used labelling theory to understand how we view and respond to the mentally ill, and observe that in the USA public attitudes have been conditioned so that such people are perceived in negative and devalued ways with the outcome being that many who need psychiatric help (and those who care for them) will either try to hide this reality from family friends, colleagues and their employers, or will withdraw from groups or people who they think might reject them.

Some have suggested that the criminal justice system and the public are increasing the stigmatization of (particularly young) offenders and thus heightening the most negative effects of labelling. De Haan (2000) observes that levels of violence in society appear to be rising – even in the Netherlands where previously there had been reasonable tolerance of such behaviour – and explains this occurrence as a process of re-labelling previously non-problematic actions as more serious. Indeed, it seems that there is an increasingly universal intolerance of violence and such behaviour is being dealt with much more harshly. Triplett (2000) claims that an increase in violent offences in the USA during the 1980s and 1990s had been accompanied by changes in the criminal justice system moving less serious offences – particularly status offences such as truancy – up the sentencing tariff, and by a change in the way in which (especially young) violent offenders come to be seen as evil. She observes that these judgements have been subsequently attached to all young offenders who have subsequently become isolated and excluded from mainstream society. Meossi (2000) argues that this demonizing of offenders – observed both in Italy and the USA – tends to correlate closely with periodic economic downturns, and Halpern (2001) asserts that the subsequent rise in crime levels leads to harsher treatment of offenders, thus devaluing people through labelling, which can itself lead to further acceleration in offending behaviour.

While many studies have been conducted to apply labelling theory to various types of deviance, Kenney (2002) considers it in relationship to the victims of crime and found that sympathy offered to a victim may be received as condescension and may result in a feeling of a loss of power. The victim may lose self-esteem as a result of this loss of power and, if he or she seeks help from friends and loved ones, they may fear feeling or being viewed as incompetent. Once the individual has been labelled as a 'victim', they may well find that work colleagues, friends and even family begin to avoid them due to feelings of guilt or not knowing how to react, which can lead to further isolation of the victim. Many victims do not receive the support they seek from loved ones and may wonder if their feelings are normal. Similarly, Li and Moore (2001) concluded from their study of the relationship between disability and illicit drug use that discrimination against persons with disabilities leads to higher rates of illegal drug use by these people.

Others have utilized the concept of labelling in a more positive mode. Braithwaite (1989) thus introduces the concept of 'reintegrative shaming', where it is proposed that offenders should be shamed not in order to stigmatize them but to make them realize the negative impact of their actions on both individual victims and the wider community and then encourage others to forgive them and accept them back into society. Reintegrative shaming is an influential concept that underpins reparation and restorative justice programmes and has been widely introduced – in particular with young offenders – in New Zealand (see Morris *et al.*, 1993), Australia (see Strang, 1993; Forsythe, 1994; Hudson *et al.*, 1996), parts of the USA (see Alford, 1997) and Britain (see Dignan, 1999; Young and Goold, 1999; Maxwell and Morris, 2001). The concept is discussed in more detail in the following chapter and Chapter 15. Some have suggested that such a policy would only work in rural communities with strong community bonds, but Braithwaite (1993) considers that it could be even more effective in cities, which are invariably constituted of many closely knit micro mechanical solidarities or communities (see Hopkins Burke and Pollock, 2004). Moreover, Braithwaite (1993) and Simpson *et al.* (2000) consider reintegrative shaming to be an appropriate response to some white-collar and corporate violations of the law and propose that its application would be a considerable advance on a long-established tradition of ignoring such cases.

Policy implications of labelling theories

The most significant policy implications of labelling theories is in the criminal justice response to early career offending, in particular by children and juveniles. Myers (2003) has observed that moves towards the sentencing of juveniles in adult courts in the spirit of 'getting tough on crime' or 'holding kids accountable' may simply exacerbate the problem of recidivism among individual offenders. Strong, automatic labelling that results in social rejection is an extreme response on the part of policy-makers (Okimoto and Wenzel, 2009; Scheff, 2010) and one that is largely unsupported as an effective method of crime control (Myers, 2003). Adolescents who are in the process of developing their identities may, in particular, be strongly affected by stigmatization and, because they are just beginning to develop their stakes in conformity, the presentation of serious social obstacles, such as difficulty finding employment, ineligibility for student loans and exclusion from conventional social networks, may affect their life-course orientation.

Rather than discourage participation in conventional activities by labelling and isolating offenders, juvenile crime policy should be remedial and foster reintegration following shame (Braithwaite, 1989; Okimoto and Wenzel, 2009). This may happen through academic mentoring, career advising or providing alternative activities. Again, if the evidence suggests that a deviant self-concept and weakened stakes in conformity contribute to further delinquent behaviour, juvenile criminal policy should be structured to weaken the influence of these variables.

Summary of main points

1. Labelling theorists argue that no behaviour is inherently deviant or criminal, but only comes to be considered so when others confer this label upon the act.
2. Becker (1963) argues that rules and laws are made by 'moral entrepreneurs', people with power, and enforced upon people without power.
3. Becker notes two closely interrelated outcomes of a successful 'moral crusade': (i) there is the creation of a new group of 'outsiders' who infringe the new rule; and (ii) there is a social control agency charged with enforcing the rule.
4. Platt (1969) showed how contemporary approaches to 'juvenile delinquency' were the outcome of a nineteenth-century moral crusade undertaken by largely upper-class women.

5. Tierney (1982) argues that 'wife battering' only emerged as an important social issue worthy of criminal justice intervention after the mid-1970s, mainly because of the increasing strength of the women's movement.
6. Erikson (1962) argues that all social systems place certain boundaries on culturally permissible behaviour and deviancy is simply that which is defined as crossing these parameters.
7. Quinney argues that society is segmentally organized and the criminal law tends to reflect the values of politically powerful sections of society.
8. The labelling perspective has also been applied at the group level and a useful analytical tool is that of the deviancy amplification feedback or spiral (Wilkins, 1964), which is central to the phenomenon known as the 'moral panic'.
9. Goode and Ben-Yehuda (1994) challenge the assumption of earlier theorists that moral panics are in some way engineered at the behest of dominant elites.
10. In more recent years, the notions and concepts of labelling theories have been modified and developed with much attention devoted to the issue of informal labelling carried out by parents, peers and teachers.

Discussion questions

1. What are 'moral entrepreneurs' and what significant role do they play in the labelling process?
2. How does Lemert differentiate between 'primary' and 'secondary' deviance?
3. What is a 'moral panic' and who are 'folk devils'?
4. Explain the process of 'informal' labelling. What is its importance?
5. Discuss whether labelling theories have any relevance in the twenty-first century.

Suggested further reading

Becker (1963) still provides an essential introduction to the labelling tradition in criminology, with Erikson (1966), Kitsuse (1962) and Lemert (1972) being other key texts. Quinney (1970) provides an early link with conflict theory. Cohen (1973) is a milestone text on 'moral panics' with the concept importantly developed from a radical/critical perspective by Hall *et al.* (1978) and revised substantially by Goode and Ben-Yehuda (1994).

10. Conflict and radical theories

Key Issues

1. Socio-economic conflict and society
2. Conflict theories
3. Radical theories
4. Peacemaking criminology
5. Criticisms of the radical tradition

Conflict and radical theories sought to explain crime and criminal behaviour in terms of the unequal nature of the socio-political structure of society. Again, this is not a homogenous theory but a diverse collection of perspectives united by a common tendency to see societies as being characterized by conflict rather than consensus. Two broad categories or groupings can be identified. First, conflict theorists take a *pluralist* stance and propose that society consists of numerous groups all involved in a struggle to promote their socio-economic interests. Second, *radical* accounts are invariably informed by various interpretations of Marxist social and economic theory. Notwithstanding these differences, writers in both camps see social consensus as a temporary situation engineered by those with substantial power in society and the main concern for both groups of writers is with the social struggle for power and authority.

Among the critics of the labelling perspective were those who argued that it had just not gone far enough and failed to account for the origins of the differential power to label or stigmatize people. It was thus in response to that critique that conflict and radical writers came to explore and apply wider ideas from economic and political science to the consideration of crime and criminal behaviour.

Conflict theories

Thorsten Sellin (1938) was influenced by the work of Georg Simmel and was the first to argue that conflict causes crime. He proposed with his *culture conflict theory* that each culture establishes its own norms – or rules of behaviour – which are then embedded into its members through the various processes of socialization they undergo. Thus, the norms learned by any individual are prescribed by the host culture to which they belong. In a healthy homogenous society, these norms are enacted into laws and upheld by the members of that society because they are accepted as representing the consensual viewpoint, but where homogeneity and consensus does not exist the outcome will be conflict. Sellin argues that conflicts over *conduct norms* can occur at both the micro and macro level in society.

At the macro level, conflicts occur between two different societal cultures and can arise because of border conflicts, territorial extension or, most typically, through migration. Secondary conflicts at the micro level occur within the macro culture, particularly when subcultures with their own conduct norms develop within the host culture. In the latter case, the laws usually represent the rules or norms of the dominant culture and, indeed, the norms – and rules of behaviour – of other groups can be in conflict with the law. Thus, society contains certain unwritten, and often unspoken, rules about what a person is supposed to do in certain circumstances, for example, if a man finds his wife in bed with another man. Thus, while some more pre-modern or traditional societies might specify exactly what a man is supposed to do in this case – kill both his cheating wife and the other man – more modern societies offer less in the way of guidance and, for Sellin, this ambiguous state of confusion and contradiction is what leads to crime. This clearly has implications in contemporary multicultural societies where different cultures may clash on how such situations should be dealt with. We should note however that – unlike the deviant subcultural tradition epitomized by Cohen (1955) or Cloward and Ohlin (1960) and discussed in Chapter 7 – the norms of the subcultures in this conceptualization do not develop in order to question or challenge dominant societal values or, for that matter, represent a different means of achieving the cultural goals of the middle or upper classes, they represent fundamentally different values and norms.

Lewis Coser (1956) was a functionalist sociologist with significantly left-wing political leanings who was also clearly influenced by the work of Simmel. Coser presents several propositions surrounding what he considers to be the key issue of the intensity of conflict. Thus, conflict is seen to actually increase when attempts are made to suppress it, when fighting takes place on behalf of a group, and when conflicting parties are in close proximity. Coser observes that closeness creates intensity because that is when love and hate occur alongside each other. Other propositions have to do with the construction of social forms, like stability and rigidity, which are drawn from comparing the membership of groups that are formed by crosscutting other group memberships. Non-realistic conflict is perceived to have safety-valve functions and Coser observes that the necessity for hierarchy has emerged from a need to manage group size and complexity. He also produces an image of an ever-present and always-emerging offender, and this is also clearly consistent with the ideas of Simmel, although Coser follows a more 'crime is functional for the needs of society' approach than his predecessor.

George Vold (1958) developed the above ideas and produced an explanation of crime and criminal behaviour that emphasized the group nature of society and stressed the fact that groups compete with each other in order to secure what they identify as their interests. He argued that groups become ever more wary and watchful of their interests vis-à-vis other groups and become engaged in a continuous struggle to improve their standing in relation to others. The whole process of law-making, law-breaking and law enforcement directly reflects deep-seated and fundamental conflicts between these group interests and the more general struggle between groups for control of the police power of the state. Since minority groups lack the power to strongly influence the legislative process, their behaviour is that most often defined as criminal, or deviant. This process of criminalization then legitimizes the use of the police and other control agencies to enforce these laws on behalf of the most powerful groups in society.

For Austin Turk, the theoretical problem of explaining crime lies not in understanding the different varieties of criminal behaviour – for he observes that definitions of what is criminal will vary over time and place – but in explaining the actual process of criminalization. Specifically, this involves examining the process of the assignment of criminal status to individuals, which results in the production of criminality. There is an obvious resonance here with labelling theory but Turk was to go much further than those working in that tradition and sought to explain why it is that labels come to be widely accepted as legitimate, often by those who are so labelled.

Turk fundamentally saw the social order as the outcome of powerful social groups who successfully control society in their own interests. He argued that social control is exercised by providing a normative – moral or value-laden – justification for law, which is then enforced by controlling agencies such as the police. In his earlier work, Turk (1969) suggested that those people who have an unclear view of how their behaviour will impact on others, especially on the powerful, and who go on to break rules, norms or laws will be the most likely to be caught and processed by control agencies. It is an argument that explains why it is that young people are more likely to fall foul of the law than most adults.

In his later work, Turk (1969) described two ways in which control is exercised in society: first, by *coercion* and second, by the *control of legal images* and *living time*. The control of society by *coercion* – or the threat and exercise of physical force – is perhaps the most obvious form of control, but the more that force is applied, the less likely it is to be accepted as legitimate and thus the more difficult it will be to control society. The control of legal images, on the other hand, is an altogether more subtle exercise. Legal systems have formal laws, breaches of which are legally punishable, and there are established procedures for exercising those laws, but there are also degrees of discretion as to how the law is exercised. Turk argues that the subtle interplay of the formal and informal allows the powerful to manipulate the legal system in their own interests, while still preserving an image of due process and impartiality. The control of living time suggests that people will become accustomed to forms of domination and control, especially if it is maintained and legitimized over generations. Later generations will gradually forget that social control conditions were ever any different from those with which they are familiar.

Richard Quinney was originally a traditional conflict theorist – heavily influenced by social reaction/labelling theory but later coming to be identified with a more radical Marxist-inspired perspective – who considered crime to be the product of legal definitions constructed through the exercise of political power. In this way, actions that may cause harm to others and be similar to forms of behaviour that are subject to the criminal law may be dealt with less seriously, or not at all, if they are conventional activities carried out by, or in the interests of, the powerful. Thus, while the causing of death by a less powerful individual may well be defined as murder or manslaughter, if committed by a corporate body, or high-status individual, it may be interpreted as a civil law violation, or simply an accident. Quinney pointed to numerous examples of harm-generating activities committed by the powerful that are not investigated, or are excused or effectively treated as misdemeanours and fail to come under the auspices of the criminal law.

Quinney – like many of the later radical criminologists – paid a good deal of attention to the role of the mass media in shaping the way in which people perceive crime. He observed that both crime and non-crime definitions are spread throughout the media. With their pervasive effect, the media select and construct a commonly held view of reality where certain actions are naturally crimes and others non-crimes.

Quinney outlined six propositions that summarize his particular version of conflict theory. First, crime is a definition of human conduct that is created by authorized agents in a politically organized society. Second, these criminal definitions are applied by those segments of society that have the power to shape the enforcement of the criminal law. Third, these criminal definitions are applied by those segments of society that have the power to shape the administration of the criminal law. Fourth, behaviour patterns are structured in segmentally organized society in relation to criminal definitions, and within this context people engage in actions that have relative probabilities of being defined as deviant. Fifth, conceptions of crime are constructed and diffused in the segments of society by various means of communication. Sixth, the social reality of crime is constructed by the formulation and application of criminal definitions, the development of behaviour patterns related to criminal definitions and the construction of criminal conceptions (Quinney, 1970: 15–23).

Criticisms of conflict theories

For the later radical criminologists, much of early conflict theory, while accepting the inevitability of social conflict, was still seen as essentially conservative and complacent about the possibility of conflict leading to more successful social integration. It was also to an extent founded on predestined actor model notions that denied the possibility that those victims of an unfair social and economic system might simply rationally choose offending behaviour as a way of coming to terms with a system that had failed to accommodate their interests. Conflict theorists had failed to explain why the law is as it is in the first place and, moreover, they proffered no acceptable explanation as to why it is that those sections of society who do not have their interests represented by established social institutions should choose to accept 'stable authority relationships' out of which they benefit little. In seeking an answer to that last criticism, Turk had argued that it is a 'lack of sophistication' among the subordinate groups that is to blame for the problems that they pose for established society. They may simply choose to break laws or norms that do not fit in with their perceptions of their situation.

By promoting the idea that offenders have a limited capacity to express themselves to authority, we are encouraged to see their subjective accounts of their actions as less valid than those of authority-holders. This is a perspective strongly countered by labelling theorists such as Howard Becker, who argued that it is the task of the social researcher to give voice to the 'underdog' in the face of more than adequate representation of the account of 'superordinate groups'. The essentially predestined actor model 'correctionalist' stance implicit in the work of Turk is illustrated by his view that deviant subcultures should be forcibly broken up by the authorities in order to coerce deviants back into an integrated consensus (Turk, 1969). This should happen, apparently regardless of whether or not the individuals concerned see such integration to be in their interests or not.

This criticism cannot be directed at Quinney, who proposes that the actions of those who are criminally labelled are not so much the outcome of inadequate socialization and personality disorders as conscientious actions taken against the established, unequal social order. Taking this rather more rational actor model-oriented approach, Quinney observed that these acts defined as criminal were perhaps the only appropriate means for expressing thoughts and feelings concerning powerlessness and inequality, and he also, somewhat romantically, considered that deviant, or criminal, behaviour provides the only possibilities for bringing about social change.

Radical theories

Radical theories – like their conflict predecessors – encompass a broad range of ideas. The seminal UK text is Taylor, Walton and Young's *The New Criminology* (1973), which was an attempt to link the concerns of labelling theory with Marxism, while in the USA the works of William Chambliss and Richard Quinney were based on somewhat different theoretical foundations.

There are many different variants of Marxism and these variants are invariably focused around different interpretations of what Marx said, wrote or meant. The basic two-class model of social stratification, while retaining some popularity as an explanation of the fiscal crisis (O'Connor, 1973) – and which might well come back into its explanatory own during the current economic recession – has been significantly criticized as a form of 'vulgar Marxism' (Poulantzas, 1969). Similarly, only another vulgar variant, 'instrumental Marxism', views the law as a simple tool of the ruling class (Chambliss, 1975), with 'structural Marxism' rejecting notions of deliberate intention by the ruling class and proposing that it rules through the creation and control of ideas (Althusser, 1966) or conspiracies (Mills, 1956). The Frankfurt School (Jay, 1973) incorporated Freudian psychoanalysis into Marxism, while neo-Marxism (Friedrichs, 1980) makes use of the suggestion that Marx implied most criminals were *lumpenproletariat* – or what we would today call the underclass – who simply could not be counted on for revolutionary purposes.

Wilhelm Bonger (1916) was a traditional Marxist who saw capitalism to be the creator of social irresponsibility with his scholarship focusing on the dialectical interplay between capitalist business cycles and crime rates. Thus, when unemployment rises during periods of economic recession, the crime rate increases. Using a two-class model, Bonger argued that conflict is likely to continue indefinitely because the inherent contradictions of capitalism create a climate of motivation for crime with offenders motivated by self-interests rather than social interests.

Rusche and Kirchheimer (1939) took a broader historical focus to examine imprisonment rates and the fluctuations of capitalism and observed that the former rates have tended to vary in accordance with our position in the business cycle. This adds some support to the surplus labour hypothesis, which proposes that prisons are simply conduits for those – usually men – who are surplus to the requirements of the economy during any given period in time. Marxist penology (Adamson, 1984) shows little interest in abolishing crime but does seek to abolish prisons, while the rehabilitation of prisoners is rejected as a strategy because it would only serve bourgeois interests (Scull, 1977). Gordon (1971) argues that crime is a rational response to the political and economic structure of institutions and claims that what are traditionally viewed as non-economic goals – status, respect – are closely tied into chances of material survival. Taking an instrumentalist view of the state, he argues that the mere token enforcement of 'upper-world crime' – which is a major concern of conflict criminology (Pearce, 1976) – is explained by the protection of power and profits.

Bill Chambliss had become interested in the socio-political context in which the criminal law had developed while undertaking a study of the development of the vagrancy laws in Britain, and observed that the origin of this body of legislation could be traced to vested interests:

> There is little question that these statutes were designed for one express purpose: to force labourers to accept employment at a low wage in order to ensure the landowner an adequate supply of labour at a price he could afford to pay.
>
> (Chambliss, 1964: 69)

It is an approach influenced by the US school of *legal realism*, which concerned itself with the distinction between the 'law in books' and the 'law in action', and in Chambliss' 1971 work *Law, Order, and Power* – written in collaboration with Robert Seidman – an almost Durkheimian argument is presented. The authors propose that the complexity that comes with technological development, and which necessitates more complicated, differentiated and sophisticated social roles, actually operates to put people at odds with one another and thus this increasing social complexity requires that sanctioning institutions be designed to keep order among the conflicting interests. In their view, the basis of the sanctioning would be organized in the interests of the 'dominant groups' in society but the actual application of the sanctions are enforced by bureaucratic institutions who have their own interests. The 'law of action' thus comes to reflect a combination of the organizations created to enforce the rules.

Chambliss (1969) had previously argued that criminal justice bureaucracies tend to deal more harshly with members of the lower social classes than with other people because the latter have little to offer in return for leniency, while they are in no position to fight the system. Chambliss and Seidman (1971) later concluded that the police act illegally and breach the norms of due process at every stage of their activities and that this occurs because they are not committed to the notion of due process in the first place, while, at the same time, they have an enormous potential for making discretionary decisions. There are also no real safeguards. Bargains struck with the prosecutor before the trial begins tend to reflect the relative political and economic power of the defendant. Additionally, considerable pressure is applied to the accused to plead guilty, leading the powerless to surrender the 'right' to trial by jury in nine cases out of ten.

Chambliss (1969) had observed that much of the criminal legal effort is devoted to processing the very people least likely to be deterred by legal sanctions. On the one hand, he observed that the use of lengthy prison sentences against drug addicts and capital punishment against murderers are instances where sanctions have little deterrent effect. On the other hand, there is a reluctance to impose severe sentences against white-collar and professional criminals, the very offenders who are deterred by sanctions. Chambliss argued that such a policy went directly against the formal logic of deterrence, but fits perfectly with the bureaucratic logic of demonstrating 'effectiveness' by harsh treatment of the powerless, while avoiding the organizational tensions that would follow from confronting the powerful.

By the mid-1970s – at a time when a number of important social theorists were returning to the Marxist tradition that had virtually disappeared during the 1940s and 1950s in the USA – there was a significant shift in the position of Chambliss. This shift is reflected in his nine propositions. First, acts are defined as criminal because it is in the interests of the ruling class to define them as such. Second, members of the ruling class will be able to violate the laws with impunity, while members of the subject class will be punished. Third, as capitalist societies industrialize and the gap between the ruling class and the working class widens, penal law will expand in an effort to coerce the latter class into submission. Fourth, crime reduces the pool of surplus labour by creating employment not only for the criminals but also for law enforcers, welfare workers, professors of criminology and a horde of people who live off the fact that crime exists. This analysis was later developed by Christie (1993), who introduced the term 'the crime industry' to describe this multitude of interested professional groups. Fifth, crime diverts the attention of the lower classes from the exploitation they experience and directs it towards other members of their own class rather than towards the capitalist class or the economic system. Sixth, crime is a reality that exists only inasmuch as those who create it in society have an interest in its presence. Seventh, people involved in criminal behaviour are acting rationally in ways that are compatible with the life conditions of their social class position. Eighth, crime varies from society to society depending on the political and economic structures of society. Ninth, socialist countries should have much lower rates of crime because the less intense class struggle should reduce the forces leading to and the functions of crime (Chambliss, 1975: 152–5).

In a complementary analysis, Spitzer (1975) focuses upon surplus populations created by capitalism and observes that 'skid-row' alcoholics and others who do not pose a threat to the system are called 'social junk', while dangerous acts and people who do pose a threat are called 'social dynamite' or proto-revolutionaries. This analysis has led to a variety of loosely connected studies on the safety net of capitalism – including welfare and mental health reforms – which some have come to term the medicalization of deviance (Liska, 1992). The contradiction is that the more capitalism seeks to control these populations, the more exposed the fiscal crisis becomes.

At this time during the late 1960s, similar concerns and conclusions were emerging among a group of radical young criminologists in the UK who were beginning to question the role of orthodox criminology in helping to legitimate unequal social relations in capitalist societies. The law, police and social workers in particular were highlighted as having an important role in preserving the status quo, and the proponents of the predestined actor model of criminal behaviour that dominated social work and probation training, the British Home Office and the Cambridge Institute of Criminology, were observed to give these crucial criminal justice agencies academic support. There thus developed among these young radicals an increased concern to restore some dignity to the deviant person. They were no longer to be seen as the 'poor wee things' of the predestined actor model, nor the inevitable and terrible pathological creatures deserving of harsh containment – or even death – proposed by a great deal of right-wing criminology. There was a concern to restore meaning to the deviant actors, to regard them as knowing people responding rationally, albeit sometimes rebelliously, to their circumstances.

This concern for the 'authenticity' of the deviant's position was combined with a concern for the nature of the state and its agencies in labelling deviance, in the passing of legislation, apportioning blame and prosecuting individuals, in the interests of those who already hold political power. The ideas were by no means new and many of them can be traced back to the Chicago School. The work of Howard Becker – discussed in the previous chapter – in such work as *Outsiders* (1963), and other symbolic interactionists and labelling theorists, was very influential, as was the entire phenomenological and ethnomethodological tradition. Further influences were the anti-psychiatry movement and radical psychology epitomized by the work of R.D. Laing (1960).

Notable practitioners in this field emerged from a series of meetings held by the New Deviancy Conference at York University in the late 1960s and early 1970s. Those involved included Paul Rock, David Downes, Laurie Taylor, Stan Cohen, Ian Taylor and Jock Young. These new criminologists – or 'sociologists of deviance' – moved from a purely symbolic interactionist, labelling theory position to one more heavily influenced by Marxism, but, at the same time, the latter was itself going through something of a revision.

There had been earlier writers, as we have seen above – in particular Wilhelm Bonger (1916) – who had attempted to explain crime and criminal behaviour from a Marxist perspective but these had tended to over-predict the amount of crime that would occur in a capitalist system by proposing that an inherently alienating social structure would inevitably lead to criminal and antisocial behaviour. Bonger's work was crudely deterministic and ignored the possible diversity of responses to adverse social conditions – such as drug taking, retreatism and ritualistic accommodations by those with little stake in society – as described by Merton and others working in the anomie theory tradition. The new criminologists thus sought a 'totalizing' explanation of crime and criminal behaviour, one that accounted for social structural power and history. They argued that they had found the solution – 'a fully social view of deviance' – in the combination of a 'sociology of deviance' based on labelling theory and a then new contemporary form of Marxism.

The classic text in this tradition is Taylor *et al.*'s *The New Criminology* (1973), which provides an impressive summary of previous criminological ideas and a provision of indicators that the authors considered would give rise to a crime-free society. The book is founded on a set of assumptions that can be summarized as follows. First, crime is a two-sided affair – the cause of criminal behaviour and the identification of the power to criminalize. Second, capitalism itself is crime producing – or criminogenic – as crime is a product of the material and social inequalities that are inherent in the logic of capitalism. Third, the only way to eliminate crime is to destroy inequality and thus the power and need to criminalize. Drawing heavily on labelling theory, it was argued that the power to criminalize, make laws and prosecute offenders, or particular groups that are perceived as offenders, was a function of the state. The state was seen to vary in form during different historical periods, and the techniques that it employs to maintain social discipline, ultimately in the interests of the powerful, also varies.

In summary, *The New Criminology* represented a 'global', 'macro' approach that locates the causes of crime and criminal behaviour within the social structure. The labelling perspective retains a great deal of importance in this explanatory model and, indeed, it appears to be at least as significant as the underlying structural considerations, but this approach does have the advantage of ensuring that there is an appreciation that individuals do possess a great deal of freedom of action within the broad social context in which they find themselves. The decision to act is nevertheless left to the rationality of the individual.

Criticisms of radical theories

The 'new criminology' provides a generalized prescription for a crime-free, socialist 'good society' and, from the standpoint of the twenty-first century, it can be seen to be utopian, reflecting the optimistic nature of the times in which it was written, while the generality of the work itself meant that it could offer very little to substantive theory at all. Indeed, it can be argued that, since its publication, very little has been achieved to produce a 'truly social view of deviance'. The subsequent text, edited by Taylor *et al.* (1975), appears to have marked something of a retreat into smaller concerns and away from the 'grand theory' and meta-vision of the original programme. Five possible not necessarily mutually exclusive explanations as to why this should have been the case can be identified.

First, some have doubted the legitimacy of merging and synthesizing labelling theory and Marxist analysis, as the philosophical underpinnings of the two traditions are fundamentally different. Hirst (1980) argues that Taylor *et al.* are simply labelling theorists who have raided the works of Marx in order to provide a synthesis of the two perspectives.

Second, others have argued that the new criminologists failed to provide an adequate definition of crime and deviance. For proponents of the predestined actor tradition, this was not a problem. Crime is either the outcome of 'pathological behaviour' or simply behaviour that transgresses against the law. The notion of crime consisting of any behaviour that causes social harm is highly problematic. The fundamental question is whether it is possible to have a theory of crime causation that legitimately encompasses such diverse activities as working-class theft, rape and 'white-collar' fraud. If we accept such an expansive definition of crime, the problem arises as to how we are to accurately measure social harm, and some have argued that, once the label 'crime' has become problematic, it becomes clear that separate areas of criminal behaviour require different explanatory frameworks. In that case, the ability to develop any central all-encompassing criminology begins to dissolve and this inevitably leads to a retreat from grand theory.

Third, the retreat from grand theory was encouraged by the diverse accounts of criminal activity emerging from sociologists and social historians. Studies carried out by researchers such as Thompson (1975) and Hay (1981) reveal that criminal behaviour is not a homogenous concept and, thus, the 'rule of law' cannot be simply conceptualized as an external coercive force repressing the working class. Indeed, it could possibly offer protection from certain abuses of power, while constraining action in the interests of maintaining order. Examples offered by these authors from the eighteenth and nineteenth centuries demonstrate that state power was a far more complex concept than the authors of *The New Criminology* had at first envisaged. In short, there are many parasitic and diverse forms of crime from which the working class seek protection in law and order.

Fourth, changes in Marxist theory during the 1970s left the first wave of new criminologists intellectually stranded. The state had traditionally been seen as the political form of class domination but, during the 1970s, the focus of Marxist theorizing changed to encompass such areas as culture, ideology and hegemony, a much more complex analysis. The law was no longer conceptualized as an entirely bourgeois concept, but as a more differentiated idea.

New criminology revisionists addressed many of these complex new issues, some working at Birmingham University's Centre for Contemporary Cultural Studies (CCCS) under its charismatic director, Professor Stuart Hall, and this group was responsible for producing the controversial *Policing the Crisis* (1978), an attempt to rework many of the utopian aspects of *The New Criminology* into a more modern and sophisticated theoretical package. Thus, ideas were incorporated from the recently available work of the Italian Marxist Antonio Gramsci – originally published during the 1920s – in a discussion of the substantive issue of street robbery or 'mugging'. In doing so, they investigated the relationship between ethnicity, class and the state, and this body of work forms a crucial element in the intellectual origins of critical criminology – one of two contemporary variants of the radical tradition – that is the focus of Chapter 12. It is a perspective that to date has had little impact outside academic criminology.

Fifth, in response to an apparent substantial increase in crime rates and a general perception among vast sections of the population that crime levels were at an unacceptable level, a great deal of popularism came to infiltrate criminological debate. We saw in Chapter 3 that the conservative populists – or 'right' realists – came to take seriously the problems that ordinary people, notably working-class people, had experienced, and in doing so managed to capture much of the electoral ground that the political left had always regarded as their natural constituency. We shall see in Chapter 18 that, in an effort to recapture the issue of crime from the political 'right', the populist socialists – or left realists – influentially came to reconsider radical criminology. This second contemporary variant of the radical tradition recognizes that capitalism may well be responsible for the relative inequality and absolute poverty that shapes so much of British culture and provides the root cause of crime. On the other hand, the bulk of that crime is predatory on the very people that they would wish to defend, the working class and the poor.

Peacemaking criminology

Introduction

Peacemaking criminology is a more contemporary variant of the radical criminology tradition that has emerged during the past twenty years in the USA, signified by the publication of Harold Pepinsky and Richard Quinney's edited text *Criminology as Peacemaking* (1991), and which draws on three peacemaking traditions: (i) religious and humanistic; (ii) feminist; and (iii) critical. The general argument presented is that the whole of the US criminal justice system is based on the continuance of violence and oppression (as seen in the prison system); war (as seen in the 'war on crime' and the 'war on drugs'); and the failure to account for how the larger social system contributes to the problem of crime (as seen in the failure to reduce poverty in society). Quinney, a long-time critic of mainstream, predominantly predestined actor model criminology, observes:

> Let us begin with a fundamental realization: No amount of thinking and no amount of public policy have brought us any closer to understanding and solving the problem of crime. The more we have reacted to crime, the farther we have removed ourselves from any understanding and any reduction of the problem. In recent years, we have floundered desperately in reformulating the law, punishing the offender, and quantifying our knowledge. Yet this country remains one of the most crime-ridden nations. In spite of all its wealth, economic development, and scientific advances, this country has one of the worst crime records in the world.
>
> (1991: 3)

Peacemaking criminology proposes that crime is connected to suffering and that, to end crime, we must end suffering. This means that poverty, racism, sexism, alienation, abuse within families, harassment and all other forms of suffering must be dealt with if crime is to be reduced. Moreover, the state itself is seen to perpetuate crime (and violence) through repressive policies of social control, such as the death penalty, lengthy prison sentences for offenders and the criminalization of non-violent drug offences, while the criminological focus on individual offenders has been at the neglect of institutional arrangements in society that contribute to a very high crime rate. Criminology should thus concern itself with promoting greater social equity and there should be a significant move away from traditional criminal justice to restorative justice.

Peacemaking criminology is thus not traditional mainstream criminology, it cannot be located in the predestined actor model tradition and it is certainly not obsessed with the detailed statistical analysis of the causes of criminal behaviour, which is very much the dominant orthodoxy in the contemporary USA (Young, 2011). This is not to say that peacemaking criminology is not interested in the causes of crime; but rather, it approaches the aetiology issue through non-traditional means. Thus, for example, in providing a summary of the intellectual foundations of peacemaking criminology, Quinney attempts to encapsulate how the aetiology issue can be framed:

(1) Thought of the Western rational mode is conditional, limiting knowledge to what is already known. (2) The truth of reality is emptiness: all that is real is beyond human conception. (3) Each life is a spiritual journey into the unknown and the unknowable, beyond the egocentric self. (4) Human existence is characterized by suffering; crime is suffering; and the sources of suffering are within each of us. (5) Through love and compassion, beyond the egocentric self, we can end suffering and live in peace, personally and collectively. (6) The ending of suffering can be attained in a quieting of the mind and an opening of the heart, in being aware. (7) Crime can be ended only with the ending of suffering, only when there is peace – through the love and compassion found in awareness. (8) Understanding, service, justice: all these flow naturally from love and compassion, from mindful attention to the reality of all that is, here and now. (9) A criminology of peacemaking, the nonviolent criminology of compassion and service, seeks to end suffering and thereby eliminate crime.

(1991: 3–4)

One of the greatest challenges for peacemaking criminology is the development of a coherent, unifying theory. The kind of theorizing that has accompanied peacemaking criminology has been more general in tone and has a broader, less systematic nature

The peacemaking pyramid paradigm

John Fuller (2003: 86–8) has developed a six-stage model of peacemaking criminology that deals with the criminal justice system:

1. *Non-violence.* Peacemaking criminology is first and foremost opposed to violence and the use of capital punishment as a criminal justice policy. The

premeditated violence of the state is viewed as just as wrong as the violence of the offender.

2. *Social justice*. Social justice considers a broader concept of justice than traditional criminal justice, and issues of sexism, racism and inequality are key concerns. For example, it is observed that a pattern of racial bias has long been apparent in capital punishment cases with the ethnicity of the offender and the victim having been shown to influence the death sentence. Minorities have been more likely to receive death penalties than whites and, while there are other reasons to argue against the death penalty, this obvious ethnic bias is quite clearly a violation of any notion of social justice. The minority offender may be guilty of a heinous crime, but the peacemaking perspective argues against the death penalty on social justice grounds when there are such extra-legal factors affecting the sentence.

3. *Inclusion*. It is argued that the criminal justice system needs to be more inclusive of the stakeholders in the community. In the current highly formalized concept of criminal justice, the offender is pitted against the state. There are nevertheless others who have an interest in the case and who can offer legitimate perspectives and alternatives. Families of the victim and the offender, as well as individuals from the neighbourhood, are all interested parties who have valuable insights. When the state takes such total control of a case, it deprives the affected parties of the opportunity to develop their own creative solution. Christie (1977) likens this situation to the state taking away the property of the offender and victim. The concept of inclusion also entails giving the offender an opportunity to negotiate the outcome. Rather than having a sentence imposed on them, the offender agrees to the conditions and takes ownership of the offence and their treatment. The peacemaking perspective proposes that such conditions of inclusion will form more satisfactory and lasting solutions than conventional sentencing.

4. *Correct means*. There is an old saying that the ends do not justify the means and this is seen to be especially true in the criminal justice system. A whole area of procedural law has been developed to ensure that criminal justice practitioners do not violate the legal and civil rights of the offender. Correct means entails ensuring that offenders and victims are not coerced into settlements of their cases with due process guarantees preserved and not sacrificed in order to ensure effectiveness. An example of this point offered is the extensive racial profiling used by many law-enforcement agencies. While targeting minorities may seem justified to the police based on their expectations and experience, such incorrect means are inherently unfair and quickly become a self-fulfilling prophecy. When minorities are excessively targeted, they become disproportionately arrested and this is used as evidence in developing suspect profiles. It becomes a vicious circle where incorrect means contributes to the violations of social justice.

5. *Ascertainable criteria*. In order for victims, offenders and community members to fully participate in the criminal justice system, they must understand what is going on. There are two types of language barriers that inhibit equal access to the law. The first is the inability of many recent immigrants to understand English. While many jurisdictions provide adequate translators, many do

not. It is clear that, when individuals cannot understand English, they cannot fully participate in the court proceedings. The second issue concerns the specialized jargon used in the criminal justice system. The language of the law is a highly specialized professional argot that is only completely understood by lawyers. The peacemaking concepts of ascertainable criteria and inclusion argue that efforts to insure that all parties fully understand the procedures are desirable. This would include education efforts aimed at non-English-speaking individuals as well as clearly written legal guidelines aimed at educating victims and offenders.

6. *Categorical imperative.* When considering the problems of crime and the criminal justice system, the peacemaking perspective aims at developing a consistent and predictable viewpoint. Using Immanuel Kant's concept of the categorical imperative, the peacemaking perspective argues that responses to crime should reflect an underlying philosophy of non-violence and social justice that is extended throughout the criminal justice system. Victims and offenders, criminal justice practitioners, as well as the public, should all be treated with the respect and dignity we all deserve. To that end, criminal justice decisions should employ Kant's axiom: 'Act only according to that maxim whereby you can at the same time will that it should become a universal law'. Thus, the peacemaking perspective is not a haphazard and inconsistent policy guide. It aims at providing true equality under the law for all people.

A few observations can be made about this 'theoretical' perspective. First, it is not a traditional criminological theory, complete with hypotheses and propositions that can be tested. Second, it does not directly address the issue of crime causation or who commits crime and why. Third, it could be considered to be less peacemaking criminology and more peacemaking criminal justice. All three observations are not necessarily criticisms. Fuller provides an alternative and welcome social justice view to the dominant criminal justice perspective, which we should note is in harmony with the radical moral communitarianism promoted by this author in Chapter 22. Moreover, his argument is a humanist and compassionate plea for human dignity, while, at the same time, reminding us that perhaps criminologists should be as interested in victims as in offenders. Finally, Fuller has clearly implied that the contemporary criminologist should be actively engaged in the various struggles for social justice.

Criticism of peacemaking criminology

Peacemaking criminology has, perhaps not surprisingly, been the recipient of significant and often vitriolic criticism, having been viewed as 'utopian', 'soft on crime', 'unrealistic' and 'just not feasible'. One of its staunchest critics is Ronald Akers, who noted in his 1997 book, *Criminological Theories: Introduction and Evaluation*, that:

> Peacemaking criminology does not offer a theory of crime or of the criminal justice system that can be evaluated empirically . . . . It may be possible to

construct a testable, parsimonious, and valid theory from peacemaking criminology, but at this point it remains a philosophy rather than a theory. It is a utopian vision of society that calls for reforming and restructuring to get away from war, crime, and violence.... This is a highly laudable philosophy of criminal justice, but it does not offer an explanation of why the system operates as it does or why offenders commit crime. It can be evaluated on other grounds but not on empirical validity.

(Akers, 1997: 183)

In a subsequent edition of the text, Akers (2000) identifies four additional short-comings. First, he argues that it is contradictory to claim Marxist/critical theory as one of the main foundations for peacemaking, because this perspective is based on class conflict and Marx himself endorsed violent revolution. Second, feminism is not consistent with peacemaking because the nurturing role of women is simply part of the patriarchal system of the oppression of women. Third, almost all of the policies recommended by peacemaking criminology have long been mainstays of the policy recommendations of traditional criminology. Thus, peacemaking criminology is not really anything new or different. Fourth, peacemaking criminology does not provide a strategy for getting beyond the limitations of criminal justice policies to suggest how large-scale structural changes can be brought about to make society less violent.

Fuller (2003: 93–4) responds to these objections. First, he observes that peace-making criminology does not share all aspects of Marxism. Thus, it is committed to that part that calls for equality and rejects that element that calls for violence, which we might observe is very much in accord with serious contemporary European thought. Second, he argues that feminism is consistent with peace-making criminology; in particular, it demonstrates how rigid gender roles have had a negative impact on society, proposing that both women and men should have a nurturing role. Third, traditional criminologists may have advocated many changes in the criminal justice system, but the 'war on crime' mentality still tends to dominate. Fourth, he argues that people practise 'peacemaking' in their everyday lives and the extent to which this occurs will mean less crime.

Akers is not the only critic who asks how peacemaking criminology would propose a structural reorganization of society. Gibbons observes that 'the Pepinsky and Quinney volume has little to say about how the grand-scale changes they propose might be achieved' (1994: 172), but peacemaking crimin-ologists have responded and point to structural innovations that could be under-taken in the USA that could arguably reduce the suffering that causes crime. Among the changes proposed are:

1. Provision of universal healthcare based on the Canadian and European models.
2. Replace the minimum wage law with one based on the idea of a liveable wage.
3. Make poverty a priority and initiate a broad and sweeping national programme to reduce poverty through a system of guaranteed child support for all poor families.

4. Provide free tuition for all students enrolled in community colleges.
5. Provide free childcare for all preschool children – with a minimal charge for affluent families.
6. De-criminalize all drug laws and expand free treatment for addicts.
7. De-institutionalize prisons and use these institutions predominantly for violent offenders.
8. Shift the tax burden from the middle and working classes to the upper economic classes and corporations.
9. Make a total commitment to the abolition of wage inequality based on sex.
10. Redirect economic and social policies to inner cities, especially in housing.
11. De-militarize the political economy of the USA.
12. Abolish the death penalty.

Some of the changes proposed are clearly more radical than others but some, such as the provision of free healthcare for all citizens and policies to help poor families become independent and productive members of society, have been in existence in Europe for some years and these societies enjoy much lower crime rates than the USA. To the average European, such policies are not radical but mainstream.

Restorative justice as an alternative to criminal justice

The single most important proposal by peacemaking criminologists centres on the notion of restorative justice, which is seen as an opportunity to restructure a significant part of the criminal justice system. It is recognized that the criminal justice system should be maintained for dealing with crimes of violence – murder, rape, robbery and assault – but it is proposed that many property and drug crimes could be dealt with through a non-criminal justice system.

Van Ness and Strong (2002: 38–43) note that restorative justice rests on three major propositions. First, justice requires that we work to restore those who have been injured: victims, communities and even offenders. Second, those most directly involved and affected by crime – victims, offenders and community – should have the opportunity to participate as fully in the intervention as they wish. Third, while the government is responsible for preserving a just social order, the role of the community in establishing and maintaining a just peace must be given special significance.

In other words, restorative justice is seen to be a justice system whose primary motive is healing, not punishment. It looks to bring victim and offender together, to promote restitution (both monetary and symbolic), to involve the community in decision-making and to seek non-violent (that is, non-custodial) solutions to crime. It is not the traditional response to crime. Thus, it is not founded on principles of retribution, nor does it ignore victims, as does the current dominant criminal justice orthodoxy in the USA. Restorative justice looks to options other than trial, plea-bargaining and imprisonment. In short, it is a peacemaking alternative to crime rather than the war model, which has come to dominate contemporary criminal justice in the USA. Rick Sarre (2003: 102–7) offers some examples of what restorative justice looks like in actual practice:

- *Family conferencing*. This is where offenders, victims, family and community members and police are brought together to negotiate a settlement. Offenders confront their wrongs, and the aim is a mutually satisfactory reconciliation.
- *Family violence court*. This is an 'interventionist' court that deals with domestic violence issues and generally seeks treatment for offenders through anger management programmes and drug abuse treatment.
- *Mental health court*. This court takes referrals from police and lower-level magistrates for people who have non-severe mental disorders, yet are in need of mental health intervention through various agencies.
- *Drug assessment and aid panels*. This is a pre-court diversionary programme now in use in South Australia that works with drug offenders to seek medical, not criminal, solutions for addiction. A 'panel' oversees the treatment regimen for these offenders.
- *Customary law*. This is the recognition of tribal and customary law among indigenous populations in solving many justice issues.
- *Victim Offender Reconciliation Program (VORP)*. This is a programme that can operate at both the pre-court and post-conviction stages. It is designed around the principles of mediation and reconciliation, bringing offender and victim together to repair the damage done by the crime and to have the offender take responsibility for that damage.

Restorative justice is perceived to be a new way of thinking about crime and the way in which society responds and intervenes. It promotes bringing together offenders and victims and expects the former to accept responsibility for their actions. It promotes victim healing through reconciliation and offender rehabilitation through treatment, restitution and reparation. It emphasizes the need to effectively reintegrate offenders back into the community and the related responsibility of the community to play a positive role in that reintegration. Restorative justice is the principal proposal of peacemaking criminology for overhauling the criminal justice system. It may not be a workable proposal for some crimes – many crimes of violence, for instance – but, for many property crimes, drug offences and young offending, it is a very reasonable alternative to incarceration and punishment, which provide the foundations of the contemporary criminal justice system in the USA.

Conclusion

Larry Siegel observes that:

> All too often criminologists forget the social responsibility they bear as experts in the area of crime and justice . . . . By accepting their roles as experts on law-violating behavior, criminologists place themselves in a position of power. The potential consequences of their actions are enormous. Therefore, they must be both aware of the ethics of their profession and prepared to defend their work in the light of public scrutiny. Major ethical issues include what to study, whom to study, and how to conduct those studies.
>
> (2002: 23)

Peacemaking criminology seeks to address these concerns in the following ways. First, crime is clearly identified as a significant part of peacemaking criminological study, but it is only part. Peacemaking criminologists should also study the institutions that comprise the social structure with attention directed to the systems of court administration, law enforcement and the penal system. In other words, the focus should not only be on offenders, but also on the societal response to crime with the peacemaking criminologist needing to examine those institutions that play a role in producing the suffering that is at the core of the crime problem. This means that criminologists should know more about economic inequality, poverty, racism, sexism and bias against gays and lesbians. It is necessary to know how schools reproduce academic and personal failure. The focus of peacemaking criminology must be on 'criminals' but also on the social dynamics that produce the suffering that causes criminals.

Second, it is proposed that peacemaking criminology must study those in positions of political and social power. It is necessary to know how law-makers function, what philosophies motivate judges, and what priorities drive police activities. Peacemaking criminologists should study those who work in mainstream corrections (prison wardens, correctional officers) and those who would be part of the restorative justice process (mediators, teachers, counsellors, therapists). It needs to explore how community activists, religious leaders and social workers can be brought into ways of reducing suffering. In short, peacemaking criminologists should be as interested in the persons and agencies that respond to crime as in the criminals.

Third, peacemaking criminology has the responsibility to engage in only ethical research, committed to the principles of confidentiality and non-violence. Peacemaking criminologists must not conduct studies that contribute to suffering; they must be attentive to the human rights of their research subjects, whether they are criminals or the police. They must not allow their research to further a system of oppression, alienation and mistreatment of law offenders or law enforcers. Whether their work is based on case studies, large-scale survey research or participant observation, peacemaking criminologists must always be dedicated to finding constructive solutions to the social problems that generate crime. Peacemaking criminologists must themselves be agents of social change and be engaged in various struggles to promote social justice.

Peacemaking criminology has had a short history, but its adherents propose that it offers a realistic cause for crime (human suffering) and a practical response (restorative justice). It broadens the vision of the criminologist to the structure and processes of the social system, thus breaking away from the narrow vision of examining only offenders and, in doing so, revives and revitalizes the radical tradition in the USA and brings it into line with contemporary radical developments in Australia and the UK.

Policy implications of conflict and radical theories

The policy implications of conflict theory are:

1. To redistribute power and wealth through a more progressive tax system or limitation of political contributions, for example.
2. For dominant group members to become more effective rulers and subordinate group members better subjects.

The policy implications of radical theory include:

1. Demonstrating that the current definition of crime supports the ruling class.
2. Redefining crime as a violation of human rights.
3. Creation of a benevolent socialist society in which the economy is regulated to promote public welfare.

The policy implications of peacemaking criminology include:

1. A mixture of anarchism, humanism, socialism, and Native American and Eastern philosophies.
2. Rejecting the idea that criminal violence can be reduced by state violence.
3. The belief that reducing suffering will reduce crime.
4. An approach that suggests that the solution to all social problems, including crime, is: (i) the transformation of human beings; (ii) mutual dependence; (iii) reduction of class structures; (iv) the creation of communities of caring people; and (v) universal social justice.

Summary of main points

1. Conflict and radical theories have sought to explain crime and criminal behaviour in terms of the unequal nature of the socio-political structure of society.
2. Thorsten Sellin (1938) proposed that each culture establishes its own norms – or rules of behaviour – which are then embedded into its members through the various processes of socialization. Conflicts over *conduct norms* can occur at both the micro and macro level in society.
3. George Vold (1958) emphasized the group nature of society and stressed the fact that groups compete with each other in order to secure what they identify as their interests.
4. Austin Turk fundamentally saw the social order as the outcome of powerful social groups who successfully control society in their own interests. Social control is exercised by providing a normative justification for law, which is then enforced by controlling agencies such as the police.
5. Richard Quinney considered crime to be the product of legal definitions constructed through the exercise of political power.
6. Radical theories – like their conflict predecessors – encompass a broad range of ideas. The seminal UK text is Taylor, Walton and Young's *The New Criminology* (1973), which was an attempt to link the concerns of labelling theory with Marxism, while in the USA the works of William Chambliss

and Richard Quinney were based on somewhat different theoretical foundations.

7. Chambliss (1969) argued that criminal justice bureaucracies tend to deal with members of the lower social classes more harshly than with other people because the latter have little to offer in return for leniency, while they are in no position to fight the system.

8. The 'new criminologists' – or 'sociologists of deviance' – moved from a purely symbolic interactionist, labelling theory position to one more heavily influenced by Marxism.

9. Peacemaking criminology is a more contemporary variant of the radical tradition, which proposes that the whole of the US criminal justice system is based on the continuance of violence and oppression (as seen in the prison system); war (as seen in the 'war on crime' and the 'war on drugs'); and the failure to account for how the larger social system contributes to the problem of crime (as seen in the failure to reduce poverty in society).

10. Peacemaking criminology has – like the earlier conflict and radical traditions – been viewed as 'utopian', 'soft on crime', 'unrealistic' and 'just not feasible'.

Discussion questions

1. How do conflict theorists explain crime and criminal behaviour in a pluralist society?
2. How do radical theorists explain crime and criminal behaviour in an inherently unequal society?
3. How do peacemaking criminologists explain crime and criminal behaviour?
4. Is peacemaking criminology 'utopian', 'soft on crime' and 'unrealistic' or does it have any practical relevance in the twenty-first century?
5. What are the identified weaknesses of the radical conflict tradition in both the past and the present?

Suggested further reading

The US conflict and radical theory approach is well represented by Chambliss (1969, 1975), Chambliss and Seidman (1971), Quinney (1970) and Turk (1969). The radical UK tradition is best represented by Taylor *et al.* (1973) and Taylor *et al.* (eds) (1975). Christie (1993) provides an excellent more recent radical discussion of the notion of crime control as industry in a tradition established by Cohen (1985).

11. The gendered criminal

Key Issues

1. Feminist perspectives
2. The feminist critique of positivism
3. The impact of feminist critiques
4. Feminism and prostitution
5. Crime and masculinities

We have seen in the previous three chapters that the victimized actor model of crime and criminal behaviour proposes that the criminal is in some way the victim of an unjust and unequal society. It is the activities of the poorer and less powerful sections of society that are criminalized, while the actions of the rich and powerful are simply ignored or not even defined as criminal. From a feminist perspective, it is men who are the dominant group in society and it is they that make and enforce the rules, which are invariably to the detriment of women.

Feminism has had a considerable impact on criminology in recent years – using feminist or critical social theories to consider the significance of gender in crime and criminal justice – and has provided both critiques of the traditional explanations of female criminality that we encountered in Chapter 8, while at the same time offering its own perspectives. We should note that a distinction can be made between the biological characteristics that define and distinguish males and females and the cultural expectations inherent in the social roles defined by societies as being applicable to men and women. 'Sex' is a biological term used to describe the anatomical differences between males and females, while the term 'gender' refers to learned behaviour associated with men and women, which is developed through the socialization process. Gender is thus the social construction of non-biological differences between men and women and this can be further explained by the identification of at least two sub-groups such as masculinity and femininity, which are partially based on physical difference.

Feminist criminologies challenge the androcentrism – or male-centredness – of criminology (Daly and Chesney-Lind, 1988) and propose that the main weakness of traditional 'malestream' criminological theory is the failure to understand the important significance of gender and sex roles (Gelsthorpe and Morris, 1990). For some, this significance is reflected in the ongoing differential in sex roles and gender inequality; for others, the inequalities are structural within patriarchy – a situation where the rights and privileges of males are superior to those of females – and are a fundamental principle of societal organization. Labelling and conflict theories – which we encountered in the preceding two chapters – recognize male–female differences in power, but feminist theory proposes that the power differential between men and women is at least as important as, if not more important than, the power differentials of race, class and age. Marxists consider class to be the fundamental divisive force in capitalist society but, from the feminist perspective, patriarchy is equally as important and may even be the dominant factor. Feminist theories explain criminal justice decisions as reflecting this male dominance and functioning to support patriarchy by discriminating against women and reinforcing traditional sex and family roles (Mann, 1984; Messerschmidt, 1986; Morris, 1987; Chesney-Lind, 1988, 1989; Daly and Chesney-Lind, 1988; Daly, 1989, 1992, 1994a, 1994b; Simpson, 1989, 1991; Gelsthorpe and Morris, 1990, Chesney-Lind and Shelden, 1992).

It is nevertheless important to recognize that feminism is not a unitary system of thought but a collection of different theoretical perspectives with each explaining the oppression of women in a different way. Consequently, there is no one feminist explanation of female criminality and, before examining these debates, it will be useful to briefly consider the different variations of feminist thought or feminisms. First, a further word of caution should be noted. The various versions of feminism tend to be united in their rejection of the term 'victim' to describe the oppression of women in a male-dominated society and there is a preference for the far more positive term 'survivor'. It is a linguistic device that suggests that, by working together in pursuit of the common cause, women can successfully contest and overcome male supremacy.

Perspectives in feminist theory

The French term *feminisme* was first used in the late nineteenth century as a synonym for the emancipation of women (Jaggar, 1983; Pilcher, 1983) and referred in the broadest sense to a 'women's movement' made up of a number of diverse groups seeking to advance the position of women in society. In the early twentieth century, when the term was introduced in the USA, its meaning was limited to referring only to a group that asserted the uniqueness of women's experience and their social and sexual purity (Jaggar, 1983). Today, the term is no longer so restricted, although there is still confusion about its exact meaning and use.

Feminism is generally perceived to have emerged in Western societies in two waves. The first emphasized equality within rational individual rights and was most notably characterized in the British context by the suffrage movement that lasted from the 1860s to the First World War. Subsequently, there was the opening up of educational opportunities, the provision of social legislation providing rights over property and the marital home. In 1928, there was the provision of the vote for those women over the age of 21. Nonetheless, while the social position of women was enhanced, they did not enjoy equality with men.

The second wave of feminism emerged in the USA and was brought to the UK in the late 1960s. The emergence of the Women's Liberation Movement in the wake of the Civil Rights and student movements demanded nothing less than the wholesale transformation of society. Consciousness-raising groups and the development of women's collectives provided the arena for debate and discussion that formed the basis of contemporary feminist thought and action.

Feminist thought has subsequently had a considerable impact on the social sciences and other academic fields and has essentially involved a challenge to traditional male-dominated perspectives, and arguments have been proposed both for the integration of women into theoretical perspectives and the development of new approaches that analyse and develop an understanding of issues specifically related to their lives. Essentially, new areas of research have been opened up designed to make previously invisible women visible.

The feminist enterprise within academia has not come without criticism or been universally welcomed with its theories, writing and research often criticized, trivialized and, in some instances, openly undermined. Despite these problems, it has challenged the dominance of traditional male-centred knowledge and can be understood as a social and political force. There are at least six main contemporary variants of feminism and we will consider each in turn.

Liberal feminism has its roots in the notions of individual rights and freedoms that were central to the rise and consolidation of modern societies in the eighteenth and nineteenth centuries. From this perspective, the subordination of women is examined as part of an analysis of the wider social structures and inequalities with the central concern to locate discrimination in social practice, specifically within the public sphere, and extend rights to women to equal those enjoyed by men through the process of legal reform. It is a perspective that has nevertheless been criticized for its inability to confront the deep-rooted levels of gender inequality. In short, there is an identified failure to challenge fundamental male values, while the solutions offered are limited and to some extent superficial. The legacy of sex discrimination and equal pay legislation can be attributed, however, to the influence of liberal feminism and there is recognition of its value to the broader feminist paradigm (Jaggar, 1983; Tong, 1988).

Radical feminism emerged in the 1970s and focuses on the importance of *patriarchy*, or the 'set of hierarchical relations between men, and solidarity between them, which enables them to control women' (Hartmann, 1981: 447). Patriarchy describes a power relationship inherent in the structures and social relations within which the subordination and exploitation of women occurs and it is used to explain the institutionalization of male power and domination over women (see Walby, 1980: 173–201). The slogan 'the personal is political' has been used to identify the basis of women's oppression within the private realm of personal relationships and private lives. Thus, the need to expose the hidden secrets of personal relationships and social practice within the private sphere is recognized by radical feminists and has led to the examination of issues such as reproductive freedom, pornography, domestic violence and child abuse. Radical feminists advocate separatism from men to different degrees and this can be seen either partially, in the provision of women-only institutions or events, or wholly, including the withdrawal of women from personal and sexual relationships with men.

Radical feminism has been criticized for its biological determinism, that is, the belief that by nature all men are the same and so are all women. Further criticism is directed at the notion that patriarchy is an all-pervasive universal principle operating in the same way in all places at all times and thus fails to recognize differences in the experiences of women across time and space including class and ethnic differences (Jaggar, 1983).

Marxist feminists argue that the subordination of women is located in the capitalist exploitation of their domestic role and they identify the existence of a dominant ideology that presents women as primarily carers within the domestic sphere and that is used to justify low wages, low status and part-time jobs, and is, in turn, used to deny women the right to economic independence (Beechey, 1977). Women are also considered to be part of a reserve army of labour, available to be drawn into the workforce when the needs of capitalism demand it and to be easily rejected when there is surplus labour (Bruegel, 1978).

Marxist feminists have nevertheless been criticized for their overuse of economic explanations of women's oppression, while failing to examine the complexity of family relationships. Tong (1988) notes, however, the increasing relevance of the Marxist feminist critique, as more and more women have become employed in the market economy, a process that has accelerated during the intervening years.

Socialist feminism provides a synthesis of the radical and Marxist feminist perspectives with recognition that both capitalist and patriarchal systems play a part in the subordination of women. This 'dual systems theory' recognizes the systems of capitalism and patriarchy to be separate but, at the same time, mutually accommodating systems of oppression, while 'unified system theorists' have developed unifying concepts as central categories of analysis. Jaggar (1983), for example, identified the concept of 'alienation' that provides a theoretical synthesis of Marxist, radical and liberal feminist thought. The potential of socialist feminism to bring together the diverse accounts of different feminist approaches is significant but it has nevertheless been criticized by black feminists for the tendency to deny the diversity of experiences that different women encounter.

Black feminism examines the structures of domination prevalent in the personal, cultural and institutional levels and experiences of the lives of black women, and the axes of race, gender and class are identified as forming the basis of their oppression within which, it is argued, there exists a 'more generalized matrix of domination'. This matrix was described by bell hooks (the writer spells her name in the lower case) (1988: 174–6) as a 'politic of domination', which is grounded in a hierarchical, ideological belief system. In their critique of feminist accounts of the family, education, reproduction and patriarchy, black feminist writers have identified the relationship of black women to the structures, ideologies and institutions of oppression. Accusations of racism made by black feminists towards the broader, often white middle-class feminist movement have been productive for this has opened up a discourse of difference, recognizing the diversity of female experience.

The notion of difference is also central to any understanding of the relationship of feminism to *postmodernism* (see the fifth part of this book). We shall see later that a prominent feminist Carol Smart has welcomed postmodernism, while others have found it problematic. Radical feminists have criticized the emphasis on – and celebration of – individual difference by arguing that it is the collective voice that makes women strong, but others argue that the challenge is to find a way to think both women *and* 'women' recognizing diversity and collective experience.

It has been the purpose of this section to sensitize the reader with little or no knowledge of contemporary feminism to the diversity of thought that co-exists within that paradigm. The main differences between these accounts centre on factors identified as providing the basis of the oppression of women and the proposed solutions. Black feminism and postmodernist feminism provide both critiques of other feminist accounts and also their own perspectives that recognize the different experiences of women and of their subordination. We now return to our discussion of women and criminality.

The feminist critique of early explanations of female criminality

Late twentieth-century criminology was described as the 'most masculine of all the social sciences, a speciality that wore six-shooters on its hips and strutted its machismo' (Rafter and Heidensohn, 1985: 5). Thus, the most significant characteristic of feminist work has been its critique of traditional or 'malestream' criminology with the main concern being the 'intellectual sexism in theories of female crime and the institutional sexism in the juvenile and criminal justice systems' (Daly and Chesney-Lind, 1988: 508).

Bertrand (1967), Heidensohn (1968) and Klein (1973) were among the first feminists to draw attention to the relative neglect of women in the study of crime and the stereotypical distortions imposed on females in those studies that did address the issue, and we should note that a more traditional woman criminologist – Barbara Wootton (1959) – first made similar observations during the 1950s. It was nevertheless the publication of Carol Smart's *Women, Crime and Criminology* (1977) that is widely acknowledged to be the turning point, highlighting the failure of much traditional criminology to recognize women, while – at the same time – identifying the sexual stereotypes imposed on women and girls in those studies that did consider female criminality and which we encountered in Chapter 8 of this book. The agenda was thus set for future feminist work.

Early feminists criticized traditional criminology for assuming women to be controlled by their biology and incapable of rational action, observing that, while the rest of the criminological world had moved on from a slavish adherence to the prescriptions of the biological variant of predestined actor model, female crime had been cut off from most of this development (Heidensohn, 1994). At the same time, as Downes and Rock note, 'policies and attitudes towards female criminality mirrored such determinisms and lent undue prominence to "sexual deviance" as the focus of enquiry' (1998: 274–5). Early feminists emphasized these undesirable consequences to be a direct outcome of the approach to the study of female criminality adopted by traditional criminological theorists, where the common theme – regardless of whether biological, psychological, anomie, control, differential association, conflict, labelling, social disorganization or social learning theories – is that they are designed to explain only male criminality and have been tested only with male populations (Einstadter and Henry, 1995). It is acknowledged that there may be certain elements of these theories that are useful, but neither one single theory nor all the theories combined are capable of explaining female criminality or the male–female differences in crime (Leonard, 1983).

Some feminist theorists nevertheless disagree with this general critical assessment of all traditional criminological theories. Alison Morris (1987) argues that, although biological and psychological theories are undoubtedly mistaken, traditional sociological explanations of crime have the potential to explain female crime and why it occurs less frequently than male crime:

> Special theories for women's crimes have not been particularly successful ... One implication of this ... is that we need to reconsider the relevance to women of general criminological theories. [T]here is no reason to suppose that explanations of women's crime should be fundamentally different from explanations for men's crimes, though gender must play a part in any such explanation ... There are a number of criminological theories, however, which, though not originally developed for women, do contribute to our understanding of women's crime.
>
> (Morris, 1987: 75)

Morris thus finds anomie, differential association and social bonding theories to be particularly relevant, and concludes that 'differential opportunity structure, associations, socialisation, and social bonding can aid our understanding of crimes committed both by men and women and can take account of differences in the nature and extent of their crimes' (Morris, 1987: 76).

There is still not a well-developed, uniquely feminist explanation of criminal behaviour that can answer the generalizability or gender ratio questions. Feminist theorists have approached the task of constructing such a theory by paying close attention to the dimensions of gender and sex roles that they believe other theorists have ignored or misunderstood, and this includes not only sex-role expectations, but the significance of the underlying patriarchal structures that permeate all aspects of society. As Chesney-Lind observes:

> It is increasingly clear that gender stratification in patriarchal society is as powerful a system as class. A feminist approach to delinquency means construction of explanations of female behaviour that are sensitive to its patriarchal context. Feminist analysis of delinquency would also examine ways in which agencies of social control ... act in ways to reinforce women's place in male society.
>
> (1989: 19)

The impact of feminist critiques

An area where feminism has been particularly influential has been in focusing our attention on the nature of crimes committed against women by men with the two areas most frequently studied being rape and domestic violence. In the former case, feminists have campaigned for anonymity and protection for women against having their character tested in court – although, in practice, it is still possible to agree with Adler (1982) that few women are actually protected – and the setting up of specialist rape suites in police stations where victims can be dealt with in a sympathetic manner. These changes have encouraged some improvement in the reporting of offences to the police, although the incidence of rape continues to be greater than officially recorded (Jones *et al.*, 1994).

In the case of domestic violence, the whole issue is now considered far more serious than previously by the criminal justice system. As recently as 1984, Sir Kenneth Newman, then Metropolitan Police Commissioner, had tried to exclude the police, invariably the first port of call for victims of domestic violence, from responding to such cases, as he called this 'rubbish work' akin to dealing with 'lost dogs'. It was not proper police work (Radford and Stanko, 1994: 149–58). There are now special legal provisions established in order to protect women and children from domestic violence, although some critics have argued that this body of legislation has actually made matters worse, for it allows these offences to be dealt with less seriously than would be the case in incidents of street violence. Second, although there is now a greater emphasis than before in dealing with these cases, domestic violence remains under-reported (see Hanmer and Saunders, 1984; Dobash and Dobash, 1992; Heidensohn, 2003).

Separate studies of women and their experiences of crime have had a threefold influence in criminology. First, there has been the development of different explanations of female criminality and conformity. Second, there has been a general 'gendering' of crime, which includes gendered explanations of certain male criminality. Indeed, we might note that, in some respects, men have also been gender-stereotyped previously by criminology and this point is addressed later in this chapter. Third, there has been recognition of different female 'experiences' of crime, victimization and the criminal justice system and, in particular, feminist criminologists have been very influential in the development of the left realism, which is the focus of Chapter 18, in particular the emphasis on the use of victim studies, even though the application of the information is not always acceptable to feminists (see Schwartz and DeKeseredy, 1991; Carlen, 1992).

Downes and Rock (1998) identify three specific areas where the feminist perspective has contributed to theoretical criminology: (i) the 'female emancipation leads to crime' debate; (ii) the invalidation of the 'leniency hypothesis'; and (iii) the emergence of gender-based theories.

The 'female emancipation leads to crime' debate

Freda Adler (1975) and Rita Simon (1975) focused their attention on increases in female crime that had occurred during the late 1960s and early 1970s and the increasing aggression involved in much female offending. Both claimed that such variations could be explained by the influence of the emerging Women's Liberation Movement.

Adler (1975) argued that there is very little actual difference between the potential propensity for criminality between men and women, and previous variations in actual criminal involvement can be explained by sex-role differences. Changes in the social position of women in the legitimate sphere have a correlation in the illegitimate social world, which has brought about greater involvement in crimes such as robbery and violence previously solely associated with men.

Simon (1975) argued rather differently that female emancipation has led to an increase in opportunities for women to commit crime, particularly in the area of financial or property crimes. Simon disagrees with Adler on two important issues: first, she argues that emancipation will make women less violent as the frustration associated with victimization and exploitation is reduced both inside and outside the home; and, second, instead of arguing that women are competing with men to become criminals, she proposes that increases in criminality are the outcome of the increased opportunities that liberation brings.

Regardless of their differences, both Adler and Simon argued that liberation, or emancipation, causes crime. Box and Hale (1983) neatly summarize the many and varied criticisms by noting merely an historical overlap between women's liberation and an increase in female crime. It has also been noted that the rate of male violent crime has continued to rise faster than the female rate (Mukherjee and Fitzgerald, 1981) and, thus, the 'new violent' female is considered to be a myth (Box, 1983). Walklate (1995) concludes that men and women commit similar types of crime, although the latter offend at a much lower rate and commit far less serious crimes than men less frequently.

Heidensohn (2000/1) observes that offences committed by women tend to be concentrated in the areas of theft, handling stolen goods and drug offences with little involvement in acts of violence, while Graham and Bowling (1995) found that female offending tends to peak at the age of 13 to 14, a much earlier age than for males. We might note that none of the above observations totally refutes the propositions of Adler and Simon that, in short, a reduction in the extent of informal social controls for girls and young women has provided them with opportunities to engage in previously less thinkable criminal activities, although a simple causal relationship between female emancipation and criminality was never likely to exist.

The invalidation of the 'leniency hypothesis'

The 'leniency hypothesis' was first proposed by Pollak (1950). Much subsequent feminist work has examined how women are dealt with by the criminal justice system in an attempt to discover whether or not they are treated more leniently for reasons of 'chivalry'. Farrington and Morris (1983), for example, found that court leniency towards women was an outcome of their lesser criminal records, while Carlen (1983) found that Scottish sheriffs justified imprisonment more readily for female offenders whom they viewed as having 'failed' as mothers.

Downes and Rock conclude that, rather than being treated leniently by the courts, 'women – by comparison with men – are under-protected and over-controlled' (1998: 285–6).

The emergence of gender-based theories

Some writers, in seeking to understand female criminality, have modified the 'control theory' originally proposed by Hirschi (1969) – and discussed more fully in Chapter 15 – and applied this to the situation of women. Heidensohn (1985) argues that the reason why there are so few women criminals is because of the formal and informal controls that constrain them within male-dominated society and proposes that, in order to understand more about the transmission of gender inequality and the control of women by familial roles, it is necessary to consider the practical and ideological constraints imposed by family life. It is these very practices and policies that limit the involvement of women in activities outside of the home and that propel them back into the family where they are subject to greater control. Heidensohn observes that, while women can be seen as responsible for the behaviour of others within the home and within the community, they are acting as the agents of male authority when carrying out that control function; there, thus, exists the stereotype of the mother reprimanding a child by saying 'wait until your father gets home'.

Heidensohn notes that, while women may act as agents of control on behalf of men, they are themselves controlled both at home and outside. The sexual division of labour is related to the notion of separate spheres – public and private – for men and women, and the latter are expected to function chiefly within the 'private' sphere of the home. Moreover, the privacy afforded this sphere is a contributing factor in the oppression that women experience, for it is within the home that they are vulnerable to isolation and its consequences. Lacking alternative definitions of themselves and their roles, they are affected by those around them, particularly their husbands. Male dominance may result in the subtle undermining of the woman's confidence and self-esteem and this may lead to overt violence and bodily harm (Dobash and Dobash, 1980). Wives who are housebound, isolated and dependent, are also the major victims of neurosis and depression (Brown and Harris, 1978). Furthermore, paid employment for women often means subjection to male power and supervision. Heidensohn argues that, in short, their socialization and the conditions of their existence effectively control women. It is thus little wonder that so few women engage in criminal activity. An area of criminality in which women are involved, while at the same time clearly being controlled by men – although this latter point is challenged by some – is that of prostitution, and feminism has been at the forefront of challenging the notion of this being a victimless crime.

Feminism and prostitution

We saw in Chapter 8 that the influential structural functionalist Kingsley Davis (1961 originally 1937) argued from a traditional malestream perspective that prostitution is a structural necessity for society and will continue to be universally inevitable all the while sexual repression remains essential to the functioning of society. Liberal feminists are not entirely antagonistic to this traditional perspective, and observe that prostitution involves choice for women and indeed often some form of 'liberation' (economic or sexual). The contract between the prostitute and her client is seen as a consensual relationship between two adults and these writers highlight the fact that many women work independently from pimps. Any violence and oppression that they experience can be seen to be exacerbated by the present legal system of regulation, which stigmatizes, marginalizes and criminalizes the prostitute. Thus, for liberal feminists, prostitution is perceived as being a private business transaction. Where radical feminists view the prostitute as a human being who has been reduced to a piece of merchandise or a commodity, liberals propose that a woman is free to enter into contracts or not, as she so wishes. Radical feminists nevertheless do not believe that the desire of a prostitute to enter into such a 'contract' is done of her own free will and argue that prostitution is an exploitative relationship in which the customer is interested only in the services of the prostitute and has no interest in her personal welfare. But the liberal responds to this by pointing out that, when one seeks out a professional such as a doctor, lawyer, plumber or mechanic, one is not centrally concerned in the person doing the professional work – only his or her services (Weisberg, 1996).

Liberal feminists believe that personal 'rights' should predominate over concerns for the social good, and this is a political view that goes back to the utilitarianism of John Stuart Mill, who argued that government should stay out of the private affairs of its citizens (Weisberg, 1996). The oppression identified by liberal feminists focuses on the injustices fostered by gender roles that favour men to the disadvantage of women, but this does not necessarily mean that they all approve of prostitution in a moral sense.

Marxist feminists identify poverty as the crucial motivation for women involved in prostitution. Thus, the extreme economic misery under capitalism and within the system of marriage, which provides it with crucial support, makes prostitution a rational choice for women (see Bonger, 1916). Prostitution is identified as a particular corrupt form of labour and Marx himself asserted that 'prostitution is only a specific expression of the general prostitution of the labourer' (cited by Pateman, 1995) and, therefore, can be seen as standing as a symbol of all that is wrong with capitalist society. Prostitutes may well feel that they are free to make rational choices, but in objective terms they are oppressed workers reinforcing and perpetuating an exploitative capitalist scheme. Carol Pateman nevertheless – and perhaps rather surprisingly – appears to agree with the liberal feminists and argues that prostitutes are not wage labourers but rather independent contractors:

> The objection that the prostitute is harmed or degraded by her trade misunderstands the nature of what is traded. The body and the self of the prostitute are not offered in the market; she can contract out use of her services without detriment to herself.
>
> (1995: 191)

Marxists and Marxist feminists observe a significant reduction in the spiritual qualities of life in the capitalist system with people reduced to being mere cogs in an invariably economically determined machine. There is, moreover, a tendency in some feminist writings to discuss the relationship between feminism and prostitution in very much the same terms, thus removing the transcendent and spiritual qualities of prostitutes and leaving only a mechanistic view of their involvement in prostitution (Bromberg, 1997).

Radical feminists argue that prostitution is the product of patriarchal society and point to the inequality and unequal power relations that structure interaction between the sexes. Women are thus exploited by pimps, clients, and sometimes official agencies like the police, in a patriarchal society dominated by male privilege. Prostitution is evidence of the sexual and economic oppression and exploitation of all women by men. Edwards observes that, with radical feminism, 'the focus of attention has been turned on its head, and the obsession with prostitutes' sexuality has been abandoned for a concern with the sexuality and psychology of men' (1993: 113).

Radical feminists thus do not view prostitution as a harmless private transaction and victimless crime, but, on the contrary, they argue that it reinforces and perpetuates the objectification, subordination and exploitation of women (Weisberg, 1996), while, at the same time, men are perceived to universally believe two significant myths regarding their own sexuality. The first myth is that men need more sex than women and, second, that they are genetically the stronger sex and should therefore be dominant in relationships with women (Jaggar, 1980). Men believe that they have no choice but to respond to their sexual urges, which thus creates a self-validating tautology of belief predicated on the notion that their aggressive behaviours are linked to inherited traits. Radical feminists disagree with this male mythology and view the source of male sexuality to be derived in part from culture and not exclusively from biology. Prostitution and pornography as factors in male experience only exacerbate his self-serving belief in the primacy of his sexuality and thus, his role as the 'dominant' sex is reinforced in his mind as something very real, when, in fact, it is not. In this sense, influences such as prostitution and pornography can be viewed as degrading to all women as acceptance of these events reinforces and perpetuates a cruel fantasy of women as weak and submissive. Weisberg observes that:

> According to the radical feminist view, men are socialised to have sexual desires and to feel entitled to have those desires met, whereas women are socialised to meet those desires and to internalise accepted definitions of femininity and sexual objectification.
>
> (1996: 71)

As men cling to the idea that their sexuality is an absolute expression of their need and dominance, they prevent women from effecting new attitudes, self-realizations and behaviours (Bromberg, 1997). The issue of male masculinity is discussed in some detail in the final section of this chapter.

Is there a feminist criminology?

Some writers have observed the existence of an identifiable feminist criminology (Brown, 1986), while others have argued that to have a few writers calling their work feminist does not constitute a 'feminist criminology' (Smart, 1977). Moreover, where attempts to create such a 'feminist criminology' have been made, there has not been any consensus about its success. Pat Carlen (1988) identified two problems with the endeavour: first, most feminists, she suggests, identify crime as a male problem, ironically agreeing with the great body of traditional criminology; and, second, where there has been an attempt to identify a universal explanation of crime that applies to both men and women, it has been theoretically unsound.

Other feminist writers have identified the wider feminist debate as the ideal location for examining the position of women in society and their social control. They argue that a feminist analysis should be central to any examination of women and crime, rather than the development of a 'feminist criminology' as a separate discipline (Heidensohn, 1985). Alison Morris (1987) takes this point further, suggesting that, since the nature of feminism, like criminology itself, is diverse, the very idea of a unified feminist criminology is suspect. Gelsthorpe and Morris (1988) suggest that a more appropriate position is to talk about feminist perspectives within criminology, thereby recognizing the diversity within both feminism itself and among the writers examining women as subjects within criminology.

For postmodern feminists, all-encompassing feminist theory is itself of concern as it draws together and attempts to provide, in some instances, a universalistic account or grand theory of the experience of all women. However, the rejection of malestream assumptions of truth and reality – an essential feature of feminist postmodernism – has been identified as a potential weakness.

We have seen that Carol Smart (1977) had considered the possibility of creating a 'feminist criminology' but a few years later she had decided that this was an unnecessary task, as there were 'more important goals to achieve than the one of constructing a sub-discipline to rank alongside other criminologies' (Smart, 1981: 86). She took this argument a step further in a later article entitled 'Feminist Approaches to Criminology or Postmodern Woman Meets Atavistic Man' (1990), where she argues that feminism has actually transgressed, or gone beyond, criminology. Smart observes the positive and emancipatory advances made in feminist thought and contrasts these with the perceived limited horizons of criminology and argues that 'the core enterprise of criminology is problematic, that feminists' attempts to alter criminology have only succeeded in revitalising a problematic enterprise' (1990: 70). She focuses on 'the continuing "marriage" of criminology to . . . positivistic paradigms' and 'highlights criminology's isolation from some of the major theoretical and political questions which are engaging feminist scholarship elsewhere' and observes that 'for a long time we have been asking "what does feminism have to contribute to criminology?" when the question should be rephrased to read "what has criminology got to offer feminism?"' (1990: 83). In this case, her reply is that criminology actually has very little to offer.

Gender issues have nevertheless broadened the field of criminological enquiry, opening up opportunities for the examination of female criminality but at the same time the useful possibility of an examination of masculinity, male power and violence drawing upon broader feminist debates. Pat Carlen (1992) – although critical of what she describes as the anti-criminology and libertarian, gender-centric and separatist tendencies of contemporary feminist 'criminologists' – also recognizes the benefits of a feminist perspective to an understanding of women, law and order. She advocates the recognition of women's crimes as those of the powerless, of the stereotypical notions of femininity integral to women's oppression, and observes the active contributions of some feminist writers to campaigns around women and crime. The influence of these can be observed in the 'left realism' that is the focus of Chapter 18.

Heidensohn (2012) identifies ideas and concepts that are currently being explored within feminist criminology, which she predicts will have a major impact in the future and which will be an area of fruitful research for the next generation of scholars. First, there is the area of human rights, which has had a major impact in recent years in criminology and which holds real promise for achieving justice for women (Silvestri, 2006). Britain already has in place legislative requirements for gender equality, which impose duties on public bodies to comply. It is evident, however, that these laws are not being respected, when, for instance, children are penalized because their parent – usually their mother – receives a custodial sentence (Epstein, 2011).

Second, comparatively little work has looked at the media representations of deviant women or deployed the approaches of contemporary cultural studies to do so. Certainly, a few topics – in particular, those relatively rare women who kill – have been the focus of some attention and individual cases such as Myra Hindley, the 'Moors Murderer', have been studied, but this is an area that lacks and, it is proposed, needs major analysis. It is observed that some of the fictional depictions of women offenders and women in the criminal justice system have been disproportionate to their lives – think of the TV show *Bad Girls* – and, while other topics have been closer to 'reality', analyses of these aspects and their significance are very limited. *Dixon of Dock Green*, a very early TV police series, has been accorded iconic status by serious, male police researchers who have explored its importance at great length (McLaughlin, 2006; Reiner, 2004), while *Cagney and Lacey* and *Prime Suspect*, major US and British female cop shows, have not attracted anything like the same attention, despite their massive success (Heidensohn and Brown, 2012). This is an important area of study because the mass media have played a vital role in promoting gender stereotypes of and to women – and men – but they are also the route through which most people learn about feminism and where significant debates occur.

Third, there is the continued and long-term issue of the paucity of theories of female criminality. It is proposed that some of the most high-profile current criminological concepts should be tested to see how far they can account for gender and gender differences. Thus, the thriving debate on penality and the state – the punishments inflicted on convicted offenders – needs more than just an added section on women; it needs to be proved against the old generalizability notion.

Fourth, it is observed that research on gender and crime, and especially feminist perspectives in this area, has been one of the most robust, resilient and important features of modern criminology but it is not exactly clear why this has been the case. While there have been various descriptions of phases of that development, there has to date been no in-depth history or sociology of knowledge. This is partly an archival and partly an empirical project, which it is observed is urgently needed and which it is proposed will be a major project for the next generation of feminist scholars.

Crime and masculinities

Maureen Cain (1989, 1990) agrees with Smart (1990) that feminism has 'transgressed criminology' and thus proposed from that perspective a significant need to answer the fundamental question of what it is about 'maleness' that leads a disproportionate number of men to become criminals. It was thus in response to this feminist discourse that a growing literature began to emerge that sought to 'take masculinity seriously'. Central to this development was the work of the Australian academic Bob Connell (1987, 1995), who – in response to the one-dimensional notion of male dominance presented by radical feminism – recognized the existence of 'multiple masculinities'. In short, he argued that masculinities could be black as well as white, homosexual or heterosexual, working class or middle class, with all subject to challenge and change over time. Connell accepts that there is a dominant masculinity in society, which is based on the notions of heterosexual power and authority, but proposes that other forms can challenge this and that male power is not absolute but is historically variable and thus a social construction.

James Messerschmidt (1993) applied this analysis of diverse and contested masculinities to youth crime, arguing that the types of offences committed by young males are patterned through various interpretations of masculinity generated by 'structures of labour and power in class and race relations'. In an apparent development of Robert Merton's anomie theory, he argues that crime provides a means of 'doing masculinity' when there is no access to other resources. The nature of the actual offence committed takes on different forms according to how different class and ethnic groups define their masculinities.

Thus, for white working-class youth, masculinity is constructed around physical aggression and, for some, hostility to all groups considered to be inferior in a racist and heterosexual society. Lower working-class ethnic minorities, on the other hand, find their masculinity in the street gang. Whereas the white middle class may envisage a future in mental labour and the white working class in manual labour, both of these routes are seen as inaccessible to many youths from ethnic minority backgrounds, and, therefore, offences, such as robbery, provide the opportunity to accomplish a particular form of masculinity based on toughness and physical power. Messerschmidt argues that each form of masculinity represents an attempt to meet the cultural ideal of the dominant form of masculinity that is denied to young people elsewhere, whether it is in the home, school or even work.

Jefferson (1997) is nevertheless critical of such structurally determinist arguments, which he observes tell us little of why it is that only a particular minority of young men from a given ethnic group or social class choose to accomplish their masculinity by 'doing crime', while the majority do not. He follows Katz (1988) and Presdee (1994) in noting that criminological knowledge has repeatedly failed to recognize the pleasure that is involved in 'doing masculinity' and 'doing crime'. Both these writers argue that, unless we come to understand these pleasures, we will never have a complete picture of why it is that particularly young people become involved in criminal behaviour. The work of these cultural criminologists and notions of the attractions and seduction of criminal behaviour are explored in more depth in the final part of this book. However, if masculinity – or at least different variants of masculinity – is a social construction and hence not a characteristic biologically inherent in the male sex, it follows logically that there is a false duality between the male and female gender with the outcome that women may well do masculinity. Connell observes that, 'unless we subside into defining masculinity as equivalent to men, we must acknowledge that sometimes masculine conduct or masculine identity goes together with a female body' (2000: 16). If this is the case, it therefore becomes necessary to analyse how crime and violence committed by women and girls is related to masculinities.

Messerschmidt (2005) argues that both traditional malestream pre-feminist and liberal feminist criminological theories create an artificial dualism in gender constructions and reduce all masculinities and femininities to one normative standard case for each – the 'male sex role' and the 'female sex role' – with the outcome being a reification of gender. He observes that these criminological theories require that we examine masculinity exclusively done by men and boys and femininity by women and girls, while ignoring the creation of masculinities and femininities by people. Messerschmidt observes that, as masculinities and femininities are not determined biologically, it is important to identify and examine possible masculinities by women and girls (and femininities by men and boys) and their relation to crime. Indeed, there remains a necessity in criminological research to uncover not only gender diversity among girls/women, but also girls'/women's relations to crime and violence and whether or not such social action constructs masculinity or femininity. Thus, Jody Miller (2001, 2002) shows that certain girls involved in gangs identify with the boys and describe such groupings as 'masculinist enterprises':

> To be sure, 'one of the guys' is only one part of a complex tapestry of gender beliefs and identities held by the gang girls I spoke with – and is rarely matched by gendered actions – but it remains significant nonetheless.
>
> (Miller, 2002: 442)

Miller observes that, while gender inequality is rampant in the mixed-gender gangs of which the girls were members – for example, male leadership, a double standard with regard to sexual activities, the sexual exploitation of some girls and the exclusion of most of the girls from serious gang crime – some of the girls differentiated themselves from others through a construction of being 'one of the guys'. In other words, the notion 'one of the guys' is not fashioned by being similar to boys – because of the inequalities – but, rather, certain girls are perceived and perceive themselves as being different from other girls.

Messerschmidt (2004) conducted a life-history study of adolescent involvement in violent assault and found numerous gender constructions by violent girls and that some of them 'do' masculinity by in part displaying themselves in a masculine way, by engaging primarily in what they and others in their milieu consider to be authentically masculine behaviour, and by an outright rejection of most aspects of femininity. Messerschmidt (2005) observes that the task of contemporary criminologists is not therefore to reify gender by concentrating research and theory solely on gender differences in crime but proposes that the goal should be to examine and explain both gender differences and gender similarities – that is, gender diversity – in the commission of crime.

Policy implications of the gendered criminal

Gender plays a critical role throughout the criminal justice process. A review of the life circumstances and of the backgrounds of female offenders in the system would suggest that there are more effective ways to prevent and address the criminal behaviour of women than are currently in use. Feminists thus propose that criminal justice practice could be improved by addressing the pathways that women take into the criminal justice system, the differences in their patterns of offending from those of male offenders, their experiences in the criminal justice system and their responses to programmes.

Feminists argue, for example, that it is important to re-examine the gendered effects of public policies that criminalize substance abuse, which often results in the over-representation of women in prison. Mandatory minimum-sentencing statutes for drug offences in the USA, in particular, have had a devastating effect on women and have unfairly punished them as well as their children. Standard gender-neutral correctional procedures have also disadvantaged women in that such procedures do not take into account the histories of abuse of many female offenders. The criminal justice system, it is argued, must become trauma-informed in order to provide effective interventions and services for women.

At present, both the availability of programming for women offenders and the types of services offered fall short of what is needed. For example, because women in treatment find recovery complicated by trauma, childcare issues, inadequate social support systems and lack of financial resources, proposed strategies must take these issues into account. Additionally, it is critical that programmes provide appropriate screening and assessment of the needs – not risks – of individual clients, along with a range of services designed to meet those needs.

In creating appropriate services that truly take into account and respond to gender and cultural factors it is necessary to first re-examine our current criminal justice policies. We can then work to adjust those policies so that the response to offending by women is one that emphasizes human needs, specifically those that reflect the realities of the lives of women.

Rather than focusing solely on punitive sanctions, a feminist-inspired policy perspective would propose that we begin to systematically consider the least restrictive appropriate alternatives to incarceration. The savings to society from a reduction in the imprisonment of women and from the improved reintegration of female offenders into the community would be of benefit, it is argued, not only to the women themselves, but also to future generations.

Summary of main points

1. Feminists argue that it is men who are the dominant group in society and it is they who make and enforce the rules, which are invariably to the detriment of women.
2. Feminism has had a considerable impact on criminology in recent years and has provided both critiques of the traditional explanations of female criminality while offering its own perspectives.
3. Feminist criminologies challenge the male-centredness of criminology and propose that the main weakness of traditional 'malestream' criminological theory is the failure to understand the important significance of gender and sex roles.
4. Feminism is not a unitary system of thought but a collection of different theoretical perspectives with each explaining the oppression of women in a different way.
5. An area where feminism has been particularly influential has been in focusing our attention on the nature of crimes committed against women by men with the two areas most frequently studied being rape and domestic violence.
6. Separate studies of women and their experiences of crime have had a three-fold influence in criminology: (i) the development of different explanations of female criminality and conformity; (ii) a 'gendering' of crime which includes gendered explanations of certain male criminality; and (iii) a recognition of different female 'experiences' of crime, victimization and the criminal justice system.
7. There are three specific areas where the feminist perspective has contributed to theoretical criminology: (i) the 'female emancipation leads to crime' debate; (ii) the invalidation of the 'leniency hypothesis'; and (iii) the emergence of gender-based theories.
8. Different feminist perspectives have differing perspectives on prostitution.
9. It was in response to feminist discourse that a growing literature began to emerge that sought to 'take masculinity seriously'.
10. Messerschmidt observes that, as masculinities and femininities are not determined biologically, it is important to identify and examine possible masculinities by women and girls (and femininities by men and boys) and their relation to crime.

Discussion questions

1. What are the different versions of feminist thought?
2. Discuss the feminist critiques of traditional 'malestream' criminology.
3. Discuss the notion that feminist criminology has had no impact on the law and criminal justice system.
4. In what ways do feminists explain increasing female involvement in crime?
5. What impact has feminism had on the study of male criminality?

Suggested further reading

Key feminist texts in the field of explaining crime and criminal behaviour are Carlen (1988, 1992), Gelsthorpe and Morris (1988), Heidensohn (1985, 1994), Leonard (1983) and Smart (1977, 1981, 1990). Dobash and Dobash (1992) and Hanmer and Saunders (1984) are essential reading on violent crime against women. For key texts on masculinity and crime, consult Connell (1987, 1995), Messerschmidt (1993, 2004, 2005), Miller (2001, 2002) and Jefferson (1997).

12. Critical criminology

Key Issues

1. The origins of critical criminology
2. Crimes of the powerful
3. Crimes of the less powerful
4. Critical race theory
5. The challenge of zemiology

There are two contemporary manifestations of the radical criminological tradition we encountered in Chapter 10. One variant, 'left realism', is the focus of Chapter 18. The other, critical criminology – or 'left idealism' as it has been termed by their former colleagues and now 'realist' opponents – is the only version that can be argued to have unequivocal foundations in the victimized actor model of crime and criminal behaviour. There are a number of different variations of critical criminology but, in general, it can be said to be a perspective where crime is defined in terms of the concept of oppression. Thus, some groups in society – the working class (in particular, the poorer sections), women (especially those who are poor, sole parents and socially isolated) and ethnic minority groups (especially those from non-English-speaking backgrounds and refugees) – are seen to be the most likely to suffer oppressive social relations based upon class division, sexism and racism.

Critical criminologists focus their attention on both the crimes of the powerful and those of the less powerful. Crime is viewed as associated with broad processes of the political economy that affect both groups but in quite different ways. For the powerful, there are pressures associated with the securing and maintenance of state and corporate interests in the context of global capitalism. In the case of the less powerful, criminal behaviour is seen to be the outcome of the interaction between the marginalization or exclusion from access to mainstream institutions and criminalization by the state authorities, with particular attention paid to the increasing racialization of crime, in which the media and police, in the 'war against crime' and public disorder, target certain invariably ethnic minority communities. In short, critical criminologists link offending behaviour to a social context that is structurally determined by the general allocation of societal resources and by the specific nature of police intervention in the lives of its citizens.

The origins of critical criminology

From the late 1960s onwards, many radical criminologists in the UK came to develop an idealist view of the working class that allowed them to appreciate and even condone deviant acts committed by members of this group. It was thus argued that offenders do not respond mindlessly to stimuli as suggested by the then dominant predestined actor model-inspired criminology, but are engaged in activity that is meaningful to them and that so happens to have been labelled as criminal by the dominant groups in society. Thus, Stan Cohen argued that 'our society as presently structured, will continue to generate problems for some of its members – like working class adolescents – and then condemn whatever solution these groups find' (1980: 1).

The labelling and deviant subculture perspectives with their tradition of ethnographic observation were a considerable influence on this 'new idealism'. Actual day-to-day contact with so-called deviant adolescents convinced researchers that these young people were simply involved in activities regarded as legitimate by the perpetrators, but that had been prohibited by the state. In stigmatizing sections of young people, the legislature was responding to a moral panic fanned by sensational and exaggerated media reporting. Cohen (1973) had written about the stigmatization of mods and rockers and the exaggerated newspaper and television reports of their behaviour, the damage they caused and the holidaymakers they terrorized back in 1964. Today, critical criminologists might claim that diverse groups ranging from recreational drugs users and 'binge' consumers of alcohol to asylum seekers and a welfare-dependent underclass are the new 'folk devils' and the targets of an overly enthusiastic and criminalizing criminal justice intervention. Thus, critical criminologists have argued that crime rates are far from being a perfect measure of the actual amount of criminality in society – being more a measure of the level of police activity – and thus can create a misleading image of horrific rises in certain types of crime. Figures purporting to show that black people are responsible for a disproportionate number of street robberies, for example, may be seen to reflect racist police stereotyping rather than reality (Hall *et al.*, 1978).

During the 1970s, orthodox criminology with its roots firmly founded in the predestined actor model was undergoing a crisis of confidence or aetiology (Young, 1994) because it had failed to explain why the crime statistics seemed to increase ever upwards even during periods of societal affluence. Criminologists, as we have seen in this book, had proposed many – varied, apparently incompatible and sometimes even more impractical – solutions to an ever-increasing crime problem for many years without any visible success. A cynic might have observed that the numbers of books offering explanations of crime and criminal behaviour – and indeed ways of successfully responding to the crime problem – had grown accordingly on the shelves of academia in direct proportion to the ever-increasing crime figures. Indeed, one of their own had influentially noted that 'nothing works' (Martinson, 1974), an observation subsequently eagerly seized upon at the British Home Office (Mayhew *et al.*, 1976) and which was to become the new official orthodoxy. This new 'administrative criminology' (Young, 1994) was to supposedly bring an end to grandiose projects to change and rehabilitate criminals, with the emphasis now on reducing the opportunity to offend, while catching and incarcerating those who still managed to transgress. This new way of thinking was heavily influenced by contemporary manifestations of the rational actor model discussed in the first part of this book. A new and 'useful' role was nevertheless found for academic criminologists who could now be employed in assessing and evaluating the success of these usually small-scale situational crime prevention schemes. Explaining crime and criminal behaviour – and thus developing extravagant and expensive proposals for its elimination – was now dismissed as an academic exercise without practical application and not worthy of support.

If the 'nothing works' argument was becoming increasingly popular with politicians, critical criminologists nevertheless had their own answers to the aetiological crisis. They argued that an analysis of the processes and situations within which the labelling of certain individuals and groups takes place simply does not go far enough. It is necessary to examine the structural relations of power in society and to view crime in the context of social relations and political economy (Scraton and Chadwick, 1996 originally 1992) and it was at this point that much work was done from a Marxist perspective to identify the causal basis of crime, and to make the link between dominant institutions and ruling-class interests. There was, nevertheless, a tendency either to romanticize crime – as acts of rebellion or resistance – or to see the issue solely in economic terms. Later work was to explore in more detail the specific contexts and lived experiences of people involved with the criminal justice system (Hall and Scraton, 1981). The issues of racism, sexism and masculinity had been virtually ignored by much of academic Marxism, while, at the other end of the spectrum, there was a perceived need to keep the focus on the actions of those in power, not only in relation to those marginalized in society but also more generally in the area of what has come to be known as white-collar crime or crimes of the powerful.

Crimes of the powerful

We saw in Chapter 6 that Edwin Sutherland (1940) was the first person to use the term 'white-collar crime' when he launched an attack on the actions of the respectable in society, which, had they been performed by the less powerful in a different context, would have been labelled as criminal. Sutherland basically observed a need to address the inequalities in the treatment of people who engaged in harmful behaviour between those in power and those without power. This pioneering work was to lead to a steady increase in research and writing – in particular, as we have seen, among those working in the differential association, anomie and deviant subculture traditions – initially in the USA and then world-wide (Geis and Goff, 1983). Critical criminology subsequently identified and built upon that earlier tradition, but has situated it firmly in the context of a contemporary critique of the nature of global capitalist society.

Swartz (1975: 18) has observed that, because capitalism involves the maximization of corporate profits, 'its normal functioning produces ... deaths and illnesses' and the commission of business crime is linked to the values of capitalism and legitimate business goals. In the same vein, Mars (1982) observes that there is only a fine line between 'entrepreneurialism and flair' and 'sharp practice and fraud'. Indeed, many such activities are not greeted with widespread disapproval, for example, an electrician who overcharges for services is often not perceived as a thief but an entrepreneur, and in this way such behaviour is excused and distinguished from the activities of 'real' crimi-nals. Corporations can practise a policy of law evasion and this may include the setting up of factories in countries that do not have pollution controls or stringent safety legislation – for example, the Union Carbide plant in Bhopal (Pearce and Tombs, 1993) – or the selling of goods that have been banned by the developed nations to markets in the developing world (Braithwaite, 1984). An example of this involved the Dalkon Shield intrauterine (contraceptive) device that was sold overseas for a considerable period when it had been declared unsafe in the USA (Hagan, 1994). In other words, multinationals dump some of their products, plants and practices, illegal in industrialized countries, onto undeveloped or underdeveloped countries (Box, 1987).

Such practices occur because the recipient nations are dependent on the capital investment of multinationals, they have fewer resources to check the claims of manufacturers and their government officials are more susceptible to bribery and corruption (Braithwaite, 1984). Corporations therefore export their illegal behaviour to where it is legal or at least where laws are not so rigorously enforced. In addition, multinational corporations often have sufficient economic resources and political influence to instigate or curtail legislation or at least its enforcement. In fact, many of the world's multinationals are wealthier than some of the less developed countries where they have a subsidiary, which means that they hold tremendous economic and political influence in those locations (Carson, 1980; Box, 1983). Box (1983) observes a need to penetrate the process of mystification that perpetuates the myth that corporate crime is both not serious and harmless and which protects the powerful segments of society who benefit from such crime. He himself provides a readable account of the ability of corporate crime to kill, injure and rob, while arguing forcefully that the competitive environment in which businesses operate actively encourages employees to break the law:

> Not only does the promotion system mean that people who rise to the top are likely to have just those personal characteristics it takes to commit corporate crime, but these are reinforced by the psychological consequences of success itself, for these too free a person from the moral bind of conventional values.
>
> (Box, 1983: 39)

In short, critical criminologists argue that working-class crime is insignificant when compared to the 'crimes of the powerful' that largely go unpunished. Price-fixing, tax evasion, white-collar crime, environmental pollution, deaths at work and other offences, they contend, cost society far more than, for example, youth offending, a regular source of societal condemnation and moral panic. Moreover, the powerful perpetrators of these offences stand to gain far more material advantage from their misdemeanours, while fewer resources are used to combat white-collar crime and some questionable activities are not even criminalized, but are instead portrayed as examples of wealth creation and enterprise. In addition, offenders in this category can hire accountants and lawyers to protect them and have powerful friends to lobby on their behalf.

Crimes of the less powerful

Critical criminologists recognized that – although the general level of affluence as measured by gross domestic product per head, public spending and welfare benefits had increased – relative deprivation still existed among a substantial minority of society, who were well below 'the average' and accepted standard of living of the majority. Now the definition of relative deprivation changes over time and between societies. Absolute poverty was admittedly being eliminated, but relative poverty continued to exist, as the rich claimed a seemingly unfair slice of the larger cake. Thus, according to critical criminologists, attempts by the less powerful to claim their just rewards, or to protest about their lot, were simply criminalized. Reiman (1979) claimed that 'the rich get richer and the poor get prison'.

Critical criminologists explain crime among the less powerful in society by reference to an interaction between *marginalization*, or the exclusion from access to mainstream institutions, and *criminalization*, which occurs with the intervention of the state authorities. The latter involves a process in which the law, agencies of social control and the media come to associate crime with particular groups who are subsequently identified, sought out and targeted as a threat. Scraton and Chadwick (1996) argue that this process is used to divert attention from economic and social conditions, particularly at times of acute economic change that could provide the impetus for serious political unrest. Moreover, overtly political protests are criminalized and political terrorists termed 'common criminals' in order to neutralize the political nature of their actions. Hillyard (1987) observes that this criminalization process helps to engender public support for anti-terrorist measures, as it is easier to mobilize state intervention against criminal acts than for the repression of what might be seen as a just political cause.

Criminalization can therefore be used to justify harsher social control measures that are often taken against economically and politically marginalized groups who have few means of resisting these initiatives. Major economic changes occurred during the last quarter of the twentieth century in most advanced industrial societies and, in particular, in the UK, that were to impoverish many in the lower, and less powerful, social classes, while critical criminologists observe that it is this group that has always been seen, since at least the beginning of the modern era, as the 'dangerous classes'. It is through the criminalization of their activities that their situation can be attributed to their own weaknesses, thus justifying harsher control measures.

Crime, according to some critical criminologists, is, therefore, a reassuring sign that the perpetual struggle against inequality continues and this is an idea with its origins in the writings of Durkheim, who claimed that crime could be 'functional' for the needs of society:

> Crime must no longer be conceived as an evil that cannot be too much suppressed. There is no occasion for self-congratulation when the crime rate drops noticeably below the average level, for we may be certain that this apparent progress is associated with some social disorder.
>
> (1964: 72)

Durkheim's concept of the functionality of crime has survived in those 'conflict theories' that depict crime as symptomatic of an ongoing struggle between powerful groups and the weak. This conflict essentially needs to take place so that social control does not become an unchecked oppression of citizens by the state.

Critical criminology or 'left idealism'

For critical criminologists – such as Scraton and Chadwick (1996) – the growing disparities between rich and poor and the expansion in the sheer number of the latter constitute a legitimation crisis for the capitalist system as a whole. *Actual* deprivation is again seen as the cause of working-class crime with the perceived state response involving a substantial move towards 'law-and-order' politics, which has exacerbated the process of identifying and punishing members of particular groups within the working class and ethnic minorities.

Critical criminologists propose that a legitimate response to crime must be built upon a strategy of social empowerment. This means involving people directly in decisions about their future through direct participatory democracy but also crucially requires a redistribution of economic resources to communities on the basis of social need and equity. To counter crimes committed by the powerful, there must be open and public accountability of all state officials and, as part of wealth redistribution, there has to be a transfer of wealth from private hands to public ownership under community control. As a general crime prevention measure, and to reduce the prevalence of certain crimes, there needs to be anti-racist and anti-sexist campaigns, including the re-education and retraining of agents of the state such as the police. Strong emphasis is given to extending and protecting basic human rights and institutionalizing these by means of watchdog agencies and developmental policies.

Critical criminologists argue that the true function of the criminal justice system is not to solve crime but to unite the people against a rump in their midst – defined as deviant – and hence in this way maintain the legitimacy of the existing social order. The true function of prisons, it is argued, is not to reform criminals but rather to stigmatize them and cause them to be seen as the enemy in our midst (Foucault, 1980). Likewise, it is not the real function of the police to prevent crime and apprehend criminals but rather to maintain the social order, being used to control industrial disputes, political demonstrations or any other activities that may threaten the community. They are also used to widen the net of social control so that the state – in the form of the criminal justice system – brings under surveillance and control more of those individuals and groups that can be considered potentially deviant (Cohen, 1985). In order to achieve this overall intention, the authorities, in particular the police, will require the necessary powers and be relatively free of control by local and central governments (Scraton, 1985).

Many would consider this view of social order, the law and the criminal justice system to be too simplistic and a denial of the reality that most people experience and, moreover, the individual nature of criminality cannot simply be regarded as a construction of the state. Critical criminologists have nevertheless posed a number of important questions and have attempted to critically interrogate dominant and orthodox perceptions of crime and criminal behaviour, arguing that crime should not be perceived as a problem of individual offenders in society but as a process related to the wider economic and social structures of power. This is nevertheless a problematic analysis. Most criminal behaviour is not targeted against the dominant social order, while the criminal law is not just directed at keeping the less powerful in their place. Indeed, many of the weaker and poorer sections of our society need both the law and its agents in the criminal justice system to protect them from criminal elements living in their midst (Hopkins Burke, 1998b), and some former radical criminologists came to recognize that reality and eventually came to reconsider their stance and the very meaning of radicalism. These subsequently highly influential 'left realists' came to constitute the second variant of the former radical tradition – terming their former radical colleagues as 'left idealists' – and are themselves the focus of attention in Chapter 18.

Critical race theory

Critical race theory refers to an historical and contemporary body of scholarship that aims to interrogate the discourses, ideologies and social structures that produce and maintain conditions of racial injustice. Critical race theory analyses how race and racism are foundational elements in historical and contemporary social structures and social experiences.

In defining critical race theory, it is important to make a distinction between the long-established historical tradition of critical theorizing about race and racism and a specific body of US legal scholarship that emerged during the 1970s and 1980s in response to the successes and failures of the Civil Rights movement struggles for the freedom and liberation of black people during the 1950s and

1960s. While this new school of legal thought created the term 'critical race theory' to indicate a new critical analysis of the role of the law in propagating and maintaining racism, this movement is nevertheless part of a broader intellectual tradition of critical theories of race and anti-racist struggle that has political roots in the work of pioneering scholar-activists like Frederick Douglass, Ida Wells-Barnett and W.E.B. Du Bois. Using this broader framework, critical race theory can be viewed as a diagnostic body of 'intellectual activism' scholarship that seeks to identify the pressure points for anti-racist struggle. Given the historical scope of critical race theories, this chapter highlights several core themes that bring together this eclectic body of explicitly political theorizing.

The first core theme deals with how critical race theories frame their two focal objects of study: race and racism. First, critical race theory understands the concept of race as a social construction that is produced as a result of the cultural and political meanings ascribed to it through social interactions and relationships across multiple levels of social organization. Thus, since the seventeenth century, race has been a constitutive feature of global social, political, economic and cultural organization. Critical race theories demonstrate how race concepts and their accompanying racisms were foundational to the administration of colonial social systems, the rise and expansion of global capitalism, and emergence of the human biological sciences and medicine of the eighteenth, nineteenth and twentieth centuries.

Second, critical race theorists have rejected the notion that racism is limited to malign individual prejudice and have embraced a more structural understanding of racism. An organizing theme of critical race theory is that there is not, and has never been, one monolithic and universal form of racism. In 1967, black radicals Stokely Carmichael and Charles V. Hamilton devised the term 'institutional racism' to identify how racism is embedded in social structures and multiple institutions. In highlighting the structural dynamics of racism, critical race theorists challenge the idea that black people are solely responsible for their own oppression. Drawing on these formulations, contemporary critical race theories understand racism as a vast and complicated system of institutionalized practices that structure the allocation of social, economic and political power in unjust and racially coded ways.

The second core theme is that critical race theories are grounded in the lived experiences, unique experiential knowledge and narrative voice of racialized and subordinated communities. Strongly influenced by previous freedom movements against colonialism, segregation and racial violence, these theorists engaged pragmatically in 'intellectual activism' that aimed not only to theorize, but also to resist these conditions of racial oppression. These lived experiences are not always reflected in the activities of scholars located in professional academia. Critical race theorists have helped to produce and have drawn upon social and intellectual movements for liberation and empowerment in the USA and elsewhere, such as the Harlem Renaissance, Black Nationalism and Afrocentrism. Not only have critical race theorists tended to emerge from subordinated social groups, but also their theories attempt to use the voices and experiences of black people in the pursuit of social and economic justice.

The third core theme is that critical race theory has traditionally used and continues to represent an interdisciplinary approach to the study of race and racism. The interdisciplinary and, indeed, extra-disciplinary nature of critical race theory enables the analysis of a wide range of social, economic and political phenomena that shape race and racism as social structures. Critical race theory draws upon an interdisciplinary body of scholarship that has intellectual roots and practitioners in sociology (Brown *et al.*, 2003), critical legal studies (Bell, 2004; Matsuda *et al.*, 1993), political theory and philosophy (Goldberg, 1993, 2002), neo-Marxist British cultural studies (CCCS, 1982; Hall, 1992), African American literary criticism (Murray, 1970; Carby, 1998), history (Fredrickson, 2002; Marable, 2000) and philosophy (Outlaw, 1996; West, 1999). In sociology, critical race theories draw heavily upon the theoretical and philosophical orientations of Marxism, pragmatism and poststructuralism. Drawing on psychoanalytic and literary theories, critical race theorists have analysed the relationships between forms of cultural racism and colonial domination and have also documented and critiqued the role of nation-states in the formation of racial categories in the enactment of different forms of political oppressions. From these various disciplinary locations, critical race theories entail the illumination and critique of these discursive and institutional relationships between social constructions of race and the social practices of racism in terms that make opposition to these racial discourses and racist practices possible.

A fourth core theme is that critical race theories embrace and deploy quantitative, qualitative and discursive methodologies to illuminate different aspects of race and racism as social structural phenomena. Critical race theorists have used quantitative methodologies to map the contours of economic and spatial segregation, racist attitudes and ideologies, and racially coded health disparities. They have also deployed qualitative methodologies to understand the lived experiences and narratives of racially designated peoples and discursive approaches to investigate the relationships between racial discourses and the construction of racial subjects. As will be discussed later, critical race theories also draw heavily upon historical and comparative frameworks that allow for the analysis of race and racism as historically embedded social phenomena. This methodological pluralism, partly a consequence of the interdisciplinary scope of critical race theory, has enabled the formulation of a response to the dominant social, political and scientific practices and ideas that constitute race and racism in different historical periods.

Fifth, critical racial theories have long recognized and opposed the centrality of science to the construction of racial meanings and practices. In fact, in what might be considered the first treatise of critical race theory, the detailed analysis produced by W.E.B. Du Bois in *The Philadelphia Negro* (1899) was intended to refute the claims that rates of poverty and destitution among the black population of that city were the result of inherent biological and cultural inferiorities. Scientific racism consists of ideas of race based on presumed physiological, biological and/or genetic differences and the practices of deploying such ideas as essentialist explanations for racial stratification and oppression. Critical race theory has long contested these scientific claims that upheld racial hierarchies and justified ideologies of white supremacy. Whereas science had long been a tool of racial oppression, it emerged as the spearhead and epistemic foundation of the critical race theories of the post-Second World War era.

While critical race theories have relied on a wide range of theoretical approaches, a core theoretical framework embraced by many contemporary critical race theorists is that of racial formation, which emerged in the 1990s as an explicitly historical and political approach to analysing race as an organizing system of knowledge and power that combines both discursive and institutional elements (Omi and Winant, 1994; Winant, 2001). The racial formation framework stands in stark contrast to demographic approaches to race that conceptualize race as a quantitative variable trait in population studies, biological approaches that view race as something rooted in biology and/or genetics, and colourblind approaches that wish to abandon the study of race concepts altogether. The racial formation understands the construct of race as 'a concept that signifies and symbolises socio-political conflicts and interests in reference to different types of human bodies' (Omi and Winant, 1994: 72). Analytically, this means always interpreting the meaning of race in relation to the discursive practices that produce the idea of race, the social processes through which racial categories are created, embodied, transformed and destroyed, and the institutionalized power relations that are brought to bear in shaping racial conflicts and interests (Omi and Winant, 1994).

These discursive and institutional elements form what are called 'racial projects' in which social and political conflicts and interests are waged over race bodies and racialized groups. The idea of racial projects is central to the racial formation approach because it draws the discursive and institutional elements of race and racism together into a single analytic framework. Omi and Winant (1994: 56) define racial projects as the discursive and institutional deployments of race that are both an interpretation, representation or explanation of racial dynamics and/or an effort to organize and distribute resources using racial categories. Racial projects combine what race means in a particular discursive practice and the ways in which both social structures and everyday experiences are racially organized based upon that meaning (Winant, 2001, 2004).

Some critical race theorists, particularly black feminist theorists, have also articulated an intersectional theoretical approach to analysing the ways in which systems of gender, sexuality and nationalism are implicated in the production and maintenance of racial subordinations (Collins, 1990, 1998; Matsuda *et al.*, 1993). Drawing on this earlier work, critical race theorists continued to turn their attention to the ways in which the formulation, production and dissemination of cultural images and representations are placed in the service of white supremacy (Collins, 2005; hooks, 1981, 1990).

In the post-Civil Rights era, critical race theorists have exposed and criticized the ways in which the myths of US democracy, meritocracy and progress and the ideology of individualism function to justify changing forms of racial domination. In particular, critical race theorists have analysed new forms of colourblind racism that enable and conceal the reproduction of racial inequality without direct reference to social constructions of race (Bonilla-Silva, 2003; Williams, 1997). Colourblind racisms assume that racial inequalities are the outcome of natural, economic and/or cultural differences between racialized groups, and advocate that not using constructions of 'race' is necessary for the principled end of racism.

A major trajectory in this analysis of colourblind racism is the analysis of the law and legal institutions as crucial sites for the production of colourblind policies and practices. Legal scholar Derrick Bell (2004), considered to be the intellectual inspiration for the consolidation of critical race theories of the law, has demonstrated that conditions of racial segregation have ideological and pragmatic foundations in the speech about socially denigrated groups. His primary target of critique is the absolutist position on the First Amendment protection of free speech and how this strong position allows racist speech ideology to ripple throughout society, especially in universities. Bell and his followers have also targeted the assumption that racial progress has been achieved in the post-Civil Rights era. Bell illuminates the partial truths of racial progress in the American society by a close rereading of American political and legal history armed with the notion of silent covenant, a backdoor agreement among white elites to advance black interests and civil rights if and only if they will also benefit whites. The implication of his analysis is that political freedom for oppressed racial groups is only achieved when it can be accomplished in the context of furthering white political domination. Bell recounts key moments in American social history that illustrate this relationship: the signing of the Constitution, the Emancipation Proclamation and, most importantly, the Brown decision, the landmark US Supreme Court case where state laws establishing separate public schools for black and white students were declared unconstitutional. Bell argues that conditions of racial injustice are so entrenched in the United States that, when modest gains for racial equality are achieved, they are too often interpreted as evidence that the struggle for racial equality is complete.

A final theme is illustrated in a recent exemplar of contemporary critical race theory. Many critical race theories go beyond diagnosis and critique to offer arguments and proposals for specific social policies that, if implemented, can work to undo the systemic disadvantages that impair the life chances and conditions of black people in the USA. These theories continue to challenge entrenched racial inequalities in health, education, criminal injustice, political representation and economic opportunity (Brown et al., 2003; Guiner and Torres, 2002; Shapiro, 2004). In a recent exemplar of contemporary critical race theory, a group of prominent sociologists attacked racial realism, a variant of colourblind ideology, in which it is claimed that racism is largely over and the racial inequalities that remain are the result of the natural proclivities and cultural pathologies of black people (Brown et al., 2003).

Michael Coyle (2010) argues that we can build on the use of language critique, which is fundamental to the critical justice theory research tradition, to develop critical race criminology. Specifically, language studies can unmask the racism of modern 'criminal justice' discourse and modern 'criminal justice system' practices. Thus, it is proposed that researchers can identify the construction and maintenance of race work in the discourse and practices of 'criminal justice' in at least two important ways. The first is to conduct individual investigations into any word or phrase commonly used in 'criminal justice discourse'. It is exactly because everyday justice discourse takes place within a body of interpretations, metaphors, rhetorical frames and, ultimately, ideology that can be and sometimes is racist that the study of the very words and phrases used in 'criminal justice discourse' will disclose the presence of racism. Second, it is proposed that researchers can engage in a critical examination of the language they encounter in their research, regardless of its topic. Thus, for example, an ethnography of incarcerated black youth in a juvenile facility in the USA can not only unveil the voice and meanings that these young people give to their experience, but can also trace what the very words they use show about racism in incarcerated and everyday life.

Critical criminology and the challenge of zemiology

A significant contemporary variant of critical criminology has been zemiology or the study of social harm. The intention from this perspective is to significantly extend the legitimate parameters of criminological study away from a limited focus on those injurious acts defined as such by the criminal law – for example, theft, burglary and criminal damage – and to establish that a vast range of harms – for example, sexism, racism, imperialism and economic exploitation – could and should be included as the focal concern of criminological investigation (Schwendinger and Schwendinger, 1970), and these contemporary critical criminologists observe that their former colleagues and now left realists remain trapped within a legal definition of 'crime'. It is the intention of these new zemiologists to look beyond 'crime' to discover where the most dangerous threats and risks to our person and property lie, for example, poverty, malnutrition, pollution, medical negligence, breaches of workplace health and safety laws, corporate corruption, state violence, genocide and human rights violations all have more widespread and damaging consequences than most of the behaviours and incidents that currently make up the 'problem of crime' (Muncie, 2000).

By the 1990s, recognition of these social harms was beginning to be identified as a legitimate focus of criminological inquiry (Muncie and McLaughlin, 1996) and the issue of human rights denial was entered on the agenda, not simply through extending definitions of what actually constitutes crime, but through recognition of the legal transgressions routinely employed by those wielding political and economic power and their ability to deny or conceal the harms they unleash under the protection of the law (Cohen, 1993). Similarly, it had taken some twenty years of feminist enquiry to establish that violence, danger and risk lie not just on the streets or in the corridors of power, but in the sanctity of the home. Recognizing male violence and opening up the vexed question of 'violent masculinities' further extended our conception of what actually does constitute the 'crime problem' (Segal, 1990; Campbell, 1993; Jefferson, 1997).

In other areas, we can witness an at least partial emergence of 'hidden crime' onto the mainstream agenda. The murder of Stephen Lawrence and the unrelenting campaign by his family to expose police and judicial racism was to catapult racial violence and hate crime to the forefront of issues to be addressed by law-enforcement and community safety agencies in the early twenty-first century. The concept of state crime – in the form of illegal arms dealings, genocide and torture – has been consistent front-page news following successive wars in the Balkans, Afghanistan, Iraq and the establishment of the War Crimes Tribunal in The Hague. A long campaign against the transportation of live animals from Britain to Europe entered the issue of animal rights into legitimate crime discourse, as has the recognition of the culpable negligence of tobacco and food companies in knowingly marketing unsafe and life-threatening substances. It has also become increasingly likely that one will find numerous aspects of social policy (in particular, housing policy and youth homelessness), environmental policy (in particular, road building and pollution) and economic policy (in particular, third world debt, the arms trade and corporate greed) being described within a crime discourse.

For zemiologists, a conception of crime without a corresponding conception of power is meaningless. The power to cause certain harmful acts to become visible and define them as 'crime', while maintaining the invisibility of others – or defining them as beyond criminal sanction – lies at the heart of the problem of working within notions of 'the problem of crime'. It is perceived to be a notion with a particularly limited vision of the range of misfortunes, dangers, harms, risks and injuries that are a routine part of everyday life. If the criminological intent is to reveal such misfortunes, risks and harms, then the concept of 'crime' has to be rejected as its sole justification and object of enquiry.

Muncie (2000) observes that the first stage in what he terms 'decriminalising criminology' is to recognize that a great number of damaging events are far more serious than those that make up the 'crime problem'. Moreover, many of these incidents – such as petty theft, shoplifting, recreational drug use, vandalism, brawls, antisocial behaviour – would not seem to score particularly high on a scale of serious harm. It is nevertheless these 'minor' events that take up much of the time and preoccupation of law-enforcement agencies and the criminal justice system. Conversely, the risk of suffering many of those crimes defined by the state as 'serious' would seem negligible compared to such everyday risks as workplace injury and avoidable disease. What has remained unclear is how far the zemiological project of recoding crime as harm is capable of challenging and overthrowing legal definitions. Nelken (1994) has argued that campaigns to extend the criminal label so that it includes new forms of injury continually run the risk of reinforcing the concept of crime even when it is seemingly being attacked. From a different, left realist, perspective, Matthews and Young (1992) observed that a comprehensive expansion of the notion of criminality can only lead to nihilism and cynicism, and that by removing the principal object of criminology – crime – the subject is evaporated into larger disciplines such as sociology. Henry and Lanier (1998) respond by proposing the need for an integrated definition of crime that recognizes the legally defined and the legally ignored, the serious and the trivial, and the visible and the invisible located on a continuum dependent on the seriousness of the harm.

Critical criminologists argue that the redefining of crime as harm opens up the possibility of dealing with pain, suffering and injury as conflicts and troubles deserving negotiation, mediation and arbitration rather than as criminal events deserving guilt, punishment and exclusion. Bianchi (1986) proposed that crime should be defined in terms of tort and dispute with the criminal law replaced by reparative law. From this perspective, questions of crime control are subordinated to those of a wider social justice agenda in which governments and the wider community recognize disadvantage, difference and diversity, and acknowledge that they have a responsibility for enhancing personal and social development. While a concept of harm encourages conceptions of victimization as universal, it enables recognition of its most damaging forms beyond those which are currently recognized by media, law and the state. Perceptions of seriousness frequently reveal the differential placed on human life dependent on social status and position within the hierarchy of power. Muncie (2000) thus observes that, for example, the death of Princess Diana and the TV presenter Jill Dando were portrayed in the media to be more serious than the regular and continuing murders experienced by Nationalist and Loyalist communities in Northern Ireland at the time.

Zemiologists propose that the concept of harm enables injury to be addressed by a wide variety of social responses and without necessarily the involvement of the criminal justice system. Thus, the concept of *redress* has an extensive set of formal definitions and meanings from 'to put right, repair, rectify something suffered or complained of' to 'correct, amend, reform or do away with a bad or faulty state of things' (De Haan, 1990: 158). It provides an opportunity for dealing with social problems or conflicts – such as crime – through neighbourhood rather than criminal courts and the pursuit of compensation or reconciliation, rather than retaliation or blame allocation:

> To claim redress is merely to assert that an undesirable event has taken place and that something needs to be done about it. It carries no implications of what sort of reaction would be appropriate; nor does it define reflexively the nature of the initial event ... It puts forth the claim for a procedure rather than a specific result. Punitive claims already implied in defining an event as a 'crime' are opened up to rational debate.
>
> (De Haan, 1990: 158)

In short, the zemiological aim is to integrate, rather than exclude; to reduce or, if possible, abolish deliberately inflicted pain; to seek restoration rather than retribution (Cohen, 1994). Muncie (1998) observes that working within established criminological or criminal justice discourses essentially excludes any possibility of imaginative rethinking and, therefore, important work needs to be done to expose the ways that these orthodox 'knowledges' of 'crime', criminal justice and criminology are constructed and used in order to open up challenging alternatives.

Muncie (2000) sounds a note of caution for the zemiological project by observing that the successful incorporation of a social harm agenda into mainstream criminological discourse could lead to the unwelcome and totally unintended criminalization of all 'undesirable behaviour' by the criminal justice system, noting that, for example, notions of community safety were first promoted as a means of liberalizing crime prevention policy but were subsequently appropriated by New Labour as a means of targeting the 'antisocial' and used to justify all manner of punitive interventions from curfews to custody. From a zemiological perspective, these emergent discourses do not challenge the notion of 'crime', but have become incorporated by it because they continue to fail to recognize the multifaceted nature of harm.

While the concept of harm has clear potential for broadening what for critical criminologists is a traditionally conservative criminological agenda it nevertheless continues to operate within a negative discursive framework. Harm is not only a source of fear, but also a source of *fascination, pleasure* and *entertainment*. Simple observation of television programme listings, the contents of mass-circulation newspapers or the shelves of fiction in bookshops will confirm the extent to which an audience perceives crime not just as a social problem but as a major source of entertainment. The way we enjoy violence, humiliation and hurt casts doubt on the universal applicability of harm as always connoting trouble, fear and loss. For participants, too, the pleasure in creating harm or doing wrong or breaking boundaries is also a significant part of the equation and is the focus of study for cultural criminologists, which we will examine further in Chapter 20.

Critical criminology revisited

Critical criminology had been able to respond to the suggestion that criminology was unable to offer a convincing explanation of the ever-increasing crime problem, but, with the arrival of mass unemployment at the end of the 1970s and the beginning of the 1980s, these radical criminologists were able to return to their traditional argument that deprivation is the main cause of working-class crime. At the time of writing, the major economies of the world are undergoing a major 'correction' and multiple recessions, which have not been seen since the 1930s and which were the outcome of a 'credit crunch' where boom conditions were artificially sustained for some years by banks loaning large sums of money that did not really exist to people with a dubious ability to repay. The Chancellor of the Exchequer at the time, Alistair Darling, felt it was his duty to tell the public that the UK faced its worst economic crisis in sixty years (BBC News, 2008a) and not long afterwards a leaked draft letter from the Home Office advised that crime levels would inevitably increase because of the downturn. Rising property crime and violent crime, and increased hostility to migrants, were also considered likely. Home Office Minister Tony McNulty told the media that the letter was a 'statement of the blindingly obvious' as it was clear that crime would probably go up during the economic slowdown, and this argument about property crime, such as burglary, and violent crime was based on the experience of the recession in the early 1990s (BBC News, 2008b), when we might observe that conditions were nowhere near as severe as those that existed during the 1930s.

Such changed socio-economic circumstances should provide fruitful conditions for critical criminological research and analysis, and indeed provide support for recent arguments for a return to traditional Marxist analysis. Russell (2006) observes that, since the early 1990s, the 'new directions' in critical criminology that we encountered above have simply excluded Marxism on the grounds that it is an outdated mode of analysis. He argues that Marxism remains as relevant as ever for analysing crime, criminal justice and the role of the state, and we might observe that, in the current economic crisis, whole groups of 'white-collared' professionals, among many others, previously not considered to be members of the working class, not least by themselves, and thus immune to the negative extremes of the trade cycle, have become increasingly proletarianized victims of the downturn with both their homes and jobs at risk. The effect on the psyche of those with strong bonds to the conventional social order and socio-economic status world suddenly cast adrift in unfamiliar and significantly impoverished changed circumstances can have major implications for crime and criminality.

Policy implications of critical criminology

Critical criminology is a more recent contemporary version of the earlier conflict and radical theories we encountered in Chapter 10. The policy implications of critical criminology are thus very similar to these earlier variants with the major priority being a significant restructuring of society to address the inherent inequalities based on socio-economic exclusion, gender and ethnic discrimination. Thus, contemporary policy implications can include the promotion of research to clearly demonstrate that current definitions of crime and the function of the criminal justice system act to support the interests of the capitalist class and the powerful to the detriment of the powerless and socially excluded, which is detri-mental to the civil and human rights of the latter groups. The main implication of the critical criminological agenda is the creation of a benevolent socialist society in which the economy is regulated to promote public welfare and social equality.

Fichtelberg and Kupchik (2011) note that the policy implications of the critical approach to criminology have a limited utility for those who are charged with making practical, pragmatic criminal justice policy in the contemporary world.

As Young (1997) and Currie (1992) have pointed out in their realist critiques of critical approaches to crime and justice, the reality of crime is overlooked when analysts become focused on broader justice issues. This leaves the formation of criminal justice policy to other, often less progressive figures. Moreover, the harsh realities of crime, issues of great concern to the public, particularly to those living in disadvantaged communities, are ignored by scholars. As Currie describes this problem in relation to drug use:

> Too many well-meaning progressives simply do not get it when it comes to the trauma of drugs in the cities. A world-view that cannot even acknow-ledge the seriousness of a social problem is necessarily unable to come up with anything approaching a credible remedy for it; in the absence of any effort to provide a remedy, there are plenty of other takers. Minimalism thus effectively ceded the political terrain on illicit drugs and violent crime to the political right.
>
> (1992: 92)

And further to cite Young:

> Thus we have the characteristic syndrome of left idealism: great emphasis is placed on the criminal justice system as an autonomous agent which shapes and causes problems. Crime itself is played down, marginalized, and is not the focus of attention. Pathology and dysfunction within oppressed groups is minimalized or denied.
>
> (1997: 479)

Fichtelberg and Kupchik (2011) observe that, while it is undoubtedly true that the formation of criminal justice policy deserves critical scrutiny, the failure of much critical criminology to engage with the subject of crime as a real problem that ought to be addressed scientifically is problematic for the development of public criminology and we will return to these issues in the concluding chapter.

Summary of main points

1. There are different variations of critical criminology, but, in general, it is a perspective where crime is defined in terms of the concept of oppression.
2. The focus of attention is on both the crimes of the powerful and those of the less powerful, with crime associated with the broad processes of the political economy that affect both groups but in quite different ways.
3. For the powerful, there are pressures associated with the securing and maintenance of state and corporate interests in the context of global capitalism.
4. Critical criminologists argue that working-class crime is insignificant when compared to the 'crimes of the powerful' that largely go unpunished.
5. Crime among the less powerful in society is explained by reference to an interaction between marginalization, and the exclusion from access to mainstream institutions, and criminalization, which occurs with the intervention of the state authorities.
6. Criminalization can be used to justify the harsher social control measures that are often taken against economically and politically marginalized groups who have few means of resisting these initiatives.
7. The recent growing disparities between rich and poor and the expansion in the number of the latter constitute a legitimation crisis for the capitalist system as a whole. Actual deprivation is again seen as the cause of working-class crime.
8. Critical race theory refers to an historical and contemporary body of scholarship that aims to interrogate the discourses, ideologies and social structures that produce and maintain conditions of racial injustice.
9. A significant contemporary variant of critical criminology has been zemiology. The intention is to significantly extend the legitimate parameters of criminological study away from a limited focus on those injurious acts defined as such by the criminal law.

10. Critical criminologists argue that the redefining of crime as harm opens up the possibility of dealing with pain, suffering and injury as conflicts and troubles deserving negotiation, mediation and arbitration rather than as criminal events deserving guilt, punishment and exclusion.

Discussion questions

1. How do critical criminologists explain crimes of the powerful?
2. How do critical criminologists explain crimes of the less powerful?
3. What is the real purpose of prison from a critical criminology perspective?
4. What value does critical race theory bring to the study of crime and criminal behaviour?
5. Is zemiology a legitimate area of research and scholarship for criminologists to pursue?

Suggested further reading

Box (1987), Cohen (1980, 1985), Hall et al. (1978), Reiman (1979), Scraton and Chadwick (1996) and Van Swaaningen (1999) all make essential contributions to critical criminological explanation of crime and criminal behaviour. Those interested in the crimes of the powerful should consult the following body of work not necessarily written by those identifying themselves as critical criminologists: Braithwaite (1984), Geis (1968), Mars (1982) and Pearce and Tombs (1993). Schwendinger and Schwendinger (1970) provide an early and paradigm-forming introduction to notions of social harm, with Shearing (1989) and Tifft (1995) more recently providing significant discussions. Russell (2006) and Cowling (2008) provide a good discussion of the continuing relevance of Marxism for critical criminology – and, indeed, criminology in general – while the latter provides an interesting 'toolkit' for utilizing Marxist theories in the analysis of crime and criminal justice. Delgado and Stefancic (2001) provide an excellent introduction to critical race theory.

Part Four

Integrated theories of crime and criminal behaviour

As positivism evolved, it eventually encompassed, under the term 'deviance', the many forms of behaviour left behind by the Classical tradition. Lacking the Classical theory of behaviour, however, positivists have not been able to deal with the connections among the many acts that make up deviance and crime. Consequently, they have tended to develop behaviour-specific theories and to treat the relations between deviance and crime as cause and effect rather than as manifestations of a single cause. One purpose of this [theory] is to reunite deviance and crime under a general theory of behaviour.

(Gottfredson and Hirschi, 1990: 3–4)

The first three parts of this book each considered a different model of explaining crime and criminal behaviour. The first, the rational actor model, proposed that people choose to engage in criminal behaviour in the same way that they choose to become involved in any other form of activity. The second, the predestined actor model, proposed that the behaviour of the person is in some way determined by factors, either internal or external to them, in ways over which they have very little or no control. Criminal behaviour is thus the destiny of that person. The third, the victimized actor model, proposes that the offender is the victim of an unequal society that has in some way chosen to target and criminalize his or her activities, while ignoring those of other invariably more powerful individuals and groups.

Within the parameters of these models, there are a range of different theories that have sought to explain criminality and there are essentially three principal ways in which these can be developed and their predictability value validated. The first is to consider each theory on its own. If the data obtained by empirical research confirms the predictions of the theory, then it is generally accepted. If the data fails to support those predictions then the theory can be either modified or rejected.

The second, theory competition, involves the logical, conceptual, or empirical comparison of two or more theories to determine which offers the best explanation of the phenomenon to be studied (Liska *et al.*, 1989). In the first three parts of this book, the focus has been on single-theory explanation, albeit in the context of the particular model – or tradition – of criminal behaviour in which it can be best located. Moreover, it should be noted that theory building – like the development and acquisition of knowledge in general – is usually incremental, each theory thus building on its predecessors.

Evaluation of the evidence on a single theory has rarely led to its total rejection but, on the other hand, no one theory cited has been able to explain all incidences or forms of crime. In reality, the evidence to support, or challenge, most theories lies somewhere in between these two extremes.

The central issue is how well a theory performs when compared with others either internal or external to its model of behaviour. Criticism of one approach from the perspective of another is common, and direct competitive testing of rival perspectives often occurs. For example, the older biological variants of the predestined actor model have been largely discredited. Even the more recent and sophisticated biological explanations of criminal behaviour have tended to perform badly in comparison with sociological theories. Psychological approaches that rely on emotional disturbance or personality traits have also been found to be less successful than sociological or social-psychological explanations (Akers, 1997).

The third way to assess and construct an explanation of crime and criminal behaviour is through theoretical integration. The objective is to identify commonalities in two or more theories to produce a synthesis that is superior to any one individual theory (Farnsworth, 1989). However, while theory integration often involves such deliberate attempts to fuse together two closely related theories, it may well also stem from theory competition. Upon closer examination, two theories may not be as compatible as at first thought.

Certainly, all of the theories discussed in the first three parts of this book have been subjected, to some degree, both to competition and integration. For example, there has long been competition between the proponents of biological, sociological and social learning theories as to which approach best provides an explanation of criminal families. On the other hand, most theories have come to at least tacitly – but usually more explicitly – incorporate concepts and notions from their supposed competitors. For example, Cesare Lombroso, that much-maligned early biological positivist, came to accept social factors to such an extent that, by the fifth edition of *L'Uomo Delinquente* (*On Criminal Man*), they account for 80 per cent of his explanation of criminal behaviour.

Moreover, when a theory is first formulated, it tends to build upon other explanations within the context of the particular model of criminal behaviour in which it is situated; for example, critical criminologists provide a radical reworking of labelling perspectives incorporating structural concepts. At the same time, each theory tends to draw upon a range of different sources, for example, labelling theorists incorporate ideas and concepts from symbolic interactionism, phenomenology and ethnomethodology.

All theories have been revised to some degree after their original formulations. These revisions almost always borrow from the insights and explanations found in other theories and the sources can be both internal and external to their host model of criminal behaviour. For example, later criminologists working within the predestined actor tradition came increasingly to recognize that people are capable of making – albeit limited – choices. On the other hand, the converse is also true, later rational actor model theorists came to recognize the limitations of individual rationality. At the same time, the proponents of each theory implicitly or explicitly compare its explanatory power with that of alternative explanations.

Liska *et al.* (1989) identify different types of theoretical integration. First, there is *conceptual* integration where concepts from one theory are shown to have meanings similar to those within another theory, for example, there has been a long debate about the similarities between Durkheim's concept of anomie and Marx's notion of alienation. Second, *propositional* integration relates propositions from different theories. This can be accomplished by showing how two or more theories make the same predictions about crime, even though each begins with different concepts and assumptions, for example, both anomie theory and conflict theories predict higher crime rates among the lower social classes. This form of integration can also be achieved by placing the explanatory variables from different theories into some kind of causal or explanatory sequence. The sequence starts with the variables from one theory (for example social disorganization) to explain the variations in variables from another theory (for example, attachment to family) that can be used to explain offending behaviour. Theoretical integration can be *within level* (only micro-level or only macro-level), *across level* (micro–macro), as well as *within model* or *across model*.

Both theory competition and integration have been rigorously defended (see the various contributors to Messner *et al.*, 1989). Hirschi and Gottfredson (Hirschi, 1979, 1989; Gottfredson and Hirschi, 1990) are strong proponents of the oppositional strategy of pitting theories against one another, whereas Elliott advocates theoretical integration (Elliott, 1985; Elliott *et al.*, 1985). Hirschi argues that what passes for theoretical integration in criminology usually involves ignoring crucial differences between the theories undergoing integration. He observes that some 'integrated theories are merely oppositional theories in disguise, theories that pretend to open-mindedness while in fact taking sides in theoretical disputes' (Hirschi, 1989: 41–2):

> I do not favour efforts to link theories together unless it can be shown that they are for all intents and purposes the same theory. . . .
>
> The first purpose of oppositional theory construction is to make the world safe for a theory contrary to currently accepted views . . . Therefore, oppositional theorists should not make life easy for those interested in preserving the status quo. They should instead remain at all times blind to the weaknesses of their own position and stubborn in its defense. Finally, they should never smile.
>
> (Hirschi, 1989: 44–5)

Akers (1989) agreed with Hirschi that the integration of theories, if done without regard to incompatibilities, can result in useless 'theoretical mush'. On the other hand, regarding a strictly oppositional strategy that often overlooks important comparabilities between theories, he stated:

> [T]he insistence on keeping theories separate and competing carries . . . the risk of ignoring similarities and overlap between two theories even when they are different . . .
>
> If concepts and propositions from two or more theories are essentially the same, why pretend they are different and ignore the similarities merely for the sake of retaining separate theories? Such an attitude results in theories that are different in name only.
>
> (Akers, 1989: 24–5)

Bernard and Snipes (1995) argued that Hirschi's opposition to integration is based on his characterization of theories as falling into three main categories: 'control, strain and cultural deviance'. Hirschi believed that these are inherently incompatible theories resting on irreconcilable assumptions. Bernard and Snipes (1995) maintained that Hirschi reached this conclusion because he misinterpreted and distorted both strain and cultural deviance theory. A clear example of this is the way in which Gottfredson and Hirschi (1990; see also Gottfredson and Hirschi, 2004) mistakenly described social learning theory as cultural deviance theory and a pure 'positivist' theory that led them to ignore the many similarities between control and learning theories (see Akers, 1991, 1996).

The following chapters in this fourth part of the book consider some of those explanations of crime and criminal behaviour where theorists have deliberately set out to integrate different approaches in order to provide what they consider to be a stronger explanatory tool than that offered by one individual theory.

13. Sociobiological theories

Key Issues

1.   Biosocial theory
2.   Biosocial theory and poverty
3.   Biosocial theory and the 'new right'
4.   Sociobiological theories of rape
5.   Sociobiological explanations of childhood delinquency

Biology is the key to human nature, and social scientists cannot afford to ignore its rapidly tightening principles. But the social sciences are potentially far richer in content. Eventually they will absorb the relevant ideas of biology and go on to beggar them by comparison.

(Wilson, 1990: 260)

We saw in Chapter 5 that proponents of the biological variant of the predestined actor model sought explanations of crime and criminal behaviour in the measurable physiological part of individuals, their bodies and brains. It was acknowledged that some of the studies reviewed in that chapter really do point to biological explanations of criminality but only in a tiny minority of offenders, for a closer investigation of individual cases suggests that social and environmental background is at least equally as important. Consequently, in recent years, there has been a concerted attempt to rehabilitate biological explanations by incorporating social and environmental factors into a 'multifactor' approach to explaining criminal behaviour (Vold *et al.*, 1998; Walsh and Ellis, 2006). Thus, from this contemporary perspective, it is argued that the presence of certain biological factors may increase, but not determine absolutely, the likelihood of an individual engaging in criminal behaviour. These physiological factors generate criminal behaviours when they interact with psychological or social factors.

Biosocial theory

An interest in biological explanations of crime and criminal behaviour was revived during the 1970s following the publication of Edmund O. Wilson's book *Sociobiology*, where Wilson argued that people are biosocial organisms whose behaviours are influenced by both their physical characteristics and the environmental conditions in which they live. Thus, rather than viewing criminals as people whose behaviours are totally controlled or predetermined by their biological traits, modern biosocial theorists believe that physical, environmental and social conditions interact in complex ways to produce human behaviour (see Englander, 2007; Ellis, 2005; Fishbein, 2001; Yaralian and Raine, 2001).

Biosocial thinkers ask why it is that, when faced with the same environmental stressors, some people engage in violence yet most people do not, and they maintain that it is the presence of certain biological abnormalities or physical disabilities that makes some individuals more prone to violence or aggression than others. The perspective of many sociobiologists was neatly captured by Van den Bergle:

> What seems no longer tenable at this juncture is any theory of human behaviour which ignores biology and relies exclusively on sociocultural learning. Most scientists have been wrong in their dogmatic rejection and blissful ignorance of the biological parameters of our behaviour.
>
> (1974: 779)

Biosociology is thus an emerging paradigm that seeks to understand human behaviour by integrating relevant insights from the natural sciences into traditional sociological thinking. It is not a 'biological' perspective but conversely a biosocial perspective that recognizes 'the continuous, mutual, and inseparable interaction between biology and the social environment' (Lancaster *et al.*, 1987: 2). Biosociology proposes no ultimate causes of human behaviour but rather seeks to understand how biological factors interact with other factors to produce observed behaviour. It does not seek to 'reduce' complex behaviour to the level of biological processes in isolation from environmental influences but merely insists that such processes must be recognized and included in any analysis of behaviour.

The work of Sarnoff Mednick and associates (1977, 1987) provides a good example of the orientation of criminological biologists working in the context of the biosocial paradigm. Mednick *et al.* (1987) thus argue that the biological characteristics of an individual are only part of the explanation of criminal behaviour, with other factors involved being the physical and social environment:

> Where the social experiences of the antisocial individual are not especially antisocial, biological factors should be examined. The value of the biological factors is more limited in predicting antisocial behaviour in individuals who have experienced criminogenic social conditions in their rearing.
>
> (Mednick *et al.*, 1987: 68)

Mednick proposes in his *biosocial theory* that all individuals must learn to control natural urges that drive us towards antisocial and criminal behaviour. It is acknowledged that the learning process takes place in the context of the family and during the course of interaction with peer groups, and is based on the punishment of undesirable behaviours. The punishment response is mediated by the autonomic nervous system. If the reaction is short-lived, the individual is said to have rewarded him- or herself, and criminal behaviour is inhibited. A slow physiological recovery from punishment nevertheless does little to teach the individual to refrain from undesirable behaviour. Mednick ultimately proposes that criminals are those who have slow autonomic nervous system responses to stimuli.

Jeffery (1977) has argued strongly that this new biological criminology is not 'neo-Lombrosian' and is highly critical of those criminological theories that ignore or reject biological components. He proposes that biological, psychological and sociological characteristics should be seen as interacting together in a systems model to produce criminal behaviour. Central to his argument is the notion that individuals are born with particular biological and psychological characteristics that not only may predispose them to, but also may actually cause, certain forms of behaviour. This 'nature' is independent of the socialization process present in the social environment. There is, however, a good deal of interaction between nature and nurture through the physical environment and the feedback mechanisms that exist in human biochemical systems.

Jeffery (1977) further notes that it is poor people who tend to experience a poor-quality, vitamin-deficient diet and are more likely to be geographically exposed to pollutants. The resulting nutrients and chemicals are transformed by the biochemical system into neurochemical compounds within the brain, which can have a significant impact on their behaviour. Bio-criminologists maintain that minimum levels of vitamins and minerals are required for normal brain functioning and medical research suggests that proper nutrition is especially important during early childhood. Nutritional deficiencies at this stage in child development can result in serious physical, mental and behavioural problems (Liu and Wuerker, 2005; Neisser, 1996). Research also suggests that improving diet quality can reduce delinquency and dramatically improve the mental functioning and the academic performance of adolescents (see Schoenthaler and Bier, 2000). Other studies indicate that diets that are deficient in potassium, calcium, amino acids, sodium, peptides and other nutrients can lead to depression, mania and cognitive problems. Such mental health issues can, in turn, significantly increase the probability of violent behaviour. Similarly, studies have found a strong link between antisocial behaviour and insufficient quantities of vitamins B3, B6 and C (Siegel and McCormick, 2006; Liu and Wuerker, 2005).

Diets that are high in sugar and carbohydrates have also been linked to violence, aggression and other behavioural issues (Gans, 1991). One experiment with incarcerated youths, for example, found that reducing sweet foods and drinks in the prison diet produced a 45 per cent decline in institutional violence (Schoenthaler and Doraz, 1983). However, other, more recent studies suggest that most people with high-sugar/carbohydrate diets never engage in serious violence and that, for some individuals, sugar actually has a calming effect that reduces aggression (Gray, 1986).

Other studies have explained that apparent discrepancy by suggesting that it is how the brain metabolizes glucose that may determine whether sugar causes anti-social behaviour. Hypoglycaemia, for example, is a condition that causes glucose to fall below the level needed to maintain normal brain functioning (the brain is the only organ that obtains all of its energy from glucose). Symptoms of hypogly-caemia include anxiety, depression, insomnia, nervousness, mood swings, phobias and temper tantrums. A number of studies have found a significant rela-tionship between hypoglycaemia and violence – including assault, homicide and rape. Furthermore, studies of prison populations have found higher than normal rates of hypoglycaemia among habitually violent inmates (Virkkunen, 1986).

Sociobiological researchers have also established a connection between expo-sure to dangerous contaminants – including copper, mercury, chlorine, artificial colouring, food dyes, etc. – and both aggressive and antisocial behaviour (see Rappaport and Thomas, 2004; Ellis, 2005), while a great deal of recent research has focused on the possible relationship between lead poisoning and violence. One study, for example, found that communities with the highest concentrations of lead in the air also reported the highest levels of homicide and other forms of violence (Stretesky and Lynch, 2001). A number of studies have also found that lead poisoning is one of the most significant predictors of male delinquency and persistent adult criminality (see Denno, 1993; McCall and Land, 2004). Needleman *et al.* (1996), for example, tracked several hundred boys from the age of seven to eleven and found that those with high concentrations of lead in their bones were much more likely to demonstrate attention deficit problems, poor language skills, delinquency and aggression. High lead ingestion is also linked to lower IQ scores – a factor that can contribute to youth violence (Neisser, 1996).

In short, the sociobiological perspective proposes that poverty leads to behav-ioural differences through the interaction of individual and environment and it is an argument that has been taken up and developed by key 'right realist' crimino-logical theorists in sometimes highly contentious formulations.

Biosocial theory and the 'new right'

James Q. Wilson was – as we noted in Chapter 3 – a major influence on the devel-opment of the 'right realist' perspective on crime and criminal behaviour that was so influential in the rehabilitation of the rational actor model after many years in the explanatory wilderness. His work with Richard Herrnstein (Wilson and Herrnstein, 1985) offers a more definitive account of what they consider to be the underlying causes of crime.

Their theory contains three key elements. First, there are constitutional factors, which, although not necessarily genetic, have some biological origin. Observing that crime is an activity disproportionately undertaken by young men, Wilson and Herrnstein observe that:

It is likely that the effect of maleness and youthfulness on the tendency to commit crime has both constitutional and social origins: that is, it has something to do with the biological status of being a young male and with how that young man has been treated by family, friends and society.

(1985: 69)

It is therefore an explanation of criminal behaviour that is not solely rooted in biology. There is a concern to construct an explanation in which factors such as gender, age, intelligence, body type and personality are inserted as potential biological givens of human beings projected into a social world. But these factors are not necessarily determiners of human action. It is a social world in which the individual learns what kind of behaviour is rewarded in what circumstances. This is the second element of the theory.

Wilson and Herrnstein are heavily influenced by the psychological behaviourism of B.F. Skinner – which we encountered in Chapter 6 – and thus propose that individuals learn to respond to situations in accordance with how their behaviour has been rewarded and punished on previous occasions. From this 'operant conditioning' perspective, it is proposed that the environment can be changed to produce the kind of behavioural response most wanted from an individual. Thus, in order to understand the propensity to commit crime, it is important to understand the ways in which the environment might operate on individuals – whose constitutional disposition might be different – to produce this response. Within this general learning framework, the influence of the family, the school and the wider community is located.

The third element in the theory is that of the conscience. Wilson and Herrnstein (1985: 125) support the conjecture made by Eysenck that 'conscience is a conditioned reflex' by proposing that some people during childhood have so effectively internalized law-abiding behaviour that they could never be tempted to behave otherwise. For others, breaking the law might be dependent upon the particular circumstances of a specific situation, suggesting less effective internalization of such rules. For yet others, the failure to appreciate the likely consequences of their actions might lead them into criminal behaviour under any conditions. In other words, the effectiveness of something termed 'the conscience' may vary in terms of the particular constitution of the individual and the learning environment in which people find themselves.

These three elements – constitutional factors, the presence and/or absence of positive and negative behavioural reinforcement, alongside the strength of the conscience – provide the framework in which Wilson and Herrnstein seek to explain crime. For them, the interplay between these factors can explain why crime rates may increase in times of both prosperity and recession since the equation between the social and the individual is a complex one. They suggest that:

Long-term trends in crime rates can be accounted for primarily by three factors. First, shifts in the age structure of the population will increase or decrease the proportion of persons – young males in the population who are likely to be temperamentally aggressive and to have short horizons. Second, changes in the benefits of crime . . . and in the cost of crime will change the rate at which crimes occur, especially property crimes . . . Third, broad social and cultural changes in the level and intensity of society's

investment (via families, schools, churches, and the mass media) incul-
cating an internalised commitment to self-control will affect the extent to
which individuals at risk are willing to postpone gratification, accept as
equitable the outcomes of others, and conform to rules.

(Wilson and Herrnstein, 1985: 437)

Sociobiological theories of rape

Evolutionary theory has long been used to explain gender differences in
both violent behaviour and sexual activity and this tradition has become very
influential with sociobiological criminologists. Some evolutionary theorists
argue that, in order to ensure their genetic legacy, it is advantageous for males to
mate with as many females as possible. On the other hand, because of the physical toll of a long gestation period, it is advantageous for females to mate with
only a few males, especially those who are thought to be nurturing or carry the
best genetic material. Because of these different mating strategies, it has been
argued that the most aggressive males have historically been able to mate with
the largest number of women. From an evolutionary perspective, violence is
thought to have developed as a male reproductive strategy because it can:
(1) eliminate or deter genetic competition, that is, prevent rival males from
getting the opportunity to mate; (2) serve as a method for displaying physical
strength – genetic superiority – and attracting females; and (3) deter females from
leaving and mating with other males. Thus, in the distant past, male aggression
may have frequently led to reproductive success. If so, aggressive traits would be
more likely than passive traits to be passed on to the next generation of males.
Thus, it is often assumed by biosocial researchers, heavily influenced by
evolutionary psychology, that the descendants of aggressive males account for
the fact that, even in modern society, men continue to be more violent than
women (Ellis and Walsh, 1997).

Probably the most contentious sociobiological criminological theories to
emerge in recent years have been those proposed to explain the act of rape.
These explore what role, if any, evolutionary-psychological adaptations play in
causing the act of rape in animals and humans and are highly controversial, as
traditional sociologically based theories do not consider rape to be a behavioural
adaptation. Furthermore, and perhaps not surprisingly, some have objected to
such theories on ethical, religious, feminist or political as well as scientific
grounds. Evolutionary psychology proposes that human and primate cognition
and behaviour should be understood in the context of human and primate
evolutionary history.

It has long been observed that some animals appear to show behaviour resem-
bling rape in humans, such as combining sexual intercourse with violent assault,
often observed in ducks and geese (Abele and Gilchrist, 1977; Barash, 1977).
Sometimes an animal is sexually approached and penetrated while it is clear that
it does not want to be, but it is not these observations that are controversial but
the interpretation of these – and the extension of the theories based on them – to

human beings. It is because rape sometimes results in reproduction that some sociobiologists have argued that it may be genetically advantageous for rapists and thus prospers as a psychological adaptation.

The idea that rape evolved as a genetically advantageous behavioural adaptation was popularized by Thornhill and Palmer (2000), who propose that all human behaviours are, no matter how indirectly, the result of some evolutionary adaptation (see also Thornhill and Thornhill, 1983). They argue that, since the human brain itself, and thus all capacities for any kind of action whatsoever, evolved from natural selection, the only point of dispute is whether rape is only a by-product of some other unrelated adaptation – such as a desire for aggression, domination, etc. – or if rape itself is an adaptation favoured because it increases the number of descendants of rapists. It is argued that the latter is true.

Thornhill and Palmer (2000) argue that the underlying motivations of rapists evolved because they were at one time conducive to reproduction and observe that the overwhelming majority of rape victims are of childbearing age and suggest that childbearing ability is involved in the victims chosen by rapists. Women, they argue, have evolutionary-psychological adaptations that protect their genes from would-be rapists and cite a study that claims that victims of childbearing age suffer more emotional trauma from rape than older women do. They present this case as evidence consistent with their theory and propose that women beyond their reproductive years have less to lose – in terms of genetic progeny – by being raped.

Thornhill and Palmer (2000) present rape as an evolutionary inclination but they stress that they are doing so primarily to reveal better ways to combat rape and not to excuse rapists in contemporary society. Rape can only be eliminated, they argue, once a society is fully aware of its evolutionary origins and they discuss a range of rape-prevention methods – including chemical castration – and advocate harsher sentences for rapists than those currently used (see also Chavanne and Gallup, 1998).

Many biologists have declared themselves to be strongly opposed to these sociobiological theories of rape and three crucial arguments can be identified. First, it is difficult to determine to what extent the idea of rape can be extended to intercourse in other animal species, as the defining attribute of rape in humans is the lack of informed consent, which is a legal condition whereby a person can be said to have given their permission for the act to take place based upon an appreciation and understanding of the facts and implications of any actions. This concept is difficult to determine in other animals and it is thus argued that these theories are founded on anthropomorphic interpretations of animal behaviour, which means the attribution of a human form, characteristics or behaviour to non-human things. Second, it is claimed that forced sex in animals is ineffective as a means of reproduction because males will attack other males, or groups of males will attack lone females, killing them in the process. Third, others do not deny the generally observed attempts to control female sexuality and reproduction, but see these as being culturally conditioned, rather than as a product of evolution (Fausto-Sterling, 1992; Travis, 2003).

Recent sociobiological explanations of childhood delinquency

There has been substantial interest among sociobiological researchers in the USA in recent years in antisocial behaviour that is seen to emerge early in childhood in some individuals and persists into adulthood. Contributing to that research interest has been the growing evidence that 5–6 per cent of the most persistent offenders are responsible for 50 per cent of known crimes (Aguilar *et al.*, 2000) and that these individuals are difficult – if not impossible – to rehabilitate and most likely to become recidivists (Kazdin, 1987; Moffitt, 1993a). It is argued that identifying risk factors of early antisocial behaviour has important implications for improving both intervention and prevention.

Raine (2002) has proposed the development of a biosocial model to account for the contribution of both biologically and environmentally related risk factors in the development of antisocial behaviour. One group of studies that has sought to test this model has focused on perinatal complications and environmental adversity, noting a consistent interaction between the presence of both of these factors and the development of serious antisocial behaviour in adulthood (Raine *et al.*, 1997; Piquero and Tibbetts, 1999; Arseneault *et al.*, 2002).

Research has suggested that there are multiple risk factors and pathways associated with the development of antisocial behaviour during early and middle childhood (Cicchetti and Rogosch, 1996). One such risk factor is the health status of the mother, which, when compromised during pregnancy, has been associated with impaired functioning of the central nervous system of the child and subsequent problems in its well-being (Moffitt, 1993a, 1993b). Complications during the prenatal – conception to seventh month of pregnancy – and perinatal – seventh month of pregnancy through to 28 days after birth – periods have been found to be early factors affecting the development of the central nervous system and have been tested individually as predictors of deviant outcomes (see Brennan and Mednick, 1997). The most consistent correlation has been found between complications during the perinatal stage and later antisocial behaviour (Kandel and Mednick, 1991). Direct relations between perinatal complications and antisocial behaviour have not typically been demonstrated (Cohen *et al.*, 1989; Rantakallio *et al.*, 1992). However, in the context of family adversity, high levels of perinatal complications have been associated with increased risk of child antisocial behaviour (Drillien, 1964; Werner *et al.*, 1971; Broman *et al.*, 1975).

Recent empirical research testing the biosocial interaction hypothesis has clearly suggested that the correlation between perinatal complications and later antisocial behaviour is moderated by environmental adversity (Brennan and Mednick, 1997; Piquero and Tibbetts, 1999; Laucht *et al.*, 2000; Arseneault *et al.*, 2002). In their study of a Danish male birth cohort, Raine *et al.* (1997) found that boys who suffered both perinatal complications and early maternal rejection were most likely to become violent offenders in adulthood. Arseneault *et al.* (2002) also found support for the biosocial model in a low-income sample of 849 boys, with their results suggesting that a combination of perinatal complications posing imminent harm to the infant predicted increased rates of physical aggression at ages six to seventeen years when the children were reared in impoverished environments.

A whole body of research has linked aspects of the environment inhabited by the child – such as the quality of parenting and marital conflict – to the development of antisocial behaviour. Several studies suggest that the quality of early parental care – such as unresponsiveness and rejection – plays a significant role in the development of early-onset antisocial behaviour (Campbell *et al.*, 2000; Shaw *et al.*, 2003). Parental responsiveness, sensitivity to social cues and emotional availability are all associated with positive outcomes in young children, such as behavioural regulation and social competence (Martin, 1981; Bost *et al.*, 1998; Wakschlag and Hans, 1999). A lack of parental responsiveness during infancy, however, has been associated with negative outcomes, such as antisocial behaviour later in childhood (Shaw *et al.*, 1994a; Shaw *et al.*, 1998b; Wakschlag and Hans, 1999). Parental rejection, the combination of harsh and controlling parenting practices coupled with unacceptance of the child, also has been linked with the development of later antisocial behaviour (Dishion, 1990; Dodge *et al.*, 1994; Campbell *et al.*, 1996; Younge *et al.*, 1996). A number of studies support a 'cumulative risk hypothesis' wherein the number of environmental stressors rather than the particular combination of stressors has been associated with child behaviour problems both in the short and long term (Rutter *et al.*, 1975a; Rutter *et al.*, 1975b; Sameroff *et al.*, 1987; Sanson *et al.*, 1991; Shaw *et al.*, 1994b; Shaw *et al.*, 1998a; Deater-Deckard *et al.*, 1998).

In what is now widely considered to be a classic study, Rutter and his colleagues (1975a, 1975b) found a dramatic rise in the probability of child adjustment difficulties as the number of family stressors increased. Sameroff *et al.* (1987) thus tested the impact of three sets of variables on the behaviour of the children in their sample and found that those with high multiple environmental risk scores had much worse outcomes than children with low multiple risk scores.

There thus does seem to be research evidence to demonstrate a close correlation between biological factors, multiple environmental factors, in particular poor parenting skills, poverty and inadequate living conditions, and the onset and persistence of antisocial behaviour. Whether possession of these factors can be legitimately considered to be the fault or responsibility of the family involved – as would be suggested by right realists such as Wilson and Herrnstein (1985) – or at least partially the responsibility of wider society and government is considered in the discussion of left realism in Chapter 18.

Conclusions

Biologically oriented and sociologically oriented criminologists have in the past been in fundamental disagreement. Both have tended to defend their own positions and disciplines, while completely refusing to acknowledge those of their adversaries. Increasingly, there has been recognition of the need for biological theories that examine the interaction of sociological, psychological and biological phenomena in the production of criminal behaviour. Vold *et al.* pertinently observe that:

This emerging synthesis of perspectives will probably benefit biological criminology, since extreme biological views often raise images of determinism among some audiences, who subsequently react negatively to the furthering of such research and to any policies based on it.

(1998: 87)

In short, the future of biological explanations of crime and criminal behaviour probably only lies in its rejection of its old predestined actor model pretensions and a willingness – however grudgingly – to incorporate notions from the other two models.

Policy implications of sociobiological theories

Biosocial criminologists advocate a wide variety of nurturing strategies such as pre- and post-natal care, the monitoring of infants and young children through the early developmental years, paid maternity leave and comprehensive nutritional awareness and intervention strategies.

The fundamental nature of the response is to prioritize proactive prevention interventions rather than reactive cures and, at the same time, indeterminate sentencing, in accordance with predestined actor notions of treatment, is favoured.

Another favoured policy intervention is to provide challenging and risky legal alternatives to the excitement provided by involvement in antisocial behaviour.

Summary of main points

1. In recent years, there has been a concerted attempt to rehabilitate biological explanations by incorporating sociological factors into a 'multifactor' approach to explaining criminal behaviour.
2. It is argued that the presence of certain biological factors may increase, but not determine absolutely, the likelihood of an individual engaging in criminal behaviour.
3. Mednick proposes in his biosocial theory that all individuals must learn to control natural urges that drive us towards antisocial and criminal behaviour.
4. Jeffery (1977) argues that individuals are born with particular biological and psychological characteristics that not only may predispose them to, but also may actually cause, certain forms of behaviour.
5. Jeffery (1977) further observes that it is poor people who tend to experience a poor-quality, vitamin-deficient diet and are more likely to be geographically exposed to pollutants.
6. Sociobiological researchers have also established a connection between exposure to dangerous contaminants and both aggressive and antisocial behaviour.

7. The sociobiological argument has been taken up and developed by key 'right realist' theorists. Thus, Wilson and Herrnstein (1985) propose a definitive account of the underlying causes of crime which contains three key elements: (i) constitutional factors; (ii) social learning factors; and (iii) the 'conscience'.
8. Probably the most contentious sociobiological criminological theories to emerge in recent years have been those proposed to explain the act of rape. These explore what role, if any, evolutionary-psychological adaptations play in causing the act of rape.
9. Thornhill and Palmer (2000) argue that the underlying motivations of rapists evolved because they were at one time conducive to reproduction, although many biologists are strongly opposed to these sociobiological theories of rape.
10. There has been substantial interest among sociobiological researchers in the USA in recent years in antisocial behaviour that is seen to emerge early in childhood in some individuals and persists into adulthood.

Discussion questions

1. Explain the fundamental focus of sociobiological theories of crime.
2. Why are poor people more likely to be involved in criminality from this perspective?
3. How do 'new right' criminologists use sociobiological theories to explain crime?
4. How do sociobiologists such as Thornhill and Palmer explain rape?
5. How do sociobiologists link problems in early childhood with later antisocial behaviour?

Suggested further reading

Jeffery (1977), Mednick (1977) and Mednick *et al.* (1987) provide essential introductory readings for those interested in sociobiology. Wilson and Herrnstein (1985) provide the links between this approach and right realism. Thornhill and Palmer (2000) provide a contentious biosociological argument for rape as an adaptive behaviour for those with interests in that area, while Travis (2003) edits a collection of critiques of that argument.

14. Environmental theories

Key Issues

1. Early environmental theories
2. British environmental theories
3. North American environmental theories
4. Environmental design
5. Environmental management

The environmental criminologists Brantingham and Brantingham (1981) argue that criminal incidents essentially occur when four different dimensions of crime – a law, an offender, a target and a place – are all in concurrence. They describe environmental criminology as the study of the fourth dimension, the study of where and when crimes occur. However, while academic interest in environmental explanations of crime and criminal behaviour has grown considerably since the 1970s, the recognition of the relevance of geographical location to levels of crime is far from new.

Early environmental theories

The earliest environmental explanations of crime and criminal behaviour appeared during the nineteenth century. In France, Guerry (1833) and Quételet (1842) had analysed conviction rates for crimes committed in different geographical areas and had made a number of important findings. First, they found that crime rates varied greatly in different geographical areas. Second, when violent crimes and property crimes were separated, a further variation in patterning was found. Third, these patterns remained stable over time.

Similar studies were carried out in England and these also showed variations in crime rates between different counties, towns and villages (Plint, 1851; Mayhew, 1968 originally 1862). Mayhew (1968) conducted a study of parts of London and identified the existence of areas – known as 'rookeries' – with a high proportion of criminal residents and, moreover, the tendency of crime levels to persist over time in these areas was confirmed by later studies. In short, the significance of geographical location to the incidence of crime was confirmed, while the tendency for spatial patterns to persist suggested an element of predictability and therefore the possibility of adopting preventive policies.

The later Chicago School variant of environmental criminology – which we encountered in Chapter 7 – also proposed that social disorganization and social pathology tend to be more prevalent in certain geographical areas. Researchers in that tradition argued that crime and delinquency are transmitted by frequent contact with criminal traditions that have developed over time in disorganized areas of the city (see Shaw and McKay, 1972 originally 1931).

British environmental theories

A number of British studies conducted during the 1950s (Mays, 1954; Morris, 1957; Wootton, 1959) made repeated attempts to explain the relatively high incidence of crime in urban working-class areas. What was distinctive about this approach was the attempt to combine three different sociological explanatory perspectives. First, there was the ecological approach, which considers why people live where they do. Second, there was the deviant subculture approach, which considers the development of distinctive life-patterns and their relationship to local and environmental factors. Third, there was the social reaction, or labelling, approach, which considers the effects of classifying certain individuals and residential groups as being different or simply bad (Gill, 1977).

In reality, this integrated theoretical perspective had rather unequivocal theoretical foundations in the predestined actor model. The notion that aspects of social disorganization and anomie characterized the 'criminal areas' led to the familiar determinist tautology that proposed crime was caused by levels of social pathology already in existence in these areas, but this was by no means a simple or crude environmental determinism. It was rendered more 'open' and complex by adding the rational actor model notion of 'free will' to the environmental predestined actor model 'influences' affecting the city, and ordering and disordering its behaviour patterns. In short, from this perspective, influences such as the varying indices of social disorganization are seen to affect group and individual action, but in the last resort it is the individuals themselves who decide whether or not to become criminal. Thus, they can choose to disregard the surrounding influences, even if – as Rex and Moore (1967) have shown – there is little real choice over their area of residence in the ecological struggle between the city 'housing classes'.

A summary of the significant features of this post-Second World War reconstitution of the ecological approach to crime in a British context includes the following points. First, there was a modified use of the core Chicago School concept of the 'struggle for space' in studies of city life. Second, the focus of this concept was on studies of housing allocation and 'housing classes', thus, in ecological terms, the competition and differential access to residential space

(Morris, 1957). Third, there was an emphasis on the importance of market situation, race relations and the 'class struggle for housing' in the work of Rex and Moore (1967) in Sparkbrook, Birmingham, a study that broke with the determinism of the Chicago School while still retaining its distinction of differential urban areas.

Fourth, there was the further theoretical refinement of Lambert (1970), who revealed how high crime rates in inner Birmingham were not primarily instigated by the arrival of new and unemployed black immigrants, but through the activities of the permanent black and white residents. Newcomers merely adjusted the nature of their activities to fit in with those already taking place in the locality. Again, explanations for crime are located in the market for jobs, housing and leisure. The problems culminating in the Bristol, Brixton and Toxteth (Liverpool) disturbances in 1981 provide good examples of this type of explanation.

Fifth, there was the existence by the early 1970s of two further significant theoretical developments. Taylor *et al.* (1973) proposed that criminal area delinquency reflects the availability of opportunities/gratifications that exist in particular urban contexts, rather than being a natural outgrowth of the demoralization of the less able, the biologically inferior or the individually pathological. At the same time, a more dynamic view of culture was being developed, where the notions of change, conflict and struggle were coming to replace the static, predestined actor model notion of a social disorganization-induced 'pathology' disturbing a harmonious and monolithic 'normal' culture.

Sixth, area studies conducted since the mid–1970s show a changed focus on 'the manufacture of neighbourhood reputation', notably in the work by Damer (1974) and Gill (1977). The focus of these studies remains on the housing area and the neighbourhood unit but now includes new notions such as 'hierarchies of desirability' of housing area 'types' and types of tenant, the ideology of manufactured reputation, as in 'dreadful enclosures' (Damer, 1974), and the differential policing of such areas as prime agents in the production of offending behaviour.

These British ecological analyses did not in themselves purport to provide a causal explanation. Morris (1957) thus stresses their importance as a method of calculating the likelihood of offending behaviour taking place in a particular area, while Baldwin and Bottoms (1976) critically observe these studies to be strong on description without providing any theoretical explanation. Later North American studies sought a more sophisticated explanation of the geographical distribution of crime and criminals.

North American environmental theories

Brantingham and Brantingham (1981) observe a distinct break between earlier ecological research and the later environmental criminology, and this is characterized by at least three shifts in perspective. First, there was a significant move away from the tendency for academics to keep their research contained within the parameters of their own specific discipline with the new environmental criminologists prepared to incorporate techniques and knowledge from different perspectives. Second, there was a move away from the traditional predestined actor model search for causes of criminal motivation. Environmental criminologists simply assume that there are some people who are criminally motivated with the focus now on the actual criminal event, to find patterns in where, when and how crimes occur. Third, there has been a shift in emphasis away from the sociological imagination to the geographical imagination. This does not mean a simple replacement of the former by the latter but the two are now used together in an attempt to gain a more comprehensive understanding of crimes and ultimately an increased capacity to control them.

The contemporary field of environmental criminology includes studies of: the spatial patterning of crime at different levels of aggregation; the 'journey to crime', or the processes by which potential offenders recognize potential crime sites and specific opportunities; and the creation and maintenance of areas of criminal residence. Moreover, environmental criminology should not be equated with a crude environmental determinism; rather, the sequence by which potential criminals recognize and act on criminal opportunities is seen as a 'multi-staged decision process situated within a more general environmental learning and evaluation process' (Brantingham and Brantingham, 1981: 25).

Contemporary environmental criminology incorporates elements from three theoretical perspectives: first, routine activities theory (Cohen and Felson, 1979); second, rational choice theory (Cornish and Clarke, 1986); and, third, crime pattern theory (Brantingham and Brantingham, 1984). The first two perspectives were both identified as contemporary variants of the rational actor model and were discussed in detail in Chapter 4 but will be briefly revisited here.

Cohen and Felson (1979) developed routine activities theory in order to explain the changing nature of predatory crimes, in particular burglary. They propose that there are three elements necessary for a crime to occur – a motivated offender, a suitable target and the absence of a capable guardian – and these must converge 'in time and space' (Felson and Clarke, 1998). They argue that crime is dependent on the changing routine activities of victims and changes to the durability and manufacture of products; for example, televisions, computers and stereos have become commonplace in most homes as they are manufactured in large quantities and readily available to consumers. Moreover, these products have become more attractive targets because they are lighter and easier to steal – for example, during the 1970s, a computer occupied an entire room, whereas, in the early twenty-first century, a laptop computer with more power than its predecessor can be easily carried. At the same time, the changing routine activities of people in the last quarter of the twentieth century – for example, women entering the workforce in unprecedented numbers, which has left a great number of homes unoccupied during the day – has led to a temporal change in the distribution of burglary and this has now become a daytime rather than night-time phenomenon. It could also mean that recent decreases in the burglary rate might be at least partially explained by the increase in the number of households with economically inactive residents present much of the day.

Felson and Clarke explain that 'the rational choice perspective focuses upon the offender's decision making. Its main assumption being that offending is purposive behavior, designed to benefit the offender in some way' (1998: 7). The emphasis is on the need to consider the cost-benefit analysis process of the offender, although it is recognized that decisions reached are rarely purely rational because offenders do not factor in all possible risks, relative to rewards, involved in committing a criminal act. There is a long tradition of ethnographic research that has focused on this issue and the recognition that offenders use limited risk cues has led some researchers to propose that offenders operate in terms of a constrained or limited rationality invariably heavily influenced by illicit drugs and alcohol use (Bennett and Wright, 1984; Cromwell *et al.*, 1991; Feeney, 1999; Jacobs, 2000; Wright and Decker, 1997).

Although offenders demonstrate a limited form of rationality in the planning and execution of their offences – for example, many offenders are opportunists – there is much research to support the proposition that they do develop and utilize cues and crime templates in the selection of targets/victims (Brantingham and Brantingham, 1978, 1981; Bennett and Wright, 1984; Cromwell *et al.*, 1991; Wright and Decker, 1997; Feeney, 1999; Jacobs, 2000).

Brantingham and Brantingham (1978) propose a five-part model of victim selection. First, offenders undertake a 'multi-staged decision process which seeks out and identifies, within the general environment, a target or victim positioned in time and space' (1978: 107). Second, the cues used to make these decisions are taken from the environment in which an offender is operating. Third, an offender uses these cues for target selection and these are learned 'through experience' or 'social transmission' from other experienced offenders. Fourth, through experience, an offender develops 'individual cues, clusters of cues, and sequences of cues associated with "good" targets' (1978: 108) and these develop into crime templates. Crime targets are accepted when they correspond strongly to a crime template. Fifth, although a single offender may possess a multitude of crime selection templates, 'once the template is established, it becomes relatively fixed and influences future searching behaviour' (1978: 107).

Much of the research dedicated to the understanding of cue and template use in target selection has focused on robbery offenders (Wright and Decker, 1997; Feeney, 1999; Jacobs, 2000) and burglary offenders (Bennett and Wright, 1984; Cromwell *et al.*, 1991). Research on robbery shows that repeat offenders prefer to select targets that are vulnerable, have an outward appearance that indicates the highest potential pay-off and are in specific density areas with good escape routes (Wright and Decker, 1997). Burglary research shows that burglars use similar cues when selecting a residence to victimize. Cromwell *et al.* found that the burglars in their study used cues 'to indicate the surveillability of the target', used occupancy probes to avoid personal contact, a substantial proportion preferred to burgle a residence during the day – to avoid personal contact – and they used cues that signified 'the degree of difficulty that might be expected' in entering a home (1991: 40). Although these ethnographic studies indicate that offenders use cues and develop crime templates for victim/target selection, it is shown that offenders rarely incorporate all preferred cues. Instead, due to drug use and cash-intensive lifestyles, offenders chose victims that 'appeared to meet their minimal subjective criteria for an acceptable victim' (Wright and Decker, 1997: 87–8).

Crime pattern theory was originally developed by Brantingham and Brantingham (1984) and proposes that crime is the result of the interaction of people – both offenders and potential victims – and movement in the urban landscape in space or time. The researchers note that different crime types, offenders and victims/targets are not evenly distributed across the urban landscape in space or time and the importance of zoning and population flows in a city is observed. Thus, offenders interested in commercial burglary have a limited area to search for suitable attractive establishments, as these tend to cluster along major transportation routes in commercial zones. Moreover, offenders must take time into account as shops have definitive hours of operation that determine when a target will be left unguarded.

Brantingham and Brantingham (1984) emphasize three interrelated concepts to explain the pattern of personal and property crimes, which focus on the movement patterns of both potential victims and offenders. First, *activity nodes* are centres of high activity where individuals 'spend the majority of their time', such as the home, school, work, places of entertainment and shopping areas (Brantingham and Brantingham, 1998: 36). Second, *pathways* are the routes that connect the activity nodes of a person, such as streets, pavements or sidewalks and footpaths that may be travelled by foot, public transport or automobile. As people travel these paths from activity nodes with some regularity, the 'paths and narrow areas surrounding them become known spaces to the people who travel them' (1998: 36). Third, an *edge* is a boundary that cannot easily be traversed and this can be both physical and perceptual. A physical edge includes rivers, forests and bridges. A perceptual edge includes areas that people are afraid of, such as a rival gang territory or areas with a large discrepancy in socio-economic status, for example, a middle-class person may experience discomfort when entering high-crime inner-city areas, while, conversely, an inner-city offender might wish to choose lucrative targets in affluent areas, but generally would not venture into such localities because anonymity is absent (Brantingham and Brantingham, 1995).

These three concepts interact to form what Brantingham and Brantingham refer to as an awareness space, or cognitive map, where people – offender and non-offender – feel most comfortable because they have intimate knowledge of the area. This is the case with offenders and non-offenders. Crime pattern theory predicts that, all else being equal, offenders will commit crimes in their awareness spaces, either along a path, along an edge or around an activity node. An offender who commits offences outside their awareness space runs the risk of becoming lost because they are not familiar with escape routes, they are unaware of the location of attractive targets and they would have to devote much time and attention to the routines of guardians. All these tasks are accomplished by committing crimes within the awareness space of an offender because this knowledge is developed through their daily routines.

Contemporary environmental criminology has focused its attention on repeat or chronic offenders who, research has shown, commit a disproportionate amount of crime (Cromwell et al., 1991; Horney and Marshall, 1991; Wright and Decker, 1997), while studies indicate that some offenders develop a preference for certain offences (Cromwell et al., 1991; Wright and Decker, 1997; Schwaner,

2000). These findings are significant for environmental criminologists because it is proposed that these offenders have the most developed and fixed crime templates for target selection. Moreover, by targeting law-enforcement resources on these offenders, it should be possible to significantly increase detection rates.

Environmental criminologists have found that certain places experience a disproportionate amount of crime (Sherman *et al.*, 1989; Brantingham and Brantingham, 1995; Spelman, 1995). Spelman found that 'the worst 10 per cent of locations reliably account for some 30 per cent of all calls' for the police service (1995: 142). Brantingham and Brantingham (1995) refer to places with a dispro-portionate level of criminal activity as crime generators and crime attractors. *Crime generators* are places or areas 'to which large numbers of people are attracted for reasons unrelated to any particular level of criminal motivation they might have or to any particular crime they might end up committing' (Brantingham and Brantingham, 1995: 7). These areas or places 'produce crime by creating particular times and places that provide appropriate concentrations of people and other targets in settings that are conducive to particular types of criminal acts' (1995: 7). Examples include the development of new rapid transit routes and stations, the opening of a new bar or new shopping centre. *Crime attractors*, on the other hand, 'are particular places, areas, neighborhoods, districts which present well-known criminal opportunities to which strongly motivated intending criminal offenders are attracted because of the known opportunities for particular types of crime' (1995: 8). These places or areas include inner-city ghettos and the opening of a needle-exchange clinic in a high-crime area. Often the difference between these two concepts is blurred. However, the major differentiator is that a crime generator produces crime in an area that was absent prior to the establishment of the place, while a crime attractor intensifies criminal activities already present in a particular area.

The concepts of environmental criminology have significantly informed crime mapping and analysis, which has become increasingly central to the work of the police service and analogous agencies during the past thirty years. In the early days, most agencies used maps with coloured pins to visualize individual crime events and crime-plagued areas. Today, with the rapid advancement of tech-nology, computer-based techniques for exploring, visualizing and explaining the occurrences of criminal activity have been essential. One of the more influential tools facilitating exploration of the spatial distribution of crime has been Geographical Information Systems or GIS (Ratcliffe and McCullagh, 1999; Harries, 1999). Murray *et al.* (2001) observe that it is the ability to combine spatial information with other data that makes GIS so valuable. Moreover, the consider-able quantity of information available to most analysts necessitates an intelligent computational system, able to integrate a wide variety of data and facilitate the identification of patterns with minimal effort.

The research cited above indicates that certain areas are more prone to higher concentrations of crime than others. Widely labelled as 'hot spots', such areas are often targets of increased resources from law-enforcement agencies in an effort to reduce crime. The identification of hot spots is helpful because most police departments have limited resources and the ability to prioritize intervention through a geographic lens is appealing (Levine, 1999).

Operationally, the delineation of hot spot boundaries is somewhat arbitrary. Levine (1999) notes that crime density is measured over a continuous area and the boundaries separating hot spots of crime from areas without enough activity to merit that label are perceptual constructs. Moreover, depending on the scale of geographic analysis, a hot spot can mean very different things (Harries, 1999).

Recent studies by the Crime Mapping Research Center at the National Institute of Justice in the USA categorize hot spot detection and methods of analysis as follows: *visual interpretation, choropleth mapping, grid cell analysis, spatial autocorrelation* and *cluster analysis*. Furthermore, twelve different variations on the five classes of hot spot identification techniques were systematically documented and evaluated. However, while there are a variety of methods for detecting hot spots in crime event data, no single approach has been found to be superior to others. What has become apparent is that combining cartographic visualization of crime events with statistical tools provides valuable insights.

Environmental design

Closely linked with environmental criminology are the notions of environmental design and environmental management. It is through the work of writers like Jane Jacobs (1961), Oscar Newman (1972, 1976) and C. Ray Jeffery (1977) that the concept of preventing crime through environmental design was to become influential. These various writers propose that the nature of the built environment can affect the level of crime both by influencing potential offenders and by affecting the ability of a person to exercise control over their surroundings. There is essentially a powerful belief in the capacity of surveillance to help control crime.

Jane Jacobs (1961) was the first person to propose a new way of looking at the relationship between the physical environment and crime, and her work was essentially an attack on the urban planning practices in the USA during the 1950s, such as the urban renewal and slum clearance programmes, which she perceived to be the unnecessary destruction of a number of the older urban neighbourhoods. Jacobs argued that these structures provided a number of natural security techniques – such as being close to the street, with porches and street-level windows – that could be useful for enabling a sense of community and social bonding. She argued that the removal of such structures would decrease the social interaction, the ability to identify strangers and the overall sense of security felt by inhabitants.

Oscar Newman (1972, 1976) likewise suggests that part of the explanation for urban crime lies in a breakdown of the social mechanisms that once kept crime in check, while the inability of communities to come together in collective action hampers crime prevention. In his study of low-cost housing projects in New York City, he found that higher crime rates were associated with high-rise apartment buildings than with those of three or five storeys in comparable social settings. In the former, 55 per cent of the crimes were committed in interior public spaces, such as hallways, lifts, stairwells and lobbies, as opposed to only 17 per cent in the low-rise buildings (Newman, 1972). The proposed solution was to restructure 'the residential environments of our cities so they can again become liveable and controlled ... not by the police but by a community of people sharing a common terrain' (Newman, 1976: 2).

Newman advocated action to foster (i) territoriality; (ii) natural surveillance; (iii) a safe image; and (iv) a protected milieu. First, the notion of *territoriality* is defined as the 'capacity of the physical environment to create perceived zones of influence' (Newman, 1976: 51) that is, the ability and desire of legitimate users to claim control of an area. It is claimed that the design of buildings and their sites can encourage residents to adopt ownership attitudes, and also that certain layouts inform outsiders that particular areas are for the private use of residents. Newman argues that such design features as narrowed street entrances – real and psychological boundaries – and the use of cul-de-sacs to project a 'private' image can enhance the environment. The use of raised, coloured paving on residential streets provides such an example. Territoriality is diminished by the existence of public thoroughfares and open spaces that provide access to and from residential areas, while giving the impression that they are owned and cared for by nobody.

Second, design features such as overlooked entrance lobbies and well-placed windows, which allow residents to identify and observe strangers, provide *natural surveillance*. Newman urged the avoidance of high-rise blocks to which outsiders can gain easy access, and enclosed entrances where offenders can operate unseen.

Third, the *safe image* good design should seek to convey an impression of a safe and invulnerable neighbourhood in which residents know and look after each other. Where the distinctive image is negative, 'the project will be stigmatised and its residents castigated and victimised' (Newman, 1976: 102). It is suggested that public sector housing is particularly affected because such estates or projects are designed to stand out. This image combines with other design features that reduce territoriality and surveillance opportunities and with the socio-economic characteristics of the population to make this type of housing particularly vulnerable to crime.

Fourth, a *protected milieu* is a neighbourhood situated in the middle of a wider crime-free area, which is thus insulated from the outside world by a 'moat' of safety. Jacobs (1961) had suggested that residential areas should be sited alongside commercial areas in the expectation of enhancing safety because of increased activity. Newman argued that the success of a particular mixture of land uses 'depends as much on the degree to which residents can identify with and survey activity in the related facility as it does on the nature of the users of that facility and the activities they indulge in' (1976: 112).

Attempts by researchers to evaluate the effectiveness of the 'defensible space' thesis have often proved problematic because environmental design usually involves the simultaneous implementation of a number of measures. One initiative that was tested – in Hartford, Connecticut – featured enhanced police patrols and citizen mobilization as well as design improvements. Large reductions in the relative rates of burglary and robbery were achieved in the redesigned area (Fowler et al., 1979), but a follow-up study found that the effects of the scheme on offence rates were short-lived (Fowler and Mangione, 1982).

Other studies have found even less support for the effectiveness of environmental design schemes (Evans *et al.*, 1992). Merry (1981), for example, has noted that the advantages of 'defensible space' are largely dependent on the residents who must report or challenge strangers. Thus, in order to reduce crime, 'defensible' space must actually be defended.

Other features of environmental design may have a secondary impact on crime. Traffic-calming measures, increasingly seen in residential areas, prevent a quick exit for offenders, as well as giving the impression of ownership. Moreover, systems of barriers and one-way schemes to prevent traffic using residential areas as short cuts have the same effect. They also reduce easy and casual access to the area and lessen the chance that a burglar, for example, will select a house in the area while passing through.

The idea of offenders being products of their environment has – as we have seen – firm foundations in the predestined actor model, but it has enjoyed a renaissance through collaboration between 'routine activity theorists' and rational choice/opportunity theorists located theoretically within the rational actor tradition (Felson, 1998). Brantingham and Brantingham have commented extensively on Canadian experiments that have sought to curb crime through environmental design and have noted – as we have seen above – that many of these initiatives have stemmed from the observation that people travelling from one place to another, normally between home, school/work and place of entertainment, commit much crime.

Similar to environmental design is the notion of Design Against Crime (DAC), which as an approach to innovation emerged at the University of the Arts London during the first decade of this century. DAC has four stated aims. First, to reduce the incidence and adverse consequences of crime through the design of products, services, communications and environments that are 'fit for the purpose' and that are contextually appropriate in all other respects. Second, to equip design practitioners with the cognitive and practical tools and resources to design out crime. Third, to prove and promote the social and commercial benefits of designing out crime to manufacturing and service industries, as well as to local and national government, and society at large. Fourth, to address environmental complicity with crime in the built environment and to reduce crime and improve individual and community well-being.

DAC thus brings together designers, researchers, criminologists, manufacturers, the police and other stakeholders to design out opportunities for crime and is theoretically informed by the notions of situational crime prevention and opportunity theory, which considers 'opportunities' – linked to objects/environments and sources as well as users and abusers – to be among the main explanations of crime (Felson and Clarke, 1998). Closely linked to these notions is the recent 'hot products' theory (Clarke, 1999).

Clarke (1999) had argued that significant benefits for crime prevention could arise from focusing policy and research attention on 'hot products' or those items that are most likely to be stolen by criminals, which he observes include not just manufactured goods, but also food, animals and works of art. The ultimate hot product is nevertheless cash, which helps determine the distribution of many kinds of theft, including commercial robberies, muggings, burglaries and thefts from ticket machines and public phone boxes. Clarke argues that a better understanding of which products are 'hot', and why, would help businesses protect themselves from theft and would help the police in advising them how to do this. It would help governments in seeking to persuade business and industry to protect their property or to think about ways of avoiding the crime waves that are sometimes generated by new products and illegal use of certain drugs. It would furthermore help consumers avoid purchasing items – such as particular models of car – that put them at risk of theft and might well lead them to demand greater built-in security. Finally, improved understanding of hot products would assist police in thinking about ways to intervene effectively in markets for stolen goods.

Clarke (1999) conducted a review of the most stolen items for a variety of theft types and this led to some important conclusions. First, for each kind of theft, specific items were consistently chosen by criminals. In residential burglaries, for example, criminals were most likely to pick jewellery, videos, cash, stereos and televisions. In shoplifting, the items at risk depend on the store but bookshops in the USA were most likely at the time to lose magazines and cassette tapes, while groceries, supermarkets and convenience stores were most likely to lose cigarettes, video tapes, beauty aids and non-prescription medicines. Second, there was some consistency across the different settings in the goods stolen. Certain items were at risk of being shoplifted wherever they were sold and these included cassettes, cigarettes, alcoholic drinks and fashion items, such as Hilfiger jeans and Nike training shoes. Third, the type of car that is most likely to be stolen will depend on the motivation for the theft. Thus, 'joyriders' (or 'twockers' in the British context) tend to prefer sporty models. Those criminals stealing cars to sell prefer expensive luxury models. Offenders who were looking to steal components to sell preferred models with easily removable, good-quality radios. Fourth, vehicle body type helped determine which commercial vehicles were stolen. Vehicles used by the construction industry, such as tippers, seemed to be particularly at risk, which might well be the result of a thriving second-hand market, which would make these vehicles easier for thieves to sell. Fifth, it was concluded that relatively few hot products may account for a large proportion of all thefts. For example, theft insurance claims for new cars in the USA were twenty times higher for models with the worst theft record than those with the best. Clarke (1999) observes that policy-makers need research assistance help in anticipating and assessing technological developments that could result in new hot products and new ways of preventing theft. Moreover, the existence of large quantities of unprotected attractive property might both encourage habitual thieves to steal more, and tempt more people to try their hand at theft. If theft is made easy, there is likely to be more of it, and making it more difficult may lead to a more orderly, law-abiding society.

Environmental management

The concept of 'environmental management' rests largely on the premise that – apart from encouraging offending by their 'indefensibility' – certain districts may suffer simply because they give the impression that their residents no longer care. The difference between environmental design and environmental management is subtle but nevertheless important. The former requires implementation at the planning stage, before a district is built or developed, while the latter can be practised on an existing neighbourhood and also commercial environments where there is less prospect of using informal surveillance.

Essentially, the theory that informs the notion of environmental management proposes that evidence that crime has been committed, if allowed to remain in place, will lead to further offences being committed. The argument is applied especially to such offences as vandalism, public drunkenness, vagrancy and begging: offences which are collectively known as 'incivilities'. Wilson and Kelling describe the problem as witnessed in urban America in their 'broken windows' thesis:

> A piece of property is abandoned, weeds grow up, and a window is smashed. Adults stop scolding rowdy children; the children, emboldened, become more rowdy. Families move out, unmarried adults move in. Teenagers gather in front of the corner store. The merchant asks them to move, they refuse. Fights occur. Litter accumulates. People start drinking in front of the grocery store, in time; an inebriate drunkard slumps to the sidewalk and is allowed to sleep it off. Pedestrians are approached by panhandlers.
>
> (Wilson and Kelling, 1982: 32)

Incivilities, according to this hypothesis, lead to crime, the evidence of which causes further incivilities. Environmental management involves striving to remove the evidence of incivilities by, for example, cleaning up graffiti and other signs of vandalism, cleaning the streets and avoiding property falling into decay. This thesis has relevance beyond residential areas, for example, refusing to allow its effects to accumulate could reduce vandalism in schools (Knights, 1998). The attraction of 'broken windows' theory has been its plausibility. In fact, it is so plausible that it has been accepted despite very little research support. One study, nevertheless, suggested that the immediate removal of graffiti from subway cars in New York deprived the 'artists' of the expressive benefits of seeing their work travelling around the system, and substantially reduced the problem (Felson, 1998).

Matthews (1992) questions whether the Wilson and Kelling hypothesis should have been so readily accepted and observes that, according to British Crime Survey data, incivilities such as drunks, beggars, litter and vandalism seem to be linked more to the fear of crime than its actuality. He also notes that some inner-city areas have attracted young professional people searching for an exciting and vibrant place in which to live, with street musicians and performers, noisy bars and the other trappings of inner-city life being as attractive to some people as they are a cause of fear to others.

Hopkins Burke (1998c, 2000) nevertheless notes the ambiguity surrounding the issue of street incivilities. Beggars invariably choose specific urban areas where their close proximity to the public enables them to use tacit intimidation as an aid to their activities and different groups undoubtedly differentially receive the resultant aura of menace. Old people may be fearful and genuinely scared, while cosmopolitan young professionals might consider it to be just a colourful segment of the rich tapestry of life. Likewise, drunken vagrants gathered menacingly in a bus shelter may force by their presence – albeit silently – young mothers with pushchairs outside into the rain. Those openly urinating in the street after a hard day's drinking in the full view of mothers collecting their young children from a nearby nursery should surely experience some regulation, management and restriction placed upon their activities (Hopkins Burke, 1998c). Radical proponents of the victimized actor model would recognize that these people are among the poorest and most disadvantaged people in society and are invariably targeted by agents of the criminal justice system; on the other hand, the wider public surely deserve some protection from their more antisocial activities. This latter 'left realist' perspective is revisited in Chapter 18.

'Broken windows' theory was to become very influential in the introduction and implementation of 'zero tolerance' and 'problem-oriented policing', with the former receiving considerable attention from politicians and the media both in the USA and the UK during the last years of the twentieth century. This version of 'broken windows' theory proposed that the police can arrest a tendency towards serious criminal behaviour in a neighbourhood by proactively and assertively confronting antisocial behaviour, minor offenders and 'quality of life' offences (Hopkins Burke, 1998b), but was to go out of favour in most constituencies because of identified difficulties in sustaining hard-line strategies in the long term (Hopkins Burke, 2002).

Problem-oriented policing (POP) is an altogether more subtle and sustainable policing strategy, which requires police forces to analyse the problems that they are routinely called upon to deal with and to devise more effective ways to respond to them. It was first introduced by Herman Goldstein (1977, 1979) during the 1970s and developed during the 1990s. Goldstein (1990) argued most influentially for the replacement of the reactive, law-enforcement-based model of police work by proactive 'bottom-up' approaches, which emphasize tackling the underlying conditions that create the problems that the police have to deal with. Police forces should thus analyse patterns of crime incident clusters to identify underlying causes and problems and formulate appropriate responses most successfully in partnership with other criminal justice, welfare and voluntary groups in the locality (Leigh et al., 1998).

Policy implications of environmental theories

Environmental criminological theories focus on the criminal event and the geographical location in which it takes place. Policies to reduce crime will thus involve some way of changing or regulating identified problematic environments. Policies to help design out crime will emphasize designing and building homes and shop premises, which have easily recognizable defensible space, excellent natural surveillance and promote neighbourhoods that project an image of collective community ownership. Policies to promote environmental management will actively encourage private and public owners to carry out immediate repairs to damaged property and to enhance the attractiveness of neighbourhoods by encouraging the setting out and maintenance of trees and plants. The activities of beggars and vagrants should be strictly monitored and those engaging in street drinking and other incivilities should be targeted by regular patrols of formal guardians, such as the police and private security.

Summary of main points

1. Environmental criminologists Brantingham and Brantingham (1981) argue that criminal incidents essentially occur when four different dimensions of crime – a law, an offender, a target and a place – are all in concurrence. Environmental criminology is the study of the fourth dimension, the study of where and when crimes occur.

2. Brantingham and Brantingham (1981) observe a distinct break between earlier ecological research and the later environmental criminology. The contemporary field includes studies of: (i) the spatial patterning of crime; (ii) the 'journey to crime'; and (iii) the creation and maintenance of areas of criminal residence.

3. Contemporary environmental criminology incorporates elements from three theoretical perspectives: first, routine activities theory; second, rational choice theory; and, third, crime pattern theory.

4. Brantingham and Brantingham (1978) propose a five-part model of victim selection: (i) offenders seek and identify a target or victim; (ii) the cues used to make these decisions are taken from the environment; (iii) offenders use these cues for target selection; (iv) an offender develops cues associated with 'good' targets; and (v) a single offender may possess a multitude of crime selection templates.

5. Crime generators are places or areas to which large numbers of people are attracted for reasons unrelated to any particular level of criminal motivation, while crime attractors are places that present well-known criminal opportunities to which strongly motivated criminal offenders are attracted.

6. Closely linked with environmental criminology are the notions of environmental design and environmental management.

7. Jane Jacobs (1961) was the first person to propose a new way of looking at the relationship between the physical environment and crime, and her work was essentially an attack on the urban planning practices in the USA during the 1950s.

8. Oscar Newman (1972, 1976) likewise suggests that part of the explanation for urban crime lies in a breakdown of the social mechanisms that once kept crime in check. Action was advocated to foster (i) territoriality; (ii) natural surveillance; (iii) a safe image; and (iv) a protected milieu.

9. The concept of 'environmental management' rests largely on the premise that certain districts may suffer because they give the impression that their residents no longer care.

10. 'Broken windows' theory proposes that incivilities lead to crime, the evidence of which causes further incivilities. Environmental management involves striving to remove the evidence of incivilities.

Discussion questions

1. According to Brantingham and Brantingham, how do offenders choose their victims?
2. How can an architect 'design out' crime?
3. Explain the difference between 'crime generators' and 'crime attractors'.
4. Explain the concept of environmental management.
5. Explain 'broken windows' theory.

Suggested further reading

Key texts in environmental criminology are Brantingham and Brantingham (1981, 1984), Jacobs (1961), Jeffery (1977) and Newman (1972, 1976). Felson (1998) provides links between this approach and routine activities theory. Wilson and Kelling (1982) provide a classic text on environmental criminology with a left realist critique from Matthews (1992). Hopkins Burke (1998c, 2000) discusses this approach in terms of the policing of begging and vagrancy. Ekblom (2005) provides a good introduction to designing products against crime. Hopkins Burke (1998a, 2004a) provides comprehensive discussions of 'zero tolerance' policing, and Leigh *et al.* (1998) provide a good introduction to 'problem-oriented' policing in practice.

15. Social control theories

Key Issues

1. Early social control theories
2. Later social control theories
3. Integrated theoretical perspectives
4. A general theory of crime
5. Developments in social control theories

Social control theories of crime and criminal behaviour have a long and distinguished pedigree with strong foundations in both the rational actor and predestined actor models. Later variants have entailed explicit attempts to integrate notions from both models, while even more recently elements from the victimized actor model have been incorporated.

The origins of social control theories

The origins of social control theories – or at least the underlying assumptions on which they are founded – can be traced back to the work of Hobbes (1968 originally 1651) in the rational actor tradition, Freud (1927) and Durkheim (1951 originally 1897) from, respectively, the psychological and sociological variants of the predestined actor model.

Hobbes had been concerned with the apparent incompatibility between human nature and the notion of legal restraint. The answer to his question 'why do men obey the rules of society?' was, however, simple enough. 'Fear . . . it is the only thing, when there is appearance of profit or pleasure by breaking the laws that makes men keep them' (Hobbes, 1968: 247).

One of the central ideas of Freud that deviant impulses arise naturally when the id is not sufficiently constrained by the other components of the personality, the ego and superego, is also apparent in much of the work on control theory. This is particularly true of those earlier models that draw more explicitly on

293

psychological rather than sociological factors (Reiss, 1951; Nye, 1958; Reckless, 1961).

The roots of the more sociologically oriented control theories can be found partly in the work of Durkheim (1951), who had argued that needs, desires or aspirations arise naturally within the individual, are unlimited and restrained only by the socialized moral norms of a given society. At the same time, it is society itself that creates needs and ambitions that are incapable of realization in the particular social framework of the time. Merton (1938) later developed this idea in his analysis of *anomie* as a cause of crime.

Social control theory is fundamentally derived from a conception of human nature that proposes that there are no natural limits on elementary human needs and desires. People will always want and seek further economic reward and it is thus not necessary to look for special motives for engaging in criminal activity. Human beings are born free to break the law and will only refrain from doing so under particular circumstances. It is these fundamental assumptions that provide the foundations of later social control theories.

Most of the explanations of crime and criminal behaviour that we have encountered previously in this book view conformity as the normal or natural state of humanity. Criminal behaviour is simply abnormal. It is this orthodox way of thinking about crime that social control theory seeks to challenge. Therefore, in taking deviance for granted and treating conformity as problem-atic, social control theory offers not so much a theory of *deviance* but one of *conformity*. The central question asked is not the usual 'why do some people commit crimes?' but rather: 'why do most of us conform?'

The unifying factor in the different versions of control theory is thus the assumption that crime and deviance is only to be expected when social and personal controls are in some way inadequate. Primacy is given to relationships, commitments, values, norms and beliefs that, it is proposed, explain why people do not break laws, in contrast to those theories we have seen in this book that accord primacy to motivating forces thought to explain why people do break laws. From this perspective, it is thus recognized that law-breaking is often the most immediate source of gratification or conflict resolution, and that no special motivation is required to explain such behaviour. Human beings are active, flexible organisms who will engage in a wide selection of activities, unless the range is limited by processes of socialization and social learning.

Some writers in the rational actor tradition, for example Hobbes (1588–1678) and Bentham (1748–1832), had viewed human nature in general as essentially amoral and self-serving, but later social control theories do not, on the whole, depict people in this way. They merely reject the underlying assumption contained in many of the theories discussed earlier in this book – for example anomie and subcultural theories – that people are basically moral as a result of having internalized pro-social norms and values during socialization.

Because they remove the assumption of morality and the positively socialized individual, control theories are not dependent on explanations such as 'relative deprivation', 'blocked opportunities', 'alienation' or 'status-frustration' to account for the motivated deviant. Crime is seen as a product of the weaknesses of the forces restraining the individual rather than of the strength of the impulse to deviate. It is the *absence* of control and the fact that delinquent or criminal behaviour 'usually results in quicker achievement of goals than normative behaviour' that leaves the individual free to calculate the costs of crime (Hirschi, 1969). Again, the influence of the rational actor model is apparent in this core idea of the 'rational' individual choosing crime only after a careful appraisal of the costs and benefits of such activity.

Early social control theories

It was observed above that social control theories draw on both social and psychological factors in order to explain conformity and deviance. Probably the earliest sociological control theory was Durkheim's theory of anomie where it is proposed that inadequate forms of social control are more likely during periods of rapid modernization and social change because new forms of regulation cannot evolve quickly enough to replace the declining force of social integration. The outcome is *anomie* – or even the complete collapse of social solidarity – when the insatiable desires and aspirations of individuals can no longer be adequately regulated or controlled by society. Many of Durkheim's central concerns and ideas were also present in the work of the Chicago School – particularly in its use of the concept of social disorganization – a theoretical perspective that influenced many of the later theories encountered in this book. There have nevertheless been fundamental differences in how these different theorists have used the concept. For example, anomie theorists argued that social disorganization generates pressure, which, in turn, *produces* crime and deviance (a predestined actor model argument). Social control theorists, on the other hand, consider that social disorganization causes a weakening of social control, making crime and deviance more *possible* (a rational actor model argument).

The early control theories reviewed in the remainder of this section attach much more importance to psychological factors in their analysis of deviance and conformity. Albert Reiss (1951) thus distinguished between the effects of 'personal' control and 'social' control, proposing that the former comes about when individuals internalize the norms and rules of non-deviant primary groups to such an extent that they become their own. The latter are founded in the ability of social groups or institutions to make rules or norms effective. Thus, conformity derived from social control tends to involve mere submission to the norms in question and does not necessarily require the internalization of these within the value system of the individual. Reiss tested his theory on 1,110 children between the ages of 11 and 17 who were subject to probation orders and found that personal controls were much more important in preventing deviance than social controls. He did not specify the specific control mechanisms that lead to conformity but did identify the failure of such primary groups as the family to provide reinforcement for non-delinquent roles and values as being crucial to the explanation of delinquency. His perspective was nevertheless true to control theory logic in that no specific motivational sources leading to delinquency were identified.

Jackson Toby (1957) argued that the adolescent without commitment to conventional society is a candidate for 'gang socialization', which he acknowledged was part of the causal, motivational, dynamic leading to delinquency, but introduced the concept of 'stakes in conformity' to explain 'candidacy' for such learning experiences. Thus, young people who had few stakes or investments in conformity were more likely to be drawn into gang activity than those who had more to lose. A variety of conventional social relationships and commitments could be jeopardized by involvement in delinquency, and thus young people without such stakes were free to be recruited into gangs. This notion of 'stakes in conformity' was to be similar to concepts developed in later versions of social control theory.

Ivan Nye (1958) developed a much more systematic version of control theory and, in attempting to locate and identify the factors that encourage conformity in adolescents, he focused on the family, which, because of the affectional bonds established between members, was considered to be the most important mechanism of social control. He identified four modes of social control generated by the family. First, *direct control* is imposed through external forces such as parents, teachers and the police using direct restraint and punishment. Second, individuals themselves in the absence of external regulation exercise *internalized control*. Third, *indirect control* is dependent upon the degree of affection that an individual has for conventional significant others. Fourth, *control through alternative means of needs satisfaction* works by reducing the temptation for individuals to resort to illegitimate means of needs satisfaction. Though independent of each other, these four modes of control were considered mutually reinforcing and to work more effectively in tandem. The focus on the family as a source of control was in marked contrast to the emphasis on economic circumstances as a source of criminogenic motivation at the time. Although he acknowledged motivational forces by stating that 'some delinquent behaviour results from a *combination* of positive learning and weak and ineffective social control', he nevertheless adopts a control theory position when he proposes that 'most delinquent behaviour is the result of insufficient social control' (Nye, 1958: 4). Hirschi (1969) was critical of Nye's use of concepts such as internal control, but, together with Gottfredson (Gottfredson and Hirschi, 1990), was to propose 'self-control' as a key explanatory variable over thirty years later. Nye's work was the first major presentation of research from a social control perspective and most of his findings were to be found consistent with subsequent research using survey data.

Walter Reckless's (1967) containment theory sought to explain why – despite the various 'push' and 'pull' factors that may tempt individuals into criminal behaviour, for example, psychological factors such as restlessness or aggression, or adverse social conditions, such as poverty and unemployment – most people resist these pressures and remain law-abiding citizens. Reckless argued that a combination of control factors, both internal and external to the individual, serve as insulators or 'containments' against these 'push' and 'pull' factors. The factors involved in outer containment were identified as being i) reasonable limits and expectations; ii) meaningful roles and activities; and iii) several complementary variables, such as a sense of belonging and identity, supportive relationships especially in the family and adequate discipline.

Reckless nevertheless attached much more importance to factors in inner containment, as he argued that these would tend to control the individual irrespective of the extent to which the external environment changed. Four key components of inner containment were identified. First, individuals with a strong and favourable *self-concept* are better insulated against those 'push' and 'pull' factors that encourage involvement in criminal activity. Second, *goal orientation* is the extent to which the individual has a clear direction in life oriented towards the achievement of legitimate goals such as educational and occupational success. Third, *frustration tolerance* is where contemporary society – with its emphasis on individualism and immediate gratification – might generate considerable frustration and, moreover, individuals were observed to have different capacities for coping with this factor. Fourth, *norm retention* is the extent to which individuals accept, internalize and are committed to conventional laws, norms, values and rules, and the institutions that represent and uphold these. Reckless described the process by which norm retention is undermined, thus making deviance more possible, as one of norm erosion, which involves 'alienation from, emancipation from, withdrawal of legitimacy from and neutralisation of formerly internalised ethics, morals, laws and values' (1967: 476).

This idea of individuals being able to neutralize formerly internalized norms and values to facilitate deviant or offending behaviour had been a prominent element in Matza's drift theory (see Chapter 7), where it was proposed that delinquent youth were 'neither compelled nor committed to' their offending activities but were 'partially unreceptive to other more conventional traditions' (Matza, 1964: 28). In short, delinquent youth could be depicted as 'drifters' who were relatively free to take part in offending behaviour, and this was to become a significant challenge to other theories in the 1960s that emphasized status frustration and the adoption of oppositional values by delinquent youth. Matza proposed, in contrast to the previously orthodox determinism, that the delinquent merely 'flirts' with criminal and conventional behaviour, while drifting among different social worlds. No specific constraints or controls were identified that keep young people from drifting, but those that did so were those who have few stakes in conformity and are free to drift into delinquency.

Scott Briar and Irving Piliavin (1965) presented one of the clearest statements of control theory rationale and they specifically challenged other theoretical perspectives of the 1960s by emphasizing transitory, situational inducements as the motivating forces for involvement in delinquency in contrast to deviant subcultural or contra-cultural value systems and socially structured status problems. They found that motivation did not differentiate delinquent and non-delinquent young people as much as variable commitments to conformity and argued that the 'central process of social control' was 'commitments to conformity'; they included fear of material deprivations if apprehended, self-image, valued relationships, current and future statuses and activities. In his version of social control theory to which we now turn our attention, Hirschi (1969) was to limit the concept of commitment to the rational and emotional investments that people make in the pursuit of shared cultural goals.

Later social control theories

Travis Hirschi (1969) made the most influential contribution to the development of later social control theory and asserts that, at their simplest level, all share the assumption that 'delinquent acts result when an individual's bond to society is weak or broken' (Hirschi, 1969: 16). He identified four elements of the social bond: *attachment, commitment, involvement* and *belief*, but, unlike other control theorists who had emphasized the internal psychological dimension of control, these terms were employed in a much more sociological sense. The idea that norms and attitudes can be so deeply internalized as to constitute part of the personality is simply rejected and an individual's bonds to conventional society are much more superficial and precarious.

First, *attachment* refers to the capacity of individuals to form effective relationships with other people and institutions – in the case of adolescents, with their parents, peers and school. When these attachments are sufficiently strong, individuals are more likely to be concerned with the opinions and expectations of others and thus more likely to behave in accordance with them. Since this bond of attachment is considered by Hirschi to lie not in some psychological 'inner state', but in ongoing social relationships with significant others, the strength of these attachments can and may vary over time.

Second, *commitment* refers to the social investments made by the individual to conventional lines of action that could be put at risk by engaging in deviant behaviour. This is essentially a rational actor model cost-benefit type of argument where it is proposed that those investing most in conventional social life have a greater stake in conformity, and thus most to lose by breaking the rules. Third, *involvement* again refers not to some psychological or emotional state but to the more mundane reality that a person may be too busy doing conventional things to find time to engage in deviant activities. Fourth, *beliefs* are not – as we might expect – a set of deeply held convictions but rather a set of impressions and convictions in need of constant reinforcement. In this context, beliefs are closely bound up with – and dependent upon – the pattern and strength of attachments an individual has with other people and institutions. These four variables, though independent, are also highly interrelated and are theoretically given equal weight: each helps to prevent law-breaking activities in most people.

For many, the main strength of Hirschi's work is empirical rather than theoretical (see Box, 1981; Downes and Rock, 1998). This view tends to be based on the results of a large-scale study conducted by Hirschi of over 4,000 adolescents from mixed social and ethnic backgrounds, where a variety of propositions derived from control, strain and cultural diversity theories were tested and for the most part it was the control variables that appeared to correlate most closely and consistently with offending behaviour. Hirschi's data indicate that the closer the relationship a child enjoys with its parents, the more it is attached to and identifies with them, the less likelihood there is of involvement in delinquent behaviour. Moreover, it is those who do not like school and do not care what teachers think of them who are more likely to commit delinquent acts. Not that attachment to delinquent peers is, in itself, found to undermine conventional bonds and lead to offending behaviour. It is rather, weak social bonds and a low stake in conformity that lead to the acquisition of delinquent friends. The data showed that high aspirations give a stake in conformity that ties an individual to the conventional social order and not the reverse suggested by the anomie theory tradition. Moreover, social class and ethnic background were found to be 'very weakly' related to offending behaviour.

Numerous other attempts have been made to test the theoretical and empirical adequacy of Hirschi's original theory and the models derived from it. One notable example is Thomas and Hyman's (1978) study, which is particularly illuminating as it employed a much more sophisticated methodology than Hirschi's original. The authors concluded that, 'while control theory does not appear to provide anything like a full explanation, its ability to account for a significant proportion of delinquency cannot be ignored' (1978: 88–9). Thompson et al. (1984) later conducted a survey among hundreds of high school students and juveniles in correctional institutions and found that variations in offending behaviour between the two groups were better explained when the role of delinquent peers was introduced as a variable to the original theoretical formulation. Indeed, their findings were found to be more representative of social learning or differential association theory than social control theory.

Overall, subsequent research has tended to find that the aspects of the social bond most consistently related to offending behaviour are those of the family and the school. There is substantial evidence that juveniles with strong attachments to their family are less likely to engage in delinquency. The evidence on the association between attachment and commitment to the school, particularly poor school performance, not liking school and low educational and occupational aspirations and delinquency, is even stronger.

Despite its impressive empirical support, Hirschi's original formulation of control theory has not escaped criticism. He himself conceded that it overestimated the significance of involvement in conventional activities and underestimated the importance of delinquent friends. Moreover, both of these problems appeared to have stemmed from the same conceptual source, the taken-for-granted assumption of a natural motivation towards offending behaviour (Box, 1981; Downes and Rock, 1998). There have been other criticisms. First, the theory cannot account for the specific form or content of deviant behaviour, or 'why some uncontrolled individuals become heroin users, some become hit men, and others price fixing conspirators' (Braithwaite, 1989: 13). Second, there is a failure to consider the underlying structural and historical context in which criminal behaviour takes place (Elliott et al., 1979; Box, 1981, 1987). Third, while it plainly considers primary deviance among adolescents, habitual 'secondary deviance' appears to be outside its conceptual boundaries (Box, 1981). Subsequently, other researchers have sought a remedy for these various identified defects by integrating control theory with other theoretical perspectives.

Integrated theoretical perspectives

Elliott et al. (1979) developed a model that sought to expand and synthesize anomie theories, social learning and social control perspectives into a simple explanatory paradigm. They begin with the assumption that individuals have different early socialization experiences, leading to variable degrees of commitment to, and integration into, the conventional social order, in other words, strong and weak social bonds. These initial bonds can be further reinforced or attenuated by such factors as positive experiences at school and in the wider community, positive labelling in these new settings and continuing stability in the home.

The structural dimension of Elliott *et al.*'s model is most explicit in their analysis of the factors that serve to loosen social bonds. Limited or blocked opportunities, negative labelling experiences at school, for example, streaming, social disorganization at home and in the wider community – high rates of geographic mobility, economic recession and unemployment – are all identified as experiences that may weaken or break initially strong ties to the conventional order.

Such structural impediments to achieving conventional success goals will constitute a source of strain, and can, of themselves – where commitment to conventional goals is strong enough – provide *the* motivational stimulus to delinquency. In most cases, however, and specifically for those whose ties and commitments to conventional groups and goals are weak in the first place, some further motivation is necessary for sustained involvement in delinquent behaviour. For Elliott *et al.*, it is 'access to and involvement in delinquent learning structures that provides this positive motivation and largely shapes the form and content of delinquent behaviour' (1979: 15).

Elliott *et al.* propose two primary explanatory routes to delinquency. The first and probably most frequent represents an integration of control theory and social learning theory, and involves weak bonds to conventional society and exposure and commitment to groups involved in delinquent activity. The second path represents an integration of traditional strain and social learning perspectives, and this involves strong bonds to conventional society, conditions and experiences that accentuate those bonds and, in most cases, exposure and commitment to groups involved in delinquency.

Stephen Box (1981, 1987) sought to explain the discrepancy between the findings of self-report studies – such as those conducted by Hirschi – and which suggest only a weak relationship between social class and delinquency, and official statistics that show strong links. By integrating control theory with a labelling/conflict perspective – incorporated from the victimized actor model – Box showed how the 'primary' deviants of the self-report studies become the largely economically disadvantaged and minority group 'secondary' deviants of the official statistics. He argues that differential policing practices and institutional biases at different stages of the criminal justice system all operate in favour of the most advantaged sections of society and to the detriment of its less favoured citizens. However, this is not merely a product of discriminating decision-making criteria made on the basis of the individual characteristics of the suspect. Employing a more macro and historical view of the criminalization process, Box suggested that it may be plausible to view such outcomes as a response to social problems of which the individual is merely a symbol:

Thus, the economically marginalised and the oppressed ethnic minorities – because they will also be economically marginalised – will be treated more harshly by the judicial system not simply because of who they are, but also because of what they symbolise, namely the perceived threat to social order posed by the growth of the permanently unemployed. This relationship is viewed as being fully interactive as the stigma, disadvantage and sense of injustice engendered by the criminalisation process, particularly when it is perceived as discriminatory, provides a further impetus towards criminal behaviour.

(1981: 20)

In his later work, Box (1987) showed how the impact of economic recession – such as that experienced in Britain during the 1980s – could lead to an increase in criminal activity. First, by further reducing legitimate opportunities and increasing relative deprivation, recession produces more 'strain' and thus more individuals with a motive to deviate, particularly among the economically disadvantaged. Thus, the commitment of a person to society is undermined because his or her access to conventional modes of activity has been seriously reduced. Second, by undermining the family and conventional employment prospects, the ability and motivation of an individual to develop an attachment to other human beings, who might introduce a controlling influence in his or her life, is substantially reduced.

John Braithwaite's (1989) theory of 'predatory' crime – that is, crimes involving the victimization of one party by another – builds upon and integrates elements of control, labelling, strain and subcultural theory, and argues that the key to crime control is a cultural commitment to shaming in ways that are described as 'reintegrative'; thus, 'societies with low crime rates are those that shame potently and judiciously' (1989: 1). Braithwaite makes a crucial distinction between shaming that leads to stigmatizing, 'to outcasting, to confirmation of a deviant master status' and shaming that is 'reintegrative, that shames while maintaining bonds of respect or love, that sharply terminates disapproval with forgiveness. The latter controls crime while the former pushes offenders toward criminal sub-cultures' (1989: 12–13).

Braithwaite argues that criminal subcultures become attractive to those who have been stigmatized by their shaming because they can provide emotional and social support. Participation in these groups can also supply criminal role models, knowledge on how to offend and techniques of 'neutralization' (see Matza, 1964) that, taken together, can make the choice to engage in crime more attractive and likely. Therefore, a high level of stigmatization in a society is a key factor in stimulating the formation of criminal subcultures. The other major societal variable that encourages this configuration is the 'systematic blockage of legitimate opportunities for critical fractions of the population' (Braithwaite, 1989: 103).

Braithwaite claims that individuals are more susceptible to shaming when they are enmeshed in multiple relationships of *interdependency* and, furthermore, societies shame more effectively when they are *communitarian*. It is such societies or cultures – constituted of dense networks of individual interdependencies characterized by mutual help and trust – rather than individualistic societies that are more capable of delivering the required potent reintegrative shaming. This is a crucial observation.

Both Box and Braithwaite have significantly sought to rescue the social control theory perspective from its emphasis on the individual – or, more accurately, family – culpability that had made it so popular with conservative governments both in the UK and the USA during the 1980s. Box (1981, 1987) located his radical reformulation of social control theory within the victimized actor model but it is the notion of 'reintegrative shaming' developed by Braithwaite that has been central to the left realist perspective that is the focus of Chapter 18. Significantly, neither Box nor Braithwaite – like Hirschi, upon whom they sought to improve – manages to offer a satisfactory explanation of all crime and criminal behaviour. Hirschi sought subsequently – in collaboration with Michael Gottfredson – to do just that.

A general theory of crime

In their *General Theory of Crime*, Gottfredson and Hirschi (1990) manage to combine rational actor model notions of crime with a predestined actor model theory of criminality. In line with the hedonistic calculus of rational actor model thinking, crime is defined as acts of force or fraud undertaken in the pursuit of self-interest. The authors propose that the vast bulk of criminal acts are trivial and mundane affairs that result in little gain and require little in the way of effort, planning, preparation or skill, and their 'versatility construct' points to how crime is essentially interchangeable. The characteristics of ordinary criminal events are simply inconsistent with notions of specialization or the 'criminal career'. Since the likelihood of criminal behaviour is also closely linked to the availability of opportunity, the characteristics of situations and the personal properties of individuals will also affect the use of force or fraud in the pursuit of self-interest. This concept of criminality – low self-control – is not confined to criminal acts but is also causally implicated in many 'analogous' acts, such as promiscuity, alcohol use and smoking, where such behaviour is portrayed as the impulsive actions of disorganized individuals seeking quick gratification.

Gottfredson and Hirschi turn to the predestined actor model in order to account for the variation in self-control among individuals, arguing that the main cause is 'ineffective parenting' and this failure to instil self-control early in life cannot easily be remedied later, any more than effective control, once established, can be later undone. According to this 'stability postulate', levels of self-control will remain stable throughout the life course and 'differences between people in the likelihood that they will commit criminal acts persist over time' (1990: 107).

The *General Theory of Crime* is essentially a radical restatement of the control theory set out by Hirschi in his earlier work, successfully addressing many of the key criticisms aimed at the original. It is more explicitly grounded in a rational actor model conception of crime and thus offers a more consistent notion of criminal motivation than has been the case with previous control theories. By asserting that crime is essentially interchangeable, while the propensity to commit crime remains stable throughout the life course, the theory has no need to provide separate explanations for different *types* of crime, nor for *primary* or persistent *secondary* deviation.

The theory does nevertheless deny the relevance of structural or sociological variables, including those in Hirschi's original theory. The types of bonds an individual establishes with other people and institutions are now said to be a function of that same individual's level of self-control. Thus, those who have self-control are more likely to form constraining social relationships, whereas those who lack it will tend to 'avoid attachments to or involvement in all social institutions' (1990: 168).

Gottfredson and Hirschi describe their theory as 'general', claiming that it 'is meant to explain all crime, at all times' (1990: 117). Whether it does or not depends on the extent to which the observed nature of crime corresponds with that presented as typical by the authors. Depicting all crime as impulsive, unplanned and of little or no real benefit to the perpetrator poses particular problems in the case of white-collar – or business – crime. There is much evidence that high-ranking governmental and corporate officials, acting independently or on behalf of the organizations they serve, use fraud and force in carefully planned ways to enrich themselves and maintain their positions. Barlow observes that, 'compared to low-end crime, high-end crime is much more likely to involve planning, special expertise, organisation, delayed gratification, and persistence – as well as considerably larger potential gains' (1991: 238).

The existence of high-level crime also seems to cast considerable doubt on Gottfredson and Hirschi's 'stability postulate', that is, the notion that levels of self-control remain constant throughout the life course. Since low self-control is also incompatible with the discipline and effort normally required to attain high office, it is difficult to see how business offenders managed to climb the corporate ladder in the first place!

Even if the proposition that low self-control is a causal factor in some – or even most – types of crime is accepted, can we also accept the straightforward association Gottfredson and Hirschi propose between low self-control and ineffective parenting? Although the literature discussed elsewhere in this book does suggest a relationship between parenting and delinquency, this is compromised and complicated when structural factors are considered; for example, while her study of socially deprived families in Birmingham did find that parental supervision was an important factor in determining adolescent offending behaviour, Harriet Wilson warned against the misinterpretation of her findings:

> The essential point of our findings is the very close association of lax parenting methods with severe social handicap. Lax parenting methods are often the result of chronic stress . . . frequent or prolonged spells of unemployment, physical or mental disabilities amongst members of the family, and an often-permanent condition of poverty. It is the position of the most disadvantaged groups in society, and not the individual, which needs improvement in the first place.
>
> (1980: 320–1)

These findings show quite clearly that, even by relocating the source of control from the nature of an individual's bond to society back to within the individual him- or herself, Gottfredson and Hirschi cannot escape the need to incorporate some sense of underlying structural context into their analysis. Their work has, however, been influential and Hirschi has himself subsequently outlined the policy implications of the general theory. Hirschi (1995) argues that policies designed to deter (the rational actor model) or rehabilitate (the predestined actor model) will continue to have little success in reducing criminal behaviour. Effective state policies are those that support and enhance socialization within the family by improving the quality of child-rearing practices with the focus on the form, size and stability of the family unit. Thus, there should always be two parents for every child, no more than three children in a family and the relationships between parents and children strong and durable. Furthermore, it is not young teenage mothers who are a problem that causes delinquency in children. It is having a mother without a father. Therefore, effective policies are those that focus not on preventing teenage pregnancies, but on maintaining the involvement of the father in the life of the child. It is proposed that these policy reforms would strengthen family bonds, increase socialization and create greater self-control in the child that will make it unlikely that they will become involved in offending behaviour (1995: 138–9).

Developments in social control theories

Various developments in and modifications to social control theories have occurred in the USA in the later decades of the twentieth and the first decade of the twenty-first century. We will here consider three of the most significant: power control theory, control balance theories and differential coercion theory.

Power control theory developed by John Hagan (Hagan et al., 1985, 1987, 1990; Hagan, 1989) combines social class and control theories of criminal behaviour in order to explain the effects of familial control on gender differences in crime. Hagan et al. (1987) argue that parental position in the workforce affects patriarchal attitudes in the household and these, in turn, result in different levels of control placed on boys and girls in the home. Moreover, differing levels of control affect the likelihood of the children taking risks and ultimately becoming involved in deviant behaviour. In other words, because of the greater levels of control placed on girls in patriarchal households, boys are more delinquent than girls.

Power control theory begins with the assumption that mothers constitute the primary agents of socialization in the family. In households in which the mother and father have relatively similar levels of power at work – 'balanced households' – the former will be less likely to differentially exert control over their daughters, and both sons and daughters will experience similar levels of control, thus leading them to develop similar attitudes regarding the risks and benefits of engaging in deviant behaviour. It is thus assumed that balanced households will experience fewer gender differences in deviant behaviour. In contrast, households in which mothers and fathers have dissimilar levels of power in the workplace – 'unbalanced households' – are more 'patriarchal' in their attitudes to gender roles and parents will place greater levels of control on their daughters than their sons. Therefore, the former will develop attitudes unfavourable towards deviant behaviour identifying higher levels of apparent risk and fewer supposed benefits of engaging in such activities. Thus, significant gender differences in unbalanced households are predicted with male children more likely than females to engage in deviant activity.

Research studies suggest that gender differences in criminal behaviour arise because girls are differentially controlled in the household. Thus, in other words, female offending increases or decreases depending on the level of patriarchy (see Bates *et al.*, 2003). McCarthy *et al.* (1999) suggest that gender differences in delinquency and offending behaviour probably decrease because *both* male and female delinquents are affected. Moreover, in less patriarchal households, sons are shown to have more controls placed on them, thus decreasing their levels of delinquency.

Charles Tittle (1995, 1997, 1999, 2000) proposes a general theory of deviant behaviour – control balance theory – which provides a definition of deviancy that goes well beyond that of traditional notions of criminality and into the realm of social harms that preoccupies zemiologists. From this perspective, deviancy is simply any activity that the majority find unacceptable and/or disapprove of and occurs when a person has either a surplus or deficit of control in relation to others. Those people whose position in society allows them to exert more control over others and their environment than is exerted over them enjoy a control surplus. A control deficit arises where people are controlled more by others than they are able to control. Tittle proposes that any control imbalance – surplus or deficit – is likely to lead to deviancy. A deficit of control could well lead to resentment, envy and the loss of any stake in society, thus removing any incentive to conform; a surplus, on the other hand, can lead to corruption, a desire to extend the surplus, enhance autonomy and increase domination. The link with criminal behaviour is founded on the supposition that the subservience of others largely removes the risk of being caught. A more specific claim is that any breakdown of acquiescence provokes angry outbursts and this has been used to explain some incidents of domestic violence (see Hopkins and McGregor, 1991). The dual aspect of the theory seems to provide explanations of street crime – most likely to be associated with a control deficit – and corporate crime – most likely to be associated with a control surplus.

Tittle does not assume that an imbalance alone will inevitably lead to criminality but emphasizes the drive for autonomy. Criminal motivation arises for those with a control surplus because they want to extend it (greed) and for those with a deficit (need) because they want to alleviate it. For criminal behaviour to occur, motivation has to be triggered by provocation and facilitated by both opportunity and an absence of constraint.

Linking crime with power is not new. Violent crime invariably involves an element of control or power over the victim and sex crimes have often been explained in this way (see Lansky, 1987; Scheff and Retzinger, 1991). Property offences can also be explained in this manner, thus burglars have power over their victims, the power to decide what to take and leave, how much mess and trauma to cause, and for some this is part of the attraction of burglary (Katz,

1988). Control balance theory is nevertheless helpful in explaining gender differentials in offending rates for there is still a tendency for women to be controlled to a greater extent than men and in more spheres of their lives. Women experience control deficits more frequently than men and become easily enmeshed in the full range of submissive deviancy without access to predatory criminal opportunity. In contrast, fewer women are presumed to have a control surplus so they would be under-represented in the areas of exploitation, plunder and decadence, the converse being true for a considerably higher proportion of males.

Braithwaite (1997) proposes a policy strategy of redistributing control imbalances and argues that a more egalitarian society will reduce both control surplus and deficit, with the outcome that deviance in general and offending behaviour in particular will be reduced. He acknowledges that some form of control will be inevitable to maintain order in even the most equal of societies but proposes that this should be exercised in ways that respect those who are subjected to the control.

Differential coercion theory developed by Mark Colvin (2000) seeks to extend our existing understanding of the coercion–crime relationship. Other recent criminological theories have also highlighted the theme of coercion. Athens (1997) thus describes coercive interpersonal relations as primary forces in the creation of dangerous violent criminals. Regoli and Hewitt (1994) argue that coercive acts by adults in their quest for order play a major role in creating an oppressive environment for young people that produces delinquency. Tittle (1995) contends that repression – a concept similar to coercion – creates control deficits that, depending on the strength and consistency of the repression, produce predatory, defiant or submissive forms of deviance. Hagan and McCarthy (1998) focus on the coercive forces in both the background and foreground in their explanation of delinquency among homeless, street youth.

Colvin (2000) observes that coercion has multiple sources – including families, schools, peer relations and neighbourhoods – and then specifies how each of these coercive experiences fosters criminal involvement. He uses the term 'differential' because individuals vary in the extent to which they are exposed to coercion and it is a central premise of his perspective that criminal involvement will be positively related to the degree of duress experienced by individuals.

There are two proposed dimensions of differential coercion: the *degree* of the coercive force – on a continuum from none to very strong coercion – and the *consistency* with which it is applied or experienced. In most ordinary circumstances – in families, schools, peer groups and a neighbourhood, for example – coercion is most likely to be experienced on an inconsistent basis, in which case, the extent, or degree, of the coercion is the most significant element in producing delinquency.

Coercion, it is argued, produces a set of 'social-psychological' deficits that are conducive to greater involvement in delinquency. Thus, to the degree that individuals experience coercion, they are more likely to have higher levels of anger, lower self-control, weaker social bonds and a high degree of 'coercive ideation' (Colvin, 2000). The latter concept refers to a world view in which the individual perceives that the social environment is filled with coercive forces that can only be overcome through coercion. This set of 'social-psychological deficits' mediates the relationship between coercion and delinquency.

Colvin (2000) differentiates between interpersonal and impersonal forms of coercion: the former occurs within direct interpersonal relations of control in various settings, such as the family, while the latter is connected to pressures from impersonal forces that create an indirect experience of coercion. Interpersonal coercion involves the use or threat of force and intimidation aimed at creating compliance in an interpersonal relationship. These micro-level coercive processes of control can involve the actual or threatened use of physical force and/or the actual or threatened removal of social supports. Impersonal coercion is experienced as pressure arising from larger circumstances beyond the control of the individual and these macro-level sources of coercion can include economic and social pressures created by structural unemployment, poverty or violent competition among groups.

An example of impersonal coercion discussed by Colvin (2000: 124) is the violent environment within neighbourhoods created by gang rivalries. Such neighbourhoods – perceived as dangerous and violent by the young people who live in them – are a strong, impersonal force that creates an environment of threat (Decker and Van Winkle, 1996), which enhances 'coercive ideation' and other social-psychological deficits that Colvin (2000) argues are conducive to delinquency. Moreover, the school setting can be perceived as coercive if school administrators fail to curtail a threatening school environment created by bullying and other forms of aggression.

In summary, for Colvin (2000), the accumulated coercion that juveniles experience in their families, schools, peer relations and neighbourhoods creates social-psychological deficits that make involvement in delinquent activities more likely. The logic of differential coercion theory is that the effects of coercion are general and thus are implicated in most, if not all, forms of criminality, including white-collar and corporate crime.

Unnever et al. (2004) sought to test the core propositions of differential coercion theory and collected data from 2,472 middle school students at 6 different public (state) schools in a metropolitan area of Virginia. Variables included demographic information including gender, measures of economic status, race and grade level, as well as various measures of coercion, such as parental coercion, peer coercion, school coercion and neighbourhood coercion. Other variables included four measures of social-psychological factors: anger, parental social bonds, school social bonds and coercive ideation. Their results largely supported the general proposition that different types of coercion would be positively associated with delinquent involvement. Parental coercion, including verbal abuse, threats and physical punishment, were significantly related to delinquency. School and neighbourhood coercion were also significantly related to delinquency, although the associations were less strong than parental coercion. Peer coercion was found to have no relationship to delinquency. Unnever et al. (2004) conclude from their data that students exposed to coercive environments develop social-psychological deficits, which may lead them to engage in delinquent activities.

Conclusions

In the forty-plus years since Hirschi introduced his control theory, it has gained in popularity and influence and this is not difficult to understand. First, social control theory lends itself remarkably well to empirical research and has become the most tested theory of crime causation. Moreover, it is very well supported empirically. Second, because it avoided implicating social structural issues such as poverty and unemployment as a cause of criminal behaviour, it was to become very popular with the 'right wing' in the USA and thus extremely attractive for research funds. It was on the basis of these factors that Box (1987) justified his inclusion of control theory in his integrated theory.

While 'popular' support for a particular perspective on crime is, of itself, no proof of worth, extensive empirical support clearly is. Despite its impressive empirical support vis-à-vis other theories, one could nevertheless argue, as Downes and Rock (1998) have done, that control theory is not addressing the same problems as its rivals. Alternative sociological theories attempt to account for the character of offending behaviour and to construct models of motivation that account for its typical forms. In control theory, by contrast, deviance has no meaning other than as a means of gratifying basic appetites, be they acquisitive, aggressive or sexual.

Even if we can accept the underlying assumptions of control theory about human nature, that we would all be deviant but for the controls that rein in our natural tendencies, the question still remains: 'in what ways would we be deviant?' By redefining the problem of motivation out of existence, it becomes difficult, if not impossible, for control theory to account for the very phenomena that other theories specifically set out to address. In other words, 'why delinquency is so often non-utilitarian; why aggression is so frequently ritualised and non-violent in its outcome; why sexual gratification takes such complex forms. In short, control theorists make far too little of both deviance and conformity' (Downes and Rock, 1998: 238).

There is little doubt that, in redirecting attention to the previously overlooked issue of conformity, and how this is 'caused' and sustained, control theory has made a significant contribution to the project of explaining crime and criminal behaviour. It nevertheless fails to supply the complete explanation claimed by Gottfredson and Hirschi, but there is research evidence to suggest that some of the more recent developments in social control theories, such as power control theories, control balance theory and differential coercion theory, have helped extend the parameters of explanation without necessarily being able to provide a comprehensive explanation of all forms of deviancy and criminal behaviour. The recently formulated situational action theory we encounter in the following chapter seeks to address these issues further but, at the same time, locate these in the context of situational and motivational factors, thus providing a more comprehensive explanation of crime causation.

Policy implications of social control theories

Social control theory emphasizes opportunity as well as self-control, thus some of the same policies advocated by routine activities and rational choice theorists

– target hardening – are recommended from this perspective but the main emphasis is on social programmes.

Due to the great emphasis placed on the role of self-control – or the lack of it – in causing criminal behaviour, social programmes aimed at intervening in the lives of young people at an early stage of their development are promoted. These have included initiatives aimed at enhancing parenting skills in order to help parents instil self-control within young children. Such policies have been fuelled by the notion that, beyond early intervention, little can be done to later curb criminality (Gottfredson and Hirschi, 1990). As such, these types of social policies can be seen as serving a crime prevention function, rather than as a reactive means of addressing crime within society. Thus, from this perspective, programmes directed at influencing parenting practices would be promoted rather than those aimed at the rehabilitation of the offender, which are seen as a futile approach to addressing crime (Akers and Sellers, 2004). Consequently, policies that have arisen from the general theory of crime have been surrounded by controversy. As the theory asserts that rehabilitation is not an effective mechanism by which to address criminality, the theory has been used in the USA, where it has been very influential, to support the implementation of policies focused on the prolonged incarceration of offenders. This increasingly punitive approach to crime has been questioned by those who disagree with the notion that offenders cannot change and therefore should be incapacitated to avoid future criminality. Finally, Gottfredson and Hirschi suggest that '[e]ffective policy must deal with the attractiveness of criminal events to potential offenders' (1990: 274). While a secondary aspect of the general theory of crime and a potential area for policy development, in actuality, how such policies would look in practice is unclear. It is not surprising, then, that the authors and supporters alike have continued to stress the importance of early interventions in the lives of young people in minimizing the likelihood of future criminality.

Summary of main points

1. Social control theories have a long and distinguished pedigree with strong foundations in both the rational actor and predestined actor models. Later variants have incorporated elements from the victimized actor model.
2. The unifying factor in the different versions of control theory is the assumption that crime and deviance is only to be expected when social and personal controls are inadequate.
3. Travis Hirschi (1969) made the most influential contribution to the development of later social control theory and asserts that, at their simplest level, all share the assumption that individuals become involved in criminality when their bond to society is weak or broken.
4. Hirschi found that the closer a relationship a child enjoys with its parents, the more it is attached to and identifies with them, the less likelihood there is of involvement in delinquent behaviour.

5. Box (1987) showed how the impact of economic recession could lead to breakdown in social bonds and an increase in criminal activity.
6. John Braithwaite (1989) builds on and integrates elements of control, labelling, strain and subcultural theory and argues that the key to crime control is a cultural commitment to shaming in ways that are described as 'reintegrative'.
7. Gottfredson and Hirschi (1990) combine rational actor model notions of crime with a predestined actor model theory of criminality. They propose that the vast bulk of criminal acts are trivial and mundane affairs that result in little gain and require little in the way of effort, planning, preparation or skill, and their 'versatility construct' points to how crime is essentially interchangeable.
8. Power control theory combines social class and control theories of criminal behaviour in order to explain the effects of familial control on gender differences in crime.
9. Control balance theory defines deviancy as any activity that the majority find unacceptable and/or disapprove of and occurs when a person has either a surplus or deficit of control in relation to others.
10. Differential coercion theory developed by Mark Colvin (2000) seeks to extend our existing understanding of the coercion–crime relationship.

Discussion questions

1. What are the fundamental assumptions of all social control theories?
2. How does Travis Hirschi (1969) explain involvement in criminality?
3. What contribution has Stephen Box made to social control theories?
4. Explain control balance theory.
5. Explain differential coercion theory.

Suggested further reading

Key texts in social control theory written from a US perspective are Gottfredson and Hirschi (1990) and Hirschi (1969). Wilson (1980) provides a classic use of the theory in a UK context. Box (1981, 1987), Braithwaite (1989) and Elliott *et al.* (1979) have all produced important texts that have integrated social control theory with other theoretical perspectives. Heidensohn (1985) discusses the value of social control theory in the study of women and crime. For more recent developments in social control theory, Hagan *et al.* (1985) provide an excellent introduction to their power control theory, Tittle (2000) outlines his control balance theory and Colvin (2000) his differential control theory.

16. Situational action theories

Key Issues

1. Crime as moral action
2. Rules and rule guidance
3. The role of motivation
4. Environment and exposure
5. Broader social conditions

Per-Olof Wikström (2005) identifies two central themes in criminological theory, which propose that involvement in crime is dependent on, first, who the person is and what are their personal characteristics and life experiences; and, second, where they are and what are the features of the environments in which the criminal behaviour takes place. Thus, while many of the criminological theories we have encountered in this book have contributed considerably to our understanding of the role of person and environmental differences in crime causation, these two strands of criminological theorising are rarely brought together in a developed integrated theoretical framework.

Most criminological theory lacks a developed theory of action that outlines how person and environmental characteristics, and, in particular, their interaction, impact on action, and specifically acts of crime. Without knowledge of the process whereby person and environmental factors are supposed to influence acts of crime, it is difficult to evaluate their potential role and relative importance in crime causation. In short, it is problematic to properly integrate person and environmental influences in explaining individual crime involvement and why the likelihood of criminal participation changes.

A further identified problem with many criminological theories is that they fail to provide a clear non-ambiguous definition of crime and criminality. Since a theory is always an explanation of something, it is difficult to develop an effective account of the causes of crime without a clear definition of crime, which is, of course, what the theory is seeking to explain. It is these issues that situational action theory seeks to address.

Situational action theory

Situational action theory (SAT) is a general theory of moral action and crime which was devised by the Scandinavian criminologist Per-Olof Wikström during the first decade of the twenty-first century. It aims to produce a theory that integrates person and environmental explanatory perspectives within the framework of a situational action theory (Wikström, 2004, 2005, 2006; Wikström and Sampson, 2003; Wikström and Treiber, 2007, 2009).

Situational action theory thus seeks to address identified problems in mainstream criminological theory. First, there is the imprecise definition of what actually constitutes 'crime'. Second, there is the limited understanding of causal mechanisms that link the individual to the crime event. Third, there is the poor integration of criminological explanation at different levels of the social world. Fourth, there is the inadequate understanding of the role of individual development and change (Wikström, 2004, 2005, 2007c). Wikström is not proposing that all criminological theories fail to address all these points, simply that they fail on one or more of these points. Situational action theory nevertheless seeks to build upon insights from various conventional criminological theories and is based on five key propositions:

1. Acts of crime are *moral actions* that are guided by what is considered to be the right or wrong thing to do – or not to do – in particular circumstances.
2. It is recognized that people engage in acts of crime because they (i) come to see such acts as a viable *action alternative*; and (ii) choose either habitually or deliberately to carry them out.
3. The likelihood that a person will come to see an act of crime as a valid action alternative and choose to carry this out is ultimately dependent on their crime *propensity*. The latter is grounded in their action-relevant moral values and emotions and their capability to exercise self-control and its *interplay* with their *exposure* to criminogenic settings. These are defined by their action-relevant moral rules and the level of their enforcement.
4. The role of *broader social conditions* and their changes, for example, social integration and segregation, and the role of *individual development and change*, the life-history of the individual, should be analysed as the wider causes of criminal involvement.
5. The relevant causes of crime are only those social conditions and aspects of life-histories that can be demonstrated to directly influence the development of the individual propensity (morality and ability to exercise self-control) and influence the emergence of, and the differential exposure of individuals to, settings that contain particular criminogenic features, which may encourage, or discourage, acts of crime (Wikström, 2005).

Situational action theory thus seeks to provide causal explanations that tell us why and how acts of crime occur and it is based on a realist perspective. Wikström (2007c) observes two important assumptions of realism. First, the world exists independent of us and our theorising about it – for example, in science, we do not invent causal relationships, we discover them. Second, many important explanatory processes are unobservable, or partly unobservable, that is, scientific knowledge is not only what can be observed.

A realist perspective does not deny that different people may perceive the same reality differently but it insists that such differences can be rationally explained by factors such as the variations in skills, knowledge, values and experiences held by individuals. For example, why some people in a particular setting will see crime as an action alternative while others will not can be attributed to differences in their moral values and moral habits.

From a realist perspective, simply establishing causation – that is, demonstrating that if we manipulate x then y will change in predicted ways – is not enough to provide a scientific explanation. We also have to demonstrate the *process* through which the causal relationship occurs. Thus, a proper theory of crime causation provides explanation by suggesting plausible causal processes or a mechanism that links the supposed cause and the effect. It tells us *how* the outcome is produced and, in doing so, answers the question of why people engage in acts of crime.

Crime as moral action

There is little doubt that when explaining crime we seek to explain human actions. The latter are sequences of bodily movements – or withheld bodily movements – under the guidance of the individual, for example, speaking or hitting. However, any particular action can, in principle, be defined as a crime and there are, as we have seen in this book, variations over time and geographical location as to what kinds of action are regarded as crime. Moreover, specific actions like hitting, or even shooting, another person may be considered crimes in some circumstances but not in others, as the labelling tradition discussed in Chapter 9 has made us aware (see Lemert, 1951; Becker, 1963).

What defines crime is thus not any particular type of action, but the fact that carrying out a particular action – or refraining from carrying out an action – in a particular circumstance is regarded as breaching a rule of conduct stated in the law. The question of explaining why some acts are regarded as crime and others are not is an important question, which has been addressed elsewhere in this book, but situational action theory is only concerned with why people breach rules of conduct and the law. Not why we have these rules in the first place.

Situational action theory proposes that crime is best considered as *moral action*, which is defined as action guided by moral rules about what is right or wrong in a particular circumstance. Crime is defined as breaches of moral rules defined in law. The latter is a set of moral rules of conduct, but far from all moral rules are regulated by law. Acts of crime are thus viewed as a special case of moral rule-breaking. The advantage of conceptualising crime as breaches of moral rules defined in law is that it focuses on what all kinds of crime, in all places, at all times, have in common, namely, moral *rule-breaking*. A theory of moral action thus seeks to explain why it is that people follow and breach moral rules.

From this perspective, any action that is guided by rules of what it is right or wrong to do in particular circumstances is a moral action. There is no perceived difference between, for example, lying to a friend, stealing an iPod in a shop or blowing up a person with a roadside bomb. All are examples of moral actions and all can be explained within the same theoretical framework. What may differ in the explanation of different kinds of moral action (acts of crime) is not the process (the perception–choice process) leading up to the action, but the content of the moral context (the action-relevant moral rules) and a person's morality (the action-relevant moral values and emotions), which drive the process and the broader social processes (the wider causes) that generate particular moral contexts (contents) in which people develop and act. In all cases, for example, lying, shoplifting or roadside bombing, the individual has to perceive the particular action as a viable alternative and choose to carry out the act. However, the specific moral background that guides whether, for example, an act of shoplifting is perceived as an action alternative will differ from that which guides whether an act of roadside bombing is considered an action alternative (Wikström, 2005).

Rules and rule guidance

Situational action theory is based on explicit assumptions about human nature and its relation to social order. Humans are viewed as essentially rule-guided actors and social order is fundamentally based on the adherence to common rules of conduct. From this perspective, the social order is essentially a moral order. Explaining human moral action and crime is thus about making sense of the interaction between common moral rules of conduct and those to which an individual adheres in shaping their moral development and which provides the grounds for their moral actions.

Wikström (2004) observes that most criminological theory does not have an explicit theory of action, although the rational actor model theories – which we encountered in the first part of this book – do generally allude to the importance of choice as guided by self-interest and rationality. They nevertheless fail to provide any further detail of its role in explaining the actual crime event. Situational action theory accepts that rationality and self-interest do on occasion play a role in guiding human action, but observes that, on a more fundamental level, humans are rule-guided actors. Human actions – including acts of crime – ultimately have to be explained as rule-guided action.

Most criminological theory focuses on the role of either the person or the environment in the explanation of crime (Wikström, 2004, 2005). Situational action theory has thus been developed with the intention of overcoming this divide between person and environmental explanations of moral action and crime and this has been achieved by proposing a situational mechanism (a perception–choice process), which links the person and their environment to their actions. All action, including acts of crime, is seen ultimately to be an outcome of (i) what action alternatives a person perceives they have; and, on that basis, (ii) what choices they make. In contrast to most choice-based theories, which focus on how people choose among predetermined alternatives, situational action theory emphasizes the importance of why people perceive certain action alternatives and not others in the first place. Perception of action alternatives thus plays a more fundamental role in explaining action than the process of choice, which is considered to be a secondary factor.

Situational action theory provides a clear differentiation criterion for evaluating which person and environmental factors are potential causes, or are merely correlates. Only those person and environmental factors that can be demonstrated to influence – directly or indirectly – how a person perceives their action alternatives and makes choices are causally relevant in the explanation of moral action and acts of crime.

One of the most difficult problems in explaining human action is reconciling the role of deterministic and voluntaristic forces in the explanation of action, and situational action theory seeks to integrate the two in its explanation of moral action and crime. It does so by recognising that human action is caused either by *habit* or rational *deliberation*, and this includes law abidance and acts of crime.

The individual is the source of his or her action and to say that people have agency means that they have causal powers to make things happen. Situational action theory contends that people exercise agency within the context of rule-guided choice and the latter can take the form of either deliberation or habit. Habitual action involves automatically applying experience-based moral rules of conduct in a setting without reflection or thought; deliberation involves taking moral rules of conduct into consideration when actively choosing between action alternatives. The former is oriented towards the past, while the latter is oriented towards the future. When people act habitually they routinely apply past experiences to guide current action; when they act deliberately, they try to anticipate future consequences of perceived action alternatives and choose what they consider to be the best course of action.

Wikström (2006) observes that it is only when people make deliberate choices that they exercise free will. The choices they make will be influenced by their ability to exercise self-control – internal control – or respond to deterrence cues – external controls. Whether or not a choice of action tends to be an outcome of deliberation or habit depends on the familiarity of the individual with the circumstances in which they operate. Habits are created by repeated exposure to particular circumstances, which leads to action becoming automated, rather than deliberate, in these and other similar circumstances.

The role of motivation

People commit acts of crime for all sorts of reasons, for example, greed, anger or simply boredom. Moreover, there are no particular motives, for example, desires, needs or wants, that make people breach moral rules and commit acts of crime. It would be incorrect nevertheless to claim that motivation has no role in crime causation. It is a necessary but not sufficient cause of moral action: it is part of the process that moves people to action and has a general directional influence on what kinds of acts of moral rule-breaking a person may perceive and consider.

From the situational action theory perspective, the two main categories of motivation in crime causation are temptation and provocation and these come about as an outcome of the person–setting interaction. A *temptation* occurs (a) when there is a connection between the desires of a person, that is, their wants or needs, and an opportunity to fulfil a desire; or (b) when there is an opportunity for a person to fulfil a commitment they have made. A *provocation* occurs when a friction, that is, an unwanted external interference, causes a person to feel anger or annoyance (Wikström, 2006).

While acknowledging that motivation – temptations or provocations – has a general directional influence on moral action, situational action theory proposes that the crucial factor in the explanation of moral action is the interplay between the morality of a person – their values or emotions – and the moral context in which they operate. The outcome of this interaction will serve as a moral filter, determining whether or not they will act upon temptations or provocations. Many people are, for example, disadvantaged and frustrated for various reasons, without breaking moral rules, or committing acts of crime, but they do not have a propensity to commit crime.

Propensity is a key term in situational action theory and may be defined as the tendency of a person to see crime – or a particular type of crime – as a legitimate action alternative for them to make and to act upon that alternative. The idea that people have different propensities to engage in acts of crime is that, if different people encounter the same setting, they will respond differently. Some are more likely than others to engage in acts of crime.

Individuals will vary in their propensity to engage in a particular moral action depending on their moral values and emotions. Thus, moral emotions – shame or guilt – attached to violating a particular moral rule may be regarded as a measure of the strength with which a person adheres to their propensity to engage in moral action. For example, while many people may think it is wrong to steal something from another person, some may feel very strongly about this, while others may not. Those who feel less strongly about stealing from others may be regarded as having a higher propensity to engage in such action.

The ability of an individual to exercise self-control, that is, to act in accordance with their morality in the face of temptations and provocations, can also significantly affect their crime propensity. The ability of an individual to exercise self-control is influenced by both relatively stable individual characteristics and momentary influences, such as high levels of stress and/or intoxication (Wikström and Treiber, 2007). However, the ability to exercise self-control is only important when an individual perceives crime – or moral rule-breaking – as a legitimate alternative, because self-control exerts its effects through the process of choice. Thus, when an individual deliberates over whether or not they should commit an act of crime, their ability to exercise self-control will influence the process of choice and will play a causal role in their decision to offend or not to offend.

Environment and exposure

People do not act in a social vacuum and it is thus important to bear in mind that propensities always need some environmental inducement to become activated. Individuals will vary in their exposure to *moral contexts*, which are external moral rules and their enforcement, which is linked to particular settings. The extent to which moral rule-following in a particular context is enforced – supervised and breaches sanctioned – may be regarded as the strength of the moral context. The idea that settings vary in their criminogenic features is the idea that the same person will respond differently to different kinds of settings. A person will be more likely to engage in acts of crime in some settings than in others.

It is a key assumption of situational action theory that human action and development is directly influenced only by the settings in which people take part. A setting may be defined as the part of the environment that an individual, at a particular moment in time, can access with their senses, including any media present. The key environmental factor that determines whether or not a setting is criminogenic is its *moral context*, which is the moral rules that apply to the particular setting and their levels of enforcement. The configuration of the settings a person takes part in, during a specific period of time, may be referred to as their *activity field*, for example, a daily or weekly activity field. A person's activity field is the environment to which they are exposed during a specific period.

In terms of analysing action, the moral context of settings is significant because it is within such a context that opportunity may create temptation, if connecting to the particular desires and needs of a person and their commitment, and friction may create provocation, if evoking feelings of annoyance or anger in a person. Temptation and provocation are key motivational elements emerging from the person–setting interaction. However, it is the moral context of the setting, its moral rules and deterrent qualities, and its interaction with the morality of a person and their ability to exercise self-control by acting as a 'moral filter', that will determine whether or not a person will act upon a particular temptation or provocation.

The importance of causal interaction

Situational action theory proposes that the *causes* of moral actions and acts of crime are the factors that influence the moral perception of action alternatives and influence the process of moral choice. Causes of crime are thus factors which influence a person to see an act of crime – a particular crime – as an action alternative and factors that influence a person's process of choice to carry out such an action alternative. All human action is a result of the interaction between people and the environment and, according to situational action theory, all moral actions are an outcome of a person's propensity to engage in the particular moral action and their exposure to environmental inducements to engage in the particular moral action. Thus, a simple equation:

Propensity × *Exposure* = *Action*

		Moral rules of setting	
		Encouraging	Discouraging
Morality	Encouraging	Action likely, controls irrelevant	Action dependent on level of deterrence
	Discouraging	Action dependent on capability to exercise self-control	Action unlikely, controls irrelevant

Figure 16.1 What makes a particular moral action likely.

Source: Adapted from Wikström, 2005.

Situational action theory does not propose a simple additive model of propensity and exposure but proposes that the two interact to determine the crime involvement of a person (Figure 16.1). Specific combinations of propensity and exposure are thus likely to produce specific outcomes in terms of the level of crime involvement of a particular individual.

The *action relevant propensity* is those moral values and emotions that are supported or undermined by the capability of the person to exercise self-control and which are relevant to a particular moral action. For example, if we aim to explain acts of shoplifting, all those moral values and emotions relevant to seeing acts of shoplifting as an action alternative and relevant to choosing such an alternative for action constitute the action relevant propensity.

The *action relevant exposure* includes those criminogenic features of the moral context of a setting – or the perceived moral rules and their level of enforcement – that are linked to acting upon a particular *temptation* or *provocation*. The causal process that links the interplay of propensity and exposure to action is the 'moral perception–moral choice process', which was discussed earlier. This process can, depending on the familiarity of the circumstances, be predominantly *habitual*, expressing moral habits, or *deliberative*, expressing moral judgements, in nature.

To say that the interaction of propensity and exposure are causes of action, including acts of crime, does not deny the role of agency. Propensity and exposure set the context within which people exercise agency, that is, they act deliberately or by habit. Agency is exercised through the perception–choice process. The interaction of propensity and exposure is the input to this process. To say that propensity and exposure are causal factors means that changes in propensity and exposure will lead to changes in action through their impact on the perception–choice process.

At the core of the proposed propensity–exposure interaction in situational action theory is the principle of *moral correspondence*, which states that moral action is guided by the interplay between the morality of an individual and the moral rules of the setting in which they operate. The values and emotions that constitute the morality of a person can either encourage or discourage a particular moral action, while the moral rules of the setting in which they take part can either encourage or discourage a particular moral action. The combination of the two gives four ideal type possibilities:

1. In the case where both the morality of the person and the moral rules of the setting encourage a particular moral action, this action is likely to take place; that is, assuming that the person is tempted or provoked to act in this way.
2. In the case in which both the morality of the person and the moral rules of the setting discourage a particular moral action, it is unlikely that this action will take place.
3. In the case where the morality of the person discourages a particular action, but the moral rules of the setting encourage it, their capability to exercise self-control, that is, internal control, will play a crucial role in determining whether or not the act will take place. For example, the capability to exercise self-control may come into play in the action choice for a young person who does not think it is right to smoke cannabis but may be tempted to try it out because they attend a 'coffee shop' – a place where smoking pot is legal – in Amsterdam with a group of friends who all want to and think it is okay to do so.
4. In the case where the morality of a person encourages a particular moral action, but the moral rules of the setting discourage it, the level of deterrence, that is, external controls, may play a key role in the action choice of the individual (see Wikström, 2007a). For example, if an act is illegal but the person does not have a moral problem with carrying it out, the perceived risk of getting caught and the perceived consequences thereof may come into play as a causally relevant factor in their choice process.

Controls will thus come into play only when there is a discrepancy between the morality of a person and the moral rules of the setting. This may be referred to as the principle of the *conditional relevance of controls* because internal and external controls are only causally relevant under certain moral conditions.

All of this depends on there being an initial motivation, that is, temptation or provocation, to act in a certain manner. If a person is not tempted or provoked to carry out a certain kind of act, their moral values and emotions and the moral rules of the setting that apply to this particular kind of action, and the controls in place, lack relevance for their actions.

Development and change

Situational action theory proposes that changes in the actions of individuals arise from changes in their propensity, that is, changes in their morality and ability to exercise self-control, and/or changes in their exposure, that is, changes in the time the person spends in criminogenic settings (Wikström, 2005; Wikström and Treiber, 2009). Changes in propensity and exposure cause changes in action – for example, engagement in acts of crime – by bringing about change in the moral perception–moral choice process that guides moral action.

$$(Change)\ Propensity + (Change)\ Exposure = (Change)\ Action$$

Changes in propensity and exposure are not unrelated from a developmental perspective. Changes in exposure may lead to changes in propensity through changes in the processes of socialization and habituation. For example, if a person spends increasing amounts of time in moral contexts favouring a certain kind of moral rule-breaking, this may, through the processes of moral education and moral habituation, affect their propensity to engage in such acts. Changes in propensity may lead to changes in exposure through changes in setting selection. For example, if a person comes to find a certain moral action, for example recreational drug use, morally acceptable and is thus motivated to commit that action, they may be more likely to seek out settings that support that action. However, in the explanation of crime causation, it is crucial not to confuse the question of why a person chooses to be in a certain setting and the effect this setting has on their actions. Why people are exposed to certain environments and how these environments influence their actions are two different questions (Wikström, 2006). The former is a question that belongs to the explanation of the causes of the causes, and the latter to the explanation of the causes of a person's engagement in acts of crime.

Broader social conditions

Situational action theory maintains that, to be able to explain the role in crime causation of broader social factors and social change, as well as individual development and life-histories, one first has to understand what moves people to action or to engage in acts of crime. Knowing what moves people to engage in acts of crime gives us guidance as to which broader social conditions, and aspects of the life-histories of people, are important candidates as the causes of the causes – or indirect causes – that move people to action.

People act and develop in settings. Situational action theory proposes that the key to understanding the potential role of broader social conditions such as social disadvantage, levels of social integration and segregation in crime causation, as possible causes of the causes, is to understand how these social conditions and their related social processes help create particular kinds of settings, with particular moral contexts and levels of enforcement, in which people develop, that is, form their morality and ability to exercise self-control and act.

Societies vary in their levels of social integration and moral integration, that is, the level of homogeneity of moral values held by the population and their correspondence to moral rules or laws expressed by the larger society. It is thus reasonable to assume that societies that have higher degrees of social and moral integration will have less moral rule-breaking and crime because there will be less room for a discrepancy between individual and collective moral rules.

Changes in the broader social environment, in which the daily lives of people are embedded, for example political, economic and social changes of relevance to moral actions, may instigate changes in the kinds of moral contexts present in a society and the processes of exposure of different groups of people to particular moral contexts. This, in turn, may impact on, in the longer term, the moral education of the population, or segments of the population, and, in the short term, the moral contexts in which people, or groups of people, act.

Reflections on situational action theories

We have seen in this chapter that situational action theory proposes a way to unify empirical and theoretical concepts that have become widely accepted in the sociological, criminological and behavioural sciences literature in an attempt to explain moral actions. In short, it attempts to determine just why it is that people choose to break the law (Bouhana and Wikström, 2011). It is proposed that 'moral rules and emotions' feed into the perceptions and choices confronting an individual, thus providing a moral context to their actions. It seeks to explain many aspects of crime ranging from the lowest level of petty street crime to large-scale white-collar criminal enterprises and perhaps even international terror organizations. Thus, the criminal act, no matter how large or small, may be motivated by the moral lexicon of the individual, and defined by the situational context in determining if an action is a viable option.

Situational action theory rather ambitiously proposes that social scientists can predict individual behaviours by the systematic collection of empirical data, which enables them to correlate their traits and actions to situational factors that serve as the causation of the act. It also identifies the process via which an individual first becomes motivated and is subsequently transformed from a law-abiding citizen to a person who, due to the situation, perceives a criminal act to be a viable alternative and a legitimate means to achieve a desired result. It is a central premise of this theory that human beings are products of the society in which they live and as such follow the social contract established in the 'rules' or 'norms' of their society. Social scientists must first locate the complex motivations of why an individual will carry out a particular action. If the motive behind their action cannot be empirically established, then research to establish the environmental factors resulting from the individual situation will be artificially founded.

Situational action theory seeks to explain the behaviour of the individual as a meeting at a crossroads between that of a human being and their interaction with their environment. Wikström contends that previous criminological theories have tended to focus on *either* contextual and environmental factors, such as culture or community, *or* explained behaviours through the innate proclivities of the individual. Situational action theory seeks to integrate the individual reactions of the individual person to a unique situation with the two sets of dynamics *connected*.

It is through examining this connection that researchers working in the situational action theory tradition can use an analysis of variance (ANOVA), which is based upon the known causal factors to predict future criminal action. At its root, the primary act of the perceived crime is a moral action. The causal action is the interaction between the individual and the environment in which the individual is acting. Individuals decide to act when that action becomes a feasible option through their individual 'crime propensity' developed through the moral guidelines and enforced within the environment in which they exist. Wikström (2009) expressed this as the 'interplay with his or her exposure to criminogenic settings' and developed the idea that it is a perception and choice process that links the participant to the environment in which they act, and that all actions can fall under the outcomes of (a) what the actor perceives as a rational choice for action; and (b) the action of making that choice and carrying through with the desired action.

Situational action theory is also based on the notions that humans are able to think rationally and are guided by the rules of the society in which they live. In explaining the criminal or deviant acts a person decides to commit, the actions can be explained as the interplay between the perception of the rules of society and the perception of the personal moral guidelines to which the person adheres. People are thus seen as using internal controls to restrain their behaviour, and applying external controls when they choose to act for or against the norms of society. Sometimes the choice of deviance is based upon a determined preference for the action; however, when an individual is exposed to a particular situation repeatedly, the choice made by the individual is no longer seen as a result of free will and is instead viewed as a habitual act based on a history of repetition, which creates an automated tendency of humans to default to a learned action (Wikström, 2009).

An important question for many social scientists when measuring the validity of a theory is whether it is able to address fragmented and hard to account for controls, such as external influences on the subject being tested. It could be argued that such theories as situational action theory can be of little use to policy-makers because of an inability to control for outside factors affecting the actions of the individual other than the environment. Despite this apparent limitation, situational action theory attempts to build on the rational choice theory we encountered in the first part of this book in order to explain the mechanisms by which an individual acts, as well as the process that triggers the response, rather than focus only on the outcome of the choices or consequences that arise. Situational action theories have thus been tested by allowing for multiple variations of the crime, the propensity of the actors, the moral context of the individual and society, as well as the human and social capital for various situations used for study.

Wikström *et al.* (2012) conducted a longitudinal study of criminal environments located in disadvantaged neighbourhoods and found a close correlation to the offending behaviours of the individuals living in these deprived localities. The researchers concluded that it was not living in a disadvantaged area that triggered involvement in criminality in itself, but it was the prolonged exposure to the disadvantaged and criminogenic environment that led to criminal involvement for most individuals. These findings suggest that this data point could be used to combat the growing crime problem within disadvantaged neighbourhoods and in the development of programmes designed to reduce the level of criminality within a particular locality. It is argued that recognition of the correlation between two data points assists criminologists in understanding potential triggers, allowing them to work towards amending current policies and developing future legislation for effective community or state intervention strategies.

It is also proposed that situational action theory could be used on a national or multinational level to study the radicalization process that leads to active involvement in terrorism. Furthermore, it plays a role in the body of knowledge that seeks to understand the role society plays in promoting or discouraging terrorist activities through its moral context or environment in which the individual operates.

Situational action theorists argue that, by applying this theory to the study of criminal justice, criminologists are better able to enhance crime prevention initiatives through an increased understanding of the root causes of crime that certainly impact differentially on particular individuals. It is proposed that, when elements such as criminal propensity, exposure and other social criminal correlations can be better understood and identified, methods of crime prevention can be developed and employed in response.

Policy implications of situational action theories

Wikström *et al.* (2011) reconsider the core rational actor model question that is posed by deterrence theory, which asks whether people choose to comply with the law because they fear getting caught, in terms of situational action theory. Their findings support the assumption that one important reason why many people do not engage in acts of crime – or particular types of crime – is that they do not see crime – or a particular crime – as an action alternative; rather they abstain from involvement because they fear the consequences following their assessment of the risk of getting caught. On the other hand, people who do not see crime to be an action alternative do not tend to engage in crime, regardless of whether they assess the risk of getting caught as very high or very low. The findings of the researchers also indicate that, among those who more regularly see crime – a particular crime – as an action alternative, their level of involvement is generally influenced by their assessment of the risk of getting caught (their deterrence sensitivity): those who assess the risk of getting caught as higher tend to commit crime less frequently. Such studies are important because they empirically interrogate the central rational actor issue of under what circumstances people will choose to become involved in crime – if at all – and, if so, what are the risks of them actually doing so. Situational action theory thus provides a sophisticated basis for discovering who is likely to offend and under what circumstances and, in doing so, considers key predestined actor model motivational issues long neglected by rational choice theorists. Policies should thus target these issues and provide likely criminal candidates with legitimate action choices, while, at the same time, making illegitimate action choices less attractive.

Summary of main points

1. Situational action theory (SAT) is a general theory of moral action and crime that aims to integrate person and environmental explanatory perspectives.

2. Situational action theory seeks to provide causal explanations that tell us why and how acts of crime occur and is based on a realist perspective.
3. It is proposed that crime is best considered as moral action, which is defined as action guided by moral rules about what is right or wrong in a particular circumstance.
4. Humans are viewed as essentially rule-guided actors and social order is fundamentally based on the adherence to common rules of conduct. It is essentially a moral order.
5. People exercise agency within the context of rule-guided choice and the latter can take the form of either deliberation or habit. It is only when people make deliberate choices that they exercise free will.
6. People commit acts of crime for all sorts of reasons and there are no particular motives that make people breach moral rules and commit acts of crime.
7. There are two main categories of motivation in crime causation – temptation and provocation – and these are the outcome of the person–setting interaction.
8. Individuals will vary in their propensity to engage in a particular moral action depending on their moral values and emotions.
9. The ability of an individual to exercise self-control can also significantly affect their crime propensity.
10. People do not act in a social vacuum, and thus propensities always need some environmental inducement to become activated.

Discussion questions

1. Explain the concept of moral action in situational action theory.
2. How is free will explained in situational action theory?
3. What is the crime propensity?
4. How are crime propensities activated?
5. Explain the notion of moral correspondence.

Suggested further reading

Situational action theory was devised in the first decade of the twenty-first century and subsequently developed by its creator P.-O. Wikström. To date, there are no secondary sources, commentary or published critiques, thus the student who wishes to pursue these issues further will need to consult the original primary sources. The following are recommended: Wikström (2005, 2006, 2009); Wikström and Sampson (2003); Wikström and Treiber (2007, 2009); and Wikström et al. (2011).

17. Desistance theories

Key Issues

1. The ontogenetic and sociogenic paradigms
2. Understanding change in adulthood
3. Personality traits
4. The narrative identity
5. Narratives of desistance and change

Maruna (1997) observes that the fact that most young offenders eventually grow out of offending behaviour is one of the most well-known findings in criminology (see Rutherford, 1992), and notes that what is less well known is what this change process actually involves; he argues that this lack of understanding stems from the shortcomings of the traditional criminological framework for examining desistance. The good news is that most juvenile delinquents are leading quite successful lives by the age of 32 (Farrington, 1995).

Maruna thus observes that few phenomena in criminology have been as widely acknowledged and as poorly understood as why it is people desist from doing crime. It is recognized that, for most individuals, participation in 'street crimes' generally begins in the early teenage years, peaks in late adolescence or young adulthood, and ends before the person reaches 30 or 40 years of age. This pattern emerges in studies using a wide range of different methodologies (see Farrington, 1986; Hindelang, 1981; Rowe and Tittle, 1977; Sullivan, 1996), while some have argued that this pattern has remained virtually unchanged for at least 150 years (Gottfredson and Hirschi, 1990). At least as far back as 1915, Goring – whom we encountered in Chapter 5 – called this identified age–crime relationship a 'law of nature'. Criminal behaviour thus seems to be largely an activity engaged in by the young.

At some stage in their life course, usually between 18 and 35 years of age, even serious offenders tend to undergo what Wolfgang *et al.* (1972) described as 'spontaneous remission', where criminal behaviour seems to cease. Yet, traditional criminological theories have no easy explanation for the process of desistance from crime and, in fact, they tend to imply that a person's involvement in criminal behaviour should increase over time (Gove, 1985; Moffitt, 1993a); certainly, the dominant twentieth-century criminological orthodoxy of the predestined actor model would suggest this to be the case. Hirschi and Gottfredson argue that the relationship between age and crime 'easily qualifies as the most difficult fact in the field' (1995: 126), while Moffitt calls the 'mysterious' age–crime relationship 'at once the most robust and least understood empirical observation in the field of criminology' (1993a: 675).

This chapter completes a criminological sequence of three closely linked perspectives in recent integrated criminology theory, which have a considerable correspondence between them. Thus, Chapter 15 discussed the social bonds that bind individuals to society and, it is argued, discourage them from offending, as well as the consequences when those bonds break down and criminality becomes an attractive option for the individual. Chapter 16 takes that argument a step further and considers the complex processes whereby the individual comes to consider that a particular course of criminal action is a viable action alternative in a particular situation. This chapter completes the trilogy by addressing the 'social and cognitive processes' (Graham and Bowling, 1995) and the 'complex interplay between objective and subjective contingencies' (Gartner and Piliavin, 1988) involved in 'going straight' or when the offender decided to desist from crime.

Graham and Bowling (1995) addressed the question of who is most likely to desist from offending (whites/non-whites; males/females) and when this change is likely to occur in the life course, but much less is known about how and why desistance is possible for those individuals who do eventually desist, and how criminologists and other social scientists can conceptualize this process. In one of the most thorough analyses of the topic, Rand suggested that 'the phenomenon of desistance has received no specific theoretical or empirical attention' (1987: 134), and, although this observation is overstated, studies of desistance tended to exist in relative isolation from each other and most were not theoretically informed. There is certainly no consensus for understanding why it is that young offenders desist from crime. Shover observed that, 'although it is conventional wisdom that most offenders eventually desist from criminal behaviour, criminology textbooks have little or nothing to say about this process' (1985: 15).

Mulvey and LaRosa conclude that, 'in short, we know that many youth "grow out" of delinquent activity, but we know very little about why' (1986: 213). Maruna (1997) observed that this gap in the literature is a result of both methodological and theoretical weaknesses in existing research and that most of the leading desistance explanations continued to fall into the dichotomy of *ontogenetic* and *sociogenic* paradigm, and we will consider each of these two paradigms below. Lewin (1935) observed many years ago that the notion that behaviour is a product of an interaction between persons and environments had become a virtual truism in criminology, but, on the other hand, this acknowledgement did not lead to a wealth of interactionist theories and research on the topic of desistance. The outcome was a polarized debate as to whether or not the phenomenon of desistance can be explained at all (see, for example, Gottfredson and Hirschi, 1990).

The ontogenetic paradigm

One of the first social scientists to address the question of desistance from offending was Adolphe Quételet (1833), who argued that the predilection for crime diminishes with age 'due to the enfeeblement of physical vitality and the passions' (cited in Brown and Miller, 1988: 13). Sheldon and Eleanor Glueck (1940) were to develop this proposition into their theory of 'maturational reform', in which they argue that intrinsic criminality naturally declines after the age of 25. The Gluecks (1940: 105) suggest that, with the 'sheer passage of time', juvenile delinquents 'grow out' of this transitory phase and 'burn out' physiologically. Significantly, they conclude that 'ageing is the only factor which emerges as significant in the reformative process'.

Although the Gluecks explicitly urged future researchers to 'dissect maturation into its components' (1940: 270), Shover (1985) observes that explanatory efforts of criminology had not progressed appreciably beyond the work of the Gluecks. Thus, maturational reform continued to be the most influential theory of desistance in criminology (Maruna, 1997). Wilson and Herrnstein, for instance, argue that none of the possible correlates of age, such as employment, peers or family circumstances, explains crime as well as the variable of age itself. 'That is to say, an older person is likely to have a lower propensity for crime than a younger person, even after they have been matched in demographic variables' (1985: 145). Similarly, Gottfredson and Hirschi suggest that, 'spontaneous desistance is just that, change in behaviour that cannot be explained and change that occurs regardless of what else happens' (1990: 136). According to this view, the effect of age on crime is 'natural', direct and invariant across social, temporal and economic conditions.

Similarly, efforts have been made to use normative patterns of human development to explain desistance as a natural or normal process of ageing (Gove, 1985; Jolin, 1985). In his bio-psychosocial theory of desistance, Gove observes that:

> As persons ... move through the life cycle, (1) they will shift from self-absorption to concern for others; (2) they will increasingly accept societal values and behave in socially appropriate ways; (3) they will become more comfortable with social relations; (4) their activities will increasingly reflect a concern for others in their community; and (5) they will become increasingly concerned with the issue of the meaning of life.
>
> (1985: 128)

Borrowing largely from Levinson's linear model of normative adult development,[1] such theories generally suggest that desistance from criminal behaviour is a natural 'stage' in personality development, parallel to the questioning of roles and identity that supposedly takes place for all adults at mid-life (Jolin, 1985).

According to all these maturational theories it is ageing that 'causes' desistance. Yet, as Sutton suggests, 'to say that age influences everything is to say nothing' (1994: 228). Developmentalists are increasingly beginning to view biological age as an 'ambiguous' and 'irrelevant' variable, with little meaning except that which is socially attached to it (Dannefer, 1984; Havighurst, 1973; Neugarten and Neugarten, 1986; Rutter, 1989). Maruna observes that few criminologists would be satisfied with the assessment: 'criminal behaviour peaks at age seventeen, therefore crime is *caused* by turning seventeen' (1997: 72). Yet, he observes, ageing continues to be seen as an adequate explanation for desistance.

Sampson and Laub (1992) observe that age is clearly a very strong correlate of desistance, but, on the other hand, criminologists have generally failed to 'unpack' the 'meaning' of age. Age indexes a range of different variables, including biological changes, social and normative transitions, and life experiences, and thus, in itself, is not an explanation for change. Rutter observes that, 'it is necessary to go on to ask which features indexed by age constitute the mediating mechanisms' (1996: 608), and cites research that indicates that the effect of years of schooling outweigh the effect of chronological age on student performance on various cognitive tests, for instance.

While Gove (1985) and others have appealed to the *physiological* changes that typically accompany ageing to explain desistance, these theories also fail to produce adequate explanations. For example, although testosterone levels decrease with age, the age–testosterone curve is far from parallel to the sharply peaking age–crime curve (Farrington, 1986). Similarly, while physical strength tends to peak at age 30 (Adams, 1997), the decline in physical abilities in adulthood is nowhere near as steep as the decline in criminal behaviour.

Much of the developmental research on the age–crime relationship commits what Dannefer refers to as the 'ontogenetic fallacy' (1984: 101), by accepting that changes in behaviour reflect the natural and universal 'properties of the ageing organism' rather than social or institutional processes or the age-graded structure of social roles and social controls. As with differences in gender or ethnicity, some differences in behaviour between persons of different ages might be intrinsic to ageing itself, but it would be absurd to ignore the fact that 40-year-olds are systematically treated differently from 20-year-olds in Western society, just as men are treated differently from women (Greenberg, 1981). In fact, portraying desistance as 'natural' might actually decrease public support for the social mechanisms (such as rehabilitation and reintegration services for ex-offenders) that may be instrumental in existing patterns.

Most importantly, longitudinal studies of crime in the life course show a great variety of adult outcomes for young offenders, with far greater diversity in the ages of desistance than in the ages of onset of criminal behaviour (for example, Farrington and West, 1993). Therefore, any theory that uses age alone or a single, normative pattern of development to explain desistance fails to account for the considerable heterogeneity of developmental pathways.

In summary, most ontogenetic theories of desistance generally only restate the facts of the age–crime relationship, while doing little to increase our understanding of *how* this change takes place (Wootton, 1959). As Matza argues, a simple notion like 'burning out' also 'merely reiterates the occurrence of maturational reform – it hardly explains it' (1964: 24). We need to go beyond restating the correlates of age and begin investigating the dimensions, ingredients or facets of desistance.

The sociogenic paradigm

Beyond 'maturational reform', the next most influential explanation of desistance is the theory of social bonds or 'informal social control' (Farrington, 1992b). Social bond theory – as we saw with social control theories in Chapter 15 – suggests that varying informal ties to family, employment or educational programmes in early adulthood explain changes in criminality during the life course. Therefore, unlike maturational or developmental theories, social theories posit that the experiences that lead to desistance from crime are not necessarily universal and can often be partially under the control of the individual, as in the case of entering employment or finding a partner.

Matza (1964) – whom we encountered in Chapter 7 with the discussion of sociological theories of crime causation – was among the first to address this issue with his notion of a 'drift'. To Matza, most delinquents are caught somewhere in between the social bonds of adulthood and deviant peer subcultures without a deep attachment to either. Once adolescence has ended, and adult roles become available, the majority of young people easily move away from their weak affiliation with offending. Trasler (1979, 1980) and Sampson and Laub (1993) also describe turning points that can redirect a person's life path away from delinquency. Trasler observes that 'as they grow older, most young men gain access to other sources of achievement and social satisfaction – a job, a girlfriend, a wife, a home and eventually children – and in doing so become gradually less dependent upon peer-group support' (1980: 109). Those who lack these bonds are the most likely to stay involved in criminal and delinquent behaviour because they have the least to lose from social sanctions and ostracism. Moreover, the stronger the ties to society (that is, the higher legal income one has), the more likely a person is to desist from criminal behaviour (Pezzin, 1995).

Substantial research has confirmed that desistance from crime is strongly correlated with *finding employment* (Glaser, 1964; Mischkowitz, 1994; Sampson and Laub, 1993; Shover, 1985), *completing schooling* (Farrington *et al.*, 1986; Rand, 1987), *getting married* (Farrington and West, 1995; Gibbens, 1984; Irwin, 1970; Meisenhelder, 1977; Mischkowitz, 1994; Rand, 1987; Rutherford, 1992; Rutter *et al.*, 1990; Sampson and Laub, 1993; West, 1982; Zoccolillo *et al.*, 1992), and *becoming a parent* (Leibrich, 1993).

Still, these correlations are by no means apparent in all of the research on desistance, and treatment programmes designed to test social bonding theory experimentally have generally been viewed as failures (Uggen, 1996). Gottfredson and Hirschi conclude that differences in the rates of criminality among employed and unemployed, other factors being equal, are 'small, non-existent, or even in the wrong direction' (1990: 138–9). McCord (1990) also argues that providing work and educational opportunities for ex-offenders may not be a panacea for reform. First, improved opportunities for legitimate success have not consistently reduced criminal behaviour (see also Soothill, 1974; Haines, 1990). Secondly, the connection between low job attachment and crime does not seem to hold up for a substantial proportion of the population – namely women – who have been historically detached from employment opportunities, but remain highly underrepresented in crime statistics (see also Naffine and Gale, 1989).

Gottfredson and Hirschi similarly observe that wives, homes and children 'sound nice' as explanations for desistance but 'they do not seem to have an impact on the likelihood of crime' (1990: 140) (see also Wright and Wright, 1992). In fact, Gottfredson and Hirschi argue that young men in relationships with females are actually more likely to commit delinquent acts than unattached youth. Reviewing research on 'assortative mating', they conclude, 'the offender tends to convert these institutions (of marriage or jobs) into sources of satisfaction consistent with his previous criminal behaviour' (1990: 141) (see Caspi and Moffitt, 1993).

Individuals differ enormously in their response to social stimuli, and the same social event can affect individuals in different ways based on differences in gender, age, ethnicity, prior experiences and personality (Cowan, 1991; Rutter, 1996). Thus, Graham and Bowling (1995) found that, for females, social transitions like leaving home and forming a new family unit were highly correlated with desistance from crime; yet, for young males, these social transitions seemed to have little effect on patterns of offending. Similarly, in a reanalysis of the National Supported Work Demonstration Project data in the USA, Uggen (1996) found that the effect of providing marginal employment opportunities for ex-offenders was age-dependent. While persons aged 27 or older in the supported work project were more likely to desist from crime, the employment scheme seemed to have little effect for persons under 27. Uggen concluded that the meaning of work and crime may change as individuals move from adolescence into adulthood, indicating that desistance also has a subjective component that needs to be understood.

Uggen (1996) observes that even proponents of social bonding theory admit that the relationship between social ties and desistance has 'strings attached'. Sampson and Laub (1993: 304), for instance, argue that employment 'by itself' does not cause desistance; the relationship is conditional upon a person's 'commitment' to a particular job. Similarly, Rutter observes that 'marriage *as such* has no very predictable effect. It all depends on the sort of person whom you marry, when you marry, and the sort of relationship that is achieved' (1996: 610). Loeber *et al.* (1991: 71–3) argue that educational opportunities do not correlate with desistance, but 'attitudes towards education' do. Hence, desistance depends on not just the *existence* of social attachments, but on the perceived strength, quality and interdependence of these ties (West, 1982). Such qualifications to social bond theory only serve to reinforce the view of social bonding as an incomplete understanding of desistance.

Most importantly, the relationship between finding work (or getting married) and giving up crime, rather than being causally related, might be a spurious association, based on some common, *internal* factor, such as an underlying strength of personality (Gottfredson and Hirschi, 1990) or else a conscious *choice* on the part of individuals to change (Cusson and Pinsonneault, 1986). Individuals predisposed to committing crime for whatever reason may be unlikely to want to pursue jobs or relationships (cf. Akerstrom, 1985). Clarke and Cornish (1985) have refocused the attention of criminologists on the very old notions of choice and human agency in the determination of criminal behaviour. Certainly, rational calculations, emotions, impulses and intentional decisions play a major role in the process of 'going straight' (Cusson and Pinsonneault, 1986; Farrall and Bowling, 1997). Yet, social bonding theories of desistance portray human behaviour as largely determined by external forces.

Gottfredson and Hirschi, for instance, mock the notion that 'jobs somehow attach themselves' to individuals, and they emphasize that 'subjects are not randomly assigned to marital statuses' (1990: 188). To this criticism, Farrington and West respond, 'If we accepted this argument it would follow that most causal hypotheses in criminology could not be tested. Yet, like biological age, employment and marriage interact with psychosocial variables in a complex fashion' (1995: 225). Researchers should make every effort to understand cognitive and subjective correlates as well as the more easily measured (and quantified) social correlates of desistance if we are going to achieve a complete understanding of the process. As is reflected in the well-known aphorism among offenders that 'you rehabilitate yourself' (Meisenhelder, 1977), families, jobs, age or time cannot change a person who does not want to or make an effort to change. Presumably, individuals make a purposeful decision to marry or find work, and, if these bonds sustain desistance, the internal process involved in staying married or continuing to work needs to be understood if we want to understand how individuals can give up crime.

Understanding change in adulthood

Maruna (2001) observes that, essentially, what seems to be missing from both the ontogenetic and sociogenic approaches is 'the person' – the wholeness and subjective agency of the individual. He observes that the great French existentialist philosopher Jean-Paul Sartre (1963: 24) argued that trying to explain behaviour (and individual change in particular) by relying on 'the great idols of our epoch – heredity, education, environment, physiological constitution' allows us to 'understand nothing', the transitions, the 'becomings', the transformations, have been carefully veiled from us, and we have been limited to putting order into the succession by invoking empirically established but literally unintelligible sequences.

Sartre makes the same point as an expanding group of researchers in cognitive and personality psychology: we need a literally *intelligible* sequence, or a coherent 'story' of the individual if we want to understand changes in behaviour such as desistance. It is indeed an argument which has considerable support from critiques of traditional predominantly predestined actor model criminology. Thus, Toch argues that:

> Positivist approaches ... help us to 'understand crime.' These theories, however, do not permit us to 'understand criminals,' because they are segmental views rather than full-blooded portraits. ... [T]hese must be supplemented with portraits of offender perspectives, and with a review of unique *personal histories*.
>
> (1987: 162)

The use of such personal autobiographies in social enquiry, occasionally referred to as 'narrative studies', has been called 'a viable alternative to the positivist paradigm' in social science (Sarbin, 1986: vii). According to narrative theory, in order to achieve a contingent, temporally structured and contextualized under-standing of human behaviour, one needs to look at the self-narratives or storied self-concepts of individuals (Bruner, 1987; Giddens, 1991; McAdams, 1985). Essentially, understanding the person means understanding the person's 'story'.

We should note that narrative theories take many shapes (Gergen, 1991; Giddens, 1991; Ricoeur, 1984), but almost all of them take seriously Murray's (1938: 49) maxim, 'the history of the organism is the organism', by arguing that the 'self' is essentially a *storied construct*. In a seminal statement of the importance of narrative identity to understanding behaviour, Bruner observed:

> The heart of my argument is this: eventually the culturally shaped cognitive and linguistic processes that guide the self-telling of life narratives achieve the power to structure perceptual experience, to organise memory, to segment and purpose-build the very 'events' of a life. In the end, we *become* [emphasis added] the autobiographical narratives by which we 'tell about' our lives.
>
> (1987: 15)

Thus, the way that each of us views our own history is interesting not only because of what it reveals about our personality and our background but this subjective autobiography actually shapes our future choices and behaviour. In this framework, life narratives provide useful information about the person *and* his or her environment, and also show how the two interact to form a person's personality. McAdams (1994) argues that human behaviour is guided by three internalized domains (often called personality): (i) psychological traits; (ii) personal strategies; and (iii) identity narratives or self-stories (see also Conley, 1985). Though traits are relatively stable over the life course, the second two, more contextualized domains of personality leave open the possibility of substantial change during adulthood. To understand the desistance process from this narrative framework, therefore, one needs to analyse each of these domains of the 'whole person'.

Personality traits

Criminology has seen a revival in the study of the psychological traits of offenders over the past thirty years (Blackburn, 1992; Caspi *et al.*, 1994; Farrington, 1994). Wilson and Herrnstein (1985), for instance, argue that the primary cause of crim-inal behaviour is offenders' weak impulse control and lack of empathy for others (see Chapter 3). Eysenck (1977, 1989), on the other hand, identifies a correlation between crime and high levels of extroversion, neurosis and psychosis (see Chapter 5). The consensus reached in this psychometric research is that 'criminality' – or a 'criminal personality' – is generally constant throughout the life course, even when ex-offenders desist from criminal behaviour (Gottfredson and Hirschi, 1990; Huesmann *et al.*, 1984).

Osborn and West found that recidivist offenders who desist from crime 'retained some traits typical of delinquents, most notably their relative high scores on the scale of "anti-sociality"' (1980: 104). Similarly, Charland (1985) found that those who desist from offending, even though they have previously committed serious crimes, continued to display 'profound personality deficits' (based on numerous trait measures) long after offending had ceased.

In the trait framework, offenders are seen as 'types' of people suffering from an underlying antisocial personality disorder, with little chance of a 'cure' (see Chapter 5). Gottfredson and Hirschi, for instance, argue that the trait of low self-control is at the root of all criminal behaviour, yet they insist that differences between individuals in this trait remain constant over the life course: 'Enhancing the level of self-control appears possible in early childhood, but the record suggests that successful efforts to change the level later in life are exceedingly rare, if not non-existent' (1990: 33).

Maruna (1997) argues that this finding of continuity in the 'criminal personality' may be a methodological artefact stemming from the concentration on dispositional traits to the exclusion of other aspects of personality. The stability of basic personality traits like extroversion or aggressiveness over time and across contexts is one of the most robust findings in personality psychology (Costa *et al.*, 1983). On the other hand, people can and do 'change' even if their basic personality traits do not change radically over time (Helson and Stewart, 1994). By definition, if personality traits changed radically over time, they would not be traits, but rather temporary states or phases, and would lose their theoretical value. The study of traits provides valuable information about individual differences in disposition and personal styles, but the fact that traits are largely stable over time means they can probably tell us very little about how and why people change their behaviour. As Moffitt observes:

> [Psychological] theories typically rely on the stability of individual differences in traits such as impulsivity, neuroticism, autonomic nervous system reactivity, or low intelligence. Psychological theories cannot explain the onset and desistance of adolescent delinquency without positing compelling reasons for a sudden and dramatic population shift in criminogenic traits followed by return to baseline a few years later.
>
> (1993a: 694)

Thus, in order to understand desistance (or any significant behavioural change), researchers need to explore *other* aspects of personality, such as offender self-concepts or personal strategies (Maruna, 1997; McAdams, 1994).

McAdams' (1994) second level of personality involves the plans or goals the person is trying to accomplish. Linked to attitudes and group norms, these goal articulations are explicitly contextualized and change with situational and developmental demands. Those who desist from criminality are likely to have more spiritual and generative goals and strivings than persistent offenders. Maruna (1997) conducted an exploratory study where reformed ex-offenders frequently reported turning to a 'higher power' and making an effort to 'give something back' to their communities. This seems to be a strategy both for 'atoning' for past wrongs, as well as for advertising a new identity in an effort to alleviate the stigma faced by ex-convicts (see Meisenhelder, 1982).

The narrative identity

McAdams' (1994) third level of personality is the internalized and evolving narrative individuals construct to integrate their pasts, presents and perceived futures into a personal identity that sustains and guides behaviour. Overwhelmed with the choices and possibilities of modern society (Fromm, 1941; Manning, 1991), modern individuals internalize this autobiographical narrative in order to provide a sense of coherence and predictability to the chaos of their lives (Giddens, 1991; Sartre, 1963). According to Giddens, in modern society, 'a person's identity is not to be found in behaviour, nor – important though this is – in the reactions of others, but in the capacity to keep a particular narrative going' (1991: 54).

The *storied identity* can be seen as an active 'information-processing structure', a 'cognitive schema' or a construct system that is both shaped by and later mediates social interaction. Giddens observes that 'each of us not only "has", but lives a biography' (1991: 14). People tell stories about what they do and why they did it. These narratives explain their actions in a sequence of events that connect up to explanatory goals, motivations and feelings. Moreover, these self-narratives then act to shape and guide future behaviour, as persons act in ways that accord to the stories we have created about ourselves. Therefore, while our life goals give us a direction in which to act, our self-narratives provide the shape and coherence to our lives (Giddens, 1991).

While a variety of methods have been proposed for accessing life narratives (see Singer and Salovey, 1993), most involve intensive, non-clinical, semi-structured interviewing in field settings. Importantly, the tape-recorded and transcribed life story documents produced in such research *themselves* do not represent the self-narratives that guide the behaviour of an individual. However, the stories people tell about themselves are assumed to 'hold the outlines' of the *internalized*, ongoing self-narrative in the same way that answers to a psychological trait questionnaire are supposed to represent a person's personality traits.

Samplings of life narratives can be collected for any population of interest (for example, students, drug users or persons who have desisted from crime), content-coded, and analysed for patterns in tone, theme, plot, roles, value structure, coherence and complexity. The precise methodology of this thematic analysis varies (see Denzin, 1989), yet some of the most innovative studies have borrowed constructs from the work of semiotics, linguistics, hermeneutics and psycho-biography (for example, Manning, 1991). The accounts and explanations themselves – as well as the 'facts' or biographical events they describe – are the primary 'data' of these studies (McAdams, 1993).

Narratives of desistance and change

Personality traits are supposed to be both stable and 'transcontextual', the narrative identity, on the other hand, 'has to be routinely created and sustained in the reflexive activities of the individual' (Giddens, 1991: 52). Unlike developmental stage theorists, narrative theorists generally argue that identity is a life-long project, which individuals continuously restructure in light of new experiences and information (McAdams, 1993). Epstein and Erskine (1983) compare narrative identity change to paradigm shifts in the sciences, where past information is reorganized and understood in a new light. Individuals interpret and assimilate every emotionally salient experience into this evolving and cohesive narrative. When information is processed that does not fit into one's story, the person can either change his or her story to accommodate the new facts or distort the information to fit his or her story.

The internal changes involved in desistance from crime are likely to be charted and understood on this narrative level of personality. Erikson (1959) argues that people first begin to shape individual identities during adolescence. Consequently, teenagers go through a 'psychosocial moratorium' where they 'try on' various possible selves 'for size'. Identity theorists would argue that it is no coincidence that these 'disorganized' early narratives correspond with high rates of criminal behaviour. Canter observes that 'many acts of violence seem to erupt at a time when the perpetrator is searching for identity and personal meaning' (1994: 236). Understanding how individuals who internalize a criminal or deviant label are able to create a new self-understanding for themselves should be a priority in identity research (for example, Lofland, 1969).

Importantly, these 'structured self-images' are not created in a vacuum. Identity theorists like Erikson (1959) and Giddens (1991) argue that identity is very much shaped within the constraints and opportunity structure of the social world in which people live. The self is both socially shaped and individually constructed (Meisenhelder, 1982). Rather than stripping individuals of community and macro-historical context, narrative analysis can inform our understandings by illustrating how the person sees and experiences the world around them.

Cultural criminologist Jack Katz (1988) – whose work we will encounter in the fifth part of this book – calls this the merging of 'phenomenal foreground' with 'social background', and most narrative theorists would argue that the two are generally inseparable. Personal autobiographies are also excellent data for the analysis of the underlying economic and socio-structural relations of a population (Bertaux, 1981).

Agency and choice

Like the 'rational choice' models of criminal decision-making (Clarke and Cornish, 1985; Cusson and Pinsonneault, 1986), narrative theory provides a model of intentional and purposeful human behaviour. From the narrative perspective, when an individual desists from crime, they act as their own change agent (Adams, 1997) and are not merely the product of outside forces of social control or personality traits. This alone represents an important and radical departure from traditional, predestined model criminology which sees individual behaviour as largely determined by uncontrollable outer or inner forces (Matza, 1964). Adams observes that:

> No major investigation has ever been made of the kinds of changes adults may be seeking to make in their personalities; that is, evidently no one has systematically asked adults about this, even though adults, clearly more than children, are able to, and surely do, initiate their own socialisation.
>
> (1997: 334)

The comparison between narrative theory and 'choice' theories of desistance probably ends there. The latter theories propose that offenders weigh the risks and rewards of crime in much the same way that other economic actors decide to purchase a house or invest in a company (see contemporary rational actor theories discussed in Chapter 4). While most self-narratives certainly have an 'internal logic' (Canter, 1994), narrative theory does not see individuals in the frame of the 'rational actor model' of economics. For instance, beyond the economists' vague notions of preferences and constraints, narrative theory incorporates the attitudes, emotions and self-concepts of social psychology into its notion of choice.

Fundamentally, narrative theory explicitly tries to account for individual choices that appear to be far from 'rational', emphasising that human subjects, unlike their counterparts in the hard sciences, react differently to stimuli based on how events and constructs are 'perceived and interpreted . . . in line with pre-existing and emerging goals' (Toch, 1987). Epstein and Erskine, for instance, argue that 'behaviour that either is manifestly self-destructive or is maintained in the absence of reinforcement' can be explained and understood by first understanding the actor's "theory of reality" or guiding "construct" system' (1983: 135).

Self-stories represent personal outlooks and *theories* of reality, not necessarily an objective reality. For instance, if a person sees himself as 'backed against the wall' or feels that his dignity has been challenged by some insult, he may commit certain acts of violence that would be deemed 'senseless' by the public. Yet, these acts might be perfectly 'rational' in terms of that person's self-understanding. After all, according to narrative theory, like the symbolic interactionism that provides the theoretical foundations to the labelling theories, 'if [persons] define situations as real, they are real in their consequences' (Thomas and Thomas, 1928: 572). Maruna cites an inmate in HM Whitemoor Prison who provided the following illustration of the power of such situational definitions in his account of the theft of his gold chain:

> I said, 'Give me the fucking chain back,' and he pulled a knife out at me and his friend had got this baseball bat. . . . I went home, and I couldn't sleep. I kept waking up at 2 a.m. saying, 'I can't deal with this.' My girl was telling me to calm down, let it go. But I kept thinking to myself, 'this is going to have to be something big. This isn't going to be just a fist fight. This is going to be big. . . . Everybody in the scene knew I was looking for him. . . . Then

eventually I met him at the pub. I brought this knife and I stabbed him. . . . Unless you actually grew up in that situation, you wouldn't understand what I was going through. Common sense is just different in that situation. You just don't have the same common sense. Lying in bed, really, I think about it a lot. 'If this . . .' 'If that . . .', but then the 'ifs' go away and you just have to say, 'this is the real you.' I had little choice really. Either you do it, or you do nothing and you get written off the scene altogether. Street-wise, that's suicide – you're back to the bottom of the ladder, you're nobody. Sensible-wise, of course, that's the best thing that could happen to you. That means taking the alternative route with the suit and job and all. But I've got a rough streak in me somewhere. . . . I had to do it.

(1997: 87)

Only by understanding the way this man understood himself, his actions and the 'common sense' of the streets can one begin to understand why he attempted murder. To truly desist from crime, according to the narrative perspective, a person needs to restructure their understanding of self. If individuals chose to desist from crime as soon as they rationally decide that 'crime doesn't pay', as traditional deterrence and rational choice theories suggest, the recidivism rate of ex-convicts returning to prisons would not be nearly as high as it is (Shover, 1996). Deciding or 'choosing' to give up crime, after all, is vastly different from actual desistance from crime. Individuals can *choose* to stop getting into fights – just like smokers *choose* to quit smoking – seven times a week in some cases. Yet maintaining abstinence from crime involves more than choice. Offenders typically *decide* to 'go straight' (for quite rational reasons) many times over the course of a criminal career, but *continue* to offend – for reasons that are more to do with their perceptions of their situation (Shover, 1996; Maruna, 1997). Understanding the person's narrative can help observers understand these less than rational decisions.

Narrating desistance

Following the long tradition of autobiographical research in criminology (Becker, 1966; Bennett, 1981), several studies of ex-offenders have found indications that a systematic change in identity and self-concept may be critical to the process of reform (Burnett, 1992; Graham and Bowling, 1995; Irwin, 1970; Leibrich, 1993; Maruna, 1997, 2001; Meisenhelder, 1982; Shover, 1985, 1996). Similar indications have been found in research on the cessation of addictive behaviours such as drug use (Biernacki, 1986; Denzin, 1987; DiClemente, 1994; Waldorf, 1983). These important qualitative studies have generated consistent and empirically testable hypotheses regarding the subjective experience of the conversion experience. Still, this research remains highly disconnected and somewhat outside of mainstream criminological debates.

In one such study, Maruna (1997) analysed the autobiographical narratives of twenty ex-offenders and found substantial evidence for a 'prototypical reform story' that integrates a person's past mistakes into a generative script for the future. Ex-offenders who desisted from crime overwhelmingly attributed their delinquent pasts to environmental factors outside of their control. They attributed their radical lifestyle change to outside forces as well. Usually to the generosity of some forgiving person or persons who could see past the ex-offender's mistakes. This opportunity allowed the ex-offender to finally become his or her 'true self' (a good or non-criminal person). As a way of showing appreciation for this second chance, many ex-offenders explained, they are trying to 'give something back' to the society from which they have taken so much. The development of some variation on this coherent self-story may contribute to the process of desistance from crime and support individual efforts to go straight.

Unfortunately, like most of the other research on ex-offenders who go straight, Maruna's (1997) study did not include a comparison sample, and so may be seen as largely exploratory. Instead of asking why some individuals desist from crime while others do not, these biographical studies tend to concentrate on the experiences of *all* ex-convicts or the similarities between middle-aged offenders and middle-aged men in general (for example, Shover, 1985). In order to isolate what aspects of self-concept are *directly* related to desistance, research needs to compare those who desist with a matched sample of offenders who do not desist from crime (see Burnett, 1992, 1994; Glaser, 1964).

Developments and reflections on desistance theories

Maruna and Immarigeon argue that primary desistance happens so frequently it does not warrant further study, arguing that the focus should be on secondary desistance from crime when 'existing roles become disrupted' and 'reorganisation based on new roles occurs' (2004: 19). Maruna (2001) concluded that true desistance can only occur once the individuals' perspective of themselves changes.

We have seen that the value of the narrative perspective can provide insight into why the desire to 'go straight', and support from the probation service and other groups supporting reintegration into the community, such as NACRO, are still not enough for the process of desistance. Laub and Sampson (2003) conducted a study where they heard 52 life stories from men in their 60s, some of whom continued to offend in one way or another, while others had stopped. Their research offers an interesting perspective because the men were given time to reflect on their life of crime and provide insights into why, despite good intentions, they were unable to 'go straight' or were able to turn their lives around.

Maruna (2001) reports on a narrative study involving twenty persistent offenders and thirty who had desisted from crime, who shared similar criminogenic traits, backgrounds and environments. The research clearly demonstrated the significance of the individual's 'story' or 'script' to justify and explain their criminal career, discussing their subjective perspective on their past, present and future, and the role they played in their life story. Maruna observed that, while each story was unique to the particular individual, two common themes of *condemnation* and *redemption* were repeated and these significantly differed between those who persisted with their offending and those who had desisted. Those who persisted had adopted a condemnation script, where they saw themselves to be the victims of environmental and social circumstances beyond their control, with a lack of access to decent education, coming from a poor family background, having had a lack of financial freedom and having turned to crime and deviant behaviour as a method of taking back control and surviving; these feelings of being in a criminal career trap, in what Jock Young (1999: 395) describes as a bulimic society, where the media and society present ideals everyone should aspire to – financial success, material goods, own homes – and yet certain groups are excluded from achieving these ideals through lack of legitimate opportunities; these individuals are 'vomited' from society and excluded.

Maruna (2007) suggests that, by encouraging offenders to partake in community activities, such as providing respite care, staffing charity shops, the repair and maintenance of wheelchairs, they can combat the 'bulimic' society; thus, by taking part in long-term volunteer placements, offenders reported an improved sense of self-worth, accomplishment and purpose. Unlike formal interventions such as menial community service, short-term imprisonment or treatment programmes for anger or social skills:

> Volunteer work gives the offender the dignified position of being a help-giver rather than a passive help-receiver. Volunteering also sends a message to the community that the offender deserves further support and investment in his or her reintegration. Yet the real virtue of volunteerism might be its reversal of our bulimic value system.
>
> (Maruna, 2007)

In opposition to those who had a condemnation script, those who took on a redemption script (Maruna, 2001: 147) were individuals who had a strong sense of self-belief and control over their future and present. While they too put past criminal and deviant behaviours down to circumstances they could not control, they took responsibility for current and future successes, which is an area of psychological interest called 'learned optimism' (Maruna, 2001: 147).

Lemert (1951) had observed – working in the labelling theory tradition we encountered earlier in this book – that there is no systematic theory to specify the social mechanisms which might change the secondary deviant into a 'normal' acceptable member of society, Maruna and his narrative approach explains how the individual is able to make the transition subjectively. Over time, those who came to desist from crime were able to explain and internalize 'why they did, what they did, and why they are now "not like that" anymore' (Maruna, 2001), developing these credible stories that they and others could understand, in a way where they were able to move beyond previous identities they held. By being able to view themselves more positively when others still see the bad, those who came to desist from offending were able to utilize techniques of neutralization (see Sykes and Matza, 1957), thus justifying their past and moving forward into their present. In this way, they are separating themselves from their old social circles who expect them to live up to their old identities.

McCulloch and McNeill (2008: 157) report on a study of sixty probationers and identified the importance of a significant relationship, or 'change agents' for those who were able to successfully desist from offending. They found that those who desisted identified probation workers as a particular positive influence when the particular individuals were seemingly genuinely interested in their lives, demonstrating positive displays in well-being and offering encouragement. This suggests a return to the traditional principles of the probation role of 'advise, assist and befriend' and a move away from the new public sector management style of control, manage and monitoring, which dominates the contemporary profession.

The pessimistic view that 'nothing works', which had come to dominate criminal justice thinking in the 1970s and 1980s (see Chapter 3), returns us to the traditional predestined actor model orthodoxy that offenders and non-offenders are fundamentally different. That much maligned father of biological positivism Cesare Lombroso had observed over a century ago that 'atavism shows us the inefficiency of punishment for born criminals and why it is they inevitably have periodic relapses into crime' (Lombroso, 1875: 369). Crime was their inevitable destiny and there was no escape in the long term. It is an enduring view widely held, and, when Maruna (2001) began his study of ex-offenders who had 'gone straight', he was greeted by a 'chorus of doubt' from his peers and criminal justice practitioners, questioning 'how can he prove they are really clean?' and 'how do you know they are not just lying to you?' (Maruna, 2001: 19). But Maruna took an interest in the 'false positives', those individuals who, due to socio-economic and environmental factors, and according to all predestined actor model orthodoxy, should persist in offending, and yet go on to 'make good'.

Several significant concerns have nevertheless been raised about the theoretical veracity and implementation of desistance theories and strategies. First, there are inevitable questions about the ethical implications of probation officers and academics trying to facilitate desistance through coercion (McNeill, 2006). Second, some have argued that any probationer or parolee should be required as part of their conditions of bail to obtain work or appropriate training (Sampson and Laub, 1995), and this clearly raises the significant issue of how the criminal justice service will be able to ensure there is appropriate and suitable employment for all, particularly during a period of major economic recession. Third, it is observed that desistance theories do not really explain involvement in white-collar offending, although Maruna (2001) suggested that the peak age of offending curve could be explained in part by a transition to involvement in less risky offending such as that found in the workplace. Nevertheless, in his study of persistent offenders, none of the sample was a white-collar offender. All of them were from underprivileged and socially excluded groups, compared to the 'typical' white-collar offender, who has legitimate access to reasonable financial rewards, a respectable role within society, family and social ties. However, we might observe that convicted white-collar offenders are extremely unlikely to get further employment in that area again and that desistance from that type of offending is rather enforced. It does nevertheless seem inevitable that persistent offenders are invariably the failures – the failed criminals recycled through the criminal justice system – giving credibility to theories like life course persistent offending. What we do not know enough about is successful criminal enterprise and that poses a methodological minefield.

Policy implications of desistance theories

Eight central themes can be identified from the above discussion of desistance theories, which have significant policy implications. First, desistance for people who have been involved in persistent offending is clearly a difficult and complex process, and one that is likely to involve lapses and relapses. There is thus value in criminal justice supervision being realistic about these difficulties and seeking ways to manage setbacks and difficulties constructively. It may take considerable time for supervision and support to exercise a positive effect (Farrall and Calverley, 2006; Weaver and McNeill, 2007). Second, since desistance is an inherently individualized and subjective process, approaches to criminal justice social work supervision must accommodate and exploit issues of identity and diversity. One-size-fits-all interventions will not work (Weaver and McNeill, 2010). Three, the development and maintenance not just of motivation but also of hope become key tasks for criminal justice social workers (Farrall and Calverley, 2006). Fourth, desistance can only be understood within the context of human relationships; not just relationships between workers and offenders (though these matter a great deal), but also between offenders and those who matter to them (Burnett and McNeill, 2005; McNeill, 2006). Fifth, although the focus is often on the risks and needs of offenders, they also have strengths and resources that they can use to overcome obstacles to desistance – both personal strengths and resources, and strengths and resources in their social networks. Supporting and developing these capacities can be a useful dimension of criminal justice social work (Maruna and LeBel, 2003, 2009). Sixth, since desistance is in part about discovering self-efficacy or agency, interventions are most likely to be effective where they encourage and respect self-determination; this means working *with* offenders not *on* them (McCulloch, 2005; McNeill, 2006). Seventh, interventions based only on developing the capacities and skills of people who have offended – human capital – will not be enough. Probation workers also need to work on developing social capital, opportunities to apply these skills or to practise newly forming identities, such as 'worker' or 'father' (Farrall, 2002, 2004; McNeill and Whyte, 2007). Eighth, the language of practice should strive to more clearly recognize positive potential and development, and should seek to avoid identifying people with the behaviours we want them to leave behind (McNeill and Maruna, 2007). In short, the policy implications of desistance theories are to strengthen these probation service interventions.

Summary of main points

1. Maruna (1997) observes that few phenomena in criminology have been as widely acknowledged and as poorly understood as why it is people desist from doing crime.

2. For most individuals, participation in 'street crimes' generally begins in the early teenage years, peaks in late adolescence or young adulthood, and ends before the person reaches 30 or 40 years of age.
3. At some stage in their life course, usually between 18 and 35 years of age, even serious offenders tend to cease criminal behaviour.
4. Maruna (1997) observed that most of the leading desistance explanations continued to fall into the dichotomy of ontogenetic and sociogenic paradigms.
5. Such theories suggest that desistance from criminal behaviour is a natural 'stage' in personality development, parallel to the questioning of roles and identity that supposedly takes place for all adults at mid-life.
6. Narrative theory proposes that, in order to achieve a contingent, temporally structured and contextualized understanding of human behaviour, one needs to look at the self-narratives or storied self-concepts of individuals.
7. The consensus reached in psychometric research is that 'criminality' – or a 'criminal personality' – is generally constant throughout the life course, even when ex-offenders desist from criminal behaviour.
8. Unlike developmental stage theorists, narrative theorists generally argue that identity is a life-long project, which individuals continuously restructure in light of new experiences and information (McAdams, 1993).
9. From the narrative perspective, when an individual desists from crime, they act as their own change agent (Adams, 1997) and are not merely the product of outside forces of social control or personality traits.
10. Fundamentally, narrative theory explicitly tries to account for individual choices that appear to be far from 'rational', emphasising that human subjects react differently to stimuli based on how events and constructs are perceived and interpreted.

Discussion questions

1. Briefly explain the ontogenetic paradigm of desistance and its perceived weaknesses.
2. Briefly explain the sociogenic paradigm of desistance and its perceived weaknesses.
3. How does narrative theory propose that we achieve a full understanding of human behaviour?
4. Why does an individual desist from crime from the narrative perspective?
5. How in terms of the narrative perspective do individuals make choices, ultimately to desist from offending?

Suggested further reading

Desistance theories have come very much to the fore during the first two decades of the twenty-first century and the key researcher and author in this tradition is

Shadd Maruna; the reader wanting an informed introduction to the subject is advised to consult Maruna (1997, 1998, 2001), and for an extensive overview consult Maruna and Immarigeon (2004). Stephen Farrall has produced a series of valuable publications for those working with offenders (see Farrall, 2002, 2004; with Ben Bowling, 1997; and with Adam Calverley, 2006).

Note

1 Daniel Levinson (1986) suggests that there is an underlying order in the human life course. Although each individual life is unique, everyone goes through the same basic sequence. The course of a life is not a simple, continuous process. There are qualitatively different phases or seasons. Three parts have been suggested (a) an initial segment of about 20 years, including childhood and adolescence (pre-adulthood); (b) a final segment starting at around 65 (old age); and (c) between these segments, an amorphous time vaguely known as adulthood.

18. Left realism

Key Issues

1. The origins of 'left realism'
2. A balance of intervention
3. Left realism and 'New' Labour
4. Social exclusion and the 'underclass': a case study
5. Recent developments in left realism

Left realism is not like the theoretically integrated approaches discussed previously in this fourth part of the book for it is not really an attempt to integrate and synthesize elements from different theories in order to provide a stronger comprehensive theoretical tool. It is more recognition of the validity of explanatory elements contained in each of the three models of crime and criminal behaviour that we have so far encountered, and their practical value as part of a comprehensive strategy for understanding and responding to crime both at a macro societal level and at the level of practice. There is, nevertheless, a predominant emphasis on sociological explanations of criminality with recently more focus on developing an integrated theory synthesizing traditions such as labelling and subcultural theories and bringing them together within a socialist feminist framework that stresses class and gender inequality (see Mooney, 2000).

The origins of left realism

Left realism has its origins in the writings of a group of British criminologists, some of whom had been in the forefront of the radical criminology of the 1970s, and these texts emerged principally in response to four closely interconnected factors. First, there was a reaction among this group to what they considered to be 'left idealism', the utopian positions that their previous confederates in the radical/critical criminological tradition had now taken up. In the USA, Elliott Currie (1992) referred to 'progressive minimalists' or left-wing academics

frightened of entering the law and order debate for fear of adding to the preju-
dices of the public and thus promoting support for conservative crime control
strategies with the unintended outcome that, in ignoring the real problems of
serious crime and drug use in the USA:

> they help to perpetuate an image of progressives as being both fuzzy-
> minded and, much worse, unconcerned about the realities of life for those
> ordinary Americans who are understandably frightened and enraged by
> the suffering and fear crime brings to their communities and families.
>
> (Currie, 1992: 91)

Second, there was a response to the rising tide of criminal victimization that
was becoming increasingly apparent in British society and where poor people
were overwhelmingly the victims. It nevertheless seems extremely unlikely
that these writers and researchers would have so readily discovered this
new reality but for the important impetus provided by the other two factors.
Thus, third, there was the rise to prominence and power of the populist
conservatives or the 'new right' and, fourth, the simultaneous rediscovery by
right realist criminologists of the rational actor model of crime and criminal
behaviour.

This significant shift in the intellectual climate of radical criminology had
centred on a debate around the issue of policing the inner city and the notion of
moral panics. Critical criminology, it was acknowledged, had made important
contributions to the study of the crimes of the powerful, such as corporate crimes,
government wrongdoings and white-collar crimes, but most of these criminologists, it was observed, had simply chosen to ignore the causes and possible
control of crime committed by members of the working class against other
members of the working class with, of course, the exception of violence against
women, children and members of ethnic groups. This failure to acknowledge
working-class crime had, however, come at a great price to the political left
because it had allowed right-wing politicians – and right realist criminologists –
in several countries to claim opposition to street crime as their own issue, giving
them room to generate ideological support for harsh law and order policies.

It was in this context that a new perspective was to emerge among some left
criminologists that a 'new realist' view on crime was necessary and that it was
time to 'take crime seriously' (Lea and Young, 1984). From this viewpoint, it was
argued that crime is not purely a social construction, nor is the fear of crime
shared by many people. To put the latter down solely to the manipulations of the
'capitalist media' or 'the system' is, again, politically and morally irresponsible.
Moreover, as was becoming readily apparent from the findings of victimization
studies – such as the British Crime Surveys – to regard criminal statistics as mere
inventions is not acceptable either. Broad patterns of offences can be established
after all, and a disproportionate amount of personally hurtful crime is undeni-
ably committed by the more 'marginalized' sectors of the urban working class,
for example, young black males. Quite simply, the lives of many ordinary citizens are seriously disrupted by this kind of offence, and it is not 'pro-state' to
argue for effective policing in these areas.

This group of criminologists on the left of the political spectrum – such as Jock Young, John Lea and Roger Matthews – thus became increasingly worried during the 1980s that the debate on crime control was slipping away from them. Critical criminologists – by denying that working-class crime was a real problem and concentrating instead on 'crimes of the powerful' – were ignoring the plight of working-class victims of predatory crime. Successive defeats of the British Labour Party furthermore convinced them that they had allowed the political high ground to be captured by the new populist conservative theorists. The rediscovered rational actor model was gaining favour with government, while administrative criminologists in the Home Office – as we have seen elsewhere in this book – were concentrating on small-scale empirical investigation.

Young detected a need for a 'radical realist' response: one that recognized the impact of crime, but that, at the same time, addressed the context in which it occurred. The first statement of his dissatisfaction with radical orthodoxy came in a book written with his contemporary John Lea, *What is to be Done About Law and Order?* (Lea and Young, 1984). In this text, they stressed the evidence of victim studies, which showed that official statistics presented an incomplete and even inaccurate picture of the impact of crime. Victim studies had two major advantages: first, they revealed offences and incivilities, which, although not reported to the police, nevertheless caused great misery to those who suffered them; second, because many of the studies were localized, they gave a truer impression of the situation in particular areas where offending might be concentrated.

Lea and Young were concerned to highlight differences in victimization levels within groups. For example, national statistics suggest that women as a group are far less likely than men to be victims of homicide, but a closer examination shows that the chances of a black woman being murdered are greater than that of a white male. They also drew attention to the disparity between the impacts of crime on different groups: thus, men generally feel anger towards aggressors, whereas women tend to suffer shock and fear. Moreover, the impact of crime cannot be measured in absolute terms: £50 stolen from a middle-class home is likely to have less effect on the victims than the same sum taken from a poor household.

For left realists, crime is a real problem that must be addressed. Lea and Young deal with the argument that corporate crime is more important: yes, 'crimes of the powerful' do exist and are to be condemned, but the effects of corporate crime are generally widespread, while those of direct-contact crime are concentrated. Corporate crime may indeed cause financial loss and even death and danger, but the real problem for those living in high-crime areas is posed by predatory offenders in their midst. Left realism thus takes into account the immediate fears that people have and seeks to deal with them.

Lea and Young were also keen to address the peripheral problems around the central issue. People living in high-crime areas suffer individual offences that they may or may not report to the police, but they also suffer a range of incivilities, such as vandalism, where they are not directly victimized, threats, vulgarity, sexual harassment, noise and swearing, all of which taken together further reduce quality of life and increase despair.

Police excesses are also identified as causing crime. First, police harassment of minority groups causes resentment and feelings of helplessness that may actually encourage offending. Second, 'military-style policing', such as that noted in the run-up to the Brixton riots in April 1981, creates a siege mentality among the residents of an area that discourages them from assisting the police in their investigations. Moreover, aggressive policing further brutalizes crime areas, which, in turn, leads to more crime.

Left realists have also responded to the claim of critical criminologists that the apparent propensity of black youths to commit predatory crime is solely the outcome of racist police stereotyping and targeting. While recognizing that such stereotyping does exist, and deploring it, Lea and Young observe that young black males do in fact commit more of these offences. In the USA, they are more represented in this category of offenders than Asians, Hispanics and Mexicans, who suffer comparative levels of poverty and discrimination. In fact, in Britain, the police had at first refused to accept that there was a 'black crime problem', instead pointing out that young black males were over-represented in areas where crime tended to be highest.

Left realism, however, draws on the lessons of anomie theory and proposes that young second-generation African-Caribbeans in Britain committed more crime than other ethnic groups because they have been fully integrated into the surrounding culture and were consequently led to expect a fair slice of the economic cake. Not being able to achieve their promised position through legitimate means – because of discrimination – they turned to crime. Other ethnic minorities – having integrated less – retain strong family and cultural ties that subject them to stronger social control and help them to achieve without offending.

Moreover, left realists doubt the existence of the simple relationship between crime and unemployment that has been so central to the critical criminology perspective. Women, who until recently have been unable to enter the workplace in large numbers, have always been massively under-represented in the ranks of offenders. It is only now, when women are finding opportunities for work, that the female crime rate is starting to rise more quickly.

Critical criminologists are accused of being 'schizophrenic' about crime. It is observed that feminists have forced them to take seriously the fear of women about rape and sexual assault, while racial attacks are naturally deplored, but other crime is depicted as being understandable and a symptom of the class struggle. Nevertheless:

> The tide is turning for radical criminology. For over two decades it has neglected the effect of crime upon the victim and concentrated on the impact of the state – through the process of labelling – on the criminal . . . It became an advocate for the indefensible: the criminal became the victim, the state the solitary focus of attention, while the real victim remained off-stage.
>
> (Matthews and Young, 1986: Introduction)

Young also turned his sights on the limited adequacy of the 'new administrative criminology' that had come to dominate the British Home Office and the research departments of the larger universities: 'the new administrative criminologists seek to construct a system of punishment and surveillance which discards rehabilitation and replaces it with a social behaviourism worthy of the management of white rats in laboratory cages' (1986b: 28).

While criminologists had often been arguing among themselves in the pursuit of the 'holy grail' of an all-encompassing explanation of crime and criminal behaviour, there is evidence that governments had lost patience with a discipline that seemed no closer than ever to solving the crime problem. One of the world's leading criminologists, the Australian John Braithwaite, had perceptively observed as recently as 1989:

> The present state of criminology is one of abject failure in its own terms. We cannot say anything convincing to the community about the causes of crime; we cannot prescribe policies that will work to reduce crime; we cannot in all honesty say that societies spending more on criminological research get better criminal justice policies than those that spend little or nothing on criminology.
>
> (Braithwaite, quoted in Matthews and Young, 1992: 3–4)

In Britain – as we have seen elsewhere in this book – government pessimism at ever being able to solve the crime problem through understanding, and being able to deal with the origins and motivations for offending, had shifted the focus of research. Spending since the late 1970s had been devoted more to finding and evaluating pragmatic solutions to particular offences than to developing criminological theory. Most professional crime prevention practitioners enjoying government patronage had come to accept that crime is a function of opportunity. Whatever motives offenders might have, removal of opportunities for offending will, says the assumption, reduce the incidence of crime. The response of the left realists was in reality an attempt to develop an all-encompassing crime control strategy that, while accepting the need for the practical, pragmatic and certainly the empirical, managed to locate this all within both a macro and micro theoretical context.

A balance of intervention

Central to the left realist crime control strategy is the proposition that crime requires a comprehensive solution where there must be a 'balance of intervention'. Both crime and the causes of crime must thus be tackled and this argument is illustrated with the 'square of crime' (Lea, 1992; Young 1987, 1992) or what John Lea (2002) later called the 'social relations of crime control', which he observed created a framework that enabled a detailed specification of the conditions of existence of a policing and criminal justice system meeting the needs of the community.

The square of crime (Figure 18.1) is designed as a reminder that crime is the outcome of a number of lines of force, and intervention to prevent it must take place at different levels in order to be effective. Left realists propose that crime is

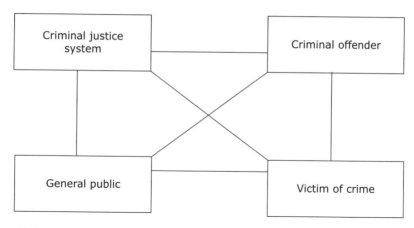

Figure 18.1 The square of crime.

a function of four factors. First, there is *the state* or the criminal justice system, principally through the capacity of its front-line agents to label individuals and groups as offenders, which is a major factor in recidivism. Second, there is *the victim* of crime who may actually encourage offenders through inadequate defence or may even precipitate crime through his or her lifestyle or personality, all of which determine the impact of crime. Third, there is *society* or the general public, through which the various forces of informal and formal social control are exercised. Fourth, there are *the criminal offenders* themselves (their number, their rate of offending, the type of crimes they commit, etc.).

Crime occurs not only as a product of these four individual factors, but also as an outcome of the relationship between them. The relationship between the police and the public that left – and, indeed, right – realists argue determines the effectiveness of the former in preventing crime can be described as state–society interplay. The actions of the criminal justice system are state–offender interplay. Fundamentally, all crime prevention efforts, of whatever type, involve some relationship between the four corners of the square. In short:

> To control crime from a realist perspective involves intervention at each part of the square of crime: at the level of the factors which give rise to the putative offender (such as structural unemployment), the informal system (such as lack of public mobilisation), the victim (such as inadequate target hardening), and the formal system (such as ineffective policing).
>
> (Young, 1986b: 41)

Essentially, all the left realists are really saying is that there is something to be said for most explanations of crime and criminal behaviour. The problem with most theorists, they argue, is that, by occupying entrenched positions on the causes of crime, they are not able to step back and look at the wider picture.

Critical criminologists accept that the 'new realist' perspective has much in common with both Engels' (1845) and Bonger's (1916) much earlier Marxist versions of 'demoralization' theory where it had been argued that capitalism is a social system that dehumanizes and alienates people, particularly sections of the working class, who inevitably become at times desperate and antisocial in their strategies for personal survival. From that perspective, crime statistics are considered to be an index of the general moral malaise of a society that – in its legitimate as well as illegitimate business – thrives on greed and self-interest. It thus follows that certain kinds of crime, criminal and victim are not to be 'explained away' as if they are somehow unreal or merely a product of repressive bourgeois law.

Consequently, both the older Marxists and the new realists see a positive element in the 'rule of law' and, in particular, some need is recognized for effective policing, for example, in declining urban areas. More positively, a socialist strategy is held to require the extension and defence of certain civil rights, which are, nominally at least, available within liberal capitalist society (Hirst, 1980). Thus, the politics of law and order, for the left, should be less to do with the denial of street crime and sympathy with marginalized groups, and more to do with the elaboration of a responsible, rights-based notion of order.

Left realism has nevertheless been criticized for presenting a caricature of a supposedly antagonistic 'left idealist' position. The equation is made that the police are part of the state, are a part of capitalism, or that in true socialism, when it comes, there will be no problems of order, crime or dissent. Critical theorists such as Phil Scraton and Joe Sim acknowledge that elements of that position crept into 1960s and 1970s theorizing but assert that virtually no one would maintain these caricatured assertions in the early twenty-first century. At the same time, they have quite serious and legitimate reservations about the drift into left realism that requires a response.

Critical criminologists have argued that, in a phase of capitalism that displays increasingly harsh traits, it is not at all 'idealist' to argue that the main focus and priority should be on the nature of police coercion and authoritarian tendencies in the state (Scraton, 1985; Sim *et al.*, 1987). They argue that the most striking fact about law and order today is not so much the fear of crime and street offences. Rather, we are seeing – if only we look in the right places – a massive growth in the powers of the armed and surveillance branches of the state, limbs of the body politic that are becoming dangerously unaccountable (see Hopkins Burke, 2004c). To concentrate on the 'problem of crime' in this context is to reverse the proper order of priorities. It would be wrong to say nevertheless, and despite some parallels, that left and right realism are the same. The left would thus strenuously dispute references to Victorian values and the virtues of traditional authority – highlighted by the right – on the grounds that a restricted conception of human autonomy has been based on historical myth. Yet the political right instigated a moral climate during its long period of electoral dominance in the 1980s and 1990s that established an apparent new social consensus. The 'New' Labour Government elected in 1997 was subsequently widely criticized by many traditionalists on the political left – in particular by critical criminologists – for merely carrying on with the law and order project instigated by their predecessors and supposedly political opponents.

Left realism and 'New' Labour

We have seen above and elsewhere in this book that during the 1980s the British Home Office came to promote what Jock Young has termed the new 'administrative criminology'. The emphasis on reducing the opportunity to offend through small-scale situational crime prevention schemes was in perfect accord with the ideological viewpoint of the Conservative Government of 1979–97 committed to notions of rational choice and making people take responsibility for their actions, but there had also been good practical reasons for this shift in emphasis.

The previous rehabilitative orthodoxy of the predestined actor model of criminal behaviour and its emphasis on treatment and changing criminals – the biological or psychological versions – or their environment – the sociological version – had been widely seen not to work. A considerable sum of money had been spent over the years on rehabilitative measures, while at the same time the ever-increasing official crime statistics painted a picture of expensive failure.

The new administrative orthodoxy proposed that, if none of these causal explanations of criminal behaviour and their corresponding policy interventions worked, then there was little point in pursuing this approach. Conservative populists – or 'right realists' – proposed reducing the opportunity to offend, while catching, incarcerating and incapacitating those who did transgress. Nonetheless, this was not an entirely successful strategy.

Evaluations of strategies of situational crime prevention measures suggested some ambiguous outcomes (Hughes, 1998), but they were not without success and crime has definitely been reduced on occasion in certain situations. Problematically, while there remains a population of potentially determined and available criminals, there will continue to be an issue of crime displacement. In short, locking all doors and bolting all windows is invariably a good idea but it is no universal panacea for the problem of crime. Situational crime prevention is thus a sensible but incomplete crime control strategy.

If we accept the latter point, then we have to recognize that some attempt has to be made to address the motivations of offenders or – to use the language of the predestined actor model – to locate the causes of crime and do something about them. The solution for the left realists is a 'balanced intervention' that addresses all sides of the crime problem. For the British 'New' Labour Government – or the populist socialists – unquestionably influenced by this criminological discourse, it was an approach to crime and criminal behaviour summarized and popularized by the oft-quoted sound bite of Prime Minister Tony Blair when Shadow Home Secretary: 'tough on crime, tough on the causes of crime'.

Being 'tough on crime' suggests that offenders should take responsibility for their actions and is in theoretical accordance with the prescriptions of the rational actor model. Taking a tough stance on the causes of crime suggests a targeting of both those individual and structural factors that in some way encourage criminality, and is thus in accordance with not only the predestined actor model but *also* – and most appropriately for a socialist political party, however much they might like to disguise that fact – rooted most firmly in the victimized actor model. The theoretical justification for that governmental approach – and it is one that sets it apart from its political opponents and predecessors in government – is offered by the following realist case study of an apparently criminal 'underclass'.

Social exclusion and the 'underclass': a case study

An analysis of a socially excluded 'underclass' whose members are over-represented among the ranks of convicted offenders conducted from a left realist perspective requires that we consider theoretical inputs from each of the three models of crime and criminal behaviour introduced in this book. Two principal academic explanations can be found for the existence of this 'underclass' (Crowther, 1998) and these encompass theoretical insights from each of the three models.

Structural accounts – for example those offered by Dahrendorf (1985), Field (1989), Jordan (1996) and, from the USA, William Julius Wilson (1987, 1991) – are normally associated with the political 'left' and have their theoretical foundations firmly located in both the conflict, radical and critical variants of the victimized actor tradition *and* the sociological tradition within the predestined actor model. Primarily various forms of social exclusion, poverty, material deprivation and patterns of inequality are highlighted. Entry into and membership of this class is explained by the inadequacy of state-provided welfare services, changes in the labour market and exclusion from full citizenship.

Behavioural accounts, on the other hand – for example, Wilson and Herrnstein (1985), Murray (1990, 1994) and Herrnstein and Murray (1995) – are normally associated with the political 'new right' or populist conservatives, and have their theoretical foundations in the rational actor model and the biological variant of the predestined actor model (see Chapter 13). This form of explanation came to prominence during the 1980s following the rise in the number of long-term unemployed, the burgeoning lone-parent population, increased welfare dependency and rising crime and disorder. From this perspective, it is argued that the provision of state welfare erodes individual responsibility by giving people incentives not to work and provide for themselves and their family. Moreover, it is argued that those 'controls' – identified in Chapter 15 (see Hirschi, 1969) – that stop individuals and communities from behaving badly, such as stable family backgrounds and in particular positive male role models – do not exist for many members of this 'underclass'.

There is no evidence to suggest that non-participation in the labour market leads to inevitable involvement in a distinctive subculture (Westergaard, 1995; Marshall *et al.*, 1996; Levitas, 1996; Crowther, 1998). People can remain unemployed for many years, surviving on a very limited income, while remaining law-abiding citizens. On the other hand, it has to be recognized that there has been a real problem of crime and antisocial behaviour inflicted on some invariably poor working-class communities by gangs of socially excluded males living in their midst (Campbell, 1993; Jordan, 1996), and this situation has been exacerbated during the early years of the twenty-first century in isolated and brutalized communities where young men have become embroiled in criminal lifestyles, amid the detritus of collapsed economic and community structures and in a wider world where consumerism has triumphed (Hall *et al.*, 2008).

This author has proposed elsewhere that a left realist analysis requires the development of a process model that both locates the *structural* preconditions for the emergence of this social grouping, while at the same time examining the nature of their *behavioural* response to their found predicament (Hopkins Burke, 1999a). It is an analysis that provides a theoretical justification for a balanced intervention in their lives.

The structural precondition for the emergence of an underclass was undoubtedly the collapse of the unwritten post-war social contract between governments and the unskilled working class in advanced industrial societies. This had been founded on the provision of full employment and a fall-back position – or safety net – of a relatively generous welfare state. However, with the major economic restructuring that occurred during the late 1970s and the 1980s, non-skilled young people – in particular young males – entering into the labour market became increasingly over-represented among the ranks of the unemployed. At the same time, changes to social security entitlement in 1988 – instigated by the populist Conservatives with the conscious intention of eradicating welfare dependency – had meant that 16- and 17-year-olds lost their automatic right to benefits while 18- to 24-year-olds saw a dramatic reduction in the amount of money they could claim. Caroline Adams from the charity 'Action for Children' estimated that this was a contributory reason why 75,000 16- to 17-year-olds had no source of income whatsoever (Hopkins Burke, 1998c). In short, the collapse of the economic basis of their existence provides the structural element of a process model of the creation of an underclass (Hopkins Burke, 2000).

The behavioural response of this group has its origins in changes to familial living arrangements encouraged by that economic upheaval. The ideal type nuclear family of industrial modernity (Parsons, 1951) had been based on a division of labour and interdependency between men and women that had made considerable sense. The man had invariably been the main breadwinner and the woman had provided the home conditions to support him, while nurturing and socializing the next generation. It was a rational arrangement because there were very few – if any – realistic alternatives available to either man or woman, but in changed socio-economic circumstances it was to become a form of social arrangement that was less of a rational choice for the potential participants.

Feminists have observed that, stripped of their role as the breadwinner, 'workless' men now had little to offer women and their children other than the erratic affection, violence and child abuse that had often been present in working-class families (Campbell, 1993). Moreover, in a situation where the modernist state was quite understandably prepared to place women and children at the head of the queue for welfare benefits and 'social' housing provision, the former had relinquished their economic dependency on men to become dependent upon an increasingly inadequate welfare state (Field, 1989).

Many young men were now stripped of the informal controls of waged employment and family responsibilities that had previously restrained their wilder excesses and brought them back into the fold of conforming non-offending by their early twenties. Unskilled and poorly educated, they were now completely superfluous to the long-term requirements of post-industrial society. Excluded from legitimate employment opportunities and presenting themselves as unattractive propositions to young women as partners in long-term relationships, many of these young men found themselves 'frozen in a state of persistent adolescence' (Pitts, 1996: 260). These restricted life chances had important implications for their involvement in crime because all the evidence suggests that 'growing up' also means growing out of crime (Rutherford, 1992). Stripped of legitimate access to adulthood, these young men were trapped in a limbo world somewhere between childhood and adulthood long after the 'developmental tasks' of adolescence had been completed (Graham and Bowling, 1995). Now into their second (or even third) generation of what is a workless underclass in some geographical localities, this widely ostracized grouping ('would you let your children play, or even go to school, with them, *now be honest*') has become stereotyped as inherently criminogenic and drug-ridden, with images that are frequently racialized (see Rose, 1999; Parenti, 2000; Bauman, 1998, 2000).

'New' Labour criminal justice policy revisited

Left realism was extremely influential with the 'New' Labour Government elected in 1997. There was a readily identified need for a balanced intervention that tackles both offending behaviour and the social and environmental conditions that supported and encouraged that behaviour. The bottom line would nevertheless be an attempt to reintegrate into included society the socially excluded 'underclass' identified above, as part of a major government project (or 'big idea') that this author has elsewhere termed 'reintegrative tutelage' (Hopkins Burke, 1999a, 2008). In order to achieve that ambition, it was necessary to incorporate theoretical insights from each of the three substantive models of crime and criminal behaviour outlined in this book, and it is the youth justice provisions, in particular, contained in that government's initial flagship criminal justice legislation (The Crime and Disorder Act 1998) that provides us with an unequivocal demonstration of that strategy (see Hopkins Burke, 2008).

The influence of the rational actor model is indicated in that legislation by the emphasis on the notion that the young offender must take responsibility for their actions. First, the rule of '*doli incapax*' that had presumed that a child under the age of 14 does not know the difference between serious right and wrong was revised. Previously the onus had been on the prosecution to prove that the child was aware that their criminal actions were seriously wrong; with the change in emphasis, it was now the task of the defence to establish that the child did not understand that their actions were significantly wrong. Second, the courts were now given powers to impose a new reparation order, requiring young offenders to make some form of reparation to their victims. It was the crucial intention of these legislative changes that young offenders would encounter the consequences of their actions and recognize the harm they had caused their victims (Home Office, 1997).

Evidence of the influence of the predestined actor model is contained in legislative strategies to identify young people at risk of becoming involved in criminal activity. First, the Child Safety Order was introduced to intervene in the lives of children aged under ten who are considered to be at risk of becoming involved in crime; for example, if they are found wandering the streets unsupervised late at night, or are failing to attend school. Second, local authorities were empowered to impose a temporary curfew on children aged under ten in a specified public area.

These legislative initiatives contained in the Crime and Disorder Act 1998 were, however, located in the context of a range of other policy initiatives devised to tackle the causes of crime and criminality among young people, while at the same time recognizing their status as victims of serious social and economic exclusion. There is a clear resonance here with the victimized actor model. First, measures were introduced to support families, including assistance for single parents to get off benefits and return to work, to help prevent marriage and family breakdown, and to deal with such breakdown. Second, policies were introduced with the intention of helping children achieve at school. These measures included the provision of nursery education for all four-year-olds; an emphasis on higher school standards, with a particular focus on literacy and numeracy skills in primary schools; with steps taken to tackle truancy and prevent exclusions; and the provision of study support out of school hours. Third, there was the provision of opportunities for jobs, training and leisure, through the New Start strategy aimed at re-engaging in education or training youngsters up to age 17 that have dropped out of the system. Moreover, there was the welfare to work New Deal for unemployed 18- to 24-year-olds. Fourth, action was taken to tackle drug misuse with new initiatives in the criminal justice system, innovative projects showing what schools and the wider community can do and through the work of the new UK Anti-Drugs Co-ordinator in putting forward a new strategy aimed at young people.

In short, there was to be a comprehensive 'balance of intervention' in the lives of young offenders – or those at serious risk of becoming offenders – with the intention of tackling their offending behaviour, while at the same time challenging the socio-economic structural conditions that had contributed to making such behaviour a rational choice for many. Hopkins Burke observes that:

> Left alone these young people face a life of social exclusion, serious offending, probable lengthy periods of incarceration and the likelihood of being involved in the raising of a further generation in their own image. Of course many of these young males may have only a tangential role in parenting their own children.
>
> (2008: 11)

The 'New' Labour 'reintegrative tutelage' crime control strategy (Hopkins Burke, 1999a) could be situated in the context of a government commitment to the socio-political notion of communitarianism where there is an emphasis on the centrality of informal, communal bonds, networks for the maintenance of social order and the rights of communities rather than the liberal emphasis on the rights of individuals (see Hughes, 1998, 2000). The US sociologist Amitai Etzioni (1993) is the most prominent contemporary proponent of a conservative communitarianism that seeks a 're-moralization of society' where people are required to accept their responsibilities to society and not just focus on their rights and entitlements. A more radical version emphasizes principles of spontaneous solidarity, rules of reciprocity and small-scale communities founded on participatory democracy (Jordan, 1996).

Communitarianism is discussed in significantly more detail in Chapter 22, but it will suffice for our purposes here to observe that 'New' Labour has been invariably associated with the more conservative version and it is the introduction of the Antisocial Behaviour Order (ASBO) that has clearly demonstrated a commitment to the rights of community even when these have impacted negatively on those of the individual (Hopkins Burke and Morrill, 2002, 2004). ASBOs are statutory measures that aim to protect the public from behaviour that causes or is likely to cause harassment, alarm or distress, contain conditions prohibiting the offender from specific antisocial acts or entering defined areas, and are effective for a minimum of two years. They are civil orders applied for by local authorities, police forces and registered social landlords, but breach is a criminal offence, which is arrestable and can lead to the imposition of custodial sentences, and it is this element that has been widely criticized by libertarians (see Von Hirsch et al., 1999; Squires and Stephen, 2005).

Hopkins Burke and Morrill (2004), in contrast, observe that people – and the communities in which they live – have a right to be protected against harassment, alarm, distress and incivilities and that it is perfectly reasonable that such behaviour is targeted by the authorities to ensure protection. From this perspective, the ASBO is a reasonable measure that has filled a prominent gap in the law; it is not a punishment but a deterrent and its purpose is to curtail behaviour before it reaches a criminal level. The authors do suggest, however, that the 'balance of intervention' may have shifted too much in favour of 'communities' at the expense of individual liberty and that there is a 'worrying potential to absorb further into a widening net a whole group of relatively non problematic young people who left pretty much alone would grow out of their antisocial activities and become respectable members of society' (2004: 240).

Hopkins Burke and Hodgson (2013) have nevertheless revisited the issue of antisocial behaviour in our communities in a study conducted in a large Midlands city in the aftermath of the case of Fiona Pilkington and her daughter Francecca Hardwick, who were found dead in a burned-out car in Leicestershire in 2007 after suffering years of abuse from gangs of youths. The researchers found that antisocial behaviour is a broad term used to describe the day-to-day incidents of crime, nuisance and disorder that make the lives of many people a misery – from litter and vandalism, to public drunkenness or aggressive dogs, to noisy or abusive neighbours. Such a wide range of behaviours means that incidents can range from the relatively minor, at one end of the spectrum, to targeted and repeated incidents at the most serious end. Interestingly, it was found that children and young people were involved in less than 20 per cent of incidents as perpetrators. It was found that antisocial behaviour is both widespread and insidious, and takes different forms, but significantly there are many very distraught victims with harrowing tales of repeated victimization which has carried on for many years without being adequately dealt with and which could quite easily have led to 'another Pilkington'. This research and proposals for responding to such cases are discussed both below and further in Chapter 23.

Recent developments in left realism

Jock Young (1999, 2001 and 2003), a key founding member of the left realist perspective, has questioned the capacity of the 'New' Labour reintegrative tutelage project to successfully tackle a crime problem so clearly identified with what is a difficult to empirically isolate socially excluded minority population. Thus, the social exclusion thesis proposes a supposed binary divide between an inclusive and largely satisfied majority and an excluded and despondent minority. Yet, the presumption of a fairly static underclass is nevertheless misleading as there is in reality a great deal of social mobility across categories (see Hills *et al.*, 2002).

Moreover, there is a supposed moral exclusion where exists a vast majority with good habits of work, virtuous conduct and stable family structures, and a minority who are disorganized, welfare dependent, criminal and criminogenic, who live in unstable and dysfunctional families. There is a supposed spatial exclusion where the excluded are geographically isolated from the included and the borderlines between the two are rarely crossed. In reality, no such spatial segregation is empirically apparent – physical mobility in and out of the ghetto, for example, is frequent – and the values of its inhabitants are shared with those of the wider society (Nightingale, 1993; Young, 1999); furthermore, the geographical localities themselves have a mixed population, many of whom are in work (Hagedorn, 1992; Newman, 1999).

Young nevertheless continues to support political demands for social integration and citizenship, noting that such policies have formed the basis of relatively successful French social inclusion policies (see Pitts, 2003) directly targeted at reducing the problems of racism and active social exclusion both within civil society and by the criminal justice system. Social policies that address both the problems of economic exclusion, on the one hand, and social and political exclusion, on the other, are proposed (Young and Matthews, 2003). These issues are again revisited in the final part of this book.

John Lea (2010) observes that, if left realism had become as influential with governments post-1997 as implied by some (including this author), then it might also be expected that the integrative potential of the square of crime would come to pre-eminence as a paradigm in criminology and criminal justice. This, he argues, has not been the case and he observes that left realism – at least in its original complete formulation – has had relatively little influence and, in fact, 'it is extremely rare to find an approach that examines the changing nature of crime by incorporating all four dimensions (of the square of crime) into the analysis' (Matthews, 2009: 346).

Lea (2010) observes that the extent to which left realism was absorbed into the 'New' Labour consensus was at the expense of the democratic imperative that had been essential to the original formulation of the theoretical perspective. Thus, while community building with a focus on crime control has been an aspect of government policy both domestically and internationally, the role of democratization has been, while not entirely absent, heavily overlaid by other concerns that were very different from those advocated by left realism. They are characterized, first, by the role of criminal justice, not as part of the democratic social relations of crime control but as an autonomous agency of social reconstruction and, second, by the exclusion and marginalization of significant groups as part of the strategy of reconstruction itself.

Lea (2010) observes that, on one level, the 'New' Labour Government was inspired by democratic motives. Thus, the 2008 UK Government White Paper 'Communities in Control: Real People, Real Power' (DCLG, 2008) proposes a responsibility on local councils – local city government – to respond to citizen petitions, to involve local people in decision-making – including 'neighbourhood level determination of priorities for council spending'. Such themes harmonize strongly with left realist themes of local democracy and police accountability. However, despite valuable work by community and voluntary agencies aimed at employment and social inclusion, there have been powerful tendencies working in other directions.

Channelling economic resources to deprived areas presupposes an ability on the part of the national state to decisively influence capital investment decisions. But, under conditions of neoliberal deregulation, this power is weakened considerably. Government policy becomes – rather than community renewal through the steering of investment into poor communities – a matter of encouraging globally mobile capital to locate in such areas by making the latter attractive locations for business and local authorities taking steps to 'convince corporate executives that their public policies are capable of supporting profitable business activities before their territories are earmarked for investment' (Hall and Winlow, 2003: 143).

Lea (2010) thus observes that community cohesion has to pre-date – and act as a prerequisite for – the inward flow of investment. It has therefore tended to be built in the face of marginalized and disorderly groups rather than through their reintegration into a democratic local public sphere. Under 'New' Labour, the mechanics of building community cohesion came to assume a mixture of ideological exhortation and coercion. Exhortation took the form of an injunction to orderly and work-seeking behaviour through a new emphasis on personal responsibility and respect (Halpern *et al.*, 2004), while coercion, it is argued, has taken the form of strategies aimed at the regulation of 'antisocial behaviour' by the marginalized poor from the standpoint of maintaining the security of middle-class residential and consumption zones. However, Hopkins Burke and Hodgson (2013) dispute the totality of that observation with their research supporting a revision of the long-established left realist sentiment that much crime (antisocial behaviour, in this case) is committed by poor people on others in their very own community.

Lea (2010) refers to the influential 'broken windows' thesis (Wilson and Kelling, 1982), which argues that the *de facto* criminalization by the police of 'incivilities' (that is, low-level antisocial behaviour, such as street drinking, begging, aggressive behaviour) can arrest the economic and social community decay by making streets and public spaces safe, so as to stop driving law-abiding citizens off the streets and out of the area. Lea (2010) observes that, in reality, antisocial behaviour is likely to be a problem precisely where more serious crime is already well established (Harcourt, 2001; Harcourt and Ludwig, 2006). Although Hopkins Burke and Hodgson (2013) support the general tenor of these observations, they have, nevertheless, identified a substantial quantity of antisocial behaviour imported into previously non-problematic geographical locations – invariably previously 'respectable' working-class social housing estates – as suggested by the 'broken windows' theory, which the researchers propose can be stemmed and reversed at an early stage before the neighbourhood undergoes terminal decline. Certainly, this thesis has been an important theoretical catalyst for the antisocial behaviour agenda in the UK (Squires and Stephen, 2005; Burney, 2005), albeit an agenda that is supposedly opposed to the position taken by left realists.

Thus, the 'democratic' elements of such development are seen to become a divisive force, mobilizing middle-class 'active citizens' around police and central government-led agendas of cleaning up the area by keeping the poor and marginalized out of sight (Fitzgibbon and Lea, 2010). Ostensible forms of democratic or consultative local initiatives, such as local Crime and Disorder Reduction Partnerships (CDRPs), in which agencies such as police, education and social services liaise with local agencies and stakeholders:

> lack significant autonomy from central government . . . Under pressure from government to prioritize national targets . . . the community safety remit of CDRPs has narrowed to a focus on crime reduction . . . By and large, their engagement with the private sector is minimal, voluntary sector input is often marginalized and community involvement largely non-existent.
>
> (Crawford, 2006: 460–2)

Lea observes that the second feature of the control of antisocial behaviour is its circumventing of the principles of criminal justice: 'Rather, regulatory ideas are being used to circumvent and erode established criminal justice principles, notably those of due process, proportionality and special protections traditionally afforded to young people' (Crawford, 2009: 810, cited in Lea, 2010).

Lea (2010) states that the due process principles (we encountered in Chapter 4), such as 'beyond reasonable doubt' and the right of the accused to cross examine all prosecution evidence, are a considerable hindrance to agencies concerned with the management of antisocial behaviour and low-level incivilities where the target is less conviction of individual offenders than the management of groups defined as risks. The role of hearsay evidence and the reduction of proof to civil law standards of 'balance of probabilities' are features of the management of antisocial behaviour. Furthermore, the key to due process is the flow of reliable information about crime to the law enforcement and prosecution agencies. Lea (2010) observes that such information is unlikely to be obtained from groups who feel their social and spatial marginality is being reinforced rather than ameliorated by official agencies, which, in the case of control of antisocial behaviour, includes not only the police but other agencies such as schools and social housing in an expanding 'police family' (Burnett, 2004).

Lea (2010) states that such arrangements are the antithesis of what left realists were advocating in the mid-1980s. Instead of social inclusion through democracy, employment and the restriction of law enforcement to issues of crime defined through an inclusive democratic process, policing has become part of a spectrum of agencies aiming to build community through a process of 'authoritarian renewal' (Scraton, 2004). A criminal justice system that depends upon the social relations of crime control is now deployed as a device with which to construct them in the interests of building communities attractive to global capital. In the process, democratic accountability is replaced by mobilization of 'respectable' elements – those with secure jobs and property who define themselves as the community and as collective potential victim, while the marginalized are externalized as a risk group. In these situations, the social relations of crime control are weak to the point of non-existence.

Lea (2010) observes that, from a left realist perspective, intervention in poor communities with high crime rates at all points of the square of crime would involve independent action to strengthen communities through the establishment of democratic organs combined with investment in employment and education to enable the reintegration of marginalized youth and reductions in antisocial behaviour and low-level incivilities. Such resilient communities would be better equipped to subject the police to a proper accountability regarding crime priorities. They would also be in a better position to deal with antisocial behaviour through various forms of rehabilitation and restorative justice. The latter would be conditional not so much on prior admission of a criminal offence, as it is in the majority of cases, but on participation in various de-marginalization projects relating to work and collective community activities. It is observed that the fundamental aim of left realism was to defend criminal justice by making it democratically accountable, not to turn it into a device for the authoritarian regulation of the poor and marginalized as a whole. Lea observes that, in the absence of such strategies, the marginalization of left realism as a theoretical and political perspective is only to be expected.

Left realist theory revisited – the historical context

Hopkins Burke (2012, 2013) has adapted and adopted left realist theory in an historical context as a significant component of his criminal justice theory, which seeks to explain the development of the criminal justice system in modern societies and in whose interest this has all occurred. From this perspective, it is observed that existing explanations of this process can be broadly located in the context of one of three models. First, there is the orthodox social progress model, which proposes that the evolution and development of criminal justice agencies and systems in modern societies has been a principally neutral process instigated by well-meaning individuals and institutions in the interests of all groups of society. Second, the radical conflict model argues that this has been a far from disinterested process, which, in reality, has occurred in the interests of a capitalist market economy in an inherently conflict-ridden society.

All changes thus occur in the final analysis in the interests of the economy. Third, the carceral society model considers that both the previous two models are too simplistic and recognizes that power is diffuse throughout society with agents and experts in criminal justice institutions having a significant role in establishing and implementing the crime control agenda. Hopkins Burke (2012, 2013) develops a fourth model (the left realist hybrid model), which essentially provides a synthesis of the orthodox social progress, radical conflict and carceral surveillance society models, but with the additional significant recognition of the interest and collusion of us – the general public – in the creation of the increasingly pervasive socio-control matrix of the carceral society (Hopkins Burke, 2004a, 2008, 2009). These models are discussed in some detail in Chapter 23.

Policy implications of left realism

John Lea and Jock Young (1984) established the fundamental credentials of left realism and set out three main policies of left realism. These are as relevant today as they were thirty years ago and are reproduced here:

1. *De-marginalization* – realists argue for legitimate alternatives to prison and advocate measures such as community service orders, victim restitution schemes and widespread release from prison, which they argue would stop the severance of the moral bond with the community. It is proposed that the institutions that are involved in controlling crime and criminals must epitomize justice.
2. *Pre-emptive deterrence* – it is observed by left realists that environmental and public precautions against crime are always dismissed by left idealists or critical criminologists as being distractions from the real concerns. On the contrary, it is argued, the organization of communities in an attempt to pre-empt crime is of the utmost importance.
3. *The minimal use of prison* – it is proposed that prisons should only be used in those circumstances where there is extreme danger to the community. Life inside prison should be as free and as 'normal' as possible. It is argued that such a demand is not simply humanitarian idealism – it is based on the simple fact that the outcome of the brutalized prison experience is to produce pitifully inadequate or hardened criminals.

Summary of main points

1. Left realism is not really an attempt to integrate and synthesize elements from different theories but is more a recognition of the validity of explanatory elements contained in each of the three models of crime and criminal behaviour and their practical value as part of a comprehensive strategy for understanding and responding to crime.

2. A new perspective was to emerge among some left criminologists who argued that a 'new realist' view on crime was necessary and that it was time to 'take crime seriously' (Lea and Young, 1984).
3. Crime is thus seen to be a real problem that must be addressed. Corporate crime is important but its effects are generally widespread, while those of direct-contact crime are concentrated.
4. People living in high-crime areas suffer individual offences that they may or may not report to the police, but they also suffer a range of incivilities, such as vandalism, threats, vulgarity, sexual harassment, noise and swearing, all of which taken together further reduce quality of life and increase despair.
5. Central to the left realist crime control strategy is the proposition that crime requires a comprehensive solution where there must be a 'balance of intervention'. Both crime and the causes of crime must thus be tackled and this argument is illustrated with the 'square of crime'.
6. Left realism was extremely influential with the 'New' Labour Government elected in 1997, and their 'reintegrative tutelage' crime control strategy (Hopkins Burke, 1999a) could be situated in the context of a government commitment to the socio-political notion of communitarianism.
7. Jock Young has nevertheless questioned the capacity of the 'New' Labour reintegrative tutelage project to successfully tackle a crime problem that it so clearly identified with what is a difficult to empirically isolate socially excluded minority population.
8. John Lea (2010) argues that the extent to which left realism was absorbed into the 'New' Labour consensus was at the expense of the democratic imperative, which had been essential to the original formulation of the theoretical perspective.
9. Hopkins Burke (2012, 2013) has adapted and adopted left realist theory in an historical context as a significant component of his criminal justice theory, which seeks to explain the development of the criminal justice system in modern societies and in whose interest this has all occurred.
10. The three main policy implications of left realism outlined by John Lea and Jock Young (1984) are as relevant today as they were thirty years ago and are (i) de-marginalization; (ii) pre-emptive deterrence; and (iii) the minimal use of prison.

Discussion questions

1. What is a 'balanced intervention'?
2. What is the 'square of crime'?
3. Explain the concept of 'reintegrative tutelage'.
4. In what ways did 'New' Labour retreat from the prescriptions of left realism?
5. In what ways has left realism been used to explain the development of the criminal justice system?

Suggested further reading

For a comprehensive introduction to the basic tenets of left realism, you should consult Lea and Young (1984), Matthews and Young (1986, 1992) and Young (1994). Hopkins Burke (1999a) extends the discussion of the process model of the underclass, while Hopkins Burke and Morrill (2004) discuss the ambiguities between the rights of individuals and communities. Hughes (1998, 2000) provides excellent introductions to communitarianism and its links to crime control and community safety. Young (1999) is essential for a contemporary discussion of social exclusion, while Young and Matthews (2003) should be readily consulted on the relationship between the former and 'New' Labour. Hopkins Burke (2004a) outlines his left realist account of the development of the police service and discusses the development of the increasing surveillance and control of young people and the emergence of the contemporary youth justice system (Hopkins Burke, 2008). Hopkins Burke (2012) provides a comprehensive introduction to criminal justice theory and its application to a wide range of institutions and processes in contemporary criminal justice, including the philosophy of law and legal ethics (including Islamic jurisprudence and Sharia Law, policing, the legal process, punishment and youth justice).

Part Five

Crime and criminal behaviour in the age of moral uncertainty

Neither liberalism, economic or political, nor the various Marxisms emerge from [the last] two centuries untainted by accusations of crimes against humanity. We can make a list of names, names of places, persons, dates, capable of illustrating and substantiating our suspicion. Following Theodor Adorno I have used the name 'Auschwitz' to signify the extent to which recent Western philosophy seems inconsistent as regards the 'modern' project of the emancipation of humanity.

Lyotard (1988: 110)

My argument is that the modern project (of realisation of universality) has not been abandoned, forgotten, but destroyed, 'liquidated'. There are several methods of destruction, several names which are symbols of it. Auschwitz can be taken as a paradigmatic name for the tragic incompletion of modernity.

Lyotard (1988: 32)

Grand narratives have become barely credible.

Lyotard (1988: 46)

This book has examined the different ways that crime and criminal behaviour have been explained during the past 200 years. While these explanations have been proposed at various times by among others legal philosophers, biologists, psychologists, sociologists, political scientists and geographers, it is possible to locate these many and varied explanations – or criminological theories – in terms of one of three different general models or traditions that were the focus of the first three parts of this book.

The first tradition – the rational actor model – proposes that human beings enjoy free will and this enables them to choose whether or not to engage in criminal activities. Crime can be controlled by making the costs of offending – that is, punishment – sufficient to discourage the pursuit of criminal rewards. In other words, the choice of criminal activity would be irrational in such circumstances.

The second tradition – the predestined actor model – proposes that criminal behaviour can be explained in terms of factors that exist either within the individual or their environment that cause that person to act in ways over which they have little or no control. Crime can be controlled by identifying and eradicating these factors through some form of treatment process. Thus, biological and psychological variants propose that the individual should be changed, while sociological versions advocate the transformation of the criminogenic environment.

The third tradition – the victimized actor model – denies neither entirely the prescriptions of the rational actor nor the predestined actor models but recognizes that people make decisions to behave in ways that may well be perfectly rational for them in the circumstances in which they find themselves but that it is the activities of the economically poor and politically powerless that are criminalized, a process which is conducted in the interests of those with power and wealth. At the micro level, individuals can be labelled and criminalized by coming into contact with front-line agents of the state working in the criminal justice and welfare systems; at the macro societal level, it is those with economic power and the control of authority that are in a position to influence the legislative agenda. From this perspective, crime is seen to be a social construction; it can be controlled or reduced by not criminalizing dispossessed unfortunates and by abolishing legislation that criminalizes their activities.

The fourth part of this book has discussed those attempts to produce a synthesis of different theoretical perspectives – some of these being internal to one particular model of criminal behaviour, others incorporating elements that cross model boundaries – with the intention of providing a bigger, better, all-encompassing theory that seeks to explain as much crime and criminal behaviour as possible. Indeed, these integrated perspectives invariably seek to explain *all* criminal behaviour, an approach clearly in line with modernist social science thinking.

It has been explained that each of the theories introduced in this book – and, indeed, their particular host model or explanatory tradition – have a common central characteristic: that is, each is a product of what has come to be termed the modern age. Prior to the rise of modernity, religion and other forms of pre-scientific knowledge had crucially influenced explanations of crime and, at that time, criminal justice and its administration was non-codified, capricious, invariably brutal and at the cynical discretion of the agents of monarchical regimes. In contrast, modern societies are secular, industrialized, rationalized, codified and rule-bound with at least some pretence to widely participative democracy. Science is the dominant – and for a long time unchallenged – form of knowledge and thus, crime and criminal behaviour have been invariably explained by reference to scientific discourses or theories, while there had been a wider modernist faith in reason, which stretches from the great liberals of the twentieth century back beyond the Enlightenment philosophers of the eighteenth century, to the Greeks:

> Man is in principle at least, everywhere and in every condition, able, if he wills it, to discover and apply rational solutions to his problems. And these solutions, because they are rational, cannot clash with one another, and will ultimately form a harmonious system in which the truth will prevail, and freedom, happiness, and unlimited opportunity for untrammelled self-development will be open to all.
>
> (Berlin, 1969: 8)

In the last decades of the twentieth century, there were increasing doubts about the sustainability of the modernist project in an increasingly fragmented and diverse social world, and this is a situation that some social scientists have come to refer to as the postmodern condition (see Lyotard, 1984; but also Baudrillard 1988; Bauman, 1989, 1991, 1993). Three main sources for the idea of the postmodern can be identified. The first is the emergence and consolidation of an intellectual current articulated by the publication of two books by Daniel Bell, *The End of Ideology* (1960) and *The Coming of Post-Industrial Society* (1973). It was an emerging world view with two sub-currents: there was the ideological exhaustion of the post-war world with the retreat from the pre-war ideologies of communism and National Socialism that had seemed to lead to only totalitarianism, world war and holocaust. At the same time, there was a growing interest in the idea of a post-industrial – or later 'post-Fordist' – society where manufacturing was giving way to the service industry, primary production was being displaced by secondary exploitation – especially of science and technology – and consumers were coming to outperform producers in the economy. In this changed context, the old radical class analyses seemed to make little sense and the intellectual categories around which modernism had been built appeared to have lost their explanatory power.

The second source is poststructuralism, a movement that had flourished mainly in France during the late 1960s and 1970s and, as its name suggests, succeeded structuralism, which had flourished a decade or so earlier, most notably in the work of Claude Levi-Strauss, but which could be traced back to the nineteenth century. While structuralists had been preoccupied with the 'deep structures' of language and society, poststructuralists were sceptical of efforts to attach meanings to words. Michel Foucault significantly contributed to the wider popular influence of poststructuralism by arguing that knowledge and language – and so the categories derived from them – cannot be regarded as anything other than subjective and relative (Foucault, 1980). Thus, by emphasizing the subjectivity of language, poststructuralism contributed to the central belief of postmodernism, that no intellectual tradition can have privileged authority over another.

The third source was an aesthetic movement with its foundations in an architectural controversy centred on the rejection of the so-called 'international style' of austere unadorned modernism epitomized by 1960s tower blocks and multi-storey car parks.

In summary, there are three significant characteristics that appear to distinguish postmodernism from modernism. First, there is an aversion to 'metadiscourses' – or grand self-legitimating theories – that it is proposed can lead to intellectual sterility and political oppression. Second, there is an awareness of the indeterminacy of knowledge and the impossibility of absolute truth inherited from poststructuralism. Third, there is an enthusiasm for eclecticism and variety derived from art, architecture and literature, but which has come to have much stronger intellectual reverberations.

The idea of the postmodern thus involves claims that modernist features of society are under challenge. This can be seen in the realm of culture, where self-proclaimed modern thinkers and artists were challenged from the mid-1960s by anti-modernist ideas which attacked the dehumanization of modern society, questioned the authority of technical experts and celebrated human diversity in place of the pressure to encourage rationalized, standardized, human conformity to systems developed by 'experts' and technicians (see Marcuse, 1964). These concerns were furthermore reflected in the social sciences field by the emergence of radical efforts to challenge orthodox, positivist forms of thought whose claims to objective scientific status were questioned and rejected.

Underlying these changes was the beginning of an economic and political transformation manifest in a breakdown of the Keynesian and Fordist practices of the post-war world in the industrial West. This had been prompted by the oil crisis of the early 1970s, an abandonment of full employment policies with a decline in economic competitiveness, and a restructuring of the world economy with the rise in the productive capacity of the nations of the Pacific Rim. Thus, in all three areas, the economy, the political system and culture, there began to emerge increasingly diverse and fragmented social structures that heralded the beginning of postmodernism.

Economically, postmodernity is often described as post-Fordism, which involves the rejection of mass production-line technology in favour of both flexible working patterns and labour force. This in turn involves a weakening of trade unions, greater reliance on peripheral and secondary labour markets, the development of a low-paid and part-time, often female, labour force, and the shift towards a service, rather than manufacturing, economy. On the side of capital owning and controlling interests, it involves a greater stress on enterprise and entrepreneurialism, corporate restructuring and the growth of small businesses acting as subcontractors to larger firms. These trends are often seen as evidence of deindustrialization and the disorganization of capitalism.

Politically, postmodernity is complex and is difficult to categorize in traditional terms. An interesting development has been Michel Foucault's (1980) poststructuralist conceptualization of power, which he argues is not simply the prerogative of the state. Strategies of power are seen to be pervasive in society with the state only one location of the points of control and resistance and, from this perspective, there should be a move away from a restricted chain of criminological references – 'state-law-crime-criminals' – to a wider chain of associations that need to be addressed. Thus, for Foucault (1971, 1976) particular areas of social life – for example, medicine, law, sexuality – are colonized and defined by the norms and control strategies which a variety of institutions and experts devise and abide by. These networks of power and control are governed as much by the *knowledge* and concepts that define them as by the definite intentions of individuals and groups.

The state, for its part, is implicated in this matrix of power-knowledge, but it is only part of it and, in this vein, it has been argued that within civil society there are numerous 'semi-autonomous' realms and relations – such as communities, occupations, organizations, families – where certain kinds of 'policing' and 'order' are indeed present, but where the state administration and police force are technically absent. These semi-autonomous arenas are often appropriately negotiated and resisted by their participants in ways over which even now the state has little jurisdiction. To some, it might seem ironic that this emphasis comes at a time when many of the traditional coercive and regulatory roles of the state are being *enhanced* politically and technologically and it is a point to which we return later in this fifth part of the book, for more recently many of these previously autonomous locations have been incorporated into multi-agency partnerships delivering the interests of the state from a distance.

Postmodernity has been expressed in neoconservative ideas, such as those promoted by the British Prime Minister Margaret Thatcher and her contemporary as US President, Ronald Reagan (and subsequently in the USA, by George Bush, father and son), and termed *Thatcherism* and *Reaganomics*. These ideologies have included the offering of tax cuts as a means to facilitating consumer choice and the dismantling of elaborate state planning and provision in the fields of welfare. At the same time, the diversity of interests that has become apparent in Western societies has placed strains on conventional representative democratic systems. Thus, long-standing democracies have had significant difficulties in representing myriad interest groups as diverse as major industrialists and financiers, small business proprietors, the unemployed and the socially excluded underclass, wide-ranging gender and sexual preference interests, environmentalists and the homeless.

Modernity was essentially an era characterized by moral certainty. There was a confidence and belief in the superiority and infallibility of natural science that had filtered through into the social sciences, in particular social and political theory. There was a confidence in the explanatory power of grand theories to solve the problems of humanity. There may be competing theories – for example, the many criminological theories introduced in this book – but the devotees of each of these had confidence in the fundamental capacity of their doctrine to solve the crime problem. This might well – as we have seen particularly in the fourth part – entail revisions to the theory, the incorporation of concepts from other theoretical perspectives and indeed other models of criminal behaviour, but in the final analysis the intention is the same: as was observed earlier, the creation of a criminological theory that explains most – if not all – criminal activity.

Postmodern societies are – in contrast to modern societies – characterized by moral ambiguity. Now this condition should not be confused with a period of moral uncertainty where the reconsideration and rebuilding of theoretical perspectives can rekindle the moral certainty of old. It is a condition characterized by a terminal loss of certainty with absolutely no expectation that it will ever return.

Postmodern social scientists thus recognize the complexity of society and the moral ambiguities that are inherent within it and there is recognition of a range of different discourses that can be legitimate and hence right for different people, at different times, in different contexts. It is a perspective founded on cultural relativism, the notion that there are a series of legitimate discourses on a particular issue and that it is difficult, if not impossible, to objectively choose between them. Essentially, the objective truth – or the competing objective realities – of modernity is replaced by recognition of the multiple realities or moral ambiguities of postmodernity. These realities are invariably complex, highly susceptible to inconsistent interpretation and are contested by individuals – politicians and members of the general public – who often make short-term, pragmatic and inconsistent judgements without reference to any coherent body of knowledge.

Whereas modernists had attempted to develop large-scale theories to explain society in terms of enduring, identifiable social structures, postmodernists have followed in the poststructuralist tradition emphasizing the redundancy and futility of such efforts and contested the entire concept of truth. The social sciences – since their very inception in modernity – had made efforts to transcend the relativity of social situations and identify 'what is going on' systematically and objectively, while philosophers had attempted to establish some rational standpoint from which reality could be described. Postmodern writers have, on the other hand, celebrated the failure of the modern project to establish rational foundations for knowledge and have themselves embraced the trend towards human diversity and social fragmentation, arguing that there is no objective reality behind the plethora of social meanings. Accounts and definitions have no objective or external reference but are merely elements in a free-floating system of images that are produced and reproduced through the medium of popular mass communication and come to define reality to consumers.

To some, postmodernism is undoubtedly a nightmare vision but others have embraced and celebrated its implications. The fragmentation of social institutions such as social class and status may have increased our uncertainty in how we understand society but, on the other hand, the same trends allow the expression of the diversity of human needs, interests and sensitivities. By challenging the validity of modern claims to privileged forms of knowledge for the powerful, postmodernism gives a voice to the less powerful and oppressed, and it is thus not surprising that some branches of feminism have embraced this approach.

Postmodernists have also celebrated the development of new social movements such as travelling communities as they make efforts to live a lifestyle outside of the constraints and dictates of the modern world. In the Western world, gay and what were formerly regarded as other unconventional sexual interest groups have also been celebrated for their efforts to break down restrictive stereotypes and 'expert' knowledge surrounding the pursuit of sexual pleasure. The ideas and interests of animal rights groups and environmental concerns have also been welcomed. These challenge the adequacy of representation in long-established representative democracies in which party systems commonly only represent the interests of people as members of a social class and, hence, give rise to a restricted form of political agenda, which fails to address other interests. The celebration and acceptance of diversity, therefore, is taken as a positive thing.

Lyotard reflects on some of the horrors of the past two centuries of modernist society when people have controlled and killed others in their pursuit of a rational, scientific world order that – in the criminological context – had led us from the biological notions of Lombroso via Goring to Auschwitz:

> The nineteenth and twentieth centuries have given us as much terror as we can take. We have paid a high enough price for the nostalgia of the whole and the one, for the reconciliation of the concept and the sensible, of the transparent and the communicable experience. Under the general demand for slackening and for appeasement, we can hear the mutterings of the desire for a return to terror, for the realisation of the fantasy to seize reality. The answer is: let us wage war on totality; let us be witness to the unrepresentable; let us activate the differences and save the honour of the name.
>
> (Lyotard, 1984: 81–2)

The philosopher of the social sciences Feyerabend also had celebrated a nonrationalist – even anarchistic – approach to the manner in which we study the world. Highly critical of efforts to unify and control the limits of science and the potential for knowledge as authoritarian and inhumane, he argues that 'science is an essentially anarchistic enterprise: theoretical anarchism is more humanitarian and more likely to encourage progress than its "law and order" alternatives' (Feyerabend, 1975: 17).

Problematically, given this general approach, we might legitimately ask how Feyerabend can legitimately judge what is 'more humanitarian' and more 'progressive'. In comparison to what is it progressive and why is this so? The Feyerabend legacy is nevertheless significant because it alerts us not to be slaves to dominant paradigms of how we see the world but be prepared to take risks – perhaps even be prepared to consider the previously unthinkable at least in terms of contemporary orthodoxy – and be prepared to consider the potential of a whole range of often neglected theoretical perspectives.

19. Crime and the postmodern condition

Key Issues

1. Sceptical and affirmative postmodernism
2. Constitutive criminology
3. Weaknesses of constitutive criminology
4. Anarchist criminology
5. Crime and postmodernism reconsidered

Postmodernism can appear to be an extremely negative and nihilistic vision, for, if there is no such thing as the 'truth of the human condition', it is clearly difficult to formulate an argument in support of basic human rights, or to locate legitimate foundations for law, if the human experience is seen to be reflexive and relative. The relativism implied by postmodernism thus denies the possibility of truth and hence of justice in anything other than a purely subjective form, which inevitably consigns us to the prospect of conflict.

Politically, postmodernism can carry us right the way across the traditional political spectrum from the libertarian right-wing assumption of a war of all against all, resonant of the work of Thomas Hobbes, to a libertarianism of the left, or even anarchism, which celebrates and tolerates all human diversity and activity. Postmodernism therefore appears contemptuous of the possibility of developing an objective normative – moral – order that human beings can translate into enforceable norms or laws. Thus, while intellectually challenging and providing a possible explanation for the nature of social change in contemporary Western societies, postmodernism has appeared extremely problematic for developing a plausible criminological strategy and this will become increasingly apparent throughout this fifth part of the book.

By regarding postmodernism in two distinct ways, it is possible that we can accept some of its power to explain the enormous diversity in contemporary society without accepting some of the baggage of philosophical relativism. Pauline-Marie Rosenau offers this option identifying what she terms *sceptical* and *affirmative* postmodernism:

The sceptical postmodernism (or merely sceptic), offering a pessimistic, negative, gloomy assessment, argues that the postmodern age is one of fragmentation, disintegration, malaise, meaninglessness, a vagueness, or even absence of moral parameters and societal chaos . . . This is the dark side of postmodernism, the postmodernism of despair, the postmodernism that speaks of the immediacy of death, the demise of the subject, the end of the author, the impossibility of truth. They argue that the destructive nature of modernity makes the postmodern age one of 'radical, unsuppressible uncertainty' . . . characterised by all that is grim, cruel, alienating, hopeless, tired and ambiguous. In this period no social or political project is worthy of commitment. If, as the sceptics claim, there is no truth, then all that is left is play, the play of words and meaning.

(1992: 15)

Acknowledging that there is no clear-cut divide between the approaches, Rosenau identifies an alternative and altogether more positive tendency in the postmodern movement:

Although the affirmative postmodernists . . . agree with the sceptical post-modern critique of modernity, they have a more hopeful, optimistic view of the postmodern age. More indigenous to Anglo-North American culture than to the [European] Continent, the generally optimistic affirmatives are oriented towards process. They are either open to positive political action (struggle and resistance) or content with the recognition of visionary, cele-bratory, personal, non-dogmatic projects that range from New Age religion to New Wave lifestyles and include a whole spectrum of postmodern social movements. Most affirmatives seek a philosophical and intellectual prac-tice that is non-dogmatic, tentative and non-ideological. These postmod-ernists do not, however, shy away from affirming an ethic, making normative choices, and striving to build issue-specific political coalitions. Many affirmatives argue that certain value choices are superior to others, a line of reasoning that would incur the disapproval of the sceptical postmodernists.

(1992: 15–16)

The essential problem for the development of legislation and explanations of crime and criminal behaviour in the postmodern condition nevertheless remains the difficulty of making any objective claims for truth, goodness and morality. This is, of course, less the case for the affirmatives than for the sceptics. On the issue of the foundations of knowledge (epistemology), Rosenau notes:

Postmodern social science . . . announces the end of all paradigms. Only an absence of knowledge claims, an affirmation of multiple realities, and an acceptance of divergent interpretations remain. We can convince those who agree with us, but we have no basis for convincing those who dissent and no criteria to employ in arguing for the superiority of any particular view. Those who disagree with us can always argue that different interpretations must be accepted and that in a postmodern world one interpretation is as good as another. Postmodernists have no interest in convincing others that their view is best – the most just, appropriate, or true. In the end the problem with most postmodern social science is that you can say anything you want, but so can everyone else. Some of what is said will be interesting and fascinating, but some will also be ridiculous and absurd. Postmodernism provides no means to distinguish between the two.

(1992: 137)

There are clearly some fundamental logical intellectual difficulties posed for those seeking to research and explain criminal behaviour. First, there is little available empirical evidence to support the assumption that we have already reached a post-ideological climate. To argue that we can achieve the position that no intellectual tradition can be considered to have privileged authority over another is seriously problematic, as the only too obvious reality is that particular traditions are usually seen to be more authoritative. We should moreover note at this juncture that many influential social scientists and theorists deny the notion of postmodern society – which for such a social formation to exist would require some substantive rupture with the modernist social formation – and thus emphasising the continuities and following the influential social theorist Anthony Giddens (1990, 1991) use the term 'late modernity'. The term 'postmodern condition' is favoured by this author and is thus used in this book, although we might note that the equally distinguished social theorist Norbert Elias (1978, 1982) had previously observed that we live in a period of late barbarism and at times it is difficult to dissent from that viewpoint.

Second, while postmodernism may advocate giving a voice to the oppressed and less powerful (and may celebrate diversity), it could be argued that, in practice, power relations and political decisions are fundamentally important and may restrict this ideal. Indeed, it could be argued that recent criminal justice policy (in both the UK and the USA and beyond) and the politics that have informed it have tended to encourage less tolerance of difference rather than more. We will now consider how constitutive criminology has sought to explain crime and criminal behaviour in the context of the postmodern condition and the proposed solutions offered by that school of criminological thought.

Constitutive criminology and postmodernism

Mark Cowling (2006) observes that, while many criminologists have used aspects of postmodernism as a critique (or as a source of inspiration), the only well-developed attempt to rethink the central issues and themes of criminology in terms of postmodernism is the constitutive criminology originally developed by Stuart Henry and Dragan Milovanovic (1996, 1999, 2000, 2001). In a critical review of their perspective, he observes that they actually produce a fairly orthodox account of postmodernism where there are no privileged knowledges and everyone or anyone is an expert, with a celebration of diversity, plurality and the subjugated. We should nevertheless note that the authors themselves actually deny they are postmodernists and that they and their subsequent followers depend on aspects of modernism in order to identify the marginalized and oppressed. The two main theoretical foundations of constitutive criminology can be identified as being an interpretation of the post-Freudian Jacques Lacan and chaos theory, which, in its original manifestation, describes the behaviour of certain dynamic systems.

Jacques Lacan and constitutive criminology

The ideas of Lacan centre on Freudian concepts such as the unconscious, the castration complex and the ego, with the focus being on the centrality of language to subjectivity. Lacan has been extremely influential in critical theory, literary studies and twentieth-century French philosophy, but it is his interpretation of clinical psychoanalysis that has been influential with constitutive criminologists.

Lacan understands psychoanalysis as a process in which there are four major discourses: (i) the discourse of the master; (ii) the university; (iii) the hysteric; and (iv) the analyst. It is invariably the role of the discourse of the analyst to help develop the discourse of the hysteric, in order to assist her through a collaborative process in articulating her desire, and in the criminological context this can be a prisoner, an oppressed community or group who are being helped by an expert activist. Williams and Arrigo (2004) cite the example of young offenders involved in restorative justice.

Constitutive criminologists argue that people who are being repressed by the criminal justice system are extremely likely to be suffering oppression and would thus benefit from assistance in articulating their needs, while, at the same time, they might well have desires that are not socially acceptable in their current form and that can get them into trouble with the law. This notion is clearly problematic because of the difficulty of reconciling individual needs with those of the group. Henry and Milovanovic acknowledge this conundrum to some extent and note that 'satisfying positions of desire can occur at another's expense' (2001: 168).

Constitutive criminologists have a strong commitment to social justice rather than merely criminal justice, and thus Henry and Milovanovic (1996: 64) aim for a 'constitutive theorising [which] is a contingently and provisionally based humanistic vision of what could be a radical super-liberalism' and where justice is held to be specific to particular sites and which cannot be linked to a desire for consensus or universally posited agreement. Tracy Young (1999) adopts a similar approach and observes that modernist criminal justice systems are concerned with the rationality, uniformity and consistency of treatment before the law, whereas the postmodern equivalent is grounded in chaos theory, which allows room for creativity. Variation and creativity are thus seen to be desirable and some of this is linked to the idea that different local justice systems can co-exist with each other. Young (1997) uses the examples of a Native American system – or one within a professional body – which she observes can co-exist within the wider state justice system.

Chaos theory and constitutive criminology

Henry and Milovanovic (1996) observe that chaos theory is a central component in much postmodernist analysis and it is therefore worth exploring this notion a little further. Chaos theory began as a field of physics and mathematics dealing with the structures of turbulence and self-similar forms of fractal geometry. As it is popularly understood, chaos deals with unpredictable complex systems and the theory originates, in part, from the work of Edward Lorenz, a meteorologist, who simulated weather patterns on a computer. Working with a computer that had limited memory and after viewing a particular pattern, he wanted to recover the data and started the program again, except he put in the values rounded off to three places instead of the original six. He was astonished to find a completely different result on his computer than previously which looked like Figure 19.1 when it was printed out:

This has become known as the 'butterfly effect' and is often used to refer to complexity and unpredictability, and in chaos theory refers to the discovery that, in a chaotic system such as the global weather, tiny perturbations – or slight disturbances of a system by a secondary influence within the system – may sometimes lead to major changes in the overall system. It is theoretically possible that a slight rise in temperature in the ocean off the coast of Peru will create tiny changes in the airflow that would eventually lead to different weather in North America and Europe. In most cases, the slight change would make no difference whatsoever, but, when the system is unpredictable at a certain stage, the future may unfold quite differently, depending upon what little difference occurred. Chaos theory has been subsequently applied to the study of management and organizations – including those within the criminal justice system – and where the constituents of a system are observed to be complex and unpredictable. Some observe parallels between chaos theory and postmodernism even to the extent of proposing that the former is postmodern science (Hayles, 1990, 1991; Brennan, 1995; Bloland, 1995; Markus, 2000) but there is also significant opposition to that notion.

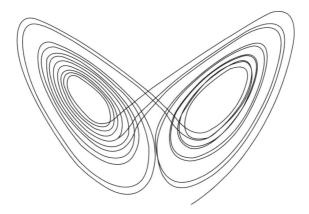

Figure 19.1 The 'butterfly effect'.

The application of the mathematics of chaos theory to society is inherently problematic (Cowling, 2006). Chaos theory tends to be seen as applicable to physical phenomena governed by deterministic laws, which are predictable in principle but which in reality are unpredictable in practice because they are so sensitive to initial conditions. This is famously expressed in the idea that a butterfly flapping its wings in Brazil might cause a hurricane in Florida three weeks from that date and this is why, although it is possible to predict roughly the sort of weather that can be expected in a particular place in three weeks' time, it is not possible to produce an accurate weather forecast. Human societies, in contrast, are complicated systems involving a vast number of variables, for which it is impossible – at least currently – to develop any legitimate equations, and thus to speak of systems in terms of chaos takes us no further than the intuition already contained in popular wisdom (Sokal and Bricmont, 1999). Thus, the sort of situation in society where a small cause can produce a large effect will also be a highly unpredictable situation and where it is not at all clear what will eventually emerge. Thus, for example, the assassination of Archduke Franz Ferdinand of Austria in Sarajevo in 1914 precipitated a complex chain of events that was to lead to the First World War and a multitude of subsequent momentous linked events, which have changed the history of the world. Few, if any, of these events could have been predicted at the time. Some of those involved in the constitutive criminology project thus use chaos theory simply as a metaphor (Simons and Stroup, 1997; Arrigo 1997; Williams and Arrigo, 2004), but in the main the authors see themselves as applying chaos theory (Cowling, 2006).

Constitutive criminologists adopt three main concepts from chaos theory: (i) the notion of undecidability or uncertainty; (ii) the idea that one individual can make a significant difference; and (iii) the analysis of conditions being far from equilibrium. The first two outcomes thus flow from the idea that a very small initial difference can have a massive causal effect, but the problem with this is that, given the very many possible initial variables, the very idea of undecidability means that social science becomes impossible. We simply cannot know what outcome we might expect from an initial set of variables. The constitutive response to this conundrum, however, is to celebrate the unexpected, surprise, ironic, contradictory and emergent (Milovanovic, 1997a) but this does seem to occur in a context where there is no background of regularity against which to contrast the unexpected.

Cowling (2006) observes that the idea that one individual can make a difference is found repeatedly in constitutive criminology and the best way of assessing the idea is to consider some ways in which it might be recognized in practice. The examples provided by the constitutive criminologists concern things such as a crossing guard who takes an interest in one particular young person, thus helping him avoid becoming delinquent when his circumstances would make this likely, or going on a demonstration, signing a petition, engaging in civil disobedience or voting (Milovanovic, 1997b).

A further use of chaos theory concerns situations where, following a great deal of replication, far from equilibrium conditions result, and the system itself may thus change dramatically. Young (1997) thus proposes that white-collar crime may be instigated by four or more unmanageable parameters. Thus, for example, a doctor might cope with a general drop in her income, the failure of investment portfolios and the reduction in rent payments from tenants if a major corporation was to move from the city, but any further losses such as patients defaulting on bills could well drive her to crime. We might call this the 'straw that broke the camel's back' argument.

A rather different use of chaos theory is the claim that truth values are 'fractal': thus, matters of right or wrong, good or bad, just or unjust are simply matters of degree (Arrigo, 1997). This claim is nevertheless over-optimistic for the practical consequence of the unpredictability that follows from chaos theory is that standard moral judgements become impossible. Cowling (2006) observes that we commend acts of charity because they help people in need, while we condemn random unpremeditated violence because it harms people who do not deserve to be harmed. The adoption of chaos theory simply undermines any confidence we might have in typical consequences and thus we have no legitimate basis for making moral judgements.

Henry and Milovanovic (1996) define crime as the power to deny others and they argue that the conventional crime control strategies, in the form of fast-expanding criminal justice institutions – the police and prisons – or as political rhetoric rehearsed in the media, fuel the engine of crime. What they seek is the development of 'replacement discourses' that fuel positive social constructions with the intention not to 'replace one truth with another' but instead invoke 'a multiplicity of resistances' 'to the ubiquity of power' (Henry and Milovanovic, 1996: ix–xiii; Milovanovic, 1997b: 91). Constitutive criminologists are thus opposed to imprisonment, which they consider to be merely incapacitation and an approach that presents a false separation between inside and outside, and observe that the incarcerated actually commit more and worse crimes in their 'new architectural spaces'. They object to expenditure on prisons, which they propose is money that might be better spent on education and welfare provision. Prison expansion is, moreover, accompanied by an increased fear of crime, with the outcome that incapacitation simply offers the fiction of a safer society but actually offers more freedom for the powerful to commit more crimes (Henry and Milovanovic, 1996: 194; Milovanovic, 1997b). Constitutive criminologists are also opposed to the war on drugs and offer some support for mediation, conflict resolution, and reconciliation programmes and the idea of relating crime more to wider society (Henry and Milovanovic, 2001: 174–5).

Mark Cowling (2006) questions these notions and asks whether the imprisonment of serial killers and rapists simply makes things worse, and queries whether it would be better for us all if the state did not interfere in domestic violence. He moreover asks whether it is an appropriate role for 'progressive' criminologists to be supporting 'resistances' by men who have been engaged in battering against the 'ubiquitous' power of the police and courts and proposes that such expansive claims need to be revealed and argued rather than merely asserted.

We might observe that, in many ways, constitutive criminology has consider-able similarities to the anarchist criminology to which we now turn, although this is part of a long-established tradition that clearly precedes postmodernity.

Anarchist criminology

> Anarchism is an orientation toward social life and social relations that is ultimately no orientation at all. In fact, anarchism might best be thought of as disorientation; that is, an approach which openly values fractured, uncertain, and unrealised understandings and practices as the emerging essence of social life.
>
> (Ferrell, 1998: 5)

Unlike most modernist intellectual orientations, anarchism and anarchist criminology do not seek to incorporate reasoned or reasonable critiques of law and legal authority, but, in contrast, argue that progressive social change requires the 'unreasonable' and the 'unthinkable'. In other words, reason and 'common sense' notions of the legal and illegal are seen to keep us trapped within the present arrangements of authority and power, and it is thus in our interest to stop making sense, to imagine the unimaginable and think the unthinkable (Ferrell, 1998).

Anarchist criminologists thus launch aggressive and 'unreasonable' critiques against law and legal authority because they argue that the latter institutions undermine human community and diversity. Anarchist criminology is therefore different from the modernist critical criminological tradition because it is not a careful criticism of criminal justice, a 'loyal opposition' to the state and state law, but stands instead as a disloyal and disrespectful attack (Mazor, 1978), a 'counterpunch to the belly of authority' (Ferrell, 1996: 197). Moreover, it aims its disrespectable gaze both high and low: it attacks the state structure and legal authority above us but also encourages those below and beyond this authority to find ways of resisting it and finding more egalitarian alternatives.

Anarchist critiques of law and legality are nothing new and have long-established foundations in early anarchism itself, with prominent writers and activists like William Godwin (1756–1836), Max Stirner (1806–56), Michael Bakunin (1814–76) and Peter Kropotkin (1842–1921) focusing some of their most significant assaults on state authority and legal control. Kropotkin (1975), for example, criticized the tendency of the law to crystallize that which should be modified and developed on a day-to-day basis and demanded the abolition of prisons and the law itself. Bakunin also called for the destruction of the state and its replacement with the spontaneous and continuous action of the masses.

Ferrell (1998) observes that such anarchist critiques have emerged not as the outcome of theoretical posturing but out of head-on confrontations between state legal authorities and anarchists attempting to construct alternative societal arrangements. Thus, for Bakunin and Kropotkin, anarchist criminology was part of revolutionary activity against the Russian oligarchy and the emerging nation states of capitalism. In fact, Bakunin's notion of 'the spontaneous and continuous action of the masses' referred to an actual case of anarchist revolt: the Paris Commune of 1871. In the USA, anarchists like Emma Goldman (1869–1940) and Alexander Berkman (1870–1936) also mixed labour and social activism with theoretical critique and spent large periods of their lives in prison. Most remarkable were the Wobblies,[1] who blended deceptive strategies to avoid legal prosecution with out-and-out defiance of the law. With allied trade unions, they invented strategies to turn the law against itself, and win labour and political victories: thus, for example, on occasion, in the workplace, they obeyed every rule and regulation so precisely as to finally grind all work to a halt and, in the streets, they systematically violated unjust laws in such great numbers as to overload courts and jails, and force dismissal of their cases (Ferrell and Ryan, 1985; Kornbluh, 1988; Ferrell, 1991).

Ferrell (1998) observes that anarchist criminology has actually flourished during the previous thirty years in the USA. Harold Pepinsky (1978) published an article advocating 'communist anarchism as an alternative to the rule of criminal law' and later transformed this approach into a 'peacemaking criminology' which is now almost mainstream in the USA – and which we encountered in Chapter 10 of this text – and is opposed to the violence seen to be inherent in the concept and practice of state law (Pepinsky, 1991; Pepinsky and Quinney, 1991). Larry Tifft (1979) developed an anarchist criminology which argued for replacing state/legal 'justice' with a fluid, face-to-face form of justice grounded in emerging human needs. Bruce DiCristina (1995) has, more recently, constructed a critique of criminology and criminal justice developed from the work of the anarchist philosopher of science Paul Feyerabend (1975), whom we encountered above in the introduction to this part of the book. Ferrell (1994, 1995a, 1995b, 1996; Ryan and Ferrell, 1986) has also developed an anarchist criminology aimed at examining the interplay between state/legal authority, day-to-day resistance to it, and the practice of criminality.

Anarchist criminology thus incorporates the sort of 'visceral revolt' (Guerin, 1970) that is characteristic of anarchism itself, the passionate sense of 'fuck authority', to quote the old anarchist slogan, that is the outcome of being pushed around by police officers, judges, bosses, priests and other authorities. Ferrell (1997) notes that anarchists agree with many feminist and postmodernist theorists that intuitive passions are important as methods of understanding and resistance outside the usual confines of rationality and respect, while, at the same time, they seek to incorporate a relatively complex critique of state law and legality, which begins to explain *why* we might benefit from defying authority, or standing 'against the law'.

Many contemporary critical criminologists agree that state law is so thoroughly lubricated by economic privilege, intertwined with patriarchal arrangements and protected by racist procedures as to constitute a mailed fist regularly brought down on the heads of women, the poor, ethnic minorities, young people, and other outsiders to economic power or state authority (Ferrell, 1998). Anarchist criminologists certainly agree with this analysis but actually go further and argue that the practice of centralized state law in fact harms people, groups and the social fabric that joins them together even if it is not aimed directly at 'the powerless'. In other words, they are arguing that the administration of centralized state authority and legality destroys community, exacerbates criminality and expands the abusive power of the state machinery throughout the contemporary social order, and then, through its discriminatory practices, doubles this harm for those pushed to the bottom of the system.

Ferrell (1998) observes four broad harms of state legality. First, there is the 'state-protection racket' (Pepinsky and Jesilow, 1984: 10), where cash and conformity are seen to be extorted from those unlucky enough to be caught up in it:

> From speed traps to parking fines, from the plethora of licensing fees to the bureaucratised bungling of the tax authorities, the state operates a vast revenue machine which serves itself and those who operate it and which is enforced by a whole range of state-sanctioned strong-arm tactics such as impoundment, seizure and imprisonment. It is a system designed to perpetuate itself and to protect the powerful in and around it, obscuring its real intentions by an ideological veil of being in the best interests of the community.
>
> (Ferrell, 1998: 13)

Second, this labyrinth of state legality grows in the absence of real human community and, once in place, suffocates any possibility of fluid and engaged human interaction:

> In a social world increasingly fractured by alienated labour and economic inequality, privatised leisure, and the paranoia of the lonely crowd, calls for police assistance and civil litigation multiply as does the sense that such disjointed, externalised tactics somehow constitute appropriate measures for solving disputes and achieving justice.
>
> (Ferrell, 1998: 14)

Third, there is recognition and acknowledgement of the crucial role of the labelling tradition we encountered in the third part of this book with the confinement of people and groups within state-administered categories of criminality and systems of punishment and retribution, which, in reality, promotes not rehabilitative humanity but rather a downward spiral of crime, criminalization and inhumanity:

> This spiral interconnects state and media sponsored fears of crime, an ideology of state-sanctioned retaliation, and thus sudden outbreaks of objectification, dehumanisation, and legal retribution. It is in this way that a system of state law and 'justice' is perpetuated within individual lives and larger social relations.
>
> (Ferrell, 1998: 15)

This acknowledgement of the enduring significance of labelling theory for the radical/critical criminological project is clearly important. Indeed, Stan Cohen (1998) in his chapter in *The New Criminology Revisited* argues that, if one re-examines labelling theory and its critique of traditional criminology, one can find the majority of the postmodern themes included within that canon of work.

Fourth, the 'rule of law' continues to proliferate, to penetrate further into all corners of social and cultural life (Cohen, 1979) – as in Max Weber's (1964) notion of the 'iron cage of bureaucracy' – while state legality constitutes a sort of bureaucratic cancer that grows on itself, that produces an ever-expanding maze of legal control, and that in turn generates an ever-expanding body of bureaucratic and legal sycophants employed to obfuscate and interpret it:

> This proliferation of legal controls finally suspends what little protection the law once may have afforded. Every facet of social and cultural life is defined by legal control, and thus by state definitions of legality and illegality, we all remain continually vulnerable to the flagrant exercise of state power.
>
> (Ferrell, 1998: 16)

Anarchist criminology thus produces a profoundly radical critique of state law as a system of inherent inhumanity and its sense of standing 'against the law' leads logically to a criminology of crime and resistance. Labour historians and sociologists of work have long documented the pattern by which systems of authoritarian, alienating work generate among workers incidents of sabotage (of intentional rule-breaking and disruption) as a means of resisting these systems and regaining some sense of humanity and control. Anarchist criminologists suggest that this pattern may be found in the interplay of state legal control and criminality. Rather than dismissing criminality as mindless misbehaviour, or worse, simply accepting the social construction of legality and illegality provided by the state as definitive of good and bad human conduct, anarchist criminologists seek to explore the situated politics of crime and criminality. In other words, anarchist criminologists argue that the political (and politically inequitable) nature of state law and criminalization means that acts of crime under such a system must also carry some degree of political meaning.

Anarchist criminologists thus seek to blur and explore the boundaries between crime and political resistance (Simon, 1991). This exploration does not, however, assume that all crime constitutes conscious resistance to state authority, nor does it ignore the often, but not always, negative consequences of criminality for people and communities, but it does, on the other hand, require that careful attention is paid to various criminal(ized) activities – graffiti writing, 'obscene' art and music performances, pirate radio broadcasts, illegal labour strikes, curfew violations, shoplifting, drug use, street cruising, gangbanging, computer hacking (Ferrell, 1995a, 1996; Ferrell and Sanders, 1995) – as a means of investigating the variety of ways in which criminal or criminalized behaviours may incorporate repressed dimensions of human dignity and self-determination, and lived resistance to the authority of state law.

Anarchist criminology calls for human communities that are decentralized, fluid, eclectic and inclusive, and it is proposed that this sense of inclusive, non-authoritarian community can benefit critical criminology itself. Ferrell (1998) observes that anarchist criminology shares much with the uncertainty and situated politics of feminist criminology, with the decentred authority and textual deconstruction of the postmodern and constitutive criminologies we encountered above, the critical pacifism of peacemaking criminology and, of course, with the broader critique of legal injustice common to all critical criminologies. He observes that even left realists share with anarchist criminology a concern with identifying and exploring the situated consequences of crime and crime control. In the spirit of eclectic inclusivity, then, anarchist criminology argues against partitioning critical criminology into a series of small intellectual cubicles, and then closing one critical cubicle to the occupants of another (Pepinsky, 1991). It instead calls for an ongoing critical conversation among perspectives, for a multifaceted critique of legal injustice made all the more powerful by its openness to alternatives. Stan Cohen writes of his 'lack of commitment to any master plan (such as liberalism, left realism, or abolitionism), a failing, I would like to think, not of my own psyche but of the social world's refusal to correspond to any one theory' (1988: 232). Anarchist criminology shares this postmodern lack of commitment to master plans or grand narratives – including its own – and embraces instead fluid communities of uncertainty and critique.

Policy implications of crime and the postmodern condition

The fundamental policy implication confronting postmodern – and in particular constitutive – criminology is how is it possible as a society to stop investing in structures of oppression whose appearance channels and sustains the very use of the power to harm, without at the same time actually exercising power? A related problem is how, given the nature of power and social structure, is it possible to change the reified products of discourse that we take to be structure, culture and nature? This is the major – some suggest insurmountable – problem facing the postmodern and constitutive criminological project.

Perhaps most disappointing from this perspective is the discussion of how to overcome the problem that local action cannot transform wider structural, state and institutional systems. While Henry and Milovanovic argue that super-liberalism and chaos theory can create an 'empowered' democracy, they provide few practical strategies to indicate how this can be achieved and many of the strategies seem little more than 'old wine in new bottles' (Croall, 1996).

In considering policy, the connection between resistance and reconstruction is vital. Unlike some relevant critiques levied against the nihilistic forms of post-modern analysis, the affirmative version sees deconstruction and reconstruction as the necessary focus of attention. Simply separate one from the other and the roads to nihilism or romanticism are seductively inviting.

Given that the basis of crime – as harm – is the socially constructed and discursively constituted exercise of power through difference, it follows that human subjects whose investment in power relations harms others have the potential to reconstitute their use of human agency to be less harmful or have the potential to be reconstituted through interactive relations with the wider culture or structure. Such a perspective, as Colvin comments, 'opens the possibility for transformation of human subjects and the social structures we construct' (1997: 1450). The problem of policy, then, is not one of merely applying strategies, but of closely linking deconstruction and reconstruction so that appreciation of difference, rather than domination based on difference, pervades the spirit of social life. Difference without domination is to be celebrated but will be inevitably difficult, indeed probably impossible to achieve.

Summary of main points

1. Postmodernism can appear to be an extremely negative and nihilistic vision, for, if there is no such thing as the 'truth of the human condition', it is clearly difficult to formulate an argument in support of basic human rights, or to locate legitimate foundations for law.
2. The relativism implied by postmodernism denies the possibility of truth and hence of justice in anything other than a purely subjective form, which inevitably consigns us to the prospect of conflict.
3. The essential problem for the development of legislation and explanations of crime and criminal behaviour remains the difficulty of making any objective claims for truth, goodness and morality.
4. Postmodernism may advocate giving a voice to the oppressed and less powerful – and may celebrate diversity – but it could be argued that, in practice, power relations and political decisions are fundamentally important and may restrict this ideal.
5. The only well-developed attempt to rethink the central issues and themes of criminology in terms of postmodernism is the constitutive criminology originally developed by Stuart Henry and Dragan Milovanovic.
6. Henry and Milovanovic (1996) define crime as the power to deny others and they argue that the conventional crime control strategies, in the form of fast-expanding criminal justice institutions – the police and prisons – or as political rhetoric rehearsed in the media, fuel the engine of crime.
7. Unlike most modernist intellectual orientations, anarchism and anarchist criminology do not seek to incorporate reasoned or reasonable critiques of law and legal authority but, in contrast, argue that progressive social change requires the 'unreasonable' and the 'unthinkable'.
8. Anarchist criminologists thus launch aggressive and 'unreasonable' critiques against law and legal authority because they argue that these institutions undermine human community and diversity.
9. Ferrell (1998) observes that anarchist criminology has actually flourished during the previous thirty years in the USA.
10. Anarchist criminology thus produces a profoundly radical critique of state law as a system of inherent inhumanity, and its sense of standing 'against the law' leads logically to a criminology of crime and resistance.

Discussion questions

1. Explain the differences between sceptical and affirmative postmodernism.
2. What are the two theoretical underpinnings of constitutive criminology?
3. What are the identified weaknesses of constitutive criminology?

4. Outline the basic prescriptions of anarchist criminology.
5. What are the policy implications of anarchist criminology?

Suggested further reading

The following texts are recommended for those seeking an introduction to the notion of the postmodern condition: Baudrillard (1988), Bauman (1991, 1993), Harvey (1989) and Lyotard (1984). Rosenau (1992) is essential reading on the relationship of postmodernity to the social sciences. Both Davis (1990) and Young (1999) provide rather different accounts of contemporary post-industrial societies and the significance for criminology. Henry and Milovanovic (1994, 1996, 1999) are the doyens of constitutive criminology and these texts give a thorough introduction to the theory and its applications. Ferrell (1994, 1995a, 1995b) should likewise be consulted on anarchist criminology.

Note

1 The Industrial Workers of the World (IWW or the Wobblies) is an international union currently with headquarters in Cincinnati, Ohio, USA. At its peak in 1923, the organization claimed some 100,000 members and could marshal the support of perhaps 300,000 workers. Its membership declined dramatically after a 1924 split brought on by internal conflict and government repression. It continues to actively organize but now numbers only about 2,000 members worldwide and membership does not require that one works in a represented workplace, nor does it exclude membership in another labour union.

20. Cultural criminology and the schizophrenia of crime

Key Issues

1. The focus of cultural criminology and the seductions of crime
2. The carnival of crime and the schizophrenia of crime
3. Crime as normal and non-pathological
4. One planet under a groove
5. Cultural criminology and the mass media

Cultural criminology seeks to explain crime and criminal behaviour and its control in terms of culture and has very close intellectual links with the post-modern and anarchist criminology we encountered in the previous chapter. From this perspective, crime and the various agencies and institutions of crime control are perceived to be cultural and creative constructs and it is argued that these should be understood in terms of the phenomenological meanings they carry. It is thus a perspective that also has clear links to the labelling tradition, which was a central component of the modernist victimized actor model and which has been so influential in providing crucial foundations of critical criminology. Cultural criminology involves a focus upon the continuous generation of meaning around interaction where rules are created and broken involving a constant interplay of moral entrepreneurship, political innovation and transgression.

The focus of cultural criminology

Cultural criminologists follow in a tradition established by Marx and the later humanist Marxists who argue that the essence of 'humanity' is not that we are rational calculating beings but that we are productive and creative beings who carry with us a 'world vision' and ideology that shapes our own version of what is right and wrong (Lukacs, 1970; Goldmann, 1970). We nevertheless live out the 'everyday' within a social world that is structured at least in part by an economic system that insists on the pursuit of scientific rationalism in order to survive. In this context, 'crime' appears to the dominant political groups in society to be endemic and simply a reflection of their world turned 'upside down'. Mike Presdee observes that the overwhelming lure of transgression for the cultural criminologist brings with it a 'fascination with the unacceptable' in scientific rational society:

> Culture delivers to us social sites where popular transgression – the breaking through of the constraints created around us – is considered a crime in itself and where order and its accompanying rationalisations actually herald the death and the destruction of spontaneous life.
>
> (2004: 276)

That spontaneity – by its very essence – defies and resists order, and this dynamic tension between order and disorder in turn creates a cultural energy that is immediately apparent in the culture of 'edge work', 'emotion work' and 'excitement', which provides a central thread in much of the work conducted by cultural criminologists. The history of cultural criminology therefore reflects the history of the discourses of 'limit' and 'transgression'; 'boundary making' and 'boundary breaking'; 'control' and 'hedonism'; 'rationality' and 'irrationality'; alongside the examination of the 'inner' experience of individuals free from moral reasoning and safe from the 'outside' world.

Garland (2001) argues that contemporary life is characterized by a 'culture of control' where we are policed at home, at work, at pleasure and in a surveillance society where we cannot escape the dominant gaze (the gaze of the dominant), as we are watched and tracked, trailed, filmed and photographed, as our 'life-trail' is picked up by the electronic panopticon of rational society. This experience of domination thus produces cultures that are characterized by the process of the dominance through which they are formed. Mainstream criminology has tended to view these cultures as non-cultural, deviant and pathological but cultural criminology approaches human behaviour through an analysis of lived everyday life, and has thus come to understand that humans have the ability to twist, modify and oppose meanings produced by dominant rational groups (Willis, 1978).

Cultural criminology thus studies the way that some cultures have come to be designated as deviant. Cultural activities, whether strategies of resistance or otherwise, represent clear attempts to find meaning in a life lived through rules proscribed by others and provided from above. These are ways of life first 'received' and then 'perceived' and acted upon as 'tastes, feelings, likes and dislikes are developed in minute articulation with the concrete world' (Willis, 1978). Presdee observes that:

> Now we can begin to see that much crime, but not all; much disorder, but not all, is no more or less than the everyday life of the oppressed and the 'excluded'. From this perspective, crime should be viewed as everyday responses to lives lived out within deprived, brutalised and often lonely

social locations. Moreover, the responses from within the structures of domination are often truly masochistic in that the reaction to such disorder is often further acts of cruelty by the dominant over the dominated.

(2004: 281)

Similar themes are very much in evidence in one of the other major social dynamics explored by cultural criminologists: the changing cultural significance of contemporary consumer cultures and their particular effect on feelings and emotions (see Hayward, 2004a). The desire to own, to have and therefore to 'be' no longer respects the limits and cultural boundaries produced in the past to protect the institution of ownership. This new and all-encompassing consumer culture creates a confused consumer psyche where anxiety and its social anti-dotes are themselves producing much so-called 'social disorder' and 'transgres-sion', as groups and individuals attempt to make sense of a life increasingly mediated through the new and distinct processes associated with consumerism in contemporary society (Presdee, 2000; Hayward, 2004b). The search for the thwarted promise of happiness through consumption thus leads many to hedonism and seemingly irrational acts.

We have seen earlier in this book that a fundamental change has occurred in the economic order during the past thirty years. Thus, where previously 'produc-tion' was the dominant culture, this has been replaced by the dominance of 'consumption' (Bauman, 1997, 1998), and in this changed world we must all now consume at all costs. Presdee explains this perspective thus:

It is no longer the creation or the making of 'things' that excites us, but the consumption of things – or more specifically, the destruction of 'things'. To destroy, use up, consume, becomes an important daily activity and hangs in our consciousness, peppering our culture and everyday lives. One of the responsibilities of 'citizenship' under contemporary social conditions is to destroy daily. The perfect consumer leaves nothing of the product and is thus made ready for further destruction, emotionally as well as economically.

(2004: 283)

In a society based on consumption, to 'have' is to exist: to have nothing is to be nothing. Presdee asks rhetorically how – in the latter case – can we emotionally live a life that is laden with such shame and observes that it is through crime we can 'have', and therefore 'be'. It is this nothingness and loss of social status that is often the wellspring of social or personal harm, the trigger for violence as self-expression, whether it is directed inwardly (self-mutilation) or outwardly (the mutilation of others):

Personal social decline isolates us as we learn where we fit; learn that we are poor, that we are ugly, that we are excluded, different, apart. Then a silence descends on the isolated and lonely within a culture of distraction that is part of everyday life and the central question becomes . . . social survival or social destruction?

(Presdee, 2004: 283)

Crime and disorder can provide a subjective solution to this conundrum and thus becomes a 'therapeutic action' to alleviate personally perceived loss and translates the nothingness of life into something, while the pain of life is translated into pleasure.

In the same way that new crimes emerged as feudalism gave way to capitalism, we have now entered a new and largely uncharted phase of globalized capitalism and hyper-consumption, and once again crime takes on new meanings that require new criminological understandings. Presdee (2004) observes that individuals work through these new tensions in the turmoil of their everyday lives, then new feelings, emotions and imperatives emerge in their culture and it is somewhere here that the new cultural criminology has established its territory.

The seductions of crime

Cultural criminology uses everyday existences, life histories, music, dance and performance as databases to discover how and why it is that certain cultural forms become criminalized. Ferrell and Sanders (1995) observe that it is the intention to expand and enliven criminology and to push back the boundaries of accepted criminological discourse, and it is in this context that Katz (1988) writes about the 'seductions of crime' in which disorder becomes in itself a 'delight' to be sought after and savoured and where the causes of crime are constructed by the offenders themselves in ways that are compellingly seductive. 'Hot-blooded' murder is thus described in terms of a triad of conditions: interpretive, emotional and practical. Interpretive conditions include the defence of morality, the role of teasing or daring the victim, the role of a supportive audience, and the role of alcohol in casual settings of last resort, for example, in the home. Emotional conditions involve a process of transcending humiliation with rage via the intermediary of righteousness. Practical conditions are a marking, or desecration, of the body of the victim, for example, when offenders can recall precisely the number of stitches it took for a victim to survive. The key term is 'humiliation', which is defined as a 'profound loss of control over one's identity, or soul' (Katz, 1988: 24).

Humiliation is also a key term for analysing other categories of crime and all forms of criminality are considered to be a moral response to this shame. The notion of 'uncertainty' eliminates inevitability in the event. Cursing by the attacker and silent prayers by the victim are treated as priestly omens and sacrificial service honouring the sacred, which must be approached by a 'leap into faith' and the final seduction into 'the unknown' (Katz, 1988: 43).

Katz (1988: 51) defines foreground as individual consciousness and associated mental processes, while the less important background involves factors such as social class and gender. Background differences can vary the experience of humiliation and open up possibilities for rituals of forgiveness, but foreground, or what is going through the head of the offender at the time of the crime, is more important. Crimes such as shoplifting and pizza theft involve attributing sensual power to an object so that the seduction is like a 'romantic encounter'. Practical conditions involve flirting with the object and a tension of being privately deviant in public places. Emotional conditions involve transcending uncontrollable feelings of thrill. Interpretive conditions involve metaphors of self (bounding immorality), game (timeouts and goal lines), religion (secret defilement), sex (like an orgasm) and the interrelationship between deviance and charisma (reaching for mysterious forces). The resonating of these metaphors makes the seduction irresistibly compelling and, thus, 'it is not the taste for pizza that makes the crime happen but the crime that makes the pizza taste good' (Katz, 1988: 91).

Gang violence requires learning to be a 'badass' by projecting symbols of impenetrability, which Katz relates to the hardness of male phallic imagery and feels that such behaviour requires a commitment to firmness of purpose so that it is left to make the rational choice calculations of costs and benefits. Badasses engage in the 'accidental bump' and hog the pavement when they walk. Practical conditions involve creation of an oppressive background image to emphasize the status of the person as a street survivor, or member of an elite. Emotional conditions involve 'getting over' from 'here' to 'there' and the personal insults involving others' violations of artificial turf space.

Katz (1988) considers robbery to be a prototypical 'breeding ground' for crime and thus those conducting hold-ups with weapons are those that seek 'continuous action' and embrace a death wish (thanatos) and they will commit any degree of violence necessary even to the point where it puts their own lives at risk. These 'stick-up men' also develop a sense of competence at superior perceptual ability – in exploiting contextual weaknesses in a target, be it victim or architecture – and claim a special morality about this. Uncertainty in this example is related to 'chaos', that is, during a hold-up, the offender is required to maintain suspense and manage the impression of coming from an alien world.

Katz (1988) argues that it is the desire to seek continuous action – for example, crime, drugs, sex and gambling – that distinguishes the persistent or career criminal. Such offenders – also known as 'heavies' or omnibus felons – will often pursue action to the point of physical and mental exhaustion and they do this by always being available for all spontaneous opportunities, maintaining permeable boundaries for associates, and reckless, super-fast spending with the proceeds from crime.

Katz observes that the main problem for criminals is the transcendence of chaos and this exists as an ongoing project. Chaos is the master dialectic, acting as both a resource and a barrier to action. Katz draws heavily upon Matza (1969) in describing the dizziness of a criminal career where – caught up in a lifestyle of frequent intoxication, compounded lies, jealous lovers, and being a constant target for rip-offs and a regular suspect for police – the arrest, or more final end to the project, almost comes as a relief. Katz depicts the project of transcending chaos as a process of imposing discipline and control on one's life and doing this often means the humiliation and physical abuse of women and children. Imposing control is seeking to get caught by sarcastically thanking the authorities, doing some moral accountancy – thus 'got away withs' exceed 'got caughts' – and looking forward to the opportunities for action in prison.

Katz (1988: 247) observes that the attractions of crime are seen as extensions, or 'celebrations', of being male and being black and cites research on childhood socialization to suggest that the main effect of being male is preparation for a life of pretensions (Lever, 1978). Being black means to live in a culture of continuous insult, even from fellow blacks, and this tradition prepares blacks for becoming 'bad' by overcoming insult with insult. Crime emerges in the process of establishing a gendered, ethnic identity.

The carnival of crime

O'Malley and Mugford (1994) propose that a new phenomenology of pleasure is needed if we are to recognize 'crime' as simply a *transgression* from the impermissible and as *transcendence* of the everyday mundane. Presdee (2000) captures this sense of the interrelationships between pleasure and pain through his notion of 'crime as carnival', where the latter is a site where the pleasure of playing at the boundaries is clearly catered for. Thus, festive excess, transgression, the mocking of the powerful, irrational behaviour and so on are all temporarily legitimated in the moment of carnival. Breaking rules is a source of joy, of humour, of celebration, and many acts that might otherwise be considered criminal are momentarily tolerated. In such acts as sado-masochism, raving, joyriding, computer hacking, recreational drug use, reclaim the streets parties, gang rituals and extreme sports, Presdee finds enduring fragments from the culture of the carnival. Moreover, as Thornton's (1995) study of 1990s youth club cultures found, there is a continual and shifting exchange between the boundaries of acceptability and illegality and between subcultural authenticity and media manufacture. Moral panics about deviancy no longer simply signify condemnation, but are something to be celebrated by the subcultural participants themselves.

Cultural criminologists argue that we need to push deeper and deeper to capture the full meaning of social harm. They accept that the traditional concept of crime does have a place but one that is subjugated to, and set against, a multiple series of alternative discourses incorporating transgression, disrespect, disorder and resistance, as well as loss, injury and troubles. Van Swaaningen (1999: 23) observes that such discourses themselves may also suggest a new sociology of deviance based on difference and 'otherness'. Once more, the discursive frame necessary to recognize these elements needs to shift not just from criminal justice to social justice, restoration and reconciliation, but to delight, drama, tolerance, celebration, transcendence and the pursuit of pleasure. It is an ambitious and for some an exhilarating agenda.

The schizophrenia of crime

Hopkins Burke (2007) introduces the term 'the schizophrenia of crime' to refer to the apparently contradictory duality of attitude to criminal behaviour that has become endemic in contemporary societies characterized by the postmodern condition. Thus, on the one hand, it is possible to observe widespread public demand for a rigorous intervention against criminality that has made the 'war against crime' a major political issue and, indeed, it is in this context that we can observe an extensive expansion in situational crime prevention strategies epitomized by the ubiquitous existence of closed-circuit television (CCTV) cameras (Hopkins Burke, 2004b), a whole raft of crime control legislation that has placed increasing restrictions on our civil liberties and human rights (Hopkins Burke, 2004c), and the introduction of rigorous 'zero-tolerance-style' policing interventions (see Hopkins Burke, 1998a, 2002, 2004a) that have occurred not as the outcome of the coercive strategies of a totalitarian regime but in response to overwhelming public demand in a liberal democratic society (Hopkins Burke, 2004b). *We* want it, *we* demand it and *we* get it (Hopkins Burke, 2007), even though we as individuals are invariably unaware of the ultimate implications for our freedom. Hopkins Burke thus has developed a left realist historical perspective we have encountered elsewhere in this book to incorporate both the embourgeoisement thesis of John Goldthorpe (1968) and the 'civilising process' of Norbert Elias (1978, 1982) in order to explain how increasing demands for improved social conditions and material rewards among the respectable working classes – or more recently the new middle classes – have occurred alongside a fast-declining tolerance for the very visible criminality and incivilities in our midst.

On the other hand, we should observe that criminality has become widespread to the virtual point of universality. Many people have consequently committed criminal offences at some stage in their life and a great many continue to do so. There is increasing empirical evidence to show that white-collar, corporate and business crime is extremely widespread as was shown in the introduction to this book and when one considers, for example, recreational drug use (far from the sole prerogative of an unemployed underclass) (see Winlow and Hall, 2006), crimes of disorder and incivility associated with alcohol use (extremely extensive in any location, urban or rural, in the UK, particularly during weekend evenings) (Hobbs *et al.*, 2000, 2005) and driving cars beyond the legal speed limit (virtually compulsory through peer group pressure on motorways) (Hopkins Burke, 2007), the notion of the virtual universality of criminality is not as implausible as it may at first seem. Hopkins Burke (2007) is clearly influenced by Mike Presdee's notion of 'second lives', where the usually law-abiding and pillars of straight society enjoy an alternative part-time existence involving walking on the wild side (Presdee, 2000). There is thus – as Jock Young (1999, 2001) has observed – a considerable 'blurring of boundaries' between the criminal and the legal and, significantly, in our perceptions and understandings of these supposedly polarized opposite behaviours, that enables us to make some sense of 'the schizophrenia of crime' in a world where crime has become both normal and indeed non-pathological.

Crime as normal and non-pathological

For many years, the crime rate rose ever upwards, although it has come down recently in the UK, and more so in the USA, but that fall has been from unprecedented high levels and crime rates remain historically high. David Garland (1996) has pertinently observed that, as crime has come to be more frequent, it has ceased to be an exceptional or pathological event that surprises us when it occurs, but has become instead a standard, normal, background feature of our lives.

This increasing blurring of boundaries has become nowhere more apparent than in the realms of organized crime, corporate crime and legitimate business. As Ruggiero (2000) observes, organized crime has become a branch of big business and is simply the illegal sector of capital. Castells (1998) notes that, by the middle of the 1990s, the 'gross criminal product' of global organized crime had made it the twentieth richest organization in the world and richer than 150 sovereign states, while De Brie (2000) notes that the total world gross criminal product is estimated at 20 per cent of world trade.

Carter (1997) proposes that the structure of criminal enterprise is no longer characterized by archaic forms of 'family' organization typified by the old Sicilian Mafia and observes that newer flexible forms of 'entrepreneurial' criminal organization and methods of operation are highly adaptive to fast-moving global networks and achieve increasing integration into the legitimate economy through sophisticated money laundering techniques. The use of encrypted electronic mail, anonymous websites and the myriad instantaneous transactions that constitute the Internet in general and financial markets in particular render the legal and the illegal increasingly indistinguishable and, where distinguished, beyond the reach of national law-enforcement agencies. As both Van Duyne (1997) and Castells (1998) note, criminality is thus normalized by these networks.

Ruggiero (1997) further observes that legitimate business both actively seeks relations with criminal organizations and adopts methods akin to those of organized crime. Thus, immigrant smuggling eases labour supply problems in a variety of manufacturing sectors such as clothing and food, construction and agriculture and in 'dirty economies' where semi-legal employment is interspersed with employment in more directly criminal activity. Moreover, as De Brie (2000) notes, the global sphere of multinational corporations enables the export of the most brutal aspects of cheap labour to convenient locations in the southern hemisphere. Meanwhile, the legal financial sector may go out of its way to attract criminal investments. Kochan and Whittington (1991) note that the closure of the Bank of Credit and Commerce International in 1991 showed how private banks and investment traders openly tout for legal and illegal funds without being too concerned about the distinction between the two. Moreover, legitimate capital has started to use the same tactics as organized crime. Thus, while drugs cartels launder their profits through 'offshore' banking facilities, legitimate capital enhances its power over governments to reduce tax burdens not only with the threat to relocate employment but also by adopting some of the tactics and resources of organized crime (Shelley, 1998). At the same time, for many states, criminality acts as a buffer against poverty and economic collapse. Cocaine production, for example, acts as a counter to the impoverishment of thousands of Latin American peasant farmers, reducing the impact of falling world prices for agricultural products and raw materials in these areas. Thus, in a world where the boundaries between criminals and non-criminals and legal and illegal activities become increasingly difficult to disentangle, the classic crime control methods of modernity become increasingly more problematic not least with a globalization of deviance. The globalization of generic crime and criminal behaviour is considered in more detail in the following chapter, which discusses new modes of governance in a risk society. We will here consider the globalization of deviant youth subcultures in the guise of a significant fast-growing club culture with clear roots in the notions of the postmodern condition, cultural criminology, the carnival of crime and beyond.

One planet under a groove

Ben Carrington and Brian Wilson (2002) observe that, like all youth cultures, and especially those formed through associations with music cultures, the evolution of 'club cultures' around the world can be attributed, in part, to the ongoing global processes of cultural borrowing. The term 'club cultures' refers to the youth cultural phenomenon that is associated with all-night dance parties at nightclubs or other venues, the production and consumption of various dance music genres – music 'mixed' or electronically created by DJs – and with the use of amphetamine drugs – particularly MDMA or 'Ecstasy' – to enhance the dance/music experience. The roots of this culture can be found in the 1970s and early 1980s American dance music scenes of New York, Chicago and Detroit, and more recently in Britain where 'rave culture' emerged in 1988 during what came to be known as the 'second summer of love'. In Britain, in particular, the subsequent criminalization of the rave scene – a partial outcome of moral panics about rave-related drug use – and the incorporation of the rave scene by the mainstream music industry led the culture to become grounded in 'nightclub venues and that is how ravers, in effect, became clubbers' (Carrington and Wilson, 2002). Chambers argues that:

> The international medium of musical reproduction underlines *a new epoch of global culture contact*. Modern movement and mobility, whether through migration, the media or tourism, have dramatically transformed both musical production and publics and intensified cultural contact.
>
> (1994: 80)

DJs and promoters thus travel to foreign countries, are exposed to fresh varieties of music and nightclubs, and ultimately integrate ideas gleaned from these experiences into their domestic dance music cultures. Touring DJs and imported albums – in turn – influence local music-makers who combine the new material with their current work, thus creating something 'new again'. Images and ideas extracted from mass and alternative media are incorporated into local music production, fashion styles and club venues. In retrospect, what has emanated from years of this cultural 'cutting and mixing' (Hebdige, 1987) is a fascinating but hazy relationship between a 'global' club culture and various 'local club cultures'.

Carrington and Wilson (2002) observe that the increasing tendency for youth to travel to foreign scenes as 'post-rave tourists' has meant that local cultures are becoming further defined by their diverse and transient membership. These mobile formations might well be described as *reflexive* communities in the extent to which they dissolve the boundary between producers and consumers, are actively entered into by their members rather than being proscribed by social location, are not delimited by simple time–space boundaries, and are based on cultural and symbolic practices.

We observed in Chapter 7 how researchers and scholars at the Centre for Contemporary Cultural Studies (CCCS) in Birmingham, UK, had shown how youth 'reactively and proactively' expressed their dissatisfaction with the status quo of post-war British society. By articulating themselves through spectacular forms of 'style' (for example, the extreme fashions of punks and skinheads), youth were believed to be symbolically and creatively resisting, and, in so doing, finding 'solutions' to their problems. CCCS theorists referred to these 'magical solutions' as a way of recognizing that subcultural involvement is only a temporary form of empowerment and escape that does not (necessarily) substantially challenge the dominance/hegemony of the ruling classes. Hopkins Burke and Sunley (1996, 1998) more recently observed the co-existence of a number of different subcultures and argued that this is the outcome of the postmodern condition where specific groups of young people have coalesced to create solutions to their specific socio-economic problems with the possibility of choice being central to their account.

Carrington and Wilson (2002) recognize that these studies were to provide significant foundations for later studies of youth culture, but among a number of identified limitations was the recognition that insufficient attention had been paid to the ways in which youth cultures were influenced by subcultural traditions in other countries. Others were simply dismissive of such developments and even announced the death of youth subcultures, while Redhead (1990) proposed that subcultural authenticity was now 'impossible' because of the tendency of contemporary culture to be self-referential, shallow, flat and hyper-real or, in other words, a culture of effervescent, spectacular, fast-moving, ever-present, 'better than real' images. Muggleton (1997, 2000) thus suggests that the postmodern condition is inhabited by 'post-sub-culturalists' whose 'neo-tribal' identities are multiple and fluid, whose consumption is no longer 'articulated through the modernist structuring relations of class, gender or ethnicity' and who are defined by their fragmented/multiple stylistic identities. They have a low degree of commitment to any subcultural group and high rates of subcultural mobility, any fascination with style and image are generally apolitical, and have a 'positive attitude toward media and a celebration of the inauthentic' (Muggleton, 2000: 52). From this perspective, dance cultures are invariably seen as the archetypal postmodern youth formation.

Appadurai (1990) provides an alternative perspective and identifies 'five dimensions of cultural flow' in order to describe the dynamics of global cultural transmission. He suggests that these five dimensions – *ethnoscapes, mediascapes, technoscapes, finanscapes* and *ideoscapes* – work in ways that prevent the construction of a homogenous culture. Ethnoscapes refers to the flow of people around the world, for example tourists, immigrants, refugees, exiles, guest-workers and other moving groups. Technoscapes refers to the flow of technology, for example the export of technology to countries as part of transnational business relocations. Finanscapes refers to the patterns of global capital transfer, and Appadurai argues that:

> The global relationship between these three scapes is deeply disjunctive and profoundly unpredictable, since each of these landscapes is subject to its own constraints and incentives . . . at the same time as each acts as a constraint and a parameter for the other.
>
> (1990: 298)

Augmenting these first three scapes are *mediascapes* and *ideoscapes*. The former refers to mass media images, to the modes of image distribution, for example electronic or print media, and to the ways that these images allow viewers to gain access to other parts of the world and thus become part of 'imagined communities'. The latter refers to images that are invested with political-ideological meaning, for example the images presented by governmental groups justifying a military action, or images created by social movements attempting to overthrow power groups. The crux of Appadurai's framework is the assumption that the various 'disjunctures' or interactions that occur between global cultural flows – as they relate to the various scapes – provide the analyst with crucial information about the complex ways that local cultures relate to global forces.

Carrington and Wilson (2002) adapt this framework to their discussion of the globalization of dance music cultures and observe that this more elaborate approach to theorizing 'the local' encourages researchers to consider the intricacies of youth tastes, for example preferences for various genres of dance music, such as house or jungle or trance; interpretations of the music, for example as an escape, as a form of resistance; and uses of it, for example making a living in dance-music-related occupations. This more flexible and integrated interpretive framework also allows the analyst to consider how youth might simultaneously be interpreters and producers of culture, creating 'alternative' media that reflects the individuals' understandings of global culture, while contributing to this same culture.

Carrington and Wilson (2002) observe that the history of rave and club culture shows how travellers – within the ethnoscape – contributed to the transmission of dance music culture from the USA and Ibiza to Britain, and then, subsequently, back from Britain to the USA and parts of Europe. The 'post-rave tourist' has also emerged, as a clubber who travels to locations around the world with the explicit purpose of experiencing the club/rave culture of the area. It is observed that British satellite and terrestrial television companies continue to make programmes such as *Ibiza Uncovered* (BSkyB) and *Around the World in 80 Raves* (Channel 4) aimed at this newly found constituency of clubbing tourists, who can now enjoy the spectacle related to the post-rave tourist gaze without ever having to engage with the old modernist tradition of actually leaving their front rooms to experience the club sensation.

Carrington and Wilson (2002) argue that it would be a mistake to simply read the consumption (and production) of young people within this scene as an index of cultural manipulation. They argue that there is a sense of agency in the ways in which young people, through their engagement with the dance scene, have developed a degree of scepticism around the truth claims made by the scientific knowledge industries. For example, the attempt to define dance cultures through a public health discourse, as inherently dangerous sites of unknown and indeterminate risk, have spectacularly failed to prevent young people from embracing, adapting and exploring the possibilities of dance culture. It is argued that this is why, despite the attempt of most Western governments to prohibit the consumption of drugs especially among the 'vulnerable' young, rates of consumption of Ecstasy – among other drugs – have remained high. Carrington and Wilson (2002) suggest that the dance scene, by the extent and degree of its normalization of drug use, has challenged the hegemony of the anti-drug discourse to the extent that a number of governmental agencies and states are having to radically rethink the effectiveness of the 'war on drugs', citing as an example the dramatic decriminalization by Portugal of its drug laws in 2001.

Carrington and Wilson (2002) recognize that, if social relations are primarily defined as being produced in the last instance by a particular set of (economic) determinants, then formations such as dance music cultures will always be seen as proxies for 'real' oppositional politics. If, however, it is acknowledged that the social field is constituted by multi-various power relations between different social groupings, none of which has an assumed claim to determinacy, then more qualified 'moments of resistance' can be traced by careful and historically situated studies. Gilbert and Pearson argue that the key questions should not be:

> how likely dance culture is to bring down capitalism or patriarchy, but at what precise points it succeeds or fails in negotiating new spaces. In particular, it is not a simple question of dance culture being 'for' or 'against' the dominant culture, but of how far its articulations with other discourses and cultures – dominant or otherwise – result in democratisations of the cultural field, how far they successfully break down existing concentrations of power, and how far they fail to do so.
>
> (1999: 160)

Thus, in a world where the boundaries between criminals and non-criminals and legal and illegal activities have become increasingly difficult to distinguish, the classic crime control methods of modernity become increasingly more problematic not least because these are invariably based on the individual nation-state and are totally inadequate to deal with global phenomena such as the dance culture and its ancillary attached illegal activities. Some criminologists have thus drawn upon the 'governmentality' literature in order to explore the links between contemporary neoliberal political policy and the growing use of 'actuarial' or 'risk-based' strategies of crime control (Stenson and Sullivan, 2001), and these theories are explored in the following chapter. We will first consider the cultural criminology analysis of the mass media and crime.

Cultural criminology and the mass media

> In multi-mediated worlds, where signs, codes and symbols constantly loop, merge and intertwine in an endless stream of simulations and (re)presentations, crime and criminal justice are fundamentally mediatised phenomena.
>
> (Greer, 2010: 8)

Chris Greer defines 'media criminology' as 'the complex and constantly shifting intersections between crime, criminalization and control, on the one hand, and media, mediatisation and representation on the other' (2010: 5). This is nevertheless an enormous and relatively unexplored territory.

Barak (2012) observes that, when it comes to actual media coverage and/or representation of crime, there have been essentially two kinds: first, the more frequent inclusion of some type of felony or street crime often involving an act of violence and, second, the less common insertion of white-collar offences, involving some type of public or private trust violation that usually concentrates its focus on individuals and their victims in contrast to societal institutions or social organizations and their victims. Not surprisingly, these mediated relations of delivering and receiving crime and justice 'information' are also reflected in the limited scholarly research, academic analysis and critical literature on media and crime. Thus, most of the documented work on the social construction of mediated crime and crime control has been restricted to the entertainment and news media spheres. In comparison, there has been a virtual absence of research when it comes to the online sphere.

Barak (2012) cites the example of one barely explored, underdeveloped and potentially profitable area of research, which involves the emergence of what some have labelled pro-abuse cyberspace male peer support groups associated with certain types of shared pornography (DeKeseredy and Olsson, 2011; Kendall, 2003). He observes that, to date, no causal relations have been established between viewing these types of pornography and engaging in abusive sexual behaviour with women but some researchers have nevertheless speculated about an increasing number of men who are sharing and consuming derogatory, denigrating, racist and sexist pornographic materials online as 'part of a broader subculture of sexual deviance that legitimizes various forms of deviant sexuality' (Stack *et al.*, 2004: 85).

Media, society and criminology

Barak (2012) observes that throughout history the various forms of media have always shown a massive interest in crime, criminals, punishment and justice. Print, sound, visual and new media alike have always depended on responsive audiences or 'ratings'. Through the processes of mass communication, these popular media have also made significant contributions, for better and worse, to the social construction of crime and justice. The media have nevertheless inconsistently mystified and demystified crime and justice, while in reflecting the status quo – as well as in its capacity to lead, follow or resist social change – have not only facilitated the targeting of certain offenders, such as drug users, sex offenders, the poor or immigrants, but they have also omitted or treated lightly other offenders, such as the habitually law-violating corporations, or those Wall Street bankers, insurers and stockbrokers who engaged in derivative Ponzi schemes[1] and subprime mortgaging,[2] or private security contractors who have thieved, raped and killed. The former category are typically portrayed as dangerous offenders who threaten the well-being of otherwise lawful societies, while the latter group are less frequently (and less) scrutinized. They are simply presented as anomalies, exceptions or glitches in the normative order with both these offenders and their offences not taken seriously or considered to be real crime or with any thought given to the systemic negative consequences for the well-being of the rest of society (Barak, 1994; Potter and Kappeler, 1998; Bohm and Walker, 2006; Surette, 2007; Marsh and Melville, 2009; Stevens, 2010).

When it comes to the concept of 'moral panic' or the 'situation in which public fears and state interventions greatly exceed the objective threat posed to society by a particular group that is claimed to be responsible for the condition' (Bonn, 2010: 5), this radical criminological theorizing has greatly influenced the studying of social problems, crime, media and collective behaviour; indeed, it has become part of mainstream journalistic and political discourse (Altheide, 2009). First used in a criminological sense by Jock Young in 1971, it was elaborated upon by Stanley Cohen in *Folk Devils and Moral Panics*, where this classic work explained that a moral panic had occurred when:

> A condition, episode, person or group of persons emerges to become defined as a threat to societal values or interests; its nature is presented in a stylized and stereotypical fashion by the mass media; [and] the moral barricades are manned by editors, bishops, politicians or other right-thinking people.
>
> (1973: 9)

Barak (2012) observes that, while these intense, media-fuelled bursts of collective concern have typically distorted the danger or threat posed by the targeted groups and have directed public outrage against those particular 'others' that are successfully labelled or identified by various 'moral entrepreneurs' (Becker, 1963) via the mass media as evil, the extent to which the new media has impacted or influenced the contemporary formation of postmodern folk devils and moral panics still remains to be discovered.

News representation and the social construction of crime

Barak (2012) argues that understanding news representation and the social construction of newsmaking requires an examination of the conscious and unconscious processes involved in the mass dissemination of symbolic consumer goods. These commodities of news production and the images of social reality that they invoke cannot be separated from their cultural histories. Moreover, mediated characterizations of crime and criminal justice, of criminals and social control, projected in news presentations are representations themselves of culturally shared visions accessed through commonly unfolding historical narratives, in which average people and most journalists come to know crime and justice in developed societies. In other words, crime and justice stories produced by news media for mass consumption reflect and reveal much about the views those societies have of themselves.

These 'crime news' stories are not objective or value-neutral. All theoretical perspectives agree that, although crime and justice representations are highly selective and unrepresentative of their subject matter, they are viewed as essential for disentangling the relationships between crime, control, justice and social order. These news stories respectively reproduce moral boundaries, legitimate law and order, and reinforce gender stereotypes. All of which helps to reify unequal power relations as well as inequality throughout society. Nevertheless, within and without the news business, there are also all kinds of sources and values that shape the processes of newsmaking in general and newsmaking criminology in particular.

Herbert Gans conducted a classic study of the national news in the USA and argued that 'news is about the economic, political, social, and cultural hierarchies' and that reporting focuses 'on those at or near the top of the hierarchies and on those, particularly at the bottom, who threaten them, to an audience, most of whom are located in the vast middle range between top and bottom' (1980: 284). News was defined as:

Information which is transmitted from sources to audiences, with journalists – who are both employees of bureaucratic commercial organizations and members of a profession – summarizing, refining, and altering what becomes available to them from sources in order to make the information suitable for their audiences.

(Gans, 1980: 80)

Gans (1980: 52) divided news stories into two categories: first, those stories about 'disorder news' that report threats to all kinds of order as well as the measures taken to restore it and, second, those about 'routine activities' that are normative and usually pose no direct threats. Despite their differences, both categories of newsmaking nevertheless help to reproduce the dominant social order.

Within the disorder category, Gans identified four subcategories, distinguishing between natural, technological, social and moral disorder. Mediated crime and justice tends to focus its reporting primarily on external activities that threaten public peace and private security, typically involving physical violence to persons and/or property (social disorder) and, secondarily, on reported transgressions of laws and mores that do not necessarily or that may or may not endanger the social order, such as many of the activities associated with 'victimless criminality' (moral disorder). The fundamental distinction between these types of disorder stories is the value of intentionality or culpability that can be attached to those who may be violating the social or moral orders.

Steve Chibnall (1977) and Yvonne Jewkes (2004) have mapped out the news values that not only shape the reporting of crime, but that also help to locate these within the larger practices of journalism. For Chibnall, these include: immediacy, dramatization, personalization, simplification, titillation, conventionalism, structured access and novelty. Jewkes has updated and expanded on this list and includes threshold, predictability, individualism, risk, sex, celebrity, proximity, violence, spectacle and graphic imagery, and children. These journalistic values that increasingly rely over time on visual imagery with respect to film/video and print have also served as a primary device for defining normative and deviant behaviour, identity and reality. They often make it difficult, if not impossible, to clearly distinguish between the perception, reaction and production of crime and justice. In the process of news crime construction, crime and crime control represents order, which 'provides people with preferred versions and visions of social order, on the basis of which they take action' (Ericson *et al.*, 1991: 239).

At the end of the newsmaking day, the mediated construction of crime and justice becomes the socially constructed reality, when, in fact, this is the socially constructed subjective reality. According to Surette (2007), there are four stages in the social construction of crime and five contemporary crime and justice frames that provide fully developed socially constructed templates, which allow claims and claims makers to succeed in making their representations of crime and justice stick to the media overload of information. Stage one consists of 'the physical world' enclosed by conditions, events and properties that establish the boundaries or background in which the other stages must frame their interactions. Stage two consists of the 'competing social constructions' or differing descriptions of the physical world of crime and justice offered up by various claims makers.

It is at stage three, 'media as social construction competition arena', that Surette (2007: 35, 40) argues that the media play their most powerful role, filtering out competing constructions, typically favouring those positions that 'are dramatic, sponsored by powerful groups, and are related to pre-established cultural themes' or to the five prevailing crime and justice frames described by Sasson (1995: 13–17). First, the 'faulty system' thematic proposes that crime stems from criminal justice leniency and inefficiency. The proposed solution is to 'get tough' and 'tighten up'. Popular symbols used have included 'handcuffed police' and 'revolving door justice'. Second, the 'blocked opportunities' thematic argues that crime arises from poverty and inequality. The proposed solution is to address the 'root causes' of crime by creating jobs, community development and reducing poverty. Popular symbols used have included 'dead-end, low-paying jobs' and high unemployment rates. Third, the 'social breakdown' thematic argues that crime stems from family and community breakdown. The proposed solution is citizen involvement and community efficacy/policing. Popular symbols used have included 'family values' and 'take back the streets'. Fourth, the 'racist system' proposes that the problem of crime arises from a criminal justice system that operates in a discriminatory fashion. The proposed solution is greater sensitivity to racial justice and to the empowerment of those groups discriminated against. Popular symbols used include 'profiling' and the 'differential application' of the criminal law. Fifth, the 'violent media' thematic proposes that crime, particularly violent crime, stems from the amount of extreme violence in the mass media. The proposed solution is more government regulation of the production and distribution of violent imagery. Popular symbols used include 'life imitating art' and 'copycat crimes'.

Stage four represents the emergence of dominant news themes or the 'winning social construction', which often drives – if not determines – criminal justice and crime control policies. Surette argues that those

> social policies supported by the public and the solutions forwarded by the policy makers are tied to the successful construction[s]. For crime and justice, the socially constructed reality will define the conditions, trends, and factors accepted as the causes of crime, the behaviours that are seen as criminal, and the criminal justice policies accepted as reasonable and likely to be successful.
>
> (2007: 36)

Crime, entertainment and the postmodern imagination

Barak (2012) observes that, regardless of the changing discourses in mediated crime and justice, in the fictional and nonfictional entertainment spheres of television soap operas and documentaries, respectively, the representations of 'good' and 'evil', 'non-violent' and 'violent', 'in control' and 'out of control' typically distort the images of perpetrators, victims, criminal justice and criminal punishment. In the case of criminal harm, depictions are primarily of individuals rather than of organizations or institutions. Though criminal victimization may be located at home, it is usually represented in the street, and rarely viewed from the executive suite. In the process, myths and stereotypes about various types of violent 'offenders' and 'non-offenders' are projected onto large and small screens alike (Barak, 2003).

Frus observes that, when it comes to fictional accounts of gender and violence, Hollywood films 'are expert at providing illusion of reality, no matter how fantastic the story, they are an important source of our mythology about family violence' (2001: 227). The portrayal of women in US cinema operates according to age-old myths, for example, wife 'batterers' are not like ordinary men, women who are abused are asking for it, beatings leave no permanent scars, women can leave their abusers and so on and so forth. In the mediums of film and literature more generally, criminal violence is often put to use through shifting mythic and ideological imperatives, in the service of constructing audience awareness and a world view sympathetic to extreme individualism and free enterprise. These themes are not so much the product of a manufactured consensus as they are the product of reflexivity, reification and reproduction, grounded in an integrating political economy and a dynamically developing collective unconscious (Barak, 2003).

Barak (2012) observes that no book or film (in this case both) has captured the dilemma of mediated criminal violence and the postmodern imagination better than *American Psycho*, Bret Easton Ellis's twisted satire on serial murder. This best-selling novel was first published in 1991, and in 1999 it was released as a semi-successful film. Despite the movie's controversial portrayal of a high-class Wall Street, wheeling and dealing serial killer – or perhaps because of it – the film became a cult classic as a video rental and is still shown regularly on cable television. In a strange way, the representations of graphic violence were of a serial killer gone mainstream, suggesting that, in accordance with the 'risk society' thesis (which we will encounter in the following chapter), harm and dangers can come from anywhere.

Media, crime and social control

Barak (2012) observes that, despite differences, all theories of communication associate the workings of the mass media with contributing to the maintenance of social conformity, order and control. Historically, the roots of mass media involvement in social control can be traced back to the 1960s with 'the success of prosocial entertainment programs and public information campaigns' and to the 'development of a number of media-based anticrime programs and the widespread adoption of media technology in the criminal justice field' a decade later (Surette, 2007: 171). Today, in addition to the anti-crime advertising, case processing using media technology and police surveillance systems based on the older technologies of audio- and videotaping, there is an abundance of newer media technologies 'capable of both facilitating and constraining communication, interaction, mobility, and the creation and realisation of fluid identities' (Greer, 2010: 491).

Greer further observes that the digitized, computerized and networked information and communication technologies exemplified by the Internet have created virtual worlds with their own changing norms, values and codes of practice, altering the ways in which 'people engage and interact in time and space', giving 'new meaning to what it is to be "social"' (2010: 491). These technological transformations have created new opportunities and risks for crime and victimization, and for surveillance and crime control. For example, CCTV, information gathering and data processing have transformed how people perceive and negotiate their social worlds with caution and reserve, aware that 'cybercrime' is all about. At the same time, while the news media, law enforcement and external observers have raised concerns over the rise of 'Big Brother' and '1984', the public has tended to resign itself to a lack of privacy and to the installation of surveillance cameras in public places to prevent crime (Surette, 2007) (see Chapter 23).

In this, the second decade of the twenty-first century, the mass media can be used to influence the attitudes people have about crime and criminal justice, for better or worse. The popular media can be used to provide the police with more crime-related information. Media technology has also become a staple used to speed the processing of criminal cases, to videotape police patrols, vehicle stops and subsequent interrogations. It can be useful in the investigation, surveillance and deterrence of crime, and in the prevention of victimization by intercepting, for example, potential terrorist bombers foiled by TSA full-body video scanners when trying to pass through airport security. In these applications of media technology to crime and social control, the question typically asked by enquiring minds is: what are the costs or benefits to the general public?

Barak (2012) observes that, while programmes designed to increase public cooperation by advertising crime have proven effective in gathering information and in solving some crimes, the overall effect on crime is not significant. Media programmes that teach the public about crime prevention techniques are quite popular. They also increase public knowledge and change attitudes about crime prevention, but not actual crime prevention behaviour. Similarly, while surveillance programmes do show deterrence effects, their ability to do so without displacement remains unproven. With these caveats in mind, Surette (2007) is ambivalent, at best acknowledging that media technologies can enhance both due process and crime control models of the administration of justice (see Chapter 2). His concern is that the message conveyed by the news media, in conjunction with the entertainment message that crime is caused by individuals, is that the resolution of crime becomes overly dependent on technological rather than social interventions. Other noted costs to the public include the potential for decreased citizen involvement; increased depersonalization of the criminal justice system and isolation of the police from the policed; increased citizen fear and suspicion of the criminal justice system; and the polarization of society due to the creation of affluent, technologically secured garrison communities.

Mediatized crime and crime control – direct and indirect effects

Barak (2012) considers whether mass communication (text and visual) can be used to stop war, abolish the death penalty, cultivate genocide, reduce ethno-political conflict or mediatize peace and non-violence. He acknowledges that is not the typical set of questions pondered by most people trying to understand the impact of mass media on non-conforming – or conforming – behaviour. Yet, he observes that in 1997 the Nobel Peace Prize was awarded to the International Campaign to Ban Landmines, recognizing the power of the Internet to mobilize and enlist worldwide support. It had all begun a few years earlier when Jody Williams, from Putney, Vermont, used her email account to coordinate the activities of more than 700 organizations from over 60 countries. Direct effect? Indirect effect? What about the ultimate cases of ethnic cleansing and the extraordinary crime of genocide or the denial of it by millions of people? Direct effect? Indirect effect? No effect? Contradictory effect? (Barak, 2012).

In terms of genocidal murder or rape, for example, or more generally in the context of collective and/or organizational violence (or non-violence), the causes of ethnic conflicts (or peace) involve 'structural factors', including economic, social and political dimensions relating to both the distribution of wealth and inter-ethnic relations, 'facilitating factors', such as the degree of politicization and ethnic consciousness, and 'triggering factors' including sharp economic shocks, intergroup tensions and collapsed central authority. In the genocidal cases of Nazi Germany, the former Yugoslavia and Rwanda, while the ethnic and national media could not be blamed directly for the creation of ethno-political conflicts, the media and mediation played an important role in negotiation across all three causal spheres, especially in shaping evil Others, messages of hatred and the need for extermination (Costy and Gilbert, 1998).

Barak (2012) observes that, since the inception of mass mediatized words and images, concerns have been selectively raised over the real and imagined impact of deviant or taboo behaviours, especially as these have been associated with graphic or explicit depictions of sex, interpersonal violence and other 'morally' transgressive behaviours involved in both crime and crime control. The issue has always been whether the various mass media and mediatized representations of these behaviours elicit fear or imitation from their audiences. Thus, whether there is a direct effect, an indirect effect, no effect, or perhaps all three. Barak observes that, despite an abundance of research studies both in the laboratory and in the field examining the effects of televised violence, sexual and non-sexual, on aggressive and non-aggressive behaviour, which tend to support the third possibility of both mixed and contradictory effects at the same time, most, if not all, of these studies are subject to a number of criticisms regarding the validity and appropriateness of the theories and methods, and, in many instances, the moral politics that have traditionally underpinned the direct-effects model of mediated research.

Importantly, media studies of violence and aggression of a sexual or non-sexual nature have been able to differentiate among media consumers. Moreover, these studies have also been able to examine the indirect effects of media in relation to the reciprocal roles of other contributing factors. In arguing for an 'indirect-effects' model of hypothesized environmental influences on the development of antisocial behaviour against women, Neil Malamuth summarized the work that he and his colleagues had conducted on sexually violent media, thought patterns and antisocial behaviour as, 'no influence works in a vacuum, and media influences are viewed as combining and interacting with a variety of other individual and cultural factors – sometimes counteracting them, sometimes reinforcing them, and at other times, not having much of any effect' (1989: 162). More specifically, the indirect-effects model or reciprocal theory of mediatized sexual violence may be thought of as follows:

> Individual conditions and the broader social climate are postulated as the originating environmental influences on the individual. The mass media are considered one of the many social forces that may, in interaction with a variety of other cultural and individual factors, affect the development of immediate attributes, such as thought patterns, sexual arousal patterns, motivations, emotions, and personality characteristics. These immediate variables, in complex interactions with each other and with situational circumstances, such as alcohol consumption or acute arousal, may precipitate behaviors ranging from passive support to actual aggression.
>
> (Malamuth, 1989: 164)

Barak (2012) observes that, as the indirect-effects model of mediatized sexual violence simply emphasizes the direct-effects model of crime and crime control, it is too simplistic for serious consideration. On the other hand, the indirect-effects model of mass media effects leaves the door wide open for exploring the reciprocal relations between media and crime, and proposes this as a useful future research agenda.

Policy implications of cultural criminology

Keith Hayward and Jock Young (2012) respond to the frequent criticisms of cultural criminology that it has little potential for crime policy. They observe that this theoretical perspective is in an appreciative approach that totally eschews 'correctionalism', although that does not inevitably mean to romanticize the offender, nor does it necessitate a non-intervention approach to crime. The emphasis is on the cultural meanings of the activities to those doing the crime.

Young (2011) recognizes the complete neglect of the cultural nature of crime in the current predestined actor model-dominated criminological orthodoxy in the USA, which invariably involves entirely inadequate attempts to measure – and sometimes the collection of – toxic data. With this in mind, Hayward and Young (2012) observe that the issue becomes not whether cultural criminology is capable of providing legitimate policy interventions but rather whether or not much of the current funding directed at positivistic intervention is simply a waste of money.

Summary of main points

1. Cultural criminology seeks to explain crime and criminal behaviour and its control in terms of culture, with the focus on the continuous generation of meaning around interaction where rules are created and broken.
2. Cultural criminology studies the way that some cultures have come to be designated as deviant and thus has been heavily influenced by labelling theories.
3. Cultural criminology uses everyday existences, life histories, music, dance and performance as databases to discover how and why certain cultural forms become criminalized.
4. Katz (1988) writes about the 'seductions of crime' in which disorder becomes in itself a 'delight' to be sought after and savoured and where the causes of crime are constructed by the offenders themselves in ways that are compellingly seductive.
5. Presdee (2000) captures the interrelationships between pleasure and pain through his notion of 'crime as carnival' where the latter is a site where the pleasure of playing at the boundaries is clearly catered for.
6. Hopkins Burke (2007) introduces the term 'the schizophrenia of crime' to refer to the apparently contradictory duality of attitude to criminal behaviour that has become endemic in contemporary societies characterized by the postmodern condition.
7. David Garland (1996) has observed that, as crime has come to be more frequent, it has ceased to be an exceptional or pathological event that surprises us when it occurs, but has become instead a standard, normal, background feature of our lives.
8. This increasing blurring of boundaries has become nowhere more apparent than in the realms of organized crime, corporate crime and legitimate business.

9. Ben Carrington and Brian Wilson (2002) observe that, like all youth cultures, and especially those formed through associations with music cultures, the evolution of 'club cultures' around the world can be attributed, in part, to the ongoing global processes of cultural borrowing.

10. Chris Greer defines 'media criminology' as 'the complex and constantly shifting intersections between crime, criminalization and control, on the one hand, and media, mediatisation and representation on the other' (2010: 5).

Discussion questions

1. Explain the focus of cultural criminology.
2. What are the 'seductions of crime' according to Jack Katz?
3. Explain the concept of 'the carnival of crime' (Presdee).
4. What is the 'schizophrenia of crime' (Hopkins Burke)?
5. How does the media present 'the crime problem'?

Suggested further reading

Ferrell and Sanders (1995), Ferrell (1999) and O'Malley and Mugford (1994) provide a good introduction to cultural criminology, while the second edition of Ferrell *et al.* (2008) is being published as this book is being written and is extremely likely to become a classic. Katz (1988) provides an excellent study of the seductions and pleasures of crime and Presdee (2000) the 'carnival of crime'. Hopkins Burke (2007) provides a more extensive discussion than here of the 'schizophrenia of crime' and Carrington and Wilson (2002) discuss the globalization of dance culture. Yvonne Jewkes (2004) provides an excellent introduction to the relationship between the media and crime.

Notes

1   The Ponzi Scheme is named after Charles Ponzi, a clerk in Boston who first orchestrated such a scheme in 1919. It is a fraudulent investing scam promising high rates of return with little risk to investors and generates returns for older investors by acquiring new investors. This scam actually yields the promised returns to earlier investors, as long as there are more new investors. These schemes usually collapse on themselves when the new investments stop.

    A Ponzi scheme is similar to a pyramid scheme in that both are based on using new investors' funds to pay the earlier backers. One difference between the two schemes is that the Ponzi mastermind gathers all relevant funds from new investors and then distributes them. Pyramid schemes, on the other hand, allow each investor to directly benefit depending on how many new investors are recruited. In this case, the person on the top of the pyramid does not at any point have access to all the money in the system.

2   A subprime mortgage is a type of mortgage that is normally made out to borrowers with lower credit ratings. As a result of the borrower's lowered credit rating, a

conventional mortgage is not offered because the lender views the borrower as having a larger-than-average risk of defaulting on the loan. Lending institutions often charge interest on subprime mortgages at a rate that is higher than a conventional mortgage in order to compensate themselves for carrying more risk.

Borrowers with credit ratings below 600 often will be stuck with subprime mortgages and the higher interest rates that go with those mortgages. Making late bill payments or declaring personal bankruptcy could very well land borrowers in a situation where they can only qualify for a subprime mortgage. Therefore, it is often useful for people with low credit scores to wait for a period of time and build up their scores before applying for mortgages to ensure they are eligible for a conventional mortgage.

21. Crime, globalization and the risk society

Key Issues

1. New modes of governance
2. Crime and the risk society
3. Penal modernism and postmodernism
4. Globalization and crime
5. Terrorism and state violence

In the previous chapter, it was recognized that, in a world permeated with the morally ambiguous postmodern condition, where the boundaries between criminals and non-criminals and legal and illegal activities have become increasingly difficult to distinguish, the classic crime control methods of modernity have become increasingly problematic. Some criminologists have thus drawn upon the 'governmentality' literature in order to explore the links between contemporary neoliberal political policy and the growing use of 'actuarial' or 'risk-based' strategies of crime control (Stenson and Sullivan, 2001). This new governmentality thesis refers to 'the new means to render populations thinkable and measurable through categorisation, differentiation, and sorting into hierarchies, for the purpose of government' (Stenson, 2001: 22–3). This chapter commences with a consideration of these new modes of governance, the wider notion of the risk society and the threats contained within it, which seem to be a significant outcome of the postmodern condition, and the debates that question the whole notion of a significant break with a penal welfare past, and will conclude by considering the internationalization of crime and risk in terms of globalization, Southern theory and the morally ambiguous notion of terrorism.

New modes of governance

The concept of governance in contemporary political theory signifies 'a change in the meaning of government, referring to a *new* process of governing; or a *changed* condition of ordered rule; or the *new* method by which society is governed' (Rhodes, 1997: 46). In criminological theory, the concept has been used to signify changes in the control of crime and to acknowledge similar objects of control such as incivility, harm, safety and security.

The principal feature of the concept of governance is a rupture with traditional perceptions that place the state at the centre of the exercise of political power. In this new Foucauldian conceptualization, power is thus not simply possessed by the state to be wielded over civil society but is tenuous, unresolved and the outcome of struggles between coalitions of public and private, formal and informal, actors. These struggles are rooted in the central paradox of power: thus, when actors possess the potential to govern, they are not powerful because they are not actually governing, but neither are they powerful when they govern because they are dependent on others to carry out their commands (Clegg, 1989).

Male as non-powerful

This all implies a new complex and fragile process of governing through negotiation, bargaining and other relationships of exchange rather than through command, coercion or normative appeals for support. Thus, in order to accomplish and sustain political authority, would-be political leaders have to appreciate their 'power-dependence' on others and recruit and retain sufficient supporters to maintain a governing coalition (Rhodes, 1997). A criminological example is the attempt to control crime through partnerships of statutory, commercial and voluntary organizations (Crawford, 1997). This multi-agency approach has accompanied official recognition of the limits to the state's capacity to reduce crime, in particular the insufficiency of criminal justice, and the consequent need to enrol expertise and resources from non-state actors including the 'responsibilization' of private citizens for their own security (Garland, 2001).

This idea of 'joined-up' government to attack multifaceted and complex problems such as youth offending, through multi-agency partnerships employing a broad spectrum of social policy interventions, represents a definite break with the methods of modern public administration. It challenges the specialization of government into discrete areas of functional expertise and, in so doing, defines new objects of governance. Youth offending, for example, ceases to be defined only in terms of 'criminality' (and thus subject to the expertise of criminal justice professionals) but becomes a problem of education, health and, in contemporary terminology, one of 'social exclusion' and 'antisocial behaviour' (Hopkins Burke, 2008).

For most of the twentieth century, crime control was dominated by the 'treatment model' prescribed by the predestined actor model of crime and criminal behaviour (which we encountered in the second part of this book) and was closely aligned to the powerful and benevolent state, which was obliged to intervene in the lives of individual offenders and seek to diagnose and cure their criminal behaviour. It was (as we have seen) the apparent failure of that interventionist modernist project epitomized by chronically high crime rates and the apparent failure of criminal justice intervention that led to a rediscovery of the rational actor model and an increased emphasis on preventive responses.

Crime and the risk society

Garland (1996) has argued that the new governmental style is organized around 'economic forms of reasoning' and it is thus reflected in those contemporary rational actor theories that view crime as simply a matter of opportunity and that require no special disposition or abnormality (see Chapter 4). The subsequent outcome has been a shift in policies from those directed at the individual offender to those directed at 'criminogenic situations' and these include 'unsupervised car parks, town squares late at night, deserted neighbourhoods, poorly lit streets, shopping malls, football games, bus stops, subway stations and so on' (Garland, 1999: 19).

Feeley and Simon (1994: 180) have influentially proposed that these changes are part of a paradigm shift in the criminal process from the 'old penology' (penal welfarism) to the 'new penology' (risk management). The former was concerned with the identification of the individual criminal for the purpose of ascribing guilt and blame, the imposition of punishment and treatment, while the latter is 'concerned with techniques for identifying, classifying and managing groups assorted by levels of dangerousness' based not on individualized suspicion, but on the probability that an individual may be an offender. Justice is thus becoming 'actuarial', its interventions increasingly based on risk assessment, rather than on the identification of specific criminal behaviour, and we are therefore witnessing an increase in, and the legal sanction of, such practices as preventive detention, offender profiling and mass surveillance (Norris and Armstrong, 1999) and indeed – when that fails – mass incarceration.

McCahill and Norris (2002) observe that the past thirty years has witnessed an ever-increasing use of surveillance technologies designed to regulate groups as part of a strategy of managing danger and these include the ubiquitous city-centre surveillance systems referred to above, the testing of employees for the use of drugs (Gilliom, 1994) and the introduction of the blanket DNA testing of entire communities (Nelken and Andrews, 1999). The introduction of these new technologies often tends to be justified in terms of their ability to monitor 'risk' groups who pose a serious threat to society, but, once introduced, the concept of dangerousness is broadened to include a much wider range of offenders and suspects (see Pratt, 1999). Thus, the National DNA Database was originally established in the UK as a forensic source to help identify those involved in serious crimes, such as murder and rape, but an amendment to the Criminal Justice and Public Order Act 1994 allows samples to be taken without consent from any person convicted or *suspected* of a recordable offence (Home Office, 1999).

For some, these trends are indicative of a broader transition in structural formation from an industrial society towards a risk society (Beck, 1992). This concept is not intended to imply any increase in the levels of risk that exist in society but rather refers to a social formation that is organized in order to respond to risks. As Anthony Giddens observes, 'it is a society increasingly preoccupied with the future (and also with safety), which generates the notion of risk' (Giddens, 1998: 3). Beck himself defines risk in such a social formation as 'a systematic way of dealing with hazards and insecurities induced and introduced by modernisation itself' (1992: 21).

Human beings have always been subjected to certain levels of risk but modern societies are exposed to a particular type that is the outcome of the modernization process itself and, as a result, this has led to changes in the nature of social organization. Thus, there are risks such as natural disasters that have always had negative effects on human populations but these are produced by non-human forces. Modern risks, in contrast, are the product of human activity, and Giddens (1998) refers to these two different categories as *external* and *manufactured* risks. Risk society is predominantly concerned with the latter.

Because manufactured risks are the product of human agents, there is the potential to assess the level of risk that is being or about to be produced. The outcome is that risks have transformed the very process of modernization. Thus, with the introduction of human-caused disasters, such as Chernobyl (in the Ukraine)[1] and the Love Canal Crisis (in New York City),[2] public faith in the modernist project has declined, leaving only variable trust in industry, government and experts (Giddens, 1990). The increased critique of modern industrial practices has resulted in a state of reflexive modernization with widespread consideration given to issues of sustainability and the precautionary principle that focuses on preventative measures to reduce risk levels. Contemporary debates about global warming and the future of the planet should be seen in the context of debates about the risk society.

Social relations have changed significantly with the introduction of manufactured risks and reflexive modernization. Risks, much like wealth, are distributed unevenly in a population and, thus, differentially, influence the quality of life. People will occupy social risk positions they achieve through aversion strategies and that differ from wealth positions that are gained through accumulation. Beck (1992) proposes that widespread risks contain a 'boomerang effect', in that individual producers of risk will at the same time be exposed to them, which suggests, for example, that wealthy individuals whose capital is largely responsible for creating pollution will suffer when, for example, contaminants seep into the water supply. This argument might appear to be oversimplified, as wealthy people may have the ability to mitigate risk more easily, but the argument is that the distribution of the risk originates from knowledge as opposed to wealth.

Ericson and Haggerty argue that, in the area of criminal justice, we are witnessing a transformation of legal forms and policing strategies that reflect the transition to the risk society:

> Risk society is fuelled by surveillance, by the routine production of knowledge of populations useful for their administration. Surveillance provides biopower, the power to make biographical profiles of human populations to determine what is probable and possible for them. Surveillance fabricates people around institutionally established norms – risk is always somewhere on the continuum of imprecise normality.

(1997: 450)

McCahill and Norris (2002) observe that, in these circumstances, policing becomes increasingly proactive rather than reactive and – given that risk assessment is probabilistic rather than determinist – it requires the assignment of individuals and events to classificatory schemes, which provide differentiated assessment of risk and calls for management strategies. Returning to the predestined actor tradition, offenders are now classified as 'prolific' rather than merely opportunistic and, having been designated as such, the individual becomes a candidate for targeting by more intensive forms of technical or human surveillance. The emphasis on risk makes everyone a legitimate target for surveillance and 'everyone is assumed guilty until the risk profile assumes otherwise' (Norris and Armstrong, 1999: 25).

Developments in the contemporary youth justice system reflect these wider trends for social policy, often focusing on children 'at risk', and the management of that risk pervades every sphere of activity within the contemporary youth justice system. The commencement of intervention itself is regulated through a detailed assessment of risk through the Asset profile, which contains a scoring system that predicts the likelihood of offending and will determine the level of intervention and surveillance the young person will experience (Youth Justice Board, 2002; Hopkins Burke, 2008).

McCahill and Norris (2002) observe that many of the programmes of practical action that flow from strategies of 'risk management' in the criminal justice system are increasingly addressed not by central-state agencies such as the police, 'but beyond the state apparatus, to the organisations, institutions and individuals in civil society' (O'Malley, 1992; Fyfe, 1995; Garland, 1996: 451). Following the demise of the Keynesian Welfare State that had epitomized for many the high point in modernity in advanced capitalist nations (Hopkins Burke, 1999a), the emphasis on individuals managing their own risk finds converts from all parts of the political spectrum (Barry et al., 1996). Thus, Pat O'Malley (1992) writes of the emergence of a new form of 'prudentialism' where insurance against future risks becomes a private obligation of the active citizen. Responsibilization strategies are thus designed to offload the responsibility for risk management from central government on to the local state and non-state agencies, hence the increasing emphasis on public/private partnerships, inter-agency cooperation, intergovernmental forums and the rapid growth of non-elected government agencies. The composition of such networks allows the state to 'govern-at-a-distance' – to utilize the norms and control strategies of those formerly autonomous institutions identified by Foucault (1971, 1976) – while leaving 'the centralised state machine more powerful than before, with an extended capacity for action and influence' (Garland, 1996: 454).

It is in this context that Hopkins Burke has directed our attention not just to the increasing pervasiveness of policing in its various disguises in society (Hopkins Burke, 2004a), including the development of the contemporary youth justice system (Hopkins Burke, 2008), but also significantly to our own contribution in the legitimization of this state of affairs, and his neo-Foucauldian left realist variation on the carceral surveillance society proposes that, in a complex fragmented dangerous global risk society, it is *we* the general public – regardless of class location, gender or ethnic origin – that have a significant material interest in the development of that surveillance matrix invariably at an international level (and this argument is developed further in Chapter 23).

Penal modernism and postmodernism

— penology *advocate.*

The risk society thesis is – like the postmodern thesis – far from universally accepted by academics, with some recognizing the survival of significant aspects of penal welfarism – penal modernism (Garland, 1996, 2001) – and rejecting the whole notion that we have seen a significant penological break with the modernist past. Before we proceed to briefly review the literature from both sides of the theoretical debate on this issue, it will be useful to reflect on our previous observations about postmodernism. Those who propose that we are living in postmodern societies (Lyotard, 1984, 1988) tend to identify significant ruptures with the past and, indeed, those who follow the late modernity thesis (Giddens, 1990, 1991) are at risk of falling into the same methodological trap. The book has taken the postmodern condition route, which suggests that there are postmodern *tendencies* apparent that challenge the dominant modernist social formations but have far from replaced them, and, indeed, as the following review of the literature clearly demonstrates, they have very much survived, albeit sometimes in different forms.

Hallsworth and Lea (2008) observe that, with the huge expansion in prison populations in the English-speaking world during the last thirty years (particularly in the USA), it has become increasingly apparent to many penologists and sociologists that the state has taken 'a punitive turn' away from penal welfarism or modernism Thus, John Pratt proposes that such developments are indicative of a process of de-civilization which is occurring 'in late modernity' (Pratt, 2002, 2005); Loïc Wacquant (2004) observes a new way of governing poverty in post-welfare state societies involving a deadly symbiosis between ghetto and penitentiary; David Garland (1996, 2001) identifies a volatile response by the state to the arrival of perennially high-crime societies. Other elaborations and theorizations of aspects of the punitive turn include John Lea (2002, 2004) and Simon Hallsworth (2000, 2005).

These various contributors to the 'punitive turn' thesis come from very different theoretical backgrounds but tend to agree on the following observations. First, a punitive turn has occurred in the criminal justice systems of many advanced capitalist societies. Second, it appears to mark a significant rupture with the penal welfarism of earlier decades. Third, it is to be understood in the context of wider changes in the socio-economic structure and political dynamics of advanced capitalist societies in an era of globalization. Four, given the nature of this shift and the social costs involved, such developments are a cause for major concern. Hallsworth and Lea (2008) observe that, while none of those who have attempted to explain the punitive turn has argued that we are all punitive, or that punitive is the only available strategy currently in use, its presence does indicate a decisive shift in the orientation of criminal justice in advanced capitalist societies.

Other academics have been highly critical of various aspects of punitive turn theory. Pat O'Malley (2000) began the process with an attack on 'criminologies of catastrophe', a term subsequently adopted and applied by Steven Hutchinson (2006); Lucia Zedner (2002) has been extremely critical of Garland's version of the punitive turn (Garland, 2001), while Roger Matthews (2005) observes the 'myth of punitiveness'. Hopkins Burke (2008) challenges the widely held notion – indeed, new orthodoxy in critical youth justice circles – of punitiveness in the 'new' youth justice system, observing a restructuring of welfarism in the context of a left realist-inspired 'balanced intervention'. Hallsworth and Lea (2008) observe that what unites these different authors is a rejection of the whole idea of a punitive turn and the proposition that recent developments in social control are largely benevolent or benign, and can thus be conceptualized in terms of the continuation of penal welfarism or modernism.

The penal turn deniers produce four distinct sets of arguments. The first, exemplified by O'Malley and Hutchinson, argues that punitive turn theorists are, by and large, chasing an illusion and, in reality, traditional penal welfarism is alive and well. The second, argued by O'Malley (1999), proposes that criminal justice policies have always been 'volatile and contradictory' and that a diversity of recent developments can be identified, which have little to do with any punitive turn arising from core changes to the structure of advanced capitalist societies. Zedner, by contrast, argues that such core socio-economic changes may well have taken place but have little to do with crime or criminal justice, which is a relatively peripheral area of social relations. Finally, Matthews directly challenges the social cost aspects of the punitive turn, seeing recent changes in crime control as 'emancipatory' rather than punitive but certainly absorbed in the context of traditional penal welfarism. The common theme in all four of these arguments is the assumption that the momentous and far-reaching socio-economic transformations that are currently taking place throughout the world have had few consequences for crime and criminal justice. From this perspective, it is proposed that the latter continues to move along as a relatively unchanged aspect of state activity, or, if changing, then it is for the better.

Hallsworth and Lea (2008) observe that perhaps the most fundamental critique of the punitive turn thesis is that it simply has not occurred. Matthews (2005) argues that, for the thesis to hold, there must be clear evidence of punitive intent. If this assumption is granted, then of course it becomes possible to counter the thesis by arguing, for example, that the prison expansion in the USA can be better explained either by unintentional features integral to the operation of the criminal justice system – in this case the recirculation of penal subjects – or by push factors external to it – such as the imprisonment of people with mental health problems following the collapse of care in the community. As both these examples lack the required punitive intent, so the punitive turn thesis appears falsified. The problem here is that no version of the punitive turn thesis has ever relied on intentionality and why it should do so is unclear. It is quite possible to explain many of the punitive trends not as a direct attempt to induce more pain but as an unanticipated consequence of social actions that are not punitive but that nevertheless deliver punitive outcomes.

Hallsworth and Lea observe that the predominant form of counter-factual critique usually takes the form of a series of snapshots of aspects of current penal regimes – usually some mix of Canada, Australia, Scandinavia and the UK – to show that penal welfarism is alive and well (see, for example, Penna and Yar, 2003). The implied assumption is that such case studies are falsifying instances as far as punitive turn theory is concerned. Thus, for example, in a discussion of

Canada, Meyer and O'Malley conclude that 'Canadian criminal justice cannot be subsumed under a general model of a global punitive turn' (2005: 213). The implication is that general theories of a punitive turn must be rejected. If such phenomena do exist, then their explanation is conditional and localized.

Hallsworth and Lea (2008) observe that critique frequently takes the form of a simple snapshot purporting to demonstrate the continued dominance of penal welfarism in a particular country. There is no general attempt to show how the current socio-economic changes in the advanced capitalist societies facilitate the survival of penal welfare or indeed disprove the existence of those changes themselves. Maybe they do exist but they are only part of the story. Perhaps there are powerful counter-tendencies that sustain penal welfarism in the face of such changes. Maybe a punitive turn is only produced in certain circumstances or is one of a number of possible adaptations depending on the history of individual countries and political systems. Thus, for example, it is observed that the relationship between what Pratt (2000) calls 'ostentatious punishment', on the one hand, and, on the other, the rise of risk management (Feeley and Simon 1992) certainly needs further clarification.

Hallsworth and Lea observe that critics of the punitive turn thesis can, of course, use other ambiguities in the opposite direction to argue that apparent punitive shifts are, in fact, continuations of penal welfarism in another form. Kelly Hannah-Moffat thus argues that the apparent decline of penal welfarism in favour of risk management strategies ignores new hybrids of the two and what Garland and punitive turn theorists 'fail to explore in sufficient detail is how risk strategies have evolved and how rehabilitation has been revived as a central feature of risk/need management and penal control' (Hannah-Moffat, 2005: 30). She rejects any notion that rehabilitation has been displaced wholesale by the 'management in place' strategies first described by Feeley and Simon (1992). What has happened, she argues, is that the two have been amalgamated in the form of the orientation to the 'transformative risk subject' in which the aim of intervention is indeed to change/rehabilitate the offender but by contemporary methods associated with the identification and management of the 'criminogenic needs' of the offender rather than older, welfarist-inspired rehabilitation strategies. She points out that the new rehabilitative strategies are not relics of penal welfare but are firmly oriented to removing individuals from risk of offending by teaching them to manage their criminogenic needs within the resources available.

Rene van Swaaningen (2007) documents what most would consider one of the clearest and most decisive punitive shifts in recent years – the transformation of Dutch society from a liberal welfare state into a punishing state that has presided over a dramatic rise in its prison population. In so doing, he does not attempt to suggest that the punitive turn is the only strategy in existence in Dutch society, rather he shows how punitive developments do occur but in conjunction with – and by no means in contradiction to – the kind of preventative turn identified by Hughes (2007) as another key feature of 'late modern society'.

Hallsworth and Lea (2008) accept that the punitive turn thesis is not immune from criticism, and its main weakness, it can be argued, is its focus on the prison system. This is not wrong but it is only part of the overall picture. Thus a much wider and, therefore, more alarming sea change in criminal justice systems as a whole is under way. Much of it is associated with changes in criminal procedure in areas such as legal proof, sentencing policy and police powers. There seems a diminishing concern with civil liberties and a view that these must be obviously compromised in the name of combating organized crime (see Lea, 2004), terrorism and a more general rebalancing of the criminal justice system in favour of the victim. At the same time, there has been an expansion of coercive policing and forms of pre-emptive criminalization directed at marginalized groups (Hopkins Burke, 1998a, 2000, 2002, 2004a). There is a real feeling that those concerned with traditions of civil liberties, due process, non-intrusive police powers, as well as rising prison numbers are swimming against the stream, and we will return to debates about the development of the criminal justice system and in whose interest this has occurred in Chapter 23.

Globalization and crime

It is evident that theorists of risk, modernity and postmodernity see many of the processes they are discussing as global transformations and thus the concept of globalization is central to these new ways of thinking. The term is, however, used in different ways. A restricted meaning of globalization widely used proposes the process to be one of global market liberalization, the product of the last three decades. Other theorists use the term in a much broader historical perspective and where it refers to a much wider set of processes.

Kinnvall and Jonsson (2002) observe that the concept of globalization is very difficult to define precisely as it appears to be an all-embracing catchword of the contemporary world, covering everything from economic and political issues to the spread of Western culture to all points of the globe. Globalization is nevertheless invariably discussed in terms of three processes: scale, speed and cognition. Scale involves a discussion of magnitudes and refers to the number of economic, political, social and human linkages between societies at the present, which are greater than at any other time in history. Speed has to do with how globalization is conceptualized in time and space, and it is observed that this is not a new phenomenon but does involve a compression of time and space never previously experienced. Cognition refers to an increased awareness of the globe as a smaller place where events elsewhere may have consequences for our everyday political, social and economic lives, which may significantly impact on our sense of individual being.

Kiely and Marfleet (1998) define globalization in reference to a world where societies, cultures, politics and economics have in some sense come closer together, thus following Giddens (1964), who observed an intensification of worldwide social relations that link distant localities in such a way that local undertakings are shaped by events occurring many miles away and vice versa. Snyder (2002) conceptualizes globalization as an aggregate of multifaceted uneven, often contradictory economic, political, social and cultural processes which are characteristic of our time.

Johannen *et al.* (2003) note that there appears to be agreement in recent academic discussion that the term 'globalization' embraces the essence of historical movement, a triumph of neoliberal and characteristically Anglo-US ideology, being a more intense stage of capitalism, a confluence of events and technologies, or some combination of these. This Anglo-US ideology brings with it rapid transformations for business, government and, indeed, ordinary people. Findlay (2000) takes this further and views globalization in a social context as the progress towards one culture on the planet or a single interdependent society. In this definition, globalization is seen as a social process whereby the constraints of geography on social and cultural arrangements recede and people become increasingly aware of this recession. The common denominator of all these various different definitions appears to focus on the increasing degree of integration among societies that plays a crucial role in most types of social change.

A review of the literature shows that the following are considered to be critical global crimes: dealing in illicit drugs; illegal trafficking in weapons; illegal trafficking in human beings; money laundering; corruption; violent crimes including terrorism; and war crimes (Braithwaite, 1979; UNDP, 1999; Bequai, 2002; UNODC, 2013). Eduardo (2002) provides an example of the interlinking of transnational crimes where the 'vast poppy fields in eastern Turkey are linked to the heroin dealer in downtown Detroit', 'the banker laundering drug money in Vienna is in league with the thriving cocaine refineries in Colombia', 'the men of the Chinese triads who control gambling and extortion in San Francisco's Chinatown work the same network as the Singapore gang that turns out millions of fake credit cards' and 'the contract hit man who flies from Moscow to kill an uncooperative store owner in New York, on behalf of the Organisation, gets his fake papers by supplying the Sicilian Mafia with Soviet Army surplus ground-to-air missiles to smuggle into the Balkans to supply the Bosnian Serbs'.

The growing influence of organized crime has been estimated to gross $1.5 trillion a year and it is a significant rival to multinational corporations as an economic power. Global crime groups have the power to criminalize politics, business and the police, developing efficient networks, extending their reach deep and wide. All have operations ranging beyond national borders, and they are now developing strategic alliances, which are linked in a global network, reaping the benefits of globalization (UNDP, 1999). Crime syndicates prefer globalization, for it creates 'new and exciting opportunities, and among the most enterprising and imaginative opportunists are the world's criminals' (UNDP, 1999: 43). The UNDP thus observes that '[t]he illegal drug trade in 1995 was estimated at $400 billion, about 8% of world trade, more than the share of iron and steel or of motor vehicles, and roughly the same as textiles (7.5%) and gas and oil (8.6%)' (1999: 41).

There are now 200 million drug users throughout the world, and in the past twenty years the production of opium has more than tripled and that of the coca leaf more than doubled in order to meet the huge demand from this illicit market. The problem of drugs is thus not restricted to a few countries but is a global phenomenon and many armed conflicts taking place in different parts of the world may be financed by illegal sources including a significant element from drugs.

Buchanan (2004) observes that, as globalization has evolved, money launderers have been able to conduct their trade with greater ease, sophistication and profitability. As new financial instruments and trading opportunities have been created and the liquidity of financial markets has improved, it has also become possible for money-laundering systems to be set up and shut down with greater ease. The latter tend to allocate dirty money around the world on the basis of avoiding national controls and thus flow to countries with less stringent controls. Globalization has also improved the ability of money launderers to communicate using the Internet and travel, allowing them to spread transactions across a greater number of jurisdictions and, in doing so, has increased the number of legal obstacles that may hinder investigations. Underground or parallel banking systems have also attracted the attention of law-enforcement and regulatory agencies.

Braithwaite (1979) observes that global money laundering imposes significant costs on the world economy by damaging the effective operations of national economies and by promoting inadequate economic policies. The outcome is that financial markets slowly become corrupted and the confidence of the public in the international financial system is eroded. Eventually, as financial markets become increasingly risky and less stable, the rate of growth of the world economy is reduced.

Eduardo (2000) observes that corruption is a significant trait of global crime with the blurring of the boundary between state and criminal power making the fight against organized crime significantly more difficult. In the countries where organized crime has asserted its political or financial power, whether it is by greed or fear, state illegality has become endemic. Interestingly, low levels of corruption are seen to promote economic growth in certain regions, but at a higher level it inhibits growth and damages the economy. Bribes are socially damaging and politically destabilizing and are harmful for the growth prospects of host countries in that they can undermine the functioning of states, lower the efficiency of production, reduce competitiveness and introduce inequities (Ackerman, 2002). Corruption is not only damaging in itself but it also furthers other criminal activities, such as drug production and trafficking and the creation of safe havens for terrorists. Russia is an example of how corruption becomes a main factor in the expansion of organized crime (Eduardo, 2000).

Global crime groups have the power to criminalize politics, business and law-enforcement agencies, developing efficient networks and pervasively extending their reach. For example, in a study published in 2002, the United Nations estimated that human trafficking was a $5–7 billion operation annually with four million persons moved from one country to another and within countries (Raymond, 2002). The traffic in women and girls for sexual exploitation – 500,000 a year to Western Europe alone – was estimated to be a $7 billion business (UNDP, 1999), and it is a worldwide phenomenon that is becoming the fastest-growing branch of organized crime (Raymond, 2002). Reliable estimates indicate that two hundred million people may be under the control of traffickers of various kinds worldwide (Eduardo, 2002).

Globalization has greatly facilitated the growth of international terrorism. The development of international civil aviation has made hijacking possible,

420

television and the Internet have given terrorists worldwide publicity and modern technology has provided an impressive range of weapons and explosives (Eduardo, 2002). International terrorist organizations would nevertheless find it hard to operate and pose a challenge to any nation-state without media publicity and requisite funding. It is the money that they obtain from money laundering, credit card frauds, securities scams and much more, that enables international terrorists to traverse the globe at will, and buy the requisite equipment and armaments (Bequai, 2002). The threat of international terrorism is multiform. First, there is the traditional state-sponsored terrorism – which is a form of global organized crime – and this is also characterized as socio-political organized crime. Second, there is a new variant of freelance terrorists who constitute an even more frightening possibility because they are not sponsored by any particular state and are loosely affiliated with extremist and violent ideologies. These terrorists have proven to be all the more dangerous precisely because of their lack of organization and the difficulties associated with identifying them (Eduardo, 2002). Terrorism and terrorist motivations are discussed in more detail below.

Computer and related criminality – cybercrime – has become the phenomenon of the early twenty-first century and this has been created by the vast expansion of computers in the global economy, the rapid increase of their use in households and, in particular, the Internet and public access cable television. There are thus countless individuals with the capacity and intent to use the medium to inflict damage (Bequai, 2002). One of the largest industries utilizing the Internet is that of pornography, a business that is estimated to exceed a $100 billion annual turnover and one that terrorists have been quick to exploit as a source of income. With a minimal investment of funds, and working through corporate fronts and money men, terrorist organizations have been reaping billions of dollars annually from pornography (Bequai, 2002).

The illegal trafficking of weapons is a fast-expanding business that destabilizes societies and governments, arming conflicts in Africa and Eastern Europe. Light weapons, which have the most immediate impact on the lives of people, have been used in every conflict around the world, and have caused 90 per cent of war casualties since 1945. In El Salvador, the homicide rate increased 36 per cent after the end of the civil war, and, in South Africa, machine guns pouring in from Angola and Mozambique are being used in more and more crimes. In Albania, there were five times as many murders in 1997 as in 1996, a rise attributed to the illegal arming of civilians (UNDP, 1999).

Organized crime is not new but criminals have been taking advantage of fast-moving technological advances, overall globalization and the freedom of circulation, and the establishment of global markets. The acceleration of the liberalization of markets has been at least partly technology-driven and, with the rapid development of travel, global networks, electronic commerce and the information economy, it has been easy for people to trade and communicate. Financial activity, services and investments are becoming increasingly mobile. These developments provide opportunities for sustained improvements in economic performance but they also raise important new challenges in the form of globalized crime. Globalization has certainly brought countries closer together through technological innovation and the integration of financial markets. The ability to conduct trade has become substantially quicker and cheaper, and the global financial system now operates on a 24-hour basis. Globalization has increased levels of cross-border investment and brought about the transfer of technology, skills and knowledge across countries. It has significantly benefited participants not only in the legal economy but also in the illegal economy (Findlay, 2000).

Findlay (2000) explains the global explosion in crime and criminal activity in terms of the market conditions that are the outcome of the internationalization of capital, the generalization of consumerism and the unification of economies that are in a state of imbalance. He observes that power and domination are simply criminogenic. The new rules of globalization focus on the integration of global markets, and the needs of people that markets cannot meet are simply neglected. The process is thus concentrating power in the hands of the rich and already powerful, while accentuating the marginalization of both poor people and poor countries.

Susan George (1999) proposes that globalization is creating a three-track society, in which there are the exploiters, the exploited and the outcasts, the latter group being people who are not even worth exploiting. She argues that the current 'corporate-driven, neo-liberal globalization' results in increasing inequalities between rich and poor, both within and between countries. Many are marginalized, specifically in the less developed world with weak state institutions and fragile economies burdened by debt payments. George (1999) observes that those marginalized do not passively wait until they starve to death, but create their own means to survive, whether in the legal economy or in the illegal one and more often in the grey area that lies in between.

Globalization excludes segments of economies and societies from the networks of information available to the dominant society. Unemployment, alienation and youth abandonment, which make up what Castells (1998) calls the 'black holes of informational capitalism', provide the ideal terrain for criminal recruitment of, for example, global drug traffickers. This phenomenon is even more acute in Russia where, following the collapse of the Soviet Union, young people became an attractive labour pool for criminal organizations (Findlay, 2000; Eduardo, 2002). Findlay (2000) argues that the globalization of markets has profoundly transformed the structures of employment, distribution of wealth and consumption through modernization, development and urbanization. Such macro-economic transformations are, moreover, accompanied by significant global changes of societal norms and values, which influence the scope and nature of local and global crime (Le Billon, 2001; Eduardo, 2002; Mehanna, 2004). This may be a result of technological transfer, information transfer or immigration.

A further significant link in the globalization process is that of the media. For example, the globalization of a culture of violence has spread through the media and has become a major focus of popular culture, from children's cartoons to investigative journalism, and has been very influential on the pattern of local crime. The over-representation and legitimization of violence by the global media is thus compounded locally by the availability of guns, the institutionalization of

422

violence by criminal justice agencies, lax parental supervision and weak parental bonding. At the cultural level, these phenomena are connected with the general dissolution of traditional norms and values that characterize the current era of globalization (Funk, 2004).

A United Nations Office on Drugs and Crime (UNODC) (2013) audit of globalized criminality showed that the global crime trends identified above are still very much in existence with new profitable crimes emerging all the time. Transnational organized crime continues to be big business. Thus, in 2009, it was estimated to generate $870 billion, which is an amount equal to 1.5 per cent of global GDP. That is more than six times the amount of official development assistance for that year and the equivalent of close to 7 per cent of total world exports of merchandise.

Transnational organized crime encompasses virtually all serious profit-motivated criminal actions of an international nature where more than one country is involved. There are many activities that can be characterized as trans-national organized crime, including drug trafficking, smuggling of migrants, human trafficking, money laundering, trafficking in firearms, counterfeit goods, wildlife and cultural property, and even some aspects of cybercrime. It threatens peace and human security, leads to human rights being violated and undermines the economic, social, cultural, political and civil development of societies around the world. The vast sums of money involved can compromise legitimate econo-mies and have a direct impact on governance, such as through corruption and the 'buying' of elections.

The UNODC (2013) report observes that, every year, countless lives are lost as a result of organized crime. Drug-related health problems and violence, firearm deaths and the unscrupulous methods and motives of human traffickers and migrant smugglers are all part of this. Millions of victims are affected each year as a result of the activities of organized crime groups, with human trafficking victims alone numbering 2.4 million.

Transnational organized crime is not stagnant, but is an ever-changing industry, adapting to markets and creating new forms of crime. In short, it is an illicit business that transcends cultural, social, linguistic and geographical bound-aries and one that knows no borders or rules.

Drug trafficking continues to be the most lucrative form of business for crimi-nals, with an estimated annual value of $320 billion. In 2009, UNODC placed the approximate annual worth of the global cocaine and opiate markets alone at $85 billion and $68 billion, respectively (UNODC, 2013).

Human trafficking continues to be a global crime in which men, women and children are used as products for sexual or labour-based exploitation. While figures vary, an estimate from the International Labour Organization (ILO) in 2005 indicated the number of victims of trafficking at any given time to be around 2.4 million, with annual profits of about $32 billion (UNODC, 2013). However, more recent and precise estimates by the ILO on overall forced labour trends show that the scope of the problem is much greater than previously thought. Thus, in Europe, the trafficking of mostly women and children for sexual exploitation alone brings in $3 billion annually and involves 140,000 victims at any one time, with an annual flow of 70,000 victims.

The smuggling of migrants is a well-organized business moving people around the globe through criminal networks, groups and routes. Migrants can be offered a 'smuggling package' by organized crime groups, and the treatment they get along the route corresponds to the price they pay to their smugglers. In the process of being smuggled, their rights are often breached and they can be robbed, raped, beaten, held for ransom or even left to die in some cases, when the risks get too high for their smugglers. Many smugglers do not care if migrants drown in the sea, die of dehydration in a desert or suffocate in a container. Every year, this trade is valued at billions of dollars (UNODC, 2013). In 2009, some $6.6 billion was generated through the illegal smuggling of 3 million migrants from Latin America to North America, while the previous year 55,000 migrants were smuggled from Africa into Europe for a sum of $150 million.

Illicit trading in firearms brings in around $170 million to $320 million annually, and puts handguns and assault rifles in the hands of criminals and gangs. It is difficult to count the victims of these illicit weapons, but in some regions (such as the Americas) there is a strong correlation between homicide rates and the percentage of homicides by firearms.

Trafficking in natural resources includes the smuggling of raw materials such as diamonds and rare metals (often from conflict zones). The trafficking of timber in South-East Asia generates annual revenues of $3.5 billion. In addition to funding criminal groups, this strand of criminal activity ultimately contributes to deforestation, climate change and rural poverty.

The illegal trade in wildlife is another lucrative business for organized criminal groups, with poachers targeting skins and body parts for export to foreign markets. Trafficking in elephant ivory, rhino horn and tiger parts from Africa and South-East Asia to Asia produces $75 million in criminal profits each year and threatens the existence of some species.

Organized crime groups also deal in live and rare plants and animals threatening their very existence to meet demand from collectors or unwitting consumers. According to the WWF, traffickers illegally move over 100 million tons of fish, 1.5 million live birds and 440,000 tons of medicinal plants per year. The sale of fraudulent medicines is a worrying business, as it represents a potentially deadly trade for consumers. Taking advantage of the rising legitimate trade in pharmaceuticals from Asia to other developing regions, criminals traffic fraudulent medicines from Asia, in particular to South-East Asia and Africa, to the value of $1.6 billion. Instead of curing people, however, they can result in death or cause resistance to drugs used to treat deadly infectious diseases like malaria and tuberculosis. In addition to traditional trafficking methods, criminals continue to build a lucrative online trade in fraudulent medicines targeting developed and developing countries alike, which can also lead to health implications for consumers.

Cybercrime encompasses several areas, but one of the most profitable for criminals is identity theft, which generates around $1 billion each year. Criminals are increasingly exploiting the Internet to steal private data, access bank accounts and fraudulently attain payment card details.

While transnational organized crime is a global threat, its effects are felt locally. When organized crime gets a foothold, it can destabilize countries and entire regions, thereby undermining development assistance in those areas. Organized crime groups can also work with local criminals, leading to an increase in corruption, extortion, racketeering and violence, as well as a range of other more sophisticated crimes at the local level. Violent gangs can also turn inner cities into dangerous areas and put the lives of ordinary people at risk.

Southern theory

Australian academic Raewyn Connell (2007) has challenged the domination of social theory – and by implication criminological theory – by those in the metropoles of Europe and North America. She argues that this has entailed a view of the world from the skewed, minority perspective of the educated and the affluent, whose views are then perpetuated globally in educational curricula. The South appears in such global theories primarily as a source of data for Northern theorists rather than as sites of knowing and self-conscious social reflection, places where important social theories are also developed. Through a survey of nineteenth- and twentieth-century 'Southern theory' from Latin America, Iran, Africa, India and Indigenous Australia, Connell aspires to restore the fullness of the world to social science, to include its many voices in a more democratic global debate.

Connell highlights the global reach of early theorists like Comte, Spencer and Durkheim in their obsessions with the process of modernity, linking European ancients and contemporaneous 'primitives' in narratives of progress, debating the origins of human differences of race, gender and sexuality: 'sociology displaced imperial power over the colonised into an abstract space of difference' (Connell, 2007: 16), a claim that she observes is equally true of early anthropology (see Fabian, 1983). Connell suggests that the more restricted focus on industrialized metropolitan societies was linked to the professional growth of sociology in the USA, from the urban ethnography of the Chicago School to the abstract social theory of Talcott Parsons. Such modern 'general' theory, from Parsons through Coleman, Giddens and Bourdieu, aspires to universals, irrespective of time and place. Yet all such theories, albeit in different ways, fail to acknowledge the specificity of their ground of knowing, they 'read from the centre', with sweeping gestures of exclusion and grand erasures: 'whenever we see the words "building block" in a treatise of social theory, we should be asking who used to occupy the land' (Connell, 2007: 47).

Connell acknowledges that, while some social theorists like Giddens (2002), Hardt and Negri (2000) strenuously detach contemporary modernity from the colonial past, she, nevertheless, detects continuity and an enduring imperial gaze in much Northern theory. Thus, theories of globalization, translated from economics into sociology in the 1990s, too often witnessed the global spread of modernity through theoretical reifications of 'culture'. Connell expertly critiques the agonizing antinomies of such literature (global and local, homogeneity and difference, dispersal and concentration) as vortices in swirling debates. Claims about abstract linkages conceal the parochial power of the metropolis, while breathless declamations about tsunamis of global transformation become performative utterances constituting the very facts being researched. Again, the 'South' is a source of data but not of ideas.

Connell (2007) looks to the South as site, or rather sites, of social theory, extending from Australia, through Africa, Latin America, Iran and India. She starts with the early use of Spencer and Gillen's ethnography of Indigenous Australians in Durkheim's theory of elementary religion to the twentieth-century canon of Australian sociology, and shows how Australia, a rich if peripheral nation, has fed, and sometimes stretched, metropolitan debates in social theory. She affords a tantalizing glimpse of how Indigenous Australian social theory, as evinced in visual art practice, can illuminate modernity.

The Australian criminologist John Braithwaite (1989) provides an excellent example of the potential value of a Southern theory perspective to the wider criminological world with his concept of 'reintegrative shaming', which was introduced in some detail in Chapters 9 and 15. Braithwaite makes a crucial distinction between the negative stigmatic shaming, which he argues is central to criminal justice systems in the industrialized West (and indeed North), and the reintegrative shaming, which he proposes was central to the pre-colonial 'criminal justice' responses of the aboriginal tribes of Australasia. Stigmatic shaming, we are told, is counterproductive and drives stigmatized individuals into the welcoming arms of subcultural groups containing people just like themselves. Reintegrative shaming, on the other hand, is seen as likely to be effective in controlling crime. It means that the offence rather than the offender is condemned and the offender is reintegrated with – rather than rejected by – legitimate society. The problem has been the difficulty of putting this ideal of reintegrative shaming into practice, and serious questions have arisen about the applicability of the theory in contemporary industrialized societies, which does alert us to the possibility that even the best criminological lessons that can be learned from the traditional pre-colonial Southern societies may be difficult to apply in the urbanized twenty-first century. This of course is not necessarily the case and it is highly probable that there are significant criminological lessons to learn from societies outside the hegemonic North. We should watch developments in Southern theory with interest. Meanwhile, it is these power imbalances between North and South, tradition and dominant economic power, that provide fertile ground for terrorism and state violence.

Terrorism and state violence

On 11 September 2001, the terrorist group al-Qaeda carried out attacks on the World Trade Center in New York City and the Pentagon in Washington DC, causing thousands of casualties, and, in doing so, garnered inevitable widespread public support for what was to be an extensive authoritarian assault on civil liberties and human rights both in the USA and the UK. Further terrorist attacks on the allies of the USA, again involving large numbers of casualties – including those in Bali on 12 October 2002, in Turkey on 20 November 2003 and the London Transport System on 7 July 2005 – and subsequently the almost constant warnings by government of failed attempts and successful interventions by the security forces against terrorists invariably living in our midst, strengthened support for measures to protect society from such attacks (see Hopkins Burke, 2004c).

There is a well-known adage that 'one man's terrorist is another man's freedom fighter' and it is clear that those involved in the aforementioned al-Qaeda terrorist attacks undoubtedly considered their actions to be justified acts of war, just as the retaliatory strikes against Afghanistan and Iraq were subsequently considered just acts in the 'war against terrorism' by the governments of the USA, UK and their allies. Contemporary politicians go to great lengths to describe terrorists as being no different from common criminals but this has not always been the case. During the nineteenth century, Britain obtained a reputation for being a safe haven for political 'agitators' and refugees from Europe, but this situation was to change significantly during the following century when 'political criminals' were to become synonymous with 'terrorists' and abhorred by governments throughout the world.

'Terrorism' is an emotive word that emphasizes the extreme fear caused by apparently indiscriminate violent actions of individuals claiming to be operating on behalf of some particular cause. Sometimes terrorist activities are funded by states (state-sponsored terrorism) and the West has been keen to accuse countries such as Libya, Iran, (previously) Iraq and Syria of this. Western states have, on the other hand, supported terrorism when it has been in their political interests to do so, and thus during the Cold War backed many right-wing movements invariably as a bulwark against communism.

Israel also readily condemns terrorism but ironically the state itself came into being as the outcome of a terrorist campaign. One of the actions of the Jewish organization Irgun Zvai Leumi was to blow up the King David Hotel in Jerusalem in July 1946 without giving any warning, killing over seventy people, many of them British. The leader of Irgun, Menachem Begin, was sought by the British as a terrorist and a murderer and was sentenced to death in his absence. He was later to become Prime Minister of Israel and was awarded the Nobel Peace Prize in 1978. Similarly, Nelson Mandela spent over 25 years in prison for acts of terrorism and subsequently became President of South Africa within five years of his release, as well as a global icon.

Most of the major theories that seek to explain terrorism – and individual and group involvement – are derived from theories of collective violence developed in the field of political science. Terrorism is not a form of governance but anarchism is. Most anarchists reject terrorism but, in a theoretical sense, anarchism justifies such actions as a form of criminal action that attacks the values of an organized, complacent society. Anarchism is (as we saw in the previous chapter) a theory of governance that rejects any form of central or external authority, preferring instead to replace it with alternative forms of organization, such as shaming rituals for deviants, mutual assistance pacts between citizens, syndicalism (any non-authoritarian organizational structure that gives the greatest freedom to workers), iconoclasm (the destruction of cherished beliefs), libertarianism (a belief in absolute liberty) and straightforward individualism. Anarchism is often referred to as providing the nineteenth-century foundations of terrorism with the actual term first introduced in 1840 by Pierre-Joseph Proudhon. Other major nineteenth-century anarchist figures – such as Karl Heinzen and Johann Most – argued that murder, especially murder-suicide, constituted the highest form of revolutionary struggle and both advocated the use of weapons of mass destruction.

It was minor figures in the history of anarchism, such as Charles Gallo, Auguste Vaillante, Emile Henry and Claudius Konigstein, who advocated the influential idea that, to be most effective, the targets must be innocents – in places such as crowded dance halls or shopping centres – or symbols of economic success – like banks and stock exchanges. It is nevertheless important to note that present-day anarchists – and certainly not the anarchist criminologists such as Ferrell and Tifft, whom we encountered in the previous chapter – do not support terrorism. Moreover, it is important to recognize that only a small minority of terrorists have ever been anarchists, and only a small minority of anarchists have ever been terrorists.

Passmore (2002) proposes that fascism – a form of government with strong links to state-sponsored terrorism – can be defined as the consolidation of an ultranationalist ideology that is unashamedly racist. The word itself comes from the Latin 'fasces', which means to use power to scare or impress people, and it generally refers to the consolidation of all economic and political power into some form of super-patriotism that is devoted to genocide or endless war. So-called islamo-fascism has links with the birth of Nazi 'national socialist' fascism in 1928 when the Muslim Brotherhood (Al Ikhwan Al Muslimun, parent organization of numerous terrorist groups) was formed in reaction to the 1924 abolition of the caliphate by the secularist Turkish government. Passmore (2002) observes that the term 'Islamic Fascism' is a better term with which to describe the agenda of contemporary radical Islam, for this captures the twin thrusts of reactionary fascism. In one sense, fascism is born out of insecurity and a sense of failure, but in another sense it thrives in a once-proud, humbled but ascendant people. Envy and false grievances are the characteristics of such reactionary fascism, while believers are subject to all kinds of conspiratorial delusions that setbacks were caused by others and can be erased through ever more zealous action.

Fascism supports terrorism at home and abroad, and its inevitably charismatic leaders are usually given supreme powers to crack down on dissidents. With the frequent wars and militaristic ventures that come with fascism, an effort is made to demonize the enemy as sub-humans who deserve extinction, while, at the same time, they are transformed into scapegoats and blamed for all the past problems a country has experienced. Fascism simply appeals to the frustrations and resentments of an ethnic group of people who think they ought to have a bigger place at the global table. When combined with an anti-Western slant (the USA as the Great Satan, the UK the lesser Satan), fascism becomes a means of social identity (Pan-Africanism, Pan-Arabism, Islamo-Fascism) as well as a facilitator of terrorism.

Hoffman (1993) notes that about a quarter of all terrorist groups and about half of the most dangerous ones on earth are primarily motivated by religious concerns, believing that God not only approves of their action but also demands it. Their cause is thus sacred and consists of a combined sense of hope for the future and vengeance for the past. Of these two components, the backward-looking desire for vengeance may be the more important trigger for terrorism because the forward-looking component – called apocalyptic thinking or eschatology – tends to produce wild-eyed fanatics who are more a danger to themselves and their own people.

The successful use of terrorism in the name of religion rests upon convincing believers or the converted that a 'neglected duty' exists in the fundamental, mainstream part of the religion. Religious terrorism is, therefore, not about extremism, fanaticism, sects or cults, but is instead about a fundamentalist or militant interpretation of the basic tenets. Most religious traditions are filled with plenty of violent images at their core and destruction or self-destruction is a central part of the logic behind religion-based terrorism (Juergensmeyer, 2001). Stitt (2003) observes that evil is often defined as malignant narcissism from a theological point of view and religion easily serves as moral cover for self-centred terrorists and psychopaths. We should note that religion has always absorbed or absolved evil and guilt in what is called theodicy or the study of how the existence of evil can be reconciled with a good and benevolent God (Kraemer, 2004).

Economics has many concepts that are relevant to an understanding of terrorism, such as supply and demand, costs and benefits, and we saw in the first part of this book that rational choice theory has become a significant component of the contemporary variant of the rational actor model of crime and criminal behaviour, which proposes that people will engage in crime after weighing the costs and benefits of their actions. Criminals thus come to believe that their actions will be beneficial (to themselves, their community or society) and they must come to see that crime pays, or is at least a risk-free way to better their situation (Cohen and Felson, 1979). It is in this theoretical context that 'the Olson 1982 hypothesis' suggests that participants in revolutionary violence base their behaviour on a rational cost-benefit calculus to pursue the best course of action given the social circumstances (Olson, 1982). Rational choice theory, in political science, follows a similar line, and holds that people can be collectively rational, even when making what appear to be irrational decisions for them as individuals, after perceiving that their participation is important and their personal contribution to the public good outweighs any concerns they may have for the 'free rider' problem (Muller and Opp, 1986).[3]

Martha Crenshaw (1998) is a rational choice theorist who argues that terrorism is not a pathological phenomenon or aberration and that the central focus of study should be on why some groups find terrorism useful and conversely why other groups do not. Thus, some groups may continue to work with established patterns of dissident action, while others may resort to terrorism because they have tried other alternatives. Still other groups may choose terrorism as an early choice because they have learned from the experiences of others that alternative strategies do not work. Crenshaw (1998) calls the latter the contagion effect and claims it has distinctive patterns similar to the copycat effect in other theories of collective violence (Gurr, 1970). There may also be circumstances in which the terrorist group wants to publicize its cause to the world, a process Crenshaw (1995) calls the globalization of civil war.

Nassar (2004) argues that the processes of globalization contribute to dreams, fantasies and rising expectations, but, at the same time, lead to dashed hopes, broken dreams and unfulfilled achievements. He observes that terrorism breeds in the gap between expectations and achievements, and this is an argument resonant with Merton's version of anomie theory, which we encountered in the second part of this book. Indeed, we might observe that the only thing unique to this version of globalization theory is that it adds a rich–poor dichotomy. Thus, rich people – or nations – are seen as wanting power and wealth, and poor people – or nations – are seen as wanting justice. From this perspective, rich people are part of the causes of terrorism, since they contribute to the conditions that give rise to it, while the perpetrators are never seen as being born or socialized with any specific predispositions towards it. In short, globalization theory proposes that, if the oppressed and disgruntled poor people of the world were simply given the chance to find peaceful means for achieving justice, terrorism would not thrive.

Modern sociological perspectives are primarily concerned with the social construction of fear or panic and how institutions and processes, especially the media, primary and secondary groups, maintain that expression of fear. O'Connor (1994) makes use of a neo-functionalist framework to chart the way terrorism impacts on the whole of society by affecting core values of achievement, competition and individualism. Thus, some societies become 'softer' targets after terrorism – especially after short-term target hardening – and other societies become stronger in the long term. It depends upon interaction patterns, stabilities and interpenetrations among the structural subsystems (economy, polity, religion, law).

O'Connor (1994) identifies five contemporary sociological theories of terrorism. First, the *frustration-aggression hypothesis* proposes that every frustration leads to some form of aggression and every aggressive act relieves that frustration to some extent. Second, the *relative deprivation hypothesis* proposes that, as a person goes about choosing their values and interests, they compare what they have and do not have, as well as what they want or do not want, with real or imaginary others. The person then usually perceives a discrepancy between what is possible for them and what is possible for others, and reacts to it with anger or an inflamed sense of injustice. Third, the *negative identity hypothesis* proposes that, for whatever reason, a person develops a vindictive and covert rejection of the roles and statuses laid out for them by their family, community or society. Thus, a child raised in an affluent family might secretly sabotage every effort to give them a good start in life, until the day comes, with some apparent life-altering experience – like engaging in terrorism – when the long-nurtured negative identity comes to the fore, and the subject can then make it feel more like a total identity transformation. Fourth, the *narcissistic rage hypothesis* is a generic explanation for all the numerous things that can go wrong in child-rearing, such as too much mothering, too little mothering, ineffective discipline, overly stringent discipline, psychological trauma and coming from a broken home, which leads to a damaged self-concept and a tendency to blame others for our own inadequacies. Fifth, the *moral disengagement hypothesis* follows the work of David Matza on 'techniques of neutralization' (encountered in the second part of this book) and proposes the ways that a person neutralizes or removes any inhibitions they have about committing acts of horrific violence. Thus, some common patterns include imagining oneself to be a hero, portraying oneself as a mere functionary with limited – or diminished – responsibility, minimizing the harm done, dehumanizing the victim or insulating oneself in routine activities. O'Connor (1994) observes that organized crime figures, for example, usually hide behind family activities with their wives and children, although we should also be aware that there are numerous other ways that violence can be rationalized and neutralized (see Hacker, 1996). Terrorist rationalizations usually involve a complete shift in the way government and civil society is perceived by the individuals and groups concerned.

Psychological explanations of terrorism have tended – with a few exceptions (Ross, 1996, 1999) – to be clinical and invariably futile attempts to find something pathological in the terrorist personality. Merari (1990) provides a good overview of psychological approaches and factors that have been implicated in the formation of supposedly terrorist personalities, and these include the familiar explanations of ineffective parenting, rebellion against parents, a pathological need for absolutism and a variety of other 'syndromes' and hypotheses, which it is observed have yielded little valid and reliable information about the psychology of terrorists other than a few generalizations. There have been several promising attempts to merge or combine psychology with sociology (and criminal justice perspectives) into what might be called terrorist profiling (Russell and Bowman, 1977; Bell, 1982; Galvin, 1983; Strentz, 1988; Hudson, 1999). When suicide bombing came to the fore, Merari (1990) conducted interviews with terrorists and found that most who commit suicide attacks are between the ages of 16 and 28. Most are male, but 15 per cent are female with that proportion increasing. Many come from poor backgrounds and have limited education, but some have university degrees and come from wealthy families.

What sociological and psychological approaches basically tell us is that individuals join terrorist organizations in order to commit acts of terrorism, and that this process is the same as when individuals join criminal subcultures in order to commit acts of crime. Moreover, there appears to be no unique terrorist personality but there do appear to be unique subcultural phenomena that develop, support and enhance an enthusiasm for cold-blooded, calculated violence, which, if not satisfied within a terrorist organization, *might* well be fulfilled elsewhere. Terrorism is a social activity and individuals join a terrorist group usually after they have tried other forms of political involvement. The emotional links between individuals and the strength of commitment to their ideology appear to become stronger by the group living in the underground and facing adversity in the form of counterterrorism.

Socialization in the terrorist underground is quite intense and the identity of an individual may become tied to the identity of the group, but it is just as likely that emotional relationships become as important as – if not more important than – the purpose of the group. This means that the distribution of beliefs among members in a terrorist group may be uneven and there may be major differences between individual and group ideology (Ferracuti, 1982). Thus, ideology may not necessarily be the main component of motivation.

431

We have observed in our discussion above how some of the traditional criminological theories that we have encountered in the first four parts of this book – in particular, the US anomie tradition as developed via deviant subculture theories but also social control theories – have helped to explain why people join terrorist groups. In other words, this is part of a long-established criminological tradition that proposes that people choose to act in certain criminal ways because of where they are born and who they associate with, and this is as much applicable to involvement in terrorism as it is to the white-collar, professional and hate crimes we identified in the second part of this book. Ruggiero (2005) follows in this sociological criminological tradition and commences his discussion with Durkheim, and we should observe that the latter's notion of the 'normality of crime', which is functional to the requirements of society, is commensurate with an understanding of terrorist activity. Terrorist activities seem to make most sense at times of rapid social change (when there is a prevailing sense of normlessness or Durkheimian anomie) and when an unfair or forced division of labour is readily apparent to many.

Terrorism and postmodernism revisited

Whether or not the terrorist activities outlined above can be considered to be 'just' wars in terms of international law in any objective sense has been widely debated, but it does seem that these can be considered perfectly normal, albeit violent and extremely unpleasant activities, which make perfect subjective sense to the participants and the groups supporting them. The significance for our discussion of terrorism is that the events of 11 September 2001 – and those which followed – seemingly signposted the end for any positive notion of a postmodern society. From that date, the very idea of societies being founded on widely accepted and legitimate moral ambiguities where 'there are a range of different discourses that can be legitimate and hence right for different people, at different times, in different contexts' has become seriously problematic.

Postmodern societies can only function successfully if there is a reciprocal acceptance of diverse values from all participant groups. It was always a deeply problematic notion in societies with a very pronounced 'forced-division-of-labour' (Durkheim, 1933) and it appears seemingly impossible when groups become so totally opposed to the values and activities of others that they are prepared to use any means to destroy them. At that point, such groups become enemies and anyone – however tangentially associated with them – will become a legitimate target for surveillance and risk assessment. Government cannot afford not to take the issue of state security seriously and the notion of the risk society becomes entrenched and virtually unassailable in public policy discourse.

Policy implications of crime, globalization and the risk society

Hazel Kemshall observes that '[t]he identification, assessment, prevention and management of risk have become big business in crime policy, practice and research' and have become the dominant orthodoxy throughout the local contemporary criminal justice system (2003: 1). However, the domination of a 'risk-based' approach to criminal justice matters does not also mean that such strategies are popularly supported, or actively demanded from below. Yet, the existence of a 'mass risk consciousness' (O'Malley, 2004: 185) is continually asserted as though it were the mainspring of the strategic direction of contemporary crime control. It is certainly common for politicians to present legislative or policy change in terms of being responsive to public concern about risk, and this is especially evident in relation to the management of serious sexual and violent offenders. If we agree with Mick Ryan (2003) that the rise of the public voice(s) within the national and local politics of risk democratizes the policy-making process, then it is clearly important to ensure that such voices are heard in their complexity and diversity. Crime – and risk – is nevertheless a far from local affair in the twenty-first century and is closely linked to the growth and expansion of the global economy.

Globalizing policies since the 1990s have fostered the creation of a global marketplace in which labour, capital, and goods and services cross borders more freely than in the past. However, these policies also have had the unintended consequence of strengthening the power of global organized crime networks. Globalization has facilitated human trafficking, narcotics smuggling, computer crimes and other offences and the outcome of these trends has required greater global cooperation among criminal justice systems around the world.

One of the major shortcomings of market-based capitalism is that it is open to corrupt influences and encourages undesirable behaviour by providing a profit for meeting a demand. Thus, as long as there is a demand for narcotics, human servitude, and other illicit goods and services, there will be a market in human misery. Given the global nature of the monetary system, one might expect an international effort to harmonize its regulation and, to a certain extent, this is happening, but, for worldwide agreement to be reached, it will be necessary to sacrifice some national interests, which are not currently readily conceded in international negotiations.

The future does suggest a greater degree of international cooperation in dealing with globalized crime with military establishments perhaps offering more support for policing efforts with concurrent concerns that 'due process' interventions will be sacrificed for the expediency of 'crime control' strategies. Modern terrorism has blurred the boundary between war and peace, and modern organized crime has blurred the distinction between law-enforcement activities and military operations.

The process of globalization is not yet complete but, as an integrated system of trade and finance, it has become very developed. The problems that we currently face with globalization as a process are the result of a system of trade and finance that has developed faster than the regulatory framework in which trade occurs. As we move into the future, we can expect to see the regulatory framework develop in accordance with the new reality of global trade and finance.

The 'war on terror' needs to focus on more than just transnational terrorism, because domestic terrorism – and home-grown terrorists – pose a greater threat in terms of lives and property loss than the former. This is also true because domestic terrorism tends to spill over into transnational terrorism as local terrorists seek greater world recognition.

For transnational terrorism, enhanced defensive counterterrorism precautions and the increasing dominance of religious fundamentalist terrorists have made the hardest-to-defend private targets the most popular. The changing targeting of transnational and domestic terrorists has made public places – shopping malls, department stores, public squares, public transport, sporting events – likely attack venues. For domestic terrorism, private parties have been the prime target for thirty years. Targeting differences between domestic and transnational terrorism can inform the allocation of security resources.

For all target types, there is an increased targeting of people over property, which makes defensive security measures more challenging. As defensive action becomes more difficult and costly, more resources must be put into proactive measures that dismantle terrorist groups and their infrastructure, and discourage membership of extremist groups. More radical measures will be those that target global inequalities and lead to a more equal global division of labour and thus remove the substantive motivation for terrorist involvement.

Summary of main points

1. Criminologists have drawn upon the 'governmentality' literature in order to explore the links between contemporary neoliberal political policy and the growing use of 'actuarial' or 'risk-based' strategies of crime control.
2. For most of the twentieth century, crime control was dominated by the 'treatment model' and was closely aligned to the powerful and benevolent state, which was obliged to intervene in the lives of individual offenders and seek to diagnose and cure their criminal behaviour.
3. Garland (1996) has argued that the new governmental style is organized around 'economic forms of reasoning', which is reflected in contemporary rational actor theories that view crime as simply a matter of opportunity and that require no special disposition or abnormality.
4. Feeley and Simon (1994) propose that these changes are part of a paradigm shift from the 'old penology' (penal welfarism) to the 'new penology' (risk management), and for some these trends are indicative of a broader transition from an industrial society towards a risk society (Beck, 1992).
5. The risk society thesis is far from universally accepted by academics with some recognizing the survival of significant aspects of penal welfarism and some academics rejecting the whole idea of a punitive turn and proposing that recent developments in social control are largely benevolent or benign.
6. Theorists of risk, modernity and postmodernity see many of the processes they are discussing as global transformations.
7. Global crime groups have the power to criminalize politics, business and the police, developing efficient networks, and their reach has extended deep and wide.

8. Cybercrime has become the phenomenon of the early twenty-first century and has been created by the vast expansion of computers in the global economy and private households.
9. Connell (2007) has challenged the domination of social theory – and by implication criminological theory – by those in the metropoles of Europe and North America.
10. Most of the major theories that seek to explain terrorism are derived from theories of collective violence developed in the field of political science. Crenshaw (1998) argues that terrorism is not a pathological phenomenon and the focus of study should be on why some groups find terrorism useful and other groups do not.

Discussion questions

1. What are the differences between the 'old penology' and the 'new penology'?
2. Explain the concept of the risk society as it is applied to crime and criminal justice.
3. What are 'penal turn' theories and what are the criticisms of these?
4. What is Southern theory?
5. How is terrorism explained by political science?

Suggested further reading

The notion of risk society in general is discussed by Beck (1992) and the significance of this analysis for controlling crime and the notion of governance with the decline of the sovereign state by Garland (1996). For an excellent discussion of 'actuarial justice' and 'risk society' as applied to criminal justice see O'Malley (1992), Feeley and Simon (1994) and Ericson and Haggerty (1997). Giddens (1994, 1998) attempts to square the circle between the postmodern condition (for him, late modernity), left realism and the 'third way' political strategy of New Labour. Hopkins Burke (2004a) discusses the pervasiveness of multi-agency 'policing' in contemporary societies and apparently contradictory demands for security and human rights. Hopkins Burke (2008) discusses the emergence and establishment of the contemporary youth justice system in the context of a risk society. Findlay (2000) provides an excellent introduction to the globalization of crime and criminality, and Ruggiero (2005) provides an equally fine socio-criminological discussion of terrorism.

Notes

1 The Chernobyl disaster was an accident at the Chernobyl Nuclear Power Plant on 26 April 1986, consisting of an explosion at the plant and subsequent radioactive contamination of the surrounding geographic area (see Davidson, 2006).

2 Love Canal is a neighbourhood in Niagara Falls, New York, the site of the worst environmental disaster involving chemical wastes in the history of the USA (see Mazur, 1998).

3 The 'free rider' problem is a classic paradox in social science and economics, which asks why anybody should do something for the public good when most likely someone else will get credit for it and everybody else will benefit merely by sitting idly and doing nothing.

22. Radical moral communitarian criminology

Key Issues

1. The communitarian agenda
2. Radical egalitarian communitarianism
3. The concept of community reconsidered
4. Durkheim, social solidarity and the French conception of individualism
5. Radical moral communitarian criminology

This fifth part of the book has discussed ways of explaining crime and criminal behaviour in a contemporary era permeated by moral ambiguity and where there have been increasing doubts about the sustainability of the modernist project in an increasingly fragmented, complex and diverse social world. Central to the notion of the postmodern condition, there has been the recognition of a range of different discourses that can be legitimate and hence right for different people, at different times, in different contexts, and where the notion of the objective truth (or the competing objective realities) of modernity has been replaced by recognition of the multiple realities or moral ambiguities of postmodernity. Many postmodernists have indeed celebrated the failure of the modernist project to establish rational foundations for knowledge and have wholeheartedly embraced this trend towards human diversity and social fragmentation.

It was nevertheless observed in the previous chapter that postmodern societies can only function successfully if there is reciprocal acceptance of diverse values from all participant groups and it has become perfectly clear that this reciprocity of goodwill does not exist outside of predominantly bourgeois intellectual circles in some of the more affluent societies on this planet. At the same time, a whole range of significant risks, some of which have been chronicled in this fifth part of the book – and of which traditional crime patterns and motivations are only part – have arisen in contemporary global but fragmented society, which threaten the health and survival of our social existence in its present form. Global terrorism has significantly focused our thoughts on these issues and (as observed in the previous chapter) government cannot afford to take serious risks with state security in such circumstances, so the inevitable outcome is expansion of the carceral and surveillance society that we collectively not only welcome but actively encourage (Hopkins Burke, 2004a, 2008), and which will be discussed further in the following chapter.

If the regular terrorist atrocities that have occurred throughout the world during the first two decades of the twenty-first century have ended any legitimate notion of a postmodern society, there would, on the other hand, seem no justifiable basis for a return to the moral certainty of high modernity. Undoubtedly, the governments of the USA and the UK have sought to present to the world a new moral certainty but the many socio-economic and political circumstances that have come to constitute the postmodern *condition* have continued to exist and thus legitimate alternative moral certainties are available. This author has previously observed that UK government support for President Bush did not actually embrace the whole neoconservative package of criminal justice interventions – or, for that matter, other public policy pronouncements – that had come to dominate official discourse in the USA in the previous few years (Hopkins Burke, 2005, 2009). There had been at that time the recent re-election of a neoconservative government, with an apparent mandate for the creation of tough right realist policies, and thus mounting a challenge to these seemed to be an appropriate strategy for liberal or critical criminologists in the USA and beyond.

The eminent liberal and left realist US criminologist Elliott Currie (1999) had done just that and had questioned the 'triumphalism' that had greeted the supposed fall in crime levels in a number of Western countries – but in particular the USA – during the 1990s. He observed that the celebrations were not so much premature as self-delusionary in that the decline in crime levels was, in fact, measured against baselines that were already astronomically high. Crime in the USA remained very much a reality and had merely returned to levels that were unacceptably high in the mid-1980s. Moreover, the fall in the crime rate could not be attributed simply to the new order in law enforcement exemplified by more imprisonment (deterrence and incapacitation) and tougher policing (crime control and zero tolerance), which had been introduced by the neoconservatives. Evidence of brutality and differential policing practices – particularly in relation to African-Americans and Hispanics in the inner city – not to mention the manipulation of official police statistics, had been identified as some of the negative consequences of these policies (see Hopkins Burke, 2002). Currie observed that this new triumphalism has gradually displaced the idea that socio-economic conditions need to be addressed if social order is to be maintained: 'The flip-side [of triumphalism] being that we've also proven that you don't, after all, need to address such problems as poverty and social exclusion or other supposed "root causes", of violent crime' (1999: 3).

Currie thus proposed two ways in which criminologists could play a more effective role in bringing about positive change in the socio-legal domain:

> The first is to push, and push relentlessly, to ensure that this nation makes those preventative social investments that can reduce violent crime in enduring and humane ways, rather than simply suppressing it, hiding it, or denying it . . . The second is to end the systems abuse in our institutions so

that they can be devoted to 'rebuilding' the lives of people in constructive and humane environments.

(1999: 6)

Currie thus called for criminologists to encourage the development of more family support programmes, improved programmes for prison inmates, and targeted anti-poverty initiatives, while clearly challenging the extremes of neoconservative judicial policy:

If there's one task that we as professional criminologists should set for ourselves in the new millennium, it's to fight to ensure that stupid and brutal policies that we know don't work are – at the very least – challenged at every forum that's available to us.

(Currie, 1999: 7)

We are living through undoubtedly difficult socio-economic times (an issue to which we will return in more detail in the concluding chapter) and it is both easy and understandable to be negative and disillusioned in such circumstances but, at the same time, there seemed great possibilities for a reformulated new-liberal criminological agenda – indeed, as part of a wider new-liberal public policy agenda – that could gather support across a wide and diverse section of the population, not just in the USA and the UK. It was previously observed by this author that the left realist approach that concluded the fourth part of this book (and was endorsed by Elliott Currie) is far from antagonistic to that new-liberal agenda (Hopkins Burke, 2005, 2009).

The theoretical foundations of left realism are of course firmly located in the modernist tradition and it is the undoubted explicit intention of left realists to build a new moral certainty – or even a new teleological project – from the contemporary condition of moral uncertainty. It was observed that a new left realist moral certainty would demand as a baseline a substantial reduction in socio-economic inequality and, at the same time, recognition and celebration of the diversity of the postmodern condition but not the apparent uncontrollable anarchy and acceptable inequalities of moral ambiguity or the rigid authoritarianism and brutalities of neoconservatism.

The left realist strategy *implicitly* suggests an enthusiasm for the postmodern notion of rejecting grand theoretical solutions and a willingness to consider explanatory elements from all perspectives in an attempt to provide a comprehensive intervention against crime. It is thus recognized that most criminological theories have something legitimate to say about some forms of crime and criminal behaviour and, thus, due consideration should be given to these in the *appropriate* circumstances.

It was a strategy that seemed to be in harmony with the election of a 'New' Labour Government in 1997, which had proposed a 'new politics' beyond doctrinal dogma and which appeared to be willing to consider policy options from a wide range of perspectives. This strategy that – while not entirely non-ideological and undoubtedly part of a much wider strategy of attempting to build a new moral certainty – fundamentally recognized that good ideas, and, for that matter, bad ones, are not the preserve of one side of the traditional left/right political dichotomy. They can emerge from many different sources and there can be a diverse range of motivations for implementing a policy or strategy (Giddens, 1994, 1998). In terms of criminology, this 'third way' would appear to be a sensible long-term approach to both understanding crime and criminal behaviour in all its many manifestations and for the development of flexible strategies for dealing with what this book has clearly demonstrated to be a multifaceted and far from straightforward social problem. For this to be a successful and a widely accepted long-term strategy that survives the vagaries of the electoral system, it must nevertheless embrace the essential tenets of a contemporary new-liberalism where there is respect for the rights and *responsibilities* of both individuals and *communities*, while, at the same time, recognition that crime is a real problem that impacts hugely and negatively on the lives of real people, be they victims or offenders, and that it is not thus inappropriate or illiberal to intervene in such activities or deal with the consequences of those actions in a rigorous way. These ideas are of course similar to those of the communitarian philosophy that emerged in the USA in the last quarter of the twentieth century.

The communitarian agenda

Communitarianism emerged in the USA during the 1980s as a response to what its advocates considered to be the limitations of liberal theory and practice. Significantly, diverse strands in social, political and moral thought, arising from very different locations on the political spectrum – such as Marxism (Ross, 2003) and traditional 'one-nation' conservatism (Scruton, 2001) – can be identified within this body of thought. The dominant themes are: (1) the individual rights that have been vigorously promoted by traditional liberals need to be balanced with social responsibilities; and (2) autonomous individual selves do not exist in isolation but are shaped by the values and culture of communities. Communitarians thus propose that, unless we redress the balance towards the pole of community, our society will continue to become normless, self-centred and driven by special interests and power seeking.

This critique of the one-sided emphasis on individual civil or human rights promoted by liberalism is the key defining characteristic of communitarianism, for it is observed that rights have tended to be asserted without a corresponding sense of how they can be achieved or who will pay for them. 'Rights talk' is thus seen to corrupt political discourse, impedes genuine discussion and is employed without a corresponding sense of responsibilities (see Emanuel, 1991; Glendon, 1991; Etzioni, 1993, 1995a, 1995b). Communitarians nevertheless do encourage the preservation of traditional liberal rights and their extension in non-democratic regimes – or those that practise discrimination – but propose that these rights need to be located in a more balanced framework.

Communitarians argue that the one-sided emphasis on rights in liberalism is related to the individual as a 'disembodied self' who has been uprooted from cultural meanings, community attachments and the life stories that constitute the full identities of real human beings. Dominant liberal theories of justice, as well as much of economic and political theory, presume such a self (see Etzioni, 1993). Communitarians, in contrast, shift the balance and argue that the 'I' is constituted through the 'We' in a dynamic tension. Significantly, this is not, in terms of this purist form of communitarianism, an argument for the restoration of traditional community, with high levels of mechanical solidarity, repressive dominance of the majority or the patriarchal family, although some on the conservative fringes do take up that position. Mainstream communitarians are, in fact, critical of community institutions that are authoritarian and restrictive and that cannot bear scrutiny within a larger framework of human rights and equal opportunities, and they accept the (post)modern condition argument that we are located within a complex web of pluralistic communities – or organic solidarity – with genuine value conflicts within them and within selves.

Amitai Etzioni, Mary Ann Glendon and William Galston (1991) outlined the basic framework of communitarianism, urging that the focus should be on the family and its central role in socialization, and thus propose that employers should provide maximum support for parents through the creation of work-time initiatives – such as the provision of crèche facilities – and they warn us against avoidable parental relationship breakdowns, in order to put the interests of children first:

> The fact is, given the same economic and social conditions, in poor neighbourhoods one finds decent and hardworking youngsters next to antisocial ones. Likewise, in affluent suburbs one finds antisocial youngsters right next to decent hardworking ones. The difference is often a reflection of the homes they come from.
>
> (Etzioni, 1995b: 70)

Etzioni refers to the existence of a 'parenting deficit' in contemporary Western societies where self-gratification is considered as much a priority for many parents as ensuring that their children are properly socialized and instilled with the appropriate moral values that act as protection against involvement in criminality and antisocial behaviour. The outcome is both inevitable and disastrous:

> Juvenile delinquents do more than break their parents' hearts. They mug the elderly, hold up stores and gas stations, and prey on innocent children returning from school. They grow up to be useless, or worse, as employees, and they can drain taxpayers' resources and patience . . . Therefore, parents have a moral responsibility to the community to invest themselves in the proper upbringing of their children, and communities – to enable parents to so dedicate themselves.
>
> (Etzioni, 1995b: 54)

In the UK, Dennis and Erdos (1992) explain the 'parenting deficit' in terms of the liberalization of sexual mores that has been endemic in Western societies since the 1960s. They observe that the illegitimate children of single parents do less well on several fronts with young males becoming involved in criminal behaviour because of the absence of a positive male role model, while, at the same time, the whole project of creating and maintaining the skills of fatherhood is being abandoned and lost.

Communitarians thus seek to reverse these trends and demand a revival of moral education in schools at all levels, including the values of tolerance, peaceful resolution of conflict, the superiority of democratic government, hard work and saving. They also propose that government services should be devolved to an appropriate level, with the pursuit of new kinds of public–private partnerships, and the development of national and local service programmes. These ideas were to become very influential and were to filter into the Clinton administration during the 1990s and beyond, and, in a pamphlet written shortly after he became Prime Minister of the UK, Tony Blair demonstrated his communitarian or 'third way' credentials:

> We all depend on collective goods for our independence; and all our lives are enriched – or impoverished – by the communities to which we belong. . . . A key challenge of progressive politics is to use the state as an enabling force, protecting effective communities and voluntary organisations and encouraging their growth to tackle new needs, in partnership as appropriate.
>
> (1998: 4)

The most familiar and resonant of the 'abstract slogans' used by Blair in the promotion of the importance of community was the idea that rights entail responsibilities and this was taken from the work of Etzioni (1993). In contrast to the traditional liberal idea that members of a society may simply be entitled to unconditional benefits or services, it is proposed from this perspective that the responsibility to care for each individual should be seen as lying, first and foremost, with the individuals themselves.

For Blair and his sociological guru Anthony Giddens (1998), community is invoked very deliberately as residing in *civil society*: in lived social relations, and in 'common-sense' notions of our civic obligations. The 'third way' is presented as avoiding what its proponents see as the full-on atomistic egotistical individualism entailed by the Thatcherite maxim that 'there is no such thing as society', and, on the other hand, the traditional social-democratic recourse to a strong state as the tool by which to realize the aims of social justice, most notably that of economic equality. For Blair, 'the grievous twentieth century error of the fundamentalist Left was the belief that the state could replace civil society and thereby advance freedom' (1998: 4). He thus came to acknowledge that the state has a role to play, but as a facilitator, rather than a guarantor, of a flourishing community life.

Dissenters have observed that the implementation of the New Labour agenda was to take a somewhat different course with its character rather more authoritarian (and, thus, centred more on the usage of the state apparatus to deliver particular outcomes) than is suggested by the rhetorical appeal to the relatively autonomous powers of civil society to deliver progress by itself (see Driver and Martell, 1997; Jordan, 1998). Hughes (1998) thus refers to the communitarianism of Etzioni and his acolytes – and pursued enthusiastically by governments in both the USA and the UK – as moral *authoritarian* communitarianism and calls for a more radical non-authoritarian variant.

Radical egalitarian communitarianism

Radical egalitarian communitarians such as Bill Jordan (1992, 1996), Elliott Currie (1993, 1996, 1997) and Jock Young (1999) focus on inequality, deprivation and the market economy as causes of crime and promote policies to eliminate poverty, which they define as a degree of deprivation that seriously impairs participation in society. Jordan (1992) has argued persuasively that, in recent years, in the UK and similar Western societies we have witnessed deterioration in social relations due to the poor being denied access to material goods and thus their experience of power is simply one of it being unjust. He observes that, following the major socio-economic transformation that occurred during the last twenty years of the twentieth century, there has been the formation of two very different opposing communities of 'choice' and 'fate'. On the one hand, 'communities of choice' are those where individuals and families have developed income security strategies, which are associated with comfortable 'safe', convenient, healthy and status-giving private environments. On the other hand, 'communities of fate' are those bound together into long-term interdependencies because of lack of opportunities to move geographical location, gain access to good education or healthcare, get decently paid legitimate ('on-the-cards') employment and share in the cultural enjoyments of mainstream society.

Jordan argues the need for an unconditional basic income for all citizens as one specific means of sharing out the common good in a more equitable fashion, although he accepts that on its own this is no policy panacea. Nevertheless, the provision of a basic income for all would also open up the possibility for individuals and groups to participate in their own chosen projects and commitments and, moreover, such a scheme would reduce the institutionalized traps and barriers to labour market participation that undermine legitimate efforts by members of 'communities of fate' to rejoin mainstream society. From this perspective, we return to the critical criminology agenda we encountered in the third part of this book, where it is argued that marginalization, inequality and exclusion provide the foundations for much crime and antisocial activity. As a consequence, the radical *egalitarian* communitarian agenda for crime prevention gives ethical priority to decisions about the redistribution of resources, which allows all members an opportunity to share adequately in the life of the community on an equal basis. This is clearly a laudable agenda but this contribution does raise the question as to whether the state has to first 'repair' the social wounds before 'the community' can be allowed to participate in an inclusive politics of crime control and social justice.

Elliott Currie (1985, 1993, 1996, 1997) has made a significant contribution to the radical communitarian debate on crime, disorder, the decline of communities in the USA and the left realist programme on crime prevention, and argues that the most serious problem in the contemporary USA is that the most disadvantaged communities are sinking into a permanent state of terror and disintegration in a society dominated by the market and consumerism. Currie (1993) outlines the complex deprivations of life in the inner city and the failure of the state to respond humanely to the drug crisis by instead implementing a mass programme of incarceration and incapacitation, while at the same time introducing huge cutbacks in welfare expenditure. He argues that what characterizes the 'under-class' in the USA is a 'surplus of vulnerability' exacerbated by the pervasive movement towards a more deprived, more stressful, more atomized and less supportive society, observing that many parents in the deprived communities are overwhelmed by multiple disadvantages and are in no position to counter the effects of family crises on their children.

Currie observes that the 'triumph' of the market society has created deprived communities characterized by the destruction and absence of legitimate liveli-hoods, significant extremes of economic inequality, the increasing withdrawal of public services, the erosion of informal/communal support networks, the spread of a materialistic and neglectful culture, the unregulated marketing of a tech-nology of violence and a weakening of social and political alternatives:

> The policies of the seventies and eighties, then, did more than merely strip individuals of jobs and income. They created communities that lacked not only viable economic opportunities, but also hospitals, fire stations, movie theatres, stores, and neighbourhood organizations – communities without strong ties of friendship or kinship, disproportionately populated by increasingly deprived and often disorganised people locked into the bottom of a rapidly deteriorating job market. In many cities these disruptive trends were accelerated by the physical destruction left by the ghetto riots of the 1960s or by urban renewal projects and freeways that split or demolished older, more stable neighbourhoods and dispersed their residents.
>
> (Currie, 1993: 70)

Radical communitarians like Currie are thus arguing that behind the growth of crime is a cultural, as well as a structural transformation of poor communities, and in this regard there are some common themes between Etzioni and the radi-cals. The situation has certainly not improved in the intervening years and, in some geographical locations, we can observe communities where there are three or four generations of welfare claimants with little or no experience of the legiti-mate labour market. The reintegration of these socially excluded groups into mainstream society was an essential and laudable New Labour strategy termed 'reintegrative tutelage' (Hopkins Burke, 1999a) and discussed in Chapter 18. Although clearly there have been some success stories, this was ultimately a flawed strategy scuppered not least by the unremitting ravages of the market economy.

Hall *et al.* (2008) have conducted a study of the criminal patterns and criminals living on the alienated housing estates of the North East of England, where in some cases there was no one in employment. The researchers observe that the significant economic downturn of the 1980s was more than a mere structural adjustment for those living in these communities. Rather, it was a radical shift in political economy and culture, a move to the unprecedented domination of life by the market, which was to create a large number of locales in permanent recession in both the UK and the USA. Hall *et al.* observe that:

> The criminal markets developing in these areas now tend to operate in the relative absence of the traditional normal insulation . . . regarded as essential to the restraint of the inherently amoral and social logic that lies at the heart of the liberal-capitalist market economy.
>
> (2008: 3)

The researchers pointedly observe that, contrary to the arguments presented by some, the 1980s was not a time of vigorous progressive cultural change, at least not in those large brutalized and inherently criminogenic communities in which they conducted their research. Indeed, we might well ask ourselves whether communities are inevitably the supportive protectors and focus of transformation that they are sometimes thought and proposed to be by some in the literature.

The concept of community reconsidered

Some commentators argue that communities can be restored and revitalized through the provision of community justice and restorative justice mechanisms and thus facilitate strong bonds of social control that are perceived as being legitimate and acceptable to their members. Strang sums up this viewpoint pertinently: 'strong communities can speak to us in moral voices' and they allow 'the policing by communities rather than the policing of communities' (1995: 20). Braithwaite (1989: 100) observes that these informal control processes such as reintegrative shaming (which we have encountered elsewhere in this book) are significantly more effective in communitarian cultures, but, at the same time, observes that in urban, individualistic and anonymous cultures, such as those that exist in most Western towns and cities, informal control mechanisms simply lack potency. He observes that the appeal to revive or transform community has arisen at exactly the time when it appears most absent and when Durkheimian anomie or normlessness is rampant and out of control.

The whole notion of community is complex and extends well beyond the more traditional definitions based on locality – or neighbourhood – and embraces a multiplicity of groups and networks to which, it is believed, we all belong (Strang, 1995: 20). This conception does not rely upon a fixed assumption of *where* a community will be found but builds upon the notion of 'communities of care' – that is, the networks of obligation and respect between the individual and everyone who cares about the person the most – and these are significantly not bounded by geography (Braithwaite and Daly, 1994: 195).

These communities of care are considered more relevant to contemporary modern living in urban societies because they provide a developed notion of 'community' where membership – or social identity – is personal and does not necessarily carry any fixed or external attributes of membership. The fact that such communities do not carry any connotations of coercion or forced membership is one of the distinctive appeals of the concept (Crawford and Clear, 2003) and, from this perspective, there is an assumption that people can move freely between communities if they disagree with their practices and values and/ or remain within a community but dissent from the dominant moral voice that exists. This is, nevertheless, a significantly problematic situation for, on the one hand, these contemporary 'light' communities are held up as examples of how they can allow sufficient space for individual or minority dissent, innovation and difference, but, on the other hand, they are also seen as insufficient with regard to informal control.

Crawford and Clear (2003) observe that this all raises the question of exactly what is meant by the claim to 'restore' or 'reintegrate' communities (see Van Ness and Strong, 1997; Braithwaite, 1998; Clear and Karp, 1999). The very notion of restoring communities suggests a return to some pre-existing state and appears to involve a nostalgic urge to return to a mythical age of genuine human identity, connectedness and reciprocity. It certainly does seem questionable that the concept of community constitutes a dynamic force for democratic renewal that challenges existing inequalities of power and the differential distribution of life opportunities and pathways to crime that characterize our society.

Crawford and Clear (2003) argue that it is important that we avoid idealistic notions and confront the empirical realities of most communities. The ideal of unrestricted entry to, and exit from, communities needs to be reconciled with the existence of relations of dominance, exclusion and differential power. The reality is that many stable communities contain very high levels of mechanical solidarity and tend to resist innovation, creation and experimentation, and shun diversity (Hopkins Burke and Pollock, 2004). These communities may well be able to come together for informal social control but the way these processes play out lacks inclusive qualities and offender-sensitive styles. These communities can be – and often are – pockets of intolerance and prejudice, which can be coercive and tolerant of bigotry and discriminatory behaviour. Weaker individuals – and minority groups – within such communities often experience them not as a home of connectedness and mutuality but as the foundations of inequalities that sustain and reinforce relations of dependence – for example, with regard to gender role and the tolerance of domestic violence or child abuse. Such communities are thus often hostile to minorities, dissenters and outsiders, and can tolerate and even encourage deviant and offending behaviour. Communities are hierarchical formations, which are structured upon lines of power, dominance and authority, and which are intrinsically exclusive – as social exclusion presupposes processes of exclusion – and many confess and define themselves around notions of 'otherness' that are potentially infused with racialized overtones.

The work of Emile Durkheim (which we encountered in the second part of this book) and his observations on the moral component of the division of labour in society provide the theoretical foundations of the 'new' liberalism, but, at the same time, provide a legitimate social context for community: that is, a political philosophy that actively promotes the rights and responsibilities of both individuals and communities but in the context of an equal division of labour. It is this latter element that deviates significantly from the orthodoxy promoted by Amitai Etzioni – and which was embraced and distorted in the UK by New

Labour with its enthusiasm for a strong dictatorial central state apparatus to enforce its agenda – and provides us with the basis of a genuine radical moral communitarianism, founded on notions of consensual interdependency with others we all recognize and identify as fellow citizens and social partners, and not as potential legitimate crime targets.

This chapter will now (1) summarize the development of the concept of individualism in Western European thought from its Christian antecedents, locating the origins of three different conceptualizations of individualism: French, Anglo-Saxon and German; (2) outline the influential German conception of individualism and its implications for political organization; (3) outline the response of Durkheim to these traditions and show how his work builds on the French conception of individualism; and (4) show how this provides the basis of a radical moral communitarianism, which is based on a more equal division of labour in society and which, it is argued, will provide the foundation for significant reductions in crime.

The development of the concept of individualism in Western Europe

The development of the concept of individualism in Western European thought arises within three different disciplines: (1) Christian theology; (2) politics; and (3) economics. Prior to Christianity, the only individual was one who renounced worldly affairs, was self-sufficient and thus fully independent in a society where the secular was the dominant political force. With the arrival of Christianity, we get a fundamental shift in the conception of man which Troeltsch (1865–1923) identifies as *man as an individual-in-relation-to-God*: where all are equal in the presence of God, while the Church emerges as a form of institutional link between the individual and the divine.

It is with Augustine (354–430) that the concept of sacred kingship is replaced by the idea that the State should be completely acquiescent to the Church. At the same time, there is a subtle advance in the concept of individualism where the State is conceived as a collection of men united through agreement on values and common utility. The Church now pretends to rule (directly or indirectly) the world, which means that the Christian individual is now committed to the world to an unprecedented degree. It is with John Calvin (1509–64) and the Protestant Reformation that the individual becomes fully part of the world and individualist values are dominant without restriction or limitation.

It was Martin Luther (1483–1546) who removed God from the world by rejecting the mediation institutionalized in the Catholic Church; God was now accessible to the individual consciousness. The ritualism of the Catholic Church and the justification of works are now replaced within Protestant theology by the concept of justification through faith, leaving to the individual some margin of freedom. Calvin goes further and maintains the complete impotence of man in the face of the power of God. At first sight, this appears a limitation rather than a development of the notion of individualism but Troeltsch warns us against interpreting Calvin in terms of unfettered atomistic individualism. Instead, there is the concept of the imposition of values: the identification of our will with the will of God. With Luther, Calvin and the Reformation, we have the origins of a Germanic conception of individualism where the individual expresses their individuality in relation to society by close identification with the group (or society).

The political perspective on individualism has two useful starting points. First, there is the combination of Christian revelation and Aristotelian philosophy in Thomas Aquinas (1225–74), where at the level of religion each man is conceptualized as a whole being, a private individual in direct relation to his creator and model, and where on a political level he is considered to be a member of the commonwealth, a part of the social body. Second, there is the theory of Natural Law that dominates in the period leading up to the French Revolution and where the idea is to establish an ideal society while starting from the individual man of nature. The device for this purpose was the idea of contract, which, in turn, involves the combination of two elements. The first, the 'social' contract, introduced the relationship characterized by equality or 'fellowship'; the second, the political contract, introduced subjection to a Ruler or a ruling agent. Subsequently, the philosophers reduced this multiplicity of contracts to one. First, Hobbes (1588–1679) makes the social contract a contract of subjection. Second, Locke (1632–1704) replaces the political contract by a Trust. Third, Rousseau (1712–78) suppresses the Ruler altogether. The 'contract social' is the contract of association: it is assumed that one enters society at large as one enters one or another particular voluntary association.

It is with the Puritans, who founded colonies in America in the seventeenth century, that we get an example of the actual establishment of a commonwealth on the basis of a contract. What the Levellers had stressed in 1647, in their Agreement of the People, the Rights of Man and religious freedom, had been enjoyed in the American colonies since the beginning. This is an abstract statement of the concept of the individual as being over and above the State, which is endorsed by the French Revolution, but which is first articulated by the Puritans. This is linked to the emergence of utilitarianism, where the ideas of Adam Smith are applied to the solution of political problems. It is here that we have the origins of the Anglo-Saxon conception of individualism.

In France, however, for Saint-Simon (1760–1825) and his followers, the French Revolution, the Rights of Man and the advent of liberalism had a purely negative, destructive value and they concluded that the time had come to organize society and to regenerate it. For the Saint-Simonians and this decidedly French conception of socialism, the State is conceived as an industrial association, which should be hierarchical. Rewards should be unequal – as performances are – but the inheritance of property should be suppressed. We have here the origins of a French secular conception of individualism where secondary groups act as intermediaries between individuals and the state. In a society spared the Protestant Reformation, it is a conception of social organization based on the medieval Catholic Church.

Meanwhile, in Protestant Germany, Hegel's (1770–1831) philosophy of the State appears as the culmination of everything that had gone before. As proposed by Hobbes and in Rousseau: the conscious individual is called to recognize in the State his higher self, and in the command of the State the expression of his own will and freedom. This indirect presentation of society in terms of the State leads to a kind of religion of the State. In the realm of the political, Hegel does for the German concept of individualism what Luther and Calvin had done in the realm of the religious.

The economic perspective on individualism arises with the reversal of the traditional idea that relations between people are more important than the relationship between people and things. In modern society, relations between people are to be subordinated to relations between people and things. At the same time, the champions of Free Trade were impatient with the mercantilist view of state intervention and there occurred a basic ideological change. The idea that, in trade, the gain of one party is the loss of the other is replaced with the concept that exchange is advantageous to both parties. This economic perspective becomes the basis of the Anglo-Saxon conception of individualism.

Beginning in the eighteenth century, German culture exhibits an unprecedented development that brings about a complete emancipation in relation to the French culture, which had previously dominated European thought. We now see the rise of the German conception of individualism. Central to this development is the work of Herder (1744–1803), who sees in history the contrasted interplay of individual cultures, each constituting a specific Volk, in which an aspect of general humanity is embodied in a unique manner. We here have a deep transformation in the definition of man: as opposed to the abstract individual, a representative of the human species, endowed with reason, man for Herder is what he is, in all his modes of thinking, feeling and acting, by virtue of his belonging to a given cultural community. In doing so, he lays the basis for what later will be called the 'ethnic theory' of nationalities as against the 'elective theory', in which the nation rests essentially on consensus. This is a peculiarly German conception of nationality and individualism.

The social and political philosophy of Fichte (1762–1814) poses some difficulties here. Ostensibly, he sets out to be the philosopher of the French Revolution but is often considered in Germany to be a precursor of pan-Germanism. His position is essentially that the German spirit is characterized by universality. The German people are destined to dominate the world, but he modifies this meaning by basing it in the identity of universality and Germanness.

There is indeed a powerful holistic trend in German ideas where the German people as a whole have been strongly inclined to obey the dominant power. In agreement with this general background, the great majority of German intellectuals have admitted the necessity of subordination in society. Combined with the ethnocentrism that is found universally – the valuation of 'us' as against 'others' or strangers – we have the social basis of what has been called 'pan-Germanism'. In this conception, a man is essentially a German, and through being a German is a social being. There is a devotion to the whole: Germans have in their blood devotion to a thing, an idea, an institution, a super-individual entity. In other words, the subject subordinates himself spontaneously to the whole; he has no feeling of alienation in doing so, and therefore all his personal qualities are given free rein in the fulfilment of his role. On the other hand, neither the French nor English tradition of individualism can see the possibility of liberty arising from that formulation, only autocracy and slavery. Troeltsch argues that this is Hegel's conception of liberty and that this is expressed, one way or another, in all the great German creations of the nineteenth century: in the Socialist Party as well as in the army. This German conception of liberty thus arises in German political movements apparently as diverse as National Socialism and Marxism.

For instance, in *Mein Kampf*, Hitler explains very clearly that he designed his movement as a sort of counter copy of the Marxist and Bolshevik movement, replacing, among other things, the class struggle by a race struggle. Thus, from this perspective, German nationalism, on the one hand, and German socialism – that is, Marxist socialism – on the other, rest on similar ideological formulas, so that a possible shift from one to the other, or from Marxist socialism to 'national socialism', is understandable. Both German nationalism and Marxism were built on an individualist, 'nominalist' foundation, and both claim to reach a collective being.

The origins of Durkheim's social theory

Durkheim was strongly opposed to both the German and Anglo-Saxon conceptions of the relationship between individuals and society, and his social theory embodies three main influences. First, there is the rationalism of Charles Renouvier (1815–1903), his concern with morality and attempt to reconcile determinism with the concept of human freedom and morality. Renouvier had accepted that progress through mastery over nature was possible, but this was conditional on moral progress based on the mastery of the individual over themselves and their actions. Renouvier combined a concern for the dignity of the individual and a theory of social cohesion based on the individual's sense of utility with and dependence on others. Second, there are Saint-Simon's ideas about economic institutions in industrial society and for the need of new forms of social and political organization. Third, there is Alfred Espinas' (1844–1922) emphasis on the superiority of the collective consciousness over the individual, his attribution of the superiority of the social over the individual, where altruism and sympathy were to predominate over egoism and find their ultimate point of focus in the national society.

Durkheim's social theory is essentially a reaction to Anglo-Saxon utilitarianism, German state socialism and French authoritarianism. First, in the case of French authoritarianism, he accepts Comte's thesis that the increasing division of labour among occupational groups leads to social solidarity but that, at the same time, it tends to extinguish any sense of community. Yet, where Comte looked for a solution in an increasing role for the State as a unifying force, Durkheim observed that this account had no regard for the naturally achieved solidarity of an independent system of activities, a spontaneous consensus of the parts that could not be maintained by force against the nature of things. But, for Durkheim, this rejection of authoritarianism did not mean an acceptance of the utilitarian tradition.

Second, Herbert Spencer, a part of the Anglo-Saxon utilitarian tradition, disagreed with Comte and argued that industrial societies had a natural coherence as a result of the unhindered play of individual interests; these required neither conformity to shared beliefs and norms nor state regulation; social solidarity would eventually develop in accordance with individual interests. Durkheim took an opposite view and contended that the free play of individual interests would lead to instability, not harmony, which would only give rise to transient relations and passing associations. Furthermore, he observed that Spencer's account of contract was misleading. A contract was the product of a society, which gave it its binding force, and defines the condition of its operation.

Third, from the tradition of German state socialism, Tönnies' concept of Gesellschaft was close to that of Spencer's concept of industrial society, emphasizing individual property, the 'free market', traditional beliefs superseded by freedom of thought, and the isolation of individuals. Tönnies nevertheless observed the need for a strong State to safeguard interests, a form of State-regulated capitalism, which was his version of socialism. Durkheim criticized the theory of Gesellschaft as accounting for social solidarity in terms of a temporary and artificial mechanism, the imposition of the State. He subsequently reversed the dichotomy between modern and traditional societies, which had been characteristic of German thought.

Durkheim, social solidarity and the French conception of individualism

Durkheim differed from the utilitarians in his belief that the 'cult of the individual' in modern society did not rest on the egoistic pursuit of self-interest that they proposed, but in the adoption of the values of the French Revolution with the welfare and self-fulfilment of every member of society to be sought.

At the centre of his social theory is a concern to find out why we live in groups. As we saw in Chapter 7, Durkheim considered that in more simple societies people are bound together by a mechanical solidarity where like are drawn to like, where we all share the same values and cultural norms. We have a common identity and share the same beliefs and interests. This arises from a collective consciousness, a common awareness shared by all.

In more complex industrial societies, we are bound together by organic solidarity. Individuals are unlike each other and perform quite different roles from each other. There is the organic analogy between society and the human body: both need regular stable ongoing functioning organs. At the centre of organic society is the continuing progress of the division of labour between groups, but with this increasing fragmentation within society there is now a likelihood that we all believe different things. There is thus at this point a fragmentation of the collective consciousness. This has both good effects, for example, we are more readily willing to tolerate the actions and beliefs of a plurality of diverse groups, and bad effects where there is an increased prospect of social conflict between these diverse groups.

The rise in organic solidarity has essentially brought about a considerable increase in individualism. The doctrines of the Rights of Man/French Revolution create a much higher degree of tolerance and there is also a greater capacity for individual development. There are nevertheless pathological developments. First, there are spectacular increases in a new form of existence (egoism) where a person is too poorly integrated into society. Second, a sense of anomie can occur whether you are in a group or not, a sense of not belonging, where you are not subject to regulative norms. This is often the result of development of social movements and rapid social change. Thus, for example, Durkheim would undoubtedly have attributed the failure of the Bolshevik Social Revolution in the years after 1917 to the widespread anomie that was the result of the abolition of such traditional institutions as the Church and family. The message for V.I. Lenin is plain: you can abolish the bourgeois institutions overnight if you wish, but you cannot change the collective consciousness of the people as quickly, whether or not a false consciousness.

Durkheim observed that it was now possible in industrial society to believe in self-indulgence – for both the bourgeoisie and proletarian – the only check would be conflict. For, if the division of labour in society is forced or unequal, some groups have more power than others, usually the product of inherited wealth or social position. Durkheim consequently considered that the division of labour works best if people are in a position where their talents are best optimized – that is, an ideal division of labour. The actual division of labour in society is nevertheless forced, egoistical, anomic and riddled with individual despair and conflict.

For Durkheim, the solution to an anomic society is thus the creation of an ideal division of labour but at the same time he recognized that this is clearly something very difficult to bring about. He nevertheless proposed a threefold political project. First, it will be necessary to clarify what are reasonable and acceptable aspirations in life for the individual. Second, the isolated and egoistical individual needs to be integrated into an interactive and inclusive social network. Third, it is necessary to remove the conditions that sustain inequality. In short, the key thing is to unite individuals into a higher community of which they feel a part and to which they feel they belong. For Durkheim, there is only one possible candidate for the higher community – the State – which is the enabling condition of our individualism, which links us all into a moral state. At the heart of Durkheim's political theory is his concept of corporations, where an administrative council would be set up for each industry, but many have criticized this perspective. Thus, there is the issue of who is to set up these corporations. For Durkheim, there is only one candidate – again the State – but that is in the hands of those who benefit from the forced division of labour, both those who own and control economic power in a capitalist society and those bureaucrats and experts who set the agenda at the mezzo level of the institution – and in the language of Durkheim – and the corporation. We will return to these observations in the following chapter when we will consider the development of the criminal justice system and in whose interest this has occurred.

Radical moral communitarian criminology

It is thus the work of Emile Durkheim and his observations on the moral component of the division of labour in society that provide the theoretical basis of radical moral communitarianism, which actively promotes the rights and responsibilities of both individuals and communities but in the context of an equal division of labour. It is this significant latter element that deviates significantly from the orthodoxy promoted by Amitai Etzioni – and which has been embraced and distorted in the UK by New Labour with its enthusiasm for a strong dictatorial central state apparatus to enforce its agenda – and provides us with the basis of a genuine moral communitarian way of life founded on notions of consensual interdependency with others we all recognize and identify as fellow citizens and social partners, and not as potential legitimate crime targets.

Radical moral communitarianism is thus a variant on the communitarian theme, which proposes that the earlier variant promoted by Etzioni and his acolytes overemphasizes responsibilities to the detriment of rights and thus calls for a rebalancing of the two. Thus, individuals have rights and responsibilities and, at the same time, so do communities, and it is important to maintain a negotiated balance between the two at both a macro level and micro level in society. This author is currently developing the concept of moral communitarianism but it has been significantly influenced by the study conducted with Phil Hodgson on antisocial behaviour in a large Midland city and referred to in Chapter 18.

Policy implications of radical moral communitarian criminology

Table 22.1 provides a summary of some of the basic rights it is proposed that a citizen should enjoy with the simultaneous responsibilities that they should have in a moral communitarian society built on mutual trust and respect (Hopkins Burke and Hodgson, 2013).

Policies should be introduced that recognize that people and communities have both rights and responsibilities and that there is a fine balance between them. This balance will invariably require negotiation and renegotiation.

First, it is proposed that all citizens should have an acceptable income level at all stages of their life and appropriate to that stage of their life. This is clearly commensurate with the current benefits system and is a reinforcement of the basic entitlement that all citizens enjoy in the appropriate circumstances. Adequate benefits should be paid to those without work, unable to work and having caring obligations, for example, that exclude them from working. Their responsibility will be to make an active contribution to society and the economy in some form. This will be more controversial because it is suggestive of 'workfare' schemes – widely introduced in the USA – and the requirement to work in order to obtain benefits, which has been strongly resisted in other countries such as the UK. Such schemes will need to be well devised. Work experience with a very strong possibility of proper employment to follow should be acceptable but not cheap labour schemes with benefit claimants expected to work unpaid for major companies. Volunteering and work in the community should be acceptable and not exclude the individual from receiving benefits, thus requiring a possible restructuring of benefit systems. Such volunteering schemes can also be made available to individuals not required to register as unemployed, such as single parents and those with disabilities. All of those taking part should be paid

Table 22.1 Rights and responsibilities in a moral communitarian society

Rights	Responsibilities
1. The provision of an adequate income on which to live appropriate to their stage of life.	1. To play an active role in the economy while fit and healthy and of working age.
2. The provision of good-quality affordable accommodation/housing of an acceptable size and proper rights of tenure.	2. Being a good neighbour and a responsible member of the community and not engaging in antisocial behaviour to the disadvantage of fellow citizens.
3. To be treated with fairness and respect by all agencies, institutions and individuals regardless of age, disability, ethnicity, gender and religion.	3. To treat others with fairness and respect regardless of age, disability, ethnicity, gender and religion.
4. The provision of good-quality healthcare.	4. To maintain a reasonable standard of natural health where possible.
5. The provision of high-quality education and training.	5. To fully engage and participate in education and training and behave appropriately.
6. To be protected from crime and antisocial behaviour in our communities.	6. Not to engage in crime and criminal behaviour.

a higher rate of benefit. There should be an expectation of involvement for all citizens.

Second, all citizens should be provided with good-quality affordable accommodation of an acceptable size and proper rights of tenure with the rent linked to the ability to pay and reviewable periodically. There should be an end to the stigmatization of local authority and housing association housing estates and the end of the term 'social housing'. Decent housing built to decent specifications with proper sound-proofing should be available to wider sections of society on proper long-term tenancy agreements at fair rents, providing the tenants do not engage in antisocial behaviour. That is the key responsibility of the tenant, who will face eviction and removal to special accommodation for the non-compliant. There should be the provision of council houses for key public sector workers with rents dependent on income, and designated accommodation should be provided in communities for recognizable serving police officers and others from the 'policing family' as part of a return to the 'police house' system.

Third, all citizens should be entitled to respect and be treated fairly and with respect by all agencies, institutions and individuals, regardless of their age, disability, ethnicity, gender, religion and sexuality. It will be the responsibility of the individual to treat all citizens fairly and with respect, again regardless of their age, disability, ethnicity, gender, religion and sexuality. Failure to do so will involve appropriate sanction.

Fourth, there should be the provision of good-quality healthcare for all citizens, which means in the UK supporting the current National Health Service. In the USA, it will mean the provision and maintenance of such a scheme out of public funds. It will be the responsibility of the citizen to actively pursue good health and the failure to do so will involve a state health and welfare – not criminal – intervention against, for example, those with alcohol, drugs and dietary (obesity) problems.

Fifth, the provision of good-quality education to all citizens is a widely recognized basic right of most citizens in countries such as the UK, and every effort should be made to ensure that standards are maintained and improved. Nevertheless, not all people take advantage of these opportunities and it is their responsibility – and the responsibility of the parents – to ensure that they do so with appropriate sanctions taken against those who do not and/or are disruptive.

Sixth, all citizens have the right to be protected from crime and antisocial behaviour, and should be able to expect this protection from the agencies of the state, but it is also proposed that there is significantly less likelihood of victimization in a society based on radical moral communitarianism where citizens are less likely to perceive each other as legitimate crime targets. It is the responsibility of citizens to not engage in criminality and antisocial behaviour. Those who do not accept this responsibility to society will be targeted and dealt with efficiently by the agencies of the criminal justice system.

Summary of main points

1. Communitarianism emerged in the USA during the 1980s as a response to what its advocates considered to be the limitations of liberal theory and practice.
2. The dominant themes are (i) the individual rights that have been vigorously promoted by traditional liberals need to be balanced with social responsibilities; and (ii) autonomous individual selves do not exist in isolation but are shaped by the values and culture of communities.
3. Communitarians thus propose that, unless we redress the balance towards the pole of community, our society will continue to become normless, self-centred and driven by special interests and power seeking.
4. Radical egalitarian communitarians focus on inequality, deprivation and the market economy as causes of crime and promote policies to eliminate poverty, which they define as a degree of deprivation that seriously impairs participation in society.
5. The whole notion of community is complex and extends well beyond the more traditional definitions based on locality – or neighbourhood – and embraces a multiplicity of groups and networks to which, it is believed, we all belong (Strang, 1995).
6. These communities of care are considered more relevant to contemporary modern living in urban societies because they provide a developed notion of 'community' where membership – or social identity – is personal and does not necessarily carry any fixed or external attributes of membership.
7. Durkheim observed that – with organic society – it was now possible to

believe in self-indulgence – for both the bourgeois and proletarian – the only check would be conflict.

8. Durkheim considered that the division of labour works best if people are in positions where their talents are best optimized – that is, an ideal division of labour. The actual division of labour in society is nevertheless forced, egoistical, anomic and riddled with individual despair and conflict. The solution is thus the creation of an ideal division of labour.

9. It is thus the work of Emile Durkheim and his observations on the moral component of the division of labour in society that provide the theoretical basis of radical moral communitarianism, which actively promotes the rights and responsibilities of both individuals and communities but in the context of an equal division of labour.

10. Policies should be introduced that recognize that people and communities have both rights and responsibilities and that there is a fine balance between them. This balance will invariably require negotiation and renegotiation.

Discussion questions

1. In what ways does communitarianism differ from traditional liberalism?
2. What is radical egalitarian communitarianism and in what ways does it differ from the variant promoted by Etzioni?
3. Briefly outline the differences between Anglo-Saxon, French and German individualism.
4. What is an 'equal division of labour' and what are its implications for radical moral communitarianism?
5. Briefly outline the main principles of moral communitarianism.

Suggested further reading

Etzioni (1993, 1995a, 1995b) should be consulted for an introduction to the notion of communitarianism, while Dennis and Erdos (1992) discuss the 'parenting deficit' in a UK context. Jordan (1992, 1996), Currie (1993, 1996, 1997) and Young (1999) should be consulted on radical egalitarian communitarianism. Hopkins Burke and Hodgson (2013) discuss radical moral communitarianism in terms of antisocial behaviour and a copy of the report can be obtained on request by contacting the author at roger.hopkins-burke@ntu.ac.uk.

23. Living in penal society

Key Issues

1. Four models of criminal justice development
2. Loïc Wacquant and the government of insecurity
3. Racial inequality and imprisonment in the contemporary USA
4. Crime, governance and insecurity
5. Living in penal society

Throughout this book, references have been made to the – invariably socio-economic – structural conditions that have a serious impact on the lives of offenders and place significant limits on the choices that they can and do make. An important structural restriction in their lives is clearly that of the criminal justice system and thus the disputed issue as to in whose interests this operates is extremely important. This last substantive chapter considers that significant issue and explains from different theoretical perspectives why it is that the various components of the 'criminal justice system' – or for some the 'criminal justice process' – have come to operate in the way that they have and in whose interests it functions in contemporary post-industrial societies. We shall commence this chapter by considering four different models of criminal justice development: (1) the orthodox social progress model; (2) the radical conflict model; (3) the carceral surveillance society model; and (4) the left realist hybrid model. We will then proceed to consider the notion that we live in a penal society (see Hopkins Burke, 2012, 2013).

Four models of criminal justice development

The orthodox social progress model

The orthodox social progress model is – as its name suggests – the standard non-critical explanation that considers the development of law and the criminal justice system to be predominantly non-contentious. These institutions are thus seen to operate neutrally in the interests of all.

The concept of progress in history is the idea that an advance occurs within the limits of the collective morality and knowledge of humanity and its environment. It is an idea often associated with the Western notion of a straight linear direction introduced by the early Greek philosophers Aristotle and Plato, and which was to have a major impact on the later Judeo-Christian doctrine. The idea spread widely during the European Renaissance that occurred between the fourteenth and sixteenth centuries and this marked the end of the static view of history and society that had been characteristic of feudalism. By the eighteenth and nineteenth centuries – and during the great Industrial Revolution that was to transform Western Europe and instigate the rise of modern society – belief in progress was to become the dominant paradigm non-critically accepted by most people. Social progress is defined as the changing of society towards the ideal and was a concept introduced in early nineteenth-century social theories, especially those of social evolutionists like August Comte (1798–1857) and Herbert Spencer (1820–1903).

The orthodox social progress model of criminal justice development should be seen in this evolutionary context. From this perspective, it proposed that the development of modern societies, their laws and criminal justice systems are the product of enlightenment, benevolence and a consensual society where the whole population shares the same core values and which develops an increasingly progressive humanitarian response to crime and disorder. Cohen (1985) observes that, from this liberal perspective, the impetus for change is seen to come from developments in ideals, visions, theories, intentions and advances in knowledge. All change is 'reform' and, moreover, this is a term without any negative connotations. All reform is motivated by benevolence, altruism, philanthropy and humanitarianism with the collective outcome of a succession of reforms being progress. Theories of criminal justice, criminology, psychology and sociology provide the scientific support or knowledge base to inform the particular reform programme, while changes occur when the reform vision becomes more refined and ideas more sophisticated.

Thus, for example, the orthodox social progress perspective on the development of the public police service observes the emergence, expansion and consolidation of a bureaucratic professionalized service to be part of a progressive humanitarian development of institutions considered necessary to respond to crime and disorder in the interests of the whole of society (Reith, 1956). The effectiveness of the pre-modern system of policing had been based on stable, homogeneous and largely rural communities where people knew one another by name, sight and/or reputation. During the eighteenth century, such communities had begun to break down in the face of the rapid transition to an industrial economy, while, at the same time, the unpaid and frequently reluctant incumbents of posts such as the parish constable and the watch failed to carry out their duties with great diligence. Many employed substitutes who were more often than not poorly paid, ignorant and too old to be effective in their duties. The local watch was also often demoralized, drunk on duty and did little to suppress crime.

The fast-expanding towns and cities were increasingly becoming a haven for the poor and those dispossessed of their land as a result of the land enclosures we encountered above, while the rookeries, slum areas and improvised shelters for the poor grew rapidly in the eighteenth century as the urban areas expanded to serve the labour needs of the growing industrial machine. These areas were extremely overcrowded, lacked elementary sanitation and were characterized by disease, grinding poverty, excessive drinking and casual violence. Prostitution and thieving were everywhere (Emsley, 1996, 2001). From the orthodox social progress perspective, the establishment of the first professional police service in 1829 and its subsequent development occurred in the interest of all groups and classes in society who needed protection from the criminality and disorder in their midst.

Similarly, contemporary notions of childhood and adolescence were formed – or socially constructed – at the outset of the modern era. Children and increasingly their families were disciplined, controlled and placed under surveillance because motivated entrepreneurial philanthropists had genuine humanitarian concerns about poor urban children and young people at risk from the numerous dangers on the streets, including criminality and a failure to find God, and were keen to do something about this problem in the interests of the whole of society and not least the children and the parents themselves.

Cohen (1985) further observes that, in terms of the orthodox social progress model, criminal justice institutions do not actually 'fail' to achieve their aims and objectives, which might seem to be almost self-evident to the neutral observer. Instead, they adapt and modify themselves in the face of changing scientific knowledge and social circumstances. This vision is nevertheless not complacent. The system is recognized to be flawed in practical and even moral terms; bad mistakes are seen to be made and abuses to occur. From the social progress perspective, all these problems can be solved, nevertheless, over time, with the provision of more resources (invariably more money), better-trained staff and improved facilities. Thus, all can be humanized and improved with the application of scientific principles and reason.

Cohen (1985) observes that the orthodox social progress model is a contemporary variant of Enlightenment beliefs in progress, and its supporters and adherents are the genuine heirs to the nineteenth-century reform tradition. It is, in many ways, the most important model, not least because it represents taken-for-granted mainstream opinion and is thus the orthodox view held by most. There is, nonetheless, a more recent, radical, cynical, ambivalent, critical variant to this liberal reform story, which has emerged from the mid-1960s onwards. Yet, while critical of the purist version of that history, it can still be conceptualized in the liberal reform tradition not least because of its tendency to propose orthodox solutions to even major significant failure. Cohen, in his discussion of the development of the penal system in modern society, observes the extent of that failure:

> The message was that the reform vision itself is potentially suspect. The record is not just one of good intentions going wrong now and then, but of continual and disastrous failure. The gap between rhetoric and reality is so

vast; that either the rhetoric itself is deeply flawed or social reality resists all such reform attempts.

(1985: 19)

This revisionist variant of the orthodox social progress model tells a less idealist account than the purist history. Ideas and intentions are still important and to be taken seriously, but not as the simple products of humanitarian caprice or even advances in knowledge. They are functional solutions to immediate social changes. Rothman (1971) discusses the establishment and development of the asylum in the USA at the end of the eighteenth century and, in doing so, provides the original revisionist variant of the social progress model. He observes that, in the aftermath of the War of Independence, there emerged a new restless, dispossessed, socially mobile potentially dangerous population, while there was a simultaneous widespread sense that the old traditional modes of social control based on small self-policing local communities were now seriously outdated. The asylum was conceived as a microcosm of the perfect social order, a utopian experiment in which criminals and the insane could be isolated from bad influences and would be changed by subjection to a regime of discipline, order and regulation.

This goal of changing the individual was clearly based on a very optimistic world view of the nature of humanity, but there was, however, soon to be a widespread proliferation of these institutions. By the late nineteenth century, it was clear that they had failed in their honourable rehabilitative intentions and had degenerated into mere custodial institutions. Rothman nevertheless observes that, regardless of their failure and widespread derogatory criticisms, these institutions were retained and sustained because of their functionality and the enduring power of the rhetoric of benevolence. They kept a dangerous population off the streets.

Rothman (1980) develops his argument further by observing degeneration in closed institutions in the early decades of the twentieth century, which had occurred regardless of the introduction of a progressive reform package. The outcome of this disappointment was a search for alternatives, which was to lead to the ideal of individual treatment, the case-by-case method and the introduction of psychiatric doctrines and attempts to humanize all closed institutions. But, yet again, none of the programmes turned out the way their designers had intended. Cohen observes that:

Closed institutions hardly changed and were certainly not humanized; the new programmes became supplements, not alternatives, thus expanding the scope and reach of the system; discretion actually became more arbitrary; individual treatment was barely attempted, let alone successful. Once again, however, failure and persistence went hand in hand: operational needs ensured survival while benevolent rhetoric buttressed a long discredited system, deflected criticism and justified 'more of the same'.

(1985: 20)

For Rothman, the crucial concept is that of 'convenience', which does not, in reality, undermine the original vision or 'conscience' but actually aids in its acceptance. The managers of the system and their staff come to actively embrace the new programmes and use them to their advantage. A useful political alliance is thus developed between the reformers and the managers and this allows the system to survive, even though it appears to be a total failure. Rothman (1980) observes that it is essential that we have a critical understanding of the origins of the original reform vision, the political interests behind them, their internal para- doxes and the nature of their appeal, for this creates a story that is far more complicated than terms such as 'reform', 'progress', 'doing good', 'benevolence' and 'humanitarianism' suggest. This revisionist account is significantly more critical than the simplistic purist version of the orthodox social progress model but it nevertheless remains a liberal model, which still believes that things can be improved if we learn the correct lessons from history and research. The radical conflict model goes much further and identifies an inherent problematic contradiction in the very nature of capitalist society.

The radical conflict model

Proponents and supporters of the social progress model – whether in its purist or revisionist form – nevertheless fundamentally agree that society is characterized by consensus. Proponents of the radical conflict model, in contrast, argue that society is inherently conflict-ridden. Max Weber (1864–1920) had influentially argued that conflict is intrinsic in society and arises from the inevitable battle within the economic marketplace – between different interest groups with different levels of power – over the distribution of scarce material resources. The radical conflict model of criminal justice development is heavily influenced by the work of Karl Marx (1818–83) who – in a simplified account of a complex and highly contested materialist philosophy – goes significantly further than Weber and argues that economic inequality is inherent in society with the outcome being an inevitable conflict between antagonistic irreconcilable social classes. Those who own and control the capitalist mode of production are also, in the final analysis, in control of the political and civil institutions in society, which, in turn, are used to maintain and sustain the capitalist system in the interests of the rich and powerful to the disadvantage of the poor and powerless or, for that matter, anyone not owning capital.

From the radical conflict perspective, it is proposed that the story of the development of the criminal justice system during the modern era is neither what it appears to be nor can it be considered to be in any way a 'failure'. For the new control system served more than adequately the requirements of the emerging capitalist order for the continued repression of recalcitrant members of the working class and, at the same time, continued to persuade everyone – including the reformers themselves – that these changes were fair, humane and progressive.

It is thus argued from this perspective that the professional police were, from their very formation at the beginning of the modern period, 'domestic mission- aries' with an emphasis on the surveillance, discipline and control of the rough and dangerous working-class elements in society in the interests of the capitalist class (Storch, 1975), while contemporary 'hard' strategies such as zero tolerance policing, which are ostensibly targeted at socially excluded groups in society, are simply a continuation of that tradition (see Crowther, 1998, 2000a, 2000b; Hopkins Burke, 1998a, 2004a). At the same time, children and their families were disciplined and controlled from the early nineteenth century in the interests of an industrial capitalism that required a fit, healthy, increasingly educated, trained, but always obedient workforce (Hopkins Burke, 2008). The motor force of history is thus the political economy and the requirements of the dominant mode of production, which is capitalism in the modern era. Ideology is only important in that it succeeds at passing off as fair, natural and just a system that is basically coercive and unfair. It is only the outside observer, uncontaminated by false consciousness, who can really know what is going on.

Rusche and Kirchheimer (1939) provide the earliest version of the radical conflict model and they begin from the principle that changes in the mode of production correspond with changing dominant forms of punishment in society. Hence, the origins and development of penal systems were determined by – and must, therefore, be studied in terms of – primarily economic and fiscal forces. Their central argument is that, in societies where workers are scarce and work plentiful, punishment is required to make the unwilling work, and when there is a surplus of labour – or a reserve army – harsh punishments are used to keep the workless under control. The status of the labour market thus determines the form and severity of punishment. The reformed prison renders docile the noncompliant members of the working class, deters others and teaches habits of discipline and order; it reproduces the lost hierarchy; it repairs defective humans to compete in the marketplace, and rehabilitation is used in the interests of capitalism. Increasingly, the state takes on a more and more active role in guiding, coordinating and planning a criminal justice system, which can achieve a more thorough, rationalized penetration of the subject population.

Melossi and Pavarini (1981) take this argument further and argue that the functional connection between the prison and society can be found in the concept of discipline. The point is to create a socially safe proletarian who has learned to accept being propertyless without threatening the very institution of property. The capitalist organization of labour shapes the form of the prison as it does other institutions and nothing can change this. The control system continues to replicate and perpetuate the forms necessary to ensure the survival of the capitalist social order.

Ignatieff (1978) produces a rather different 'softer' version of the radical conflict model and, in doing so, rejects the rather simplistic straightforward 'economic determinism' and 'left functionalism' of the purist version and observes the 'complex and autonomous structure and philosophical beliefs', which led reformers to conceive of the penitentiary. It is these beliefs and not the functional necessity of the economic system nor the 'fiction of a ruling class with a strategic conception of its functional requirements' that explains why the penitentiary was adopted to solve the 'crisis in punishment' in the last decades of the eighteenth century. Motives were complex. Driven by a perceived disintegration of the society they valued, the reformers sought a return to what they imagined to be a more stable and orderly society. They may well have acted out of political self-interest but also out of religious belief and a sense of guilt about the condition of the lower orders.

This revisionist version of the radical conflict model is very similar to that presented by Rothman but there are crucial differences. Ignatieff observes organized philanthropy to be a new strategy of class relations and both the property nature of crime and the role of the prison in containing the labour force are essential to his account. He argues that the new disciplinary ideology of the penitentiary (with its attempt to isolate the criminal class from the rest of the working class) was a response to the crisis years of industrialization. There was thus a specific class problem to be solved and not a vague sense of unease about 'social change'. Cohen observes that, from this perspective:

> The point of the new control system – reforming the individual through punishment, allocating pain in a just way – was to devise a punishment at once so humane and so just that it would convince the offender and the rest of society of the full moral legitimacy of the law.

> (1985: 24)

In this way, the system was far from the failure suggested by the orthodox social progress model, but, quite the contrary, it was remarkably successful. The carceral surveillance society model takes these arguments further.

The carceral surveillance society model

Proponents of the carceral society model do not totally disregard the arguments presented by either the proponents of the orthodox social progress model or the radical conflict model but consider the situation to be far more complex than that explained by either.

It is clear that, from the beginning of the modern period, many – if not most – philanthropists had genuine humanitarian concerns about those involved – or at risk of involvement – in crime and disorder on the streets. They also acted with the best of humanitarian intentions but, at the same time, without wholly understanding the full – especially long-term – consequences of their actions.

The labelling theorist Howard Becker (1963) helps us to understand further not only the notion of the motivated philanthropist but also the invariably obscure consequences – intentional or unintentional – of their actions. He argues that rules of conduct – including criminal laws – are made by people with power and enforced upon people without power. Thus, rules are made by the old for the young, by men for women, by white people for ethnic minorities, by the middle class for the working class. These rules are invariably imposed upon their recipients against their will and own best interests, and are legitimized by an ideology that is transmitted to the less powerful in the course of primary and secondary socialization. As an outcome of this process, most people internalize and obey the rules without realizing (or questioning) the extent to which their behaviour is being decided for them.

Becker observes that some rules may be cynically designed to keep the less powerful in their place but others have simply been introduced as the outcome of a sincere – albeit irrational and mistaken – belief on the part of high-status individuals that the creation of a new rule will be beneficial for its intended subjects. Becker termed the people who create new rules for the 'benefit' of the less fortunate 'moral entrepreneurs'.

Hopkins Burke (2008) observes that this account has resonance with the story of how philanthropic entrepreneurs came to define different categories of children and youth as acceptable and non-acceptable to respectable society, while, at the same time, developing strategies to ensure their surveillance, control, discipline and tutelage with the intention of reconstructing the non-acceptable in the form of the acceptable. But, yet again, this account is too simplistic. It is clear that not only did many of these philanthropists have little idea of the actual or potential consequences of their actions, but also they might well have become extremely concerned had they recognized that final reality. Indeed, this predominantly liberal labelling perspective fails to take into account the complexities of power and the outcomes of strategies promoted by agencies at the mezzo level of the institution that often enjoy autonomy from the political centre and implemented by those working at the micro level of the front-line who often enjoy considerable discretion in the criminal justice field. It is thus the notion of the carceral surveillance society devised by Michel Foucault (1980) and developed notably among others by Jacques Donzelot (1980), Stanley Cohen (1985) and David Garland (2001) that helps us to make sense of this situation and provides the fundamental basis of the carceral society model.

From this Foucauldian perspective, power is not simply the privilege of an all-powerful state. Strategies of power are in reality pervasive throughout society with the state only one location of the points of control and resistance. Foucault (1971, 1976) observes that particular areas of the social world are colonized and defined by the norms and control strategies devised by a variety of institutions and experts. He argues that these networks of power and control are governed as much by the knowledge and concepts that define them as by the definite intentions of groups.

Power and knowledge are inseparable. Humanism, good intentions, professional knowledge and the rhetoric of reform are neither, in the idealist sense, the producers of change nor, in the materialist sense, the mere product of changes in the political economy. They are inevitably linked in a power/ knowledge spiral. Thus, forms of knowledge such as criminology, psychiatry and philanthropy are directly related to the exercise of power, while power itself creates new objects of knowledge and accumulates new bodies of information.

The state, for its part, is implicated in this matrix of power-knowledge, but it is only part of the story, for, in this vein, it has been argued that within civil society there are numerous 'semi-autonomous' realms and relations – such as communities, occupations, organizations, families – where surveillance and control are present but where the state administration is technically absent. These semi-autonomous arenas are often appropriately negotiated and resisted by their participants in ways that, even now, the state has little jurisdiction over.

The carceral society model is thus founded on the work of Michel Foucault and, while complementary to the conflict model, recognizes that power is both diffuse and pervasive in society. Agents and experts at all levels of the social world have both access to and control of power and, although this is invariably exercised in the overall interests of the capitalist class in the long run, those involved in its application at the micro, mezzo and macro levels are not always aware of their contribution to the 'grand design'. Cohen (1985) observes that the 'great incarcerations' of the nineteenth century – which put thieves into prison, lunatics into asylums, conscripts into barracks, workers into factories, children into school – are to be seen as part of a grand design. Property had to be protected, production had to be standardized by regulations, the young segregated and inculcated with the ideology of thrift and success, the deviant subjected to discipline and surveillance. The mode of discipline that was represented by the prison belonged to an economy of power quite different from that of the direct, arbitrary and violent rule of the sovereign in the pre-modern era. Power in capitalist society had to be exercised at the lowest possible cost – economically and politically – and its effects had to be intensive and extended throughout the social apparatus in order to gain control of those populations resistant and previously invisible to the disciplinary-control-matrix.

The left realist hybrid model

Hopkins Burke (2004a, 2008, 2009, 2012 and 2013) has developed the left realist hybrid model, which essentially provides a synthesis of the orthodox social progress, radical conflict and carceral surveillance society models but with the additional recognition of *our* interest and collusion in the creation of the increasingly pervasive socio-control matrix of the carceral society.

The model is heavily influenced by left realism, which was discussed in Chapter 18, and Hopkins Burke has subsequently employed this perspective in a historical context to demonstrate that the general public has always had an interest in the development of social progress (orthodox social progress model), but this has invariably conveniently coincided with the requirements of the capitalist economy (radical conflict model) and which at the same time has contributed invariably unwittingly to the construction of the disciplinary-control-matrix that constrains the actions and rights of all (carceral surveillance society model).

First, in order to explain the development of the public police service from the beginning of the nineteenth century, it is recognized that crime was a real problem for ordinary people at the time, as it is now, and that the respectable working class has always required protection from the criminal elements in their midst, whether these were termed the 'rough working classes' (nineteenth century) or a socially excluded underclass (twenty-first century) (Hopkins Burke, 2004b).

Second, this historical variant on the left realist thesis has helped explain the increasing surveillance and control of young people on the streets and elsewhere from the nineteenth century to the present day (Hopkins Burke, 2008).

Third, it is observed that, in a complex fragmented dangerous society, it is we the general public – regardless of our social class location, gender or ethnic origin – that have a material interest in, or an enthusiasm for, the development of the carceral surveillance matrix that restricts the civil liberties or human rights of some individuals or groups (Hopkins Burke, 2004c).

The left realist hybrid perspective readily accepts the carceral society thesis that disciplinary strategies are invariably implemented by philanthropists, moral entrepreneurs, professional agents and practitioners who rarely seem to recognize how their often, but sometimes less, humble discourse contributes to the grand overall disciplinary-control-matrix. Thus, the bourgeois child tutelage project of the nineteenth – and early twentieth – century can clearly be viewed in that context.

Proponents of the radical conflict model argue that definitions of crime and criminality are class-based with the public police service agents of a capitalist society targeting the activities of the socially excluded, while at the same time ignoring the far more damaging behaviour of corporate capitalism (see Chapters 10 and 12). Left realists consider the situation to be more ambiguous, crucially recognizing that crime is a real problem for ordinary people and that it is therefore appropriate that the criminal justice system – of which the police service is a key institution – should seek to defend the weak and oppressed (see Chapter 18).

Observed from a left realist perspective, it is apparent that, from soon after the introduction of the new police in the mid-nineteenth century, there was a widespread – and admittedly at times tacit and fairly grudging – acceptance and support for this body. The police may well have targeted criminal elements within the working class and they might on occasion have taken the side of capital in trade disputes, but at the same time their moralizing mission on the streets coincided conveniently with the increasing enthusiasm for self-betterment among the great majority that has been described from differing sociological perspectives as 'embourgeoisement' (Goldthorpe, 1968–9) and 'the civilising process' (Elias, 1978, 1982).

The left realist hybrid perspective thus does not dismiss the orthodox social progress, radical conflict or carceral models of criminal justice development but instead produces a synthesis of the three. For it seems self-evident that the police are an essential necessity in order to deal with conflicts, disorders and problems of coordination necessarily generated by any complex and materially advanced society (Reiner, 2000), and hence there is a widespread demand for policing throughout society. Studies have shown that, while during the nineteenth century prosecutions for property crime emanated overwhelmingly from the more affluent groups, the poorer sections of society also resorted extensively to the law as victims (see Storch, 1989; Philips and Storch, 1999; Emsley, 1996; Taylor, 1997; Miller, 1999). Indeed, at crucial times, these poorer groups had considerable interest in the maintenance of the status quo and the isolation of a growing criminal class. For example, the end of the Crimean War and the prospect of a foot-loose army of unemployed soldiers returning – at the very time that transportation to the colonies had ended – meant that 'an organized race of criminals' would be roaming the countryside looking for criminal opportunities from whom all would need protection (Steedman, 1984; Hopkins Burke, 1998c, 1999b).

Thus, while working-class antagonism may have been exacerbated by police intervention in recreational activities and labour disputes, a close reading of the issues suggests a more complex situation than previously supposed (Hart, 1978). There seems to be little doubt that the police were closely linked with the general increase in orderliness on the streets of Victorian society (Gatrell, 1980; Taylor, 1997) and this was again widely welcomed. Indeed, it has been argued that the crucial way in which the police effect law enforcement is not by the apprehension of criminals – for that depends on many factors beyond their control – but by symbolizing the existence of a functioning legal order, by having a visible presence on the street and being seen to be doing something (Gatrell, 1980). It is a discourse that coincides neatly with a consistent widespread contemporary public demand for police on the streets frequently expressed in crime surveys and, regardless of the academic policing orthodoxy, that has repeatedly stated that the service on its own can have little effect on the crime rate (Hopkins Burke, 1998a, 1998b, 2004a, 2004b).

The left realist hybrid variation on the carceral society model proposes that there are further interests involved in the creation of the disciplinary-control-matrix and those significantly are ours and those of our predecessors. This hybrid model accepts that the orthodox social progress, radical conflict and carceral surveillance society are, to some extent, legitimate, for there were and are a multitude of motivations for both implementing and accepting the increasing surveillance and control of a potentially dangerous population on the streets and elsewhere. For the moralizing mission of the entrepreneurial philanthropist and the reforming zeal of the liberal politician and administrator corresponded conveniently with the thinking of the mill- and mine-owners and a government that wanted a fit, healthy fighting force, but it also coincided with the ever-increasing enthusiasm for self-betterment among the great majority of the working class. Those who were resistant to that moralizing and disciplinary mission – the 'rough working' class of the Victorian era – have subsequently been reinvented in academic and popular discourse as the socially excluded underclass of contemporary society, with the moral panics of today a reflection of those of the past and demands for action remarkably similar.

The radical conflict perspective nevertheless demands some prominence in the left realist hybrid model of criminal justice development because, significantly, everyone in the nineteenth century – and certainly all of us today – are subject to the requirements and demands of the economy. Attempts at self-improvement or embourgeoisement were always constrained and restricted by the opportunities provided by the economy – healthy or otherwise – and this will always be the case, as recent events following the virtual collapse of the world-wide banking system have shown. Children and young people were increasingly disciplined and controlled throughout the nineteenth – and first half of the twentieth – century in a form that was functional and appropriate to the needs of mass modern society and an industrial capitalism that required an abundant, healthy and increasingly skilled workforce. With the fragmentation of that modernity and the subsequent retreat from mass industrialism that was to occur in the last quarter of the twentieth century, the requirements for young people were to change accordingly (Hopkins Burke, 1999a, 2008).

Attempts to control the financial services industry, which is a central component of contemporary post-industrial capitalist societies such as the UK (and increasingly the USA), have certainly been popular in the past with a general population that has been the victim of financial incompetency/malpractice/criminality, but these controls that challenge the practices of market capitalism have not been that successful and only time will tell whether further attempts following the great international banking disaster of 2008–9 will be any more effective.

467

At the time of the financial scandals at Enron and WorldCom in the USA in 2002, the great economist J.K. Galbraith, then aged 93, observed that large modern corporations – as manipulated by what he terms the 'financial craftsmen' at Enron and elsewhere – have grown so complex that they are almost beyond monitoring and effective control by their owners, the shareholders (Cornwell, 2002). Noting the sheer scale of the inadequacy of the accountancy profession and some of its prominent members in the aforementioned scandals, Galbraith observed the need for the strongest public and legal pressure to get honest competent accounting as part of a greater corporate regulation and public control of the private sector. He argued that steps must be taken so that boards of directors, supine and silent for so long, are competent to exercise their legal responsibility to their shareholders.

Public motivation for the increased policing of the financial services industry – in particular the investment arm of banking – is both apparent and unquestionably understandable in view of the activities of this sector of the economy – in particular, but not exclusively, in the USA and the UK – at the end of the first decade of the twenty-first century, activities which range from gross incompetence to unequivocal criminality. Other policing, surveillance and control intrusions into various parts of the social world are at first sight equally non-problematic and acceptable both to the general public and informed opinion. Taken individually, they may seem both inoffensive and supportable by most law-abiding right-thinking people; taken collectively, they are part of an impressive matrix of social control that restricts our freedom as the following examples clearly demonstrate.

The freedom of the authorities to access information on our private lives has grown considerably in recent years. Data from a wide range of sources (the Office for National Statistics, the National Health Service, the Inland Revenue, the VAT office, the Benefits Agency, our school reports) can now be collated into a file on a citizen, without a court order showing why this should be the case. Legislative proposals in recent years have included phone and email records to be kept for seven years, the extension of child curfews, keeping DNA of those acquitted of crimes and 'ex-suspects', restrictions on travel of those convicted of drug offences, the extension of compulsory fingerprinting for those cautioned for a recordable offence and public authorities authorized to carry out speculative searches of the DNA database (Wadham and Modi, 2003). The Social Security Fraud Act 2001 allows for the compilation of a financial inventory from our bank accounts, building societies, insurance companies, telecom companies and the Student Loan Company, while every number on our phone bills may be reverse searched for an address. There may be no evidence that we are involved in fraud for us to be investigated; we may merely belong to a demographic group of people that the authorities feel is 'likely' to be involved in fraud.

The left realist hybrid model of criminal justice development thus proposes that, in a complex contemporary society, we all have interests in – and indeed a considerable enthusiasm for the introduction of – constraints and restrictions that are placed on particular activities and that restrict the civil liberties or human rights of some individuals or groups in the apparent greater interest. Taken together, these many individual restrictions contribute significantly to the ever-expanding and pervasive disciplinary-control-surveillance-matrix that constrains the lives of all in the carceral society.

Four models of criminal justice development revisited

It has been the central aim of this chapter (to date) to explain from different theoretical perspectives why the various components of the 'criminal justice system' – or 'process' – function in the way that they do and in whose interest it operates. Four different and invariably competing – but sometimes complementary – models of criminal justice development have been outlined in order to achieve that aim.

The first, the orthodox social progress model, proposes that the development of modern societies, their laws and criminal justice systems are the product of incremental enlightenment, benevolence and a consensual society, where the great majority of the population share the same core values, and are fairly uncritically accepting of an increasingly progressive humanitarian response to crime and disorder which is widely perceived to be in the interests of everyone. A revisionist variant of the model tells a less idealist account where developments occur as functional solutions to immediate social changes and problems as they arise, but this, nevertheless, remains a liberal model where it is still assumed that things can be improved if we learn the appropriate lessons from history and research.

The second, the radical conflict model, challenges the notion of consensus and recognizes, in contrast, a society characterized by conflict, where the developing criminal justice system has been used throughout the modern era to successfully support the needs of capitalism by allowing for the continued repression of uncooperative members of the working class and increasingly other outsider groups, while continuing to give the impression that the changes introduced have been fair, humane and progressive. A revisionist variant of this model nevertheless recognizes that, while the reformers may well have acted out of political self-interest, they might have had benevolent motives as well.

The third, the carceral surveillance society model, considers that both the previous two models are too simplistic and, certainly, while complementary to the latter, recognizes that power is both diffuse and pervasive in society with agents and experts at all levels of the social world having access to, and control of, significant elements of power, and, although this is invariably exercised in the overall interests of the capitalist class in the final analysis, those involved in its application at a local, micro and mezzo level are not always aware of their contribution to the 'grand design'. Indeed, often, as a result of their discretion, independence and relative autonomy in the social world, they pose significant challenges to the totality through their control of localized 'expertise', which needs to be overcome or at least accommodated for the reproduction of a successful capitalist society.

The fourth, the left realist hybrid model, does not completely dismiss any of the other three models but instead recognizes that each has significant strengths and, thus, produces a synthesis of the three, while, additionally, recognizing the interest and collusion of the general public in the creation of the increasingly pervasive socio-control matrix of the carceral society. It is thus observed that, since at least the beginning of the modern era, the general public has always had a material interest in social progress and such concerns have conveniently coincided with the requirements of capitalist society, not least while it has managed to provide people with an incrementally improved standard of living. In short, it is proposed that there are interests involved in the creation and expansion of the disciplinary-control-matrix other than those of capitalism and its various agents and experts. These are significantly ours and those of our predecessors.

The left realist hybrid model accepts that all of the other accounts offered – social progress, radical conflict and carceral society – are to some extent legitimate, for there were and are a multitude of motivations for both implementing and accepting the increasing surveillance and control of a potentially dangerous population on the streets and elsewhere in an increasingly risk-ridden world from which we all require protection. The recent work of the French sociologist Loïc Wacquant provides significant empirical support for the left realist hybrid model of criminal justice development.

Loïc Wacquant and the government of insecurity

Loïc Wacquant (2009a) identifies a significant punitive trend in penal policies which has occurred in advanced societies over the past two decades and which cannot simply be explained in terms of traditional criminal justice discourse (although we should note that this is a contested argument and was discussed in full in Chapter 22). In an analysis significantly compatible with the new modes of governance and risk society theses presented previously in this book, he argues persuasively that these changes have instigated the introduction of a new 'government of social insecurity', which is targeted at shaping the conduct of the men and women caught up in the turbulence of economic deregulation in advanced societies and the conversion of welfare into a mechanism which leads people towards precarious employment.

Wacquant observes that, within this apparently 'liberal-paternalist' apparatus, the prison has been restored to its original purpose – at the beginning of modernity – which is to discipline and control those populations and territories that are resistant to the emerging new economic and moral order, while, at the same time, ritually reasserting the resilience of the dominant groups. It was in the USA that this new politics and policy of marginality, which brings together restrictive 'workfare' and expansive 'prisonfare', was invented, in the aftermath of the social and racial upheaval of the 1970s that was to instigate the neoliberal revolution, in a response that has transformed the socio-economic situation of the USA, and which has subsequently spread to Europe in general, and the UK in particular. Crucial to this disciplinary-tutelage agenda in the USA has been the need to control an increasingly economically excluded but enduringly problematic and potentially dangerous black population.

Racial inequality and imprisonment in the contemporary USA

Wacquant (2001) has observed three significant realities about racial inequality and imprisonment in the contemporary USA. First, for the first time in US history,

African-Americans make up a majority of those entering prison each year. Second, the rate of incarceration for this ethnic group has soared to levels unknown in any other society and is higher now than the total incarceration rate in the Soviet Union at the height of the Gulag and in South Africa at the peak of the anti-apartheid struggle. Thus, since the beginning of this millennium, nearly 800,000 black men have been held in custody in federal penitentiaries, state prisons and county jails, which is 1 male out of every 21, and 1 out of every 9 between 20 and 34. An additional 68,000 black women have been incarcerated, a number higher than the *total* carceral population of any one major western European country at the time.[1] Over one-third of African-American men in their twenties find themselves behind bars, on probation, or on parole and, at the core of the formerly industrial cities of the North, this proportion often exceeds two-thirds. Third, the ratio of black to white imprisonment rates has steadily grown over the past forty years, rising from approximately five to one to eight and a half to one. In ten US states, African-Americans are imprisoned at more than 10 times the rate of European Americans and in the District of Columbia blacks are 35 times more likely than whites to be put behind bars (Donziger, 1996; Mauer, 1997).

Wacquant (1998a) argues that, to understand these phenomena, we first need to break out of the narrow 'crime and punishment' paradigm and examine the broader role of the penal system as *an instrument for managing dispossessed and dishonoured groups* and, second, it is necessary to take a longer historical view on the shifting forms of ethno-racial domination in the USA. It is by doing so that we can identify the astonishing increase in black incarceration in the past forty years to be the outcome of the obsolescence of the ghetto as a device for caste control and the correlative need for a substitute apparatus for keeping (unskilled) African-Americans in a subordinate and confined position, physically, socially and symbolically.

Wacquant agrees with George Rusche (who we observed above provided the earliest version of the radical conflict model of criminal justice development) that it is the official mission of crime control to be part of the complete system of strategies, including social policies, which are aimed at regulating the poor, but he takes a more sophisticated carceral surveillance society model perspective. Wacquant thus does *not* follow Rusche in: (i) assuming a *direct* link between brute economic forces and penal policy; (ii) reducing economic forces to the sole state of the *labour market* and still less the supply of labour; (iii) limiting the control function of the prison to the lower *classes*, as distinct from other subordinate categories (ethnic or national, for instance); and (iv) omitting the complex *symbolic* effects that the penal system exercises by drawing, dramatizing, and enforcing group boundaries (see Rusche, 1980).

Wacquant (2001) observes that, in the case of black Americans, the symbolic function of the carceral system is paramount. Thus, in the post-Civil Rights era, the remnants of the traditional black ghetto and an expanding carceral system have become linked in a single schema that entraps large numbers of younger black men, who simply move back and forth between the two institutions. This carceral mesh is seen to have emerged from two sets of convergent changes: first, there are the sweeping economic and political forces that have reshaped the mid-century 'Black Belt' to make the ghetto more like a prison and, second, the 'inmate society' has broken down in ways that make the prison more like a ghetto. Wacquant (2001) argues that the resulting symbiosis between ghetto and prison enforces the socio-economic marginality and symbolic taint of an urban black sub-proletariat. Moreover, by producing a racialized public culture that vilifies criminals, it plays a pivotal role in remaking 'race' and redefining the citizenry.

A more extensive analysis shows that this increasing use of imprisonment to sustain the caste division in US society is part of a broader 'upsizing' of the state's penal sector, which, together with the drastic 'downsizing' of its social welfare sector, aims to enforce a regime of flexible and casual wage labour as a norm for unskilled segments of the post-industrial working class (Wacquant, 1998b). This emerging *government of poverty* weds the 'invisible hand' of a deregulated labour market to the 'iron fist' of an omnipresent punitive apparatus. It is anchored not by a 'prison industrial complex', as political opponents of the policy of mass incarceration maintain (Gordon, 1999), but by a system of gendered institutions that monitor, train and neutralize populations recalcitrant or superfluous to the new economic and racial regime. Thus, men are handled by its penal wing, while (their) women and children are managed by a revamped welfare-workfare system designed to reinforce and enhance casual employment.

Wacquant (2001) thus argues that the massive expansion in the use of imprisonment is but one component of a more comprehensive restructuring of the US state to suit the requirements of neoliberalism, but, at the same time, observes that ethnicity plays a special role in this emerging system. The USA far surpasses all advanced nations in the international trend towards the penalization of social insecurity and, while the dismantling of welfare programmes has been accelerated by a cultural and political conflation of blackness and undeservingness (Gilens, 2000), so the 'great confinement' of the rejects of market society – the poor, mentally ill, homeless, jobless and useless – can be articulated as a welcome 'crackdown' on *them*, those dark-skinned criminals from a pariah group still considered to be alien to the national body. The handling of the 'underclass' question by the prison system at once reflects, reworks and reinforces the racial division of US society and plays a key role in the fashioning of a post-Keynesian US state.

Four peculiar institutions

Wacquant (2001) observes that the task of defining, confining and controlling African-Americans in the USA has been successively administered by four 'peculiar institutions': (i) slavery; (ii) the Jim Crow system; (iii) the urban ghetto; and latterly (iv) the organizational complex formed by the remnants of the ghetto and the expanding carceral system. The first three served, each in its own way, both to extract labour from African-Americans and to demarcate and ultimately seclude them so that they would not 'contaminate' the surrounding white society that viewed them as irrevocably inferior and vile.

Wacquant observes that these two goals of *labour extraction* and *social seclusion* are nevertheless in tension: thus, extracting labour from a group requires regular communication with its constituent members, which may blur the boundaries separating 'us' from 'them', while, at the same time, social isolation can make efficient labour extraction more difficult to achieve. When the tension between exploitation and exclusion reaches the point where it threatens to undermine either of them, the institution is re-stabilized through *physical violence*: the customary use of the lash and ferocious suppression of slave insurrections on the plantation, the terroristic vigilantism and mob lynchings that occurred in the South in the years following the Civil War, and periodic bombings of Negro homes and pogroms against ghetto residents (such as the six-day riot that shook up Chicago in 1919)[2] ensured that blacks kept to their appointed place in each era (Wacquant, 2001).

Wacquant (2001) observes that the built-in instabilities of un-free labour and the anomaly of caste partition in a formally democratic and highly individualistic society, such as the USA, guaranteed that each of these peculiar institutions would eventually be undermined by its internal tensions as well as by black resistance and external opposition. It would inevitably be replaced by its successor regime and, furthermore, at each new stage, the apparatus of ethno-racial domination becomes less total and less capable of encompassing all elements of the social life of the pariah group. Wacquant observes that, as African-Americans became differentiated along class lines and attained full formal citizenship, the institutional complex charged with keeping them 'separate and unequal' grew more differentiated and diffuse, allowing a rapidly increasing middle class of professionals and salary earners to *partially* compensate for the negative symbolic capital of blackness through their high-status cultural capital and proximity to centres of political power. Lower-class blacks, on the other hand, remained burdened by the triple stigma of 'race', poverty and presumed immorality, while the new middle class had an often expert interest as 'moral entrepreneurs' (Becker, 1963) in the control and indeed suppression of the unskilled and dispossessed elements of their own ethnic group, which can be explained by both the highly compatible carceral surveillance society and left realist hybrid models of criminal justice development.

This historical schema should not therefore be seen as an inescapable forward march towards ethno-racial equality as might be suggested by the social progress model. Wacquant observes that each new phase of racial domination entailed retrogression as well as progress and notes that, while it is true that there has been a civilizing of racial domination – in the sense of the term used by Norbert Elias (1978, 1982) – it remains that each regime has to be evaluated in light of the institutional possibilities it conceals, not simply by contrast to its predecessor(s), and in this way can be explained by the radical conflict model.

Carceral recruitment and authority

Wacquant observes that the prison today further resembles the ghetto for the simple reason that an overwhelming majority of its occupants originate from the racialized core of the major cities in the USA, and return there upon release, only to be soon caught again and incarcerated for ever-longer periods, in a self-perpetuating cycle of escalating socio-economic marginality and legal incapacitation. Thus, in the late 1980s, three of out of every four inmates serving sentences in the entire state of New York came from *seven black and Latino neighbourhoods* of New York City and these also happened to be the poorest areas of the city. Ellis (1993) observes that every year these segregated and dispossessed districts provide a fresh contingent of 25,000-odd inmates, while 23,000 ex-convicts are discharged, most of them on parole, back into these devastated areas. Moreover, the reality that 46 per cent of the inmates of New York state prisons come from neighbourhoods served by the sixteen worst public schools[3] of the city ensures that their clientele will continue to be replenished.

The contemporary prison system and the ghetto not only display a similarly skewed recruitment and composition in terms of class and caste, but the former also duplicates the authority structure characteristic of the latter in that it places a population of poor blacks under the direct supervision of whites, in this case, lower-class whites. In the communal ghetto of the post-war era, black residents chafed under the rule of white landlords, white employers, white unions, white social workers and white policemen (Clark, 1965). Likewise, in the new millennium, the convicts of New York City, Philadelphia, Baltimore, Cleveland, Detroit and Chicago, who are overwhelmingly African-American, serve their sentences in establishments staffed by officers who are overwhelmingly white.

The convergent changes that have 'prisonized' the ghetto and 'ghettoized' the prison in the aftermath of the Civil Rights revolution suggest that the astonishing increasing over-representation of blacks behind bars does not stem simply from the discriminatory targeting of specific penal policies such as the War on Drugs (Tonry, 1995) or from the sheer destabilizing effects of the increased penetration of ghetto neighbourhoods by the penal state (Miller, 1997). Wacquant notes that these two factors are clearly relevant but argues that they fail to capture the precise nature and full magnitude of the transformations that have interlocked the prison and the (hyper)ghetto into a *single institutional mesh* suited to fulfil anew the mission historically imparted to America's 'peculiar institutions'. The 'blackening' of the carceral population has thus closely followed the demise of the Black Belt as a viable instrument of caste containment in the urban-industrial setting.

Wacquant observes that perhaps the most important effect of this institutional mesh is the revival and consolidation of the centuries-old *association of blackness with criminality* and devious violence. The massively disproportional incarceration of blacks supplies a powerful common-sense authorization for 'using colour as a proxy for dangerousness' (Kennedy, 1997: 136), while, in recent years, the courts have consistently authorized the police to employ race as 'a negative signal of increased risk of criminality' (1997: 143) and legal scholars have rushed to endorse it as 'a rational adaptation to the demographics of crime' (1997: 146), and all of this has been justified by the blackening of the prison population. The conflation of blackness and crime in collective representation and government policy – the other side of this equation being the conflation of blackness and welfare – thus reactivates the notion of 'race' by giving a legitimate outlet to the expression of anti-black hostility in the form of the vigorous public condemnation of criminals and prisoners.

Wacquant observes that a second major effect of the penalization of the 'race question' has been to depoliticize it. Thus, reframing problems of ethno-racial division as issues of criminality and law enforcement automatically delegitimizes any attempt at collective resistance and redress. Established organizations that speak for African-Americans cannot directly confront the crisis of hyperincarceration for fear that this might reinforce the very conflation of blackness and crime in the minds of the general public. This thus fuels the crisis and, in doing so, has silenced sub-proletarian revolt.

By assuming a central role in the contemporary government of race and poverty at the crossroads of the deregulated low-wage labour market, a revamped 'welfare-workfare' apparatus designed to support casual employment and the vestiges of the ghetto, the overgrown US carceral system has become a major engine of symbolic production in its own right. Just as bondage imposed 'social death' on imported African captives and their descendants (Patterson, 1982), mass incarceration induces civic death for those it ensnares.

Wacquant (2001) observes that inmates in the USA today are the targets of three forms of significant social exclusion. First, they are denied access to valued cultural capital. At a time when university degrees are becoming a prerequisite for employment in the (semi-)protected sector of the labour market, inmates have been made ineligible for higher-education grants. The exclusion started with drug offenders in 1988, continued with convicts sentenced to death or lifelong imprisonment without the possibility of parole in 1992, and ended with all remaining state and federal prisoners in 1994. This expulsion was passed by Congress for the sole purpose of accentuating the symbolic boundary between criminals and 'law-abiding citizens' in spite of overwhelming evidence that prison educational programmes drastically cut recidivism as well as help to maintain carceral order.

Second, prisoners are systematically excluded from social redistribution and public aid in an age when work insecurity makes access to such programmes more essential than ever for those dwelling in the lower regions of the socio-economic hierarchy. Laws deny welfare payments, benefits for veterans and food stamps to anyone in detention for more than sixty days.

Third, convicts are banned from political participation via 'criminal disenfranchisement' practised on a scale and with vigour unimaginable in any other country. All but four states deny the vote to mentally competent adults held in detention facilities; thirty-nine states forbid convicts placed on probation from exercising this political right; and thirty-two states also disenfranchise parolees. In fourteen states, ex-felons are barred from voting even when they are no longer under criminal justice supervision, for life in ten of these states. The result is that nearly four million Americans have temporarily or permanently lost the ability to cast a ballot, including 1.47 million who are not behind bars and another 1.39 million who have served their sentences in full (Fellner and Mauer, 1998). A mere quarter-century after acceding to full voting rights, one black man in seven nationwide is banned from the electoral booth through penal disenfranchisement, and seven states permanently deny the vote to more than one-quarter of their black male residents.

Wacquant (2009a) observes that this triple exclusion in prison and the criminal justice system contributes to the ongoing reconstruction of the 'imagined community' of Americans around a polar opposition. On the one hand, there are praiseworthy 'working families', implicitly white, suburban and deserving; on the other hand, there is a despicable 'underclass' of criminals, loafers and leeches, by definition dark-skinned, undeserving and personified by the dissolute teenage 'welfare mother' and the dangerous street 'gang banger'. The former are exalted as the living incarnation of genuine American values: self-control, deferred gratification, subservience of life to labour. The latter is condemned as the loathsome embodiment of their abject desecration, the 'dark side' of the 'American dream' of affluence and opportunity for all, believed to flow from morality anchored in conjugality and work. And the line that divides them is increasingly being drawn, materially and symbolically, by the prison.

Conclusions

In summary, Wacquant (2009a) argues that the social policy of transition from welfare to workfare that is incrementally taking place in advanced neoliberal societies needs to be analysed in conjunction with the rise of prisonfare, that is, the mass incarceration of certain categories of the population perceived to be problematic. Workfare and prisonfare are, from this perspective, simply two sides of the same coin: they are the areas where the neoliberal state can still assert its authority once depleted of its economic and social policy functions. The combination of workfare and prisonfare is seen to fulfil both economic and symbolic functions for the neoliberal punitive state – for workfare and prisonfare are both punishments – as it fights the crisis of legitimacy that pervades all developed democracies as the state progressively loses its capacity to establish successful economic policies in an increasingly competitive world and thus has little choice but to abandon social justice and redistribution strategies. Wacquant argues that, with the assistance of the media, public attention is directed away from the massive transfer of wealth to the top of the social stratification structure towards designated 'incorrigible' deviants who can be blamed for our lack of economic competitiveness: welfare cheats and parasites, criminals and paedophiles against whom the ever-more intrusive mechanisms of the carceral surveillance society are rigorously applied.

Wacquant argues that this neoliberal crusade is based on a series of falsifications that are perpetuated and dispersed throughout society, mostly, again, through the media. Thus, the USA is said to be spending enormous quantities of money on welfare, whereas it has never accounted for more than 1 per cent of the federal budget; or crime continues to rise, perpetrated by ever younger and more dangerous 'predators', whereas the reality is that criminality has been on the decline for a long time irrespective of the policies implemented. Americans nevertheless still believe that there is more crime. We should note that the situation is similar in the UK and other countries in continental Europe.

The increasing regulation of the poor is the major outcome of these policies but there is not a large-scale conspiracy – as suggested by the radical conflict model of criminal justice development, for such an undertaking would require much more competent coordination and centralization than is available in the USA – and probably any other advanced liberal democratic society. The perceived outcome is in reality the logical conclusions and results of separately adopted neoliberal strategies: liberalization/privatization in the economic domain, the shrinking of the state in the name of efficiency, and the desocialization of waged labour – along with waves of outsourcing and off-shoring – and along with a moral cultural outlook on social deviance devised by politicians and 'experts' who may or may not be aware of their contribution to the pervasive socio-control matrix of the carceral surveillance society. Such economic policies are bound to be devastating for certain, usually poorer, segments of the population, who then need to be controlled for their individual moral failings, largely depicted in terms of a lack of self-control and responsibility.

The victims of neoliberal policies are thus targeted as irresponsible, unproductive individuals who need tutelage and discipline, and that is a job that is left to the state with recourse to partnerships with private-sector agencies, such as private welfare/child welfare administrations and private prisons. In this sense, in this punitive environment, structural conditions leave the most vulnerable members of society to fend for themselves, even though their ghettoization prevents them from improving their conditions. They are then blamed for their failure to get out of this situation. There is, of course, one form of economic activity that would lead to better material outcomes for the dispossessed poor and that is the illegal economy, and Wacquant observes that is where the policies of the War on Drugs in the USA have worked to prevent those deprived of socialized wage labour from taking this one exit from poverty, leaving them, of course, in prison, serving large sentences for which there is no parole.

Wacquant (2009b) observes that this double regulation of poverty – through workfare and prisonfare – has been exported to Europe, starting with the liberalization of the state through Thatcherism in the UK, the Kohl years in Germany and the Chirac years in France. Even the various left-of-centre parties, such as the socialist parties in Western Europe, are seen to have embraced the law-and-order view of the state and neoliberal economic 'reforms'.

The mechanisms and discourse used for targeting, marginalizing and controlling the poor and dispossessed differ in each country and there are important different historical and cultural factors in each society. Thus, while black Europeans are significantly over-represented among the 'clientele' of the criminal justice systems of their particular countries, there are important variations in the mechanisms of control that reflect historical differences from the USA. A comparison between the USA and UK provides a useful case study.

Racism is endemic in both the USA and the UK and, while there are significant similarities in the socio-economic position of black people in both countries, there are also important differences. The first difference is that the USA has had a large black population for over three hundred years, while, in contrast, the great majority of black emigration to the UK occurred following the Second World War. In the case of the USA, large numbers of black people were taken to that country in chains, having been sold as slaves, and this reality clearly posed a serious physical threat to the white population that required techniques of control and containment, which may well have become more sophisticated and 'civilized' in recent years, but still nevertheless reflect the origins of this size-able ethnic minority. Although the British were heavily involved in the slave trade to the USA and the Caribbean – and indeed much of the latter became British colonies – the black population that emigrated to Britain from the Caribbean during the 1950s was invited because of a labour shortage. Many of those involved in the first wave had fought in the British military during the war and considered Britain to be the motherland. On arrival in the UK, they experienced racism with many similarities to the USA during the 'Jim Crow' era but this was never officially sanctioned – as had been the case in the USA, in the South, in particular – and indeed a prominent member of the Conservative Government, Enoch Powell, was forced to resign because of a widely condemned racist speech, although his views were extremely popular with large sections of the white working class at the time. Policies to integrate the black population into mainstream UK society have been pursued by all subsequent governments, although racism remains significant and many black people remain jobless, in receipt of welfare and overly represented as the clients of the criminal justice system and inmates of the prison estate. Clearly, Wacquant's account of the disciplining and tutelage of the contemporary black population has significant resonance in the UK but there are crucial differences. Black people with origins in the Caribbean are far more integrated into mainstream British society with high levels of inter-'marriage' with white people, whereas in the USA there are far fewer such instances in a society that, to many visitors, appears to be characterized by apartheid.

Many black people in the UK are the targets of tutelage and discipline strategies – with many integrated into the penal society mesh that resembles that identified by Wacquant in the USA – but as part of a socially and economically excluded underclass that incorporates people from different ethnic groups, but which, at the same time, is as invidious and pervasive in its own way as the system the other side of the Atlantic. It is just different.

It is becoming increasingly apparent that the socio-control matrix of the carceral society continues to incrementally expand in close parallel with progressively insurmountable economic pressures. The outcome is that more and more groups are being absorbed into the net of surveillance and tutelage as the inevitably failing liberal economies of advanced societies come under intense pressure to make significant cuts in services and the real incomes of their citizenry. At the time of writing, public sector employment in the UK is coming under immense pressure with government policy seeking a substantial reduction in services and jobs, all of which is 'justified' by a media vilification of people who were once known, and indeed respected, as public servants. It is a long time since that descriptive language has been widely used.

The future thus looks bleak, with the carceral surveillance model of criminal justice development having increasing explanatory relevance. We should nevertheless not underestimate our own contribution to this state of affairs with those people lucky enough to still have reasonable jobs and futures – and that number is decreasing rapidly – being encouraged to buy into the language of vilification and exclusion. It is thus the left realist hybrid model of criminal justice development that makes most sense of this situation. There are those involved in these processes who do things for the best of humanitarian motives (social progress model), but these strategies and interventions are clearly taking place in the interests of capitalism or the market economy (radical conflict model), at least in the final analysis. Hopkins Burke (2012, 2013) thus argues that it is the left realist hybrid model that provides the most comprehensive explanation – or theory – of the development of the criminal justice system – or process – and significantly indicates the direction in which we are going. We will consider further the future of criminology and criminal justice in the following concluding chapter.

Policy implications of living in penal society

Wacquant (2009b) argues that the rise of the penal state in the USA and other advanced societies over the past quarter-century is a response to rising social insecurity, not criminal insecurity. Thus, changes in welfare and justice policies are interlinked as restrictive 'workfare' and expansive 'prisonfare' and are brought together in a single organizational apparatus to discipline the precarious fractions of the post-industrial working class. It is further argued that an all-inclusive pervasive carceral system is not a deviation from, but a constituent component of, the neoliberal Leviathan state. Wacquant thus proposes that we should not simply conceive of the prison as a technical implement for law enforcement but as a core political capacity, whose selective and aggressive deployment in the lower regions of social space violates the ideals of democratic citizenship. Clearly, progressive criminologists opposed to these penological trends should thus challenge policies that help to reinforce the disciplinary-control-matrix, particularly when these are being promoted by moral entrepreneurs who have little or no understanding of how their humble policy or strategy contributes to the overall surveillance schema.

Closely linked to this recognition of the role of the expert and moral entrepreneur in the construction of policies and strategies that contribute – sometimes unthinkingly – to the disciplinary-control-matrix is, of course, the role of the general public – and again invariably unthinkingly – in legitimating this state of affairs. The notion of penal populism is significant here. It is a process whereby the major political parties compete with each other to be 'tough on crime' and is generally associated with a public perception that crime is out of control and tends to manifest itself at the time of national elections, when politicians put forward hard-line policies which would remand more offenders into prison prior to their trial and impose longer sentences on conviction. Penal populism generally reflects the disenchantment felt by a distinct segment of society (crime victims and their representatives) who believe they have been ignored by justice processes that focus on the offender. Penal populism thus leads to the pursuit of policies designed to win votes – rather than reduce crime or promote justice – and helps legitimate strategies that contribute to the ever-expanding pervasive disciplinary-control-matrix. It is again the role of the progressive criminologist to challenge such policies and help in a process of educating the public.

Summary of main points

1. This chapter considers four different models of criminal justice development: (i) the orthodox social progress model; (ii) the radical conflict model; (iii) the carceral surveillance society model; and (iv) the left realist hybrid model.

2. The left realist hybrid model provides a synthesis of the orthodox social progress, radical conflict and carceral surveillance society models but with the added recognition of our interest and collusion in the creation of the increasingly pervasive socio-control matrix of the carceral society. The radical conflict perspective nevertheless demands prominence because we are all subject to the requirements and demands of the economy.

3. Wacquant (2009a) identifies a new 'government of social insecurity', which is targeted at shaping the conduct of the men and women caught up in the turbulence of economic deregulation in advanced societies.

4. Crucial to this disciplinary-tutelage agenda in the USA has been the need to control an increasingly economically excluded but enduringly problematic and potentially dangerous black population.

5. Wacquant (1998a) argues that we need to break out of the narrow 'crime and punishment' paradigm and examine the broader role of the penal system as an instrument for managing dispossessed and dishonoured groups.

6. Wacquant observes that the prison today resembles the ghetto for the simple reason that an overwhelming majority of its occupants originate from the racialized core of the major cities and return there upon release.

7. Wacquant (2009a) argues that workfare and prisonfare are simply two sides of the same coin and this double regulation of poverty – through workfare and prisonfare – has been exported to Europe.

8. Many black people in the UK are the targets of tutelage and discipline strategies as part of a socially excluded underclass that incorporates people from all ethnic groups but that, at the same time, is invidious and pervasive.

9. It is becoming increasingly apparent that the socio-control matrix of the carceral society continues to incrementally expand in close parallel with increasingly insurmountable economic pressures.

10. It is argued that progressive criminologists opposed to these penological trends should challenge policies that help to reinforce the disciplinary-control-matrix of contemporary society.

Discussion questions

1. Briefly outline the social progress and radical conflict models of criminal justice development.

2. In what ways does the left realist hybrid model build upon the carceral surveillance society model?

3. What is the purpose of the new government of insecurity according to Wacquant?

4. In what ways do government strategies differ in Europe from those in the USA?
5. What is considered to be an appropriate role for the progressive criminologist in contemporary society?

Suggested further reading

Hopkins Burke (2012) provides a comprehensive introduction to criminal justice theory and demonstrates how his four models of criminal justice development explain in whose interest the various agencies operate. Loïc Wacquant (2009a, 2009b and 2011) provides an introduction to both the penal society thesis and also the work of a fine contemporary, thought-provoking sociologist.

Notes

1 Because males compose over 93 per cent of the US state and federal prison population and 89 per cent of jail inmates, and because the disciplining of women from the lower class and caste continues to operate primarily through welfare and workfare, his analysis focuses solely on men. But a full-fledged analysis of the distinct causes and consequences of the astonishing growth in the imprisonment of black (and Hispanic) women is urgently needed, in part because the penal confinement of women has immensely deleterious effects on their children.
2 From 27 July to 2 August 1919, a race riot broke out in Chicago. When it was over, 38 people were dead, 537 injured and about 1,000 rendered homeless. The incident which sparked the riot was the drowning of a black youth after he drifted on to a white area of a beach, on a hot, 96-degree day. The reasons for the riot, however, lie with segregation, vicious racism, and the organized activities of white gangs, many of which were sponsored by Chicago's political machine. Most of the rioting, murder and arson were concentrated in the Black Belt.
3 In the USA, public schools are what the name suggests: free schools provided by the state. In the UK, the term is used to describe fee-paying private education.

24. Conclusions: criminology in an age of austerity

Key Issues

1. Criminological theory revisited
2. Competing models of a criminological future
3. Two models of public criminology
4. An alternative: democratic criminology
5. Closing thoughts: moral communitarianism and democratic criminology

The first edition of *An Introduction to Criminological Theory* was published in July 2001. It had taken several years from first thoughts to final publication and, looking back now on that experience, those were clearly very different times from those of today. For many of us in the social sciences in the UK (and criminology was no exception), these were times of great optimism. An extremely popular New Labour Government had been elected with a massive majority in May 1997 and appeared committed to pursuing progressive social policies backed up by the empirical research evidence that had been gathering dust during the long years of the previous Conservative regime. Where research findings did not exist, then resources would be made available so that the appropriate studies could be conducted. These were good times to be a researcher in the areas of criminology and criminal justice. The Crime and Disorder Act 1998 was the new government's major flagship criminal justice legislation, which was intended to transform criminal justice in the UK. In the area of young people and crime – a particular area of expertise for this author – the long-established juvenile justice system was to be replaced with a *new* youth justice system via the auspices of the newly created Youth Justice Board for England and Wales with a significantly large budget which epitomized the self-confident optimistic times. There was, of course, academic and some professional resistance to these developments. Some observed a new punitive turn (see Chapter 21) in youth justice policies, while others (such as this author) recognized a proposed 'balanced intervention' where young offenders would be required to take responsibility for their actions but, at the same time, a great emphasis would be placed on addressing the personal and social conditions that had impacted on the lives of these young people, which could encourage them to make the 'wrong' decisions in life (a welfare-oriented intervention). All of this would be located in the context of a government programme of 'reintegrative tutelage' (Hopkins Burke, 1999), which would seek to socially reintegrate into mainstream society those large sections of the population who had become economically excluded from the good life as an outcome of the *laissez-faire* free-market economic policies implemented by the previous Conservative administrations. These governments had presided over a major restructuring of the UK economy away from manufacturing to the service industries (such as banking), leaving many in the traditional working-class communities high and dry on the economic scrapyard. Never mind. New Labour socio-economic policy would sort it all out. From the vantage point of today (June 2013), all that optimism seems incredibly naive and embarrassing.

New Labour proceeded to win an unprecedented further two general elections, but, while considerable resources were spent on further reintegrative social policies, amid a continuing feeling of 'never had it so good' – to use Prime Minister Harold Macmillan's famous phrase from the 1959 General Election – being enjoyed by large sections of the middle classes (in particular among those in the burgeoning public sector), some were becoming aware that this extended (worldwide) economic boom was being unnaturally sustained through a mountain of credit. Cutbacks in government spending were occurring long before the final worldwide economic collapse in 2008, and New Labour was losing much of its natural support (to the Liberal Democrats) because of its involvement in an extremely unpopular – many said illegal – war in Iraq. The prison population was fast expanding (as detailed elsewhere in this book), even though we were advised by official statistics and criminologists working in these areas that we were in the middle of a significant worldwide 'crime drop'. Not that anyone believed the latter, perhaps because the crime that was taking place seemed nastier and more violent than ever. Certainly, the self-confidence and optimism of post-1997 UK criminology seemed to be significantly in decline. Then came 2008!

Hardly anyone had heard the term 'credit crunch' before 2008 but today it is in widespread usage and most people know that it has something to do with banks being far less inclined to lend money than they had previously been. Since 2008, many would-be first-time house buyers have found it extremely difficult to get mortgages, as lenders demand large deposits and have suddenly become very selective in whom they will lend money to. Similarly, those looking for a personal loan to buy a car or home extension or go on a foreign holiday have also discovered that the easy credit, which enabled them to live a high-consumption lifestyle in the past, is no longer as easy to obtain.

The 2008 credit crunch was one element of a global financial crisis that led to a major – indeed, unprecedented in recent times – economic recession, with many business collapses, rising unemployment and, in many countries (such as the UK), a new austerity politics aimed at reducing high and unsustainable levels of national debt. For the majority of ordinary working people, the consequences were felt directly in pay freezes, reduced hours, redundancies and an uncertain (but far from optimistic) future. This was all dramatically symbolized on

15 September 2008 when the US investment bank Lehman Brothers effectively collapsed after 158 years in business, threatening all of its 26,000 workers around the world with the loss of their jobs. But the collapse of Lehman Brothers was not a unique event.

The fifth largest US bank, Bear Sterns, valued at $18 billion in 2007, was bought by JPMorgan Chase for just $240 million in March 2008, and another household name, Merrill Lynch, agreed to be taken over by the Bank of America. The two largest US mortgage lenders, Fannie Mae and Freddie Mac, which together accounted for $5.3 trillion worth of mortgages (half of all US home loans), had to be bailed out by the US government, as their possible collapse was considered a threat to global financial stability. Another huge mortgage lender, Washington Mutual, also failed and was closed down by the US regulatory authorities and sold to JPMorgan Chase.

Financial analysts traced the origins of the US banking crisis to risky lending practices, especially on home loans. As part of their growth strategy, many US banks had provided a large number of loans to homebuyers with poor credit histories – a practice known as 'subprime lending'. These loans were then rolled into portfolios including other assets and bonds and sold to investors around the world. However, between 2004 and 2006, US interest rates rose from 1 per cent to over 5 per cent, and default rates on subprime mortgages rose to record levels, as people could not afford their rising monthly repayments. Global investors suffered huge losses as a result and the US housing market slumped as banks became very wary of lending to each other and ready credit availability ceased.

Because the financial system is now global (as we have seen elsewhere in this book), the US crisis began to spread round the world. Investment banks in Europe, China, Australia and elsewhere all suffered losses and the credit crunch – a severe shortage of credit or money – pushed the global economy into recession. In the UK, Ireland and France, major banks were effectively taken into government ownership (nationalized) to prevent them from collapse. National governments across Europe and the European Central Bank intervened, making more money available to banks, hoping that this would encourage them to start lending again. But this strategy did not work with the outcome being a major global economic recession, bringing business failures, rising unemployment, higher living costs and with the middle classes – in particular, those public-sector employees who had done so well during the previous artificially extended economic boom – being increasingly absorbed into the ranks of socio-economic exclusion, previously the preserve of those involved in manual occupations.

The 2010 British General Election produced an inconclusive result with no single party able to form a government. As a result, the first coalition government since the Second World War was formed between the Conservatives and the Liberal Democrats. The centrepiece of the subsequent coalition agreement was the Conservative Party's economic policy of eliminating the UK's structural deficit by 2015, based primarily on public spending cuts rather than on tax rises – a policy that to date appears to have been remarkably unsuccessful, although there appears to be no realistic alternative at the time of writing. The 2010 spending review announced a series of measures aimed at achieving this goal, including an average 19 per cent cut across departmental budgets, an extra £7 billion in cuts to the welfare budget on top of £11 billion already announced, and a major reform of public-sector pensions (HM Treasury, 2010).

There was an identified synergy between the Liberal Democrats' long-standing focus on localism and the decentralization of power and Prime Minister David Cameron's pre-election idea of the Big Society. The coalition announced a vision of Britain as a bottom-up 'big society' in which the state withdraws from many of its current (expensive) obligations, to be replaced by strong citizens' groups (cheap) and reinvigorated communities. In a sense, this is an extension of the idea – evident in both 1980s 'Thatcherism' and under New Labour communitarianism – that the state should promote an 'age of responsibility' that focuses on individual behaviour (Lister, 2011). Critics nevertheless see Big Society ideas as an ideological smokescreen, covering the increasing pace of privatization and enormous spending cuts. Critics also note that without the legal right to welfare – or an obligation of the state to provide it – voluntary efforts are unlikely to be sufficient to replace reliable state provision (Charlesworth, 2010). This is a remarkably different socio-economic context to social and criminal justice policy from that offered during those heady overly optimistic days when the first edition of this book was published and there appears to be little – or, indeed, no – light at the end of the tunnel. Indeed, we might need to find the tunnel.

At the time of writing, two influential think tanks have just warned that austerity measures in the UK could still be in place when the 2020 election takes place in seven years' time. The Institute for Fiscal Studies and the Institute for Government (both of them far from radical left-wing outfits) have said, 'we are still as far away from the [budget deficit] target as we were in 2010. . . . Indeed, it would not be surprising if not just 2015 but also 2020 was an "austerity" election' (BBC News, 2013). These warnings came in a briefing ahead of the Spending Review on 26 June. Chancellor George Osborne had predicted in 2010 that he could balance the budget within four years, but that is now not expected to happen until 2017/18. While the government has stuck to most of its plans from 2010, there has been less growth than expected, which has reduced the amount of money the government has taken in taxes. The think tanks have warned that whoever is chancellor after the next election will probably have to raise taxes straight away. The warning of extended austerity was based on the experience in Canada in the 1980s and 1990s, when the government needed to bring the budget deficit under control: 'If the UK experience proves to be as drawn out as the Canadian one, we should expect not just 2015 but also 2020 to be an austerity election', the briefing said (BBC News, 2013). Some of us actually think that it will take longer than that and austerity will be the economic orthodoxy in Europe for the foreseeable future. This will be the future socio-economic context in which academic and professional (applied) criminology will operate.

Criminological theory revisited

This book has examined the different ways in which crime and criminal behaviour has been explained during the past two hundred years and, while these explanations have been proposed at various times by among others

485

legal philosophers, biologists, psychologists, sociologists, political scientists and geographers, it is possible to locate these many and varied explanations – or criminological theories – in terms of one of three different general models – or traditions – that were the focus of the first three parts of this book.

The first tradition – the rational actor model – proposes that human beings possess free will and this enables them to choose whether or not to engage in criminal activities. From this perspective, crime can be controlled by making the costs of offending – that is, punishment – sufficient to discourage the pursuit of criminal rewards. In other words, in such punitive circumstances, the choice of engagement in criminal activity would be irrational.

The second tradition – the predestined actor model – proposes that criminal behaviour can be explained in terms of factors that exist either within the individual or their environment that cause – or determine – that person to act in ways over which they have little or no control. From this perspective, it is through the identification and eradication of these factors by some form of treatment process that crime can be controlled. Thus, biological and psychological variants of this model propose that the individual should be changed, while sociological versions advocate the transformation of the criminogenic environment.

The third tradition – the victimized actor model – denies neither (entirely) the prescriptions of the rational actor nor the predestined actor models. It is recognized that people make decisions to behave in ways that may well be perfectly rational for them in the circumstances in which they find themselves but it is the activities of the economically poor and politically powerless that are criminalized, and it is thus a process conducted in the interests of those with power and wealth. At the micro level, individuals can be labelled and criminalized by coming into contact with front-line agents of the state working in the criminal justice and welfare systems (or even school teachers), while, at the macro societal level, it is those with economic power and the control of authority that are in a position to influence the legislative agenda. From this perspective, crime is seen to be a social construction and can be controlled or reduced by not criminalizing dispossessed unfortunates and by abolishing legislation that criminalizes their activities.

The fourth part of this book has discussed those attempts to produce a synthesis of different theoretical perspectives – some of which are internal to one particular model of criminal behaviour, others increasingly incorporating elements that cross model boundaries – with the intention of providing a bigger, better, all-encompassing theory that seeks to explain as much crime and criminal behaviour as possible – and in some cases, ambitiously, all criminal behaviour. It is an approach clearly in line with modernist social science thinking with its emphasis on moral certainty and our ability to successfully socially engineer society in the interests of all.

This fifth part of the book has discussed ways of explaining crime and criminal behaviour in a contemporary era permeated by moral ambiguity and where there have been increasing doubts about the sustainability of the modernist project in an increasingly fragmented, complex and diverse social world. Central to the notion of the postmodern condition has been the recognition of a range of different discourses that can be legitimate and hence right for different people, at different times, in different contexts, and where the notion of the objective truth – or competing objective realities – of modernity has been replaced by recognition of the multiple realities or moral ambiguities of the postmodern condition. Indeed, many 'postmodernists' – predominantly those who propose that there has been a significant rupture or break with modernism – have celebrated the failure of the modernist project to establish rational foundations for knowledge and have wholeheartedly embraced this trend towards human diversity and social fragmentation.

It has been observed in this book that 'postmodernism' can only function successfully if there is reciprocal acceptance of diverse values from all participant groups and it has become perfectly clear that this reciprocity of goodwill does not exist outside of predominantly bourgeois intellectual circles in some of the more affluent societies on this planet. At the same time, a whole range of significant risks, some of which have been chronicled in the final part of the book – and of which traditional crime patterns and motivations are only part – have arisen in contemporary global but fragmented society, which threaten the health and survival of our social existence in its present form – regardless of whether we accept, or deny, any notion of the postmodern condition, postmodern society, late modernity or, indeed, even late barbarism. It is in this context that we will consider the future of criminology in an age of austerity.

Competing models of a criminological future

Aaron Fichtelberg and Aaron Kupchik (2011) observe a recent debate among criminological scholars who have engaged with the idea of 'public criminology', including those who contributed to a special issue of *Theoretical Criminology* (Chancer and McLaughlin, 2007; see also Garland and Sparks, 2000; Zahn, 1999), where the focus of debate has been on the growing disjunction between criminological knowledge and criminal justice policy.

It is argued that making criminological knowledge central to the provision of legitimate crime and criminal justice policy is essential if the discipline is to survive. In his 2009 Presidential Address to the American Society of Criminology, Todd Clear (2010) challenged criminologists to make a greater contribution to public policy debates, while observing that funding agencies such as the National Science Foundation (in the USA) and the Economic and Social Research Council (in the UK) require investigators to produce policy-relevant research as a condition of receiving funding. The author of this book has got in on the act with this fourth edition of *An Introduction to Criminological Theory*, by including new sections in each chapter on the policy implications of each of the theories discussed.

Fichtelberg and Kupchik (2011) focus on how criminological research can be directed to the public at large, including sensitivity to public beliefs – and attitudes – and relevance to policy debates. Rather than analysing specific strategies for how criminologists could make their contributions relevant and accessible for news media outlets or agencies of the state (as previously discussed by Barak, 2007; Stanko, 2007; Wiles, 2002), they focus on how criminologists do – and should – draw conclusions about crime and criminal justice policies and apply these conclusions to public discourse, in ways that interact with public opinion. It is proposed that work should be produced that resonates with public concerns, takes these concerns seriously, and yet uses criminological expertise to educate the public and enhance the credibility of the discipline beyond academia. Moreover, better engagement with public opinion would facilitate the policy-making enterprise, since, as Elliott Currie (2007) suggests, policy-makers at times agree with the arguments proposed by criminologists but are reluctant to act on criminological research when it contradicts public sensibilities. Fichtelberg and Kupchik thus focus on the space between criminological research and public discourse and elaborate on what a democratic model of public criminology would look like.

While the connection between criminological research and other value systems is clearly a complex one, it is clear that the social scientific discourse, depending as it does on the development of complex theories of crime and careful theory testing, makes a unique and important contribution to our thinking about crime and criminal justice. However, its insights can often run counter to popular opinion and challenge cherished views. Whatever the strength of their research and conclusions they have reached, criminologists who venture into the public sphere can expect to find themselves buffeted by political forces and their research questioned on grounds that are very different from peer review. Public sensibilities about crime and justice are influenced by many institutions and powers beyond the mere validity or invalidity of a criminological hypothesis (Beckett 1997; Garland, 1990). Public opinion and empirical social science thus use two different discourses which operate in very different ways. The issue is precisely what sort of contributions should criminologists be making to the public debate about crime and criminal justice, and what sorts of contributions can the broader public make to criminological research?

Fichtelberg and Kupchik address this issue by defending a particular conception of criminological theory and practice in relation to the broader context of public debate. This approach, which they call democratic criminology, understands that criminologists are experts with a unique contribution to make to debates on criminal justice policy but nevertheless acknowledges that this role should be shorn of its epistemological pretensions and be aware of its political limitations. Criminology has, at times, been closely linked to the formation of criminal justice policy, but, as the authors argue, the intimacy is – and should be – mediated by political processes that have their own value. This is to say that democracy as an independent value system should have an important role to play in developing social, legal and political responses to crime, even when the democratic will runs contrary to social-scientific findings.

Two models of public criminology

Fichtelberg and Kupchik (2011) observe that there are numerous models for understanding how social scientists and their findings interact with broader society and briefly outline and critique two of these models. They then contrast them with their notion of democratic criminology.

Technocracy

Fichtelberg and Kupchik propose that the most common way in which scholars understand the role of criminology in the public sphere is to see the social scientist as the expert whose knowledge should be used to formulate criminal justice policy. They can thus advise policy-makers and help them to construct effective criminal justice policies based not on ideology or opinion, but instead rooted in scientific research. From this perspective, the criminologist is an adviser who helps develop scientifically grounded criminal justice policies that, when properly applied, will result in lower crime rates or the other laudable goals that the criminologist seeks to achieve. Garland and Sparks observe that:

> The politics of modern criminology were essentially technicist and state-centred, typically offering top-down expert solutions for social problems and disorders. . . . Policy was to be based upon research findings about the causes of crime and the most effective treatments, not upon political considerations, electoral advantage or irrational public sentiment.
>
> (2000: 195)

The analogy here is with an idealized conception of natural science: a physicist, chemist or biologist provides expert knowledge – on global warming, the health effects of a certain substance, or the consequences of a particular chemical reaction – which a rational public should accept and which should serve as the basis for sound policy.

In reality, of course, this conception of natural science is hardly accurate. Whether it is the health effects of smoking, debates about global climate change or the therapeutic merits of embryonic stem cells, natural science has always been politicized when it enters into the public sphere (see Lynch et al., 2008). Moreover, as research in the sociology of science has effectively shown, scientific evidence itself is subject to various political and economic pressures as scientists seek to develop research agendas and arrive at conclusions that are politically loaded, despite being cloaked in the neutral-sounding discourse of objective research (Duster, 2003). However, the technocratic conception of the relationship between the social and natural sciences is more an ideal type than an attempt to model actual scientific practice. When scientific knowledge is questioned or criticized in the public sphere – or its recommendations are rejected – this public response is understood by technocratic criminologists as either 'irrational' or 'ideological'.

Fichtelberg and Kupchik cite the example of the position taken by many criminologists on capital punishment and note how articles in criminological journals about capital punishment are overwhelmingly opposed to the practice as racist (particularly in the USA), fraught with error in its application, of little crime control value and barbaric. Criminologists argue that the innocent may be condemned to death (Huff, 2001), that the ethnicity of offenders and victims is a significant predictor of capital punishment (Paternoster and Brame, 2008), and that it is completely out of step with international standards of decency (Schabas, 1997). Despite selected research conducted by economists, which demonstrates some deterrent value to executions (see Dezhbakhsh *et al.*, 2003), the majority of criminological work shows no relationship between capital punishment and crime rates. In contrast, and despite the criminological evidence, the majority of the public in the USA supports the use of capital punishment – this is also the case in the UK, where there currently is no capital punishment. According to a recent Gallup poll, 64 per cent of Americans surveyed support a sentence of death for a convicted murderer, with only 30 per cent opposed (Saad, 2008). Not only are criminologists and a majority of the public on opposite sides of this issue, but standard responses from criminologists can be condescending towards public views. Zimring (2003) argues that the failure of the public to take into account criminological evidence about the perceived weaknesses of capital punishment is explained by appeal to vigilante ideologies, ignorance of the weaknesses of the death penalty, or other social pathologies or fundamentally irrational aspects of human social behaviour (Zimring, 2003). A technocratic view holds that widely accepted scientific evidence is sufficient grounds for changing policy independent of the views of the body politic, and that explaining the failure of the state to do so requires appeal to irrational or pathological modes of explanation. Thus, scientific research in these cases should be considered to be superior to public opinion on criminological issues.

Fichtelberg and Kupchik (2011) observe that an important weakness of this approach to social science in general, and criminology in particular, is that it is fundamentally anti-democratic. The technocratic model reduces politics to technical, problem-solving issues, leaving out deeper discussions about the values inherent in the chosen approach. Thus, criminologists invariably write about capital punishment as if a detached, empirically driven perspective should be the only voice in the debate – avoiding normative questions about emotional and cultural elements of punishment. The views, perspectives and experiences of the democratic polity are thus deprived of their relevance because of their perceived 'irrelevance' or 'irrationality'. Given the significant role that communication and democratic practices play in ensuring legitimacy in modernity, depriving the public of a meaningful voice in the debate over criminal justice policy, and discounting popular opinion when it conflicts with social scientific knowledge, has potentially dangerous cultural and political repercussions (Habermas, 1996).

Furthermore, such a view greatly overplays the certainty of social-scientific conclusions and, thus, their value for guiding criminal justice policy. It is true that criminology provides important and useful information, but over a century of criminological research has resulted in few definite conclusions and even fewer – if any – facts. Even the most persuasive criminological conclusions have, over time, been tempered and their utility questioned (Austin, 2003; Tittle, 2004). History is thus full of penological theories that have failed to reduce prison violence and recidivism, regardless of their apparent empirical or intuitive validity. Rather than being purely objective, criminological research is – to a great extent – socially constructed, since the presuppositions and normative orientations that guide this research are products of the cultural background of the researcher, their position in the social structure and other social or individual cues. While it is too extreme to propose that criminological knowledge is without value, its insights do not have the efficacy, generalizability or certainty proposed by the technocratic model.

The genealogical approach

Fichtelberg and Kupchik (2011) observe that the second model for understanding the relationship between criminology, criminal justice policy and popular opinion swings to the extreme opposite from the technocratic model. Rather than seeing the views of the criminologist as those of a trained expert who rationally and scientifically guides policy formation, for the genealogist, the contributions of the social scientist themselves, along with criminal justice policy, are a subject of analysis. The question of whether or not these theories are 'true' is bracketed by the social scientist, as are questions about legitimacy (Fraser, 1981). Instead, the theories are historicized and placed within broader political and social discourse, and their direct and indirect consequences explored.

Classic examples of this approach include Foucault's *Discipline and Punish* (1977), Garland's *The Culture of Control* (2001) and Simon's *Governing through Crime* (2007) (and much of the literature discussed in the fifth part of this book). Each of these works is focused more on discussing the construction and implementation of criminal justice than on using science for wise policy formation. Foucault's 'genealogical' approach examines the scientific, political and legal discourses that shape the modern world, putting aside the validity of the theories themselves. Thus, his history of imprisonment is intended as 'a genealogy of the present scientifico-legal complex from which the power to punish derives its bases, justification, and rules' (1977: 23) and not as a systematic advocacy of any particular penal method. When taking such an approach, scholars study the creation and imposition of criminology and criminal justice policy, examining how criminological discourse constructs the figure of the criminal, the concept of the prison and the implementation of criminal justice policy, rather than the construction of or advocacy for new criminal justice policy (Nelken, 1994).

Fichtelberg and Kupchik propose that the most valuable contribution of such genealogical approaches is that they locate the hidden assumptions of both academic and popular thinking regarding crime, as well as the institutional and discursive structures that shape the production of knowledge of crime and criminal justice policy. This can allow policy-makers and the public at large to see the previously unseen consequences of their policies – as well as some unpleasant consequences of what was once portrayed as innocuous reform – and begin to address crime and justice problems in novel ways, exploring routes not taken. It can also critically evaluate the concept of 'crime' itself, showing the social construction of the concept as well as the misplacement of many public fears about problems such as street crime or juvenile delinquency. Thus, for example, Foucault (1977) locates the hidden agenda behind the 'humanization' of the prison system, an approach that can free penologists from the predominant humanitarian discourse.

Fichtelberg and Kupchik observe that, while the insights of the genealogical approach are important (and acknowledge that it is influential in their notion of democratic criminology, which we will encounter below), the genealogist cannot provide the full knowledge on which to base public criminology. Genealogical criminology focuses on a critical understanding of existing beliefs and practices, but does not provide any constructive guidance for policy-makers who engage in the practical problems of contemporary criminal justice. In this tradition, social science becomes a meta-discourse about criminology and criminal justice policy, primarily a history and sociology of thought and only tangentially an empirical science. The critical approach to criminology and the related suspicion of 'governmentality' (which we have encountered in the fifth part of this book) have a limited utility for policy-makers. Foucault himself recognized this and adamantly denied that there was a specific positive agenda to be directly gathered from his work; his focus on local resistances emphasizes the non-scientific character of social transformation (Fraser, 1981: 275–6).

Left realists Young (1997) and Currie (1992) have observed in their critique of similar approaches to crime and justice that the reality of crime is overlooked when analysts remain focused on justice issues. This leaves the formation of criminal justice policy to other, often less progressive figures. Moreover, the harsh realities of crime, issues of great concern to the public, particularly to those living in disadvantaged communities, are ignored by scholars. Currie describes this problem in relation to drug use:

> Too many well-meaning progressives simply do not get it when it comes to the trauma of drugs in the cities. A world-view that cannot even acknowledge the seriousness of a social problem is necessarily unable to come up with anything approaching a credible remedy for it; in the absence of any effort to provide a remedy, there are plenty of other takers. Minimalism thus effectively ceded the political terrain on illicit drugs and violent crime to the political right.
>
> (1992: 92)

While Young, in similar vein, observes:

> Thus we have the characteristic syndrome of left idealism: great emphasis is placed on the criminal justice system as an autonomous agent which shapes and causes problems. Crime itself is played down, marginalized, and is not the focus of attention. Pathology and dysfunction within oppressed groups is minimalized or denied.
>
> (1997: 479)

Fichtelberg and Kupchik observe that, while it is undoubtedly true that the formation of criminal justice policy deserves critical scrutiny (and much of this canon has been widely discussed in this book), the failure of much critical criminology to engage with the subject of crime as a problem that ought to be addressed scientifically is problematic for the development of public criminology. They thus argue that the connection between scientific knowledge and the democratic public needs to be rethought.

An alternative: democratic criminology

Fichtelberg and Kupchik (2011) observe that, in order to more effectively relate to political practice, criminological research should follow an alternative path to both the technocratic and genealogical approaches, and they outline what they term 'democratic criminology', which involves an exchange of ideas between the criminologist and the public, in which public concern helps direct criminological research and criminological research influences public opinion and policy. It requires the criminologist to take into account the concerns and beliefs of the public not solely as moral panics or social constructions that result from fear-inducing media reports, but those that are seen as important on their own terms. Democratic criminology thus communicates research results not only to scholars but to the public as well (Green, 2008). In contrast, it is observed that the technocratic model involves criminologists who speak to but do not listen to the public, and the genealogical model involves criminologists who speak to other criminologists.

This approach thus follows on from the left realist school of criminology (which we discussed in Chapter 18) which encourages criminologists – and, in particular, radical or critical criminologists – to 'take crime seriously'. Thus, it is recognized that, while crime is clearly a by-product of social conflict, it is, at the same time, pathological and a serious disruption of social life and a great concern to all members of a society. Thus, left realists have focused on street-level crime as well as crimes directed against vulnerable populations such as women and minorities (Taylor, 2007: 191). While not avoiding macro-structural explanations of criminal behaviour, left realism has sought to ground its predominant analysis in the concerns of women, the poor and minority populations, ordinary people.

Fichtelberg and Kupchik observe that, while democratic criminology shares the focus of left realism with public concerns about crime, democratic criminologists go further. Not only should crime and justice be taken seriously by criminologists, but they ought to think more deeply about the connections between social science, policy and the public. Thus, the gathering of scientific data ought to be linked with the public, but, more importantly, the conclusions and policy recommendations that criminologists devise should be seen as contributions to a larger public debate about crime and justice policy, a debate with contributors from many other backgrounds who may arrive at very different conclusions from the criminologist.

Fichtelberg and Kupchik observe that another crucial distinguishing characteristic of democratic criminology is its recognition of its own fallibility. All social-scientific knowledge, including criminological knowledge, is vulnerable to future rejection or revision, and all criminological hypotheses and conclusions are debatable (see Clear, 2010). This fallibility has two primary dimensions: at any given time, all criminological theories have both scholarly and non-scholarly critics who either question a particular set of methods or question the veracity or generalizability of the conclusions.

A democratic model also recognizes that no criminological research is value-neutral. 'Crime' itself is a normative concept, as are 'justice', 'victim' and virtually all other terms that the criminologist uses to study their subject. When the criminologist operationalizes criminal justice terms, they deploy their normative categories to study social structures. Moreover, when the criminologist is advocating a particular policy, they are taking a stand about what they consider should be the priorities of society. Whether it is in the belief that deterrence ought to be valued over vengeance, order ought to be valued over disorder, property ought to be secured, or lives ought to be protected, the criminologist is not merely reporting facts but advocating policy. Every time the criminologist commits themself to a policy based on their social-scientific findings, they have personally concluded that a particular set of ideas has value for society. This means that, to a large extent, criminologists are as engaged in normative debates about social priorities as they are about factual connections between causes and effects in the social sphere.

Fichtelberg and Kupchik observe that, in addition to better understanding public opinion, criminologists must better communicate the results of their research to the public (Barak, 2007; Currie, 2007). Thus, by engaging in research that is viewed as important by the public, and by incorporating public concerns into how one goes about conducting and interpreting the research, improved communication with the public might follow. This can, of course, be clearly problematic.

The first and perhaps most substantial obstacle that democratic criminological work might encounter is identifying who exactly are 'the public', in view of all the many potential stakeholders in the results of criminological research: policy-makers, citizens at large, parents, children, criminals, the elderly, disadvantaged communities, non-elected officials (for example, school principals), and others. One could continue to list numerous different groups and subgroups within each group (for example, parents of different ethnicities), each of which may have very different views, concerns and preferences, as well as different levels of opportunity to voice these views. Prioritizing the input of one group over another is an aspect of the value orientations of the researcher (see above), and criminologists need to be conscious of such choices and discuss their ramifications. Furthermore, when appropriate, criminologists should consult with as broad a range of public actors as their resources allow when conducting criminological enquiry, in an attempt to understand a broad array of views about crime and criminal justice issues. Moreover, disagreements among the public about criminological issues and variation in how much impact different groups have on criminal justice policy ought to be their own subjects of enquiry.

Fichtelberg and Kupchik (2011) observe that, having decided who are the 'public', the next challenge for the democratic criminologist is finding a venue for the communication of research results to this public. It is observed that academic criminology journals and books rarely reach non-academics, and there are very few public forums for discussing and debating important social issues. New journals in the USA, such as *Criminology and Public Policy* (ASC) and *Contexts* (ASA), are seen to represent progress on this front because of their intent to communicate academic research to a broad audience. It is also considered helpful when criminologists participate in local politics, through forums such as school boards and city council meetings, and when they contribute letters or opinion pieces to newspapers or contact local journalists to offer input on important criminological issues.

Another potential but significant difficulty arises when the recommendations of empirical research and public views diverge. This might occur with popular policies, such as the aforementioned capital punishment. In such a case, it is important that the criminologist communicates research results in a way that still takes seriously the desires of the public. Thus, although researchers have argued that capital punishment is ineffective as a deterrent, democratic criminologists can still discuss the importance of the beliefs and values standing behind the call for more executions: a strong communal and retributive ideal of criminal justice (Grasmick *et al.*, 1992) and a broad sense that penal decisions have been taken away from the community (Zimring, 2003). These are values that ought to be taken seriously and engaged with by the criminologist. Certainly, this does not mean that the criminologist should simply defer to public opinion or take on broad cultural presuppositions when doing research. Rather, the criminologist should show respect for public views and engage with, but still challenge, these views and presuppositions when their research contradicts them. The democratic model requires that they acknowledge the positive aspects of a criminal justice practice standing behind public support regardless of their personal and professional feelings on the subject. Thus, the criminologist may still challenge conventional understandings by offering a critique of accepted practices and provide suggestions for how the positive aspects could be reworked into a system that better resembles evidence-based practices. Moreover, democratic deliberation is an ongoing process with no terminus, meaning that popular policy decisions can always be revised after further debate.

A conflict between public opinion and criminological enquiry can also arise when public fears seem to have no basis in fact. It was observed above that the democratic criminologist must take public fears to be important on their own terms, but this is problematic when it apparently flies in the face of empirical research. A good example is rampant fears of child abduction by strangers, despite the rarity of such events (Best, 1988). Rather than writing condescendingly about an ignorant public, democratic criminology considers the source of the public fear, such as the difficulties placed on parents – and resulting anxieties – in a postmodern era marked by fragmented community ties (for example, Putnam, 2001). When communicating these research results, one can also take seriously the horror that stranger abductions evoke, despite their rarity – any social scientist who is also a parent can understand the power of this fear. In this way, democratic criminology takes public fears seriously and treats them as important parts of an empirical puzzle, even while challenging these views.

Another important difficulty to overcome is that often both policy-makers and criminologists lack a sufficient understanding of the nature of public opinions about crime and criminal justice, which tend to be far more complicated than sound-bite politics or over-simplistic penal policies would indicate (see Green, 2008). For example, consider the view of the public on transferring adolescents to criminal courts where they can be prosecuted as if they were adults. Polls in the USA have repeatedly shown that a majority of the public favour such action when adolescents are arrested for a violent offence. Thus, in one study, Daniel Mears

(2001) found that 87 per cent of respondents favoured such a response to violent youth. Yet, in an earlier study, Stalans and Henry (1994) found that, when respondents are asked slightly more complicated questions (when contextual information about these hypothetical juvenile offenders is presented), support for transfer to adult court drops considerably. After presenting respondents with short vignettes describing juveniles who have committed murder, Stalans and Henry asked whether the respondents favoured transfer to adult criminal court for the defendant. Their results suggest that the characteristics of the offender are important, such as, whether the juvenile is 14 or 16 years old, whether the homicide victim was a stranger, whether the juvenile has any prior convictions, and particularly whether the juvenile offender was the victim of childhood abuse. Despite the severity of the offence presented in these vignettes, only 49 per cent of respondents favoured transfer to adult court for a juvenile who murdered an abusive father; in contrast, 76 per cent favoured transfer for a juvenile who murdered a non-abusive stranger. Their research clearly illustrates how the types of mitigating factors that appear in many cases of juvenile offenders can substantially alter public views of the worthiness of transfer (see Kupchik, 2006). Though, at first glance, transfer for violent youth appears to be very popular, the reality of this public support is significantly more complex and nuanced than it initially appears.

Fichtelberg and Kupchik (2011) further observe that democratic criminological work must also overcome the assumption that the relation between public opinion and policy-making is unidirectional rather than bidirectional. Thus, although it is common to hear policy-makers talk about how they respond to the issues and opinions of the public who they represent, the reverse is true as well. That is, prior research illustrates how policy-makers often encourage fears among the public and highlight certain social problems for which these policy-makers are equipped with an apparent solution. In response to this manipulation, public anxiety about these social problems grows (see Beckett, 1994; Reinarman and Levine, 1997) and clever politicians capitalize on this newfound panic. It is observed that, if they are able to overcome these difficulties, then criminologists ought to consider both public opinion and criminological research, and communicate a synthesis of the two to the public and to policy-makers.

Feasibility of a democratic model

Fichtelberg and Kupchik (2011) discuss the feasibility of a democratic criminology. One important concern is whether such an approach will actually help with the problem underlying the debate about public criminology: the disconnection between criminological knowledge and policy-making in the current political climate. As others have noted, crime and criminal justice have become such important political issues that policy-makers often proceed according to political realities rather than from academic knowledge (see Garland and Sparks, 2000). If a democratic approach helps to make criminology more relevant to the concerns of the public and takes their views seriously, then improving this disjuncture certainly seems possible. As Chancer and McLaughlin (2007) note, efforts by feminist criminologists to increase the visibility of violence against women represents an example of such a success. This movement clearly orients itself according to the lived experiences of victims, rather than to official crime statistics or presumptions about violence that have been long held among criminologists (see also Stanko, 2007). The growing relevance of this movement within both academic and policy circles suggests that a criminological approach that seeks to understand the voice of the public and frame this within the context of academic knowledge can be very effective.

A second crucial challenge to the feasibility of a democratic criminology relates to the challenges facing public criminology overall: the substantial disincentives against engaging with public criminology that are currently in place at research universities. Elliott Currie (2007) observes how the reward structures of research universities – particularly in the case of universities in the USA but not exclusively – discourage the dissemination of knowledge outside of the academy, as well as the lack of professional incentives to do so. A democratic model of public criminology might risk additional professional censure for criminologists, since it seeks to balance academic knowledge with public opinion rather than prioritizing only academic research. There is thus an acknowledgement of the limitations of implementing such a model on a large scale unless, of course, the value of public criminology, public sociology and other applied knowledge helps reshape the reward structures of universities.

Closing thoughts: moral communitarianism and democratic criminology

We should observe that democratic criminology is very much in accord with the root democracy notions that underpin the radical moral communitarian programme outlined in Chapter 22, while, moreover, it is very much in harmony with the comments made in Chapter 23 about the role of the progressive criminologist in challenging policies that help to reinforce the disciplinary-control-matrix, particularly when these are being promoted by moral entrepreneurs who have little or no understanding of how their humble policy or strategy contributes to the overall surveillance schema. Part of that strategy will be both the education of and an informed discussion with the public about their concerns and priorities and, at the same time, helping them to see where certain policy agendas might take us with the probable consequences. That, it is proposed, is a legitimate task for the progressive criminologist in contemporary society.

Summary of main points

1. The first edition of *An Introduction to Criminological Theory* was published in July 2001 in a very different socio-economic climate from today's. Those were good times to be a researcher in the areas of criminology and criminal justice.
2. The 2008 credit crunch was one element of a global financial crisis that led to a major – indeed, unprecedented in recent times – economic recession, with many business collapses, rising unemployment and, in many countries (such as the UK), a new austerity politics aimed at reducing high and unsustainable levels of national debt.

3. For the majority of ordinary working people, the consequences were felt directly in pay freezes, reduced hours, redundancies and an uncertain (but far from optimistic) future.

4. At the time of writing, two influential think tanks have just warned that austerity measures in the UK could still be in place when the 2020 election takes place in seven years' time.

5. This will be the future socio-economic context in which academic and professional (applied) criminology will operate, certainly in the UK.

6. Aaron Fichtelberg and Aaron Kupchik (2011) observe a recent debate among criminological scholars who have engaged with the idea of 'public criminology'.

7. They outline and critique two models for understanding how social scientists and their findings interact with broader society: (i) the *technocratic* model; and (ii) the *genealogical* model.

8. Fichtelberg and Kupchik (2011) provide an alternative *democratic* model, which involves an exchange of ideas between the criminologist and the public, in which public concern helps direct criminological research and criminological research influences public opinion and policy.

9. A democratic model recognizes that no criminological research is value-neutral. 'Crime' itself is a normative concept, as are 'justice', 'victim' and virtually all other terms that the criminologist uses to study their subject.

10. Democratic criminology is very much in accord with the root democracy notions that underpin the radical moral communitarian programme and are in congruence with the role of the progressive criminologist from that perspective in helping to challenge policies that help to reinforce the disciplinary-control-matrix.

Discussion questions

1. Briefly outline what Aaron Fichtelberg and Aaron Kupchik (2011) mean by a technocratic model for understanding how social scientists and their findings interact with broader society.

2. Briefly outline what Fichtelberg and Kupchik mean by a genealogical model.

3. Briefly outline the basic concepts of the proposed democratic model for doing and reporting criminological research.

4. Is a democratic model of criminology feasible? Explain why or why not.

5. What are the proposed links between radical moral communitarianism and democratic criminology?

Suggested further reading

Students who want to engage in and reflect further on these issues should consult in the first instance James Austin (2003), Michael Burawoy (2005), Richard Ericson (2003) and Garland and Sparks (2000).

Criminological theory timeline

	Pre-nineteenth century	Nineteenth century	Twentieth century	Twenty-first century
Rational actor model of crime and criminal behaviour	Classical School 1760–1810	Neo-Classical School 1800s–1890s	Populist conservatives and right realism 1970s–1990s	
			Conservative criminology 1990s–present	
			Contemporary rational actor theories (contemporary deterrence theories, rational choice theories, routine activities theories) 1970s–present	
Predestined actor model of crime and criminal behaviour		The Italian School 1875–1930	Biochemistry theories 1920s–present	
			Psychodynamic theories 1920s–1980s	
		Inherited criminal characteristic theories 1870s–1940s	Behavioural learning theories 1920s–1980s	
			Anomie and strain theories 1930s–present	
		Emile Durkheim and social disorganisation theory 1890s–1920s	Criminal body-type theories 1930s–1980s	
			Deviant subculture theories 1950s–1960s	
			Genetic structure theories 1960s–present	
			Psychoses and brain injury theories 1970s–present	
			Cognitive learning theories 1980s–present	
			Autistic spectrum disorders 1980s–present	
			Altered biological states theories 1990s–present	

(Continued overleaf)

	Pre-nineteenth century	Nineteenth century	Twentieth century	Twenty-first century
Victimized actor model of crime and criminal behaviour			Labelling theories 1960s–present	
			Conflict theories 1930s–1960s	
			Critical race theories 1970s–present	
			Radical theories 1970s–1980s	
			Feminist theories 1970s–present	
			Critical theories 1980s–present	
			Masculinity theories 1990s–present	
			Peacemaking theory 1990s–present	
Integrated theories of criminal behaviour			Sociobiological theories 1970s–present	Differential coercion theory 2000s–present
			Contemporary environmental theories 1980s–present	Situational action theories 2000s–present
			Later social control theories 1960s–present	
			Integrated social control theories 1970s–present	
			Left realism 1980s–present	
			Power control theories 1980s–present	
			Reintegrative shaming 1980s–present	
			General theory of crime 1990s–present	
			Control balance theory 1990s–present	
			Desistance theories 1990s–present	

Crime in the postmodern condition

Anarchist criminology 1990s–present

Constitutive criminology 1990s–present

Cultural criminology 1990s–present

Crime and the risk society theories 1990s–present

Globalization and crime theories 1990s–present

Terrorism and state violence theories 1990s–present

Southern theory
2000s–present

Penal society theories
2000s–present

Radical moral
communitarianism
2010s–present

Theories of criminal justice
development 2010s–present

Democratic criminology
2010s–present

Glossary

actuarial justice: interventions are increasingly based on risk assessment, rather than on the identification of specific criminal behaviour.

administrative criminology: emphasis on reducing the opportunity to offend by the creation and evaluation of usually small-scale situational crime prevention schemes.

altered biological state theories: link behavioural changes in an individual with the introduction of an external chemical agent, that is, allergies and diet, alcohol and illegal drugs.

anarchist criminology: produces a radical critique of state law as a system of inherent inhumanity and its sense of standing 'against the law' leads logically to a criminology of crime and resistance.

'anatomy is destiny': Freudian notion where women are seen to be anatomically inferior to men with a consequential inferior destiny as wives and mothers.

anomie theories: there are two variants; the first developed by Emile Durkheim proposes that anomie is a condition of normlessness experienced by individuals during periods of rapid socio-economic change when previous forms of control and restraint have broken down; the second developed by Robert Merton proposes that individuals use alternative means – including criminal activities – to gain access to socially created needs that they are unable to obtain through legitimate behaviour.

Antisocial Behaviour Orders (ASBOs): statutory measures that aim to protect the public from behaviour that causes or is likely to cause harassment, alarm or distress; contain conditions prohibiting the offender from specific antisocial acts or entering defined areas.

antisocial personality disorder (APD): a relatively recent term that is interchangeable with that of psychopathy. There are various definitions of this condition that in general emphasize such traits as an incapacity for loyalty, selfishness, irresponsibility, impulsiveness, inability to feel guilt and failure to learn from experience.

autistic spectrum disorder: a relatively new term that includes the subgroups within the spectrum of autism.

balance of intervention: a left realist notion that proposes that, on the one hand, crime must be tackled and criminals must take responsibility for their actions and, on the other hand, the social conditions that encourage crime must also be tackled.

behavioural learning theories: a variant of psychological positivism that proposes that criminal behaviour is conditioned learned behaviour.

behavioural model of the underclass: associated with populist or neoconservatives and proposes that state welfare erodes individual responsibility by giving people incentives not to work and provide for themselves and their family.

biological positivism: proposes that human beings commit crime because of internal physiological factors over which they have little or no control.

biosocial theory: contemporary biologists propose that physiological characteristics of an individual are only part of the explanation of criminal behaviour; factors in the physical and social environment are also influential.

'bloody code': a body of legislation that during the seventeenth to the early eighteenth century prescribed the death penalty for a vast number of property crimes.

carnival of crime: festive excess, transgression, the mocking of the powerful, irrational behaviour are all temporarily legitimated in the moment of carnival.

Chicago School: a group of sociologists based at the University of Chicago during the 1920s and 1930s who developed the ecological explanation of crime that proposes that people engage in criminal activities because of determining factors in their immediate environment.

Classical criminology: the foundations of the rational actor model of explaining criminal behaviour; people are rational human beings who choose to commit criminal behaviour and can be dissuaded from doing so by the threat of punishment.

cognitive learning theories: reject much of the positivist psychological tradition of explaining criminal behaviour by incorporating notions of creative thinking and thus choice; in many ways more akin to the rational actor model.

communitarianism: it is proposed that the individual rights promoted by traditional liberals need to be balanced with social responsibilities.

concentric zone theory: analysis confirmed that offending behaviour flourished in the zone in transition and was inversely related to the affluence of the area and corresponding distance from the central business district.

conflict theories: a variant of the victimized actor model that proposes that definitions of criminality – and the decision to act against certain activities and groups – are made by those with control of authority in a pluralist but equal society.

constitutive criminology: crime is defined as the 'power to deny others' and proponents seek the development of 'replacement discourses' that fuel positive social constructions with the intention not to 'replace one truth with another' but instead to invoke 'a multiplicity of resistances' 'to the ubiquity of power'.

control balance theories: define deviancy as any activity that the majority find unacceptable and/or disapprove of and that occurs when a person has either a surplus or deficit of control in relation to others.

corporate crime: involves illegal acts carried out in the furtherance of the goals of an organization.

crime control: model of criminal justice that prioritizes efficiency and getting results with emphasis on catching, convicting and punishing the offender (see 'due process').

criminalization: involves a process in which the law, agencies of social control and the media come to associate crime with particular groups who are subsequently identified, sought out and targeted as a threat.

critical criminology: or 'left idealists' to their former cohorts in the radical tradition (see 'left realism') propose that crime is defined in terms of the concept of oppression; some groups in society are seen to be the most likely to suffer oppressive social relations based upon class division, sexism and racism.

cultural criminology: crime and the various agencies and institutions of crime control are seen to be cultural and creative constructs and these should be understood in terms of the phenomenological meanings they carry.

cumulative risk hypothesis: where the number of environmental stressors rather than the particular combination of stressors has been associated with child behaviour problems both in the short and long term.

delinquency and drift: delinquency is a *status* and delinquents are *role players* who occasionally act out a delinquent role; they are nonetheless perfectly capable of engaging in conventional activity.

deterrence: a doctrine that punishment must be both swift and certain in order to dissuade people not to commit crime.

deviancy amplification: a concept that suggests that the less tolerance there is to an initial act of group deviance, the more acts will be defined as deviant (see 'moral panic').

deviant subculture theories: there are many different variants – mostly positivist but latterly incorporating notions of choice – that propose that (predominantly young) people commit crime and deviant behaviour in the company of others for whom this is seen as the normal thing to do.

differential association theory: offending behaviour is likely to occur when individuals acquire sufficient inclinations towards law-breaking that outweigh their associations with non-criminal tendencies.

differential coercion theory: seeks to extend our knowledge of the relationship between coercion and crime.

due process: it is the purpose of the criminal justice system to prove the guilt of a defendant beyond a reasonable doubt in a public trial as a condition for the imposition of a sentence; the state has a duty to seek out and punish the guilty but must prove the guilt of the accused (see 'crime control').

environmental criminology: the study of where and when crimes occur.

environmental design theories: the nature of the built environment can affect the level of crime both by influencing potential offenders and by affecting the ability of a person to exercise control over their surroundings.

environmental management theories: the activities of a rational calculating individual can be restricted or curtailed by changing his or her surroundings.

ethnomethodology: a method of sociological analysis concerned with how individuals experience and make sense of social interaction.

European Enlightenment: philosophical movement that occurred in Western Europe during the seventeenth and eighteenth centuries, which proposed that the social world could be explained and regulated by natural laws; political systems should be developed that embraced new ideas of individual rationality and free will.

feminism: there are different versions but all observe that it is men who are the dominant group in society and it is privileged males who make and enforce the rules to the detriment of women.

folk devils: see 'moral panic'.

functionalist sociology: society is seen to consist of interdependent sections that work together to fulfil the functions necessary for the survival of society as a whole.

generative phases of women theory: based on biological changes connected to the menstrual cycle.

globalization: the increasing degree of integration among societies that plays a crucial role in most types of social change.

governmentality: the means to render populations thinkable and measurable through categorization, differentiation and sorting into hierarchies for the purpose of government.

hate offenders: those unaccepting of the multicultural nature of contemporary societies in which they live and who primarily characterize social groups according to their visible ethnic, racial or sexual identity rather than their personal attributes.

incapacitation: right realist notion that imprisonment is particularly effective in neutralizing or incapacitating offenders and frightening others into adopting law-abiding lifestyles.

infanticide: if a mother kills her child within its first year as a result of post-natal depression or breastfeeding, she has a partial defence to murder.

integrated criminological theories: an incorporation of elements from different approaches in an attempt to provide a stronger explanatory tool than that offered by one individual theory.

Italian School: early biological positivists who developed the influential notion that the criminal is a physical type distinct from the non-criminal.

just deserts: a philosophy that eschews individual discretion and rehabilitation as legitimate aims of the justice system; justice must be both done and seen to be done (see 'due process').

labelling theories: propose that crime is a product of the social reaction to an activity: if the action is ignored or not discovered the person does not become a criminal; this only happens when the person is processed by the criminal justice system and sets off on the path to a criminal career.

latent delinquency theory: proposed that the absence of an intimate attachment with parents could lead to later criminality.

left realism: a response to populist conservatism and right realism that proposes the need for a balance of intervention to address both the crime and the conditions that have caused it; influential with the 'New' Labour Government elected in the UK in 1997.

limited or bounded rationality: offenders will not always obtain all the facts needed to make a wise decision and the information available will not necessarily be weighed carefully.

macro level: at the level of society, the nation-state or country.

mainstream youth subcultures: their 'problem' is an alien or irrelevant education system followed by the prospect of a boring and dead-end job or, nowadays, training and the benefits queue.

mala in se: acts considered wrong in themselves or 'real' crimes.

mala prohibita: acts prohibited not because they are morally wrong but in order to protect the public.

marginalization: the exclusion from access to mainstream institutions for the poor and less powerful.

maternal deprivation theory: suggested that a lack of a close mother–child relationship in the early years could lead to criminal behaviour.

mezzo level: the intermediate level of the institution.

micro level: the lowest level of the small group.

modernism or modernity: a secular society based on rationality and reason with science as the dominant form of social explanation.

moral panic: a frenzy of popular societal indignation usually whipped up about a particular activity that is seen to threaten the very fabric of civilization; once labelled as such, those engaged in the activity become ostracized and targeted as 'folk devils'.

multiple masculinities: there are different masculinities that are all subject to challenge and change over time.

neo-Classical criminology: the recognition that there is a limitation on the level of rationality enjoyed by some people, such as children and the mentally ill, and this is a justification for mitigating circumstances in the courtroom.

new criminology: sought an explanation of criminal behaviour based on a theoretical synthesis of Marxism and labelling perspectives.

'new penology': concerned with techniques for identifying, classifying and managing groups assorted by levels of dangerousness based not on individualized suspicion, but on the probability that an individual may be an offender.

'nothing works': agenda at the British Home Office that called into serious question the effectiveness of rehabilitation as a crime-control strategy.

offender profiling: used, particularly in the USA, to help detect particular types of criminals; has been most useful in the detection of serial murders.

opportunity theory: a more formalized version of routine activities theory that considers elements of exposure, proximity, guardianship and target attractiveness as variables that increase the risk of criminal victimization.

Panoptican: a utilitarian prison designed by Jeremy Bentham as a 'mill for grinding rogues honest'. The institution should act as a model for schools, asylums, workhouses, factories and hospitals that could all be run on the 'inspection principle' to ensure internal regulation, discipline and efficiency.

phenomenology: a philosophical approach that proposes that phenomena are only 'real' if they are defined as such by individuals who then act on the basis of those definitions.

popular conservative criminology: came to prominence with the rise of the political 'new right' in the UK and USA during the late 1970s and the 1980s, based predominantly on 'right realist' theory now known in the USA as neoconservative.

positivism: a crucial element of the predestined actor model that proposes that human behaviour is determined by factors – either internal (as in the case of biological and psychological positivism) or external (as in the case of sociological positivism) – that are outside the control of the person.

postmodernism or postmodernity: a challenge to rationality, reason and science as the dominant forms of social explanation.

postmodernist interpretation of youth subcultures: recognition that individuals, and different groups of young people, have had very different experiences of the radical economic change that has engulfed British society.

power control theory: combines social class and control theories in order to explain the effects of familial control on gender differences in criminality.

predatory crime: direct contact crime, personal or involving property.

predestined actor model of crime and criminal behaviour: based on the positivist doctrine of determinism where criminal behaviour is explained in terms of factors, either internal or external to the human being, that cause people to act in ways over which they have little or no control.

pre-modernism or pre-modernity: pre-scientific society where religion and spirituality are the dominant forms of explanation.

process model of the underclass: a left realist model that proposes we identify and address the structural preconditions for the emergence of a socially excluded underclass, while at the same time considering and responding to the behavioural subcultural strategies developed by those finding themselves located in this socio-economic position.

psychodynamic theories: a variant of psychological positivism that proposes that criminal behaviour is in some way determined by the psychosexual development of the individual during childhood.

psychological positivism: people commit crime because of internal psychological factors over which they have little or no control; there is a criminal personality.

psychopathy: see 'antisocial personality disorder'.

radical criminology: usually informed by some version of Marxist socio-economic theory, this variant of the victimized actor model proposes that there are deeply inherent inequalities in society that provide those with economic and political power with the opportunity to criminalize the activities of the poor and powerless.

radical egalitarian communitarianism: focuses on inequality, deprivation and the market economy as causes of crime and promotes policies to eliminate poverty, which is defined as a degree of deprivation that seriously impairs participation in society.

radical moral communitarian criminology: a political philosophy which promotes the rights and responsibilities of both individuals and communities but in the context of an equal division of labour.

rational actor model of crime and criminal behaviour: human beings choose to commit criminal behaviour and can be deterred through the threat of punishment.

rational choice theory: human beings commit crime when the opportunity arises and this can be thwarted by removing that opportunity.

reintegrative shaming: proposes that the key to crime control is a cultural commitment to shaming in ways that are positive rather than negative.

reintegrative tutelage: New Labour social policy strategy to reintegrate those sections of society socially excluded from mainstream society.

responsibilization strategies: designed to offload the responsibility for risk management from central government on to the local state and non-state agencies.

right realism: based on a rediscovery of the rational actor model of crime and criminal behaviour and the notion that human beings choose to commit criminal behaviour just like any other and can be deterred by the threat of punishment.

risk society: a social formation that is organized in order to respond to risks.

routine activities theory: proposes that for a personal or property crime to occur there must be at the same time and place a perpetrator, a victim and/or an object of property.

schizophrenia of crime: term used to refer to the apparently contradictory attitude to criminal behaviour where, on the one hand, there is a widespread public demand for a rigorous intervention against criminality, while, on the other hand, criminality is widespread to the virtual point of universality.

seductions of crime: where disorder is a 'delight' to be sought after and savoured and where the causes of crime are constructed by the offenders themselves in ways that are compellingly seductive.

self-fulfilling prophecy: a false definition of a situation, evoking a new behaviour that makes the original false assumption come true.

serial murder: a repetitive event where the murderer kills at a number of different times, frequently spanning a matter of months or years, and often at different locations.

situational crime prevention: see 'administrative criminology'.

social construction of crime: highly influential concept within the victimized actor model that proposes that criminal behaviour only occurs because those with power and authority define certain activities – usually those engaged in by the poor and powerless – as criminal, while those of the powerful are ignored.

social contract theories: challenged the notion of the 'natural' political authority previously asserted by the aristocracy; human beings should freely enter into contracts with others to perform interpersonal or civic duties.

social control theories: contemporary versions propose that people commit crime when their social bond to society is broken.

social disorganization theory: has its origins in the notion developed by Emile Durkheim that imperfect social regulation leads to a variety of different social problems, including crime; as developed by the Chicago School, there was a call for efforts to reorganize communities to emphasize non-criminal activities.

social evolutionism: the notion that human beings develop as part of a process of interaction with the world they inhabit.

sociological positivism: people commit crime because of determining factors in their environment over which they have little or no control.

'spectacular' youth subcultures: arise at particular historical 'moments' as cultural solutions to the same structural economic problems created by rapid social change.

square of crime: a left realist notion that proposes crime is the result of a number of lines of force and that intervention to prevent it must therefore take place at different levels in order to be effective.

structural model of the underclass: associated with the liberal left and observes the collapse of manufacturing industry, traditional working-class employment and the subsequent retreat of welfare provision as providing the structural preconditions for the creation of a socially excluded class.

subculture of violence: where there is an expectation that the receipt of a trivial insult should be met with violence; failure to respond in this way is greeted with social censure from the peer group.

symbolic interactionism: primarily analyses the way individuals conceptualize themselves and others around them with whom they interact.

techniques of neutralization: the ways in which offenders may justify their deviant activities to themselves and others.

terrorism: emotive word that emphasizes the extreme fear caused by apparently indiscriminate violent actions of individuals claiming to be operating on behalf of some particular cause.

underclass theory: groups in socially isolated neighbourhoods have few legitimate employment opportunities and this increases the chance that they will turn to illegal or deviant activities for income.

utilitarianism: assesses the applicability of policies and legislation to promote the 'happiness' of those citizens affected by them.

victimized actor model of crime and criminal behaviour: people commit crime because they have in some way been the victims of an unjust society; they can have choices but these are constrained by their structural situation.

white-collar crime: occurs when an individual commits crime against an organization within which they work.

zemiology: the study of social harm: for example, sexism, racism, imperialism and economic exploitation.

zone of transition: containing rows of deteriorating tenements and often built in the shadow of ageing factories and home to a transient population of immigrants.

Bibliography

Abele, L. and Gilchrist, S. (1977) 'Homosexual Rape and Sexual Selection in Acanthocephalan Worms', *Science*, 197: 81–3.

Abram, K.M. (1989) 'The Effect of Co-occurring Disorders on Criminal Careers: Interaction of Antisocial Personality, Alcoholism, and Drug Disorders', *International Journal of Law and Psychiatry*, 12: 122–36.

Ackerman, R.S. (2002) *Corruption and Government: Human Development Report (UNDP)*. New York: Oxford University Press.

Adams, K. (1997) 'Developmental Aspects of Adult Crime', in T.P. Thornberry (ed.) *Developmental Theories of Crime and Delinquency: Vol. 6. Advances in Criminological Theory*. New Brunswick, NJ: Transaction Publishers.

Adamson, E. (1984) 'Toward a Marxian Penology', *Social Problems*, 31: 435–58.

Adler, F. (1975) *Sisters in Crime: The Rise of the New Female Criminal*. New York: McGraw-Hill.

Adler, Z. (1982) 'Rape – The Intention of Parliament and the Practice of the Courts', *Modern Law Review*, 45: 664.

Aguilar, B., Sroufe, A., Egeland, B. and Carlson, E. (2000) 'Distinguishing the Early-onset/ Persistent and Adolescent-onset Antisocial Behavior Types: From Birth to 16 Years', *Development and Psychopathology*, 12(2): 109–32.

Aichhorn, A. (1925) *Wayward Youth*. New York: Meridian Books.

Akers, R.L. (1985) *Deviant Behaviour: A Social Learning Approach*, 3rd edition. Belmont, CA: Wadsworth.

Akers, R.L. (1989) 'A Social Behaviorist's Perspective on Integration of Theories of Crime and Deviance', in S.F. Messner, M.D. Krohn and A.E. Liska (eds) *Theoretical Integration in the Study of Crime and Deviance: Problems and Prospects*. Albany, NY: State University of New York Press.

Akers, R.L. (1991) 'Self Control as a General Theory of Crime', *Journal of Quantitative Criminology*, 7: 201–11.

Akers, R.L. (1992) 'Linking Sociology and Its Specialities', *Social Forces*, 71: 1–16.

Akers, R.L. (1996) 'Is Differential Association/Social Learning Theory Cultural Deviance Theory?', *Criminology*, 34: 229–48.

Akers, R.L. (1997) *Criminological Theories: Introduction and Evaluation*, 2nd edition. Los Angeles, CA: Roxbury.

Akers, R.L. (2000) *Criminological Theories: Introduction, Evaluation, and Application*, 3rd edition. Los Angeles, CA: Roxbury.

Akers, R.L. and Sellers, C.S. (2004) *Criminological Theories: Introduction, Evaluation, and Application*, 4th edition. Los Angeles, CA: Roxbury.

Akers, R.L., Krohn, M.D., Lanza-Kaduce, L. and Radosevich, M. (1979) 'Social Learning and Deviant Behaviour: A Specific Test of a General Theory', *American Sociological Review*, 44: 635–55.

Akerstrom, M. (1985) *Crooks and Squares: Lifestyles of Thieves and Addicts in Comparison to Conventional People*. New Brunswick, NJ: Transaction Books.

Alford, S. (1997) 'Professionals Need Not Apply', *Corrections Today*, 59: 98–111.

All-Party Group on Alcohol Misuse (1995) *Alcohol and Crime: Breaking the Link*. London: HMSO.

Allsopp, J.F. and Feldman, M.P. (1975) 'Extroversion, Neuroticism and Psychoticism and Antisocial Behaviour in Schoolgirls', *Social Behaviour and Personality*, 2: 184.

Allsopp, J.F. and Feldman, M.P. (1976) 'Personality and Antisocial Behaviour in Schoolboys', *British Journal of Criminology*, 16: 337–51.

Altheide, D. (2009) 'Moral Panic: From Sociological Concept to Public Discourse', *Crime, Media, Culture: An International Journal*, 5(1): 79–99.

Althusser, L. (1966) *For Marx*. London: Penguin Press.

American Psychiatric Association (1968) *Diagnostic and Statistical Manual of Mental Disorders*. Washington, DC: American Psychiatric Association.

Anderson, E. (1990) *Street Wise*. Chicago, IL: University of Chicago Press.

Anderson, M.L. and Collins, P.H. (1992) *Race, Class and Gender: An Anthology*. Belmont, CA: Wadsworth.

Andrews, D.A. and Bonta, J. (1994) *The Psychology of Criminal Conduct*. Cincinnati, OH: Anderson.

Andry, R.G. (1957) 'Faulty Paternal and Maternal Child Relationships, Affection and Delinquency', *British Journal of Delinquency*, VIII: 34–48.

Aos, S., Phillips, P., Barnoski, R. and Lieb, R. (2001) *The Comparative Costs and Benefits of Programs to Reduce Crime*. Olympia: Washington State Institute of Public Policy.

Appadurai, A. (1990) 'Disjuncture and Difference in the Global Cultural Economy', *Theory, Culture and Society*, 7(2/3): 295–310.

Arendt, H. (1964) *Eichmann in Jerusalem: A Report on the Banality of Evil*. New York: Viking Press.

Arrigo, B.A. (1997) 'Dimensions of Social Justice in a Single Room Occupancy: Contributions from Chaos Theory, Policy and Practice', in D. Milovanovic (ed.) *Chaos, Criminology, and Social Justice: The New Orderly (Dis) Order*. Westport, CT: Praeger.

Arseneault, L., Tremblay, R.E., Boulerice, B. and Saucier, J. (2002) 'Obstetrical Complications and Violent Delinquency: Testing Two Developmental Pathways', *Child Development*, 73(2): 496–508.

Arvanites, T. (1992) 'The Mental Health and Criminal Justice System: Complementary Forms of Coercive Control', in A. Liska (ed.) *Social Threat and Social Control*. Albany, NY: SUNY Press.

Athens, L. (1997) *Violent Acts and Actors Revisited*. Urbana, IL: University of Illinois Press.

Attwood, T. (1998) *Asperger's Syndrome: A Guide for Parents and Professionals*. London: Jessica Kingsley Publishers.

Aubert, W. (1952) 'White Collar Crime and Social Structure', *American Journal of Sociology*, 58: 263–71.

Auld, J., Dorn, N. and South, N. (1986) 'Irregular Work, Irregular Pressure: Heroin in the 1980s', in R. Matthews and J. Young (eds) *Confronting Crime*. London: Sage.

Austin, J. (2003) 'Why Criminology is Irrelevant', *Criminology and Public Policy*, 2: 557–64.

Bakhtin, M. (1984) *Rabelais and His World*. Bloomington, IN: Indiana University Press.

Bakunin, M. (1974) *Selected Writings*. New York: Grove Press.

Balding, J. and Shelley, C. (1993) *Very Young Children in 1991/2*. Exeter: University of Exeter Schools Health Education Unit.

Baldwin, J.D. (1990) 'The Role of Sensory Stimulation in Criminal Behaviour, with Special Attention to the Age Peak in Crime', in L. Ellis and H. Hoffman (eds) *Crime in Biological, Social and Moral Contexts*. New York: Praeger.

Baldwin, J. and Bottoms, A.E. (1976) *The Urban Criminal*. London: Tavistock.

Bandura, A. (1973) *Aggression: A Social Learning Analysis*. Englewood Cliffs, NJ: Prentice Hall.

Bandura, A. and Walters, R.H. (1959) *Adolescent Aggression*. New York: Ronald Press.

Barak, G. (ed.) (1994) *Media, Process, and the Social Construction of Crime: Studies in Newsmaking Criminology*. New York: Garland.

Barak, G. (2003) *Violence and Nonviolence: Pathways to Understanding*. Thousand Oaks, CA: Sage.

Barak, G. (2007) 'Doing Newsmaking Criminology From Within the Academy', *Theoretical Criminology*, 11: 191–207.

Barak, G. (2012) 'Media and Crime', in W. DeKeseredy and M. Dragiewicz (eds) *Routledge Handbook of Critical Criminology*. London: Routledge.

Barash, D. (1977) 'Sociobiology of Rape in Mallards (Anas platyrhynchos): Responses of the Mated Male', *Science*, 197: 788–9.

Barkan, S. (1997) *Criminology: A Sociological Understanding*. Upper Saddle River, NJ: Prentice Hall.

Barlow, H. (1991) 'Review Essay of "A General Theory of Crime"', *Journal of Criminal Law and Criminology*, 82(1): 229–42.

Baron-Cohen, S. (1988) 'An Assessment of Violence in a Young Man with Asperger's Syndrome', *Journal of Child Psychology and Psychiatry*, 29(3): 351–60.

Barr, R. and Pease, K. (1990) 'Crime Placement, Displacement and Defections', in M. Tonry and N. Morris (eds) *Crime and Justice: A Review of Research*, 12: 277–319. Chicago: University of Chicago Press.

Barry, A., Osborne, T. and Rose, N. (1996) *Foucault and Political Reason: Liberalism, Neo-Liberalism and Rationalities of Government*. London: UCL Press.

Bates, K.A., Bader, C.D. and Mencken, F.C. (2003) 'Family Structure, Power-Control Theory and Deviance: Extending Power-Control Theory to Include Alternate Family Forms', *Western Criminology Review*, 4(3): 170–90.

Baudrillard, J. (1981) *Simulcra and Simulations*, translated by P. Foss, P. Batton and P. Beitchman. New York: Semiotext.

Baudrillard, J. (1988) *Selected Writings*. Stanford, CA: Stanford University Press.

Bauman, Z. (1989) *Modernity and the Holocaust*. Cambridge: Polity Press.

Bauman, Z. (1991) *Modernity and Ambivalence*. Cambridge: Polity Press.

Bauman, Z. (1993) *Postmodern Ethics*. Oxford: Blackwell.

Bauman, Z. (1997) *Postmodernity and Its Discontents*. Cambridge: Polity Press.

Bauman, Z. (1998) *Work, Consumerism and the New Poor*. Buckingham: Open University Press.

Bauman, Z. (2000) 'Social Uses of Law and Order', in D. Garland and R. Sparks (eds) *Criminology and Social Theory*. Oxford: Oxford University Press.

Baumhart, R.C. (1961) 'How Ethical are Businessmen', *Harvard Business Review*, 39: 156–76.

BBC News (2001) *Autistic Boy Killed Baby Brother* [Online]. Available at: http://news.bbc.co.uk/1/hi/uk/1165848.stm [accessed 6 January 2009].

BBC News (2002) *US Condemned for Youth Executions* [Online]. Available at: http://news.bbc.co.uk/1/hi/world/americas/2280250.stm [accessed 6 January 2009].

BBC News (2003) *US Prison Population Peaks* [Online]. Available at: http://news.bbc.co.uk/1/hi/world/2925973.stm [accessed 6 January 2009].

BBC News (2004) *Death Toll on UK Roads Increasing* [Online]. Available at: http://news.bbc.co.uk/1/hi/uk/3835747.stm [accessed 6 January 2009].

BBC News (2008a) *Darling Defends Economy Warning* [Online]. Available at: http://news.bbc.co.uk/1/hi/business/7589739.stm [accessed 6 January 2009].

BBC News (2008b) *Leaked Letter Predicts Crime Rise* [Online]. Available at: http://news.bbc.co.uk/1/hi/uk_politics/7591072.stm [accessed 6 January 2009].

BBC News (2008c) *World Credit Loss '£1.8 Trillion'* [Online]. Available at: http://news.bbc.co.uk/1/hi/business/7694275.stm [accessed 6 January 2009].

BBC News (2013) *Austerity 'May Last Until 2020'* [Online]. Available at: http://www.bbc.co.uk/news/business-22819843.

Beccaria, C. (1963, first English edition 1767) *On Crimes and Punishment*, translated by H. Paolucci. Indianapolis, IN: Bobbs-Merrill Educational.

Beck, U. (1992) *Risk Society*. London: Sage.

Becker, G.S. (1968) 'Crime and Punishment: An Economic Approach', *Journal of Political Economy*, 76(2): 169–217.

Becker, H. (1963) *Outsiders: Studies in the Sociology of Deviance*. New York: Free Press.

Becker, H. (1966) 'Introduction', in C. Shaw, *The Jack-Roller*. Chicago: University of Chicago Press.

Becker, H. (1967) 'Whose Side Are We On?', *Social Problems*, 14(3): 239–47.

Beckett, K. (1994) 'Setting the Public Agenda: Street Crime and Drug Use in American Politics', *Social Problems*, 41: 425–47.

Beckett, K. (1997) *Making Crime Pay: Law and Order in Contemporary American Politics*. New York: Oxford University Press.

Bedau, H. (1964) *The Death Penalty in America*. Garden City, NY: Anchor Books.

Beechey, V. (1977) 'Some Notes on Female Wage Labour in Capitalist Production', *Capital and Class*, (Autumn): 45–66.

Beinart, S., Anderson, B., Lee, S. and Utting, D. (2002) *Youth at Risk? A National Survey of Risk Factors and Problem Behaviour Among Young People in England, Scotland and Wales*. London: Communities that Care.

Beirne, P. (1991) 'Inventing Criminology: The "Science of Man" in Cesare Beccaria's Dei Delitti e Delle Pene (1764)', *Criminology*, 29(4): 777–820.

Beirne, P. (1993) *Inventing Criminology: Essays on the Rise of 'Homo Criminalis'*. Albany, NY: SUNY.

Bell, B. (1982) 'Psychology of Leaders of Terrorist Groups', *International Journal of Group Tensions*, 12: 84–104.

Bell, D. (1960) *The End of Ideology*. Glencoe, IL: Free Press.

Bell, D. (1973) *The Coming of Post-Industrial Society: A Venture in Social Forecasting*. London: Heinemann.

Bell, D.A. (2004) *Silent Covenants: Brown v. Board of Education and the Unfulfilled Hopes for Racial Reform*. New York: Oxford University Press.

Bennett, A. (1999) 'Subcultures or Neo-tribes? Rethinking the Relationship Between Youth, Style and Musical Taste', *Sociology*, 33(3): 599–617.

Bennett, J. (1981) *Oral History and Delinquency*. Chicago: University of Chicago Press.

Bennett, T. (1986) 'Situational Crime Prevention from the Offender's Perspective', in K. Heal and G. Laycock (eds) *Situational Crime Prevention: From Theory into Practice*. London: HMSO.

Bennett, T. (2000) *Drugs and Crime: The Results of the Second Developmental Stage of the New-Adam Programme*, Home Office Research Study 2005. London: Home Office.

Bennett, T. and Wright, R. (1984) *Burglars on Burglary*. Brookfield: Gower.

Bennett, T., Holloway, K. and Williams, T. (2001) *Drug Use and Offending: Summary Results From the First Year of the NEW-ADAM Research Programme*, Findings 148. London: Home Office.

Bentham, J. (1970) *An Introduction to the Principles of Morals and Legislation*, edited by J.H. Burns and H.L.A. Hart. London: Athlone Press.

Bequai, A. (2002) *How to Prevent Computer Crime: A Guide to Forensic and Technology*. San Diego, CA: Academic Press.

Berlin, I. (1969) 'Two Concepts of Liberty', in I. Berlin (ed.) *Four Essays on Liberty*. London: Oxford University Press.

Bernard, T.J. (1983) *The Consensus–Conflict Debate*. New York: Columbia University Press.

Bernard, T.J. and Snipes, J.B. (1995) 'Theoretical Integration in Criminology', in M. Tonry (ed.) *Crime and Justice*. Chicago, MI: University of Chicago Press.

Berney, T. (2004) 'Asperger Syndrome from Childhood into Adulthood', *Advances in Psychiatric Treatment*, 10: 341–51.

Bertaux, D. (1981) 'From the Life-History Approach to the Transformation of Sociological Practice', in D. Bertaux (ed.) *Biography and Society: The Life History Approach in the Social Sciences*. London: Sage.

Bertrand, M. (1967) 'The Myth of Sexual Equality Before the Law', in *Proceedings of the Fifth Research Conference on Delinquency and Criminality*. Montreal: Quebec Society of Criminology.

Besley, A.C. (2003) 'Youth Subcultural Theory', in D. Muggleton and R. Weinzierl (eds) *The Post-Subcultures Reader*. London: Berg.

Best, J. (1988) 'Missing Children, Misleading Statistics', *The Public Interest*, 92: 84–92.

Beyleveld, D. (1978) *The Effectiveness of General Deterrents Against Crime: An Annotated Bibliography of Evaluative Research*. Cambridge: Cambridge Institute of Criminology.

Beyleveld, D. (1979) 'Deterrence Research as a Basis for Deterrence Policies', *The Howard Journal*, 18: 135.

Bianchi, H. (1986) 'Pitfalls and Strategies of Abolition', in H. Bianchi and R. van Swaaningen (eds) *Abolitionism: Towards a Non-Repressive Approach to Crime*. Amsterdam: Free University Press.

Biernacki, P. (1986) *Pathways from Heroin Addiction: Recovery Without Treatment*. Philadelphia: Temple University Press.

Blackburn, R. (1992) *The Psychology of Criminal Conduct*. Chichester: Wiley.

Blackburn, R. and Maybury, C. (1985) 'Identifying the Psychopath: The Relation of Cleckley's Criteria to the Interpersonal Domain', *Personality and Individual Differences*, 6: 375–86.

Blair, T. (1998) *The Third Way: New Politics for the New Century*. London: The Fabian Society.

Bloland, H. (1995) 'Postmodernism and Higher Education', *Journal of Higher Education*, 66(5): 521–57.

Bohm, R. and Walker, J. (eds) (2006) *Demystifying Crime and Criminal Justice*. Los Angeles: Roxbury.

Bonger, W. (1916) *Criminality and Economic Conditions*, reissued 1969. Wilmington, IN: Indiana University Press.

Bonilla-Silva, E. (2003) *Racism Without Racists: Color-Blind Racism and the Persistence of Racial Inequality in the United States*. Lanham: Rowman & Littlefield.

Bonn, S. (2010) *Mass Deception: Moral Panic and the U.S. War on Iraq*. New Brunswick, NJ: Rutgers University Press.

Bost, K.K., Vaughn, B.E., Washington, W.N., Cielinski, K.L. and Bradbard, M.R. (1998) 'Social Competence, Social Support, and Attachment: Construct Domains, Measurement, and Paths of Influence for Preschool Children', *Child Development*, 69: 192–218.

Bottomley, A.K. and Coleman, C. (1981) *Understanding Crime Rates*. Farnborough: Gower.

Boudon, R. (1980) *The Crisis in Sociology: Problems of Sociological Epistemology*. London: Macmillan.

Boudreaux, C., Lord, W.D. and Jarvis, J.P. (2001) 'Behavioral Perspectives on Child Homicide: The Role of Access, Vulnerability and Routine Activities Theory', *Trauma, Violence & Abuse*, 2(1): 56–78.

Bouhana, N. and Wikström, P.-O.H. (2011) 'Al-Qa'ida-influenced Radicalisation: A Rapid Evidence Assessment Guided by Situational Action Theory', *Report to UK Office for Security and Counter-Terrorism*. London: Department of Security and Crime Science, University College London.

Bowlby, J. (1952) *Maternal Care and Mental Health*, 2nd edition. Geneva: World Health Organization.

Box, S. (1981) *Deviance, Reality and Society*, 2nd edition. London: Rinehart and Winston.

Box, S. (1983) *Crime, Power and Mystification*. London: Sage.

Box, S. (1987) *Recession, Crime and Punishment*. London: Macmillan.

Box, S. and Hale, C. (1983) 'Liberation and Female Criminality in England and Wales', *British Journal of Criminology*, 23(1).

Braithwaite, J. (1979) *Inequality, Crime and Public Policy*. London: Routledge & Kegan Paul.

Braithwaite, J. (1984) *Corporate Crime in the Pharmaceutical Industry*. London: Routledge.

Braithwaite, J. (1989) *Crime, Shame and Reintegration*. Cambridge: Cambridge University Press.

Braithwaite, J. (1993) 'Shame and Modernity', *British Journal of Criminology*, 33: 1–18.

Braithwaite, J. (1997) 'Charles Tittle's Control Balance and Criminal Theory', *Theoretical Criminology*, 1: 68–79.

Braithwaite, J. (1998) 'Restorative Justice', in M. Tonry (ed.) *Handbook of Crime and Punishment*. New York: Oxford University Press.

Braithwaite, J. and Daly, K. (1994) 'Masculinities, Violence and Communitarian Control', in T. Newburn and E.A. Stanko (eds) *Just Boys Doing Business? Men, Masculinities and Crime*. London: Routledge, pp. 189–213.

Brake, M. (1980) *The Sociology of Youth Cultures and Youth Sub-cultures*. London: Routledge & Kegan Paul.

Brake, M. (1985) *Comparative Youth Culture*. London: Routledge.

Brand, S. and Price, R. (2000) *The Economic and Social Costs of Crime*, Research Study 217. London: Home Office.

Brantingham, P.J. and Brantingham, P.L. (1978) 'A Theoretical Model of Crime Site Selection', in M. Kron and R. Akers (eds) *Crime, Law and Sanctions*, Sage Research Progress Series in Criminology: Volume 6. Beverly Hills, CA: Sage.

Brantingham, P.J. and Brantingham, P.L. (eds) (1981) *Environmental Criminology*. Beverly Hills, CA: Sage.

Brantingham, P.J. and Brantingham, P.L. (1984) *Patterns in Crime*. New York: Macmillan.

Brantingham, P.J. and Brantingham, P.L. (1994) 'Burglar Mobility and Crime Prevention Planning', in R.V.G. Clarke and T. Hope (eds) *Coping with Burglary*. Boston: Kluwer-Nijhoff.

Brantingham, P.J. and Brantingham, P.L. (1995) 'Criminality of Place: Crime Generators and Crime Attractors', *European Journal on Criminal Policy and Research*, 3(3): 5–26.

Brantingham, P.J. and Brantingham, P.L. (1998) 'Environmental Criminology: From Theory to Urban Planning Practice', *Studies on Crime and Crime Prevention*, 7(1): 31–60.

Brennan, C. (1995) 'Beyond Theory and Practice: A Postmodern Perspective', *Counselling and Values*, 39(2): 99–108.

Brennan, P. and Mednick, S.A. (1997) 'Medical Histories of Antisocial Individuals', in D.M. Stoff, J. Breiling and J. Maser (eds) *Handbook of Antisocial Behavior*. New York: John Wiley & Sons, pp. 269–79.

Briar, S. and Piliavin, I. (1965) 'Delinquency, Situational Inducements and Commitments to Conformity', *Social Problems*, 13(1): 35–45.

Broman, S.H., Nichols, P.L. and Kennedy, W.A. (1975) *Preschool IQ: Prenatal and Early Developmental Correlates*. Hillsdale, NJ: Erlbaum.

Bromberg, S. (1997) 'Feminist Issues in Prostitution', paper presented to the International Conference on Prostitution at California State University, Northridge, CA.

Brown, B. (1986) 'Women and Crime: The Dark Figures of Criminology', *Economy and Society*, 15(3): 355–402.

Brown, G.W. and Harris, T. (1978) *Social Origins of Depression*. London: Tavistock.

Brown, M.D., Carnoy, M.K., Currie, M., Duster, T., Oppenheimer, T., Shultz, D.B.M. and Wellman, D. (2003) *Whitewashing Race: The Myth of a Colorblind Society*. Berkeley, CA: University of California Press.

Brown, S. (1998) *Understanding Youth and Crime: Listening to Youth?* Buckingham: Open University Press.

Brown, W.K. and Miller, T.M. (1988) 'Following up Previously Adjudicated Delinquents: A Method', in R.L. Jenkins and W.K. Brown (eds) *The Abandonment of Delinquent Behaviour: Promoting the Turnaround*. New York: Praeger.

Bruegel, I. (1978) 'Women as a Reserve Army of Labour: A Note on Recent British Experience', *Feminist Review*, 3: 12–23.

Bruner, J.S. (1987) 'Life as Narrative', *Social Research*, 54: 11–32.

Buchanan, B. (2004) 'Money Laundering', *Journal of Research in International Business and Finance*, 18(1): 72–89.

Burawoy, M. (2005) 'For Public Sociology', *American Sociological Review*, 70: 4–28.

Burgess, E.W. (1928) 'The Growth of the City', in R. Park, E.W. Burgess and R.D. McKenzie (eds) *The City*. Chicago, IL: University of Chicago Press.

Burgess, R.L. and Akers, R.L. (1968) 'A Differential Association–Reinforcement Theory of Criminal Behaviour', *Social Problems*, 14: 128–47.

Burnett, R. (1992) *The Dynamics of Recidivism*, Research Report for the Home Office. Oxford: Centre for Criminological Research, University of Oxford.

Burnett, R. (1994) 'The Odds of Going Straight: Offenders' Own Predictions', in Sentencing, Quality and Risk. *Proceedings of the 10th Annual Conference on Research and Information in the Probation Service*, University of Loughborough. Birmingham, UK: Midlands Probation Training Consortium.

Burnett, R. (2004) 'One-to-One Ways of Promoting Desistance: In Search of an Evidence Base', in R. Burnett and C. Roberts (eds) *What Works in Probation and Youth Justice*. Cullompton: Willan Publishing.

Burnett, R. and McNeill, F. (2005) 'The Place of the Officer–Offender Relationship in Assisting Offenders to Desist From Crime', *Probation Journal*, 52(3): 247–68.

Burney, E. (2005) *Making People Behave: Anti-social Behaviour, Politics and Policy*. Cullompton: Willan Publishing.

Bursik, R., Grasmick, H. and Chamlin, M. (1990) 'The Effect of Longitudinal Arrest Patterns on the Development of Robbery Trends at the Neighborhood Level', *Criminology*, 28: 431–50.

Burt, C. (1945) *The Young Delinquent*. London: University of London Press.

Burton, R.V., Maccoby, E. and Allinsmith, W. (1961) 'Antecedents of Resistance to Temptation in Four-year-old Children', *Child Development*, 32: 689.

Cain, M. (ed.) (1989) *Growing Up Good*. London: Sage.

Cain, M. (1990) 'Towards Transgression: New Directions in Feminist Criminology', *International Journal of the Sociology of the Law*, 18(1): 1–18.

Cameron, D. (2008) 'Fixing Our Broken Society', Speech in Gallowgate, Glasgow, 7 July [Online]. Available at: http://www.conservatives.com/News/Speeches/2008/07/David_Cameron_Fixing_our_Broken_Society.aspx [accessed 20 April 2013].

Campbell, A. (1981) *Girl Delinquents*. Oxford: Basil Blackwell.

Campbell, A. (1984) *The Girls in the Gang*. New York: Basil Blackwell.

Campbell, B. (1993) *Goliath: Britain's Dangerous Places*. London: Methuen.

Campbell, D. (2002) 'Three Strikes and You're Out: Human Rights, US Style', *The Guardian*, 26 January.

Campbell, S.B., Pierce, E.W., Moore, G. and Marakovitz, S. (1996) 'Boys' Externalizing Problems at Elementary School Age: Pathways From Early Behavior Problems, Maternal Control, and Family Stress', *Development and Psychopathology*, 8(4): 701–19.

Campbell, S.B., Shaw, D.S. and Gilliom, M. (2000) 'Early Externalizing Behavior Problems: Toddlers and Pre-schoolers at Risk for Later Maladjustment', *Development and Psychopathology*, 12(3): 467–88.

Canter, D. (1994) *Criminal Shadows*. London: Harper Collins Publishers.

Carby, H. (1998) *Race Men*. Boston: Harvard University Press.

Carlen, P. (1983) *Women's Imprisonment*. London: Routledge & Kegan Paul.

Carlen, P. (1988) *Women, Crime and Poverty*. Milton Keynes: Open University Press.

Carlen, P. (1992) 'Criminal Women and Criminal Justice: The Limits to, and Potential of, Feminist and Left Realist Perspectives', in R. Matthews and J. Young (eds) *Issues in Realist Criminology*. London: Sage.

Carrington, B. and Wilson, B. (2002) 'Global Clubcultures: Cultural Flows and Late Modern Dance Music Cultures', in M. Cieslik and G. Pollock (eds) *Young People in Risk Society: The Restructuring of Youth Identities in Late Modernity*. Aldershot: Ashgate.

Carrington, B. and Wilson, B. (2004) 'Dance Nations: Rethinking British Youth Subcultural Theory', in A. Bennett and K. Kahn-Harris (eds) *After Subculture: Critical Studies in Contemporary Youth Culture*. London: Palgrave.

Carson, W.G. (1980) 'White-collar Crime and the Institutionalisation of Ambiguity: The Case of the Early Factory Acts', in G. Geis and E. Stotland (eds) *White Collar Crime: Theory and Research*. Beverly Hills, CA: Sage.

Carter, D. (1997) 'International Organized Crime: Emerging Trends in Entrepreneurial Crime', in P. Ryan and G. Rush (eds) *Understanding Organized Crime in Global Perspective*. Newbury Park, CA: Sage.

Caspi, A. and Moffitt, T.E. (1993) 'The Continuity of Maladaptive Behaviour: From Description to Understanding in the Study of Antisocial Behaviour', in D. Cicchetti and D. Cohen (eds) *Manual of Developmental Psychopathology*. New York: Wiley and Sons.

Caspi, A., Moffitt, T.E., Silva, P.A., Stouthamer-Loeber, M., Krueger, R.F. and Schutte, P.S. (1994) 'Are Some People Crime-Prone? Replications of the Personality–Crime Relationship Across Countries, Genders, Races and Methods', *Criminology*, 32: 163–95.

Castells, M. (1998) *End of Millennium (The Information Age: Economy Society and Culture III)*. Oxford: Blackwell.

CDCU (Central Drugs Co-ordination Unit) (1995) *Tackling Drugs Together: A Strategy for England 1995–1998*. London: HMSO.

Centre for Contemporary Cultural Studies (CCCS) (1982) *The Empire Strikes Back: Race and Racism in 70s Britain*. London: Hutchinson.

Chaiken, J. and Chaiken, M. (1991) 'Drugs and Predatory Crime', in M. Tonry and J. Wilson (eds) *Crime and Justice: A Review of Research*, Vol. 13. Chicago, IL: University of Chicago Press.

Chambers, I. (1994) *Migrancy, Culture, Identity*. London: Routledge.

Chambliss, W.J. (1964) 'A Sociological Analysis of the Law of Vagrancy', *Social Problems*, 12: 67–70.

Chambliss, W.J. (1969) *Crime and the Legal Process*. New York: McGraw-Hill.

Chambliss, W.J. (1975) 'Toward a Political Economy of Crime', *Theory and Society*, 2(1): 149–70.

Chambliss, W.J. and Mankoff, M. (eds) (1976) *Whose Law? What Order?* New York: Wiley & Sons.

Chambliss, W.J. and Seidman, R.T. (1971) *Law, Order, and Power*. Reading, MA: Addison-Wesley.

Chancer, L. and McLaughlin, E. (2007) 'Public Criminologies: Diverse Perspectives on Academia and Policy', *Theoretical Criminology*, 11: 155–73.

Charland, R. (1985) *La Resorption de la délinquence a l'adolescence*. Unpublished doctoral dissertation, University of Montreal, School of Criminology.

Charlesworth, L. (2010) 'England's Early "Big Society": Parish Welfare under the Old Poor Law', *History and Policy* [Online]. Available at: www.historyandpolicy.org/papers/policy-paper-108.html [Accessed 20 April 2013].

Chatterton, P. and Hollands, R. (2003) *Urban Nightscapes: Youth Cultures, Pleasure Spaces and Corporate Power*. London: Routledge.

Chavanne, T.J. and Gallup Jr., G.G. (1998) 'Variation in Risk Taking Behavior Among Female College Students as a Function of the Menstrual Cycle', *Evolution and Human Behavior*, 19: 27–32.

Chesney-Lind, M. (1988) 'Girls in Jail', *Crime and Delinquency*, 34: 150–68.

Chesney-Lind, M. (1989) 'Girls' Crime and Woman's Place: Toward a Feminist Model of Female Delinquency', *Crime and Delinquency*, 35: 5–29.

Chesney-Lind, M. and Shelden, R.G. (1992) *Girls, Delinquency, and Juvenile Justice*. Pacific Grove, CA: Brooks/Cole.

Chibnall, S. (1977) *Law and Order News: An Analysis of Crime Reporting in the British Press*. London: Tavistock.

Chilton, R.J. and Markle, G.E. (1972) 'Family Disruption, Delinquent Conduct, and the Effect of Subclassification', *American Sociological Review*, 37: 93–108.

Christiansen, K.O. (1968) 'Threshold of Tolerance in Various Population Groups Illustrated by Results from the Danish Criminologic Twin Study', in A.V.S. de Reuck and R. Porter (eds) *The Mentally Abnormal Offender*. Boston: Little, Brown.

Christiansen, K.O. (1974) 'Seriousness of Criminality and Concordance Among Danish Twins', in R. Hood (ed.) *Crime, Criminology and Public Policy*. New York: Free Press.

Christie, N. (1977) 'Conflict as Property', *British Journal of Criminology*, 17(1): 1–14.

Christie, N. (1993) *Crime Control as Industry: Towards Gulags, Western Style?* London: Routledge.

Ciba Foundation Symposium (1996) *Genetics of Criminal and Antisocial Behaviour*. Chichester: Wiley.

Cicchetti, D. and Rogosch, F.A. (1996) 'Equifinality and Multifinality in Developmental Psychopathology', *Development & Psychopathology*, 8: 597–600.

Cicourel, A. (1968) *The Social Organization of Juvenile Justice*. New York: Wiley.

Clapham, B. (1989) 'A Case of Hypoglycaemia', *The Criminologist*, 13: 2–15.

Clark, K.B. (1965) *Dark Ghetto: Dilemmas of Social Power*. Middletown, CT: Wesleyan University Press.

Clarke, R.V.G. (1980) '"Situational" Crime Prevention: Theory and Practice', *British Journal of Criminology*, 20: 132–45.

Clarke, R.V.G. (1987) 'Rational Choice Theory and Prison Psychology', in B.J. McGurk, D. Thornton and M. Williams (eds) *Applying Psychology to Imprisonment: Theory and Practice*. London: HMSO.

Clarke, R.V.G. (1999) *Hot Products: Understanding, Anticipating and Reducing Demand for Stolen Goods*, Police Research Series, Paper 112, Policing and Reducing Crime Unit, Research Development and Statistics Directorate. London: Home Office.

Clarke, R.V.G. and Cornish, D.B. (1985) 'Modeling Offender's Decisions: A Framework for Research and Policy', in M. Tonry and N. Morris (eds) *Crime and Justice: An Annual Review of Research*. Chicago: University of Chicago Press.

Clarke, R.V.G. and Mayhew, P. (eds) (1980) *Designing Out Crime*. London: HMSO.

Clear, T.R. (1994) *Harm in American Penology: Offenders, Victims and their Communities*. Albany, NY: State University of New York Press.

Clear, T.R. (2010) 'Policy and Evidence: The Challenge to the American Society of Criminology: 2009 Presidential Address to the American Society of Criminology', *Criminology*, 48: 1–25.

Clear, T.R. and Karp, D.R. (1999) *The Community Justice Ideal: Preventing Crime and Achieving Justice*. Boulder, CO: Westview.

Cleckley, H. (1976) *The Mask of Sanity*. St Louis, MO: C.V. Mosby.

Clegg, S. (1989) *Frameworks of Power*. London: Sage.

Clinard, M.B. (1952) *The Black Market: A Study of White Collar Crime*. New York: Holt, Rinehart and Winston.

Clinard, M.B. and Yeager, P.C. (1980) *Corporate Crime*. New York: Free Press.

Cloninger, C.R. and Gottesman, I.I. (1987) 'Genetic and Environmental Factors in Antisocial Behaviour Disorders', in S.A. Mednick, T.E. Moffitt and S. Stack (eds) *The Causes of Crime: New Biological Approaches*. Cambridge: Cambridge University Press.

Cloward, R.A. (1959) 'Illegitimate Means, Anomie and Deviant Behaviour', *American Sociological Review*, 24: 164–76.

Cloward, R.A. and Ohlin, L.E. (1960) *Delinquency and Opportunity: A Theory of Delinquent Gangs*. New York: Free Press.

Cohen, A.K. (1955) *Delinquent Boys: The Culture of the Gang*. New York: Free Press.

Cohen, A.K., Lindesmith, A. and Schuessler, K. (eds) (1956) *The Sutherland Papers*. Bloomington, IN: Indiana University Press.

Cohen, L.E. and Felson, M. (1979) 'Social Inequality and Predatory Criminal Victimization: An Exposition and Test of a Formal Theory', *American Sociological Review*, 44: 588–608.

Cohen, L.E., Kluegel, J. and Land, K. (1981) 'Social Inequality and Predatory Criminal Victimization: An Exposition and Test of a Formal Theory', *American Sociological Review*, 46: 505–24.

Cohen, P. (1972) 'Sub-Cultural Conflict and Working Class Community', *Working Papers in Cultural Studies*, No. 2. Birmingham: CCCS, University of Birmingham.

Cohen, P., Velez, C., Brook, J. and Smith, J. (1989) 'Mechanisms of the Relation between Perinatal Problems, Early Childhood Illness, and Psychopathology in Late Childhood and Adolescence', *Child Development*, 60: 701–9.

Cohen, S. (1973) *Folk Devils and Moral Panics: The Creation of the Mods and Rockers*. London: Paladin.

Cohen, S. (1979) 'The Punitive City: Notes on the Dispersal of Social Control', *Contemporary Crises*, 3: 339–63.

Cohen, S. (1980, new edition) *Folk Devils and Moral Panics*. Oxford: Martin Robertson.

Cohen, S. (1985) *Visions of Social Control*. Cambridge: Polity Press.

Cohen, S. (1988) *Against Criminology*. New Brunswick, NJ: Transaction.

Cohen, S. (1993) 'Human Rights and Crimes of the State: The Culture of Denial', *Australian and New Zealand Journal of Criminology*, 26(2): 7–115.

Cohen, S. (1994) 'Social Control and the Politics of Reconstruction', in D. Nelken (ed.) *The Futures of Criminology*. London: Sage.

Cohen, S. (1998) 'Intellectual Scepticism and Political Commitment: The Case of Radical Criminology', in P. Walton and J. Young (eds) *The New Criminology Revisited*. London: Macmillan.

Coid, J., Carvell, A., Kittler, Z., Healey, A. and Henderson, J. (2000) *Opiates, Criminal Behaviour and Methadone Treatment*, RDS Occasional Paper. London: Home Office.

Coleman, C. and Moynihan, J. (1996) *Understanding Crime Data*. Buckingham: Open University Press.

Collins, J.J. (1986) 'The Relationship of Problem Drinking in Individual Offending Sequences', in A. Blumstein, J. Cohen, J. Roth and C. Visher (eds) *Criminal Careers and 'Career Criminals'*, Vol. 2. Washington, DC: National Academy Press.

Collins, J.J. (1988) 'Alcohol and Interpersonal Violence: Less than Meets the Eye', in A. Weiner and M.E. Wolfgang (eds) *Pathways to Criminal Violence*. Newbury Park, CA: Sage.

Collins, P.H. (1990) *Black Feminist Thought: Knowledge, Consciousness, and the Politics of Empowerment*. New York: Routledge.

Collins, P.H. (1998) *Fighting Words: Black Women and the Search for Justice*. Minnesota: University of Minneapolis Press.

Collins, P.H. (2005) *Black Sexual Politics: African Americans, Gender, and the New Racism*. New York: Routledge.

Collins, R. (1975) *Conflict Sociology*. New York: Academic.

Colvin, M. (1997) 'Review of Stuart Henry and Dragan Milovanovic's Constitutive Criminology', *American Journal of Sociology*, 102: 1448–50.

Colvin, M. (2000) *Crime and Coercion: An Integrated Theory of Chronic Criminality*. New York: St Martin's Press.

Comte, A. (1976) *The Foundations of Sociology* (readings edited and with an introduction by K. Thompson). London: Nelson.

Conklin, J.E. (1977) *Illegal But Not Criminal*. New Jersey: Spectrum.

Conley, J.J. (1985) 'A Personality Theory of Adulthood and Aging', in R. Hogan and W.H. Jones (eds) *Perspectives in Personality*, Vol. 1. Greenwich, CT: JAI Press.

Connell, R.W. (1987) *Gender and Power*. Cambridge: Polity Press.

Connell, R.W. (1995) *Masculinities*. Cambridge: Polity Press.

Connell, R.W. (2000) *The Men and the Boys*. Sydney: Allen and Unwin.

Connell, R.W. (2007) *Southern Theory: The Global Dynamics of Knowledge in Social Science*. Sydney: Allen and Unwin.

Cornish, D.B. and Clarke, R.V.G. (1986) *The Reasoning Criminal*. New York: Springer-Verlag.

Cornwell, R. (2002) 'An Interview J.K. Galbraith', *The Independent*, 1 July.

Corrigan, P. (1979) *The Smash Street Kids*. London: Paladin.

Cortes, J.B. and Gatti, F.M. (1972) *Delinquency and Crime: A Biopsychological Approach*. New York: Seminar Press.

Coser, L. (1956) *The Functions of Social Conflict*. New York: Free Press.

Costa, P., McKrae, R. and Arenberg, D. (1983) 'Recent Longitudinal Research on Personality and Aging', in W.K. Schaie (ed.) *Longitudinal Studies of Adult Psychological Development*. New York: Guilford Press.

Costy, A. and Gilbert, S. (1998) *Conflict Prevention and European Union: Mapping the Actors, Instruments, and Institutions*. London: International Alert.

Cowan, P.A. (1991) 'Individual and Family Life Transitions: A Proposal for a New Definition', in P.A. Cowan and E.M. Hetherington (eds) *Family Transitions*. Hillsdale, NJ: Lawrence Erlbaum Associates, Inc.

Cowling, M. (2006) 'Postmodern Policies? The Erratic Interventions of Constitutive Criminology', *Internet Journal of Criminology*, November.

Cowling, M. (2008) *Marxism and Criminological Theory: A Critique and a Toolkit*. Basingstoke: Palgrave Macmillan.

Coyle, M.J. (2010) 'Notes on the Study of Language: Towards a Critical Race Criminology', *Western Criminology Review*, 11(1): 11–19.

Crawford, A. (1997) *The Local Governance of Crime: Appeals to Community and Partnerships*. Oxford: Clarendon Press.

Crawford, A. (2006) 'Networked Governance and the Post-regulatory State? Steering, Rowing and Anchoring the Provision of Policing and Security', *Theoretical Criminology*, 10(4): 449–79.

Crawford, A. (2009) 'Governing Through Anti-Social Behaviour: Regulatory Challenges to Criminal Justice', *British Journal of Criminology*, 49: 810–31.

Crawford, A. and Clear, T.R. (2003) 'Community Justice: Transforming Communities through Restorative Justice?', in E. McLaughlin, R. Fergusson, G. Hughes and L. Westmarland (eds) *Restorative Justice: Critical Issues*. London: Sage/Open University.

Crenshaw, M. (ed.) (1995) *Terrorism in Context*. University Park, PA: Pennsylvania State University Press.

Crenshaw, M. (1998) 'The Logic of Terrorism: Terrorist Behavior as a Product of Strategic Choice', in W. Reich (ed.) *Origins of Terrorism*. New York: Woodrow Wilson Center Press.

Cressey, D. (1964) *Delinquency, Crime and Differential Association*. The Hague: Martinus Nijhoff.

Croall, H. (1992) *White-collar Crime*. Buckingham: Open University Press.

Croall, H. (1996) 'Crime: Understanding More and Condemning Less?', *Reviewing Sociology*, 10: 3.

Croall, H. (1998) *Crime and Society in Britain*. Harlow: Longman.

Croall, H. (2001) *Understanding White-collar Crime, Crime and Justice Series*. Buckingham: Open University Press.

Cromwell, P.F., Olson, J. and Avary, D. (1991) 'Breaking and Entering: An Ethnographic Analysis of Burglary', *Studies in Crime, Law and Justice: Vol. 8*. Newbury Park, CA: Sage Publications.

Cromwell, P.F., Durham, R., Akers, R.L. and Lanza-Kaduce, L. (1995) 'Routine Activities and Social Control in the Aftermath of a Natural Catastrophe', *European Journal on Criminal Policy and Research*, 3: 56–69.

Crowe, R.R. (1972) 'The Adopted Offspring of Women Criminal Offenders', *Archives of General Psychiatry*, 27(5): 600–3.

Crowther, C. (1998) 'Policing the Excluded Society', in R.D. Hopkins Burke (ed.) *Zero Tolerance Policing*. Leicester: Perpetuity Press.

Crowther, C. (2000a) *Policing Urban Poverty*. Basingstoke: Macmillan.

Crowther, C. (2000b) 'Thinking About the "Underclass": Towards a Political Economy of Policing', *Theoretical Criminology*, 4(2): 149–67.

Crowther, C. (2007) *An Introduction to Criminology and Criminal Justice*. Basingstoke: Palgrave Macmillan.

Cullen, F.T., Golden, K.M. and Cullen, J.B. (1979) 'Sex and Delinquency', *Criminology*, 17: 310–25.

Currie, E. (1985) *Confronting Crime: An American Challenge*. New York: Pantheon Books.

Currie, E. (1992) 'Retreatism, Minimalism, Realism: Three Styles of Reasoning on Crime and Drugs in the United States', in J. Lowman and B. MacLean (eds) *Realist Criminology: Crime Control and Policing in the 1990s*. Toronto, ON: Toronto University Press.

Currie, E. (1993) *Reckoning: Drugs, the Cities and the American Future*. New York: Hill and Wang.

Currie, E. (1996) *Is America Really Winning the War on Crime and Should Britain Follow Its Example?* NACRO 30th Annual Lecture. London: NACRO.

Currie, E. (1997) 'Market, Crime and Community', *Theoretical Criminology*, 1(2): 147–72.

Currie, E. (1998) *Crime and Punishment in America*. New York: Metropolitan Books.

Currie, E. (1999) 'Reflections on Crime and Criminology at the Millennium', *Western Criminology Review*, 2(1) [Online]. Available at: http://wcr.sonoma.edu/v2n1/currie.html [accessed 6 January 2009].

Currie, E. (2007) 'Against Marginality: Arguments For a Public Criminology', *Theoretical Criminology*, 11: 175–90.

Curtis, L.A. (1975) *Violence, Race and Culture*. Lexington, MA: Heath.

Cusson, M. and Pinsonneault, P. (1986) 'The Decision to Give Up Crime', in D.B. Cornish and R.V. Clarke (eds) *The Reasoning Criminal*. New York: Springer-Verlag.

Dahrendorf, R. (1958) 'Out of Utopia: Toward a Reconstruction of Sociological Analysis', *American Journal of Sociology*, 67: 115–27.

Dahrendorf, R. (1959) *Class and Class Conflict in an Industrial Society*. London: Routledge & Kegan Paul.

Dahrendorf, R. (1985) *Law and Order*. London: Stevens.

Dale, D. (1984) 'The Politics of Crime', *Salisbury Review*, October.

Dalgard, S.O. and Kringlen, E. (1976) 'Norwegian Twin Study of Criminality', *British Journal of Criminology*, 16: 213–32.

Dalton, K. (1961) 'Menstruation and Crime', *British Medical Journal*, 2: 1752–3.

Dalton, K. (1984) *The Pre-menstrual Syndrome and Progesterone Therapy*. London: Heinemann Medical.

Daly, K. (1989) 'Neither Conflict Nor Labeling Nor Paternalism Will Suffice: Intersections of Race, Ethnicity, Gender, and Family in Criminal Court Decisions', *Crime and Delinquency*, 35: 136–68.

Daly, K. (1992) 'Women's Pathways to Felony Court: Feminist Theories of Lawbreaking and Problems of Representation', *Review of Law and Women's Studies*, 2: 11–52.

Daly, K. (1994a) *Gender, Crime, and Punishment*. New Haven, CT: Yale University Press.

Daly, K. (1994b) 'Gender and Punishment Disparity', in G.S. Bridges and M. Myers (eds) *Inequality, Crime and Social Control*. Boulder, CO: Westview Press.

Daly, K. and Chesney-Lind, M. (1988) 'Feminism and Criminology', *Justice Quarterly*, 5(4): 487–535.

Damer, S. (1974) 'Wine Alley: The Sociology of a Dreadful Enclosure', *Sociological Review*, 22: 221–48.

Dannefer, D. (1984) 'Adult Development and Social Theory: A Paradigmatic Reappraisal', *American Sociological Review*, 49: 100–16.

Darwin, C. (1871) *The Descent of Man*. London: John Murray.

Darwin, C. (1872) *The Expression of Emotions in Man and Animals*. London: Philosophical Library.

Darwin, C. (1968 originally 1859) *On the Origin of Species*. New York: Penguin.

Davidson, N. (2006) 'Chernobyl's "nuclear nightmares"', *Horizon* [Online]. Available at: http://news.bbc.co.uk/1/hi/sci/tech/5173310.stm [accessed 5 January 2009].

Davis, K. (1961) 'Prostitution', in R.K. Merton and R.A. Nesbit (eds) *Contemporary Social Problems*. New York: Harcourt Brace and Jovanovich. Originally published as 'The Sociology of Prostitution', *American Sociological Review*, 2(5) (October 1937).

Davis, M. (1990) *The City of Quartz: Evacuating the Future in Los Angeles*. London: Verso.

DCLG (2008) *Communities in Control: Real People, Real Power*. London: Department of Communities and Local Government.

Deater-Deckard, K., Dodge, K.A., Bates, J.E. and Pettit, G.S. (1998) 'Multiple Risk Factors in the Development of Externalizing Behavior Problems: Group and Individual Differences', *Development and Psychopathology*, 10: 469–93.

De Brie, C. (2000) 'Thick as Thieves', *Le Monde Diplomatique* (April).

Decker, S.H. and Van Winkle, B. (1996) *Life in the Gang*. New York: Cambridge University Press.

De Haan, W. (1990) *The Politics of Redress*. London: Unwin Hyman.

De Haan, W. (2000) 'Explaining the Absence of Violence: A Comparative Approach', in S. Karstedt and K.-D. Bussman (eds) *Social Dynamics of Crime and Control*. Oxford: Hart.

DeHaemer, C.A. (2013) 'Weed Penny Stocks', *Wealth Daily* – wd-eletter@angelnexus.com, 27 February.

DeKeseredy, W. and Olsson, P. (2011) 'Adult Pornography, Male Peer Support, and Violence Against Women: The Contribution from the "Dark Side" of the Internet', in M.V. Martin, M.A. Garcia-Ruiz and A. Edwards (eds) *Technology for Facilitating Humanity and Combatting Social Deviation: Interdisciplinary Perspectives*. Hershey, PA: IGA Global.

Delgado, R. and Stefancic, J. (2001) *Critical Race Theory: An Introduction*. New York: New York University Press.

Dell, S. (1984) *Murder into Manslaughter*, Maudsley Monograph Series No. 27. London: Institute of Psychiatry.

De Luca, J.R. (ed.) (1981) *Fourth Special Report to the US Congress on Alcohol and Health*. Rockville, MD: National Institute on Alcohol Abuse and Alcoholism.

Dennis, N. and Erdos, G. (1992) *Families Without Fatherhood*. London: Institute for Economic Affairs.

Denno, D. (1993) 'Considering Lead Poisoning as a Criminal Defence', *Fordham Urban Law Journal*, 20: 377–400.

Denzin, N. (1987) *The Alcoholic Self*. Newbury Park, CA: Sage.

Denzin, N. (1989) *Interpretive Biography*. Newbury Park, CA: Sage.

Department of Health (2005) *Smoking, Drinking and Drug Use Among Young People in England in 2004*. London: Department of Health.

Dezhbakhsh, H., Rubin, P.H. and Shepherd, J.M. (2003) 'Does Capital Punishment Have a Deterrent Effect? New Evidence From Postmoratorium Panel Data', *American Law and Economics Review*, 5: 344–76.

DiClemente, C.C. (1994) 'If Behaviors Change, Can Personality Be Far Behind?', in T.F. Heatherton and J.L. Weinberger (eds) *Can Personality Change?* Washington, DC: American Psychological Association.

DiCristina, B. (1995) *Method in Criminology: A Philosophical Primer*. New York: Harrow and Heston.

Dignan, J. (1999) 'The Criminal Justice Act and the Prospect for Restorative Justice', *Criminal Law Review*, 44–56.

Dishion, T.J. (1990) 'The Family Ecology of Boys' Peer Relations in Middle Childhood', *Child Development*, 61: 874–92.

Ditton, J. (1979) *Controlology: Beyond the New Criminology*. London: Macmillan.

Dobash, R.E. and Dobash, R.P. (1980) *Violence Against Wives*. London: Open Books.

Dobash, R.E. and Dobash, R.P. (1992) *Women, Violence and Social Change*. London: Routledge & Kegan Paul.

Dodge, K.A., Pettit, G.S. and Bates, J.E. (1994) 'Socialization Mediators of the Relation between Socioeconomic Status and Child Conduct Problems', *Child Development*, 65: 649–65.

Donzelot, J. (1980) *The Policing of Families: Welfare Versus the State*. London: Hutchinson.

Donziger, S.R. (1996) *The Real War on Crime: The Report of the National Criminal Justice Commission*. New York: Harper Perennial.

Doob, A. and Cesaroni, C. (2004) *Responding to Youth Crime in Canada*. Toronto, ON: University of Toronto Press.

Doob, A. and Webster, C. (2003) 'Sentence Severity and Crime: Accepting the Null Hypothesis', in M. Tonry (ed.) *Crime and Justice: A Review of Research*, 30: 143–95. Chicago: University of Chicago Press.

Dorn, N. and South, N. (1990) 'Drug Markets and Law Enforcement', *British Journal of Criminology*, 30: 165–76.

Downes, D. (1966) *The Delinquent Solution*. London: Routledge & Kegan Paul.

Downes, D. and Rock, P. (1998) *Understanding Deviance*, 3rd edition. Oxford: Oxford University Press.

Drillien, C.M. (1964) *The Growth and Development of the Prematurely Born Infant*. Edinburgh: Livingstone.

Driver, S. and Martell, L. (1997) 'New Labour's Communitarianisms', *Critical Social Policy*, 52: 27–46.

Du Bois, W.E.B. (1899) *The Philadelphia Negro: A Social Study*. Philadelphia: University Press.

Dugdale, R.L. (1877) *The Jukes*. New York: Putnam.

Duncan Smith, I. (2007) 'Being Tough on the Causes of Crime: Tackling Family Breakdown to Prevent Youth Crime', *Policy Exchange*, February [Online]. Available at: http://www.centreforsocialjustice.org.uk/UserStorage/pdf/Pdf%20reports/causes_of_crime.pdf [accessed 15 Jauuary 2013].

Durkheim, E. (1933 originally 1893) *The Division of Labour in Society*. Glencoe, IL: Free Press.

Durkheim, E. (1951 originally 1897) *Suicide*. New York: Free Press.

Durkheim, E. (1964 originally 1915) *The Elementary Forms of Religious Life*. Glencoe, IL: Free Press.

Duster, T. (2003) *Backdoor to Eugenics*, 3rd edition. New York: Routledge.

Edmunds, M., Hough, M. and Turnbull, P.J. (1999) *Doing Justice to Treatment: Referring Offenders to Drug Treatment Services*, Drugs Prevention Initiative Paper No. 2. London: Home Office.

Eduardo, F. (2000) 'International Money Information Network for Money Laundering Investigators', *Journal of Money Laundering Control*. New York: Cambridge University Press.

Eduardo, F. (2002) 'Combating Money Laundering and Financing of Terrorism', *International Monetary Fund*, 39(3): 126–39.

Edwards, S. (1988) 'Mad, Bad or Pre-Menstrual?', *New Law Journal*, 456.

Edwards, S. (1993) 'England and Wales', in N.J. Davis (ed.) *Prostitution: An International Handbook on Trends, Problems and Policies*. Westport, CT: Greenwood.

Ehrenkranz, J., Bliss, E. and Sheard, M.H. (1974) 'Plasma Testosterone: Correlation with Aggressive Behaviour and Social Dominance in Man', *Psychosomatic Medicine*, 36: 469–83.

Ehrlich, I. (1975) 'The Deterrent Effect of Capital Punishment: A Question of Life or Death', *American Economic Review*, 65: 397.

Einstadter, W. and Henry, S. (1995) *Criminological Theory*. Fort Worth, TX: Harcourt Brace.

Ekblom, P. (2001) 'Situational Crime Prevention', in E. McLaughlin and J. Muncie (eds) *The Sage Dictionary of Criminology*. London: Sage.

Ekblom, P. (2005) 'Designing Products Against Crime', in N. Tilley (ed.) *Handbook of Crime Prevention and Community Safety*. Cullompton: Willan Publishing.

Elias, N. (1978) *The Civilising Process, Vol. 1: The History of Manners*. Oxford: Blackwell.

Elias, N. (1982) *The Civilising Process, Vol. 2: State-Formation and Civilisation*. Oxford: Blackwell.

Elliott, D.S. (1985) 'The Assumption that Theories Can be Combined with Increased Explanatory Power', in R.F. Meier (ed.) *Theoretical Methods in Criminology*. Beverly Hills, CA: Sage.

Elliott, D.S., Ageton, S.S. and Canter, J. (1979) 'An Integrated Theoretical Perspective on Delinquent Behaviour', *Journal of Research in Crime and Delinquency*, 16: 3–27.

Elliott, D.S., Huizinga, D. and Ageton, S.S. (1985) *Explaining Delinquency and Drug Use*. Beverly Hills, CA: Sage.

Ellis, E. (1993) *The Non-Traditional Approach to Criminal Justice and Social Justice*. New York: Community Justice Center.

Ellis, L. (1990) 'The Evolution of Violent Criminal Behaviour and its Non-Legal Equivalent', in L. Ellis and H. Hoffman (eds) *Crime in Biological, Social and Moral Contexts*. New York: Praeger.

Ellis, L. (2005) 'Theory Explaining the Biological Correlates of Criminality', *European Journal of Criminology*, 2(3): 287–314.

Ellis, L. and Crontz, P.D. (1990) 'Androgens, Brain Functioning, and Criminality: The Neurohormonal Foundations of Antisociality', in L. Ellis and H. Hoffman (eds) *Crime in Biological, Social, and Moral Contexts*. New York: Praeger.

Ellis, L. and Walsh, A. (1997) 'Gene Based Evolutionary Theories in Criminology', *Criminology*, 35: 229–76.

Emanuel, E. (1991) *The Ends of Human Life: Medical Ethics in a Liberal Polity*. Cambridge, MA: Harvard University Press.

Emsley, C. (1996) *The English Police: A Political and Social History*. Harlow: Longman.

Emsley, C. (2001) 'The Origins and Development of the Police', in E. McLaughlin and J. Muncie (eds) *Controlling Crime*. London: Sage with the Open University.

Engels, F. (1845) *Karl Marx/Frederick Engels: Collected Works*. New York: International Publishers.

Englander, M. (2007) 'Persistent Psychological Meaning of Early Emotional Memories', *Journal of Phenomenological Psychology*, 38: 181–216.

Epstein, R. (2011) 'Mothers in Prison: The Rights of the Child', *Criminal Justice Matters*, 86: 12–13.

Epstein, S. and Erskine, N. (1983) 'The Development of Personal Theories of Reality from an Interactional Perspective', in D. Magnusson and V.L. Allen (eds) *Human Development: An Interactional Perspective*. New York: Academic Press.

Ericson, R.V. (2003) 'The Culture and Power of Criminological Research', in L. Zedner and A. Ashworth (eds) *The Criminological Foundations of Penal Policy: Essays in Honour of Roger Hood*. Oxford: Oxford University Press.

Ericson, R.V. and Haggerty, D. (1997) *Policing the Risk Society*. Oxford: Clarendon Press.

Ericson, R.V., Baranek, P. and Chan, J. (1991) *Representing Order: Crime, Law, and Justice in the News Media*. Toronto, ON: University of Toronto Press.

Erikson, E. (1959) *Identity and the Life Cycle*. New York: W.W. Norton and Company.

Erikson, K. (1962) 'Notes on the Sociology of Deviance', *Social Problems*, 9: 309–14.

Erikson, K. (1966) *Wayward Puritans: A Study in the Sociology of Deviance*. New York: Wiley.

Escobales, R. (2008) 'Police "Unequivocally" Support Reclassification of Cannabis', *The Guardian*, 5 February.

Etzioni, A. (1961) *A Comparative Analysis of Complex Organizations*. Glencoe, IL: Free Press.

Etzioni, A. (1993) *The Spirit of Community: The Reinvention of American Society*. New York: Touchstone.

Etzioni, A. (ed.) (1995a) *New Communitarian Thinking: Persons, Virtues, Institutions and Communities*. Charlottesville, VA: University of Virginia Press.

Etzioni, A. (1995b) *The Parenting Deficit*. London: Demos.

Etzioni, A., Glendon, M.A. and Galston, W. (1991) *The Responsive Communitarian Platform*. Washington, DC: The Communitarian Network.

Evans, D.J., Fyfe, N.R. and Herbert, D.T. (eds) (1992) *Crime, Policing and Place: Essays in Environmental Criminology*. London: Routledge.

Eysenck, H.J. (1959) *Manual of the Maudsley Personality Inventory*. London: University of London Press.

Eysenck, H.J. (1963) 'On the Dual Nature of Extroversion', *British Journal of Social Clinical Psychology*, 2: 46.

Eysenck, H.J. (1970) *Crime and Personality*. London: Granada.

Eysenck, H.J. (1977) *Crime and Personality*, 3rd edition. London: Routledge & Kegan Paul.

Eysenck, H. (1989) 'Personality and Criminality: A Dispositional Analysis', in W.S. Laufer and F. Adler (eds) *Advances in Criminological Theory*, Vol. 1. New Brunswick, NJ: Transaction Publishers.

Eysenck, H.J. and Eysenck, S.B.J. (1970) 'Crime and Personality: An Empirical Study of the Three-factor Theory', *British Journal of Criminology*, 10: 225.

Eysenck, S.B.J., Rust, J. and Eysenck, H.J. (1977) 'Personality and the Classification of Adult Offenders', *British Journal of Criminology*, 17: 169–70.

Faberman, H.A. (1975) 'A Criminogenic Market Structure: The Automobile Industry', *Sociological Quarterly*, 16: 438–57.

Fabian, J. (1983) *Time and the Other: How Anthropology Makes its Object*. New York: Columbia University Press.

Fagan, J. (1990) 'Intoxication and Aggression', in M. Tonry and J.Q. Wilson (eds) *Crime and Justice: A Review of Research*, Vol. 13. Chicago, IL: University of Chicago Press.

Farnsworth, M. (1989) 'Theory Integration Versus Model Building', in S.F. Messner, M.D. Krohn and A.E. Liska (eds) *Theoretical Integration in the Study of Deviance and Crime*. Albany, NY: State University of New York Press.

Farrall, S. (1995) 'Why Do People Stop Offending?', *The Scottish Journal of Criminal Justice Studies*, 1(1): 51–9.

Farrall, S. (2002) *Rethinking What Works With Offenders*. Cullompton: Willan Publishing.

Farrall, S. (2004) 'Social Capital, Probation Supervision and Desistance from Crime', in S. Maruna and R. Immarigeon (eds) *After Crime and Punishment: Ex-offender Reintegration and Desistance from Crime*. Cullompton: Willan Publishing.

Farrall, S. and Bowling, B. (1997) 'Structuration, Human Development and Desistance from Crime', paper presented at British Society of Criminology Conference, Belfast, United Kingdom.

Farrall, S. and Calverley, A. (2006) *Understanding Desistance From Crime, Crime and Justice Series*. Open University Press: London.

Farrington, D. (1986) 'Age and Crime', in N. Morris and M. Tonry (eds) *Crime and Justice: An Annual Review of Research*, Vol. 7. Chicago, MI: Chicago University Press.

Farrington, D.P. (1992a) 'Juvenile Delinquency', in J.C. Coleman (ed.) *The School Years*, 2nd edition. London: Routledge.

Farrington, D. (1992b) 'Explaining the Beginning, Progress, and Ending of Antisocial Behaviour from Birth to Adulthood', in J. McCord (ed.) *Facts, Frameworks, and Forecasts: Advances in Criminological Theory*, Vol. 3. New Brunswick, NJ: Transaction Publishers.

Farrington, D.P. (1994) 'Introduction', in D.P. Farrington (ed.) *Psychological Explanations of Crime*. Aldershot: Dartmouth.

Farrington, D.P. (1995) 'The Development of Offending and Antisocial Behaviour from Childhood: Key Findings from the Cambridge Study in Delinquent Development', *Journal of Child Psychology and Psychiatry*, 36: 929–64.

Farrington, D.P. (2005) 'Introduction to Integrated Developmental and Life-course Theories of Offending', in D. Farrington (ed.) *Integrated Developmental and Life-course Theories of Offending*. Edison, NJ: Transaction Publishers.

Farrington, D.P. and Morris, A.M. (1983) 'Sex, Sentencing and Reconviction', *British Journal of Criminology*, 23(3): 229–48.

Farrington, D.P. and West, D.J. (1993) 'Criminal, Penal and Life Histories of Chronic Offenders: Risk and Protective Factors and Early Identification', *Criminal Behaviour and Mental Health*, 3: 492–523.

Farrington, D.P. and West, D.J. (1995) 'Effects of Marriage, Separation and Children on Offending by Adult Males', in Z.S. Blau and J. Hagan (eds) *Current Perspectives on Aging and the Life Cycle, Vol. 4: Delinquency and Disrepute in the Life Course*. Greenwich, CT: JAI Press.

Farrington, D.P., Gallagher, B., Morley, L., St Ledger, R.J. and West, D.J. (1986) 'Unemployment, School Leaving and Crime', *British Journal of Criminology*, 26: 335–56.

Farrington, D.P., Loeber, R. and Van Kammen, W. (1990) 'Long-term Criminal Outcomes of Hyperactivity-Impulsivity-Attention Deficit and Conduct Problems in Childhood', in L. Robbins and M. Rutter (eds) *Straight and Devious Pathways from Childhood to Adulthood*. Cambridge: Cambridge University Press.

Fausto-Sterling, A. (1992) 'Putting Woman in Her (Evolutionary) Place', in A. Fausto-Sterling (ed.) *Myths of Gender*. New York: Basic Books.

Feeley, M. and Simon, J. (1992) 'The New Penology: Notes on the Emerging Strategy of Corrections and its Implications', *Criminology*, 30(4): 449–74.

Feeley, M. and Simon, J. (1994) 'Actuarial Justice: The Emerging New Criminal Law', in D. Nelken (ed.) *The Futures of Criminology*. London: Sage.

Feeney, F. (1999) 'Robbers as Decision Makers', in P. Cromwell (ed.) *In Their Own Words: Criminals on Crime*, 2nd edition. Los Angeles, CA: Roxbury.

Feldman, M.P. (1977) *Criminal Behaviour: A Psychological Analysis*. Bath: Pitman Press.

Fellner, J. and Mauer, M. (1998) *Losing the Vote: The Impact of Felony Disenfranchisement in the United States*. Washington, DC: Human Rights Watch and The Sentencing Project.

Felson, M. (1998) *Crime and Everyday Life*, 2nd edition. Thousand Oaks, CA: Pine Forge.

Felson, M. and Clarke, R.V.G. (1998) *Opportunity Makes the Thief*. London: Home Office.

Ferguson, N. (2004) 'The Depressing Reality of This Messianic President's New Empire', *The Independent*, 4 November.

Ferracuti, F. (1982) 'A Sociopsychiatric Interpretation of Terrorism', *Annals of American Academy of Political & Social Science*, 463: 129–41.

Ferrell, J. (1991) 'The Brotherhood of Timber Workers and the Culture of Conflict', *Journal of Folklore Research*, 28: 163–77.

Ferrell, J. (1994) 'Confronting the Agenda of Authority: Critical Criminology, Anarchism, and Urban Graffiti', in G. Barak (ed.) *Varieties of Criminology: Readings from a Dynamic Discipline*. Westport, CT: Praeger.

Ferrell, J. (1995a) 'Urban Graffiti: Crime, Control, and Resistance', *Youth and Society*, 27: 73–92.

Ferrell, J. (1995b) 'Anarchy Against the Discipline', *Journal of Criminal Justice and Popular Culture*, 3: 86–91.

Ferrell, J. (1996) *Crimes of Style: Urban Graffiti and the Politics of Criminality*. Boston, MA: North-eastern University.

Ferrell, J. (1997) 'Criminological Verstehen: Inside the Immediacy of Crime', *Justice Quarterly*, 14: 3–23.

Ferrell, J. (1998) 'Against the Law: Anarchist Criminology', *Social Anarchism*, 25: 5–23.

Ferrell, J. (1999) 'Cultural Criminology', *Annual Review of Criminology*, 25: 395–418.

Ferrell, J. and Ryan, K. (1985) 'The Brotherhood of Timber Workers and the Southern Lumber Trust: Legal Repression and Worker Response', *Radical America*, 19: 55–74.

Ferrell, J. and Sanders, C.R. (eds) (1995) *Cultural Criminology*. Boston, MA: North-eastern University Press.

Ferrell, J., Hayward, K. and Young, J. (2008) *Cultural Criminology: An Invitation*. Beverly Hills, CA: Sage.

Ferri, E. (1895) *Criminal Sociology*. London: Unwin.

Ferri, E. (1968 originally 1901) *Three Lectures by Enrico Ferri*. Pittsburgh, PA: University of Pittsburgh Press.

Feyerabend, P. (1975) *Against Method: Outline of an Anarchistic Theory of Knowledge*. London: New Left Books.

Fichtelberg, A. and Kupchik, A. (2011) 'Democratic Criminology', *Journal of Theoretical and Philosophical Criminology*, 3(1): 57–88.

Field, F. (1989) *Losing Out: The Emergence of Britain's Underclass*. Oxford: Blackwell.

Fielding, N. (1988) *Joining Forces*. London: Routledge.

Figueira-McDonough, J. (1984) 'Feminism and Delinquency: In Search of an Elusive Link', *British Journal of Criminology*, 24: 325–42.

Findlay, M. (2000) *The Globalisation of Crime*. London: Cambridge University Press.

Fishbein, D. (2001) *Biobehavioural Perspectives in Criminology*. Belmont, CA: Wadsworth.

Fishbein, D.H. and Pease, S.E. (1990) 'Neurological Links between Substance Abuse and Crime', in L. Ellis and H. Hoffman (eds) *Crime in Biological, Social and Moral Contexts*. New York: Praeger.

Fishbein, D.H. and Pease, S.E. (1996) *The Dynamic of Drug Abuse*. Boston, MA: Allyn Bacon.

Fitzgibbon, D.W. (2007) 'Institutional Racism, Pre-emptive Criminalisation and Risk Analysis'. *Howard Journal of Criminal Justice*, 46(2), 128–44.

Fitzgibbon, W. and Lea, J. (2010) 'Police, Probation and the Bifurcation of Community', *Howard Journal of Criminal Justice*, 49(3): 215–30.

Flanzer, J. (1981) 'The Vicious Circle of Alcoholism and Family Violence', *Alcoholism*, 1(3): 30–45.

Forsythe, L. (1994) 'Evaluation of Family Group Conference Cautioning Program in Wagga, NSW', paper presented to the Australian and New Zealand Society of Criminology, 10th Annual Conference.

Foucault, M. (1971) *Madness and Civilisation: A History of Insanity in the Age of Reason*. London: Tavistock.

Foucault, M. (1976) *The History of Sexuality*. London: Allen Lane.

Foucault, M. (1977) *Discipline and Punish – the Birth of the Prison*. London: Allen Lane.

Foucault, M. (1980) *Power/Knowledge: Selected Interviews and Other Writings 1972–77*, edited by C. Gordon. Brighton: Harvester Press.

Fowler, F.J. and Mangione, T.W. (1982) *Neighborhood Crime, Fear and Social Control: A Second Look at the Hartford Program*. Washington, DC: US Government Printing Office.

Fowler, F.J., McCall, M.E. and Mangione, T.W. (1979) *Reducing Residential Crime and Fear: The Hartford Neighborhood Crime Prevention Program*. Washington, DC: US Government Printing Office.

Fraser, N. (1981) 'Foucault on Modern Power: Empirical Insights and Normative Confusions', *Praxis International*, 1: 272–87.

Fredrickson, G.M. (2002) *Racism: A Short History*. Princeton, NJ: Princeton University Press.

Freisthler, B., Midanik, L. and Gruenewald, P.J. (2004) 'Alcohol Outlets and Child Physical Abuse and Neglect: Applying Routine Activities Theory to the Study of Child Maltreatment', *Journal of Studies on Alcohol*, 65(5): 586–92.

Freud, S. (1920) *A General Introduction to Psychoanalysis*. New York: Boni and Liveright.

Freud, S. (1927) *The Ego and the Id*. London: Hogarth.

Freud, S. (1933) *New Introductory Lectures on Psychoanalysis*. New York: W.W. Norton.

Friedlander, K. (1947) *The Psychoanalytic Approach to Juvenile Delinquency*. London: Kegan Paul.

Friedlander, K. (1949) 'Latent Delinquency and Ego Development', in K.R. Eissler (ed.) *Searchlights on Delinquency*. New York: International University Press, pp. 205–15.

Friedrichs, D. (1980) 'Radical Criminology', in J. Inciardi (ed.) *Radical Criminology*. Beverly Hills, CA: Sage.

Frisby, D. (1984) *Georg Simmel*. New York: Tavistock.

Frith, U. (2003) *Autism, Explaining the Enigma*, 2nd edition. Oxford: Blackwell.

Fromm, E. (1941) *Escape from Freedom*. New York: Rinehart & Company.

Frus, P. (2001) 'Documenting Domestic Violence in American Films', in J.D. Slocum (ed) *Violence and American Cinema*. New York: Routledge.

Fuller, J. (2003) 'Peacemaking Criminology', in M.D. Schwartz and S.E. Hatty (eds) *Controversies in Critical Criminology*. Cincinnati: Anderson.

Funk, D.G. (2004) *Globalisation and Social Polarisation in Hong Kong*. New York: Routledge.

Fyfe, N.R. (1995) 'Law and Order Policy and the Spaces of Citizenship in Contemporary Britain', *Political Geography*, 14(2): 177–89.

Gabe, J. (2001) *Violence Against Professionals in the Community*. London: Royal Holloway.

Galvin, D. (1983) 'The Female Terrorist: A Socio-Psychological Perspective', *Behavioral Science & Law*, 1: 19–32.

Gamble, A. (1989) *The Free Economy and the Strong State: The Politics of Thatcherism*. Basingstoke: Macmillan.

Gans, D. (1991) 'Sucrose and Unusual Childhood Behaviour', *Nutrition Today*, 26: 8–14.

Gans, H. (1980) *Deciding What's News: A Study of CBS Evening News, NBC Nightly News, Newsweek and Time*. New York: Vintage.

Garfinkel, H. (1967) *Studies in Ethnomethodology*. Oxford: Basil Blackwell.

Garland, D. (1990) *Punishment and Modern Society: A Study in Social Theory*. Chicago: University of Chicago Press.

Garland, D. (1996) 'The Limits of the Sovereign State: Strategies of Crime Control in Contemporary Society', *British Journal of Criminology*, 34(4): 445–71.

Garland, D. (1997) 'The Development of British Criminology', in M. Maguire, R. Morgan and R. Reiner (eds) *The Oxford Handbook of Criminology*. Oxford: Clarendon Press.

Garland, D. (1999) '"Governmentality" and the Problem of Crime', in R. Smandych (ed.) *Governable Places: Readings on Governmentality and Crime Control*. Aldershot: Ashgate.

Garland, D. (2001) *The Culture of Control*. Oxford: Oxford University Press.

Garland, D. and Sparks, R. (2000) 'Criminology, Social Theory and the Challenge of Our Times', *British Journal of Criminology*, 40: 189–204.

Garofalo, R. (1914) *Criminology*. Boston, MA: Little, Brown.

Gartner, R. and Piliavin, I. (1988) 'The Aging Offender and the Aged Offender', in P.B. Baltes, D.L. Featherman and R.M. Lerner (eds) *Life-Span Development and Behaviour*, Vol. 9. Hillsdale, NJ: Lawrence Erlbaum Associates.

Gatrell, V. (1980) 'The Decline of Theft and Violence in Victorian and Edwardian England', in V. Gatrell, B. Lenman and G. Parker (eds) *Crime and the Law: The Social History of Crime in Europe Since 1500*. London: Europa.

Geis, G. (1967) 'The Heavy Electrical Equipment Anti-trust Cases of 1961', in M.B. Clinard and R. Quinney (eds) *Criminal Behaviour Systems*. New York: Holt, Rinehart & Winston.

Geis, G. (1968) *White-collar Crime: The Offender in Business and the Professions*. New York: Atherton.

Geis, G. and Goff, C. (1983) 'Introduction', in E. Sutherland, *White-collar Crime: The Uncut Version*. New Haven, CT: Yale University Press.

Geis, G. and Maier, R.F. (eds) (1977) *White-collar Crime: Offences in Business, Politics and the Professions – Classic and Contemporary Views*. New York: Free Press.

Gelsthorpe, L. and Morris, A. (1980) *Feminist Perspectives in Criminology*. Milton Keynes: Open University Press.

Gelsthorpe, L. and Morris, A. (1988) 'Feminism and Criminology in Britain', *British Journal of Criminology*, 28: 83–110.

Gelsthorpe, L. and Morris, A. (eds) (1990) *Feminist Perspectives in Criminology*. Milton Keynes: Open University Press.

George, S. (1999) 'The Crisis of Global Capitalism', *Business Week*, 19 December.

Gergen, K.J. (1991) *The Saturated Self*. New York: Basic Books.

Ghaziuddin, M. (2005) *Mental Health Aspects of Autism and Asperger's Syndrome*. London: Jessica Kingsley Publishers.

Gibbens, T.C.N. (1963) *Psychiatric Studies of Borstal Lads*. Oxford: Oxford University Press.

Gibbens, T.C.N. (1984) 'Borstal Boys After 25 Years', *British Journal of Criminology*, 24: 46–59.

Gibbens, T.C.N. and Prince, J. (1962) *Shoplifting*. London: Institute for the Study of Delinquency.

Gibbons, D.C. (1970) *Delinquent Behaviour*. Englewood Cliffs, NJ: Prentice Hall.

Gibbons, D.C. (1994) *Talking About Crime and Criminals: Problems and Issues in Theory Development in Criminology*. Englewood Cliffs, NJ: Prentice Hall.

Gibbs, J. (1966) 'Conceptions of Deviant Behaviour', *Pacific Sociological Review*, 9: 9–14.

Gibbs, J. (1975) *Crime, Punishment, and Deterrence*. New York: Elsevier.

Giddens, A. (1964) *Structuration and Related Theories of Social Life and Communication*. London: Routledge.

Giddens, A. (1990) *The Consequences of Modernity*. Cambridge: Polity Press.

Giddens, A. (1991) *Modernity and Self-Identity*. Cambridge: Polity Press.

Giddens, A. (1994) *Beyond Left and Right: The Future of Radical Politics*. Cambridge: Polity Press.

Giddens, A. (1998) *The Third Way: The Renewal of Social Democracy*. Cambridge: Polity Press.

Giddens, A. (2002) *Runaway World: How Globalisation is Reshaping Our Lives*, 2nd edition. London: Profile Books.

Gilbert, J. and Pearson, E. (1999) *Discographies: Dance Music, Culture and the Politics of Sound*. London: Routledge.

Gilens, M. (2000) *Why Americans Hate Welfare: Race, Media, and the Politics of Anti-Poverty Policy*. Chicago: The University of Chicago Press.

Gill, M. and Matthews, R. (1994) 'Robbers on Robbery: Offender Perspectives', in M. Gill (ed.) *Crime at Work: Studies in Security and Crime Prevention*, Vol. 1. Leicester: Perpetuity Press.

Gill, O. (1977) *Luke Street: Housing Policy, Conflict and the Creation of the Delinquency Area*. London: Macmillan.

Gilliom, J. (1994) *Surveillance, Privacy and the Law: Employee Drug Testing and the Politics of Social Control*. Ann Arbor, MI: University of Michigan Press.

Giordano, P.C. and Rockwell, S.M. (2000) 'Differential Association Theory and Female Crime', in S.S. Simpson (ed.) *Of Crime and Criminality*. Thousand Oaks, CA: Pine Forge Press.

Glaser, D. (1964) *Effectiveness of a Prison and Parole System*. Indianapolis, IN.: Bobbs-Merrill.

Glendon, M.A. (1991) *Rights Talk: The Impoverishment of Political Discourse*. New York: Free Press.

Glueck, S. and Glueck, E. (1940) *Juvenile Delinquents Grown Up*. New York: Commonwealth Fund.

Glueck, S. and Glueck, E. (1950) *Unravelling Juvenile Delinquency*. Oxford: Oxford University Press.

Goddard, H.H. (1914) *Feeblemindedness: Its Causes and Consequences*. New York: Macmillan.

Godfrey, C., Eaton, G., McDougall, C. and Culyer, A. (2002) *The Economic and Social Costs of Class A Drug Use in England and Wales, 2000*. London: Home Office.

Goldberg, D.T. (1993) *Racist Culture: Philosophy and the Politics of Meaning*. Oxford: Blackwell.

Goldberg, D.T. (2002) *The Racial State*. Malden: Blackwell.

Goldmann, L. (1970) 'The Sociology of Literature: Status and the Problem of Methods', in M.C. Albrecht, J.H. Barnett and M. Griff (eds) *The Sociology of Art and Literature: A Reader*. London: Duckworth.

Goldstein, H. (1977) *Policing a Free Society*. Cambridge, MA: Ballinger.

Goldstein, H. (1979) 'Improving Policing: A Problem-Oriented Approach', *Crime and Delinquency*, 25: 236–58.

Goldstein, H. (1990) *Problem-Oriented Policing*. New York: McGraw-Hill.

Goldthorpe, J.H. (1968–9) *The Affluent Worker in the Class Structure, 3 Vols*. Cambridge: Cambridge University Press.

Goode, E. and Ben-Yehuda, N. (1994) *Moral Panics: The Social Construction of Deviance*. Oxford: Blackwell.

Goodwin, D., Schulsinger, F., Hermansen, L., Guze, S. and Winokur, G. (1973) 'Alcohol Problems in Adoptees Raised Apart from Alcoholic Biological Parents', *Archives of General Psychiatry*, 28: 238–43.

Gordon, A.F. (1999) 'Globalism and the Prison Industrial Complex: An Interview with Angela Davis', *Race and Class*, 40: 145–57.

Gordon, D. (1971) 'Class and the Economics of Crime', *Review of Radical Economics*, 3: 51–75.

Gordon, R.A. (1986) 'Scientific Justification and the Race-IQ-Delinquency Model', in T. Hartnagel and R. Silverman (eds) *Critique and Explanation: Essays in Honor of Gwynne Nettler*. New Brunswick, NJ: Transaction.

Goring, C. (1913) *The English Convict: A Statistical Study*. London: HMSO.

Gottfredson, M.R. (1984) *Victims of Crime: The Dimension of Risk*, Home Office Research Study No. 81. London: HMSO.

Gottfredson, M.R. and Hirschi, T. (1990) *A General Theory of Crime*. Stanford, CA: Stanford University Press.

Gouldner, A. (1968) 'The Sociologist as Partisan: Sociology and the Welfare State', *The American Sociologist*, May: 103–16.

Gouldner, A. (1970) *The Coming Crisis of Western Sociology*. New York: Basic Books.

Gove, W. (1985) 'The Effect of Age and Gender on Deviant Behavior: A Biopsychosocial Perspective', in A.S. Rossi (ed.) *Gender and the Life Course*. New York: Aldine.

Graham, J. and Bowling, B. (1995) *Young People and Crime*, Home Office Research Study No. 145. London: HMSO.

Gramsci, A. (1977, 1978) *Selections from the Political Writings*. London: Lawrence & Wishart.

Grasmick, H. and Bursik, R. (1990) 'Conscience, Significant Others and Rational Choice: Extending the Deterrent Model', *Law and Society Review*, 24: 837–61.

Grasmick, H., Davenport, E., Chamlin, M. and Bursik, R. (1992) 'Protestant Fundamentalism and the Retributive Doctrine of Punishment', *Criminology*, 30: 21–46.

Gray, G. (1986) 'Diet, Crime and Delinquency: A Critique', *Nutrition Reviews Supplement*, 44: 89–94.

Green, D.A. (2008) *When Children Kill Children: Populism and Popular Culture*. New York: Oxford University Press.

Greenberg, D.F. (1981) 'Delinquency and the Age Structure of Society', in D.F. Greenberg (ed.) *Crime and Capitalism: Readings in Marxist Criminology*. Palo Alto, CA: Mayfield Publishing Company.

Greenberg, D.F. (1985) 'Age, Crime, and Social Explanation', *American Journal of Sociology*, 91: 1–21.

Greer, C. (ed.) (2010) *Crime and Media: A Reader*. London: Routledge.

Gregory, J. (1986) 'Sex, Class and Crime: Towards a Non-Sexist Criminology', in R. Matthews and J. Young (eds) *Confronting Crime*. London: Sage.

Gross, E. (1978) 'Organisations as Criminal Actors', in J. Braithwaite and P. Wilson (eds) *Two Faces of Deviance: Crimes of the Powerless and the Powerful*. Brisbane: University of Queensland Press.

Grosser, G.H. (1951) quoted in D.C. Gibbons (1981) *Delinquent Behaviour*, 3rd edition. Englewood Cliffs, NJ: Prentice Hall.

Grygier, T. (1969) 'Parental Deprivation: A Study of Delinquent Children', *British Journal of Criminology*, 9: 209.

Guerin, D. (1970) *Anarchism*. New York: Monthly Review.

Guerry, A.M. (1833) *Essai sur la Statistique Morale de la France*. Paris: Crochard.

Guiner, L. and Torres, G. (2002) *The Miner's Canary: Enlisting Race, Resisting Power, Transforming Democracy*. Cambridge, MA: Harvard University Press.

Gurr, T. (1970) *Why Men Rebel*. Princeton, NJ: Princeton University Press.

Habermas, J. (1989) *The New Conservatism*. Cambridge: Polity Press.

Habermas, J. (1996) *Between Facts and Norms*. Boston: MIT Press.

Hacker, F. (1996) *Crusaders, Criminals, Crazies: Terror and Terrorists in Our Time*. New York: Norton.

Hagan, J. (1989) *Structural Criminology*. New Brunswick, NJ: Rutgers University Press.

Hagan, J. (1994) *Crime and Disrepute*. Thousand Oaks, CA: Pine Forge Press.

Hagan, J. and McCarthy, B. (1998) *Mean Streets: Youth Crime and Homelessness*. Cambridge: Cambridge University Press.

Hagan, J., Gillis, A.R. and Simpson, J. (1985) 'The Class Structure of Gender and Delinquency: Toward a Power-Control Theory of Common Delinquent Behavior', *American Journal of Sociology*, 90(2): 1151–78.

Hagan, J., Gillis, A.R. and Simpson, J. (1987) 'Class in the Household: A Power-Control Theory of Gender and Delinquency', *American Journal of Sociology*, 92(4): 788–816.

Hagan, J., Gillis, A.R. and Simpson, J. (1990) 'Clarifying and Extending Power-Control Theory', *American Journal of Sociology*, 95(4): 1024–37.

Hagedorn, J. (1992) 'Gangs, Neighbourhoods, and Public Policy', *Social Problems*, 38(4): 529–42.

Haines, K. (1990) *After-care Services for Released Prisoners: A Review of the Literature*. London: Home Office.

Hall, S. (1992) 'New Ethnicities', in H.A. Baker, Jr., M. Diawara and R.H. Lindeborg (eds) *Black British Cultural Studies: A Reader*. Chicago: University of Chicago Press.

Hall, S. and Jefferson, T. (eds) (1976) *Resistance Through Rituals*. London: Hutchinson.

Hall, S. and Scraton, P. (1981) 'Law, Class and Control', in M. Fitzgerald, G. McLennan and J. Pawson (eds) *Crime and Society: Readings in History and Theory*. London: Routledge & Kegan Paul and The Open University Press.

Hall, S., Critcher, C., Jefferson, T., Clarke, J. and Roberts, B. (1978) *Policing the Crisis*. London: Macmillan.

Hall, S. and Winlow, S. (2003) 'Rehabilitating Leviathan: Reflections on the State, Economic Regulation and Violence Reduction', *Theoretical Criminology*, 7(2): 139–62.

Hall, S., Winlow, S. and Ancrum, C. (2008) *Criminal Identities and Consumer Culture: Crime, Exclusion and the New Culture of Narcissism*. Cullompton: Willan Publishing.

Hallsworth, S. (2000) 'Rethinking the Punitive Turn: Economies of Excess and the Criminology of the Other', *Punishment and Society*, 2(2): 145–60.

Hallsworth, S. (2002) 'The Case for a Postmodern Penality', *Theoretical Criminology*, 6(2): 145–63.

Hallsworth, S. and Lea, J. (2008) 'Confronting the Criminology of Complacency: A Rejoinder to Some Recent Critiques of the "Punitive Turn"' [Online]. Available at: http://www.bunker8.pwp.blueyonder.co.uk/misc/complacency.html [accessed 15 February 2013].

Halpern, D. (2001) 'Moral Values, Social Thrust and Inequality', *British Journal of Criminology*, 41: 230–44.

Halpern, D., Bates, C., Mulgan, G., Aldrige, S., Beales, G. and Beales, A.H.,(2004) *Personal Responsibility and Changing Behaviour*. London: Cabinet Office.

Hanmer, J. and Saunders, S. (1984) *Well-Founded Fear*. London: Hutchinson.

Hannah-Moffat, K. (2005) 'Criminogenic Needs and the Transformative Risk Subject: Hybridisation of Risk/Need in Penality', *Punishment and Society*, 7(1): 29–51.

Harcourt, B.E. (2001) *Illusion of Order: The False Promise of Broken Windows Policing*. New York: Harvard University Press.

Harcourt, B.E. and Ludwig, J. (2006) *Broken Windows: New Evidence from New York City and a Five-City Social Experiment*, 73(1): 271–316.

Hardt, M. and Negri, A. (2000) *Empire*. Cambridge, MA: Harvard University Press.

Hare, R.D. (1970) *Psychopathy: Theory and Research*. New York: Wiley.

Hare, R.D. (1980) 'A Research Scale for the Assessment of Psychopathy in Criminal Populations', *Personality and Individual Differences*, 1: 111–19.

Hare, R.D. (1982) 'Psychopathy and Physiological Activity During Anticipation of An Aversive Stimulus in a Distraction Paradigm', *Psychophysiology*, 19: 266–80.

Hare, R.D. (2003) *The Hare Psychopathy Checklist*, revised, 2nd edition. Toronto, ON: Multi-Health Systems.

Hare, R.D. and Jutari, J.W. (1986) 'Twenty Years of Experience with the Cleckley Psychopath', in W.H. Reid, D. Dorr, J.I. Walker and J.W. Bonner (eds) *Unmasking the Psychopath: Antisocial Personality and Related Syndromes*. New York: Norton.

Harries, K. (1999) *Mapping Crime: Principle and Practice*. Washington, DC: National Institute of Justice (NCJ 178919).

Harris, A. (1977) 'Sex and Theories of Deviance: Toward a Functional Theory of Deviant Typescripts', *American Sociological Review*, 42: 3–16.

Harris, T.G. and Rice, E.M. (2006) 'Treatment of Psychopathy: A Review of Empirical Findings', in C.J. Patrick (ed.) *Handbook of Psychopathy*. New York: Guilford Press.

Hart, J. (1978) 'Police', in W. Cornish (ed.) *Crime and Law*. Dublin: Irish University Press.

Hartjen, C. (1974) *Crime and Criminalization*. New York: Praeger.

Hartl, E., Monnelly, E. and Elderkin, R. (1982) *Physique and Delinquent Behaviour*. New York: Academic Press.

Hartmann, H. (1981) 'The Family as a Locus of Class, Gender and Political Struggle: The Example of Housework', *Signs*, 6: 360–94.

Harvey, D. (1989) *The Condition of Postmodernity: An Enquiry into the Origins of Cultural Change*. Oxford: Blackwell.

Havighurst, R.J. (1973) 'History of Developmental Psychology: Socialization and Personality Development through the Life-span', in P. Baltes and W. Schaie (eds) *Life-span Developmental Psychology: Personality and Socialization*. New York: Academic Press.

Hay, D. (1981) 'Property, Authority and the Criminal Law', in M. Fitzgerald, G. McLennan and J. Pawson (eds) *Crime and Society: Readings in History and Theory*. London: Open University Press/Routledge.

Hayles, K. (1990) *Chaos Bound*. Ithaca, NY: Cornell University Press.

Hayles, K. (1991) *Chaos and Order: Complex Dynamics in Literature and Science*. Chicago, IL: University of Chicago Press.

Hayward, K.J. (2004a) *City Limits: Crime, Consumer Culture and the Urban Experience*. London: Glass House Press.

Hayward, K.J. (2004b) 'Crime and Consumer Culture in Late Modernity', in C. Sumner (ed.) *The Blackwell Companion to Criminology*. Oxford: Blackwell.

Hayward, K.J. and Young, J. (2012) 'Cultural Criminology', in M. Maguire, R. Morgan and R. Reiner (eds) *The Oxford Handbook of Criminology*, 5th edition. Oxford: Oxford University Press.

Heal, K. and Laycock, G. (eds) (1986) *Situational Crime Prevention – From Theory into Practice*. London: HMSO.

Healy, W. and Bronner, A.F. (1936) *New Light on Delinquency and its Treatment*. New Haven, CT: Yale University Press.

Hebdige, D. (1976) 'The Meaning of Mod', in S. Hall and T. Jefferson (eds) *Resistance Through Rituals: Youth Sub-cultures in Post-war Britain*. London: Hutchinson, pp. 118–43.

Hebdige, D. (1979) *Subculture: The Meaning of Style*. London: Methuen.

Hebdige, D. (1987) *Cut 'n' Mix: Culture, Identity and Caribbean Music*. London: Comedia.

Heidensohn, F. (1968) 'The Deviance of Women: A Critique and an Enquiry', *British Journal of Criminology*, 19(2): 160–76.

Heidensohn, F.M. (1985) *Women and Crime*. London: Macmillan.

Heidensohn, F. (1987) 'Women and Crime: Questions for Criminology', in P. Carlen and A. Worrall (eds) *Gender, Crime and Justice*. Buckingham: Open University.

Heidensohn, F. (1994) 'Gender and Crime', in M. Maguire, R. Morgan and R. Reiner (eds) *The Oxford Handbook of Criminology*. Oxford: Oxford University Press.

Heidensohn, F. (1996) *Women and Crime*. London: Macmillan.

Heidensohn, F. (2000/2001) 'Women and Violence: Myths and Reality in the 21st Century', *Criminal Justice Matters*, 42: 20.

Heidensohn, F. (2003) 'Gender and Policing', in T. Newburn (ed.) *Handbook of Policing*. Cullompton: Willan Publishing.

Heidensohn, F. (2012) 'The Future of Feminist Criminology', *Crime Media Culture*, 8: 123–34.

Heidensohn, F. and Brown, J. (2012) 'From Juliet to Jane: Women Police in TV Cop Shows, Reality, Rank and Careers', in J. Peay and T. Newburn (eds) *Festschrift for Robert Reiner*. Oxford: Hart Publishing.

Heimer, K. and Matsueda, R.L. (1994) 'Role-taking, Role Commitment, and Delinquency: A Theory of Differential Social Control', *American Sociological Review*, 59: 365–90.

Helson, R. and Stewart, A. (1994) 'Personality Change in Adulthood', in T.F. Heatherton and J.L. Weinberger (eds) *Can Personality Change?* Washington, DC: American Psychological Association.

Henle, M. (1985) 'Rediscovering Gestalt Psychology', in S. Koch and D.E. Leary (eds) *A Century of Psychology as a Science*. New York: McGraw-Hill.

Henry, S. and Lanier, M.M. (1998) 'The Prism of Crime: Arguments for an Integrated Definition of Crime', *Justice Quarterly*, 15(4): 609–27.

Henry, S. and Milovanovic, D. (1994) 'The Constitution of Constitutive Criminology', in D. Nelken (ed.) *The Futures of Criminology*. London: Sage.

Henry, S. and Milovanovic, D. (1996) *Constitutive Criminology: Beyond Postmodernism*. London: Sage.

Henry, S. and Milovanovic, D. (1999) *Constitutive Criminology at Work: Applications to Crime and Justice*. New York: State University of New York Press.

Henry, S. and Milovanovic, D. (2000) 'Constitutive Criminology: Origins, Core Concepts, and Evaluation', *Social Justice*, 27(2): 260–76.

Henry, S. and Milovanovic, D. (2001) 'Constitutive Definition of Crime: Power as Harm', in S. Henry and M.M. Lanier (eds) *What is Crime? Controversies over the Nature of Crime and What to Do about It*. Lanham, MA: Rowman and Littlefield.

Herrnstein, R.J. and Murray, C. (1994) *The Bell Curve*. New York: Basic Books.

Heywood, A. (1992) *Political Ideologies*. London: Macmillan Press.

Hill, E. and Frith, U. (2004) *Autism: Mind and Brain*. Oxford: Oxford University Press.

Hills, J., LeGrand, J. and Pichaud, D. (eds) (2002) *Understanding Social Exclusion*. Oxford: Oxford University Press.

Hillyard, P. (1987) 'The Normalisation of Special Powers: From Northern Ireland to Britain', in P. Scraton (ed.) *Law, Order and the Authoritarian State*. Milton Keynes: Open University Press.

Hindelang, M.J. (1979) 'Sex Differences in Criminal Activity', *Social Problems*, 27: 15–36.

Hindelang, M.J. (1981) 'Variations in Sex-Race-Age-Specific Incidence Rates of Offending', *American Sociological Review*, 46: 461–75.

Hindelang, M.J. and Weis, J.G. (1972) 'Personality and Self-reported Delinquency: An Application of Cluster Analysis', *Criminology*, 10: 268–94.

Hirschi, T. (1969) *Causes of Delinquency*. Berkeley, CA: University of California Press.

Hirschi, T. (1979) 'Separate and Unequal is Better', *Journal of Research in Crime and Delinquency*, 16: 34–8.

Hirschi, T. (1989) 'Exploring Alternatives to Integrated Theory', in S.F. Messner, M.D. Krohn and A.E. Liska (eds) *Theoretical Integration in the Study of Deviance and Crime*. Albany, NY: State University of New York Press.

Hirschi, T. (1995) 'The Family', in J.Q. Wilson and J. Petersilia (eds) *Crime*. San Francisco, CA: ICS Press.

Hirschi, T. and Gottfredson, M. (1995) 'Control Theory and the Life Course Perspective', *Studies on Crime and Crime Prevention*, 4: 131–42.

Hirschi, T. and Gottfredson, M. (2004) 'Self Control and Crime', in R.F. Baumeister and K.D. Vohs (eds) *Handbook of Self-Regulation, Theory and Application*. New York: Guilford.

Hirschi, T. and Hindelang, M.J. (1977) 'Intelligence and Delinquency: A Revisionist Review', *American Sociological Review*, 42: 572–87.

Hirst, P.Q. (1980) 'Law, Socialism and Rights', in P. Carlen and M. Collinson (eds) *Radical Issues in Criminology*. Oxford: Martin Robertson.

HM Treasury (2010) *Spending Review 2010*. London: HMSO.

Hobbes, T. (1968 originally 1651) *Leviathan*, edited by C.B. Macpherson. Harmondsworth: Penguin.

Hobbs, D., Lister, S., Hadfield, P., Winlow, S. and Hall, S. (2000) 'Receiving Shadows: Governance and Liminality in the Night-time Economy', *British Journal of Sociology*, 51(4): 701–17.

Hobbs, D., Winslow, S., Lister, S. and Hadfield, P. (2005) 'Violent Hypocrisy: Governance and the Night-time Economy', *European Journal of Criminology*, 42(2): 352–70.

Hodge, J. (1993) 'Alcohol and Violence', in P. Taylor (ed.) *Violence in Society*. London: Royal College of Physicians.

Hoffman, B. (1993) *Holy Terror*. Santa Monica, CA: RAND.

Hoffman, M.L. and Saltzstein, H.D. (1967) 'Parent Discipline and the Child's Moral Development', *Journal of Personality and Social Psychology*, 5: 45.

Hoffman Bustamante, D. (1973) 'The Nature of Female Criminality', *Issues in Criminology*, 8: 117.

Hogg, R. and Brown, D. (1998) *Rethinking Law and Order*. Sydney: Pluto Press.

Hoghughi, M.S. and Forrest, A.R. (1970) 'Eysenck's Theory of Criminality: An Examination with Approved Schoolboys', *British Journal of Criminology*, 10: 240.

Holdaway, S. (1983) *Inside the British Police: A Force at Work*. Oxford: Blackwell.

Hollin, C.R. (1989) *Psychology and Crime: An Introduction to Criminological Psychology*. London: Routledge.

Hollin, C.R. (1990a) 'Social Skills Training with Delinquents: A Look at the Evidence and Some Recommendations for Practice', *British Journal of Social Work*, 20: 483–93.

Hollin, C.R. (1990b) *Cognitive-Behavioural Interventions with Young Offenders*. Elmsford, NY: Pergamon Press.

Holmes, R.M. and De Burger, J. (1989) *Serial Murder*. Newbury Park, CA: Sage.

Home Office (1997) *Aspects of Crime: Young Offenders*. London: Home Office.

Home Office (1999) *Proposals for Revising Legislative Measures on Fingerprints, Footprints and DNA Samples*. London: Home Office.

Home Office (2000) *British Crime Survey*. London: HMSO.

Home Office (2001) *Confidence in the Criminal Justice System*. London: HMSO.

Home Office (2004) *Anti-social Behaviour Orders and Acceptable Behaviour Orders*. London: HMSO.

Home Office (2009) *Controlled Drugs: Reclassification of Cannabis*. London: HMSO.

hooks, b. (1981) *Ain't I a Woman: Black Women and Feminism*. Boston, MA: South End Press.

hooks, b. (1988) *Talking Back, Thinking Feminist, Thinking Black*. Boston, MA: South End Press.

hooks, b. (1990) *Yearning, Race, Gender, and Cultural Politics*. Boston, MA: South End Press.

Hooton, E.A. (1939) *The American Criminal: An Anthropological Study*. Cambridge, MA: Harvard University Press.

Hopkins, A. and McGregor, H. (1991) *Working for Change: The Movement Against Domestic Violence*. Sydney: Allen & Unwin.

Hopkins Burke, R.D. (ed.) (1998a) *Zero Tolerance Policing*. Leicester: Perpetuity Press.

Hopkins Burke, R.D. (1998b) 'The Contextualisation of Zero Tolerance Policing Strategies', in R.D. Hopkins Burke (ed.) *Zero Tolerance Policing*. Leicester: Perpetuity Press.

Hopkins Burke, R.D. (1998c) 'Begging, Vagrancy and Disorder', in R.D. Hopkins Burke (ed.) *Zero Tolerance Policing*. Leicester: Perpetuity Press.

Hopkins Burke, R.D. (1999a) *Youth Justice and the Fragmentation of Modernity*. Scarman Centre for the Study of Public Order Occasional Paper Series, The University of Leicester.

Hopkins Burke, R.D. (1999b) 'The Socio-Political Context of Zero Tolerance Policing Strategies', *Policing: An International Journal of Police Strategies & Management*, 21(4): 666–82.

Hopkins Burke, R.D. (2000) 'The Regulation of Begging and Vagrancy: A Critical Discussion', *Crime Prevention and Community Safety: An International Journal*, 2(2): 43–52.

Hopkins Burke, R.D. (2002) 'Zero Tolerance Policing: New Authoritarianism or New Liberalism?', *The Nottingham Law Journal*, 2(1): 20–35.

Hopkins Burke, R.D. (2003) 'Policing Bad Behaviour: Interrogating the Dilemmas', in J. Rowbotham and K. Stevenson (eds) *Behaving Badly? Offensive Behaviour and 'Crime'*. London: Ashgate.

Hopkins Burke, R.D. (ed.) (2004a) *'Hard Cop/Soft Cop': Dilemmas and Debates in Contemporary Policing*. Cullompton: Willan Publishing.

Hopkins Burke, R.D. (2004b) 'Policing Contemporary Society', in R.D. Hopkins Burke, *'Hard Cop/Soft Cop': Dilemmas and Debates in Contemporary Policing*. Cullompton: Willan Publishing.

Hopkins Burke, R.D. (2004c) 'Policing Contemporary Society Revisited', in R.D. Hopkins Burke, *'Hard Cop/Soft Cop': Dilemmas and Debates in Contemporary Policing*. Cullompton: Willan Publishing.

Hopkins Burke, R.D. (2005) *An Introduction to Criminological Theory*, 2nd edition. Cullompton: Willan Publishing.

Hopkins Burke, R.D. (2007) 'Moral Ambiguity, the Schizophrenia of Crime and Community Justice', *British Journal of Community Justice*, 5(1): 43–64.

Hopkins Burke, R.D. (2008) *Young People, Crime and Justice*. Cullompton: Willan Publishing.

Hopkins Burke, R.D. (2012) *Criminal Justice Theory: An Introduction*. Abingdon, Oxon: Routledge.

Hopkins Burke, R.D. (2013) 'Theorizing the Criminal Justice System: Four Models of Criminal Justice Development', *Criminal Justice Review*, September (38): 335–53.

Hopkins Burke, R.D. and Hodgson, P. (2013) 'Responding to Repeat Anti-social Behaviour and Moral Communitarianism', paper given to the British Society of Criminology Conference 2013, 'Criminology on Trial', University of Wolverhampton, 1st–4th July.

Hopkins Burke, R.D. and Morrill, R. (2002) 'Anti-social Behaviour Orders: An Infringement of the Human Rights Act 1998?', *The Nottingham Law Journal*, 2(2): 1–16.

Hopkins Burke, R.D. and Morrill, R. (2004) 'Human Rights v. Community Rights: The Case of the Anti-Social Behaviour Order', in R.D. Hopkins Burke, *'Hard Cop/Soft Cop': Dilemmas and Debates in Contemporary Policing*. Cullompton: Willan Publishing.

Hopkins Burke, R.D. and Pollock, E. (2004) 'A Tale of Two Anomies: Some Observations on the Contribution of (Sociological) Criminological Theory to Explaining Hate Crime Motivation', *Internet Journal of Criminology*, November.

Hopkins Burke, R.D. and Sunley, R. (1996) *'Hanging Out' in the 1990s: Young People and the Postmodern Condition*, Occasional Paper 11, COP Series. Scarman Centre for the Study of Public Order, University of Leicester.

Hopkins Burke, R.D. and Sunley, R. (1998) 'Youth Subcultures in Contemporary Britain', in K. Hazlehurst and C. Hazlehurst (eds) *Gangs and Youth Subcultures: International Explorations*. New Brunswick, NJ: Transaction Press.

Horney, J. and Marshall, I. (1991) 'Measuring Lambda through Self-Reports', *Criminology*, 29(3): 471–95.

Hough, M., Clarke, R.V.G. and Mayhew, P. (1980) 'Introduction', in R.V.G. Clarke and P. Mayhew (eds) *Designing Out Crime*. London: HMSO.

Howlin, P. (1997) *Autism: Preparing for Adulthood*. Oxford: Routledge.

Howlin, P. (2004) *Autism and Asperger Syndrome: Preparing for Adulthood*, 2nd edition. Oxford: Routledge.

Hudson, J., Morris, A., Maxwell, G. and Galway, B. (1996) *Family Group Conferences*. Annandale, NSW: Federation Press.

Hudson, R. (1999) *Who Becomes a Terrorist and Why*. Guilford, CT: Lyons Press.

Huesmann, L.R., Eron, L.D., Lefkowitz, M.M. and Walder, L.O. (1984) 'Stability of Aggression Over Time and Across Generations', *Developmental Psychology*, 20: 1120–34.

Huff, R. (2001) 'Wrongful Conviction and Public Policy: The American Society of Criminology 2001 Presidential Address', *Criminology*, 40: 1–18.

Hughes, G. (1998) *Understanding Crime Prevention: Social Control, Risk and Late Modernity*. Buckingham: Open University Press.

Hughes, G. (2000) 'Communitarianism and Law and Order', in T. Hope (ed.) *Perspective on Crime Reduction*. Dartmouth: Ashgate.

Hughes, G. (2007) *The Politics of Crime and Community*. Basingstoke: Palgrave/Macmillan.

Hutchings, B. and Mednick, S.A. (1977) 'Criminality in Adoptees and their Adoptive and Biological Parents: A Pilot Study', in S.A. Mednick and K.O. Christiansen (eds) *Biosocial Bases of Criminal Behaviour*. New York: Gardner.

Hutchinson, S. (2006) 'Countering Catastrophic Criminology: Reform, Punishment and the Modern Liberal Compromise', *Punishment and Society*, 8(4): 443–67.

Ignatieff, M. (1978) *A Just Measure of Pain: The Penitentiary and the Industrial Revolution*. London: Macmillan.

Institute of Alcohol Studies (2005) *Adolescents and Alcohol*. St Ives, Cambridgeshire: IAS.

Institute of Race Relations (1987) *Policing Against Black People*. London: Institute of Race Relations.

Irwin, J. (1970) *The Felon*. Englewood Cliffs, NJ: Prentice Hall.

Irwin, J. and Austin, J. (1994) *It's About Time: America's Imprisonment Binge*. Belmont, CA: Wadsworth.

Jacobs, B. (2000) *Robbing Drug Dealers*. New York: Aldine de Gruyter.

Jacobs, J. (1961) *The Death and Life of Great American Cities*. New York: Vintage.

Jaggar, A.M. (1980) *'Prostitution' in Readings in the Philosophy of Sex*. Totowa, NJ: Littlefield, Adams & Co.

Jaggar, A.M. (1983) *Feminist Politics and Human Nature*. Lanham, MD: Rowman and Littlefield.

Jarvis, G. and Parker, H. (1989) 'Young Heroin Users and Crime', *British Journal of Criminology*, 29: 175.

Jay, M. (1973) *The Dialectical Imagination: A History of the Frankfurt School*. Boston, MA: Little, Brown.

Jefferis, B.J.M.H., Power, C. and Manor, O. (2005) 'Adolescent Drinking Level and Adult Binge Drinking in a National Cohort', *Addiction*, 100(4): 543–9.

Jefferson, T. (1997) 'Masculinities and Crime', in M. Maguire, R. Morgan and R. Reiner (eds) *The Oxford Handbook of Criminology*, 2nd edition. Oxford: Clarendon.

Jeffery, C.R. (1977) *Crime Prevention Through Environmental Design*. Beverly Hills, CA: Sage.

Jenkins, P. (1989) *Mrs Thatcher's Revolution*. London: Pan Books.

Jensen, A.R. (1969) 'How Much Can We Boost IQ and Scholastic Achievement?', *Harvard Educational Review*, 39: 1–23.

Jewkes, Y. (2004) *Media and Crime*. London: Sage.

Johannen, U., Steven, G. and Gomez, J. (2003) *Social and Economic Impacts of Globalisation in Latin America*. New York: Routledge.

Johnston, S. (1997) 'Forensic Psychiatry and Learning Disability', in O. Russell (ed.) *Seminars in the Psychiatry of Learning Disabilities*. London: The Royal College of Psychiatrists.

Jolin, A. (1985) *Growing Old and Going Straight: Examining the Role of Age in Criminal Career Termination*. PhD Thesis, Portland State University.

Jones, G. (1980) *Social Darwinism and English Thought – The Interaction between Biological and Social Theory*. Brighton: Harvester Press.

Jones, S. (1993) *The Language of the Genes*. London: Harper Collins.

Jones, T., Newburn, T. and Smith, D. (1994) *Democracy and Policing*. London: Policy Studies Institute.

Jordan, B. (1992) 'Basic Income and the Common Good', in P. van Parisjs (ed.) *Arguing for Basic Income*. London: Verso.

Jordan, B. (1996) *A Theory of Social Exclusion and Poverty*. Cambridge: Polity Press.

Jordan, B. (1998) 'New Labour, New Community?', *Imprints*, 3(2): 113–31.

Juergensmeyer, M. (2001) *Terror in the Mind of God: The Global Rise of Religious Violence*. Berkeley, CA: University of California Press.

Kandel, E. and Mednick, S. (1991) 'Perinatal Complications Predict Violent Offending', *Criminology*, 29(3): 519–29.

Karmen, A. (2004) 'Zero Tolerance in New York City: Hard Questions for a Get-Tough Policy', in R.D. Hopkins Burke, *'Hard Cop/Soft Cop': Dilemmas and Debates in Contemporary Policing*. Cullompton: Willan Publishing.

Katz, J. (1988) *Seductions of Crime: Moral and Sensual Attractions in Doing Evil*. New York: Basic Books.

Kazdin, A.E. (1987) *Conduct Disorder in Childhood and Adolescence*. Newbury Park, CA: Sage.

Keane, C., Maxim, P.S. and Teevan, J.T. (1993) 'Drinking and Driving, Self-Control, and Gender: Testing a General Theory of Crime', *Journal of Research in Crime and Delinquency*, 30: 30.

Kelling, G. (1999) 'Broken Windows, Zero Tolerance and Crime Control', in P. Francis and F. Penny (eds) *Building Safer Communities*. London: Centre for Crime and Justice Studies.

Kelling, G., Pate, T., Dieckman, D. and Brown, C. (1974) *The Kansas City Preventive Patrol Experiment: A Summary Report*. Washington: Police Foundation.

Kelly, T. (2006) 'Judge Tells McDonald's Killer: You Didn't Know It Was Wrong', *The Daily Mail*, 10 December.

Kemshall, H. (2003) *Understanding Risk in Criminal Justice*. Milton Keynes: Open University Press

Kendall, L. (2003) 'Cyberporn', in M.S. Kimmel and A. Aronson (eds) *Men and Masculinities: A Social, Cultural, and Historical Encyclopedia*. Santa Barbara, CA: ABC-CLIO.

Kendler, H.H. (1985) 'Behaviourism and Psychology: An Uneasy Alliance', in S. Koch and D.E. Leary (eds) *A Century of Psychology as Science*. New York: McGraw-Hill.

Kennedy, H. (1992) *Eve Was Framed*. London: Chatto & Windus.

Kennedy, R. (1997) 'Race, Law and Suspicion: Using Color as a Proxy for Dangerousness', *Race, Crime and the Law*. New York: Pantheon.

Kenney, J.S. (2002) 'Victims of Crime and Labelling Theory: A Parallel Process?', *Deviant Behavior: An Interdisciplinary Journal*, 23: 235–65.

Kershaw, C., Budd, T., Kinshott, G., Mattinson, J., Mayhew, P. and Myhill, A. (2000) *The 2000 British Crime Survey*. London: Home Office.

Keverne, E.B., Meller, R.E. and Eberhart, J.A. (1982) 'Social Influences on Behaviour and Neuroendocrine Responsiveness in Talapoin Monkeys', *Scandinavian Journal of Psychology*, 1: 37–54.

Kiely, R. and Marfleet, P. (1998) *Globalisation and the Third World*. New York: Routledge.

King, M. (1981) *The Framework of Criminal Justice*. London: Croom Helm.

Kinnvall, C. and Jonsson, K. (2002) *Globalization*. New York: Routledge

Kinsey, R., Lea, J. and Young, J. (1986) *Losing the Fight Against Crime*. Oxford: Basil Blackwell.

Kitsuse, J.I. (1962) 'Societal Reaction to Deviant Behaviour: Problems of Theory and Method', *Social Problems*, 9: 247–56.

Kitsuse, J.I. and Dietrick, D.C. (1959) 'Delinquent Boys: A Critique', *American Sociological Review*, 24: 208–15.

Klein, D. (1973) 'The Aetiology of Female Crime: A Review of the Literature', in L. Crites (ed.) *The Female Offender*. Lexington, MA: Lexington Books.

Klepper, S. and Nagin, D. (1989) 'The Deterrent Effect of Perceived Certainty and Severity of Punishment Revisited', *Criminology*, 27(4): 721–46.

Klinefelter, H.F., Reifenstein, E.C. and Albright, F. (1942) 'Syndrome Characterized by Gynecomastia, Aspermatogenesis without Aleydigism and Increased Excretion of Follicle-Stimulating Hormone', *Journal of Clinical Endocrinology*, 2: 615–27.

Knights, B. (1998) '"The Slide to Ashes": An Antidote to Zero Tolerance', in R.D. Hopkins Burke (ed.) *Zero Tolerance Policing*. Leicester: Perpetuity Press.

Kochan, N. and Whittington, B. (1991) *Bankrupt: The BCCI Fraud*. London: Victor Gollancz.

Koestler, A. and Rolph, C.H. (1961) *Hanged by the Neck*. Harmondsworth: Penguin.

Kolvin, I., Miller, F.J.W., Scott, D.M., Gatzanis, S.R.M. and Fleeting, M. (1990) *Continuities of Deprivation?* Aldershot: Avebury.

Konopka, G. (1966) *The Adolescent Girl in Conflict*. London: Prentice Hall.

Kornbluh, J. (ed.) (1988) *Rebel Voices: An IWW Anthology*. Chicago, IL: Charles H. Kerr.

Kozol, H.L., Boucher, R.J. and Garofalo, R.F. (1972) 'The Diagnosis and Treatment of Dangerousness', *Crime and Delinquency*, 18: 371–92.

Kraemer, E. (2004) 'A Philosopher Looks at Terrorism', in A. Nyatepe-Coo and D. Zeisler-Vralsted (eds) *Understanding Terrorism*. Upper Saddle River, NJ: Prentice Hall.

Kramer, R.C. (1984) 'Corporate Criminality: The Development of an Idea', in E. Hochstetler (ed.) *Corporations as Criminals*. Beverly Hills, CA: Sage.

Kramer, R.C. (1985) 'Humanistic Perspectives in Criminology', *Journal of Sociology and Social Welfare*, 12: 469–87.

Kretschmer, E. (1964) *Physique and Character*, translation by W.J.H. Sprott. New York: Cooper Square.

Kreuz, L.E. and Rose, R.M. (1972) 'Assessment of Aggressive Behaviour and Plasma Testosterone in a Young Criminal Population', *Psychosomatic Medicine*, 34: 321–33.

Krisberg, B. (1974) 'Gang Youth and Hustling: The Psychology of Survival', *Issues in Criminology*, 9: 115–31.

Kropotkin, P. (1975) *The Essential Kropotkin*. New York: Liveright.

Kupchik, A. (2006) *Judging Juveniles: Prosecuting Adolescents in Adult and Juvenile Courts*. NY: New York University Press.

Lacey, N., Wells, C. and Meure, D. (1990) *Reconstructing Criminal Law: Critical Social Perspectives on Crime and the Criminal Process*. London: Weidenfeld & Nicolson.

Ladner, J. (1972) *Tomorrow's Tomorrow: The Black Woman*. New York: Doubleday.

Ladouceur, C. and Biron, L. (1993) 'Ecouler La Merchandise Volé, Une Approche Rationelle?', *Canadian Journal of Criminology*, 35(2): 169–82.

Laing, R.D. (1960) *The Divided Self*. Harmondsworth: Penguin.

Lambert, J.R. (1970) *Crime, Police and Race Relations*. London: Institute of Race Relations/ Oxford University Press.

Lancaster, J.B., Sherrod, L., Rossi, A.S. and Altmann, J. (1987) *Parenting Across the Life Span*. Piscataway, NJ: Aldine Transaction.

Lange, J. (1930) *Crime as Destiny*. London: Allen and Unwin.

Lansky, M. (1987) 'Shame and Domestic Violence', in D. Nathanson (ed.) *The Many Faces of Shame*. New York: Guilford.

Laub, J.H. and Sampson, R.J. (2003) 'Understanding Desistance from Crime', *Crime and Justice*, 28: 1–58.

Laucht, M., Esser, G., Baving, L., Gerhold, M., Hoesch, I., Ihle, W., Steigleider, P., Stock, B., Stoehr, R., Weindrich, D. and Schmidt, M. (2000) 'Behavioral Sequelae of Perinatal Insults and Early Family Adversity at 8 Years of Age', *Journal of the American Academy of Child and Adolescent Psychiatry*, 39: 1229–37.

Lea, J. (1992) 'Left Realism: A Framework for the Analysis of Crime', in J. Young and R. Matthews (eds) *Rethinking Criminology: The Realist Debate*. London: Sage.

Lea, J. (1999) 'Social Crime Revisited', *Theoretical Criminology*, 3(5): 307–25.

Lea, J. (2002) *Crime and Modernity*. London: Sage Publications.

Lea, J. (2004) 'Hitting Criminals Where it Hurts: Organised Crime and the Erosion of Due Process', *Cambrian Law Review*, 35: 81–96.

Lea, J. (2010) 'Left Realism, Community and State-Building', *Crime, Law and Change*, 54: 141–58.

Lea, J. and Young, J. (1984) *What is to be Done About Law and Order?* Harmondsworth: Penguin.

Le Billon, P. (2001) 'Fuelling War or Buying Peace: The Role of Corruption in Conflicts', *Journal of International Development*, 13: 951–64.

LeBlanc, M. and Frechette, M. (1989) *Male Criminal Activity from Childhood through Youth: Multilevel and Development Perspectives.* New York: Springer-Verlag.

Leibrich, J. (1993) *Straight to the Point: Angles on Giving Up Crime.* Otago, New Zealand: University of Otago Press.

Leigh, A., Read, T. and Tilley, N. (1998) *Brit Pop 11: Problem Oriented Policing in Practice,* Police Research Series, Paper 93. London: Home Office.

Lemert, E. (1951) *Social Pathology: A Systematic Approach to the Theory of Sociopathic Behavior.* New York: McGraw-Hill.

Lemert, E. (1972) *Human Deviance, Social Problems and Social Control,* 2nd edition. Englewood Cliffs, NJ: Prentice Hall.

Leonard, E. (1983) *Women, Crime and Society.* London: Longmans.

Lerner, G. (1998) *The Creation of Patriarchy.* Oxford: Oxford University Press.

Lesser, M. (1980) *Nutrition and Vitamin Therapy.* New York: Bantam.

Lever, J. (1978) 'Sex Differences in the Complexity of Children's Play and Games', *American Sociological Review,* 43: 476–88.

Levin, J. and McDevitt, J. (1993) *Hate Crimes: The Rising Tide of Bigotry and Bloodshed.* Boston, MA: Plenum.

Levine, N. (1999) *CrimeStat: A Spatial Statistics Program for the Analysis of Crime Incident Locations.* Washington, DC: Ned Levine & Associates/National Institute of Justice.

Levitas, R. (1996) 'The Concept of Social Exclusion and the New Durkheimian Hegemony', *Critical Social Policy,* 16(1): 5–20.

Lewin, K. (1935) *A Dynamic Theory of Personality.* New York: McGraw-Hill.

Li, L. and Moore, D. (2001) 'Disability and Illicit Drug Use: An Application of Labeling Theory', *Deviant Behavior: An Interdisciplinary Journal,* 22: 1–21.

Liazos, A. (1972) 'The Poverty of the Sociology of Deviance: Nuts, Sluts and Perverts', *Social Problems,* 20: 103–20.

Lilienfeld, S.O. (2005) 'Scientifically Unsupported and Supported Interventions for Childhood Psychopathology: A Summary', *Paediatrics,* 115: 761–4.

Lilly, J.R., Cullen, F.T. and Ball, R.A. (1986) *Criminological Theory: Context and Consequences.* London: Sage.

Lindqvist, P. (1986) 'Criminal Homicide in Northern Sweden, 1970–1981 – Alcohol Intoxication, Alcohol Abuse and Mental Disease', *International Journal of Law and Psychiatry,* 8: 19–37.

Link, B. (1987) 'Understanding Labelling Effects of Mental Disorders: An Assessment of the Effects of Expectations of Rejection', *American Sociological Review,* 54: 395–410.

Link, B., Cullen, F., Frank, J. and Wozniak, J. (1987) 'The Social Reaction of Former Mental Patients: Understanding Why Labels Work', *American Journal of Sociology,* 92: 145–67.

Link, B., Cullen, F., Struening, E., Shrout, P. and Dohrenwend, B. (1989) 'A Modified Labelling Theory Approach to Mental Disorders: An Empirical Assessment', *American Sociological Review,* 54: 400.

Liska, A.E. (1987) *Perspectives on Deviance.* Englewood Cliffs, NJ: Prentice Hall.

Liska, A.E. (ed.) (1992) *Social Threat and Social Control.* Albany, NY: SUNY Press.

Liska, A.E., Krohn, M.D. and Messner, S.F. (1989) 'Strategies and Requisites for Theoretical Integration in the Study of Crime and Deviance', in S.F. Messner, M.D. Krohn and A.E. Liska (eds) *Theoretical Integration in the Study of Deviance and Crime.* Albany, NY: University of New York.

Lister, R. (2011) 'The Age of Responsibility: Social Policy and Citizenship in the Early 21st Century', in C. Holden, M. Kilkey and G. Ramia (eds) *Analysis and Debate in Social Policy, 2011.* Bristol: Policy Press.

Little, A. (1963) 'Professor Eysenck's Theory of Crime: An Empirical Test on Adolescent Offenders', *British Journal of Criminology*, 4: 152.

Liu, J. and Wuerker, A. (2005) 'Biosocial Bases of Aggressive and Violent Behaviour: Implications for Nursing Studies', *International Journal of Nursing Studies*, 42(2): 229–41.

Locke, J. (1970 originally 1686) *Two Treatise of Government*, edited by P. Laslett. Cambridge: Cambridge University Press.

Locke, J. (1975 originally 1689) *An Essay Concerning Human Understanding*, edited by P.M. Nidditch. Oxford: Clarendon Press.

Loeber, R. and Dishion, T. (1983) 'Early Predictors of Male Delinquency: A Review', *Psychological Bulletin*, 94(1): 68–91.

Loeber, R. and LeBlanc, M. (1990) 'Toward a Developmental Criminology', in M. Tonry and N. Morris (eds) *Crime and Justice: An Annual Review of Research*, Vol. 12. Chicago: University of Chicago Press.

Loeber, R., Stouthamer-Loeber, M., Van Kammen, W. and Farrington, D.P. (1991) 'Initiation, Escalation and Desistance in Juvenile Offending and Their Correlates', *Journal of Criminal Law and Criminology*, 82: 36–82.

Lofland, J. (1969) *Deviance and Identity*. Englewood Cliffs, NJ: Prentice Hall.

Lofland, L.H. (1973) *A World of Strangers: Order and Action in Urban Public Space*. New York: Basic Books.

Lombroso, C. (1875) *L'uomo delinquente (The Criminal Man)*. Milan: Hoepli.

Lombroso, C. (1920) *The Female Offender*. New York: Appleton.

Lombroso, C. and Ferrero, W. (1885) *The Female Offender*. London: Unwin.

Luckhaus, L. (1985) 'A Plea for PMT in the Criminal Law', in S. Edwards (ed.) *Gender, Sex and the Law*. London: Croom Helm.

Lukacs, G. (1970) *Writer and Critic*. London: Merlin Press.

Lynch, M., Cole, S.A., McNally, R. and Jordan, K. (2008) *Truth Machine: The Contentious History of DNA Fingerprinting*. Chicago, IL: University of Chicago Press.

Lyng, S. (1990) 'Edgework: A Social Psychological Analysis of Voluntary Risk Taking', *American Journal of Sociology*, 95: 851–86.

Lyons, J. (2005) *Troubled Inside: Meeting the Mental Health Needs of Men in Prison*, Press Release. London: Prison Reform Trust.

Lyotard, J.-F. (1984) *The Post-Modern Condition: A Report on Knowledge*. Manchester: Manchester University Press.

Lyotard, J.-F. (1988) *The Differend*. Minneapolis, MN: University of Minnesota Press.

McAdams, D.P. (1985) *Power, Intimacy and the Life Story: Personological Inquiries into Identity*. New York: The Guilford Press.

McAdams, D.P. (1993) *The Stories We Live By: Personal Myths and the Making of the Self*. New York: William Morrow and Co.

McAdams, D.P. (1994) 'Can Personality Change? Levels of Stability and Growth in Personality Across the Life Span', in T.F. Heatherton and J.L. Weinberger (eds) *Can Personality Change?* Washington, DC: American Psychological.

McBride, D. and McCoy, C. (1982) 'Crime and Drugs: The Issues and Literature', *Journal of Drug Issues*, Spring: 128–43.

McBurnett, K., Lahey, B., Rathouz, P. and Loeber, R. (2000) 'Low Salivary Cortisol and Persistent Aggression in Boys Referred for Disruptive Behaviour', *Archives of General Psychiatry*, 57: 38–43.

McCahill, M. and Norris, C. (2002) 'Literature Review: Working Paper Number Two' [Online]. Available at: http://www.urbaneye.net/results/ue_wp2.pdf [accessed 15 September 2008].

McCall, P. and Land, K. (2004) 'Trends in Environmental Lead Exposure and Troubled Youth', *Social Science Research*, 33(2): 339–59.

McCarthy, B., Hagan, J. and Woodward, T. (1999) 'In the Company of Women: Structure and Agency in a Revised Power-Control Theory of Gender and Delinquency', *Criminology*, 37: 761–88.

McCord, J. (1990) 'Problem Behaviors', in S.S. Feldman and G.R. Elliott (eds) *At the Threshold: The Developing Adolescent*. Cambridge, MA: Harvard University Press.

McCord, W. and McCord, J. (1964) *The Psychopath: An Essay on the Criminal Mind*. New York: Van Nostrand Reinhold.

McCord, W., McCord, J. and Zola, I.K. (1959) *Origins of Crime: A New Evaluation of the Cambridge-Somerville Youth Study*. New York: Columbia University Press.

McCormack, A., Janus, M. and Burgess, A.W. (1986) 'Runaway Youths and Sexual Victimisation: Gender Differences in an Adolescent Runaway Population', *Child Abuse and Neglect*, 10: 387–95.

McCulloch, T. (2005) 'Probation, Social Context and Desistance: Retracing the Relationship', *Probation Journal*, 52(1): 8–22.

McCulloch, T. and McNeill, F. (2008) 'Desistance-focused Approaches', in S. Green, E. Lancaster and S. Feasy (eds) *Addressing Offending Behaviour: Context, Practice and Values*. Cullompton: Willan Publishing.

McEwan, A.W. (1983) 'Eysenck's Theory of Criminality and the Personality Types and Offences of Young Delinquents', *Personality and Individual Differences*, 4: 201–4.

McEwan, A.W. and Knowles, C. (1984) 'Delinquent Personality Types and the Situational Contexts of Their Crimes', *Personality and Individual Differences*, 5: 339–44.

McGurk, B.J. and McDougall, C. (1981) 'A New Approach to Eysenck's Theory of Criminality', *Personality and Individual Differences*, 13: 338–40.

McLaughlin, E. (2006) *The New Policing*. London: Sage Publications.

McNeill, F. (2006) 'A Desistance Paradigm for Offender Management', *Criminology and Criminal Justice*, 6: 39–62.

McNeill, F. and Maruna, S. (2007) 'Giving Up and Giving Back: Desistance, Generativity and Social Work with Offenders', in G. McIvor and P. Raynor (eds) *Developments in Social Work with Offenders, Research Highlights in Social Work 48*. London: Jessica Kingsley.

McNeill, F. and Whyte, B. (2007) *Reducing Reoffending: Social Work and Community Justice in Scotland*. Cullompton: Willan Publishing.

McRae, L. (2004) 'The Redhead Review: Popular Cultural Studies and Accelerated Modernity', *History of Intellectual Culture*, 6(1).

McRobbie, A. and Thornton, S. (1995) 'Rethinking "Moral Panic" for Multi-mediated Social Worlds', *British Journal of Sociology*, 46(4): 559–74.

Maginnis, R.L. (1997) *Single-Parent Families Cause Juvenile Crime*. Farmington Hills, MI: Greenhaven Press.

Maguire, J. (2001) *Cognitive Behavioural Approaches: An Introduction to Theory and Research*. London: Her Majesty's Inspectorate of Probation, Home Office.

Maier-Katkin, D. and Ogle, R. (1993) 'A Rationale for Infanticide Laws', *Criminal Law Review*, 903.

Malamuth, N. (1989) 'Sexually Violent Media, Thought Patterns, and Antisocial Behavior', *Public Communication and Behavior*, 2: 159–204.

Mann, C.R. (1984) *Female Crime and Delinquency*. Birmingham, AL: University of Alabama Press.

Mannheim, H. (1948) *Juvenile Delinquency in an English Middletown*. London: Kegan Paul, Turner, Trubner and Co. Ltd.

Mannheim, H. (1955) *Group Problems in Crime and Punishment*. London: Routledge & Kegan Paul.

Manning, P.K. (1991) 'Critical Semiotics', in B.D. MacLean and D. Milovanovic (eds) *New Directions in Critical Criminology*. Vancouver, Canada: The Collective Press.

Mannuzza, S., Klein, R., Konig, P. and Giampino, T. (1989) 'Hyperactive Boys Almost Grown Up: IV. Criminality and its Relation to Psychiatric Status', *Archives of General Psychiatry*, 46: 1073–9.

Marable, M. (2000) *How Capitalism Underdeveloped Black America: Problems in Race, Political Economy, and Society*. Boston, MA: South End Press.

Marcuse, H. (1964) *One-Dimensional Man*. Boston, MA: Beacon.

Marion, N.E. and Oliver, W.M. (2006) *The Public Policy of Crime and Criminal Justice*. Upper Saddle River, NJ: Pearson.

Mark, V.H. and Ervin, F.R. (1970) *Violence and the Brain*. New York: Harper Row.

Marks, M.N. and Kumar, R. (1993) 'Infanticide in England and Wales', *Medicine, Science and the Law*, 33: 324–38.

Markus, M. (2000) 'A Scientist's Adventures in Postmodernism', *Leonardo*, 33(3): 179–86.

Mars, G. (1982) *Cheats at Work: An Anthology of Workplace Crime*. London: George Allen and Unwin.

Marsh, I. and Melville, G. (2009) *Crime, Justice and the Media*. London: Routledge.

Marsh, P. (1978) *Aggro: The Illusion of Violence*. London: Dent.

Marshall, G., Roberts, S. and Burgoyne, C. (1996) 'Social Class and the Underclass in Britain and the USA', *British Journal of Sociology*, 47(10): 22–44.

Martin, G. and Pear, J. (1992) *Behaviour Modification: What It Is and How to Do It*, 4th edition. Englewood Cliffs, NJ: Prentice Hall.

Martin, J. (1981) 'A Longitudinal Study of the Consequences of Early Mother–Infant Interaction: A Microanalytic Approach', *Monographs of the Society for Research in Child Development*, 190: 46.

Martin, J.-P. and Schumann, H. (1997) *The Global Trap: Globalization and the Assault on Democracy and Prosperity*. London: Zed Books.

Martin, J.P. and Webster, D. (1971) *The Social Consequences of Conviction*. London: Heinemann.

Martinson, R. (1974) 'What Works? – Questions and Answers About Prison Reform', *The Public Interest*, 35: 22–54.

Maruna, S. (1997) 'Going Straight: Desistance from Crime and Self-Narratives of Reform', *Narrative Study of Lives*, 5: 59–97.

Maruna, S. (1998) 'The Social Psychology of Desistance from Crime', in D.V. Canter and L.J. Alison (eds) *The Social Psychology of Crime*. Aldershot, UK: Dartmouth.

Maruna, S. (2001) *Making Good: How Ex-convicts Reform and Rebuild Their Lives*. Washington DC: American Psychological Society.

Maruna, S. (2007) *Public Opinion*, 27th April [Online]. Available at: http://business.timesonline.co.uk/tol/business/industry_sectors/public_sector/article1693275.ece [accessed 18 January 2013].

Maruna, S. and Immarigeon, R. (2004) *After Crime and Punishment: Pathways to Offender Reintegration*. USA and Canada: Willan Publishing.

Maruna, S. and LeBel, T. (2003) 'Welcome Home? Examining the "Re-entry Court" Concept from a Strengths-Based Perspective', *Western Criminology Review*, 4: 91–107.

Maruna, S. and LeBel, T. (2009) 'Strengths-based Approaches to Re-entry: Extra Mileage Toward Reintegration and Destigmatization', *Japanese Journal of Sociological Criminology*, 34: 58–80.

Maruna, S., Porter, L. and Carvalho, I. (2004) 'The Liverpool Desistance Study and Probation Practice: Opening the Dialogue', *The Journal of Community and Criminal Justice*, 51(3): 221–32.

Marx, K. (1859) *Critique of Political Economy*. New York: International Library.

Marx, K. (1867) *Capital*. London: Lawrence & Wishart.

Matravers, M. (ed.) (1999) *Punishment and Political Theory*. Oxford: Hart Publishing.

Matsuda, M.J., Lawrence III, C.R., Delgado, R. and Crenshaw, K.W. (1993) *Words that Wound: Critical Race Theory, Assaultive Speech, and the First Amendment*. Boulder, CO: Westview Press.

Matsueda, R.L. (1992) 'Reflected Appraisals, Parental Labeling, and Delinquency: Specifying a Symbolic Interactionist Theory', *The American Journal of Sociology*, 97(6): 1577–611.

Matthews, R. (1992) 'Replacing "Broken Windows": Crime, Incivilities and Urban Change', in R. Matthews and J. Young (eds) *Issues in Realist Criminology*. London: Sage.

Matthews, R. (1996) *Armed Robbery: Police Responses, Crime Detection and Prevention Series*, Paper 78. London: Home Office, Police Research Group.

Matthews, R. (2005) 'The Myth of Punitiveness', *Theoretical Criminology*, 9(2): 175–201.

Matthews, R. (2009) 'Beyond "So What?" Criminology: Rediscovering Realism', *Theoretical Criminology*, 13(3): 341–62.

Matthews, R. and Young, J. (eds) (1986) *Confronting Crime*. London: Sage.

Matthews, R. and Young, J. (eds) (1992) *Issues in Realist Criminology*. London: Sage.

Matza, D.M. (1964) *Delinquency and Drift*. New York: Wiley.

Matza, D.M. (1969) *Becoming Deviant*. Englewood Cliffs, NJ: Prentice Hall.

Mauer, M. (1997) 'Racial Disparities in Prison Getting Worse in the 1990s', *Overcrowded Times*, 8: 8–13.

Maxson, C.L. and Klein, M.W. (1990) 'Street Gang Violence: Twice as Great or Half as Great?', in C.R. Huff (ed.) *Gangs in America*. Newbury Park, CA: Sage.

Maxwell, G. and Morris, A. (2001) 'Putting Restorative Justice Into Practice for Adult Offenders', *Howard Journal of Criminal Justice*, 40: 46–58.

Mayhew, H. (1968 originally 1862) *London Labour and the London Poor, Vol. IV: Those That Will Not Work, Comprising Prostitutes, Thieves, Swindlers and Beggars*. New York: Dover Publications.

Mayhew, P. (1984) 'Target-Hardening: How Much of an Answer?', in R.V.G Clarke and T. Hope (eds) *Coping with Burglary*. Boston, MA: Kluwer-Nijhoff.

Mayhew, P., Clarke, R.V.G., Sturman, A. and Hough, J.M. (1976) *Crime as Opportunity*. London: HMSO.

Mays, J.B. (1954) *Growing Up in the City: A Study of Juvenile Delinquency in an Urban Neighbourhood*. Liverpool: Liverpool University Press.

Mazor, L.J. (1978) 'Disrespect for Law', in R.J. Pennock and J.W. Chapman (eds) *Anarchism*. New York: New York University.

Mazur, A. (1998) *A Hazardous Inquiry: The Rashemon Effect at Love Canal*. Cambridge, MA: Harvard University Press.

Mead, G. (1934) *Mind, Self and Society*. Chicago, IL: University of Chicago Press.

Mears, D.P. (2001) 'The Immigration–Crime Nexus: Toward an Analytic Framework for Assessing and Guiding Theory, Research, and Policy', *Sociological Perspectives*, 44(1): 1–19.

Mears, D.P. (2007) 'Towards Rational and Evidence-based Crime Policy', *Journal of Criminal Justice*, 35: 667–82.

Mednick, S.A. (1977) 'A Biosocial Theory of the Learning of Law-Abiding Behavior', in S.A. Mednick and K.O. Christiansen (eds) *Biosocial Bases of Criminal Behavior*. New York: Gardner.

Mednick, S.A. and Volavka, J. (1980) 'Biology and Crime', in N. Morris and M. Tonry (eds) *Crime and Justice: An Annual Review of Research*, Vol. 2. Chicago, IL: University of Chicago Press.

Mednick, S.A., Pollock, V., Volavka, J. and Gabrielli, W.F. (1982) 'Biology and Violence', in M.E. Wolfgang and N.A. Weiner (eds) *Criminal Violence*. Beverly Hills, CA: Sage.

Mednick, S.A., Gabrielli, T., William, F. and Hutchings, B. (1984) 'Genetic Influences on Criminal Convictions: Evidence from an Adoption Cohort', *Science*, 224.

Mednick, S.A., Moffitt, T.E. and Stack, S. (eds) (1987) *The Causes of Crime: New Biological Approaches*. Cambridge: Cambridge University Press.

Mehanna, A.R. (2004) 'Poverty and Economic Development: Not as Direct as it May Seem', *Journal of Socio-Economics*, 33(1): 76–89.

Meisenhelder, T. (1977) 'An Exploratory Study of Exiting from Criminal Careers', *Criminology*, 15: 319–34.

Meisenhelder, T. (1982) 'Becoming Normal: Certification as a Stage in Exiting from Crime', *Deviant Behaviour: An Interdisciplinary Journal*, 3: 137–53.

Melossi, D. (2000) 'Changing Representations of the Criminal', *British Journal of Criminology*, 40: 290–305.

Melossi, D. and Pavarini, M. (1981) *The Prison and the Factory: Origins of the Penitentiary System*, translated by G. Cousin. London and Basingstoke: Macmillan.

Menard, S. and Morse, B. (1984) 'A Structuralist Critique of the IQ-Delinquency Hypothesis: Theory and Evidence', *American Journal of Sociology*, 89: 1347–78.

Merari, A. (1990) 'The Readiness to Kill and Die: Suicidal Terrorism in the Middle East', in W. Reich (ed.) *Origins of Terrorism*. Cambridge: Cambridge University Press.

Merry, S.E. (1981) 'Defensible Space Undefended', *Urban Affairs Quarterly*, 16: 397–422.

Merton, R.K. (1938) 'Social Structure and Anomie', *American Sociological Review*, 3: 672–82.

Merton, R.K. (1957) *Social Theory and Social Structure*. New York: The Free Press.

Merton, R.K. (1966) 'Social Problems and Sociological Theory', in R.K. Merton and R. Nisbet (eds) *Contemporary Social Problems*. New York: Harcourt Brace Jovanovich.

Mesibov, G., Shea, V. and Adams, L. (2001) *Understanding Asperger's Syndrome and High Functioning Autism*. New York: Kluwer Academic/Plenum Publishers.

Messerschmidt, J.W. (1986) *Capitalism, Patriarchy and Crime: Toward a Socialist Feminist Criminology*. Totowa, NJ: Rowman and Littlefield.

Messerschmidt, J.W. (1993) *Masculinities and Crime*. Lanham, MD: Rowman and Littlefield.

Messerschmidt, J.W. (2004) *Flesh and Blood: Adolescent Gender Diversity and Violence*. Lanham, MD: Rowman and Littlefield.

Messerschmidt, J.W. (2005) 'Masculinities and Crime: Beyond a Dualist Criminology', in C. Renzetti, L. Goodstein and S. Miller (eds) *Gender, Crime, and Criminal Justice: Original Feminist Readings*. Los Angeles, CA: Roxbury.

Messner, S.F. and Rosenfeld, R. (1994) *Crime and the American Dream*. Belmont, CA: Wadsworth.

Messner, S.F., Krohn, M.D. and Liska, A.E. (eds) (1989) *Theoretical Integration in the Study of Deviance and Crime*. Albany, NY: State University of New York Press.

Meyer, J., and O'Malley, P. (2005) 'Missing the Punitive Turn? Canadian Criminal Justice, "Balance" and Penal Modernism', in J. Pratt, D. Brown, M. Brown, S. Hallsworth and W. Morrison (eds) *The New Punitiveness: Trends, Theories, Perspectives*. Cullompton: Willan Publishing.

Miles, S. (2000) *Youth Lifestyles in a Changing World*. Buckingham: Open University Press.

Mill, J.S. (1963–84 originally 1859) *The Collected Works of John Stuart Mill*, edited by F.E.L. Priestly. Toronto, ON: University of Toronto Press.

Miller, E.M. (1986) *Street Women*. Philadelphia, PA: Temple University Press.

Miller, J.G. (1997) *Search and Destroy: African-American Males in the Criminal Justice System*. Cambridge: Cambridge University Press.

Miller, J. (2001) *One of the Guys: Girls, Gangs, and Gender*. New York: Oxford University Press.

Miller, J. (2002) 'The Strengths and Limits of "Doing Gender" for Understanding Street Crime', *Theoretical Criminology*, 6(4): 433–60.

Miller, W.B. (1958) 'Lower Class Culture as a Generalising Milieu of Gang Delinquency', *Journal of Social Issues*, 14: 5–19.

Miller, W.B. (1990) 'When the United States Has Failed to Solve its Youth Gang Problem', in C.R. Huff (ed.) *Gangs in America*. Newbury Park, CA: Sage.

Miller, W. (1999) *Cops and Bobbies*, 2nd edition. Columbus, OH: Ohio State University Press.

Millett, K. (1970) *Sexual Politics*. New York: Doubleday and Company.

Mills, C.W. (1956) *The Power Elite*. New York: Oxford University Press.

Milovanovic, D. (ed.) (1997a) *Chaos, Criminology, and Social Justice: The New Orderly (Dis) Order*. Westport, CT: Praeger.

Milovanovic, D. (1997b) *Postmodern Criminology*. New York: Garland Publishing.

Mind (2004) *Understanding Psychotic Experiences*. London: Mind.

Mind (2006) *Statistics 8: The Criminal Justice System*. London: Mind.

Ministry of Justice (2013) *Population and Capacity Briefing*. London: Ministry of Justice. 1 March.

Mirrlees-Black, C. (1999) *Domestic Violence: Findings from a New British Crime Survey Self-completion Questionnaire*. London: HMSO.

Mirrlees-Black, C., Mayhew, P. and Percy, A. (1996) *The 1996 British Crime Survey*, Home Office Statistical Bulletin 19/96. London: Home Office.

Mischkowitz, R. (1994) 'Desistance from a Delinquent Way of Life?', in E.G.M. Weitekamp and H.J. Kerner (eds) *Cross-National Longitudinal Research on Human Development and Criminal Behaviour*. London: Kluwer.

Moffitt, T.E. (1993a) 'Adolescent-Limited and Life-Course-Persistent Antisocial Behavior: A Developmental Taxonomy', *Psychological Review*, 100: 674–701.

Moffitt, T.E. (1993b) 'The Neuropsychology of Conduct Disorder', *Development and Psychopathology*, 5: 135–51.

Mokhiber, R. (1988) *Corporate Crime and Violence*. San Francisco, CA: Sierra Club.

Monahan, J. (1981) *Predicting Violent Behaviour*. Beverly Hills, CA: Sage.

Monahan, T.P. (1957) 'Family Status and the Delinquent Child: A Reappraisal and Some New Findings', *New Forces*, 35: 250–66.

Money, J. and Ernhardt, A.A. (1972) *Man and Woman: Boy and Girl*. Baltimore, MD: Johns Hopkins University Press.

Mooney, J. (2000) *Gender, Violence and the Social Order*. London: Macmillan.

Moore, J.W. (1991) *Going Down to the Barrio*. Philadelphia, PA: Temple University Press.

Morash, M. and Rucker, L. (1989) 'An Exploratory Study of the Connection of Mother's Age at Childbearing to her Children's Delinquency in Four Data Sets', *Crime and Delinquency*, 35: 45–58.

Morgan, P. (1975) *Child Care: Sense and Fable*. London: Temple Smith.

Morgan, P. (1978) *Delinquent Fantasies*. London: Temple Smith.

Morgan, R. and Newburn, T. (1997) *The Future of Policing*. Oxford: Clarendon Press.

Morris, A. (1987) *Women, Crime and Criminal Justice*. Oxford: Blackwell.

Morris, A., Maxwell, G.M. and Robertson, J.P. (1993) 'Giving Victims a Voice: A New Zealand Experiment', *Howard Journal of Criminal Justice*, 32: 304.

Morris, R. (1964) 'Female Delinquency and Relational Problems', *Social Forces*, 43: 82–8.

Morris, R. (1965) 'Attitudes to Delinquency by Delinquents, Non-Delinquents and Their Friends', *British Journal of Criminology*, 5: 249–65.

Morris, T. (1957) *The Criminal Area: A Study in Social Ecology*. London: Routledge & Kegan Paul.

Morris, T. and Blom-Cooper, L. (1979) 'Murder in England and Wales Since 1957', *The Observer*, 17 June.

Morrison, W. (1995) *Theoretical Criminology: From Modernity to Post-modernity*. London: Cavendish.

Mott, J. (1990) 'Young People, Alcohol and Crime', *Home Office Research Bulletin (Research and Statistics Department)*, 28: 24–8.

Muggleton, D. (1997) 'The Post-Subculturalist', in S. Redhead (ed.) *The Clubcultures Reader: An Introduction to Popular Cultural Studies*. Malden, MA: Blackwell.

Muggleton, D. (2000) *Inside Subculture: The Postmodern Meaning of Style*. New York: Berg.

Mukherjee, S.K. and Fitzgerald, M.K. (1981) 'The Myth of Rising Crime', in S.K. Mukherjee and J.A. Scutt (eds) *Women and Crime*. London: Allen & Unwin.

Muller, E. and Opp, K.-D. (1986) 'Rational Choice and Rebellious Collective Action', *American Political Science Review*, 80: 471–87.

Mulvey, E.P. and LaRosa, J.F. (1986) 'Delinquency Cessation and Adolescent Development: Primary Data', *American Journal of Orthopsychiatry*, 56(2): 212–24.

Muncie, J. (1998) 'Deconstructing Criminology', *Criminal Justice Matters*, 34(1): 4–5.

Muncie, J. (1999) *Youth Crime: A Critical Introduction*. London: Sage.

Muncie, J. (2000) 'Decriminalising Criminology', *British Criminology Conference: Selected Proceedings*, Vol. 3.

Muncie, J. and McLaughlin, E. (1996) *The Problem of Crime*. London: Sage/Open University.

Murray, A. (1970) *The Omni Americans: Black Experience and American Culture*. New York: Outerbridge & Dienstfrey.

Murray, A.T., McGuffog, I., Western, J.S. and Mullins, P. (2001) 'Exploratory Spatial Data Analysis Techniques for Examining Urban Crime', *British Journal of Criminology*, 41: 309–29.

Murray, C. (ed.) (1990) *The Emerging British Underclass*. London: Institute of Economic Affairs Health and Welfare Unit.

Murray, C. (1994) *Underclass: The Crisis Deepens*. London: Institute of Economic Affairs.

Murray, H.A. (1938) *Explorations in Personality*. Oxford: Oxford University Press.

Myers, D.L. (2003) 'The Recidivism of Violent Youths in Juvenile and Adult Courts', *Youth Violence and Juvenile Justice: An Interdisciplinary Journal*, 1(1): 79–101.

NACRO (2003) *Some Facts About Young People Who Offend – 2001*, NACRO Youth Crime Briefing. London: NACRO.

Naess, S. (1959) 'Mother–Child Separation and Delinquency', *British Journal of Delinquency*, 10: 22.

Naess, S. (1962) 'Mother–Child Separation and Delinquency: Further Evidence', *British Journal of Criminology*, 2: 361.

Naffine, N. (1987) *Female Crime*. Sydney: Allen and Unwin.

Naffine, N. and Gale, F. (1989) 'Testing the Nexus: Crime, Gender and Unemployment', *British Journal of Criminology*, 29(2): 144–56.

Nassar, J. (2004) *Globalization and Terrorism*. Lanham, MD: Rowman and Littlefield.

National Autistic Society (2005) *Autism: A Guide for Criminal Justice Professionals* [Online]. Available at: http://www.autism.org.uk/cjs [accessed 6 January 2009].

Nayak, A. (2003) *Race, Place and Globalization: Youth Cultures in a Changing World*. Oxford: Berg.

Needleman, H., Reiss, J., Tobin, M., Biesecker, G. and Greenhouse, J. (1996) 'Bone Lead Levels and Delinquent Behaviour', *Journal of the American Medical Association*, 275: 363–69.

Neisser, U. (1996) 'Intelligence: Knowns and Unknowns', *American Psychologist*, 51: 77–101.

Nelken, D. (1994) 'Reflexive Criminology?', in D. Nelken (ed.) *The Futures of Criminology*. London: Sage.

Nelken, D. and Andrews, L. (1999) 'DNA Identification and Surveillance Creep', *Sociology of Health and Illness*, 21(5): 689–706.

Neugarten, B.L. and Neugarten, D.A. (1986) 'Changing Meanings of Age in the Aging Society', in A. Pifer and L. Bronte (eds) *Our Aging Society*. New York: W.W. Norton.

Newman, K. (1999) *No Shame in My Game*. New York: Knopf.

Newman, O. (1972) *Defensible Space: Crime Prevention Through Urban Design*. New York: Macmillan.

Newman, O. (1976) *Defensible Space: People and Design in the Violent City*. London: The Architectural Press.

Nightingale, C. (1993) *On the Edge*. New York: Basic Books.

Norris, C. and Armstrong, G. (1999) *The Maximum Surveillance Society: The Rise of CCTV*. Oxford: Berg.

Nye, F.I. (1958) *Family Relationships and Delinquent Behaviour*. New York: Wiley.

The Observer (2003) 'The Last Resort (Part One)' [Online]. Available at: http://www.guardian.co.uk/education/2003/jun/29/schools.uk1 [accessed 6 January 2009].

O'Connor, J. (1973) *The Fiscal Crisis of the State*. New York: St Martin's Press.

O'Connor, T. (1994) 'A Neofunctional Model of Crime and Crime Control', in G. Barak (ed.) *Varieties of Criminology*. Westport, CT: Greenwood Press.

Office for National Statistics (2001) *Psychiatric Morbidity Among Adults Living in Private Households, 2000*. London: ONS.

Okimoto, T. and Wenzel, M. (2009) 'Punishment as Restoration of Group and Offender Values Following a Transgression: Value Consensus Through Symbolic Labeling and Offender Reform', *European Journal of Social Psychology*, 39: 346–67.

Olson, M. (1982) *The Rise and Decline of Nations*. New Haven, CT: Yale University Press.

Olwens, D. (1987) 'Testosterone and Adrenaline: Aggressive and Antisocial Behaviour in Normal Adolescent Males', in S.A. Mednick, T.E. Moffitt and S. Stack (eds) *The Causes of Crime: New Biological Approaches*. Cambridge: Cambridge University Press.

O'Malley, P. (1992) 'Risk, Power and Crime Prevention', *Economy and Society*, 21(3): 252–75.

O'Malley, P. (1999) 'Volatile and Contradictory Punishment', *Theoretical Criminology*, 3(2): 175–96.

O'Malley, P. (2000) 'Criminologies of Catastrophe: Understanding Criminal Justice on the Edge of the New Millennium', *Australian and New Zealand Journal of Criminology*, 33(2): 153–67.

O'Malley, P. (2004) *Risk, Uncertainty and Government*. London: Glasshouse Press.

O'Malley, P. and Mugford, S. (1994) 'Crime, Excitement and Modernity', in G. Barak (ed.) *Varieties of Criminology*. Westport, CT: Praeger.

Omerod, D. (1996) 'The Evidential Implications of Psychological Profiling', *Criminal Law Review*, 863.

Omi, M. and Winant, H. (1994) *Racial Formation in the United States*. New York: Routledge.

Osborn, A. (2003) 'Belgium to Legalise Cannabis', *The Guardian*, 29 March.

Osborn, S.G. and West, D.J. (1978) 'Do Young Delinquents Really Reform?', *Journal of Adolescence*, 3: 99–114.

Outlaw, Jr., L.T. (1996) *On Race and Philosophy*. New York: Routledge.

Packer, H. (1968) *The Limits of the Criminal Sanction*. Stanford, CA: Stanford University Press.

Painter, K. and Farrington, D. (1999) 'Improved Street Lighting: Crime-reducing Effects and Cost-benefit Analysis', *Security Journal*, 12(4): 17–31.

Painter, K. and Farrington, D. (2001) 'Evaluating Situational Crime Prevention Using a Young People's Survey', *British Journal of Criminology*, 41: 244–66.

Pakes, F. and Winstone, J. (2007) *Psychology and Crime: Understanding and Tackling Offending Behaviour*. Cullompton: Willan Publishing.

Pantazis, C. and Gordon, D. (1997) 'Television Licence Evasion and the Criminalisation of Female Poverty', *Howard Journal of Criminal Justice*, 36: 170.

Parenti, C. (2000) *Lockdown America*. London: Verso.

Park, R.E. (1921) *Introduction to the Study of Sociology*. Chicago, IL: University of Chicago Press.

Parker, H. (1974) *View From the Boys*. Newton Abbot: David and Charles.

Parsons, T. (1937) *The Structure of Social Action*. New York: McGraw-Hill.

Parsons, T. (1947) 'Certain Primary Sources and Patterns of Aggression in the Social Structure of the Western World', *Psychiatry*, X: 158–71.

Parsons, T. (1951) *The Social System*. London: Routledge & Kegan Paul.

Parsons, T. (1954) *Essays in Sociological Theory*. Glencoe, IL: Free Press.

Passmore, K. (2002) *Fascism: A Very Short Introduction*. New York: Oxford University Press.

Pateman, C. (1995) *The Sexual Contract*. Stanford, CA: Stanford University Press.

Paternoster, R. and Brame, R. (2008) 'Reassessing Race Disparities in Maryland Capital Cases', *Criminology*, 46: 971–1007.

Patterson, O. (1982) *Slavery and Social Death*. Cambridge, MA: Harvard University Press.

Pearce, F. (1976) *Crimes of the Powerful*. London: Pluto.

Pearce, F. and Tombs, S. (1993) 'US Capital Versus the Third World: Union Carbide and Bhopal', in F. Pearce and M. Woodiwiss (eds) *Global Crime Connections*. Basingstoke: Macmillan.

Penna, S. and Yar, M. (2003) 'From Modern to Postmodern Penality?: A Response to Hallsworth', *Theoretical Criminology*, 7: 469–82.

Pepinsky, H.E. (1978) 'Communist Anarchism as an Alternative to the Rule of Criminal Law', *Contemporary Crises*, 2: 315–27.

Pepinsky, H.E. (1991) 'Peacemaking in Criminology', in B.D. MacLean and D. Milovanovic (eds) *New Directions in Critical Criminology*. Vancouver, BC: The Collective Press.

Pepinsky, H.E. and Jesilow, P. (1984) *Myths That Cause Crime*, 2nd edition. Cabin John, MD: Seven Locks.

Pepinsky, H.E. and Quinney, R. (eds) (1991) *Criminology as Peacemaking*. Bloomington, IN: Indiana.

Perlin, M.L. and McClaln, V.R. (2010) 'Unasked (and Unanswered) Questions About the Role of Neuroimaging in the Criminal Trial Process', *American Journal of Forensic Psychology*, 28(4): 5–22.

Perry, B. (2001) *In the Name of Hate*. London: Routledge.

Persky, H., Smith, K.D. and Basu, G.K. (1971) 'Relation of Psychological Measures of Aggression and Hostility to Testosterone Production in Man', *Psychosomatic Medicine*, 33: 265–75.

Peston, R. (2008) 'A Fairer Society?', *BBC News Blog*, 20 October.

Petrosino, A., Turpin-Petrosino, C. and Buehler, J. (2002) *'Scared Straight' and Other Juvenile Awareness Programs for Preventing Juvenile Delinquency*. Cochrane Database Syst Rev. (2): CD002796.

Pezzin, L.E. (1995) 'Earnings Prospects, Matching Effects, and the Decision to Terminate a Criminal Career', *Journal of Quantitative Criminology*, 11: 29–50.

Pfohl, S. (1994) *Images of Deviance and Social Control: A Sociological History*, 2nd edition. New York: McGraw-Hill.

Phelan, J. (1940) *Jail Journey*. London: Secker & Warburg.

Philips, D. and Storch, R. (1999) *Policing Provincial England, 1829–1856*. Leicester: Leicester University Press.

Piaget, J. (1980) *Adaptation and Intelligence: Organic Selection and Phenocopy*, translated by W. Mays. Chicago, IL: University of Chicago Press.

Pihl, R.O. (1982) 'Hair Element Levels of Violent Criminals', *Canadian Journal of Psychiatry*, 27: 533–45.

Pihl, R.O. and Peterson, J.B. (1993) 'Alcohol/Drug Use and Aggressive Behaviour', in S. Hodgins (ed.) *Moral Disorder and Crime*. Newbury Park, CA: Sage.

Pilcher, J. (1983) 'I'm not a Feminist, But . . . Understanding Feminism', *Sociology Review*, 3: 2.

Piliavin, I. and Briar, B. (1964) 'Police Encounters with Juveniles', *American Journal of Sociology*, 70(2): 206–14.

Piliavin, I., Gartner, R., Thornton, C. and Matsueda, R. (1986) 'Crime, Deterrence and Rational Choice', *American Sociological Review*, 51: 101–19.

Piquero, A. and Tibbetts, S. (1999) 'The Impact of Pre/Perinatal Disturbances and Disadvantaged Familial Environment in Predicting Criminal Offending', *Studies on Crime and Crime Prevention*, 8: 52–70.

Pitts, J. (1986) 'Black Young People and Juvenile Crime: Some Unanswered Questions', in R. Matthews and J. Young (eds) *Confronting Crime*. London: Sage.

Pitts, J. (1996) 'The Politics and Practice of Youth Crime', in E. McLaughlin and J. Muncie (eds) *Controlling Crime*. London: Sage.

Pitts, J. (2003) *The New Politics of Youth and Crime*. Lyme Regis: Russell House.

Pizarro, J.M., Corsaro, M. and Yu, S.V. (2007) 'Journey to Crime and Victimization: An Application of Routine Activities Theory and Environmental Criminology to Homicide', *Victims & Offenders*, 2(4): 375–94.

Plant, M. (1990) *AIDS, Drugs and Prostitution*. London: Routledge.

Platt, A.M. (1969) *The Child Savers: The Invention of Delinquency*. Chicago, IL: University of Chicago Press.

Platt, T. (1974) 'Prospects for a Radical Criminology in the U.S.', *Crime and Social Justice*, 1: 2–10.

Plint, T. (1851) *Crime in England*. London: Charles Gilpin.

Plummer, K. (1975) *Sexual Stigma*. London: Routledge & Kegan Paul.

Plummer, K. (1979) 'Misunderstanding Labelling Perspectives', in D. Downes and P. Rock (eds) *Deviant Interpretations*. London: Martin Robertson.

Pollak, O. (1950) *The Criminality of Women*. New York: Barnes.

Pontell, H. and Geis, G. (eds) *International Handbook of White-collar and Corporate Crime*. New York: Springer-Verlag.

Potter, G. and Kappeler, G. (eds) (1998) *Constructing Crime: Perspectives on Making News and Social Problems*. Prospect Heights, IL: Waveland.

Poulantzas, N. (1969) 'The Problems of the Capitalist State', *New Left Review*, 58: 67–78.

Pratt, J. (1999) 'Governmentality, Neo-Liberalism and Dangerousness', in R. Smandych (ed.) *Governable Places: Readings on Governmentality and Crime Control*. Dartmouth: Ashgate.

Pratt, J. (2000) 'Emotive and Ostentatious Punishment: Its Decline and Resurgence in Modern Society', *Punishment and Society*, 2: 417–39.

Pratt, J. (2002) *Punishment and Civilization: Penal Tolerance and Intolerance in Modern Society*. London: Sage.

Pratt, J., Brown, D. Brown, M., Hallsworth, S. and Morrison, W. (eds) (2005) *The New Punitiveness: Trends, Theories, Perspectives*. Cullompton: Willan Publishing.

Presdee, M. (1994) 'Young People, Culture and the Construction of Crime: Doing Wrong Versus Doing Crime', in G. Barak (ed.) *Varieties of Criminology*. Westport, CT: Praeger.

Presdee, M. (2000) *Cultural Criminology and the Carnival of Crime*. London: Routledge.

Presdee, M. (2004) 'Cultural Criminology: The Long and Winding Road', *Theoretical Criminology*, 8(3): 275–85.

Price, W.H. and Whatmore, P.B. (1967) 'Behaviour Disorders and Patterns of Crime Among XYY Males Identified at a Maximum Security Hospital', *British Medical Journal*, 1: 533.

Prinz, R.J., Roberts, W.A. and Hantman, E. (1980) 'Dietary Correlates of Hyperactive Behaviour in Children', *Journal of Consulting and Clinical Psychology*, 48: 760–85.

Prison Reform Trust (2002) *The Prisons League Table 2000–1: Performance Against Key Indicators*. London: Prison Reform Trust.

Prison Reform Trust (2004) *England and Wales – Western Europe's Jail Capital*, Press Release, 2 February.

Pryce, K. (1979) *Endless Pressure: A Study of West Indian Life-styles in Bristol*. Harmondsworth: Penguin.

Putnam, R.D. (2001) *Bowling Alone: The Collapse and Revival of American Community*. New York, NY: Simon and Schuster.

Quételet, M.A. (1833) *Recherches Sur le Penchant au Crime aux Différents Ages*. Belgium: Hayez.

Quételet, M.A. (1842) *A Treatise on Man*. Edinburgh: William and Robert Chalmers.

Quinney, R. (1965) 'A Conception of Man and Society for Criminology', *Sociological Quarterly*, 6: 119–27.

Quinney, R. (1970) *The Social Reality of Crime*. Boston, MA: Little, Brown.

Quinney, R. (1974) *Critique of Legal Order*. Boston, MA: Little, Brown.

Quinney, R. (1977) *Class, State and Crime*. New York: David McKay.

Quinney, R. (1991) 'The Way of Peace: On Crime, Suffering, and Service', in H. Pepinsky and R. Quinney (eds) *Criminology as Peacemaking*. Bloomington: Indiana University Press.

Rada, R. (1975) 'Alcoholism and Forcible Rape', *American Journal of Psychiatry*, 132: 444–6.

Radford, J. and Stanko, E.A. (1994) *The Contradictions of Patriarchal Crime Control*. London: Routledge.

Radzinowicz, L. (1948–86) *A History of English Criminal Law and its Administration from 1750* (5 volumes): i) (1948) *The Movement for Reform*; ii) (1956) *The Clash Between Private Initiative and Public Interest in the Enforcement of the Law*; iii) (1956) *Cross Currents in the Movement of the Reform of the Police*; iv) (1968) *Grappling for Control*; v) (with R. Hood, 1986) *The Emergence of Penal Policy in Victorian and Edwardian England*. London: Stevens and Sons.

Rafter, N.H. and Heidensohn, F. (eds) (1985) *International Feminist Perspectives: Engendering a Discipline*. Buckingham: Open University Press.

Raine, A. (2002) 'Biosocial Studies of Antisocial and Violent Behavior in Children and Adults: A Review', *Journal of Abnormal Child Psychology*, 30(4): 311–26.

Raine, A. and Yang, Y. (2006) 'The Neuroanatomical Bases of Psychopathy: A Review of Brain Imaging Findings', in C.J. Patrick (ed.) *Handbook of Psychopathy*. New York: Guilford Press.

Raine, A., Brennan, P. and Mednick, S. (1994) 'Birth Complications Combined with Early Maternal Rejections at Age 1 Year Predispose to Violent Crime at Age 18 years', *Archives of General Psychiatry*, 51: 984–8.

Raine, A., Brennan, P. and Mednick, S. (1997) 'Interaction Between Birth Complications and Early Maternal Rejection in Predisposing Individuals to Adult Violence: Specificity to Serious, Early-Onset Violence', *American Journal of Psychiatry*, 154(9): 1265–71.

Raine, A., Lencz, T., Bihrle, S., LaCasse, L. and Colletti, P. (2000) 'Reduced Pre-Frontal Gray Matter Volume and Reduced Autonomic Activity in Antisocial Personality Disorder', *Archives of General Psychiatry*, 57: 119–27.

Raloff, J. (1983) 'Locks – A Key to Violence', *Science News*, 124: 122–36.

Ramsay, M. (1996) 'The Relationship Between Alcohol and Crime', *Home Office Research Bulletin*, 38: 37–44.

Rand, A. (1987) 'Transitional Life Events and Desistance from Delinquency and Crime', in M. Wolfgang, T.P. Thornberry and R.M. Figlio (eds) *From Boy to Man: From Delinquency to Crime*. Chicago: University of Chicago Press.

Rantakallio, P., Koiranen, M. and Moettoenen, J. (1992) 'Association of Perinatal Events, Epilepsy, and Central Nervous System Trauma with Juvenile Delinquency', *Archives of Disease in Childhood*, 67: 1459–61.

Rappaport, N. and Thomas, C. (2004) 'Recent Research Findings on Aggressive and Violent Behaviour in Youth: Implications for Clinical Assessment and Intervention', *Journal of Adolescent Health*, 35(4): 260–77.

Ratcliffe, J.H. and McCullagh, M.J. (1999) 'Hotbeds of Crime and the Search for Spatial Accuracy', *Journal of Geographical Systems*, 1: 385–98.

Raymond, G.J. (2002) *A Comparative Study of Women Trafficked in the Migration Process: Patterns, Profiles and Health Consequences of Sexual Exploitation in Five Countries*. New York: United Nations Convention Against Transnational Organized Crime.

Reckless, W. (1961) *The Crime Problem*, 3rd edition. New York: Appleton Century Crofts.

Reckless, W. (1967) *The Crime Problem*, 4th edition. New York: Appleton Century Crofts.

Redhead, S. (1990) *The End-of-the-Century Party: Youth and Pop Towards 2000*. New York: St Martin's Press.

Redhead, S. (ed.) (1993) *Rave Off: Politics and Deviance in Contemporary Youth Culture*. Aldershot: Arena.

Redhead, S., O'Connor, J. and Wynne, D. (eds) (1997) *The Clubcultures Reader: Readings in Popular Cultural Studies*. Oxford: Basil Blackwell.

Redl, F. and Wineman, D. (1951) *Children Who Hate*. New York: Free Press.

Regoli, R. and Hewitt, J. (1994) *Delinquency in Society*, 2nd edition. Boston, MA: McGraw Hill.

Reiman, J. (1979) *The Rich Get Richer and the Poor Get Prison*. New York: John Wiley.

Reiman, J. and Headlee, S. (1981) 'Marxism and Criminal Justice Policy', *Crime and Delinquency*, 27: 24–47.

Reinarman, C. and Levine, H.G. (eds) (1997) *Crack in America: Demon Drugs and Social Justice*. Berkeley, CA: University of California Press.

Reiner, R. (2000) 'Crime and Control in Britain', *Sociology*, 34(1): 71–94.

Reiner, R. (2004) *The Politics of Policing*. Oxford: Oxford University Press.

Reiss, A.J. (1951) 'Delinquency as the Failure of Personal and Social Controls', *American Sociological Review*, 16: 213–39.

Reiss, A.J. (1960) 'Sex Offences: The Marginal Status of the Adolescent', *Law and Contemporary Problems*, 25: 302–23.

Reith, C. (1956) *A New Study of Police History*. London: Oliver and Boyd.

Rex, J. and Moore, R. (1967) *Race, Community and Conflict: A Study in Sparkbrook*. London: Institute of Race Relations/OUP.

Rhodes, R.A.W. (1997) *Understanding Governance: Policy Networks, Governance, Reflexivity and Accountability*. Buckingham: Open University Press.

Ricoeur, P. (1984) *Time and Narrative*, Vol. 1. Chicago: University of Chicago.

Robins, L.N. (1966) *Deviant Children Grown Up*. Baltimore, MD: Williams and Wilkins.

Robinson, M.B. and Zaitzow, B.H. (1999) 'Criminologists: Are We What We Study? A National Self-Report Study of Crime Experts', *The Criminologist*, 24(2): 17–19.

Rock, P. (1973) *Deviant Behaviour*. London: Hutchinson.

Rosaler, M. (2004) *Coping with Asperger's Syndrome*. New York: The Rosen Publishing Group.

Rose, N. (1999) *Powers of Freedom: Reframing Political Thought*. Cambridge: Cambridge University Press.

Rose, N. (2000) 'The Biology of Culpability: Pathological Identity and Crime Control in Biological Culture', *Theoretical Criminology*, 4(1): 4–19.

Rose, R.M., Holoday, J.W. and Bernstein, S. (1971) 'Plasma Testosterone, Dominance, Rank and Aggressive Behaviour in Male Rhesus Monkeys', *Nature*, 231: 366–8.

Rose, R.M., Bernstein, I.S., Gorden, T.P. and Catlin, S.E. (1974) 'Androgens and Aggression: A Review and Recent Findings in Primates', in R.L. Holloway (ed.) *Primate Aggression: Territoriality and Xenophobia*. New York: Academia Press.

Rosenau, P.-M. (1992) *Post-Modernism and the Social Sciences: Insights, Inroads and Intrusions*. Princeton, NJ: Princeton University Press.

Ross, J.I. (1996) 'A Model of the Psychological Causes of Oppositional Political Terrorism', *Peace and Conflict: Journal of Peace Psychology*, 2–11.

Ross, J.I. (1999) 'Beyond the Conceptualization of Terrorism: A Psychological-Structural Model', in C. Summers and E. Mardusen (eds) *Collective Violence*. New York: Rowen and Littlefield.

Ross, P. (2003) 'Marxism and Communitarianism', *Imprints*, 6(3): 215–43.

Rothman, D. (1971) *The Discovery of the Asylum: Social Order and Disorder in the New Republic*. Boston: Routledge and Kegan Paul.

Rothman, D. (1980) *Conscience and Convenience: The Asylum and its Alternatives in Progressive America*. Boston: Little, Brown.

Rousseau, J. (1964 originally 1762) *First and Second Discourses*, edited by R.D. Masters. New York: St Martin's Press.

Rousseau, J. (1978 originally 1775) *The Social Contract*, edited by R.D. Masters. New York: St Martin's Press.

Rowe, A. and Tittle, C. (1977) 'Life Cycle Changes and Criminal Propensity', *Sociology Quarterly*, 18: 223–36.

Rowe, D.C. (1990) 'Inherited Dispositions toward Learning Delinquent and Criminal Behaviour: New Evidence', in L. Ellis and H. Hoffman (eds) *Crime in Biological, Social and Moral Contexts*. New York: Praeger.

Rowe, D.C. and Rogers, J.L. (1989) 'Behaviour Genetics, Adolescent Deviance, and "d": Contributions and Issues', in G.R. Adams, R. Montemayor and T.P. Gullotta (eds) *Advances in Adolescent Development*. Newbury Park, CA: Sage.

Ruggiero, V. (1997) 'Trafficking in Human Beings: Slaves in Contemporary Europe', *International Journal of the Sociology of Law*, 25(3): 231–44.

Ruggiero, V. (2000) *Crimes and Markets: Essays in Anti-Criminology*. Oxford: Oxford University Press.

Ruggiero, V. (2005) 'Political Violence: A Criminological Analysis', in M. Natarajan (ed.) *Introduction to International Criminal Justice*. New York: McGraw Hill.

Ruggiero, V. and South, N. (1995) *Eurodrugs: Drug Use, Marketing and Trafficking in Europe*. London: University College London.

Rumbelow, D. (1987) *The Complete Jack the Ripper*. London: Star Books.

Ruparel, C. (2004) *The Nature of Rape of Females in the Metropolitan Police District*, Home Office Findings No. 247. London: Home Office.

Rusche, G. (1980) 'Labor Market and Penal Sanction: Thoughts on the Sociology of Punishment', in T. Platt and P. Takagi (eds) *Punishment and Penal Discipline*. Berkeley, CA: Crime and Social Justice Associates.

Rusche, G. and Kirchheimer, O. (1939) *Punishment and Social Structure*. New York: Russell & Russell.

Russell, C. and Bowman, M. (1977) 'Profile of a Terrorist', *Terrorism: An International Journal*, 1(1): 17–34.

Russell, S. (2006) 'The Continuing Relevance of Marxism to Critical Criminology', *Critical Criminology*, 11(2): 113–35.

Rutherford, A. (1992) *Growing Out of Crime: The New Era*, 2nd edition. London: Waterside Press.

Rutter, M. (1981) *Maternal Deprivation Reassessed*. Harmondsworth: Penguin.

Rutter, M. (1989) 'Age as an Ambiguous Variable in Developmental Research: Some Epidemiological Considerations from Developmental Psychopathology', *International Journal of Behavioural Development*, 12: 1–134.

Rutter, M. (1996) 'Transitions and Turning Points in Developmental Psychopathology: As Applied to the Age Span between Childhood and Mid-adulthood', *Journal of Behavioural Development*, 19(3): 603–26.

Rutter, M., Cox, A., Tupling, C., Berger, M. and Yule, W. (1975a) 'Attainment and Adjustment in Two Geographical Areas: 1. The Prevalence of Psychiatric Disorder', *British Journal of Psychiatry*, 126: 493–509.

Rutter, M., Yule, B., Quinton, D., Rowlands, O., Yule, W. and Berger, W. (1975b) 'Attainment and Adjustment in Two Geographical Areas: 3. Some Factors Accounting for Area Differences', *British Journal of Psychiatry*, 126: 520–33.

Rutter, M., Quinton, D. and Hill, J. (1990) 'Adult Outcome of Institution-Reared Children: Males and Females Compared', in L.N. Robins and M.R. Rutter (eds) *Straight and Devious Pathways to Adulthood*. New York: Cambridge University Press.

Ryan, K. and Ferrell, J. (1986) 'Knowledge, Power, and the Process of Justice', *Crime and Social Justice*, 25: 178–95.

Ryan, M. (2003) *Penal Policy and Political Culture in England and Wales*. Winchester: Waterside Press.

Saad, L. (2008) 'Americans Hold Firm to Support for Death Penalty', Gallup Inc. [Online]. Available at: http://www.gallup.com/poll/111931/americans-holdfirm-support-death-penalty.aspx [accessed 7 June 2013].

Sameroff, A., Seifer, R., Zax, M. and Barocas, R. (1987) 'Early Indicators of Developmental Risk: The Rochester Longitudinal Study', *Schizophrenia Bulletin*, 13: 383–94.

Sampson, R.J. and Laub, J. (1992) 'Crime and Deviance in the Life Course', *Annual Review of Sociology*, 18: 63–84.

Sampson, R.J. and Laub, J. (1993) *Crime in the Making: Pathways and Turning Points Through Life*. Cambridge, MA: Harvard University Press.

Sampson, R.J. and Laub, J. (1995) 'Understanding Variability in Lives through Time: Contributions of Life-Course Criminology', *Studies on Crime and Crime Prevention*, 4: 143–58.

Sanson, A., Oberklaid, F., Pedlow, R. and Prior, M. (1991) 'Risk Indicators: Assessment of Infancy Predictors of Pre-school Behavioural Maladjustment', *Journal of Child Psychology and Psychiatry*, 32(4): 609–26.

Sarbin, T.R. (ed.) (1986) *Narrative Psychology: The Storied Nature of Human Conduct*. New York: Praeger.

Sarre, R. (2003) 'Restorative Justice: A Paradigm of Possibility', in M.D. Schwartz and S.E. Hatty (eds) *Controversies in Critical Criminology*. Cincinnati: Anderson.

Sartre, J.-P. (1963) *Search for a Method*, translation by Knopf Barnes. London: Methuen.

Sasson, T. (1995) *Crime Talk: How Citizens Construct a Social Problem*. New York: Aldine de Gruyter.

Saunders, W. (1984) *Alcohol Use in Britain; How Much is Too Much?* Edinburgh: Scottish Health Education Unit.

Scarmella, T.J. and Brown, W.A. (1978) 'Serum Testosterone and Aggressiveness in Hockey Players', *Psychosomatic Medicine*, 40: 262–75.

Schabas, W. (1997) *The Abolition of the Death Penalty in International Law*. Cambridge: Cambridge University Press.

Schalling, D. (1987) 'Personality Correlates of Plasma Testosterone Levels in Young Delinquents: An Example of Person-Situation Interaction', in S.A. Mednick, T.E. Moffitt and S.A. Stack (eds) *The Causes of Crime: New Biological Approaches*. Cambridge: Cambridge University Press.

Scheff, T. (2010) 'Normalizing Symptoms: Neither Labeling nor Enabling', *Ethical Human Psychology and Psychiatry*, 12(3): 232–7.

Scheff, T. and Retzinger, S. (1991) *Emotions and Violence: Shame and Rage in Destructive Conflicts*. Lexington, VA: Lexington Books.

Schlapp, M.G. and Smith, E. (1928) *The New Criminology*. New York: Boni and Liveright.

Schlossman, S., Zellman, G. and Shavelson, R. (1984) *Delinquency Prevention in South Chicago: A Fifty-Year Assessment of the Chicago Area Project*. Santa Monica, CA: Rand.

Schoenthaler, S.J. (1982) 'The Effects of Blood Sugar on the Treatment and Control of Antisocial Behaviour: A Double-Blind Study of an Incarcerated Juvenile Population', *International Journal for Biosocial Research*, 3: 1–15.

Schoenthaler, S.J. and Bier, I. (2000) 'The Effect of Vitamin-Mineral Supplementation on Juvenile Delinquency Among American Schoolchildren: A Randomized Double-Blind Placebo-Controlled Trial', *Journal of Alternative and Complementary Medicine*, 6: 7–18.

Schoenthaler, S.J. and Doraz, W. (1983) 'Diet and Crime', *International Journal of Biosocial Crime*, 4: 74–94.

Schraeger, L.S. and Short, J.F. (1978) 'Towards a Sociology of Organisational Crime', *Social Problems*, 25: 407–19.

Schur, E. (1971) *Labelling Deviant Behaviour: Its Sociological Implications*. New York: Harper and Row.

Schutz, A. (1962) *The Problem of Social Reality*. The Hague: Martinus Nijhoff.

Schwaner, S. (2000) '"Stick 'em Up, Buddy": Robbery, Lifestyle, and Specialization within a Cohort of Parolees', *Journal of Criminal Justice*, 28: 371–84.

Schwartz, M.D. and DeKeseredy, W.S. (1991) 'Left Realist Criminology: Strengths, Weaknesses and the Feminist Critique', *Crime, Law and Social Change*, 15: 51.

Schwendinger, H. and Schwendinger, J. (1970) 'Defenders of Order or Guardians of Human Rights', *Issues in Criminology*, 7: 72–81.

Scraton, P. (1985) *The State of the Police*. London: Pluto.

Scraton, P. (2004) 'Streets of Terror: Marginalization, Criminalization and Authoritarian Renewal', *Social Justice*, 31(1 & 2): 130–58.

Scraton, P. and Chadwick, K. (1996 originally 1992) 'The Theoretical Priorities of Critical Criminology', in J. Muncie, E. McLaughlin, and M. Langan (eds) *Criminological Perspectives: A Reader*. London: Sage.

Scruton, R. (1980) *The Meaning of Conservatism*. Harmondsworth: Pelican.

Scruton, R. (1985) *Thinkers of the New Left*. London: Longman.

Scruton, R. (2001) *The Meaning of Conservatism*, 3rd edition. Houndmills: Palgrave.

Scull, A. (1977) *Decarceration*. Englewood Cliffs, NJ: Prentice Hall.

Segal, L. (1990) *Slow Motion: Changing Masculinities, Changing Men*. London: Virago.

Sellin, T. (1938) *Culture, Conflict and Crime*. New York: Social Research Council.

Sellin, T. (1959) *The Death Penalty*. Philadelphia, PA: American Law Institute.

Sellin, T. (1973) 'Enrico Ferri', in H. Mannheim (ed.) *Pioneers in Criminology*, 2nd edition. Montclair, NJ: Patterson-Smith.

Shah, S.A. and Roth, L.H. (1974) 'Biological and Psychophysiological Factors in Criminality', in D. Glaser (ed.) *Handbook of Criminology*. London: Rand McNally.

Shapiro, T.M. (2004) *The Hidden Costs of Being African American: How Wealth Perpetuates Inequality*. New York: Oxford University Press.

Shaw, C.R. (1930) *The Jack-Roller: A Delinquent Boy's Own Story*. Chicago, IL: University of Chicago Press.

Shaw, C.R. (1931) *The Natural History of a Delinquent Career*. Chicago, IL: University of Chicago Press.

Shaw, C.R. (1938) *Brothers in Crime*. Chicago, IL: University of Chicago Press.

Shaw, C.R. and McKay, H.D. (1972 originally 1931) *Juvenile Delinquency and Urban Areas*. Chicago, IL: University of Chicago Press.

Shaw, D.S., Keenan, K. and Vondra, J.I. (1994a) 'Developmental Precursors of Externalizing Behavior: Ages 1 to 3', *Developmental Psychology*, 30(3): 355–64.

Shaw, D.S., Vondra, J.I., Hommerding, K., Keenan, K. and Dunn, M. (1994b) 'Chronic Family Adversity and Early Child Behavior Problems: A Longitudinal Study of Low Income Families', *Journal of Child Psychology and Psychiatry*, 35(6): 1109–22.

Shaw, D., Winslow, E., Owens, E. and Hood, N. (1998a) 'Young Children's Adjustment to Chronic Family Adversity: A Longitudinal Study of Low-Income Families', *Journal of the American Academy of Child and Adolescent Psychiatry*, 37(5): 545–53.

Shaw, D., Winslow, E., Owens, E., Vondra, J., Cohn, J. and Bell, R. (1998b) 'The Development of Early Externalizing Problems Among Children from Low-Income Families: A Transformational Perspective', *Journal of Abnormal Child Psychology*, 26(2): 95–107.

Shaw, D.S., Ingoldsby, E., Gilliom, M. and Nagin, D. (2003) 'Trajectories Leading to School-Age Conduct Problems', *Developmental Psychology*, 38: 480–91.

Shearing, C. (1989) 'Decriminalising Criminology', *Canadian Journal of Criminology*, 31(2): 169–78.

Sheldon, B. (1995) *Cognitive-Behavioural Therapy: Research, Practice and Philosophy*. London: Routledge.

Sheldon, W.H. (1949) *Varieties of Delinquent Youth*. London: Harper.

Shelley, L. (1998) 'Crime and Corruption in the Digital Age', *Journal of International Affairs*, 51(2): 605–20.

Sherman, L., Gartin, P. and Buerger, M. (1989) 'Hot Spots of Predatory Crime: Routine Activities and the Criminology of Place', *Criminology*, 27: 27–55.

Shildrick, T. and MacDonald, R. (2006) 'In Defence of Subculture: Young People, Leisure and Social Divisions', *Journal of Youth Studies*, 9(2): 120–8.

Shockley, W. (1967) 'A "Try Simplest Cases" Approach to the Heredity-Poverty-Crime Problem', *Proceedings of the National Academy of Sciences*, 57: 1767–74.

Shover, N. (1985) *Aging Criminals*. Beverly Hills, CA: Sage Publications.

Shover, N. (1996) 'The Later Stages of Ordinary Property Offender Careers', *Social Problems*, 31: 208–18.

Shover, N., Norland, S., James, J. and Thornton, W. (1979) 'Gender Roles in Delinquency', *Social Forces*, 58: 158–71.

Sibbitt, R (1999) *The Perpetrators of Racial Harassment and Racial Violence*, Home Office Research Study 176. London: Home Office.

Siegel, L.J. (2002) *Criminology: The Core*. Belmont, CA: Wadsworth/Thomson Learning.

Siegel, L.J. and McCormick, C. (2006) *Criminology in Canada: Theories, Patterns, and Typologies*, 3rd edition. Toronto, ON: Thompson, Nelson.

Silvestri, M. (2006) 'Gender and Crime: A Human Rights Perspective', in F. Heidensohn (ed.) *Gender and Justice*. Cullompton: Willan Publishing.

Sim, J., Scraton, P. and Gordon, P. (1987) 'Introduction: Crime, the State and Critical Analysis', in P. Scraton (ed.) *Law, Order and the Authoritarian State: Readings in Critical Criminology*. Milton Keynes: Open University Press.

Simmel, G. (1900) *The Philosophy of Money*. London: Routledge & Kegan Paul.

Simmel, G. (1906) 'The Sociology of Secrecy', *American Journal of Sociology*, 11: 441–98.

Simmel, G. (1908) *Conflict and the Web of Group Affiliations*. New York: Free Press.

Simon, J.K. (1991) 'Michel Foucault on Attica: An Interview', *Social Justice*, 18: 26–34.

Simon, J.K. (2007) *Governing Through Crime: How the War on Crime Transformed American Democracy and Created a Culture of Fear*. New York: Oxford University Press.

Simon, R.J. (1975) *Women and Crime*. London: Lexington Books.

Simons, G.L. and Stroup II, W.F. (1997) 'Law and Social Change: The Implications of Chaos Theory in Understanding the Role of the American Legal System', in D. Milovanovic (ed.) *Chaos, Criminology and Social Justice: The New Orderly (Dis) Order*. Westport, CT: Praeger.

Simpson, S.S. (1989) 'Feminist Theory, Crime and Justice', *Criminology*, 27: 605–27.

Simpson, S.S. (1991) 'Caste, Class and Violent Crime: Explaining Differences in Female Offending', *Criminology*, 29: 115–35.

Simpson, S.S., Lyn Exum, M. and Smith, N.C. (2000) 'The Social Control of Corporate Criminals: Shame and Informal Sanction Threats', in S.S. Simpson (ed.) *Of Crime and Criminality: The Use of Theory in Everyday Life*. Thousand Oaks, CA: Pine Forge Press.

Singer, J.A. and Salovey, P. (1993) *The Remembered Self: Emotion and Memory in Personality*. New York: Free Press.

Skinner, B.F. (1938) *The Behaviour of Organisms*. New York: Appleton Century Crofts.

Skinner, B.F. (1981) 'Selection by Consequences', *Science*, 213: 501–4.

Smart, C. (1977) *Women, Crime and Criminology*. London: Routledge & Kegan Paul.

Smart, C. (1981) 'Response to Greenwood', in A. Morris and L. Gelsthorpe (eds) *Women and Crime*. Cambridge: Cropwood Conference Series.

Smart, C. (1990) 'Feminist Approaches to Criminology; or Postmodern Woman Meets Atavistic Man', in L. Gelsthorpe and A. Morris (eds) *Feminist Perspectives in Criminology*. Buckingham: Open University Press.

Smart, J. (1981) 'Undernutrition and Aggression', in P.F. Brain and D. Benton (eds) *Multidisciplinary Approaches to Aggression Research*. Amsterdam: Elsevier/North Holland.

Smith, A. (1910) *The Wealth of Nations*. London: Dent.

Smith, D. and Gray, J. (1986) *Police and People in London*. London: Policy Studies Institute.

Smith, D.E. and Smith, D.D. (1977) 'Eysenck's Psychoticism Scale and Reconviction', *British Journal of Criminology*, 17: 387.

Smith, G. (2004) 'What's Law Got to Do With It? Some Reflections on the Police in the Light of Developments in New York City', in R.D. Hopkins Burke (ed.) *'Hard Cop/Soft Cop': Dilemmas and Debates in Contemporary Policing*. Cullompton: Willan Publishing.

Snyder, F. (2002) *Globalisation and Power Disparities*. London: Butterworths LexisNexis.

Sokal, A. and Bricmont, J. (1999) *Intellectual Impostures*. London: Profile Books.

Soothill, K. (1974) *The Prisoner's Release*. London: Allen and Unwin.

Spalek, B. (2004) 'Policing Financial Crime: The Financial Services Authority and the Myth of the "Duped Investor"', in R.D. Hopkins Burke *'Hard Cop/Soft Cop': Dilemmas and Debates in Contemporary Policing*. Cullompton: Willan Publishing.

Spelman, W. (1995) 'The Criminal Careers of Public Places', in J. Eck and D. Weisburd (eds) *Crime and Place: Crime Prevention Studies*, Vol. 4. Monsey, NY: Criminal Justice Press.

Spencer, H. (1971) *Structure, Function and Evolution*, readings, edited with an introduction by S. Andreski. London: Nelson.

Spergel, I.A. (1964) *Racketsville, Slumtown, Haulburg*. Chicago, IL: University of Chicago Press.

Spergel, I.A. (1995) *The Youth Gang Problem: A Community Approach*. Oxford: Oxford University Press.

Spitzer, S. (1975) 'Towards a Marxian Theory of Deviance', *Social Problems*, 22: 638–51.

Squires, P. (2006) *Understanding Community Safety*. Bristol: The Policy Press.

Squires, P. and Stephen, D.E. (2005) *Rougher Justice: Anti-social Behaviour and Young People*. Cullompton: Willan Publishing.

Stack, W., Wasserman, I. and Kern, R. (2004) 'Adult Social Bonds and Use of Internet Pornography', *Social Science Quarterly*, 85: 75–88.

Stalans, L.J. and Henry, G.T. (1994) 'Societal Views of Justice for Adolescents Accused of Murder', *Law and Human Behavior*, 18: 675–96.

Stanko, E.A. (1985) *Intimate Intrusions: Women's Experience of Male Violence*. London: Routledge & Kegan Paul.

Stanko, E.A. (2007) 'From Academia to Policy Making: Changing Police Responses to Violence Against Women', *Theoretical Criminology*, 11: 209–19.

Staw, B.M. and Szwajkowski, E. (1975) 'The Scarcity-Munificence Component of Organizational Environments and the Commission of Illegal Acts', *Administrative Science Quarterly*, 20: 345–54.

Steedman, C. (1984) *Policing the Victorian Community*. London: Routledge & Kegan Paul.

Stenson, K. (2001) 'The New Politics of Crime Control', in K. Stenson and R.R. Sullivan (eds) *Crime, Risk and Justice: The Politics of Crime Control in Liberal Democracies*. Cullompton: Willan Publishing.

Stenson, K. and Sullivan, R.R. (2001) *Crime, Risk and Justice: The Politics of Crime Control in Liberal Democracies*. Cullompton: Willan Publishing.

Stevens, D. (2010) *Media and Criminal Justice: The CSI Effect*. Boston: Jones and Bartlett.

Stewart, D., Gossop, M., Marsden, J. and Rolfe, A. (2000) 'Drug Misuse and Acquisitive Crime Among Clients Recruited to the National Treatment Outcome Research (NTORS)', *Criminal Behaviour and Mental Health*, 10: 13–24.

Stitt, G.B. (2003) 'The Understanding of Evil: A Joint Quest for Criminology and Theology', in R. Chairs and B. Chilton (eds) *Star Trek Visions of Law and Justice*. Dallas, TX: Adios Press.

Storch, R. (1975) 'The Plague of the Blue Locusts: Police Reform and Popular Resistance in Northern England 1840–57', *International Review of Social History*, 20: 61–90.

Storch, R. (1989) 'Policing Rural Southern England before the Police: Opinion and Practice 1830–1856', in D. Hay and F. Snyder (eds) *Policing and Prosecution*. Oxford: Clarendon Press.

Strang, H. (1993) 'Conferencing: A New Paradigm in Community Policing', paper delivered to the Annual Conference of the Association of Chief Police Officers.

Strang, H. (1995) 'Replacing Courts With Conferences', *Policing*, 11(3): 20.

Strentz, T. (1988) 'A Terrorist Psychological Profile', *Law Enforcement Bulletin*, 57: 11–18.

Stretesky, P. and Lynch, M. (2001) 'The Relationship Between Lead Exposure and Homicide', *Archives of Paediatric Adolescent Medicine*, 155: 579–82.

Stumpfl, F. (1936) *Die Ursprunge des Verbrechens im Lebenslauf von Zwillingen*. Leipzig: Verlag.

Sullivan, M. (1996) 'Developmental Transitions in Poor Youth: Delinquency and Crime', in J.A. Graber, J. Brooks-Gunn and A.C. Petersen (eds) *Transitions through Adolescence*. Mahwah, NJ: Lawrence Erlbaum.

Sullivan, R.F. (1973) 'The Economics of Crime: An Introduction to the Literature', *Crime and Delinquency*, 19: 138–49.

Surette, R. (2007) *Media, Crime, and Criminal Justice: Images, Realities, and Policies*, 3rd edition. Belmont, CA: Thomson Wadsworth.

Sutherland, E.H. (1937) *The Professional Thief: By a Professional Thief*. Chicago, IL: University of Chicago Press.

Sutherland, E.H. (1940) 'White-collar Criminality', *American Sociological Review*, 5: 1–12.

Sutherland, E.H. (1947) *Principles of Criminology*, 4th edition. Philadelphia, PA: Lippincott.

Sutherland, E.H. and Cressey, D.R. (1960) *Criminology*, 5th edition. Philadelphia, PA: Lippincott.

Sutherland, E.H. and Cressey, D.R. (1978) *Criminology*, 10th edition. Philadelphia, PA: Lippincott.

Sutton, J.R. (1994) 'Children in the Therapeutic State: Lessons for the Sociology of Deviance and Social Control', in G.S. Bridges and M.A. Myers (eds) *Inequality, Crime and Social Control*. Boulder, CO: Westview Press.

Sutton, M. (1995) 'Supply by Theft: Does the Market for Second-hand Goods Play a Role in Keeping Crime Figures High?', *British Journal of Criminology*, 38(3): 352–65.

Sutton, M. (1998) *Handling Stolen Goods and Theft: A Market Reduction Approach*, Home Office Research Study 178. London: Home Office.

Sutton, M. (2004) 'Tackling Stolen Goods Markets is "Root-Level" Situational Crime Prevention', R.D. Hopkins Burke (ed.) *'Hard Cop/Soft Cop': Dilemmas and Debates in Contemporary Policing*. Cullompton: Willan Publishing.

Sutton, M. (2014, forthcoming) 'Fencing/Receiving Stolen Goods', *Encyclopedia of Criminology and Criminal Justice*. New York: Springer.

Swartz, J. (1975) 'Silent Killers at Work', *Crime and Social Justice*, 3: 15–20.

Sykes, G. and Matza, D. (1957) 'Techniques of Neutralization: A Theory of Delinquency', *American Sociological Review*, 22(6): 664–70.

Syndulko, K. (1978) 'Electrocortical Investigations of Sociopathy', in R.D. Hare and D. Schalling (eds) *Psychopathic Behaviour: Approaches to Research*. Chichester: Wiley.

Tallis, R. (2007) 'My Brain Made Me Do It: Biology and Freedom at the Battle of Ideas', *The Sunday Times Online*. Available at: http://www.timesonline.co.uk/tol/comment/columnists/guest_contributors/article2726643.ece [accessed 23 January 2008].

Tannenbaum, F. (1938) *Crime and the Community*. New York: Columbia University Press.

Tappan, P.W. (1960) *Crime, Justice and Correction*. New York: McGraw-Hill.

Taylor, C.S. (1990) *Dangerous Society*. East Lansing, MI: Michigan State University Press.

Taylor, D. (1997) *The New Police in Nineteenth-Century England: Crime, Conflict and Control*. Manchester: Manchester University Press.

Taylor, I. (1981) *Law and Order: Arguments for Socialism*. London: Macmillan.

Taylor, I. (2007) 'New Directions in Critical Theory', in R. Lilly, F.T. Cullen and R.A. Ball (eds) *Criminological Theory: Context and Consequences*. London: Sage Publications.

Taylor, I., Walton, P. and Young, J. (1973) *The New Criminology: For a Social Theory of Deviance*. London: Routledge & Kegan Paul.

Taylor, I., Walton, P. and Young, J. (eds) (1975) *Critical Criminology*. London: Routledge & Kegan Paul.

Thambirajah, M.S. (2007) *Case Studies in Child and Adolescent Mental Health*. Oxford: Radcliffe Publishing.

Thomas, D.W. and Hyman, J.M. (1978) 'Compliance, Theory, Control Theory and Juvenile Delinquency', in M. Krohn and R.L. Acker (eds) *Crime, Law and Sanctions*. London: Sage.

Thomas, W.I. (1907) *Sex and Society*. Boston, MA: Little, Brown.

Thomas, W.I. (1923) *The Unadjusted Girl*. New York: Harper & Row.

Thomas, W.I. and Thomas, D. (1928) *The Child in America*. New York: Knopf.

Thompson, E.P. (1975) *Whigs and Hunters*. London: Allen Lane.

Thompson, W.E., Mitchell, J. and Doddler, R.A. (1984) 'An Empirical Test of Hirschi's Control Theory of Delinquency', *Deviant Behavior*, 5: 11–22.

Thornhill, R. and Palmer, C. (2000) *A Natural History of Rape: Biological Bases of Sexual Coercion*. Cambridge, MA: MIT Press.

Thornhill, R. and Thornhill, N. (1983) 'Human Rape: An Evolutionary Analysis', *Ethology and Sociobiology*, 4: 137–73.

Thornton, S. (1995) *Club Cultures*. Cambridge: Polity Press.

Thrasher, F. (1947) *The Gang*. Chicago, IL: University of Chicago Press.

Tierney, K. (1982) 'The Battered Women Movement and the Creation of the Wife Beating Problem', *Social Problems*, 29 (February): 207–20.

Tifft, L. (1979) 'The Coming Redefinition of Crime: An Anarchist Perspective', *Social Problems*, 26: 392–402.

Tifft, L. (1995) 'Social Harm Definitions of Crime', *Critical Criminologist*, 7(1): 9–12.

Tittle, C.R. (1995) *Control Balance: Towards a General Theory of Deviance*. Boulder, CO: Westview Press.

Tittle, C.R. (1997) 'Thoughts Stimulated by Braithwaite's Analysis of Control Balance', *Theoretical Criminology*, 1: 87–107.

Tittle, C.R. (1999) 'Continuing the Discussion of Control Balance', *Theoretical Criminology*, 3: 326–43.

Tittle, C.R. (2000) 'Control Balance', in R. Paternoster and R. Bachman (eds) *Explaining Criminals and Crime: Essays in Contemporary Theory*. Los Angeles, CA: Roxbury.

Tittle, C.R. (2004) 'The Arrogance of Public Criminology', *Social Forces*, 82: 1639–43.

Toby, J. (1957) 'Social Disorganization and Stake in Conformity: Complementary Factors in the Behavior of Hoodlums', *American Sociological Review*, 22(5): 505–12.

Toch, H. (1987) 'Supplementing the Positivist Approach', in M. Gottfredson and T. Hirschi (eds) *Positive Criminology*. Beverly Hills, CA: Sage Publications.

Tolman, E.C. (1959) 'Principles of Purposive Behaviour', in S. Koch and D.E. Leary (eds) *A Century of Psychology as a Science*. New York: McGraw-Hill.

Tolson, N. (2006) *Violence against Clergy in Willesden Archdeaconry*. London: National Churchwatch.

Tolson, N. (2007) *Clergy Lifestyle Theory: Assessing the Risk of Violence to Clergy*. London: National Churchwatch.

Tong, R. (1988) *Feminist Thought: A Comprehensive Introduction*. London: Routledge.

Tonry, M. (1995) *Malign Neglect: Race, Crime, and Punishment in America*. New York: Oxford University Press.

Trasler, G.B. (1967) *The Explanation of Criminality*. London: Routledge & Kegan Paul.

Trasler, G.B. (1979) 'Delinquency, Recidivism and Desistance', *British Journal of Criminology*, 19: 314–22.

Trasler, G.B. (1980) 'Aspects of Causality, Culture, and Crime', paper presented at the Fourth International Seminar at the International Centre of Sociological, Penal and Penitentiary Research and Studies, Messina, Italy.

Trasler, G.B. (1986) 'Situational Crime Control and Rational Choice: A Critique', in K. Heal and G. Laycock (eds) *Situational Crime Prevention: From Theory into Practice*. London: HMSO.

Travis, C.B. (ed.) (2003) *Evolution, Gender and Rape*. Cambridge, MA: MIT Press.

Triplett, R. (2000) 'The Dramatisation of Evil: Reacting to Juvenile Delinquency During the 1990s', in S.S. Simpson (ed.) *Of Crime and Criminality: The Use of Theory in Everyday Life*. Thousand Oaks, CA: Pine Forge Press.

Tunnell, K. (1996) 'Choosing Crime: Close Your Eyes and Take Your Chances', in B.W. Hancock and P.M. Sharp (eds) *Criminal Justice in America: Theory, Practice, and Policy*. Englewood Cliffs, NJ: Prentice Hall.

Turk, A.T. (1969) *Criminality and the Social Order*. Chicago, IL: Rand-McNally.

Tzannetakis, T. (2001) 'Neo-Conservative Criminology', in E. McLaughlin and J. Muncie (eds) *The Sage Dictionary of Criminology*. London: Sage.

Uggen, C. (1996) 'Age, Employment and the Duration Structure of Recidivism: Estimating the "True Effect" of Work on Crime', paper presented at the 1996 American Sociological Association Conference, New York.

UKADCU (United Kingdom Anti-Drugs Co-ordinating Unit) (1998) *Tackling Drugs to Build a Better Britain: The Government's 10-year Strategy for Tackling Drug Misuse*. London: The Stationery Office.

United Nations Development Programme (UNDP) (1999) *Human Development Report 1999: Globalization with a Human Face*. Oxford: Oxford University Press.

United Nations Office on Drugs and Crime (UNODC) (2013) Transnational Organized Crime: The Globalized Illegal Economy [Online]. Available at: www.unodc.org/toc [accessed 9 October 2013].

Unnever, J.D., Colvin, M. and Cullen, F.T. (2004) 'Crime and Coercion: A Test of Core Theoretical Propositions', *Journal of Research in Crime and Delinquency*, 41(3): 244–68.

Van den Bergle, P. (1974) 'Bringing the Beast Back In: Towards a Biosocial Theory of Aggression', *American Sociological Review*, 39: 779.

Van Den Haag, E. (1975) *Punishing Criminals: Concerning a Very Old and Painful Question*. New York: Basic Books.

Van Duyne, P. (1997) 'Organized Crime, Corruption and Power', *Crime Law and Social Change*, 26: 201–38.

Van Ness, D. and Strong, K.H. (1997) *Restoring Justice*. Cincinnati, OH: Anderson Publishing.

Van Ness, D. and Strong, K.H. (2002) *Restoring Justice*. Cincinnati, OH: Anderson Publishing.

Van Swaaningen, R. (1999) 'Reclaiming Critical Criminology', *Theoretical Criminology*, 3(1): 5–28.

Van Swaaningen, R. (2007) 'Bending the Punitive Turn', paper presented at the 6th International Conference of the European Society of Criminology.

Virkkunen, M. (1986) 'Reactive Hypoglycaemic Tendency Among Habitually Violent Offenders', *Nutritional Reviews Supplement*, 44: 94–103.

Virkkunen, M. (1987) 'Metabolic Dysfunctions Amongst Habitually Violent Offenders: Reactive Hypoglycaemia and Cholesterol Levels', in S.A. Mednick, T.E. Moffitt and S.A. Stack (eds) *The Causes of Crime: New Biological Approaches*. Cambridge: Cambridge University Press.

Volavka, J. (1987) 'Electroencephalogram Among Criminals', in S.A. Mednick, T.E. Moffitt and S.A. Stack (eds) *The Causes of Crime: New Biological Approaches*. Cambridge: Cambridge University Press.

Vold, G.B. (1958) *Theoretical Criminology*. Oxford: Oxford University Press.

Vold, G.B., Bernard, T.J. and Snipes, J.B. (1998) *Theoretical Criminology*, 4th edition. Oxford: Oxford University Press.

Von Hirsch, A. (1976) *Doing Justice: The Choice of Punishments*. Report of the Committee for the Study of Incarceration. New York: Hill and Wang.

Von Hirsch, A., Ashworth, A., Wasik, M., Smith, A.T.H., Morgan, R. and Gardner, J. (1999) 'Overtaking on the Right', *New Law Journal*, 1501.

Wacquant, L. (1998a) 'Crime et châtiment en Amérique de Nixon à Clinton', *Archives De Politique Criminelle*, 20: 123–38.

Wacquant, L. (1998b) 'Negative Social Capital: State Breakdown and Social Destitution in America's Urban Core', *The Netherlands Journal of the Built Environment*, 13: 25–40.

Wacquant, L. (2001) 'The New "Peculiar Institution": On the Prison as Surrogate Ghetto', *Theoretical Criminology*, 4: 382–5.

Wacquant, L. (2009a) *Urban Outcasts: A Comparative Sociology of Advanced Marginality*. Cambridge: Polity Press.

Wacquant, L. (2009b) *Prisons of Poverty*. Minneapolis: University of Minnesota Press.

Wacquant, L. (2011) *Deadly Symbiosis: Race and the Rise of the Penal State*. Cambridge: Polity Press.

Waddington, P.A.J. (1986) 'Mugging as a Moral Panic: A Question of Proportion', *British Journal of Criminology*, 32(2): 245–59.

Wadham, J. and Modi, K. (2003) 'National Security and Open Government in the United Kingdom', *National Security and Open Government: Striking the Right Balance*. Syracuse, NY: Campbell Public Affairs Institute.

Wahlund, K. and Kristiansson, M. (2009) 'Aggression, Psychopathy and Brain Imaging – Review and Future Recommendations', *International Journal of Law and Psychiatry*, 32(4): 266–71.

Wakschlag, L.S. and Hans, S.L. (1999) 'Relation of Maternal Responsiveness during Infancy to the Development of Behavior Problems in High-Risk Youths', *Developmental Psychology*, 35(2): 569–79.

Walby, S. (1980) *Theorizing Patriarchy*. Oxford: Basil Blackwell.

Walby, S. and Allen, P. (2004) *Inter-personal Violence: Findings from 2001 British Crime Survey*, Home Office Research Study No. 276. London: Home Office.

Waldorf, D. (1983) 'Natural Recovery from Opiate Addiction: Some Social-Psychological Processes of Untreated Recovery', *Journal of Drug Issues*, 13: 237–80.

Walker, N. (1980) *Punishment, Danger and Stigma: The Morality of Criminal Justice*. Oxford: Basil Blackwell.

Walker, N. (1985) *Sentencing: Theory, Law and Practice*. London: Butterworths.

Walklate, S. (1995) *Gender and Crime: An Introduction*. Hemel Hempstead: Prentice Hall/ Harvester.

Walklate, S. (1998) *Understanding Criminology: Current Theoretical Debates*. Buckingham: Open University Press.

Walsh, A. and Ellis, L. (2006) *Criminology: An Interdisciplinary Approach*. Newbury Park, CA: Sage Publications.

Watney, S. (1987) *Policing Desire: Pornography, Aids and the Media*. London: Methuen.

Weaver, B. and McNeill, F. (2007) *Giving up Crime: Directions for Policy*. Scottish Consortium on Crime and Criminal Justice: Edinburgh.

Weaver, B. and McNeill, F. (2010) 'Travelling Hopefully: Desistance Research and Probation Practice', in J. Brayford, F. Cowe and J. Deering (eds) *What Else Works? Creative Work With Offenders*. Cullompton: Willan Publishing.

Weber, M. (1964) *The Theory of Social and Economic Organization*. New York: Free Press.

Weber, M. (1975) 'Religious Rejections of the World and their Directions', in H. Gerth and C.W. Mills (eds) *From Max Weber: Essays in Sociology*. Oxford: Oxford University Press.

Weisberg, D.K. (ed.) (1996) *Applications of Feminist Legal Theory to Women's Lives: Sex, Violence and Reproduction*. Philadelphia, PA: Temple University Press.

Wells, C. (1993) *Corporations and Criminal Responsibility*. Oxford: Clarendon Press.

Werner, E.E., Bierman, J.M. and French, F.E. (1971) *The Children of Kauai: A Longitudinal Study from the Prenatal Period to Age Ten*. Honolulu, HI: University of Hawaii Press.

West, C. (1999) *The Cornell West Reader*. New York: Basic Civitas Books.

West, D.J. (1969) *Present Conduct and Future Delinquency*. London: Heinemann.

West, D.J. (1982) *Delinquency: Its Roots, Careers, and Prospects*. London: Heinemann.

West, D.J. and Farrington, D.P. (1973) *Who Becomes Delinquent?* London: Heinemann.

Westergaard, J. (1995) *Who Gets What? The Hardening of Class Inequality in the Late Twentieth Century*. Cambridge: Polity Press.

Widom, C.S. (1979) 'Female Offenders: Three Assumptions About Self-esteem, Sex Role Identity and Feminism', *Criminal Justice Behaviour*, 6: 358–72.

Wikström, P.-O.H. (2004) 'Crime as an Alternative: Towards a Cross-level Situational Action Theory of Crime Causation', in J. McCord (ed.) *Beyond Empiricism: Institutions and Intentions in the Study of Crime: Advances in Criminological Theory*. New Brunswick: Transaction.

Wikström, P.-O.H. (2005) 'The Social Origins of Pathways in Crime: Towards a Developmental Ecological Action Theory of Crime Involvement and its Changes', in D.P. Farrington (ed.) *Integrated Developmental and Life-Course Theories of Offending: Advances in Criminological Theory*. New Brunswick: Transaction.

Wikström, P.-O.H. (2006) 'Individuals, Settings and Acts of Crime: Situational Mechanisms and the Explanation of Crime', in P.-O.H. Wikström and R.J. Sampson (eds) *The Explanation of Crime: Context, Mechanisms and Development*. Cambridge: Cambridge University Press.

Wikström, P.-O.H. (2007a) 'Deterrence and Deterrence Experiences: Preventing Crime Through the Threat of Punishment', in S.G. Shoham, O. Beck and M. Kett (eds) *International Handbook of Penology and Criminal Justice*. London: CRC Press.

Wikström, P.-O.H. (2007b) 'The Social Ecology of Crime: The Role of the Environment in Crime Causation', in H.J. Schneider (ed.) *Internationales Handbuch der Kriminologie*, Volume 1. Berlin/New York: de Gruyter.

Wikström, P.-O.H. (2007c) 'In Search of Causes and Explanations of Crime', in R.D. King and E. Wincup (eds) *Doing Research on Crime and Justice*, 2nd edition. Oxford: Oxford University Press.

Wikström, P.-O.H. (2009) 'Violence as Situational Action', *International Journal of Conflict and Violence*, 3(1): 75–96.

Wikström, P.-O.H. (2013) 'Explaining Crime as Moral Actions', in S. Hitlin and S. Vaisey (eds) *Handbook of the Sociology of Morality*. Springer: New York, pp. 211–39.

Wikström, P.-O.H. and Sampson, R.J. (2003) 'Social Mechanisms of Community Influences in Crime and Pathways in Criminality', in B.B. Lahey, T.E. Moffitt and A. Caspi (eds) *The Causes of Conduct Disorder and Serious Juvenile Delinquency*. New York: Guilford Press.

Wikström, P.-O.H. and Treiber, K. (2007) 'The Role of Self-Control in Crime Causation: Beyond Gottfredson and Hirschi's General Theory of Crime', *European Journal of Criminology*, 4: 237–64.

Wikström, P.-O.H. and Treiber, K. (2009) 'What Drives Persistent Offending: The Neglected and Unexplored Role of the Social Environment', in J. Savage (ed.) *The Development of Persistent Criminality*. Oxford: Oxford University Press.

Wikström, P.-O.H., Tseloni, A. and Karlis, D. (2011) 'Do People Comply with the Law Because They Fear Getting Caught?', *European Journal of Criminology*, 8(5): 401–20.

Wikström, P.-O.H., Oberwittler, D., Treiber, K. and Hardie, B. (2012) 'Breaking Rules: The Social and Situational Dynamics of Young People's Urban Crime', *Policing: A Journal of Policy and Practice*. [Online]. Available at: www.oxfordscholarship.com/.../9780199697 243MacLeodGroveFarrington [accessed 25 June 2012].

Wilczynski, A. and Morris, A. (1993) 'Parents Who Kill Their Children', *Criminal Law Review*, 26–44.

Wiles, P. (2002) 'Criminology in the Twenty-first Century: Public Good or Private Interest?', *Australian and New Zealand Journal of Criminology*, 35: 238–52.

Wilkins, L. (1964) *Social Deviance*. London: Tavistock.

Williams, C.R. and Arrigo, B.A. (2004) *Theory, Justice and Social Change: Theoretical Integrations and Critical Applications*. New York: Kluwer.

Williams, P.J. (1997) *Seeing a Color-Blind Future: The Paradox of Race*. New York: Noonday.

Williams, T. (1989) *The Cocaine Kids: The Inside Story of a Teenage Drug Ring*. Reading, MA: Addison-Wesley Publishing Co.

Willis, P. (1977) *Learning to Labour*. London: Saxon House.

Willis, P. (1978) *Profane Culture*. London: Routledge & Kegan Paul.

Wilmott, P. (1966) *Adolescent Boys in East London*. London: Routledge & Kegan Paul.

Wilson, E.O. (1990) *Success and Dominance in Ecosystems: The Case of the Social Insects.* Oldendorf/Luhe: Inter Research.

Wilson, H. (1980) 'Parental Supervision: A Neglected Aspect of Delinquency', *British Journal of Criminology*, 20: 315–27.

Wilson, J.Q. (1975) *Thinking About Crime.* New York: Basic Books.

Wilson, J.Q. (1985) *Thinking About Crime*, 2nd edition. New York: Basic Books.

Wilson, J.Q. and Herrnstein, R.J. (1985) *Crime and Human Nature.* New York: Simon and Schuster.

Wilson, J.Q. and Kelling, G.L. (1982) 'Broken Windows', *Atlantic Monthly*, March: 29–38.

Wilson, J.Q. and Kelling, G.L. (1989) 'Making Neighborhoods Safe', *Atlantic Monthly*, February: 46–58.

Wilson, W.J. (1987) *The Truly Disadvantaged.* Chicago, IL: Chicago University Press.

Wilson, W.J. (1991) 'Public Policy Research and the Truly Disadvantaged', in C. Jencks and P.E. Peterson (eds) *The Urban Underclass.* Washington, DC: The Brookings Institution.

Wilson, W.J. (1996) *When Work Disappears.* New York: Knopf.

Winant, H. (2001) *The World is a Ghetto: Race and Democracy Since World War II.* New York: Basic Books.

Winant, H. (2004) *The New Politics of Race.* Minneapolis: University of Minnesota Press.

Wing, L. (1998) 'The History of Asperger Syndrome', in E. Schopler, G. Mesibov and L. Kunce (eds) *Asperger Syndrome or High-Functioning Autism?* New York: Plenum Press.

Winlow, S. and Hall, S. (2006) *Violent Night: Urban Leisure and Contemporary Culture.* Oxford: Berg.

Witkin, H.A., Mednick, S.A. and Schulsinger, F. (1977) 'XYY and XXY Men: Criminality and Aggression', in S.A. Mednick and K.O. Christiansen (eds) *Biosocial Bases of Criminal Behaviour.* New York: Gardner Press.

Wolff, K. (ed.) (1950) *The Sociology of Georg Simmel.* New York: Free Press.

Wolfgang, M.E. and Ferracuti, F. (1967) *The Sub-culture of Violence: Towards an Integrated Theory in Criminology.* Beverly Hills, CA: Sage.

Wolfgang, M.E., Figlio, R.M. and Sellin, T. (1972) *Delinquency in a Birth Cohort.* Chicago, MI: University of Chicago Press.

Wood, E. (2004) 'Displacement of Canada's Largest Public Illicit Drug Market in Response to a Police Crackdown', *Canadian Medical Association Journal*, 170(10): 1551–6.

Wootton, B. (1959) *Social Science and Social Pathology.* London: Allen & Unwin.

Wootton, B. (1962) 'A Social Scientist's Approach to Maternal Deprivation', in M.D. Ainsworth (ed.) *Deprivation of Maternal Care: A Reassessment of its Effects.* Geneva: World Health Organization.

Wright, K.N. and Wright, K.E. (1992) 'Does Getting Married Reduce the Likelihood of Criminality? A Review of the Literature', *Federal Probation*, 61(3): 50–6.

Wright, M. (1982) *Making Good: Prisons, Punishment and Beyond.* London: Burnett.

Wright, R.A. (1993) 'A Socially Sensitive Criminal Justice System', in J.W. Murphy and D.L. Peck (eds) *Open Institutions: The Hope for Democracy.* Westport, CT: Praeger.

Wright, R.A. and Decker, S. (1997) *Armed Robbers in Action: Stickups and Street Culture.* Boston, MA: North-eastern University Press.

Yablonsky, L. (1962) *The Violent Gang.* New York: Macmillan.

Yaralian, P. and Raine, A. (2001) 'Biosocial Approaches to Crime: Psychophysiology and Brain Dysfunction', in R. Paternoster and R. Bachman (eds) *Explaining Criminals and Crime.* Los Angeles: Roxbury Publishing.

Young, J. (1971) *The Drug Takers: The Social Meaning of Drugtaking.* London: Paladin.

Young, J. (1986a) 'The Failure of Criminology: The Need for a Radical Realism', in R. Matthews and J. Young (eds) *Confronting Crime.* London: Sage.

Young, J. (1986b) 'Ten Points of Realism', in R. Matthews and J. Young (eds) *Issues in Realist Criminology*. London: Sage.

Young, J. (1987) 'The Tasks Facing a Realist Criminology', *Contemporary Crises*, 11: 337–56.

Young, J. (1992) 'Realist Research as a Basis for Local Criminal Justice Policy', in J. Lowman and B. MacLean (eds) *Realist Criminology: Crime Control and Policing in the 1990s*. Toronto, ON: University of Toronto Press.

Young, J. (1994) 'Incessant Chatter: Recent Paradigms in Criminology', in M. Maguire, R. Morgan and R. Reiner (eds) *The Oxford Handbook of Criminology*. Oxford: Clarendon Press.

Young, J. (1997) 'Left Realist Criminology: Radical in its Analysis, Realist in its Policy', in M. Maguire, R. Morgan and R. Reiner (eds) *Oxford Handbook of Criminology*, 2nd edition. Oxford: Oxford University Press.

Young, J. (1999) *The Exclusive Society: Social Exclusion, Crime and Difference in Late Modernity*. London: Sage.

Young, J. (2001) 'Identity, Community and Social Exclusion', in R. Matthews and J. Pitts (eds) *Crime, Disorder and Community Safety*. London: Routledge.

Young, J. (2003) 'Merton with Energy, Katz with Structure', *Theoretical Criminology*, 7(3): 389–414.

Young, J. (2011) *The Criminological Imagination*. Oxford: Polity Press.

Young, J. and Matthews, R. (2003) 'New Labour, Crime Control and Social Exclusion', in R. Matthews and J. Young (eds) *The New Politics of Crime and Punishment*. Cullompton: Willan Publishing.

Young, M. (1991) *An Inside Job: Policing and Police Culture in Britain*. Oxford: Oxford University Press.

Young, M. (1993) *In the Sticks*. Oxford: Oxford University Press.

Young, R. and Goold, B. (1999) 'Restorative Police Cautioning in Aylesbury – From Degrading to Shaming Ceremonies', *Criminal Law Review*, 123–34.

Young, T.R. (1997) 'The ABCs of Crime: Attractors, Bifurcations, and Chaotic Dynamics', in D. Milovanovic (ed.) *Chaos, Criminology, and Social Justice: The New Orderly (Dis) Order*. Westport, CT: Praeger.

Young, T.R. (1999) 'A Constitutive Theory of Justice: The Architecture of Affirmative Postmodern Legal Systems', in S. Henry and D. Milovanovic (eds) *Constitutive Criminology at Work: Applications to Crime and Justice*. New York: State University of New York Press.

Younge, S.L., Oetting, E.R. and Deffenbacher, J.L. (1996) 'Correlations Among Maternal Rejection, Dropping Out of School, and Drug Use in Adolescents', *Journal of Clinical Psychology*, 52(1): 96–102.

Youth Justice Board (2002) *Key Elements of Effective Practice – Assessment, Planning Interventions and Supervision*, edition 1. London: Youth Justice Board.

Zahn, M.A. (1999) 'Thoughts on the Future of Criminology – The American Society of Criminology 1998 Presidential Address', *Criminology*, 37: 1–16.

Zedner, L. (2002) 'Dangers of Dystopias in Penal Theory', *Oxford Journal of Legal Studies*, 22(2): 341–66.

Zimring, F. (2003) *The Contradictions of American Capital Punishment*. Oxford: Oxford University Press.

Zimring, F. and Hawkins, G. (1968) 'Deterrence and Marginal Groups', *Journal of Research in Crime and Delinquency*, 5: 110–15.

Zimring, F. and Hawkins, G. (1973) *Deterrence*. Chicago, IL: University of Chicago.

Zoccolillo, M., Pickles, A., Quinton, D. and Rutter, M. (1992) 'The Outcome of Childhood Conduct Disorder: Implications for Defining Adult Personality Disorder and Conduct Disorder', *Psychological Medicine*, 22: 971–86.

Index

abuse 70, 91, 242
actuarial justice 410, 412, 502
Adler, Freda 233–4
administrative criminology 247, 346,
    347–8, 351, 502
adopted children studies 11, 88–9, 107
adrenaline sensitivity 100
African-Americans 470–6
African-Caribbeans 115, 158, 347
age 19, 197, 271, 325–31
agency 38, 318, 330, 341
aggression 90, 93–4, 148, 172, 179, 240;
    biochemical theories 98–9, 100; diet 101;
    frustration-aggression hypothesis 430;
    sociobiological theories 268, 269–70, 272,
    274
Akers, Ronald 70, 125, 220–1, 266
alcohol 6, 11, 40, 101–3, 302, 393;
    hypoglycaemia 100; sociobiological
    perspective 17; treatment 105, 109
alienation 199, 217, 224, 230, 265
allergies 101
al-Qaeda 426–7
altered biological state theories 100–5, 499,
    502
American Dream 140, 145–6, 476
American Psycho 403–4
amphetamines 101, 104, 395
anarchism 373, 427–8
anarchist criminology 21, 380–4, 501, 502
'anatomy is destiny' 13, 171, 502
anomie 13, 18, 137, 164, 445, 499, 502;
    American Dream 145–6; 'anomie gap'
    150; Durkheim 133, 135, 265, 295, 452;
    environmental theories 279; feminism
    232; left realism 347; Merton 140–5, 149,

176, 215, 294, 430; relative deprivation
    16; women 177
anti-authoritarianism 191
antisocial behaviour 99–100, 101, 257, 358,
    411; ASBOs 356, 502; 'broken windows'
    thesis 290, 358; left realism 358–9, 360;
    protection from 454, 455; sociobiological
    theories 17, 268–9, 270, 274–5, 276
antisocial personality disorder (APD) 12,
    95, 102, 118, 119–20, 121, 333, 502
Appadurai, A. 396–7
Aquinas, St Thomas 2, 448
area studies 17, 280
aristocracy 3, 4, 9; *see also* ruling class
armed conflicts 421
arousal 100
arson 65–6, 122
ascertainable criteria 219–20
Asperger's Syndrome 11, 96, 97
assaults 63, 91
asylums 460, 465
attention deficit disorder 95–6
austerity measures 25, 485
Australia 204, 426
authority 47, 190, 211, 350
autistic spectrum disorders 11, 96–8, 499,
    502
autonomic nervous system (ANS) 94, 120,
    269
awareness space 283

balanced intervention 19, 348, 351, 354,
    356, 416, 482–3, 502–3
Barak, G. 399–400, 403–6
Beccaria, Cesare 30, 35–8, 42, 43, 52, 73
Becker, Gary 65, 198–9

Becker, Howard 194–5, 202, 211, 214, 463–4
begging 48, 57, 289–90, 291, 358
Begin, Menachem 427
behaviour modification 125–6, 127
behaviour therapy 126
behavioural learning theories 12, 20, 116–22, 127, 271, 499, 503
beliefs 298
Bell, Daniel 367
Bell, Derrick 255
benperidol 105–6
Bentham, Jeremy 30, 32, 35, 37–40, 42, 73, 294
Big Society concept 485
binge drinking 103
biochemical theories 11, 98–100, 101, 499
biological determinism 13, 230
biological deviants 134
biological positivism 10–11, 12, 81, 83–110, 167–70, 180–1, 264, 503
biology 1, 9, 81
biosocial theory 17, 48, 267–77, 503
Birmingham School 159–61, 162, 216, 396
Black Civil Rights movement 191–2, 251–2
black feminism 230–1, 254
'black holes of informational capitalism' 422
black people 24, 152, 191–2, 246, 345, 392; broken homes 115; deviant subcultures 158; imprisonment in the USA 50, 52, 470–6; left realism 347; United Kingdom 477–8; victim studies 346
Blair, Tony 19–20, 351, 442
Bleuler, Eugen 96
blood sugar levels 99–100
'bloody code' 3, 503
body/soul dualism 132
body type theories 11, 91–3, 499
Bonger, Wilhelm 212, 214–15, 349–50
born criminals 84
boundary maintenance mechanisms 195–6
bounded rationality 66, 505
Bowlby, John 113–14, 172
Box, Stephen 144, 156, 185, 234, 248, 300–1, 302, 308
brain injuries and disorders 11, 93–5, 499
Braithwaite, John 204–5, 301–2, 306, 348, 420, 426, 445
Briar, Scott 297
broken homes 12, 115–16, 180, 197, 430
'broken windows' thesis 289–90, 358–9

'bulimic' society 339
bureaucracy 187, 382–3
Burgess, Ernest 125, 138
burglary 6, 62, 66, 104, 259, 281–2, 283, 286, 287–8, 305
Bush, George 53, 369, 438

Calvin, John 447–8, 449
Cambridge Study in Delinquent Development 92–3, 95–6
Cameron, David 55, 485
cannabis 6, 11, 101, 104, 319
'canteen culture' 151–2
capable guardians, absence of 68, 70
capital punishment 2, 3, 52, 213, 218, 489–90; Classical criminology 35–6, 37; deterrence 61–2; peacemaking criminology 222; public opinion 490, 495; racial bias 219
capitalism 57, 80, 187, 202, 217, 433; 'black holes of informational capitalism' 422; carceral surveillance society model 469; critical criminology 250; left realist hybrid model 469–70; Marxism 189, 190, 212–15, 350; Marxist feminism 230, 236–7; radical conflict model 360, 461–2, 466; white-collar crime 248
carceral surveillance society model 24, 25, 361, 414, 463–5, 467, 469, 471, 473, 476, 478
carnival, crime as 21, 392, 503
Carrington, Ben 163, 395–8
castration 10, 54, 105, 109, 273
categorical imperative 220
celerity of punishment 60, 74
Centre for Contemporary Cultural Studies (CCCS) 159–61, 162, 216, 396
certainty of punishment 10, 49–50, 60–1, 74, 128
Chambliss, William 211, 212–13
chaos 391
chaos theory 21, 376, 377–9
chemotherapy 105–6, 109
Chicago Area Project (CAP) 139–40
Chicago School 18, 137–40, 146, 147, 214, 279–80, 295, 425, 503
child-rearing practices 12, 114–15, 275, 304, 430
children 40, 122, 459, 467; adopted children studies 11, 88–9, 107; attention deficit disorder 95–6; behaviour modification

126; body type theories 93; capital punishment 52; fear of abduction 495; learning disabilities 96; legislation 354–5; psychodynamic theories 112–13; sociobiological theories 274–5; trafficking of 423

chivalry 174–5, 234

choice 9, 38, 55, 127, 135–6, 162, 265; Classical criminology 42; conservatism 58; desistance theories 330, 335–7; labelling theories 202; neo-Classical criminology 41; situational action theory 314–15, 316, 322; subcultural theory 163; *see also* rational choice theory

Christianity 4, 447–8

chromosomal abnormalities 90, 94

civil society 442

class 139, 159, 177, 228; black people in the USA 473; intelligence linked to 89; labelling theories 196–7, 203; left realism 344; peacemaking criminology 222; power control theory 18; proletarianization 260; radical conflict model 462, 463, 466; radical theories 14, 213; right realism 49; victim studies 346; *see also* middle class; working class

Classical criminology 9–10, 35–45, 71, 263, 499, 503

classification of criminals 84

Clear, Todd 74, 446, 487

Clergy Lifestyle Theory 70–1

Clinton, Bill 53

Cloward, Richard 149–50, 153, 157, 178

club culture 21, 161, 162, 392, 395–8

cocaine 11–12, 101, 104

coercion 18, 209, 306–7, 358

cognitive behavioural methods 126, 128

cognitive learning theories 12, 122–6, 127, 499, 503

cognitive maps 283

Cohen, Albert 147–8, 153, 157, 177, 178

Cohen, L.E. 67–9, 281–2

Cohen, Stanley 160, 200, 214, 246, 382, 384, 400, 458, 459–60, 463, 464–5

collective consciousness 135, 195, 450, 451, 452

Colvin, Mark 306–7, 384

commitment 298

communitarianism 23–4, 25, 220, 301, 355–6, 437–56, 485, 497, 501, 503

communities of choice and fate 443

community, concept of 445–7

community cohesion 358

community empowerment 164

compassionate conservatism 55

Comte, Auguste 82, 132, 425, 450, 458

concentric zone theory 138, 503

condemnation 339

conditional relevance of controls 319

conditioned learning 12, 116–17, 122–3, 124–5, 271

conduct norms 208

conflict 187–8, 190

conflict subcultures 149, 150

conflict theories 14, 15, 190–1, 207–11, 224–5, 500, 503; gender issues 228; radical conflict model 24, 360–1, 461–3

conformity 18, 133, 141, 144, 153, 179, 205, 294–9, 308

Connell, Raewyn (Bob) 23, 240, 241, 425–6

conscience 112, 113, 117, 132–3, 271

conscience collectives 135

consensus 133–4, 187, 207

conservatism 10, 15, 19–20, 43, 46–59, 217, 345–6, 351, 352, 440, 499, 506; *see also* new right; right realism

Conservative Party 54–6, 351, 353, 483, 484

constitutive criminology 375–9, 384, 501, 503

consumption 162, 389

control, culture of 388

control balance theory 18, 305, 500, 503

control theory *see* social control

controlology 203

corporal punishment 3, 57, 61

corporate crime 7, 56, 59n2, 143–4, 155–6, 248, 393, 503; control balance theory 305; deviant subcultures 151; differential coercion theory 307; left realism 346; reintegrative shaming 205; *see also* white-collar crime

correct means 219

correctionalism 22, 211, 407

corruption 22, 419, 420, 425

cortisol 99

Coser, Lewis 208

cost-benefit calculus 65, 74, 76, 282, 429

counterterrorism 434

Cowling, Mark 375–6, 378–9

crack 11–12, 104, 105

Crawford, A. 358, 446

Crenshaw, Martha 23, 429
crime: Classical criminology 41; cultural
    criminology 21–2; defining 5–7, 216, 256,
    257–8, 311, 312; fear of 201, 382;
    genealogical approach 491; perception
    of 210; pre-modern 2–3; situational
    action theory 18–19; social construction
    of 131, 194–6, 345, 366, 402, 486, 508
Crime and Disorder Act (1998) 354, 355,
    482
Crime and Disorder Reduction
    Partnerships (CDRPs) 359
crime attractors 284
crime control 21–2, 42–3, 54, 56, 72, 197,
    398, 410, 433, 438, 471, 504
crime generators 284
'crime industry' 213
crime pattern theory 281, 283
crime prevention 22, 40, 65; Classical
    criminology 36; conservatism 10, 58;
    drug use 54; media programmes 405;
    situational action theory 323; situational
    crime prevention 63–4, 75, 125, 287, 351,
    393
crime rates 75, 80, 131, 217, 246, 271,
    278–80, 393–4, 438
criminal behaviour 11, 125, 263; biosocial
    theory 268–9; Classical criminology 36;
    conservatism 48, 56; deviant subcultures
    146–63; sociological positivism 13
criminal culture 139
criminal family studies 86–7
'criminal gene' 107
criminal justice system 24, 152, 155, 202,
    233, 417–18; chivalry 174–5; critical race
    theory 255–6; depersonalization 405; left
    idealism 261; left realism 360; models
    360–1, 457–70; peacemaking criminology
    15, 217, 221, 222, 224; right realism 50;
    'square of crime' 349; women 242
criminal mind 12, 111, 127
criminality 14, 20, 302; female 13, 167–81,
    231–2, 234, 239; modern accounts of 4–5;
    racial inequality in the USA 474–5
criminalization 15, 227, 258, 300–1, 358,
    418, 486; conflict theories 209; critical
    criminology 245, 249–50; definition of
    504; labelling theories 195, 200, 203;
    peacemaking criminology 218; radical
    theories 215
criminaloids 84

criminogenic situations 412
criminology: democratic 488, 493–7, 501;
    genealogical approach 491–3; purpose of
    8; relationship to policy 25, 487–8, 489,
    491–2, 493–4; technocratic model 489–91
critical criminology 16, 20, 216, 245–62,
    265, 345–7, 349–50, 383–4, 492, 500, 504
critical race theory 16, 251–6, 500
CS gas 106
cultural capital 164, 473, 475
cultural criminology 21–2, 387–409, 501,
    504
cultural goals 140–3, 144, 145–6, 176–7, 297
cultural studies 159–61, 253
cultural transmission theory 139, 146, 147,
    149
culture 4, 13, 189, 280
culture conflict theory 207–8
cumulative risk hypothesis 275, 504
Currie, Elliott 260, 344–5, 438–9, 443–4,
    488, 492, 497
customary law 223
cybercrime 421, 423, 424

Dahrendorf, Ralph 190, 191, 352
Darwin, Charles 81
data collection 468
Davis, Kingsley 13, 172, 173–4, 235–6
deception 174, 188
Declaration of the Rights of Man (1789) 40
'defensible space' thesis 286–7
definitions, of behaviour 125
deliberation 315, 316, 318
delinquency 128, 200, 504; delinquent
    subcultures 13, 124, 147–51, 153–4, 177;
    differential coercion theory 306–7; drift
    theory 153–5, 329; feminist approach
    232; gender differences 304–5; labelling
    theories 195, 196–7, 203; latent
    delinquency theory 12, 113, 505; parental
    responsibility 441; social control theories
    295–6, 298–9, 300; sociobiological
    theories 274–5
de-marginalization 361
democratic criminology 25, 488, 493–7, 501
demoralization theory 349–50
denial 154, 155–6
Denmark 87, 89, 105
Design Against Crime (DAC) 287
desistance theories 19, 325–43, 500
desperation 155

detection 62

determinism 10, 13, 41, 80–1, 152, 163, 215, 230, 276

deterrence 9, 72, 73–4, 76, 213, 304, 323, 438, 499; capital punishment 490; Classical criminology 35–6; conservatism 10, 50–1, 54, 55; contemporary theories 60–3; crime control model 43; definition of 504; pre-emptive 361; surveillance 64

deviance 136, 138, 263, 266, 477; amplification 14, 199, 200, 504; anomie theory 141; anti-determinist critique 152–6; deviant subcultures 13, 146–63, 177, 211, 246, 279, 499, 504; Durkheim on 134–5; globalization of 21, 395; labelling theories 14, 195, 196–7, 201–2; medicalization of 214; primary and secondary 198, 299; social control theories 18, 295, 305, 308; sociology of 143, 214–15; symbolic interactionism 186

diabetes mellitus 99

dialectical historical materialism 189

diet 101, 269–70

difference 375, 384–5, 392, 486–7

differential association theory 53, 123–5, 139, 147, 149, 178–80, 232, 504

differential coercion theory 18, 306–7, 500, 504

differential conditioning 116, 117

differential opportunity theory 178

disability 108, 204

disasters 6, 69, 413

disciplinary-control-matrix 25, 203, 465–6, 467, 469, 479, 497

discipline 114, 462, 465

discretion 42, 43, 209, 213

discrimination 109, 199, 260, 402; disabled people 204; feminism 229; racial 158, 347; *see also* racism

disenfranchisement 475

dissociation 157

division of labour 133, 134–5, 434, 446, 450, 452

DNA 412, 468

doli incapax 354

domestic violence 16, 101, 102, 180, 233; control balance theory 305; criminalization of 195; Hollywood representations 403; restorative justice 223

Downes, David 157, 202, 214, 231–2, 233, 235, 308

'dramatization of evil' hypothesis 198

drift theory 153–5, 297, 329

drives 112–13

drugs 6, 67, 68, 75, 101, 104–5, 143, 393; club culture 395, 398; criminalization of 218; delinquent subcultures 149, 150; desistance 337; deterrence 54; disabled people 204; effects of 11–12; globalization 22–3, 419, 423; ignored by scholars 260; labelling theories 195; media coverage 399–400; peacemaking criminology 222; prevention campaigns 10; in prison 63; punishment 213; restorative justice 222, 223; right realism 51; sociobiological perspective 17; treatment 105, 109; 'war on drugs' 379, 474, 477; women 234, 242; zemiology 257

drunkenness 48, 123, 131, 289, 291, 358

Du Bois, W.E.B. 252, 253

dual systems theory 230

due process 10, 42–3, 71, 197, 213, 219, 359, 504

Durkheim, Emile 24, 132–7, 140, 144, 159, 164, 195–6, 250, 265, 293–5, 425–6, 432, 446, 450–2, 499

ecological approach 279, 280

economic crisis 59n2, 137, 259, 301, 467–8, 483–5

economic policies 477

economics 4, 145–6, 189, 449

Ecstasy 101, 104, 395, 398

education 164, 330, 355, 454, 455, 481n3; left realism 360; moral 442; peacemaking criminology 222; of prisoners 475

EEG abnormality 94, 119

egalitarian communitarianism 443–5, 507

ego 112, 113, 293

egoism 133, 134, 135, 137, 451–2

electro-control 106

Elias, Norbert 375, 393, 473

embourgeoisement 466, 467

emotional immaturity 101

emotions 316, 318, 321

empathy, lack of 119

employment 20, 132, 133, 159, 164; desistance from crime 329, 330, 331, 340; left realism 360; women 180, 230;

workfare schemes 24, 453, 470, 472, 475, 476, 477, 479
Enlightenment 4, 40, 44, 367, 459, 504–5
entertainment 403–4
environmental design 285–8, 290, 504
environmental factors 9, 84, 311, 321–2; situational action theory 314–15, 317, 320; social evolutionism 82; sociobiological theories 17, 268–9, 271, 274–5; twin studies 88
environmental management 17, 288–91, 504
environmental theories 17, 278–92, 500, 504
epidemic encephalitis 93
epilepsy 93
epistemology 188–9, 374–5
equal opportunity policies 164
equal rights 191–2
equality 30, 42, 220, 221, 228, 239, 260, 306, 454
Erikson, K. 195–6, 198–9
Espinas, Alfred 450
ethical issues 108, 126, 127, 223
ethnic minorities 24, 72, 185, 301; critical criminology 16, 245–6, 250; labelling theories 203; masculinity 240–1; see also black people
ethnicity 108, 158, 177; capital punishment 489–90; hate crime 136; intelligence linked to 89; labelling theories 197; see also race
ethnographic research 138, 282
ethnomethodology 14, 186–7, 214, 265, 504
Etzioni, Amitai 24, 355–6, 441, 442, 444, 446–7, 453
eugenics 107, 109
evolutionary theory 11, 81–2, 91, 272
excitement 154–5, 388
experts 108, 368, 452, 479, 489; carceral surveillance society model 361, 464–5, 469, 477; in court 40, 41; criminologists 223; scientific 86
exploitation 213
exposure 312, 317–18, 319–20, 322, 323
extroversion 117–19, 120, 332, 333
Eysenck, Hans 94, 100, 117–19, 120, 271, 332

family 298, 304, 353, 402; broken homes 12, 115–16; communitarianism 441;

conservatism 55–6; criminal family studies 11, 86–7; middle-class socialization 157; social control theories 18, 296; sociobiology 48; women and the 173, 178, 179, 180, 235; see also parents
family conferencing 223
fascism 85, 428
fatalism 155
fathers 114, 116, 146–7, 148, 304, 441–2
fear 33, 430; of crime 56, 58, 201, 382; public 495
'feeble-mindedness' 40, 86
Felson, M. 50, 67–9, 281–2
female emancipation 16, 233–4
femininity 171–2, 179, 227
feminism 221, 227–44, 347, 353, 500, 505
feminist criminology 15–16, 227–8, 231–5, 238–40, 256, 383, 496
Ferrell, J. 380–3, 390
Ferri, Enrico 79, 83, 84, 85, 86
Feyerabend, Paul 371, 381
Fichte, Johann Gottlieb 449
Fichtelberg, Aaron 25, 261, 487–96
'fiddles' 6
financial sector 394, 420, 421–2, 467–8, 484
'focal concerns' 148, 154
'folk devils' 6, 14, 246, 400
food 101, 269–70
forensic neuropsychology 94–5
forgiveness 10, 47, 301, 390
Foucault, Michel 2, 39, 203, 367, 368–9, 414, 464, 491–2
France 80, 448, 477
Frankfurt School 211
fraud 6, 104, 144, 216, 303, 468
free will 4, 9, 80, 153, 155, 186; Classical criminology 36, 37–8, 41–2, 43–4; environmental theories 279; neo-Classical criminology 40, 41; situational action theory 315; social contract theories 30, 32; subcultural theory 163
French Revolution 4, 40, 71, 448, 449, 451
Freud, Sigmund 13, 111–12, 132–3, 146, 171–2, 173, 174, 293–4
frustration-aggression hypothesis 430
frustration tolerance 297
Fuller, John 218–19, 220, 221
functional rebels 135
functionalism 173, 196, 250, 505

Galbraith, J.K. 468
gangs 147, 152, 159, 296, 391; delinquent
    subcultures 13, 148, 150, 177; women
    178, 241–2
Gans, Herbert 401
Garland, David 4–5, 21, 388, 394, 412, 415,
    417, 464, 489, 491
Garofalo, Raffaele 83, 84, 85, 86
gender 16, 177, 227–44; control balance
    theory 306; hate crime 136; labelling
    theories 197; left realism 344; power
    control theory 18, 304–5; sentencing
    differences 170; see also femininity;
    masculinity; women
genealogical approach 25, 491–3
general deterrence 61, 74, 76
'general theory of crime' 18, 302–4,
    500
general will 32
generative phases of women theory 169,
    505
genetic selection 107, 108
genetic structure theories 11, 90–1, 107–8,
    499
genocide 405
Geographical Information Systems (GIS)
    284
geography 17, 278, 281
Germany 448–50, 477
Gestalt psychology 122
ghettos 471–2, 473, 474
Giddens, Anthony 334, 335, 375, 412, 413,
    418, 425, 442
globalization 21, 22–3, 162, 395, 418–25,
    430, 432–4, 501, 505
Glueck, Sheldon and Eleanor 327
goal orientation 297
goals 140–3, 144, 145–6, 176–7, 187, 300,
    333–4
God 30, 31, 447–8
Goring, C. 87, 107, 325, 371
Gottfredson, M.R. 18, 53, 263, 266, 296,
    302–4, 308–9, 326–7, 329–31, 333
governance, new modes of 22, 410–11
'government of social insecurity' 24, 470,
    479
governmentality 398, 410, 492, 505
group conflicts 188, 208–9
guilt (criminal) 36, 42–3, 213
guilt (emotional) 112, 114, 153, 154, 155,
    316

habit 315, 318
Hall, Stuart 200, 201, 216, 444–5
Hallsworth, Simon 415, 416–18
handling stolen goods 67, 234
happiness 32, 37
harm 256–9, 392
hate crime 72, 136, 144–5, 151, 156, 505
Hayward, Keith 22, 407
healthcare 221, 222, 454–5
hedonism 33, 36, 37, 121, 148
Hegel, G.W.F. 189, 448–50
Heidensohn, F. 231, 234, 235, 239
Henry, Stuart 20–1, 375–6, 377–9, 384
Herder, Johann Gottfried 449
heroin 101, 104, 105
Herrnstein, Richard 17, 48, 50, 270–2, 275,
    327, 352
hidden crime 174–5, 256–7
Hindley, Myra 239
Hirschi, Travis 18, 53, 89–90, 235, 263,
    265–6, 296, 298–9, 300, 302–4, 308–9,
    326–7, 329–31
Hitler, Adolf 450
Hobbes, Thomas 30, 31, 32, 293, 294, 373,
    448
Hodgson, Phil 356, 358, 359, 453
Holocaust 108
homosexuality 90, 108, 175, 196, 224, 370
Hopkins Burke, R.D. 20–1, 72, 136, 144–5,
    151–2, 156, 160–1, 289–90, 355–6, 358–61,
    392–3, 396, 414, 416, 464–5, 479
hormones 98–9, 169, 170
'hot products' 287–8
'hot spots' 284–5
household activity ratio 68–9
housing 454
Howard, John 39
human nature 132, 170–1, 188, 294, 308, 314
human rights 4, 7, 86, 225, 239, 250, 256,
    393, 440–1; see also rights
human trafficking 419, 420, 423–4
humanism 4, 24, 189, 220, 387, 464
humiliation 390, 391
Huntingdon's chorea 93
hyperactivity 95, 101
hypoglycaemia 99–100, 101, 169, 270

id 112, 293
idealism 16, 19, 24, 189, 245, 246, 250–1,
    261, 350
identity 136, 334–5, 341, 392, 396;

masculine identity crisis 146–7, 148;
negative identity hypothesis 430;
procedural self 186; terrorists 431
Ignatieff, Michael 38–9, 462–3
illegitimate opportunity structure 149
imitation 123, 125
immigrants 107, 136, 137–8, 144, 188, 190,
219–20, 394, 399–400, 424
imprisonment 6, 86, 213, 218, 309, 438;
Classical criminology 35–6;
conservatism 10, 49–52, 54, 55; left
realism 361; life 61, 62; penal society 479;
pre-modern 2–3; 'punitive turn' 416;
racial inequality in the USA 470–6;
women 242, 243; see also prisons
impulsivity 118–19
incapacitation 10, 54, 438, 505
incivilities 289–90, 291, 346, 358, 359
inclusion 219
individual factors 85
individualism 53–4, 85, 134, 254, 297, 430,
451–2; American Dream 146;
development of concept 447–50;
methodological 135–6; reintegrative
shaming 301–2
induction 114–15
Industrial Revolution 3, 458
industrialization 3–4, 80, 132, 134, 213,
463
inequality 30–1, 47, 53, 125, 143, 162–3, 173,
190; capitalism 202; Chicago School 139;
critical criminology 260; egalitarian
communitarianism 443; feminism 228,
229, 237; global 422, 434; left realism 344,
439; Marxist approaches 215, 461; media
constructions of crime 401, 402;
peacemaking criminology 219, 222, 224;
relations of dependence 446
infanticide 169–70, 181, 505
informal control systems 68, 69, 329
informal labelling 14–15, 202–3
inherited criminal characteristics 86–90, 92,
499
innovation 142, 177
the insane 40, 84
'insecurity, government of social' 24, 470,
479
insider dealing 142
institutionalized means 140, 176
integrated theories 16–17, 263–6, 366, 486,
500, 505

intelligence 86, 89–90, 107–8
interactionism 14, 186, 199, 202, 214, 265
Internet 394, 404, 420, 421, 424
involvement 298
Islam 428
Israel 427
Italian School 11, 83, 499, 505
Italy 85, 86

Jacobs, Jane 285, 286
Jamaica 126
Jordan, Bill 443
journalism 22, 401–2
judges 3, 36, 40
just deserts 10, 42, 505
juvenile delinquency see delinquency

Kanner, Leo 96
Kant, Immanuel 220
Katz, Jack 21, 241, 335, 390–2
Kelling, George 48, 51, 289
Kirchheimer, O. 212, 462
Kitsuse, J.I. 196, 198–9
Klinefelter's syndrome 90
knowledge 367, 368–9, 370, 374–5, 464, 487,
490–1, 496–7
Konopka, Gisela 172
Kupchik, Aaron 25, 261, 487–96

labelling theories 14–15, 18, 62, 149, 186,
193–206, 246, 265, 464, 500; anarchist
criminology 382; conflict theories 209,
211; cultural criminology 387; definition
of 505; environmental theories 17, 279;
gender issues 228; new criminology 214,
215–16; social control 300
labour extraction 472–3
Lacan, Jacques 21, 376
language 219–20, 255, 367
latent delinquency theory 12, 113, 505
law 5–6, 194; anarchist criminology 21,
380–3; Classical criminology 36–7, 41;
conflict theories 209, 210; culture conflict
theory 208; customary 223; labelling
theories 193, 196, 203; reparative 258;
Rousseau on 31–2
'law of action' 212
Lawrence, Stephen 256
Le Pen, Jean Marie 136
Lea, John 346, 348, 357–60, 361, 415, 416–18
lead poisoning 270

learning 12, 140, 180, 269; *see also* behavioural learning theories
learning disabilities 96
left idealism 245, 250–1, 261, 350
left realism 16, 19–20, 54, 344–63, 383–4, 439, 500; critical criminology 245, 251, 256; definition of 505; democratic criminology 493; environmental theories 290; feminist criminology 233; labelling theories 201; left realist hybrid model 24, 361, 465–70, 473, 478–9; radical criminology 217
legal images, control of 209
legal realism 212
Lemert, Edwin 198
leniency 16, 170, 213, 234–5
Leonard, Eileen 176–7, 178
Leviathan 30, 31
liberal authoritarianism 54
Liberal Democrats 483, 484–5
liberal feminism 229, 236, 241
liberalism 47, 51, 365, 440; *see also* 'new liberalism'
limbic system 93–4
living time, control of 209
Locke, John 30–1, 37, 448
Lombroso, Cesare 13, 83–4, 86, 93, 106, 152–3, 167–8, 170–2, 174, 265, 340, 371
love withdrawal 114–15
LSD 101, 104
Luther, Martin 447–8, 449
Lyotard, J.F. 365, 371

McAdams, D.P. 332, 333, 334
mace 106
McKay, Henry 138–9, 140
Macpherson Report (1999) 151, 152
macro level 136, 145, 208, 265, 486, 506
mainstream youth subcultures 160, 506
mala in se 5, 506
mala prohibita 5, 506
male role models 20, 352
malestream criminology 227–8, 231, 235–6, 238, 241
Mandela, Nelson 427
manslaughter 169, 170
mapping techniques 284–5
marginalization 199, 200, 245, 249, 301, 358, 443, 506
marijuana 195
marriage 177, 329, 330, 331

Maruna, S. 19, 325–6, 328, 331, 333–4, 336–40
Marx, Karl 188–90, 221, 236, 265, 461
Marxism 188–90, 228, 247, 253, 349–50, 365, 450; communitarianism 440; conflict theories 209–10; critical criminology 259–60; cultural criminology 387; moral panics 200; new criminology 15; peacemaking criminology 221; radical theories 14, 207, 211–16
Marxist feminism 230, 236–7
masculinity 16, 168, 179, 181, 227, 240–2, 247, 500; chromosomal abnormalities 91; masculine identity crisis 146–7, 148; multiple masculinities 240, 506; sociological positivism 154, 158, 160; violent masculinities 256
master status 199
materialism 24, 37, 189, 191
maternal deprivation theory 12, 113–14, 172, 506
Matthews, Roger 56, 62, 346, 347, 415–16
maturational reform 327, 328
maturity 154
Matza, David 152–6, 297, 328, 329, 391, 430
Mays, John 157
MDMA 101, 395
Mead, George Herbert 186
mechanical solidarity 133–4, 136, 151, 152, 156, 159, 196, 204, 441, 446, 451
media 6, 21–2, 128, 156, 259, 476; conflict theories 210; cultural criminology 399–406; globalization 422–3; mediascapes 397; moral panics 14, 201, 400; women 239
Mednick, Sarnoff 89, 100, 268–9
mens rea 42
menstruation 169, 174
mental health problems 73, 203, 223, 269
Merton, Robert 137, 140–6, 149, 150, 159, 176, 196, 215, 240, 294, 430
Messerschmidt, James 240, 241–2
methodological collectivism 135
methodological individualism 135–6
methodological pluralism 253
mezzo level 136, 145, 452, 464, 506
micro level 136, 145, 208, 265, 486, 506
middle class 147–8, 157, 171, 175, 359, 393, 483, 484
Mill, John Stuart 32, 33, 236

Miller, Walter 148, 154, 157, 158–9, 178
Milovanovic, Dragan 20–1, 375–6, 377–9, 384
minimal brain dysfunction (MBD) 93
modernity 3–5, 20, 23–4, 46, 108, 365–7, 369–70, 375, 415, 425, 437, 506
modernization 18, 135, 412–13
mods and rockers 200, 246
money 30, 31, 146, 179, 188
money laundering 22–3, 394, 419, 420, 421, 423
moral authority 132, 133
moral context 317, 320–1
moral disengagement hypothesis 430–1
moral disorder 401
moral entrepreneurs 194, 200, 400, 463–4, 465, 473, 479, 497
moral panics 14, 199–201, 392, 400, 467, 506
moral statisticians 131
moral uncertainty 369–70, 486–7
morality 5, 85, 153, 173, 294; conservatism 53, 58; postmodern condition 20–1; radical moral communitarianism 23–4; situational action theory 18–19, 312, 313–14, 316, 318–19; utilitarianism 32
Morris, Alison 232, 238
Morris, Terence 157, 280
motivation 63, 66–7, 71–2, 351; EEG motivation 94; hate crime 144–5; routine activities theory 69; serial killers 121; situational action theory 315–16, 321
mugging 149, 200, 201
multi-agency approach 411
multinational corporations 248, 394
multiple masculinities 240, 506
Muncie, J. 257–9
murder 98, 103, 123, 142, 194, 390; anarchism 428; capital punishment 61–2, 213; murderers 85, 94, 102, 121; offender profiling 121, 122; public opinion 496
Muslim Brotherhood 428
Mussolini, Benito 85, 86

narcissistic rage hypothesis 430
narrative 19, 332, 334–6
natural crimes 85
natural law 2, 4, 30–1, 106, 448
'natural man' 31
Nazi Germany 108
negative identity hypothesis 430
neighbourhood organization 138–9

neo-Classical criminology 40–2, 51, 499, 506
neoconservatism 10, 20, 59n1, 369, 438, 439
neoliberalism 358, 410, 419, 470, 472, 476–7, 479
neo-Marxism 159, 211, 253
'neotribes' 162
Netherlands 417
neuropsychology 94–5
neuroticism 117–19, 332
neutralization, techniques of 154, 155, 301, 339, 430–1, 509
new criminology 15, 214–16, 506
New Labour 19–20, 24, 53–6, 258–9, 350–1, 354–8, 439, 442, 444, 446–7, 453, 482–3, 485
'new liberalism' 24, 439, 440, 446
new penology 22, 412, 506
new right 10, 43, 46–7, 71, 270–2, 345, 352; see also right realism
New Zealand 204
NEW-ADAM research programme 104
Newman, Oscar 75, 285–6
news 22, 400–3
'noble savages' 31
non-intervention 10, 47
non-violence 218–19, 220, 224
normality of crime 432
norms 131, 147–8, 164, 187, 190; culture conflict theory 207–8; labelling theories 201–2; norm retention 297; social control theories 295
Northern Ireland 192
'nothing works' 47, 60, 247, 340, 506
Nye, Ivan 296

occasional criminals 84
O'Connor, T. 430–1
offender profiling 121–2, 412, 506
Ohlin, Lloyd 149–50, 153, 157, 178
'Olson 1982 hypothesis' 429
ontogenetic paradigm 326, 327–8
operant conditioning 117, 122–3, 124–5, 271
opiates 11, 101, 104
opium 106, 419
opportunity to offend 64, 74, 124, 287, 506; environmental theories 280, 281; opportunity theory 17, 69–70, 178; women 234

oppression 16, 128, 224, 230, 236, 245, 253, 261, 376, 384
organic solidarity 133–4, 136, 196, 441, 451
organized crime 23, 394, 419–21, 423–5, 433
orthodox social progress model 24, 360, 457–61, 465, 467, 469, 479
orthomolecular medicine 101
otherness 392, 446
outsiders 195
over-determinism 135

pain 32–3, 44, 73–4
Palmer, C. 273
Panopticon 38–40, 506
parents 87, 298, 309, 329; adopted children studies 88–9; behaviour modification of children 126; coercion 307; deficient parenting 96, 302, 303, 441; fear of child abduction 495; informal labelling 202–3; lack of affection from 119; latent delinquency theory 12; parental responsibility 55–6; power control theory 304–5; psychodynamic theories 112, 113–16; sociobiological theories 275; see also family
Park, Robert 137
Parker, Howard 157–8
Parsons, Talcott 146–7, 148, 179, 425
particularistic obligations 151
passion, crimes of 84, 124
passivity, female 169, 172, 179
patriarchy 221, 228, 229–30, 232, 237, 304–5
Pavlov, Ivan Petrovich 116
peacemaking criminology 15, 217–24, 225, 383, 500
peer counselling 140
'penal harm movement' 74
penal modernism 22, 415–16
penal populism 479
penal society 457–81, 501
penal welfarism 22, 415–16, 417
Pepinsky, Harold 217, 221, 381
perinatal complications 274
person characteristics 311, 314–15, 321
personal histories 331–2, 334, 335
personality 112, 117–19, 332–4; corporate managers 144; disorders 12; personality typing 121–2; terrorists 431; traits 91, 124, 127
pervasive developmental disorders (PDDs) 11, 97

phenomenology 14, 21, 186–7, 214, 265, 506
philanthropy 463, 464, 465, 467
physical factors 85
Piaget, Jean 122
Piliavin, Irving 297
Pilkington, Fiona 356
pity 85
pleasure 32–3, 37, 73
pluralist view of society 14, 190, 207
police 43, 44, 213, 465; accountability 57, 358, 360; 'canteen culture' 151–2; conflict theories 209; critical criminology 245–6, 251; labelling theories 196–7; left realism 347, 349, 350, 359–60, 466–7; new technologies 404; orthodox social progress model 459; problem-oriented policing 290; radical conflict model 461–2, 466; right realism 48, 50, 51
policy: biological positivism 108–9; Classical criminology 43–4; conflict theories 224–5; contemporary rational actor theories 73–6; criminology's relationship to 25, 487–8, 489, 491–2, 493–4; critical criminology 260–1; cultural criminology 407; desistance theories 341; economic 477; environmental theories 290–1; family 304; gender 242–3; globalization 432–4; labelling theories 205; left realism 354–7, 361; neoconservative 439; peacemaking criminology 221, 225; penal society 479; populist conservatism 57–8; postmodernism 384–5; psychological positivism; 127–8; radical moral communitarianism 453–5; radical theories 225; situational action theory 323; social constructions 403; social control theories 308–9; sociobiological theories 276; sociological positivism 163–4; women 181; zemiology 257
Pollak, Otto 169, 172, 174–5, 234
Pollock, E. 72, 136, 144–5, 151, 156
Ponzi schemes 400, 408n1
populism, penal 479
populist conservatism 10, 15, 19, 20, 43, 46–59, 217, 345, 346, 351, 352, 499, 506
populist socialism 15, 16, 217, 351
pornography 399, 421
positivism 9, 10–11, 14, 80–1, 238, 263, 331, 507; see also biological positivism;

predestined actor model; psychological positivism; sociological positivism
post-Fordism 367, 368
postmodernism 20–1, 23, 367–70, 373–86, 396, 437–8, 486–7; definition of 507; deviant subcultures 13, 161; feminism 231, 238; left realism 439; penal modernism 415; terrorism 432; timeline of theories 501
post-natal depression 169–70
poststructuralism 253, 367, 368
post-subcultural theory 161–3
poverty 5, 24, 249, 303, 352, 438; biosocial theory 270; conservatism 55, 56; deviant subcultures 158–9; double regulation of 477; egalitarian communitarianism 443; government of 472; labelling theories 197; media constructions of crime 402; neighbourhood organization 138; peacemaking criminology 15, 217, 221, 224; prostitution 236
Powell, Enoch 136, 478
power 21, 139, 368–9, 384, 401, 411; carceral surveillance society model 24, 464–5, 469; conflict theories 210, 225; critical race theory 254; feminism 228, 229; peacemaking criminology 224; radical theories 207; serial killers 121; social construction of crime 194; state 203; zemiology 257
power assertion 114–15
power control theory 18, 304–5, 500, 507
powerlessness 189
predatory crime 7, 49, 301, 346, 347, 507
predestined actor model 9, 10–13, 71, 79–82, 127, 186, 264, 366, 486; biological explanations 276; conflict theories 210, 211; conservatism 10, 47, 48–9, 54; critiques of 10, 14, 122, 152–3, 163, 187; definition of 507; Eysenck's theory 117; 'general theory of crime' 18; integrated theories 265; Marxist rejection of 189; neo-Classical criminology 41; rational choice theory 66; rehabilitation 351; situational action theory 19; structural factors 20; timeline 499; treatment model 22, 411; underclass 352; see also positivism
premenstrual tension (PMT) 169, 181
pre-modernity 2–3, 507
preparation, state of 155

Presdee, Mark 21, 241, 388–90, 392, 393
prevention see crime prevention
primitive rebellion thesis 189–90
prisons 10, 22, 52, 54, 72–3, 251, 379; adrenaline sensitivity 100; alcohol use 103; assaults on staff 63; carceral surveillance society model 465; chemotherapy in 106; Marxist penology 212; Panopticon 38–40; peacemaking criminology 222; radical conflict model 462, 463; rehabilitation in 47; 'Scared Straight' programme 128; see also imprisonment
probation 47, 197, 340, 341
probity 85
problem-oriented policing (POP) 290
procedural self 186
process model of the underclass 20, 507
profiling 121–2, 219, 412, 506
promiscuity 173, 179, 302
propensity 312, 316, 317–18, 319–20, 322, 323
property crime 3, 64, 69, 99, 173, 259, 466; control balance theory 305; drug use linked to 104, 105; genetic structure theories 91; restorative justice 222, 223; women 175, 234; see also burglary; robbery
property rights 30, 31, 85, 168
proportionality 42, 60
prostitution 13, 48, 51, 67, 68, 84, 459; drug use linked to 105; feminism 235–7; women and positivism 171, 173–4, 177
provocation 316, 317, 318, 319
prudentialism 414
Pryce, Ken 158
psychiatric disorders 90–1
psychoanalysis 111–12, 127–8, 376
psychodynamic theories 12, 111–16, 127, 499, 507
psychological positivism 10–11, 12, 81, 111–30, 170–6, 181, 264, 507
psychology 1, 9, 12
psychopathy 12, 94, 95, 97, 119–20
psychosexual development 12, 112
psychosis 93, 332, 499
psychoticism 117–19
'public criminology' 25, 487–97
public opinion 25, 479, 487–8, 490, 493–6
public order offences, policing 57
punishment: administrative criminology

348; biosocial theory 269; Classical
criminology 35–6, 37, 41, 42, 43;
conservatism 49–50, 52, 57, 58;
deterrence 60–3, 74; Durkheim on 133–4;
fear of 33; neo-Classical criminology 41;
parental 114–15; pre-modern 2–3; radical
conflict model 462, 463; rational actor
theories 72, 75–6, 486; retributive 47;
social contract theories 30, 32; *see also*
capital punishment; imprisonment
'punitive turn' 22, 415–18, 482
Puritans 448

Quinney, Richard 191, 196, 197, 209–11,
217–18, 221

race 115, 177, 196–7; black feminism 230–1;
critical race theory 16, 251–6; hate crime
136, 156; inequality and imprisonment
in the USA 470–6; racial profiling 219;
racial projects 254; Social Darwinism
107; *see also* ethnicity
racism 16, 92, 136, 175, 347, 357, 481n2;
African-Caribbean youths 158; black
feminism 230–1; critical criminology 245,
247; critical race theory 251–6;
institutional 151, 152, 252, 256; media
constructions of crime 402; peacemaking
criminology 217, 219, 224; subcultures
163; UK/USA comparison 477, 478;
zemiology 256
racket subcultures 150
radical conflict model 24, 360–1, 461–3,
465, 466, 467, 469, 473, 479
radical criminology 14–16, 19, 191, 202,
207, 211–17, 500; definition of 507;
deviant subcultures 159–61; left realism
345, 347; policy implications 225
radical egalitarian communitarianism
443–5, 507
radical feminism 229–30, 231, 236, 237
radical moral communitarianism 23–4,
220, 437–56, 497, 501, 507
rape 68, 91, 98, 216, 233, 347; alcohol linked
to 102, 103; offender profiling 122;
sociobiological theories 17, 272–3
rational actor model 9–10, 22, 29–33, 80,
186, 264, 366, 411, 486; administrative
criminology 247; cognitive learning
theories 127; conflict theories 211;
conservatism 52, 54, 57; contemporary

theories 60–77; definition of 507;
deterrence 63; Eysenck's theory 117;
'general theory of crime' 18; human
nature 294; integrated theories 265;
Marxist rejection of 189; opportunity
theories 17; post-subcultural theory 162;
psychology 12; social control 295;
timeline 499
rational choice theory 10, 61, 63–7, 74,
281–2, 287, 308–9, 429, 499, 507
rationality 4, 38, 42, 44, 65, 215, 314, 505
Reagan, Ronald 48, 53, 369
realism 19, 56, 189, 212, 312–13; *see also* left
realism; right realism
reason 32, 65
rebellion 143–4
recidivism 40, 50–1, 63, 71, 80, 118, 119,
128, 337
Reckless, Walter 296–7
redemption 339
redress 258
reform 458, 459–61
regicide 2
rehabilitation 42, 47, 53, 304, 351, 360;
conservatism 58; Marxist penology 212;
neo-Classical criminology 41;
questioning of 60; risk management 417
reinforcement 117, 123, 124, 125, 140
reintegration of offenders 223, 338
reintegrative shaming 204–5, 301–2, 426,
445, 500, 508
reintegrative tutelage 354, 355, 357, 444,
483, 508
Reiss, Albert 295
relative deprivation 16, 249, 301, 430
relativism 370, 373
religion 23, 136, 366, 428–9
Renouvier, Charles 450
reparation 204, 223, 258
'replacement discourses' 21
repression 306, 469
resistance 160, 383, 384
responsibility 19, 20, 155, 351, 354, 414,
508; Classical criminology 42;
communitarianism 24, 440, 442, 452–3,
454; conservatism 55, 57; denial of 154,
155–6
restorative justice 204, 218, 222–3, 224, 258,
360, 445
retreatism 141, 149
retribution 47, 52

rewards 117, 120, 124, 126
right realism 15, 17, 48–52, 57, 62, 217, 270–2, 275, 345, 350, 351, 508; *see also* conservatism; new right
rights 47, 71, 191–2; communitarianism 24, 440, 442, 452–3, 454; left realism 350; liberal feminism 236; natural law 30, 31
riots 280, 347, 481n2
risk management 413–14, 417, 432–3
risk society 22, 404, 412–14, 415, 432, 501, 508
ritualism 141–2
robbery 67, 68, 142, 234, 246, 282, 286, 391
Rock, Paul 202, 214, 231–2, 233, 235, 308
role models 20, 352
Rosenau, Pauline-Marie 373–5
Rothman, D. 460–1, 463
Rousseau, Jean-Jacques 30, 31–2, 40, 448
routine activities theory 10, 67–71, 74, 281, 287, 308–9, 499, 508
rule of law 43, 71, 216, 350, 382
rules 97, 194, 212, 392; conflict theories 208; moral entrepreneurs 463–4; situational action theory 313, 314–15, 317, 318–19, 321
ruling class 213, 225, 247
Rusche, George 212, 462, 471
Russia 420, 422

safe image/safe milieu 286
Saint-Simon, Claude Henri de Rouvroy 448, 450
'Scared Straight' programme 128
schizophrenia 101, 105
'schizophrenia of crime' 21, 392–3, 508
school 299, 307
Schutz, Alfred 187
science 2, 4, 11, 81, 253–4, 367, 371, 489
Scotland 2
'second lives' 393
sedatives 106
'seductions of crime' 21, 390–2, 508
Seidman, Robert 212–13
the self 186, 188, 332, 335, 440–1
self-concept 198, 205, 297, 332, 337, 430
self-control 48, 53, 63, 272, 333; situational action theory 312, 315, 316, 317, 319; social control theories 302–3, 304, 309
self-fulfilling prophecy 196, 198, 508
self-indulgence 47
self-interest 33, 134, 212, 302, 314, 451

Sellin, Thorsten 207–8
senile dementia 93
sentencing 40, 41, 50, 62; Classical criminology 42; gender differences 170, 176; indeterminate 109, 276; peacemaking criminology 219
serial murder 121, 508
severity of punishment 10, 60–1, 74, 75–6, 128
sex 170, 172, 173, 174
sex/gender distinction 227
sex offenders 10, 54, 63, 85, 105, 399–400
sex roles 179, 228, 232, 234, 241
sexism 16, 217, 219, 224, 231, 245, 247, 256
sexual delinquency 177
sexual exploitation 420, 423
sexual hormones 98–9
sexual violence 406; *see also* rape
sexuality 108, 111–12, 136, 173, 175–6, 237, 399
Shaw, Clifford 138–9, 140, 149
shoplifting 104, 167, 174, 175, 257, 288, 390–1
siblings 113
Simmel, Georg 188, 207–8
Simon, Rita 233–4
single-parent families 115–16, 355, 441–2
singular and segmental societies 196
situational action theory (SAT) 18–19, 308, 311–24, 500
situational crime prevention 63–4, 75, 125, 287, 351, 393
skewed deviants 135
skills training 126
skinheads 158, 159, 160
Skinner, B.F. 116, 122–3, 271
slavery 472, 473, 477–8
slum neighbourhoods 138, 139
Smart, Carol 231, 238, 240
Smith, Adam 134, 448
social bonding 232, 298–9, 300, 329, 330–1
social change 18, 21, 31, 159, 224, 295, 452; conflict theories 211; globalization 419; policies 164; sociological positivism 133, 135, 137; terrorism 432
social construction of crime 6, 22, 131, 194–6, 345, 366, 402, 486, 508
social contract theories 9, 30–2, 36, 71, 132, 448, 508
social control 17–18, 51–2, 109, 266, 293–310, 468, 500, 508; conflict theories

209; critical criminology 249, 250, 251; informal 329, 445, 446; labelling theories 199, 203; media 404–5; victimized actor model 186–7; women 235
Social Darwinism 107
social disorganization 131, 132–40, 146–7, 164, 279, 295, 499, 508
social evolutionism 11, 81–2, 508
social exclusion 20, 24–5, 55–6, 163, 352–4, 355, 357, 411, 438, 446, 475
social factors 85, 92, 163, 187, 265; Chicago School 137, 139; situational action theory 312, 320–1
social inclusion 357, 358, 360
social justice 219, 220, 224, 225, 252, 258, 376, 392
social learning theory 12, 53, 123, 266, 300
'social man' 31
social order 48, 56, 57, 209, 211, 251, 401, 462
social progress model 24, 360, 457–61, 465, 467, 469, 479
social reaction theories 14, 279; see also labelling theories
social relations of crime control 348, 360
social structures 140–1, 188, 214–15, 251, 384, 494
socialism 85, 145, 189, 190–1, 260; German 450; left realism 350; populist 15, 16, 217, 351; radical theories 213, 215, 225
socialist feminism 230, 344
socialization 18, 37, 127, 187, 336; communitarianism 441; conservatism 56, 57; culture conflict theory 208; Durkheim 133, 294; gender differences 169, 171, 179, 180; internalization of rules 194; Marxism 188; men 237; sociobiology 48–9; sociological positivism 145, 152, 154, 156, 157; terrorists 431; women 177, 235
sociation 188
societal reaction 194, 198–9, 200, 202, 203
sociobiology 17, 48–9, 267–77, 500
socio-control matrix 24–5, 361, 465, 469, 477, 478
socio-economic factors 175
sociogenic paradigm 326, 329–31
sociological positivism 10–11, 12–13, 20, 81–2, 131–66, 176–81, 264, 508
sociology 82, 187

solidarity 133–6, 151–2, 156, 159, 196, 204, 356, 441, 450–1
Southern theory 23, 425–6, 501
spatial exclusion 357
specific deterrence 61, 74, 76
'spectacular' youth subcultures 159, 160, 508
Spencer, Herbert 81, 425, 450–1, 458
Spergel, Ivan 150, 159
spirituality 2, 5
'square of crime' 348–9, 357, 509
state 347, 349, 350, 369, 414, 451, 464; anarchist critique 381–3; Big Society concept 485; Durkheim's political theory 452; Hegel's philosophy 448–9; intervention 22, 411; radical conflict model 462; role of the 191; state crime 257; 'third way' 442
state of nature 30, 31, 32
statistics 187, 197, 345, 346, 350
status 147, 187, 212
status frustration 148, 157
stereotyping 152, 198, 199, 246, 347, 354, 401
sterilization 108, 109, 127
stigmatization 15, 200, 203–4, 205, 246, 251, 301, 426
stilboestrol 105–6
stimulation, need for 154–5
stimulus control 125
stolen goods market 67
storied identity 334
strain theory 13, 140, 300, 499; see also anomie
street crime 6, 7, 19, 51, 63, 345; conservatism 56; control balance theory 305; left realism 493; media coverage 21
stress 100
structural factors 20, 56, 196, 303, 353, 457
structuralism 187, 367
subcultures 18, 21, 124, 392, 396; anti-determinist critique 152–6; culture conflict theory 208; deviant 13, 146–63, 177, 211, 246, 279, 499, 504; of violence 158, 509
subterranean values 154–5
suffering 217–18, 221, 224, 225; see also harm
suicide 68, 73, 131
suicide bombing 431
superego 112, 113, 293

Surette, R. 402–3
surgical intervention 105, 109
surplus labour hypothesis 212, 213
surveillance 4, 22, 25, 75, 348, 350, 432;
    controlology 203; culture of control 388;
    deterrence 64; environmental design
    285, 286; expansion of 438, 470; new
    technologies 404, 412; Panopticon 38;
    risk society 413–14; *see also* carceral
    surveillance society model
Sutherland, Edwin H. 7, 123–4, 139, 147,
    149, 178, 247
symbolic interactionism 14, 186, 188, 214,
    265, 509

Tannenbaum, Frank 198
Tarde, Gabriel 123
target hardening 64, 308–9, 349
target selection 282, 284
target suitability 68, 69, 74
Taylor, Ian 41, 132, 202, 211, 214, 215, 216,
    280
technocracy 25, 489–91
technology 404, 405, 421–2
temptation 316, 317, 318, 319
territoriality 286
terrorism 23, 419, 426–32, 437–8, 501, 509;
    definition of 509; globalization 420–1;
    policy implications 433–4; radicalization
    323
testosterone 98–9, 328
Thatcher, Margaret 46, 53, 54, 55, 59n1, 369
Thatcherism 55, 369, 477, 485
theft 67, 123, 150, 177, 179, 216, 234, 257,
    287–8, 459
theory competition 16, 264–5
thieves 85
'third way' 440, 442
Thomas, W.I. 170–1, 172, 173, 174–5
Thornhill, R. 273
'three strikes and you're out' policy 51–2
thrill-seeking 121
Toby, Jackson 296
token economies 126
Tolman, Edward 122
Tönnies, Ferdinand 134, 451
torture 2, 35, 37
trafficking, illegal 22–3, 419, 420, 421, 423,
    424
Tranquility Bay 126
tranquilizers 106

transcendence 392
transgression 388, 389, 392
treason 2
treatment 22, 47, 86, 351, 411, 486;
    biological positivism 12, 105–6, 109;
    conservative critique of 48; ethical issues
    108; psychological 127–8; restorative
    justice 223; women 242
triumphalism 438
Turk, Austin 191, 209, 210–11
twin studies 11, 87–8, 107

uncertainty 20, 369–70, 374, 377–8, 384,
    390, 391
unconscious tensions 112
underclass 57, 159, 211, 467, 472, 503; black
    people 24–5, 476, 478; critical
    criminology 246; definition of 509;
    deprived communities 444; left realism
    352–4, 357; process model 20, 507
unemployment 158, 185, 212, 259, 300, 347,
    422; economic crisis 483; left realism 349,
    352, 353; media constructions of crime
    402
unified system theorists 230
United Kingdom: alcohol use 11, 102–3;
    anomie 137; assaults on prison staff 63;
    austerity measures 25; black people 24,
    477–8; broken homes 115–16; capital
    punishment 490; club culture 395, 397;
    conservatism 54–5; crime prevention 64;
    deprived communities 444–5; deviant
    subcultures 157–8; drug use 104;
    economic crisis 484–5; environmental
    theories 278–80; feminism 228–9;
    healthcare 454; left realism 19–20, 344,
    348; mods and rockers 200; new
    criminology 15; 'nothing works' agenda
    60; optimism 482–3; populist
    conservatism 46; poverty 56; prisons 39,
    50, 52, 72–3; radical moral
    communitarianism 24; reintegrative
    shaming 204; Social Darwinism 107;
    terrorism 426–7; torture 2
United Nations Office on Drugs and Crime
    (UNODC) 23, 423
United States: American Dream 140, 145–6,
    476; anarchist criminology 380–1;
    anomie theory 141, 176; anti-marijuana
    campaign 195; anti-socialist attitude
    190–1; asylums 460; black offenders 24,

347, 470–6; capital punishment 62, 490; Chicago School 137–40; club culture 395, 397; communitarianism 440; conservatism 54; crime rates 438; criminal justice system 15, 50, 217, 223; critical race theory 255; deprived communities 443–4; deviant subcultures 147–52, 158–9; drugs trade 105; feminism 228, 229; financial crisis 484; healthcare 454–5; labelling theories 204; left realism 344–5; natural law 30; 'penal harm movement' 74; populist conservatism 46; prison population 10, 49, 52, 54, 72–3, 470–1, 473–4; reintegrative shaming 204; 'Scared Straight' programme 128; sex offenders 105; sex roles 179; Social Darwinism 107; terrorism 426–7; 'three strikes and you're out' policy 51–2; UK compared with 477–8; white-collar crime 7

universalistic obligations 151

urban areas 131–2, 137–40, 279–80, 283, 285–8, 459

urbanization 3–4, 80, 84, 139, 180

utilitarianism 9, 32–3, 37, 41, 49, 134, 236; conservative approach 54; definition of 509; Durkheim's critique of 132, 133

vagrancy 57, 212, 289, 290, 291

values 13, 136, 139, 143, 164; American Dream 140, 145, 146, 476; communitarianism 440; middle-class 147–8; resistance 160; singular and segmental societies 196; situational action theory 312, 316, 318, 320; social control theories 297; subterranean 154–5; Victorian 46, 350

Van Den Haag, Ernest 57

vandalism 65, 119, 148, 149, 257, 289, 346

Victim Offender Reconciliation Programs (VORPs) 223

victim studies 346

victimized actor model 10, 13–16, 18, 41, 131, 185–92, 264, 290, 366, 486; area studies 17; conservative critique of 47, 49; critical criminology 245; definition of 509; deviant subcultures 159; left realism 351, 355; timeline 500; underclass 352

victims of crime 43, 49, 202, 233; alcohol use 102, 103; denial of the victim 154, 156; labelling theories 204; left realism 345; restorative justice 222–3; routine activities theory 67, 70–1, 282; 'square of crime' 349

violence 6, 93, 120–1, 234, 259, 391, 405; alcohol linked to 101–2, 103; autistic spectrum disorders 97–8; control balance theory 305; drugs linked to 11–12, 105; evolutionary theory 272; globalization 22–3, 419, 422–3; labelling theories 204; media coverage 21, 399, 402, 406, 422–3; organized crime 425; peacemaking criminology 15, 225; racial 473; routine activities theory 69, 70–1; sociobiological theories 268, 269–70; subculture of 149, 158, 509; terrorism 23; violent criminals 85; women 234, 242

vitamin deficiency 101

Vold, George 191, 208–9, 275–6

volunteer work 339, 453

Wacquant, Loïc 24, 415, 470–6, 478, 479

Walton, P. 132, 211

'war against crime' 245, 393

war crimes 23, 257, 419

'war on drugs' 379, 474, 477

'war on terror' 433–4

wealth 145, 146, 176, 250, 476–7

weapons, trafficking 22–3, 419, 421, 423, 424

Weber, Max 187, 382, 461

welfare 20, 49, 55, 191, 453–4, 485; shift to workfare 472, 475, 476; underclass 352, 353

white-collar crime 7, 56, 143, 213, 216, 247–9, 303, 393; chaos theory 378–9; definition of 509; desistance theories 340; deviant subcultures 151; differential association theory 124; differential coercion theory 307; media coverage 21–2, 399, 400; reintegrative shaming 205

Wikström, Per-Olof 311, 312, 314, 321–2, 323

wildlife, illegal trade in 424

Wilmott, Peter 157

Wilson, Brian 163, 395–8

Wilson, Edmund O. 267, 268

Wilson, James Q. 29, 48–51, 72, 270–2, 275, 289, 327, 352

Wilson, William Julius 17, 159, 352

'Wobblies' 380–1

women 15–16, 145, 167–83, 227–44; biological positivism 167–70; control balance theory 306; critical criminology 16; desistance from crime 330; deviant subcultures 158; domestic violence 195; employment of 347; equal rights movement 192; Hollywood representations 403; left realism 493; Lombroso on 84; mediatized sexual violence 406; peacemaking criminology 221; predestined actor model 13; psychological positivism 170–6; rape victims 103; sociological positivism 176–80; trafficking of 420, 423; victim studies 346

workfare schemes 24, 453, 470, 472, 475, 476, 477, 479

working class 6–7, 80, 91, 185, 216, 393, 465; critical criminology 16, 245, 246, 250, 259, 345, 346; deviant subcultures 13, 148, 149–50, 151, 157, 158; left realism 345; Marxism 189–90, 350; masculinity 240; peer pressure 175; police subculture 152; radical conflict model 24, 469; radical criminology 213, 217; structural factors 20

Young, Jock 22, 132, 200, 211, 214, 260–1, 339, 346–9, 351, 357, 361, 393, 400, 407, 443, 492

young people 74–5, 195, 467, 482–3; alcohol use 11, 102–3; Chicago Area Project 139–40; club culture 395–8; cognitive behavioural methods 126; critical criminology 246; desistance theories 325–6; deviant subcultures 13, 147–51, 153–4, 157–8, 160; drug use 104; labelling theories 203–4, 205; neighbourhood organization 138–9; New Labour policies 355; personality traits 118; post-subcultural theory 161–2; public opinion 495–6; recidivism 63; restorative justice 223; risk assessment 414; *see also* delinquency

zemiology 16, 256–9, 509

zero tolerance 290, 393, 438, 461–2

zones of transition 138, 139, 509

Third edition

Criminology
Theory and context

John Tierney

Criminology: theory and context, third edition, expands upon the ideas presented in previous editions, while introducing new material on critical theory, feminism, masculinities, cultural criminology and postmodernism. The text has been thoroughly updated throughout to reflect key perspectives in contemporary criminological theory. Relevant updates include discussions on New Labour's criminal justice and penal policies in its third term in office, and the latest developments in criminal justice and the politics of law and order in the UK and US. This edition revisits societal and cultural influences that have shaped the discipline and invites the reader to re-examine the phenomena of crime and deviance.

Criminology: theory and context, third edition, is presented in a logical structure and adopts an accessible framework. The text is essential reading for students of criminology, criminological theory and criminal justice and will also be of key interest to those studying sociology, law and the wider social sciences.

Selected table of contents

Introduction Part I: Preliminaries and Early History 1. Criminology, crime and deviance: some preliminaries 2. Measuring crime and criminality 3. Criminology and criminologists up to World War Two **Part II: World War Two to the Mid-1960s** 4. The discipline of criminology and its context 5. Social disorganisation and anomie 6. Strain, subcultures and delinquency 7. Criminological theory in Britain **Part III: The Mid-1960s to the Early 1970s** 8. The discipline of criminology and its context 9. New deviancy theory: the interactionist approach to deviance **Part IV: The 1970s** 10. The discipline of criminology and its context 11. Post-new deviancy and the new criminology **Part V: The 1980s to the Mid-1990s** 12. The discipline of criminology and its context 13. Criminological theory **Part VI: The Mid-1990s into the New Millennium** 14. The discipline of criminology and its context 15. Theoretical perspectives: recent developments.

November 2009 | 456pp
Pb: 978-0-273-72277-9: £33.99

For more information on this title please visit www.routledge.com/9780273722779

To order: Tel: +44 (0) 1235 400524   **Fax:** +44(0) 1235 400525
or Post: Taylor and Francis Customer Services,
Bookpoint, 130 Park Drive, Milton Park, Abingdon, Oxon, OX14 4SE
Email: book.orders@tandf.co.uk

For a complete listing of all our titles visit:
www.routledge.com